CONVERSATIONS IN CONTEXT

CONVERSATIONS IN CONTEXT

Identity, Knowledge, and College Writing

Kathryn Fitzgerald
Utah State University

Heather Bruce
University of Puget Sound

Sharon Stasney
University of Utah

Anna Vogt
University of Utah

Harcourt Brace College Publishers

Fort Worth   Philadelphia   San Diego
New York   Orlando   Austin   San Antonio
Toronto   Montreal   London   Sydney   Tokyo

Publisher	Earl McPeek
Executive Editor	Michael Rosenberg
Product Manager	Ilse Wolfe West
Developmental Editor	Camille Adkins
Production Manager	Kathleen Ferguson

Cover: Paul Cezanne, *Mont Sainte-Victoire,* 1902–04. Oil on canvas, 28¾ × 36³⁄₁₆″. Philadelphia Museum of Art: The George W. Elkins Collection. Photo: Graydon Wood, 1994.

ISBN: 0-15-503710-2

Library of Congress Catalog Card Number: 97-74006

Address for Editorial Correspondence: Harcourt Brace College Publishers, 301 Commerce Street, Suite 3700, Fort Worth, TX 76102.

Address for Orders: Harcourt Brace College Publishers, 6277 Sea Harbor Drive, Orlando, FL 32887-6777. 1-800-782-4479.

Web site address: http://www.hbcollege.com

Harcourt Brace & Company will provide supplements or supplement packages to those adopters qualified under our adoption policy. Please contact your sales representative to learn how you qualify. If as an adopter or potential user you receive supplements you do not need, please return them to your sales representative or send them to: Attn: Returns Department, Troy Warehouse, 465 South Lincoln Drive, Troy, MO 63379.

Printed in the United States of America

7 8 9 0 1 2 3 4 5 6   039   9 8 7 6 5 4 3 2 1

We dedicate this book to each other, and to the significant others and children who have moved in and out of our lives (and we theirs) as we wrote this text.

CONTENTS

PART TWO
Conversations about Knowing   89

PART THREE

Conversations about Writing   245

PART FOUR

Formal Writing Assignments   367

ALPHABETICAL
TABLE OF CONTENTS

PREFACE

PURPOSE AND RATIONALE

Conversations in Context: Identity, Knowledge, and College Writing invites students to learn about and participate in a series of related conversations about student identities, the aims of the university, and the conventions of academic writing. Rather than seeing academic writing as consisting of objective statements of "truth," the editors of this textbook view it as a social construction of knowledge that requires rhetorical choices as well as empirical research. This book represents academic writing as a sequence of continuing conversations within discourse communities and provides a variety of opportunities to engage with and participate in these conversations.

COMPONENTS

Conversations in Context differs from traditional anthologies in the following ways:

1. It organizes readings as voices participating in conversations.
2. It invites examination of the role of the individual within the university as well as the role of the university as a whole.
3. It contains an entire section of articles by compositionists that allows students to listen in on and participate in the academic conversation about their own writing in the university.
4. It presents suggestions that continually encourage consideration of how reading and writing stem from, augment, challenge, and alter notions of identity. *Conversations in Context* helps connect new ideas, languages, and forms encountered in the reading selections (and in courses beyond this writing course) with identities and knowledge brought to the university from home communities.
5. Its approach to both reading and writing is rhetorical. Its commentaries and activities address reading and writing in terms of the following questions:

- What is the author's primary purpose? What does the author want the reader to do or believe?
- Who is the author's primary audience? What rhetorical strategies in the text make it possible to identify the intended audience?
- How does the author construct an identity within the text and present him- or herself as a credible authority on the topic?
- How and why does the author conform to or transgress typical academic writing conventions?

Prereading commentaries for each reading selection include:

Reading the Context—biographical information about the author and historical information surrounding the selection.

Reading the Rhetoric—information to help the reader analyze the author's rhetorical strategies.

Reading the Conversation—aids to viewing the reader's response, the text, and related texts as participants in academic discourse.

Postreading activities for each reading selection include:

Discussing the Rhetoric—questions to help the reader consider the writer's rhetorical strategies.

Discussing the Conversation—questions to help the reader consider his or her response to the content and the relationships among selections.

Joining the Conversation—activities that help the reader move from reading, thinking, and discussing to writing.

6. *Conversations in Context* includes an Appenhdix of rhetorical terms for readers and writers to aid students and instructors in using a rhetorical approach.

7. It includes readings from diverse academic disciplines that address the discovery, definition, and dissemination of knowledge in academic communities and reflect various academic conventions for writing.

8. It features a sequence of writing assignments that anticipate the specialized forms and typical conventions of writing for audiences within various disciplines. These assignments stand alone at the end of the volume (Part Four) to encourage flexible use with readings in any one section or across several sections.

INSTRUCTOR'S MANUAL

The Instructor's Manual that accompanies *Conversations in Context* contains sample quarter and semester syllabi as well as strategies for using the textbook effectively to help students (1) write across the disciplines, (2) discern and analyze the rhetorical structures of texts, and (3) understand, participate in, and transgress the boundaries of academic conversations.

Both the main text and the *Instructor's Manual* proceed from the following assumptions: students learn to write most effectively by (1) writing and reading, (2) having multiple opportunities to draft and revise, (3) sharing initial attempts with peers and the instructor for response and feedback that can guide revision, and (4) talking about writing processes and written texts with other writers and with writing instructors.

Acknowledgments

We wish to acknowledge the contributions of the Writing 112 and Writing 101 Teaching Counselors in the University of Utah Writing Program over the past ten years whose contributions to the courses have helped shape this book. We especially want to thank Thomas N. Huckin for his directorship of the University Writing Program and Susan Miller for her insight and grounding influence. Perhaps the most helpful contributors to this text were our students at both the University of Utah and the University of Puget Sound. Their perspectives on academic writing and their thoughtful evaluations of both their own work and the reading apparatus contributed in important ways to the evolution of this text.

We are grateful to the following colleagues who offered their advice in the form of reviews: Gay Lynn Crossly, Kansas State University; Stephen Dilks, University of North Dakota; Theresa Enos, University of Arizona; Susan Jarratt, Miami University; Amy Lee, SUNY Albany; Nancy MacKenzie, Mankato State University.

Finally, we wish to express sincere appreciation to our editors. We offer our special thinks to Michael Rosenberg and Camille Adkins for their encouragement and support throughout this project.

INTRODUCTION

READING AND WRITING WITH A RHETORICAL APPROACH

To take a rhetorical approach to reading and writing requires understanding that all writing is located in particular contexts. A rhetorical approach is based on the premise that all writers make choices in their writing; their choices change as their audiences and purposes change. Learning to focus your writing around a specific purpose and audience is not an arbitrary process of finding out how your professor wants you to write and then writing that way. A rhetorical approach emphasizes that academic writing requires you always to be aware of the expectations and discursive conventions of the particular community for which you are writing, and, consequently, to make choices that demonstrate your awareness of the goals or common ground you might share in this context. If you examine the choices other writers have made in light of their audiences and purposes, you can make more informed choices in your own writing. The factors influencing these choices are what we refer to as rhetorical issues.

The need to understand a particular academic community in order to write for that audience does complicate matters. Although you can't learn everything about the academic community in a single class, as you gain experience, you can learn to uncover the underlying values and assumptions of the community in anything you read. This book will encourage you to use a rhetorical approach when you read. When you start analyzing how and why a writer said something, in addition to what he or she said and in what context, you gain valuable insight that you can apply any time you read and write.

Our rhetorical approach is particularly evident in the commentary and questions accompanying each reading selection in this book. These aids are designed to help you understand the substance of the readings in a variety of ways. They will help you become aware of how writers form arguments and how you might effectively construct your own arguments in academic settings. We have included many more discussion questions and writing invitations than you could possibly complete in a single course. We did this to give your instructor flexibility of choice in working with questions and writing assignments in ways that best promote your rhetorical development.

We have provided many alternatives for approaching the reading and writing rhetorically because it is impossible to simply hand you a formula that is successful in every situation. For example, if you were to ask every professor you encounter, "What makes good writing?" you would probably end up with a bewildering range of preferences:

- "Good writing is clear and precise, leaving no room for error on the part of the reader."
- "Good writing lets you express a part of yourself that you never knew existed. It is a journey of self-discovery."
- "Good writing is properly footnoted and documented with sources written by recognized experts in the field."

Our experience as college writing teachers has taught us that no sooner do you learn the rules for successful writing than you start to notice that those rules are broken by experts in the field every day. Any given professor will respond to your writing within the context of the goals and values of a particular course within their academic discipline. For example, Professor A (who is teaching a liberal arts course titled "Great Ideas") might value personal anecdotes because the purpose of the course is to demonstrate that many great ideas begin with thoughts that individuals find personally relevant to their lives. Professor B (who is teaching a course in business) might focus heavily on the organization and appearance of written information because written communication influences a reader's views about the quality of a company's product.

If you understand what a professor is trying to accomplish in a course and what you are expected to know or be able to do after finishing the course, you can frame your writing within that context. In doing this, you can find a common ground, something to say, and a way to say it that both you and your professor understand and value.

That is why this textbook focuses not on learning and applying formulas, but on recognizing and understanding the rhetorical issues that influence why a particular rhetorical choice is successful in one situation and not in another. Once you understand that different audiences value different kinds of writing, you understand why your success depends on whether your writing "speaks" to a particular audience. When you comprehend the rhetorical characteristics of any reading and writing situation, whether inside the classroom or beyond it, you gain rhetorical power and authority.

ARRANGEMENT OF THE CONVERSATIONS

Conversations in Context treats reading selections as voices (or perspectives) in overlapping conversations, not as isolated pieces. Many textbooks separate readings from their contexts by organizing them according to some artificial principle such as alphabetical order, rhetorical mode, or opposing viewpoints in an argument. The selections in this book are organized as conversations to demonstrate that published writing never exists in a vacuum, but always responds in some way to previous writing.

The conversations in which these selections are engaged are not so much about the substance of their discipline as about how knowledge is made and disseminated in the discipline. We believe this is the appropriate starting point for learning the conventions of academic writing because the conventions are defined by the ways in which each disciplinary community allows itself to be persuaded of the validity of new ideas. We have also included articles by professional compositionists to let you see how they view the ways students struggle and ultimately develop facility with academic conventions in a variety of disciplines.

The readings in *Conversations in Context* are included neither as examples of literary excellence nor of "right" answers, but rather as multiple perspectives in continuing written conversations. The book's conversational arrangement invites you to examine the subtleties of continuing written discussions in which writers agree or disagree with, build upon, exemplify, explain, and elaborate each other's ideas. The complex interrelationships among readings encourage you to move beyond simplistic two-sided notions of argument.

FORMAL AND INFORMAL WRITING

In this book, we distinguish between formal and informal responses to various writing invitations and assignments. We call the writing invitations under "Joining the Conversation" following each reading "informal" responses while the assignments in Part Four of the book are labeled "formal." By this, we do not mean simply a difference of appearance or presentation, as between casual dress and formal wear, although these various writing responses will likely produce different appearances. Nor do we mean that informal writing is solely generative, for getting your thinking going, and that formal writing is only writing that has been reworked and revised. Formal writing, in this book, refers to writing that is tied closely to the traditional forms and genres of student writing at the university; informal writing is not necessarily connected to any particular genre, but is intended to provide opportunities for you to join in, to continue, and to transgress the more conventional forms of writing expected at the university.

The discussion questions and writing invitations following each reading selection are designed to give you a forum both for responding informally to the readings and for beginning to explore avenues for producing more formal contributions to the academic conversations represented in this book.

WRITING ASSIGNMENTS

The writing assignments in Section Four include detailed instructions, which are intended to make visible the purposes for which each assignment is typically made and the standards by which each assignment is typically evaluated. We have provided these explicit instructions to support students and instructors who find such guidelines useful, but we do not mean to suggest that they represent the single "right" approach to the assignments. On the contrary, we are attempting to give you enough information to enable you to choose the best approach to the writing assignments for the purposes you have in mind. You may want to consider treating these assignments like you might a gift—use what you need and want and store the rest away.

JOINING ACADEMIC CONVERSATIONS

All the components of this textbook work together to build analytical skills that serve a dual purpose: to help you read rhetorically within the context of academic conversations and to help you make effective choices in your own writing. Exactly what you want to accomplish in your writing is part of what you will discover as you join these conversations. Whatever you decide about your identity as a college student, your beliefs about knowledge, and your beliefs about how one should write within the university, a rhetorical approach can help you express those decisions convincingly. The goal of this textbook, therefore, is not to control or even influence *what* you say when you join these conversations, but to give you tools to help you integrate what you say with how you say it. When you can successfully synthesize these two elements for a specific audience and purpose, you will know how to write effectively within the university.

EXPANDING THE CONTEXT OF COLLEGE WRITING FROM COURSES TO DISCIPLINES

The values and goals of any college course come from a larger structure called an academic discipline. *Discipline,* in this specialized sense, is nearly synonymous with subject area. A discipline, whether it's anthropology, chemical engineering, physics, agriculture, or folklore, constructs its own criteria for what counts as knowledge. Disciplines have different goals—different work to accomplish—and these differences influence how their members use writing. As you begin to place individual pieces of writing within the specific contexts of academic disciplines, the choices writers make in their texts become more meaningful.

Academic texts are not isolated pieces of writing; rather, they are voices participating in disciplinary conversations. One text might add to, challenge, define, or agree with ideas introduced in another. In this way, writers "converse" with each other through their texts. For example, think about the ways Internet users communicate in online chat rooms. These people converse with each other because they share a common interest and want to see what others have to say about a particular topic. Paying attention to how members of a group talk among themselves, in a chat room or within an academic discipline, is part of rhetorically analyzing a context. The more you read rhetorically, the easier it will become to go beyond a writer's words to the disciplinary assumptions, goals, and values that frame those words.

ORGANIZATION OF THE BOOK

Conversations in Context opens with several readings that directly address the differences in language and belief systems between home communities and institutions of higher education. As you read this conversation about student identities in relation to the university, you may recognize that you are not alone if you feel challenged or alienated by the peculiarities of academic discourse. As you continue into the second and third sections of the book, which consist of multiple perspectives about how knowledge is made and what forms of writing are considered valid in various disciplines, you will begin to understand some of the reasons why writing takes the shapes it does. *Conversations in Context* is intended to help you discover ways to situate yourself in academic discourse by inviting you to think critically against, as well as productively within, the discourse conventions valued in scholarship.

Part One: Conversations about Identities

The readings in this section construct a conversation about relationships among student identities, home communities, and academic expectations. Writing instruction in this section begins by acknowledging differences in language and belief systems between home and academic communities. This section includes selections by a range of writers, extending from those who claim diverse, multicultural home identities to those who make no claims about their home identities. This section of readings comprises a conversation about issues of alienation from, resistance to, and compliance with academic worldviews and discourses.

The various writers in this section explore how academic conversations change and are changed by those who join them. The question, "Will entering into these academic conversations change me?" has no easy answer. Some writers in this section feel that change is a necessary aspect of education. Writers with this belief argue that students must give up prior identities and assimilate into the culture of the university. Other writers don't agree that students should assimilate at all and think that such change must be resisted, or at least tempered by one's own cultural roots and beliefs.

The counterquestion, "How does my identity affect what I bring to these conversations?" is likewise troublesome. These readings do not provide answers. Instead, they offer a rhetorical framework to use in defining your own answers to these questions.

The first two articles, "Spandex Judge" by Kent Kirkpatrick and "De-Constructive Criticism" by Elizabeth Cody Newenhuyse, introduce relationships between writing and community. They keenly represent the notion that discourse communities shape the audience, purpose and form of writing, and they reveal social and linguistic constructions of identity. Not examples of academic writing, they are included to provide informative contrasts to the academic conventions found in the majority of the book's readings.

"Liberal Education," a chapter from Allan Bloom's *The Closing of the American Mind,* is included for several reasons, none of which is necessarily intended as an endorsement of either the quality or the content of the writing. It is included because, as a voice in the discussion of what it means to be "in the university," it conveys a traditional perspective on both student identity and the *canon debate,* ongoing arguments about the selection of appropriate curricula and texts for college-educated Americans. Additionally, as a text, it exemplifies irony as a rhetorical strategy to a greater degree than any of the other selections in this section.

Authors Mike Rose, Richard Rodriguez, bell hooks, and Mary Louise Pratt oppose the representation of student identities and relationships to the university offered by Bloom. Rose's representation of the "typical" university student in "The Politics of Remediation" challenges Bloom's traditional view and calls into question commonplace ideas of what students need to know to succeed at the university. Rodriguez's "The Achievement of Desire" provides a personal account of language, race, class, and American educational issues, meditating on the gains and losses that always accompany a mainstream education for nonmainstream students. In "Keeping Close to Home," hooks proposes that diversity is to be celebrated and accommodated in the university. Her focus on the linguistic and social conflicts that arise as a result of socioeconomic class as well as ethnic diversity makes her perspective especially pertinent to this conversation.

In "Arts of the Contact Zone," Mary Louise Pratt describes the classroom as a "contact zone," a "social space where cultures meet, clash, and grapple with each other, often in contexts of highly asymmetrical relations of power." Her purpose is to rethink the power structures that lead to exclusion as well as inclusion of individuals in various communities. Pratt discusses the literate arts of the contact zone—autoethnography, critique, collaboration, bilingualism, parody, and denunciation, to name a few—and celebrates their successes while also noting their failures.

The readings in the "Conversations about Identities" section raise the question, "What impact does a traditional view of the student have on student success?" Rhetorically analyzing the relationships between writing and community enables you to locate yourself and your writing within academic communities.

Part Two: Conversations about Knowledge

This section introduces what may be a new way to think about university work. Many students believe that college or university work is similar to high school work except harder. However, professors see their work quite differently. Although teaching is a major part of professors' work, equally important are research and scholarship—the construction and dissemination of new knowledge. The fact that college professors are also researchers and scholars affects their expectations for writing. Writing is essential to their work because they share it with their colleagues and the outside world through writing. Their colleagues, also experts in the same areas of research, comprise a highly critical audience that demands that assumptions, methods, results, and logical processes be explicitly described. Professors pass these demanding writing standards on to students as part of their training in how their disciplines work.

The readings in this section address questions about how knowledge is made in the university to help you understand the context that frames the expectations for your writing. Part Two introduces central threads in a continuing conversation among philosophers of science, working scientists, historians, and literary critics about how knowledge is discovered or constructed and validated. These accounts will help you understand and question the assumptions of prevailing frameworks for making knowledge, including *positivist, post-positivist,* and *social constructivist* ways of knowing.

"Science and Nonscience: An Introduction" by E.D. Klemke, Robert Hollinger, and A. David Kline provides an example of writing in the philosophy of science, and introduces positivist ways of knowing. It is included to acknowledge positivistic science's position of privilege in academic communities, to appreciate its historical significance, and to provide an example of writing typical of certain sorts of work within the philosophy of science. Brian Magee's "Scientific Method: The Traditional View and Popper's View" elaborates a post-positivist perspective. It focuses on Hume's problem, a central issue for proof in empirical science, and summarizes Sir Karl Popper's response to the problem. Magee further explains these matters in "The Criterion of Demarcation between What Is and What Is Not Science."

"The Man of Professional Wisdom" by Kathryn Pyne Addelson and "A Feeling for the Organism" by Evelyn Fox Keller offer counterpositions to traditional views of empirical science. Addelson and Keller challenge what they view as limitations on the knowledge-making potential of science imposed by allegedly reductive positivistic methods. These two articles are particularly important to the conversation of this section because they demonstrate that questions about objectivity and value-neutral research are as applicable to the so-called "hard" sciences as they are to the social sciences or the humanities.

"Animal Sexuality" by David Crews, a practicing cellular biologist, is a scientific report that exemplifies how knowledge is socially constructed and rhetorically disseminated. Nicholas Wade in a feature article for the *New York Times Magazine,* "Star-Spangled Scandal," demonstrates, in a completely different genre, that the questions about knowledge-making discussed among professional scientists can also impact the general public.

Conversations about knowledge making within the disciplines of history and literary study extend the discussion further. Bridging the gap between the sciences and history, Londa Schiebinger challenges traditional thinking about who is qualified to be a scientist in "Who Should Do Science?" In "Discovering the Clay Feet of Science," the historians Joyce Appleby, Lynn Hunt, and Margaret Jacob address controversial ways in which the history of science is currently being revised.

In the field of literary criticism, Jane Tompkins' "Indians: Texturalism, Morality, and the Problem of History" and Stanley Fish's "How to Recognize a Poem When You See One" discuss assumptions about methodology and the origins of knowledge (epistemology) that underlie reasoning and truth. In a detailed examination of how various historians and contemporaneous diarists viewed the relationship between Native Americans and settlers in colonial New England, Tompkins develops the view that the cultural identity of the historian places an impenetrable screen between the historian as observer and the historical reality observed. Fish suggests that what is considered knowledge depends upon how a certain group or community has historically related to the world; in other words, knowledge, Fish claims, is socially constructed.

This section encourages reflection upon such questions as "Is the acceptance of scientific knowledge, historical, and (or) literary understanding socially conditioned?" Kenneth Burke is included at the end of this discussion because he both summarized and predicted these conversations about the reciprocal relations between context and text.

All the readings in this section urge you to question disciplinary statements of truth rhetorically and to understand that your professors' expectations for your writing are based on the purposes, formats, conventions, language, values, and debates of researchers engaged in inquiry.

Part Three: Conversations about Writing

In the third section, professional compositionists (researchers, scholars, and teachers in the discipline of rhetoric and writing) converse about expectations for student writing in various disciplines and exchange ideas about what it means to write for academic purposes and audiences. The selections emphasize that underlying values and assumptions about what one can know and how one can know it (the topics addressed in Part Two) heavily influence expectations for student writing. This section reveals that answers to questions such as "What kinds of evidence are appropriate in an academic essay?" change depending on the writer's disciplinary framework. These reading selections are in essence about you and your writing.

The section begins with "Inventing the University." In this article, David Bartholomae discusses "commonplaces" of student writing, and how these determine a system of interpretation for the reader and the writer. He discusses what makes student writing successful, and what "assuming a position of privilege" as a writer entails.

Karen Spear identifies problems commonly experienced by students in peer response groups in composition courses. You may be able to chart a more successful collaborative course by reading about the conflicts and confusion described in this excerpt from Spear's longer work, *Sharing Writing*.

The excerpts from *Reading to Write: Exploring a Cognitive and Social Process* come from a study in which Linda Flower and several of her colleagues at Carnegie Mellon University took a detailed look at the ways first-year writers interpret and work through a writing assignment. In making the transition into academic discourse, these students represent the task before them differently in ways that affect the level of success they achieve. This reading is included to help you understand more clearly the task set before you when you are asked to write from academic sources.

Peter Elbow participates actively in discussions among compositionists about student writing. He has written textbooks for students and the general public as well. But he frequently expresses severe doubts about the writing instruction students receive in college composition courses, and his textbooks are intended for self-instruction rather than classroom use. The excerpt printed here is taken from one such text, *Writing with Power*.

The article "Learning to Read Biology: One Student's Rhetorical Development in College" by Christina Haas provides an opportunity not only to learn how to make sense of long scientific research studies but also to determine from narrative what it means to assimilate academic discourse.

In "Conversations with Texts: Reading in the Teaching of Composition," Mariolina Salvatori argues that the act of reading is a process of engaging in a conversation in which one partner is the text and the other is the interpreter or reader. When you acknowledge that reading is a dialogue between reader and text, you can begin to generate critical questions, and thus to participate in, continue, and transgress textual conversations.

Jim W. Corder argues in "Argument as Emergence, Rhetoric as Love" that when the philosophical notion of "love" shapes the rhetoric of argument, writers can work toward creating spaces that accommodate diversity. This article returns to the questions raised in Part One, not necessarily with the "right" answers to them, but with another perspective for viewing them in relation to your own writing and identity.

Part Four: Formal Writing Assignments

The sequence of assignments in this section builds on the informal writing activities that accompany each reading in Parts One, Two, and Three. This section provides detailed instructions for working through several forms of writing commonly encountered during university study. Here you will find assignments for writing a summary, an analysis, a synthesis, a review, an annotated bibliography, a researched argument, and a self-reflective essay.

The writing assignments in this section are designed to focus your attention on rhetorical issues and to teach you how to position yourself and your texts within the boundaries of academic debate. In particular, you will learn what constitutes appropriate academic claims, credible academic evidence, and critical/analytical forms of writing. The assignments will ask you to think about issues such as these:

- Who is my audience when I write for a college course?
- What does my professor expect me to learn from writing this paper?
- How do the typical genres of this discipline affect my professor's expectations?
- What do I hope to gain from writing this paper?
- What ideas or points do I want to convey in the paper?
- How much and what kind of evidence or support do I need to include?

Each of these assignments provides questions for collaborative peer responses to drafts, criteria for evaluation, and examples of other student papers written in response to the assignment.

The assignments in this section are quite different from those suggested in "Joining the Conversation" at the end of each reading selection in Parts One, Two, and Three. However, it is expected that the personal responses called for in "Joining the Conversation" will extend into, inform, and predict the academic writing called for by these assignments.

Finally, the aim of the explicit detail given in these assignments is to teach you common expectations for these specialized forms of writing and as much as possible, to make visible the processes in which writers commonly engage. However, if you encounter any examples of these genres in a published form, you will probably notice that the writer has deviated in various ways from the guidelines outlined here. Writers typically join, alter, and transgress expectations in ways that allow them to fine tune generic formats to suit their rhetorical purposes and their intended audiences. As you gain confidence in writing, you may experiment with approaches to assignments that call for these generic forms. Use the instructions flexibly and only as they seem helpful to your purposes.

Appendix: Rhetorical Terms for Readers and Writers

The final section provides a rhetorical vocabulary for thinking and talking about how people read and write. The purpose of the Appendix is not to represent the entire field of rhetoric, but to provide a practical set of concepts to use as guidelines for thinking about college reading and writing.

The Appendix omits some items rhetoricians would usually include in an overview of rhetoric and reorganizes the rest in ways we think are useful to readers and writers. As tools for analysis of writing, you can use these terms to talk both about the readings in this book and about your own and your peers' drafts. Another goal is for you to learn that you can also apply rhetorical terms outside the university to investigate writing in any situation.

We have organized the rhetorical terms to suggest which factors in the rhetorical situation control other choices. Therefore, the terms are not alphabetized as they usually would be in a glossary, but organized from those terms referring to the whole rhetorical situation to those dealing with the most minute rhetorical decisions. The rhetorical situation, including audience and purpose, begins the Appendix because once audience and purpose are known, they influence every other choice a writer makes.

PART ONE

Conversations about Identities

It's the first day of a new semester and you're sitting in class listening to the instructor go through the syllabus. It sounds familiar, tests halfway through the semester, write a paper at the end. Then the teacher sets the syllabus aside and begins to discuss what will be the "meat" of the class. You start to feel lost. She's talking about "hegemony" this and "hegemonic" that. You thought this was a class on Western American history, not "hege . . ." what was that word again?

Later that day, after the dreaded trip to the bookstore to spend your entire life's savings on books you hope you won't have to really read, you notice that, among the many textbooks, you also bought a dictionary. What was that word that had perplexed you earlier? There it is, *hegemony:* "The predominant influence of one political body over another." There's also a usage note, "Hegemony may be stressed on either the second or first syllable, though 72 percent of the Usage Panel prefers the first pronunciation." Well, who are you to argue with "The Usage Panel"; you practice saying the word a few times, carefully stressing the second syllable.

A couple of weeks into the semester, you're sitting in your Western American History class again. The class is discussing last night's reading, an account of how Native Americans were typically portrayed as passive in American art in the 1830s. For some reason, the teacher looks at you and asks what you think. "Well, that's just one more example of how the whites practiced hegemony over the Indians," you say, carefully stressing the second syllable of "the word." The teacher looks at you with an interested expression on her face. "A compelling thought," she responds. You realize you've not only learned a word but you've also discovered a key concept

1

within a particular way of talking, or discourse. Suddenly you are participating in the very conversation that seemed foreign and even overwhelming
three weeks ago.

At the end of the semester, you're sitting with a group of high school
friends discussing the latest Seinfeld episode. In the episode, a reporter is
convinced that Jerry and George are gay and prints it in the paper. Your
friends think it's great how Jerry and George always protest that they're not
gay, but then add, "Not that there's anything wrong with that." You have a
moment of insight and say "That type of condescending language is just another form of hegemony."

"Hege what?" Your friends look at you strangely.

You make a mental note never again to use four syllable words with this
particular group of friends, forgetting that less than three months ago you
had also thought hegemony was some type of shrub.

DISCOURSE COMMUNITIES

Just like your clothing or music preferences, the words you use to express
your thoughts are part of your identity. Your language marks you as a member or nonmember of certain "discourse communities." A discourse community is a group of people who share a common interest, goal, or set of values
and whose language reflects that commonality. "Browsing the web," and
"Java" mean something entirely different to a computer user than they do to
someone who is not computer "literate." "Grist" is grain about to be ground
to a farmer, while to a skier it means snow that began to melt at one point
but has re-frozen and contains ice particles. Language is also particular to a
certain geographic locale or socioeconomic status. The discourse communities you function in might include people who enjoy similar hobbies; who
have roughly the same educational background; or who are of the same ethnic group, gender, or age group.

You participate in many different discourse communities and the language you use throughout the day may shift accordingly. The human mind
makes many of these shifts unconsciously. You don't usually decide to speak
a certain way because you're now talking with other first year college students, or other Asian co-workers, or other Catholics. Conscious choices to
use a certain discourse usually occur when a speaker stands on the boundary of a community and tries to gain membership.

The "hegemony" example at the beginning of this introduction demonstrates how acquiring "academic language" can often bring admittance to
academic discourse communities. Learning to speak "like an academic" is
tricky, however. Academics don't all speak alike. Each discipline has its
own glossary of terms that an incoming student must learn. In addition, admittance into some discourse communities means that you're no longer
comfortable or allowed in others; tough choices must be made. In her essay
"Keeping Close to Home," bell hooks makes the following observation

about how allegiance to an academic discourse community can estrange one from home communities:

> When I first came to New Haven to teach at Yale, I was truly surprised by the marked class divisions between black folks—students and professors— who identify with Yale and those black folks who work at Yale or in surrounding communities. Style of dress and self-presentation are most often the central markers of one's position. I soon learned that the black folks who spoke on the street were likely to be part of the black community and those who shifted their glance were likely to be associated with Yale. Walking with a black female colleague one day, I spoke to practically every black person in sight (a gesture which reflects my upbringing), an action which disturbed my companion. Since I addressed black folks who were clearly not associated with Yale, she wanted to know whether or not I knew them. That was funny to me. "Of course not," I answered. Yet when I thought about it seriously, I realized that in a deep way, I knew them for they, and not my companion or most of my colleagues at Yale, resemble my family.

hooks believes that entering an academic community not only affects one's language, or discourse, but can even challenge one's former beliefs about self, family, and community.

READING AND WRITING OBJECTIVES

All the readings in this part explore what can happen to home identities when you encounter institutions of higher learning. The goal is not to convert or assimilate you into a certain way of representing yourself; it is to make you aware of the forces and rules already in play when you walk into a classroom. The readings will introduce you to others' experiences and their reasons for choosing either to assimilate into or to resist academic conventions.

The writing assignments encourage you to view academic writing as a set of choices that you make to affect a certain audience in a certain way. How much of your home identity you bring into your writing and how you incorporate that part of yourself into academic papers are choices you'll have to make whenever you write a paper. The words you use, the way you organize your information, what you leave in and what you leave out, are all rhetorical choices that reveal your familiarity with and degree of adherence to academic discourse.

INTRODUCTORY COMMENTS ON "SPANDEX JUDGE" BY KENT KIRKPATRICK

Reading the Context

Magazine publishers do not think of their readers as simply "everybody." Instead, they write and advertise to a particular population. That population

Spandex

Judge Tam Nomoto is sweating. I'm sweating. She's panting. I'm panting. She's scantily clad. I'm not wearing shoes. "I can't hear you breathe," she yells. I pant harder and try to increase the volume of my breathing.

No, it isn't what you think. It's just another of Tam Nomoto's twice weekly aerobics classes at the Woodbridge Community Center in Orange County, California. Being an aerobics instructor is not uncommon, but the 5-3 woman of Chinese and Japanese ancestry at the front of the class, looking good in shrink-wrapped bright orange spandex and bopping around to music by the Fine Young Cannibals, is not the image of your typical judge.

In a world where our adjudicators are thought to be sexless, crusty old White men, Nomoto's an attractive, hip young woman who two-steps in country western bars, keeps an Arab and an Appaloosa horse on her one-acre property, and is married to a man six years younger, her third husband.

"I break all the stereotypes, don't I?" Nomoto says in a soft voice.

She is a symbol of the 90s career woman, one who works in a traditionally male dominated occupation but doesn't let it reign in her zest for life or control her femineity. She earns respect by her performance in the courtroom, not by how well she imitates male behavior. In the same way Hilary Clinton brings a woman's perspective to her hard-nosed legal work on behalf of children, Nomoto refuses to bend her life to a male's view of what is important.

Nomoto's currently involved in the June election race for a superior court judgeship. If she wins, she will hear lawsuits involving sums above $25,000, and handle felony, adoption, divorce and juvenile cases. "My background is civil law and there's a greater opportunity to do civil law cases in superior court," she says. And her $91,000 salary will increase by $10,000. If she loses, she stays at her current job where she hears misdemeanor cases and lawsuits under $25,000. "I don't see any negatives to this campaign, except for the time commitment," she says. "I mean it's very, very busy and it's never any fun to ask people for contributions and to ask people to support you. That is so anti-Asian culture. It's anti-anybody's culture."

Since her campaign started in December she has engaged in at least one election-related activity every day. She used to teach four aerobics classes a week but had to drop two. The 'Friends of Judge Barbara Tam Nomoto' committee organizes dinners to raise the necessary funds. How much will she raise? "It would be nice to have $100,000, but judges have run and won on less," she says. Does she think that running for election as an Asian in Orange County, which is a predominately white area, will disadvantage her? "I hope not," she says. "We have

Authors Note: We have boxed this article to preserve the original formatting because the format itself is a rhetorical choice by the editors of the magazine *Face.*

Judge

Justice may be blind, but she's in great shape.
Judge Tam Nomoto breaks all the stereotypes.

Kent Kirkpatrick

three council people who are Asian and one Asian legislator," she says. "I think it shows the voters are not prejudiced."

But in the courtroom being Asian made it more difficult to earn respect. "There's a credibility gap," she says. "People tend to have a hard time giving you the respect they would automatically give someone who looks like what a judge should look like." Lawyers push her because she's female. They argue a little longer than necessary, testing Nomoto's courtroom control. Defendants have called her 'honey' and 'sweetie.' "I've also had flowers sent to me by defendants," she says. She laughs at the thought. "Who knows what's going through their minds?"

The characteristics Asian culture condemns in women—aggression, self-confidence, poise—are the very characteristics that make a good attorney, Nomoto says. "My Asian colleagues all have a problem with that type of cultural mindset," she says, "and they have to overcome it. They're often told by their families they've become Americanized." Early in Nomoto's career her father, an engineer, came from San Francisco to watch her in action. An elderly male attorney refused to stop arguing and Nomoto had to dress him down. "My dad was really surprised," she says. "Here I was telling this older man he couldn't do something."

Nomoto shows no bitterness about the obstacles she's had to overcome in her career. To the contrary she is extremely fair; her opinions contain a judge's balance. She even speaks highly of her two ex-husbands, although a sign hanging on her office wall reads: "Missing husband, shotgun and dog. Reward for dog."

At the University of California-Berkeley law school, where she received her legal training, Whites assumed that as an Asian, Nomoto's acceptance was due to her minority status. "That really upset me," she says, "and I think it upset a lot of my minority friends that had gotten into school on the basis of their credentials. I don't mean to imply that the minority program isn't a good idea. It's just that non-minorities would have this condescending attitude towards minorities and it was so off-base it was offensive."

Yet Nomoto quickly adds—and here comes the other side of the story—that she had many ethnic friends in college who were just as guilty of discrimination. "A lot of times my Asian friends would tell me that I shouldn't have so many Caucasian friends, or that I shouldn't date Caucasians, so it wasn't always Caucasians."

The only time Nomoto displayed anything less than an even personality is when I showed up for the aerobics class to find that the usual room had been switched. Judge Nomoto was not happy about that. "I'm extremely crabby right now," she said as she har-

Nomoto

"You hear about people getting shot, you read it in the media, you see it on television. But nothing matches having a real life victim on a witness stand pulling up his shirt and showing you the bullet scars or the knife wound. Nothing prepared me for seeing how much damage a bullet can do."

rumphed around the room setting up the tape player. "I hate this room." When I told Nomoto I'd forgotten my shoes she said I could participate barefoot but only if I did a low impact workout. "If I see you bouncing around back there, I'll come back and brain you," she said. I assume she's joking, but I make sure my feet don't leave the ground. I remember thinking I wouldn't want to be the poor sap in the defendant's chair who decides to call Judge Nomoto 'sweetie.'

Nomoto's father is Chinese and her mother is Japanese, yet Nomoto is a Japanese name. Tam Nomoto used to be Barbara Tam. At 29 she dropped Barbara, a name she long detested, and added her mother's family name. The Nomoto clan in Japan had lost many of the male kin during WWII and they expressed an interest in seeing the name continued. "My mother's family crest hangs in a castle that the Shogun used to own," she says, "so we have a great deal of family pride and heritage." Her father didn't mind as long as she used Tam, her father's family name, as her given name. "Only my mother still calls me Barbara," she says.

For someone with such a well rounded life now, Nomoto's childhood was narrowly focused on academics and achievement. As an only child growing up in San Francisco, Nomoto began taking piano lessons at four, modern dance lessons at five, and Japanese dance by seven. Her parents wouldn't let her outside to play until all her homework was done. "If there was a choice between playing with other children outside and reading a book, I was encouraged to read a book," she says.

When she graduated from High School, Nomoto toyed with the idea of a career as a pianist, and she even applied to a few music schools, but her parent's put a quick end to that thinking "Asian parents do not look with approval on a livelihood in music," she says. She entered UC, Berkeley as a premed student. In retrospect, she's grateful. "I would have been a terrible

performance artist. I used to get nervous before every concert. It's funny because I usually speak to a full room of people, or a TV camera in my court room and not be nervous, but when it comes to playing the piano, even in front of one friend, I'm a wreck."

She quit premed quite early in her degree because as she says "there was no chemistry between me and chemistry, absolutely none," and switched into history. This, of course, horrified her parents, and Nomoto says they still haven't recovered. "Even when I got appointed to the bench," she says, "they were proud of me but still would have preferred an M.D. after my name instead of an Honorable in front of it."

Nomoto finished undergraduate in three years instead of four and entered law school on a scholarship for international legal studies. She vacationed in Japan during those summers and even attended Mejin University in Tokyo for a summer, lecturing on American jurisprudence in fluent Japanese.

Nomoto graduated in 73 and dabbled in private practice for a year but hated the 60 to 70 hour weeks and the gender discrimination. "When I first started working with the law firm, the lawyer's names were all 'Mr So and So,' but I was always referred to by my first name. It was little things like that." She left the firm and joined the Orange County Counsel's office, working on everything from airport litigation to taxes. "It was a very positive experience," she says, "There was little gender bias. It was a warm atmosphere."

The Governor, who was looking for qualified women, appointed her to the bench at 28. "I just put my name in and got appointed," she says. "I didn't do any politicking or anything. I was just very, very fortunate."

After a year hearing traffic violations and misdemeanors she moved into a general trial calendar, where she received a large share of children victim

cases because her age, sex and youthful appearance comforted the kids. "12, 13, 14 years ago I had a lot of children victims say they were sure I couldn't be older than 15," she says. The cases she heard—molestation, rape, violent assaults—were and still are emotionally and psychologically stressful. "You hear about people getting shot, you read it in the media, you see it on television, but nothing matches having a real life victim on a witness stand pulling up his shirt and showing you the bullet scars or the knife wound," she says. "Nothing prepared me for seeing how much damage a bullet can do."

Last December Nomoto married her third husband, a 37-year-old White from Texas who proposed to her while they were on a horseback camping trip in the Canadian Rockies after a five-year courtship. "I resisted dating a younger man for a long time," she says. On one of their early dates, he took Nomoto to a concert by his favorite singer named Neil—Neil Young. She reciprocated by taking him to a concert by her favorite singer named Neil—Neil Diamond. "Music was a big hurdle," she says.

Of her previous two marriages, both to lawyers, Nomoto says simply that she and her husbands grew apart. Her first marriage began at 23 and lasted six years. Her second marriage began at 33 and lasted two years. She still remains good friends with both of them. "There was no bitterness, no animosity," she says of the divorces.

On her fortieth birthday Nomoto became an aerobics instructor. She had always been a self-described 'work-out-aholic,' into aerobics and dance and cycling. A student in one of her law classes told her about the certification exam and suggested Nomoto take it.

"I thought to myself 'That's ridiculous,'but then I thought 'I'm 40 years old. I'm going to do it.'" She's been doing it ever since.

may be as broad as all HO literate people with an interest in current events *(Time)* or as narrow as gauge model railroad enthusiasts. This article comes from *Face* magazine. (In journalistic jargon, this is a "popular" magazine, that is, one intended for a segment of the general public rather than for specialists in a particular field, such as physicians or mining engineers.) *Face* targets a female Asian American audience by publishing articles about successful Asian American women. The magazine costs $5.95 per issue and boasts a colorful, glossy cover. This edition's cover portrays a Chinese Canadian woman wearing a $700 hat from Neiman Marcus, a high-priced department store. Ninety-five percent of the advertisements are for jewelry or makeup.

The writer of "Spandex Judge," Kent Kirkpatrick, wrote several articles for this issue, including one titled "The Road to Stardom" about a young Chinese Hollywood star who, even though she's rich and famous, would still like to lose twelve pounds and find a man, and another one titled "Lingerie Leader" (that title speaks for itself).

Reading the Rhetoric

"Spandex Judge" is written to an entirely female audience. As you read, think about the assumptions it makes about women's interests. Why would this article seem out of place in a legal review or a news magazine? Like all the articles in this magazine this article gives physical details about its subject's height and weight, and mentions marital status and salary. Look for passages that seem to be written strictly for women readers. What is it about the language or subject matter of those passages that makes you think they're designed to appeal to women? What assumptions do they make about the interests and values of the intended audience? Are there any passages that seem to be written to appeal to male readers? If so, what role do you think these passages play in a women's fashion magazine?

Reading the Conversation

This article introduces popular culture as a force that shapes one's identity. Magazines, television, movies, popular music, and advertising all play a role in constructing who we think we are and should be, but popular culture is only one of many such influences. Family, peer, religious, regional, and academic communities also shape our concepts of self. These influences occur to a large extent in language, whether spoken, written, recited, or sung. This reading, and many of those that follow, discuss and exemplify the relationships among language, community, and individual, and are intended to encourage you to think about the communities and languages that shape your understanding of who you are.

FOLLOW-UP ACTIVITIES

These activities should be used after you have read the article "Spandex Judge."

Discussing the Rhetoric

1. What images do the opening lines elicit? Why do you think Kirkpatrick started the article this way? What does he gain by the illusion he creates?

2. What direct quotes does Kirkpatrick include from Judge Nomoto? If you knew nothing else about her, what opinion would you form by reading these quotations? How does Kirkpatrick's choice of quotes affect the entire article? Consider how Kirkpatrick brackets the quotes. How do his comments before and after the quotes shape their meaning?

3. The photographs are an important part of the article. What do the poses in each picture tell you? What aspects of Judge Nomoto's life do you see portrayed in the pictures? What do you not see?

4. Do you agree with Kirkpatrick's statement that Judge Nomoto is "breaking all the stereotypes"? In your opinion, which stereotypes does she break? Which ones, if any, does she further?

5. How many times throughout the essay does Kirkpatrick portray Nomoto as a sexual being? As a professional? What inferences can you draw from this information about Kirkpatrick's audience?

6. What does Kirkpatrick gain by giving actual dollar amounts throughout the article?

Discussing the Conversation

1. Much discussion has occurred in feminist discourse communities about the myth of the American "superwoman." (One variation of the myth claims that women who enter areas previously reserved for men are expected to excel in their new responsibilities while continuing to perform all of their previous responsibilities.) Does this article reinforce or dispel that myth? In answering this question consider whether the representation of Judge Nomoto as a successful woman depends upon (a) wealth, (b) political success, (c) beauty, (d) physical prowess, (e) sex appeal, (f) the ability to stay balanced and even-tempered, (g) obedience to her parents, (h) scholarship, (i) all of the above. Do you think this magazine condones or critiques the myth that successful women can do and be *all?* Would you consider Judge Nomoto to be a feminist? Why or why not?

2. Do you think the editors of *Face* magazine would have published this article if it had emphasized Judge Nomoto's judicial work rather than her personal life? Can you think of other examples where editorial decisions influenced a writer's choice of topic, tone, and content?

Joining the Conversation

1. You are a freelance writer assigned to profile Sidney Huffington, a female astronaut (fictitious). From your interview with Ms. Huffington, you learn that:

- She has a Ph.D. in astrophysics from MIT.
- She has been an accomplished scientist for 20 years.
- She just received a $500 thousand extension on her NSF grant to continue her research another year.
- She's a belly dancer.
- She has published 20 articles in research journals.
- She has a resting heart rate of 35 beats per minute.
- She graduated with her M.A. at the age of 20 and her Ph.D. at 23.
- She is fluent in German and Swedish.
- She is 5'1" and weighs 102 pounds.
- She is married and has 4 children.

Write a three-paragraph article about Ms. Huffington for either *Cosmopolitan* (a woman's magazine that emphasizes the sensual side of professional women) or *Discover* (a magazine for educated adults interested in new scientific pursuits and theories). Tailor your writing to interest your target audience. Then add a separate paragraph in which you discuss the rhetorical choices you made. In what order did you put your information? What details did you emphasize? Downplay? Omit? Why?

2. Examine three popular magazines that target different audiences. You may, for instance, choose *Rolling Stone, Cosmopolitan,* and *Newsweek.* Compare them on the basis of the following characteristics—vocabulary, advertised products, layout (use of photographs, charts, headlines). What do these features tell you concerning the publisher's assumptions about their intended audience? If you were to think of this audience as a discourse community, how would you describe the community?

INTRODUCTORY COMMENTS ON "DE-CONSTRUCTIVE CRITICISM" BY ELIZABETH CODY NEWENHUYSE

Reading the Context

The following article comes from *Today's Christian Woman,* a semi-monthly publication giving advice for Christian women from young-adulthood through middle age. Though it covers many of the issues you would find in any magazine targeting homemakers, like *The Ladies' Home Journal* and *Good Housekeeping,* it considers the issues from a religious angle. This issue offers Christian solutions to problems ranging from how to be a good mother-in-law to bearing a child conceived in rape. This article is written by one of the magazine's regular staff members.

Like most popular magazines, *Today's Christian Woman* depends on advertising for funding. Among the advertisers in this magazine are companies offering advice—through books or videotapes—for life problems, such as making marriage work or raising children. Advertisements for novels and picture books with a Christian message appear frequently as well.

Reading the Rhetoric

You might be surprised to find an article written for a fundamentalist Christian women's magazine among the first readings in a college composition anthology. We include this article for several reasons. One purpose of Part One, "Conversations About Identities," is to become aware of the diverse communities from which students enter the university, but our aim is not simply to acknowledge diversity, though that is important. You will learn that each community has ways of using language that differ from other communities, and that ways of using language outside the college or university differ from inside uses. We will refer to communities that have their own ways of talking (or writing) as "discourse communities."

"Discourse" is an academic word that is defined somewhat differently by different users. We define it here as the language used by a group of people, or community, when they speak among themselves about the subject that draws them together. (See Part Five, Appendix: "A Glossary of Rhetorical Terms for Readers and Writers," for a more detailed discussion.) Individuals are capable of relating to others through an infinite variety of discourses, though each discourse can only be learned by participating in the community that uses it. For instance, the same people who, as members of a fundamentalist Christian community, employ one set of terms, concepts, and linguistic patterns when talking to each other, might use language entirely differently when conversing at the office.

This article uses two terms that have great currency in the academic discourse community as well as in the religious. The terms are "criticism" and "de-constructive criticism," and the two communities use them with entirely different meanings. In this article, these terms are viewed negatively, but when you get to the readings in Part Two, "Conversations About Knowledge," you will find that "criticism" is a concept valued highly in research and scholarship.

One of the most perplexing aspects of academic discourse is that it frequently uses common words with meanings unique to the academic community or to a particular discipline within it. While this article uses the term "criticism" as it is commonly used, you will become acquainted with its academic meanings when you read articles by Brian Magee, Kathryn Pyne Addelson, and others in Part Two. The point of contrasting these uses is not to argue that one is right and another wrong, but to make you aware that specialized academic meanings and values can be different from and even at odds with common, popular meanings.

Consequently, it is important to read textual clues closely to figure out what a word denotes in a particular reading. In such cases, dictionaries may not be much help.

Reading the Conversation

At least two issues link this reading to others in the anthology. First, like "Spandex Judge," this article constructs an image of "womanhood." As you read this article, think about how the values connected to womanhood differ from or affirm those in the first article. You will read two more articles by women in this section, bell hooks' "Keeping Close to Home" and Mary Louise Pratt's "Arts of the Contact Zone." They too deal in part with constructions of womanhood. Think about where the various values attached to "womanhood" originate. Possible sources include movies, television, advertising, religious values, economic circumstances, family values, ethnic cultures—then consider how the communities you participate in shape your concept of "ideal" womanhood.

Second, as mentioned previously, the term "criticism" carries differing meanings in common language and academic discourse. After you read this article, begin to explore this concept on two levels. One *is* the level of the term itself—consider in what ways and why "criticism" is valued differently in various discourse communities. The second level is larger—consider how and why the same words come to have such different meanings and values.

De-Constructive Criticism
*Elizabeth Cody Newenhuyse**

1 Have you ever listened to yourself think? I have—and it's not always pretty.

2 For example, a few weeks ago, I had coffee with a woman I hadn't seen for quite awhile. As we caught up on each other's life, she complained about how busy she was with business travel, church meetings, a house renovation, and a new work project.

3 "Oh, I know," I responded sympathetically. "Life gets hectic sometimes, doesn't it?" But privately, I was thinking, *Why are you complaining about being so busy when you obviously enjoy it? After all, if you didn't, you could just say no to some of these things.*

4   My reaction caught me off-guard. But there it was: the nasty little imp of a critical spirit, worming its way out.

5   I like to think of myself as an encouraging person. I try to tame my tongue and let no "unwholesome talk" (Eph. 4:29) come out of my mouth. Taming my thoughts, however, is a lot more challenging.

6   Maybe you struggle with this, too. For example, do you ever catch yourself looking at a woman on the street and wondering why in the world she would ever wear those shorts? If a neighbor shares her worries about money with you, do you secretly judge her spending habits because you've noticed she's driving a late-model minivan?

7   It's easy to rationalize this behavior: *No one knows what I'm thinking. There's no harm done.* But as I read the Bible, statements such as "All a man's ways seem right to him, but the Lord weighs the heart" (Prov. 21:2) make me squirm. It reminds me that God sees deep inside us. He turns a searching light on our thoughts and feelings (Ps. 139), and He wants our *inside* to be as pure as our *outside.*

8   There are times, too, when our critical thoughts can spill into our speech. Several years ago, I spoke at a women's retreat. Over breakfast, the talk turned to a well-known Christian personality. A couple of the women made disparaging remarks about this individual. I defended the person, but I couldn't resist a half-funny, half-critical comment of my own. Then I remembered Jesus' words: "Do not judge, or you too will be judged. For in the same way you judge others, you will be judged, and with the measure you use, it will be measured to you" (Matt. 7:1,2)—and I was ashamed.

9   I have this one kitchen cabinet that's a jumbled, hopeless catchall. No one knows about it except members of the immediate family. The rest of my kitchen is tidy. Counter tops and table are kept clutter-free; dirty dishes are immediately stowed in the dishwasher. Outwardly, the kitchen looks clean—but there's a hidden messy place.

10   That's what a critical spirit is: a hidden messy place in our Christian life. The difference is, my disorganized cabinet doesn't hurt anyone. A critical spirit hurts me, hampers my Christian walk—and may end up hurting others as well. I can keep my kitchen mess out of sight—but I can't hide my attitudes forever. If we're not alert to this tendency to be critical, that nasty little imp can take up permanent residence in our soul. Rea32cting critically to others can become an unthinking reflex, a pattern we can become trapped by without even realizing it. Eventually, this pattern will affect our relationships with others.

11   How do we root out a critical spirit? First, we have to recognize where these attitudes come from, what person or situation triggers critical thoughts and speech. Then, equipped with this understanding, we can move toward true wholeness in Christ. In my experience and that of other women I've talked to, a critical spirit has several sources:

12   **We see something in others that hits too close to home.** "The things we criticize in others tend to be the things we criticize in ourselves," my friend Anne observed. "My daughter has a friend I'm critical of, and for the

longest time I couldn't figure out why. She's only ten, and she's not a bad kid. But then I realized this little girl reminds me of my worst traits as a kid—kind of whiny and hypochondriacal. I look at her and want to say, 'Snap out of it!'"

13   Anne's right. When I analyzed why I reacted critically to my friend's recitation of busyness, I realized it's because sometimes I do the same thing when I'm trying to impress others—and I don't like that in myself.

14   **We tear down others in order to build ourselves up.** Many of us tend to be more critical of others when our own self-esteem is low. "When things are going well for me, I can overlook a multitude of sins," Anne said. "When they're not going well, I fixate on negatives in other people." I've noticed that when I'm busy and contented, or have a decent haircut, or feel good about myself as a mother, I'm more inclined to think and act charitably toward others.

15   **We learned it in childhood.** Like so many other psychological patterns, a critical spirit may stem from our own upbringing—lessons our parents unwittingly taught us. If you often overheard your father criticizing his boss or your mother speaking disparagingly of a relative, you may have grown up mimicking his or her behavior without even realizing it. Or perhaps you absorbed your parents' negative attitudes just by being around them. A wise friend of mine, the mother of grown children, recently told me that she's concluded we don't even have to say anything to our children for them to know what we're feeling: "They're so attuned to us, they just pick it up."

16   **We're dealing with a difficult relationship.** Sometimes, there's one person who brings out the worst in us. It could be a particular friend, coworker, sister, or mother-in-law with whom we have a prickly relationship— anyone whom, as my friend Linda put it, "we perceive *has* hurt us or *could* hurt us in some way." Because we're so preoccupied with our own feelings, we may not be aware that we're hurting that person, too.

17   **We're too quick to judge.** A critical spirit is closely related to a judgmental spirit. Do you ever think something like, *If she were really walking with the Lord, she would . . .*

18   I confess my own shortcomings in this area. Sometimes, when I see someone who looks sloppy, I'll inwardly criticize that person for not taking better care of her appearance. But how do I know what her circumstances might be? Maybe she can't afford to dress well, or she was up all night with sick children, or she's rushed for time, or in an emergency situation. We have to be careful not to rush to condemn when we don't know the particulars of someone's life.

GETTING RID OF THE GRINCH

19 If you're struggling to overcome a critical spirit, there's hope. I've come a long way in my efforts to be a little more charitable, a little more compassionate, a little more merciful. I still have lapses but I've recognized the pattern in myself and I'm working at it. Changing a deeply ingrained behavior

pattern is a hard, step-by-step process, but God, who loves us and wants us to live out that love, is with us through every step. Here's how to begin.

20   **Listen to yourself think.** Over a period of several weeks, try to be alert to your responses to various situations. Do you tend to be more negative when you're feeling fatigued or overworked, or even at certain points in your hormonal cycle? Are there other stressors you're dealing with? It's important to realize that you may be more vulnerable to this behavior at certain times than at others. On the other hand, it may simply be a habit you've fallen into.

21   Kathy, who is very active in her church, shared how she has dealt with this habit: "There have been times when I'll come away from a meeting fuming. I'll think, *How could this person, as a caring Christian, come to that conclusion?* Then I realize I'm being overly critical. What has helped me is to remind myself that we're both working toward the same goal—ministering to people. We just have different ways of approaching it."

22   **Mentally substitute a "sweet" for a "sour."** The other day, a rather shabbily dressed young woman walked by our house while I was working in the yard. I literally thought to myself *Be kind.* I smiled and said hello, and noticed that she gave me a beautiful smile in return. It just lit up her face. It was a small but significant encounter, because it represented a victory over my old negative pattern of judging people by external appearances.

23   When you're tempted to think or act critically, stop and consciously substitute a positive response. Smile at someone. Pay a compliment. It may seem artificial at first, but after awhile, it will become a habit, and a God-honoring habit at that.

24   **Identify your "sore spot" and work to heal it.** One of the things you may discover is an underlying issue that releases that critical imp. For me, it's competitiveness. I'm more likely to be inwardly negative toward someone who seems to be achieving a goal I've been working to attain. Here's a verse that has helped me in this area: "Each one should test his own actions. Then he can take pride in himself, without comparing himself to somebody else" (Gal. 6:4).

25   If a difficult relationship triggers your critical attitude, ask God for discernment in dealing with this person. If there's a need for forgiveness and reconciliation, you may want to seek guidance from your pastor as to how to begin the process.

26   **Admit your struggle to a person you trust.** Barb, a dear friend from church, and I have covenanted to be prayer partners. We meet weekly over the noon hour, and this issue is one of the things I've asked her to pray about on my behalf. There's something very comforting about knowing that one trusted fellow believer is acting as your spiritual cheerleader, encouraging and championing your efforts to change. And you, in turn, can serve as *her* cheerleader.

27   **Cultivate humility—and humor.** One mom of three I talked to about this issue said laughingly, "How can I be critical of anyone else when I'm so critical of myself?" Well, some of us manage to do both. But it's a

good reminder. When I was tempted to judge the shabbily dressed woman who passed by, all I had to do was look at myself in jeans and no makeup, hair frizzing from humidity, and think, *Since when are YOU the fashion expert?* Nobody's perfect—so when you're tempted to be critical of another, sometimes, the healthiest thing you can do is laugh about your own imperfections.

28   **Trust God to do His work in you.** Start by delving into His Word and perhaps doing a serious study of passages relevant to this issue. Here are just a few: Psalm 51; 1 Corinthians 13; Galatians 5:22-23; and much of 1 John. Read these Scriptures in an attitude of prayerful openness to what the Holy Spirit is saying; commit a few to memory.

29   Then pray, and pray some more! If a sibling or in-law brings out that critical imp in you, pray before a family gathering for an affirming spirit. If you struggle in a work setting, pray before a meeting. When you fail, confess it to God. But also note your victories, times when you *could* have been critical but were charitable instead. Share those with God too—and thank Him for working in you, helping you truly begin to walk in His light.

NOTE

*Elizabeth Cody Newenhuyse is a TCW contributing editor and author of *Am I the Only Crazy Mom on This Planet?* (Zondervan).

FOLLOW-UP ACTIVITIES

Discussing the Rhetoric

1. How would you describe the audience Newenhuyse seems to have in mind for this article?

2. What is Newenhuyse's purpose?

3. Often writers convince their audiences by citing authorities who are valued and respected in their discourse communities. Rhetoricians refer to the authorities valued in a certain community or by a particular writer as "privileged"—another one of those terms used with a twist in the academic community. What authorities does Newenhuyse privilege? Why do you think they would be effective given her audience?

4. What other kinds of evidence, besides citing authority, does Newenhuyse use to support her argument? [See "Appendix: Rhetorical Terms for Readers and Writers" for more information about kinds of evidence.] Why would these kinds of evidence be effective with her audience? Do you think they would be convincing in an academic setting? Why or why not?

5. If you are not a Christian, what words and phrases in this article were unfamiliar? Or, as a Christian, what phrases do you recognize as familiar? In what ways does the language make you feel included or excluded?

Discussing the Conversation

1. What authorities, both texts and persons, are most highly valued in religious settings? How does this differ in secular academic settings? For example, whom do you expect to be cited as authorities, and what kinds of evidence do you expect to be valued in a science or social science class?

2. Do you think the expectations set for women in "Spandex Judge" and "Deconstructive Criticism" are advantageous or disadvantageous for female students?

3. What words and phrases does Newenhuyse use to indicate that, to her, "criticism" is a term with severely negative connotations? What positive uses of criticism can you think of? In which discourse communities do they operate? What are the interests and goals of the people in those communities? How do those interests or goals affect their attitude toward the meaning and use of the term "criticism"?

Joining the Conversation

1. Write an informal paper in which you consider your own religious beliefs in relation to the university. Have you found in the past that your religious beliefs conflicted with what you were taught in school? How did you handle the conflict? How do you expect to handle it if this happens in the university?

2. Did you go to a high school in which a single religious or ethnic group was clearly dominant? If so, were you a member of the dominant group or the minority? Write an informal paper in which you describe the role of language in including or excluding you from the group.

3. If you are in any classes that allow discussion, take notes on the following questions, and write an informal paper about your observations.

Do men or women usually talk more in class? (Don't rely on intuition for this. Count the male and female turns for a couple of class periods.)

Do men or women talk for longer periods of time? (Time discussion turns for 15 minutes or so.)

Do men or women interrupt more?

You might conclude by relating your findings about what characteristics constitute the "ideal" woman and man, and considering whether the "ideal" works to the advantage or disadvantage of individual men and women.

4. Write an informal paper in which you discuss the sources of values: Are people born with a sense of values? Do they learn them from their surroundings? What aspects of their surroundings are most important in shaping their values?

INTRODUCTORY COMMENTS ON "LIBERAL EDUCATION" BY ALLAN BLOOM

Reading the Context

The next articles in this part are about students and their uneasy relationship to an academic environment. Most are written by professors about their own lives as students or about the students in their classrooms. In this article, Bloom describes a typical student and outlines the kind of education he thinks will benefit him most.

To understand Bloom's perspective, you need to know a little about the controversial history of American education. Up until 1876, when Johns Hopkins University was established, there were no research universities in the United States. Before then the most prestigious higher education was provided by private liberal arts colleges whose curriculum was "classical" in the strictest sense: it consisted of studies of Greek and Latin, classical history and literature, mathematics, theology, and rhetoric. Classes were even taught in Latin. Only after the Civil War did English become the common language of higher education.

The almost revolutionary changes from a classical curriculum to the modern curriculum in the sciences, social sciences, and professional areas (engineering, nursing, education, agriculture, etc.) during the latter half of the nineteenth century demonstrate that the college curriculum is not static. Though the changes since 1900 have not been as dramatic as those in the nineteenth century, they have nonetheless been controversial. Allan Bloom is one of the critics of modern education's tendency to focus on ever-more specialized professional programs rather than on a broader, "liberal" education more akin to the unified curriculum of classical nineteenth-century colleges.

This reading is a chapter from Bloom's controversial best-selling book *The Closing of the American Mind: How Higher Education Has Failed Democracy and Impoverished the Souls of Today's Students* published in 1987. We include it here because it represents one perspective of the continuing conversation within the broad community of college graduates, professors, and students about the relationship of students' cultures and backgrounds to the curriculum. Each of the succeeding articles in Part One provides a different, though not necessarily diametrically opposed, view of these issues. Like Bloom's original readers, you may find yourself avidly supporting or strongly contesting Bloom's opinions.

Bloom (1930–1992) received his bachelor's, master's, and doctorate degrees from the University of Chicago. He edited and translated several works, including *Politics and the Arts: Letters to M. D'Alembert on the Theatre* by Jean-Jacques Rouseau (1960) and *The Republic of Plato* (1968) in addition to writing *The Closing of the American Mind.*

Reading the Rhetoric

As you read this chapter, consider the author and his audience. What social class do you think Bloom comes from? Are his intended readers from the same class? Do you think you are part of the audience Bloom had in mind when he wrote this? Look for linguistic features that Bloom uses to include or exclude various groups from his readership. Be especially watchful for his use of irony.

Reading the Conversation

As you read other selections in Part One, you will see that this conversation about the relationship of students to the curriculum of higher education has attracted a wide variety of participants. These writers are trying to answer the same questions in different ways: "Which students 'belong' in college?" "Should there be a standard liberal education curriculum for all students?" "To what extent should the liberal education curriculum be focused on Western European traditions?" Sometimes these other writers name Bloom specifically; sometimes their responses are less direct. After reading several selections in this part, you will be familiar enough with the issues to become an informed participant yourself.

Liberal Education
Allan Bloom

1 What image does a first-rank college or university present today to a teenager leaving home for the first time, off to the adventure of a liberal education? He has four years of freedom to discover himself—a space between the intellectual wasteland he has left behind and the inevitable dreary professional training that awaits him after the baccalaureate. In this short time he must learn that there is a great world beyond the little one he knows, experience the exhilaration of it and digest enough of it to sustain himself in the intellectual deserts he is destined to traverse. He must do this, that is, if he is to have any hope of a higher life. These are the charmed years when he can,

if he so chooses, become anything he wishes and when he has the opportunity to survey his alternatives, not merely those current in his time or provided by careers, but those available to him as a human being. The importance of these years for an American cannot be overestimated. They are civilization's only chance to get to him.

2   In looking at him we are forced to reflect on what he should learn if he is to be called educated; we must speculate on what the human potential to be fulfilled is. In the specialties we can avoid such speculation, and the avoidance of them is one of specialization's charms. But here it is a simple duty. What are we to teach this person? The answer may not be evident, but to attempt to answer the question is already to philosophize and to begin to educate. Such a concern in itself poses the question of the unity of man and the unity of the sciences. It is childishness to say, as some do, that everyone must be allowed to develop freely, that it is authoritarian to impose a point of view on the student. In that case, why have a university? If the response is "to provide an atmosphere for learning," we come back to our original questions at the second remove. Which atmosphere? Choices and reflection on the reasons for those choices are unavoidable. The university has to stand for something. The practical effects of unwillingness to think positively about the contents of a liberal education are, on the one hand, to ensure that all the vulgarities of the world outside the university will flourish within it, and, on the other, to impose a much harsher and more illiberal necessity on the student—the one given by the imperial and imperious demands of the specialized disciplines unfiltered by unifying thought.

3   The university now offers no distinctive visage to the young person. He finds a democracy of the disciplines—which are there either because they are autochthonous or because they wandered in recently to perform some job that was demanded of the university. This democracy is really an anarchy, because there are no recognized rules for citizenship and no legitimate titles to rule. In short there is no vision, nor is there a set of competing visions, of what an educated human being is. The question has disappeared, for to pose it would be a threat to the peace. There is no organization of the sciences, no tree of knowledge. Out of chaos emerges dispiritedness, because it is impossible to make a reasonable choice. Better to give up on liberal education and get on with a specialty in which there is at least a prescribed curriculum and a prospective career. On the way the student can pick up in elective courses a little of whatever is thought to make one cultured. The student gets no intimation that great mysteries might be revealed to him, that new and higher motives of action might be discovered within him, that a different and more human way of life can be harmoniously constructed by what he is going to learn.

4   Simply, the university is not distinctive. Equality for us seems to culminate in the unwillingness and incapacity to make claims of superiority, particularly in the domains in which such claims have always been made— art, religion and philosophy. When Weber found that he could not choose

between certain high opposites—reason vs. revelation, Buddha vs. Jesus—he did not conclude that all things are equally good, that the distinction between high and low disappears. As a matter of fact he intended to revitalize the consideration of these great alternatives in showing the gravity and danger involved in choosing among them; they were to be heightened in contrast to the trivial considerations of modern life that threatened to overgrow and render indistinguishable the profound problems the confrontation with which makes the bow of the soul taut. The serious intellectual life was for him the battleground of the great decisions, all of which are spiritual or "value" choices. One can no longer present this or that particular view of the educated or civilized man as authoritative; therefore one must say that education consists in knowing, really knowing, the small number of such views in their integrity. This distinction between profound and superficial—which takes the place of good and bad, true and false—provided a focus for serious study, but it hardly held out against the naturally relaxed democratic tendency to say, "Oh, what's the use?" The first university disruptions at Berkeley were explicitly directed against the multiversity smorgasbord and, I must confess, momentarily and partially engaged my sympathies. It may have even been the case that there was some small element of longing for an education in the motivation of those students. But nothing was done to guide or inform their energy, and the result was merely to add multilife-styles to multidisciplines, the diversity of perversity to the diversity of specialization. What we see so often happening in general happened here too; the insistent demand for greater community ended in greater isolation. Old agreements, old habits, old traditions were not so easily replaced.

5   Thus, when a student arrives at the university, he finds a bewildering variety of departments and a bewildering variety of courses. And there is no official guidance, no university-wide agreement, about what he *should* study. Nor does he usually find readily available examples, either among students or professors, of a unified use of the university's resources. It is easiest simply to make a career choice and go about getting prepared for that career. The programs designed for those having made such a choice render their students immune to charms that might lead them out of the conventionally respectable. The sirens sing *sotto voce* these days, and the young already have enough wax in their ears to pass them by without danger. These specialties can provide enough courses to take up most of their time for four years in preparation for the inevitable graduate study. With the few remaining courses they can do what they please, taking a bit of this and a bit of that. No public career these days—not doctor nor lawyer nor politician nor journalist nor businessman nor entertainer—has much to do with humane learning. An education, other than purely professional or technical, can even seem to be an impediment. That is why a countervailing atmosphere in the university would be necessary for the students to gain a taste for intellectual pleasures and learn that they are viable.

6   The real problem is those students who come hoping to find out what career they want to have, or are simply looking for an adventure with themselves. There are plenty of things for them to do—courses and disciplines enough to spend many a lifetime on. Each department or great division of the university makes a pitch for itself, and each offers a course of study that will make the student an initiate. But how to choose among them? How do they relate to one another? The fact is they do not address one another. They are competing and contradictory, without being aware of it. The problem of the whole is urgently indicated by the very existence of the specialties, but it is never systematically posed. The net effect of the student's encounter with the college catalogue is bewilderment and very often demoralization. It is just a matter of chance whether he finds one or two professors who can give him an insight into one of the great visions of education that have been the distinguishing part of every civilized nation. Most professors are specialists, concerned only with their own fields, interested in the advancement of those fields in their own terms, or in their own personal advancement in a world where all the rewards are on the side of professional distinction. They have been entirely emancipated from the old structure of the university, which at least helped to indicate that they are incomplete, only parts of an unexamined and undiscovered whole. So the student must navigate among a collection of carnival barkers, each trying to lure him into a particular sideshow. This undecided student is an embarrassment to most universities, because he seems to be saying, "I am a whole human being. Help me to form myself in my wholeness and let me develop my real potential," and he is the one to whom they have nothing to say.

7   Cornell was, as in so many other things, in advance of its time on this issue. The six-year Ph.D. program, richly supported by the Ford Foundation, was directed specifically to high school students who had already made "a firm career choice" and was intended to rush them through to the start of those careers. A sop was given to desolate humanists in the form of money to fund seminars that these young careerists could take on their way through the College of Arts and Sciences. For the rest, the educators could devote their energies to arranging and packaging the program without having to provide it with any substance. That kept them busy enough to avoid thinking about the nothingness of their endeavor. This has been the preferred mode of not looking the Beast in the Jungle in the face—structure, not content. The Cornell plan for dealing with the problem of liberal education was to suppress the students' longing for liberal education by encouraging their professionalism and their avarice, providing money and all the prestige the university had available to make careerism the centerpiece of the university.

8   The Cornell plan dared not state the radical truth, a well-kept secret: the colleges do not have enough to teach their students, not enough to justify keeping them four years, probably not even three years. If the focus is careers, there is hardly one specialty, outside the hardest of the hard natural sciences,

which requires more than two years of preparatory training prior to graduate studies. The rest is just wasted time, or a period of ripening until the students are old enough for graduate studies. For many graduate careers, even less is really necessary. It is amazing how many undergraduates are poking around for courses to take, without any plan or question to ask, just filling up their college years. In fact, with rare exceptions, the courses are parts of specialties and not designed for general cultivation, or to investigate questions important for human beings as such. The so-called knowledge explosion and increasing specialization have not filled up the college years but emptied them. Those years are impediments; one wants to get beyond them. And in general the persons one finds in the professions need not have gone to college, if one is to judge by their tastes, their fund of learning or their interests. They might as well have spent their college years in the Peace Corps or the like. These great universities—which can split the atom, find cures for the most terrible diseases, conduct surveys of whole populations and produce massive dictionaries of lost languages—cannot generate a modest program of general education for undergraduate students. This is a parable for our times.

9   There are attempts to fill the vacuum painlessly with various kinds of fancy packaging of what is already there—study abroad options, individualized majors, etc. Then there are Black Studies and Women's or Gender Studies, along with Learn Another Culture. Peace Studies are on their way to a similar prevalence. All this is designed to show that the university is with it and has something in addition to its traditional specialties. The latest item is computer literacy, the full cheapness of which is evident only to those who think a bit about what literacy might mean. It would make some sense to promote literacy literacy, inasmuch as most high school graduates nowadays have difficulty reading and writing. And some institutions are quietly undertaking this worthwhile task. But they do not trumpet the fact, because this is merely a high school function that our current sad state of educational affairs has thrust upon them, about which they are not inclined to boast.

10   Now that the distractions of the sixties are over, and undergraduate education has become more important again (because the graduate departments, aside from the professional schools, are in trouble due to the shortage of academic jobs), university officials have had somehow to deal with the undeniable fact that the students who enter are uncivilized, and that the universities have some responsibility for civilizing them. If one were to give a base interpretation of the schools' motives, one could allege that their concern stems from shame and self-interest. It is becoming all too evident that liberal education—which is what the small band of prestigious institutions are supposed to provide, in contrast to the big state schools, which are thought simply to prepare specialists to meet the practical demands of a complex society—has no content, that a certain kind of fraud is being perpetrated. For a time the great moral consciousness alleged to have been fostered in students by the great universities, especially their vocation as gladiators who fight war and racism, seemed to fulfill the demands of the collective

university conscience. They were doing something other than offering preliminary training for doctors and lawyers. Concern and compassion were thought to be the indefinable X that pervaded all the parts of the Arts and Sciences campus. But when that evanescent mist dissipated during the seventies, and the faculties found themselves face to face with ill-educated young people with no intellectual tastes—unaware that there even are such things, obsessed with getting on with their careers before having looked at life—and the universities offered no counterpoise, no alternative goals, a reaction set in.

11   Liberal education—since it has for so long been ill-defined, has none of the crisp clarity or institutionalized prestige of the professions, but nevertheless perseveres and has money and respectability connected with it—has always been a battleground for those who are somewhat eccentric in relation to the specialties. It is in something like the condition of churches as opposed to, say, hospitals. Nobody is quite certain of what the religious institutions are supposed to do anymore, but they do have some kind of role either responding to a real human need or as the vestige of what was once a need, and they invite the exploitation of quacks, adventurers, cranks and fanatics. But they also solicit the warmest and most valiant efforts of persons of peculiar gravity and depth. In liberal education, too, the worst and the best fight it out, fakers vs. authentics, sophists vs. philosophers, for the favor of public opinion and for control over the study of man in our times. The most conspicuous participants in the struggle are administrators who are formally responsible for presenting some kind of public image of the education their colleges offer, persons with a political agenda or vulgarizers of what the specialties know, and real teachers of the humane disciplines who actually see their relation to the whole and urgently wish to preserve the awareness of it in their students' consciousness.

12   So, just as in the sixties universities were devoted to removing requirements, in the eighties they are busy with attempts to put them back in, a much more difficult task. The word of the day is "core." It is generally agreed that "we went a bit far in the sixties," and that a little fine-tuning has now become clearly necessary.

13   There are two typical responses to the problem. The easiest and most administratively satisfying solution is to make use of what is already there in the autonomous departments and simply force the students to cover the fields, i.e., take one or more courses in each of the general divisions of the university: natural science, social science and the humanities. The reigning ideology here is *breadth,* as was *openness* in the age of laxity. The courses are almost always the already existing introductory courses, which are of least interest to the major professors and merely assume the worth and reality of that which is to be studied. It is general education, in the sense in which a jack-of-all-trades is a generalist. He knows a bit of everything and is inferior to the specialist in each area. Students may wish to sample a variety of fields, and it may be good to encourage them to look around and see if

there is something that attracts them in one of which they have no experience. But this is not a liberal education and does not satisfy any longing they have for one. It just teaches that there is no high-level generalism, and that what they are doing is preliminary to the real stuff and part of the childhood they are leaving behind. Thus they desire to get it over with and get on with what their professors do seriously. Without recognition of important questions of common concern, there cannot be serious liberal education, and attempts to establish it will be but failed gestures.

14   It is a more or less precise awareness of the inadequacy of this approach to core curricula that motivates the second approach, which consists of what one might call composite courses. These are constructions developed especially for general-education purposes and usually require collaboration of professors drawn from several departments. These courses have titles like "Man in Nature," "War and Moral Responsibility," "The Arts and Creativity," "Culture and the Individual." Everything, of course, depends upon who plans them and who teaches them. They have the clear advantage of requiring some reflection on the general needs of students and force specialized professors to broaden their perspectives, at least for a moment. The dangers are trendiness, mere popularization and lack of substantive rigor. In general, the natural scientists do not collaborate in such endeavors, and hence these courses tend to be unbalanced. In short, they do not point beyond themselves and do not provide the student with independent means to pursue permanent questions independently, as, for example, the study of Aristotle or Kant as wholes once did. They tend to be bits of this and that. Liberal education should give the student the sense that learning must and can be both synoptic and precise. For this, a very small, detailed problem can be the best way, if it is framed so as to open out on the whole. Unless the course has the specific intention to lead to the permanent questions, to make the student aware of them and give him some competence in the important works that treat of them, it tends to be a pleasant diversion and a dead end—because it has nothing to do with any program of further study he can imagine. If such programs engage the best energies of the best people in the university, they can be beneficial and provide some of the missing intellectual excitement for both professors and students. But they rarely do, and they are too cut off from the top, from what the various faculties see as their real business. Where the power is determines the life of the whole body. And the intellectual problems unresolved at the top cannot be resolved administratively below. The problem is the lack of any unity of the sciences and the loss of the will or the means even to discuss the issue. The illness above is the cause of the illness below, to which all the good-willed efforts of honest liberal educationists can at best be palliatives.

15   Of course, the only serious solution is the one that is almost universally rejected: the good old Great Books approach, in which a liberal education means reading certain generally recognized classic texts, just reading them, letting them dictate what the questions are and the method of approaching

them—not forcing them into categories we make up, not treating them as historical products, but trying to read them as their authors wished them to be read. I am perfectly well aware of, and actually agree with, the objections to the Great Books cult. It is amateurish; it encourages an autodidact's self-assurance without competence; one cannot read all of the Great Books carefully; if one only reads Great Books, one can never know what a great, as opposed to an ordinary, book is; there is no way of determining who is to decide what a Great Book or what the canon is; books are made the ends and not the means; the whole movement has a certain coarse evangelistic tone that is the opposite of good taste; it engenders a spurious intimacy with greatness; and so forth. But one thing is certain: wherever the Great Books make up a central part of the curriculum, the students are excited and satisfied, feel they are doing something that is independent and fulfilling, getting something from the university they cannot get elsewhere. The very fact of this special experience, which leads nowhere beyond itself, provides them with a new alternative and a respect for study itself. The advantage they get is an awareness of the classic—particularly important for our innocents; an acquaintance with what big questions were when there were still big questions; models, at the very least, of how to go about answering them; and, perhaps most important of all, a fund of shared experiences and thoughts on which to ground their friendships with one another. Programs based upon judicious use of great texts provide the royal road to students' hearts. Their gratitude at learning of Achilles or the categorical imperative is boundless. Alexandre Koyré, the late historian of science, told me that his appreciation for America was great when—in the first course he taught at the University of Chicago, in 1940 at the beginning of his exile—a student spoke in his paper of Mr. Aristotle, unaware that he was not a contemporary. Koyré said that only an American could have the naive profundity to take Aristotle as living thought, unthinkable for most scholars. A good program of liberal education feeds the student's love of truth and passion to live a good life. It is the easiest thing in the world to devise courses of study, adapted to the particular conditions of each university, which thrill those who take them. The difficulty is in getting them accepted by the faculty.

16   None of the three great parts of the contemporary university is enthusiastic about the Great Books approach to education. The natural scientists are benevolent toward other fields and toward liberal education, if it does not steal away their students and does not take too much time from their preparatory studies. But they themselves are interested primarily in the solution of the questions now important in their disciplines and are not particularly concerned with discussions of their foundations, inasmuch as they are so evidently successful. They are indifferent to Newton's conception of time or his disputes with Leibniz about calculus; Aristotle's teleology is an absurdity beneath consideration. Scientific progress, they believe, no longer depends on the kind of comprehensive reflection given to the nature of

science by men like Bacon, Descartes, Hume, Kant and Marx. This is merely historical study, and for a long time now, even the greatest scientists have given up thinking about Galileo and Newton. Progress is undoubted. The difficulties about the truth of science raised by positivism, and those about the goodness of science raised by Rousseau and Nietzsche, have not really penetrated to the center of scientific consciousness. Hence, no Great Books, but incremental progress, is the theme for them.

17   Social scientists are in general hostile, because the classic texts tend to deal with the human things the social sciences deal with, and they are very proud of having freed themselves from the shackles of such earlier thought to become truly scientific. And, unlike the natural scientists, they are insecure enough about their achievement to feel threatened by the works of earlier thinkers, perhaps a bit afraid that students will be seduced and fall back into the bad old ways. Moreover, with the possible exception of Weber and Freud, there are no social science books that can be said to be classic. This may be interpreted favorably to the social sciences by comparing them to the natural sciences, which can be said to be a living organism developing by the addition of little cells, a veritable body of knowledge proving itself to be such by the very fact of this almost unconscious growth, with thousands of parts oblivious to the whole, nevertheless contributing to it. This is in opposition to a work of imagination or of philosophy, where a single creator makes and surveys an artificial whole. But whether one interprets the absence of the classic in the social sciences in ways flattering or unflattering to them, the fact causes social scientists discomfort. I remember the professor who taught the introductory graduate courses in social science methodology, a famous historian, responding scornfully and angrily to a question I naively put to him about Thucydides with "Thucydides was a fool!"

18   More difficult to explain is the tepid reaction of humanists to Great Books education, inasmuch as these books now belong almost exclusively to what are called the humanities. One would think that high esteem for the classic would reinforce the spiritual power of the humanities, at a time when their temporal power is at its lowest. And it is true that the most active proponents of liberal education and the study of classic texts are indeed usually humanists. But there is division among them. Some humanities disciplines are just crusty specialties that, although they depend on the status of classic books for their existence, are not really interested in them in their natural state—much philology, for example, is concerned with the languages but not what is said in them—and will and can do nothing to support their own infrastructure. Some humanities disciplines are eager to join the real sciences and transcend their roots in the now overcome mythic past. Some humanists make the legitimate complaints about lack of competence in the teaching and learning of Great Books, although their criticism is frequently undermined by the fact that they are only defending recent scholarly interpretation of the classics rather than a vital, authentic understanding. In their

reaction there is a strong element of specialist's jealousy and narrowness. Finally, a large part of the story is just the general debilitation of the humanities, which is both symptom and cause of our present condition.

19   To repeat, the crisis of liberal education is a reflection of a crisis at the peaks of learning, an incoherence and incompatibility among the first principles with which we interpret the world, an intellectual crisis of the greatest magnitude, which constitutes the crisis of our civilization. But perhaps it would be true to say that the crisis consists not so much in this incoherence but in our incapacity to discuss or even recognize it. Liberal education flourished when it prepared the way for the discussion of a unified view of nature and man's place in it, which the best minds debated on the highest level. It decayed when what lay beyond it were only specialties, the premises of which do not lead to any such vision. The highest is the partial intellect; there is no synopsis.

FOLLOW-UP ACTIVITIES

Discussing the Rhetoric

1. Bloom describes the differences between a student's life before, after, and during his student years in antithetical terms. What are the characteristics of life outside of university, according to Bloom? Inside? How do you respond to this characterization? (Antithesis—the juxtaposition of contrasting ideas—is a common rhetorical device. Look for it in future readings.)

2. The final sentence in the second paragraph provides another antithesis. What two versions of college education are juxtaposed here? Note that throughout the selection Bloom continues to contrast these opposing alternatives.

3. How would you describe the register that Bloom uses in this selection? To help you describe it, you might compare it to the register (refer to the Appendix for a definition of this term) of "Spandex Judge" or "De-Constructive Criticism."

4. Pick one paragraph and examine its sentence structure closely. What schemes and tropes do you find? What do you notice about the length of sentences? The use of coordination and subordination? What is the overall effect of Bloom's sentence structure on you as a reader? What does his sentence structure tell you about his assumptions concerning his audience? (The fourth paragraph is an interesting one to analyze.)

5. How does Bloom convince you that he is an authority on his subject matter? (In rhetorical terms, one would ask, how does Bloom establish a credible ethos in this selection?) Consider style as well as content to answer this question.

6. Bloom uses irony as a rhetorical device in this selection. Identify at least two sentences that are ironic. What clues in the surrounding text indicate that they are ironic?

Sometimes Bloom's use of irony makes readers misunderstand his meaning. Do you think Bloom's intended audience would recognize the irony? What assumptions did Bloom make about his readers when he chose to use an ironic tone? What background knowledge must the reader have to understand Bloom's intended irony? Why would Bloom (or any writer) use a rhetorical device that caused some readers to misunderstand him?

7. One might say that this essay follows the problem-solution organizational pattern. Assuming this is the case, what problem is Bloom addressing? What is his solution?

Discussing the Conversation

1. How does Bloom describe the "typical" college student? What can you surmise about that student's social class? Economic status? Gender? Are you one of Bloom's "typical" students? According to Bloom, what sort of student "belongs" in the university?

2. According to Bloom, what are the purposes of the typical modern university as represented, in the extreme, by Cornell University? Again, according to Bloom, what *should* the purpose of the university be?

3. What are the two types of liberal education that Bloom identifies in most colleges? What curriculum does Bloom recommend instead? Does your university's liberal education program fit into any of Bloom's categories of liberal education curricula? In what ways?

Joining the Conversation

1. Write an informal paper in which you consider the problem of defining the "typical" college student. Is such a definition possible? If you think it's possible, write your own definition. You might include examples of students you know.

You might find that writing a definition of a typical college student is more difficult than it first appeared. What problems arise as you attempt such a definition? You could choose instead to write a paper explaining why it is impossible to define a "typical" college student.

2. Write an informal paper responding to Bloom's contention that every student should be required to take the same liberal education courses and that those courses should consist of reading the "Great Books" of the Western tradition. Do you agree or disagree with Bloom? If you agree, name several books you think are essential to everyone's education, and discuss why they should be included.

Conversely, you might agree that students do need a broad liberal education, but disagree that courses in the Great Books will meet the need.

Argue for the courses that you think should be included as part of a liberal education.

Alternatively, write a short paper arguing the opposite position from Bloom's—that students need specialized education in which they learn about their major field in great depth without taking the first two years to study liberal education.

3. Write an informal paper in which you respond to the issue of who decides what the college curriculum will be. Before you write, consider these questions: Had you thought of the curriculum as the result of decisions made by committees? If not, how did you think a college curriculum came into existence?

In fact, the curriculum usually is decided within the individual university by committees made up of administrators and professors. Do you think that is the way such decisions should be made? If so, who should be on those committees? What disciplines should be represented? What issues should they take into account when they make curriculum decisions?

If you think such decisions should not be made by committees of administrators and professors, what other possibilities can you suggest? Students? Administrators? State legislators? The U.S. Department of Education? If you want to argue that some of these other voices should be heard, what are your reasons?

These questions should help you think through the issue of who should decide the college curriculum. In your paper, come to your own conclusion and argue for it as though you were a student body representative speaking to the university administration.

INTRODUCTORY COMMENTS ON "THE POLITICS OF REMEDIATION" BY MIKE ROSE

Reading the Context

Mike Rose, the son of Italian immigrants, never thought about going to college as a young boy. Rose attended a parochial school and had been tracked into a remedial course of study because of a clerical mistake in recording his IQ scores. When he was in high school, the error was discovered and he was moved into college preparatory classes. However, his remedial background had not prepared him well to succeed as a student. With the help of a dedicated teacher, Mike Rose was able to discover the challenges and joys of learning. He completed his bachelors degree at Loyola University in Los Angeles, and he holds masters degrees in Education and English and a doctorate in Educational Psychology—all from UCLA.

Today, Mike Rose is a professor of Education at The University of California—Los Angeles. He has taught in and administered a number of university writing programs. Rose works with students who have been characterized by university placement assessments as "basic writers," students who are underprepared for college work. Rose has investigated ways to better help all students succeed at the university; he has written on composition, pedagogy, curriculum development, and policy. Mike Rose is widely considered to be an extraordinary teacher.

In his highly acclaimed book, *Lives on the Boundary: The Struggles and Achievements of America's Underprepared* (1989), from which the next selection is excerpted, Rose discusses the effects his own underpreparation had on his ability to succeed in college. He compares his experiences as a student with his experiences as a teacher of college writing students who likewise are considered underprepared by common university standards. Although he writes primarily about the experiences of underprepared students, his message about entering the university resonates with many new university students.

Mike Rose wrote *Lives on the Boundary* to provide an alternative response to the literacy crises of the 1980s, which typically called for "a return to the basics." Rose believed that those calling for "back to the basics" reforms were not taking into account the social factors that seemed to influence the academic success of the students with whom he worked.

Rose discusses extensively what he calls the "canonical curriculum," and the struggles the canon can create for underprepared students. He argues that student problems are not necessarily problems with ability, although they are often labeled as such. Rose implies that different teaching strategies and variations on the "canonical curriculum" may need to be used in order to help underprepared students succeed. In the final chapter of his book, which does not appear here, Rose addresses the arguments made by Allan Bloom and others that call for a university curriculum based on the Great Books (a.k.a. the "canonical curriculum"), books that seem to cause so much trouble for the students Rose describes. He warns that a curriculum based on the European tradition encourages teachers to ignore the cultural and linguistic potential of students from diverse backgrounds. He suggests that students read the texts now in the canon, but that the criteria for including books in the canon be revised to include the works of more diverse writers.

In addition to *Lives on the Boundary,* Rose has recently published a book that extends his work in *Lives.* His new book is called *Possible Lives: The Promise of Public Education in America.* It recounts case studies of successful experiences in public schools.

Reading the Rhetoric

In this excerpt, Rose describes several students with whom he has worked. As you read this selection, notice how Rose describes these students. He compares the experiences of these students with his own floundering experiences and discusses "five overlapping problem areas—both cognitive and social—that could be used to explain the difficulties experienced by students" who struggle. Identify the five overlapping problem areas around which Rose organizes his argument. It might be helpful to think about why he portrays these as political issues involving organizational structures, rather than simply as issues of individual student abilities and performances.

As you read, look for rhetorical strategies that Rose uses to open the door for his readers to question, for example, their own assumptions about students who struggle at the university. Pay particular attention to his use of evidence. How does he assemble his evidence to support his position and convince his audience? What types of appeals is he attempting to make? Does he convince you? Why or why not? What characteristics would you ascribe to a reader who may be convinced by Rose's argument? Not convinced?

Both the organizational pattern of Rose's excerpt and his choice of evidence help to present his position to his readers. Think about how you formulate a position and organize your evidence to convince your readers. Think also about the underlying "beliefs" a reader must accept before being convinced by a writer's position.

Reading the Conversation

Rose is explicitly responding to writers like Allan Bloom who assert that the failure of students to know the great works of Western civilization has left them and "our" culture impoverished. Rose challenges such arguments. As you read, look for passages that suggest differences between Rose's understanding of a "typical" university student and Bloom's. Consider how Bloom might respond to Rose's argument, his organizational choices, and his use of evidence.

Many additional readings in this Part discuss student difficulties with entering a university environment. Imagine an interview with Rose, hooks, Rodriguez, and Pratt in which they answer the following questions:

- What do students need to do/be to have a "successful" academic experience?
- What factors outside the student determine whether a student will have a successful academic experience?

How would their answers compare?

The Politics of Remediation
Mike Rose

1   The counselor's office was always dusky, the sun blocked by thick trees outside the windows. There was an oversize easy chair by his desk. In it sat Marita, thin, head down, hands in her lap, her shiny hair covering her face. The counselor spoke her name, and she looked up, her eyes red in the half-light. The counselor explained that the graduate student who taught her English had accused Marita of plagiarism and had turned her paper over to the director of Freshman English. He asked her to continue, to tell me the story herself.

2   Marita had been at UCLA for about three weeks. This was her first writing assignment. The class had read a discussion of creativity by Jacob Bronowski and were supposed to write papers agreeing or disagreeing with his discussion. What, Marita wondered, would she say? "What is the insight with which the scientist tries to see into nature?" asked Bronowski. Marita wasn't a scientist, and she didn't consider herself to be a particularly creative person, like an artist or an actress. Her father had always been absolute about the expression of opinion, especially with his daughters: "Don't talk unless you know." "All science is the search for unity in hidden likenesses," asserted Bronowski. "The world is full of fools who speak in ignorance," Marita's father would say, and Marita grew up cautious and reticent. Her thoughts on creativity seemed obvious or, worse yet, silly next to this man Bronowski. What did it mean anyway when he said: "We remake nature by the act of discovery, in the poem or in the theorem"? She wanted to do well on the assignment, so she went to the little library by her house and looked in the encyclopedia. She found an entry on creativity and used some selections from it that had to do with mathematicians and scientists. On the bottom of the last page of her paper, she listed the encyclopedia and her English composition textbook as her references. What had she done wrong? "They're saying I cheated. I didn't cheat." She paused and thought. "You're supposed to use other people, and I did, and I put the name of the book I used on the back of my paper."

3   The counselor handed me the paper. It was clear by the third sentence that the writing was not all hers. She had incorporated stretches of old encyclopedia prose into her paper and had quoted only some of it. I couldn't know if she had lifted directly or paraphrased the rest, but it was formal and dated and sprinkled with high-cultural references, just not what you'd find in freshman writing. I imagined that it had pleased her previous teachers that she cared enough about her work to go find sources, to rely on experts. Marita had come from a tough school in Compton—an area to the southeast of where I'd grown up—and her conscientiousness and diligence, her commitment to the academic way, must have been a great joy to those who taught her. She

shifted, hoisting herself back up from the recesses of the counselor's chair. "Are they going to dismiss me? Are they going to kick me out of school?"

4   Marita was adrift in a set of conventions she didn't fully understand; she offended without knowing why. Virtually all the writing academics do is built on the writing of others. Every argument proceeds from the texts of others. Marita was only partially initiated to how this works: She was still unsure as to how to weave quotations in with her own prose, how to mark the difference, how to cite whom she used, how to strike the proper balance between her writing and someone else's—how, in short, to position herself in an academic discussion.

5   I told Marita that I would talk with her teacher and that I was sure we could work something out, maybe another chance to write the paper. I excused myself and walked slowly back to my office, half lost in thought, reading here and there in the Bronowski excerpt. It was typical fare for Freshman English anthologies, the sort of essay you'd originally find in places like *The New Yorker.* Bronowski, the eminent scientist, looking back on his career, weaving poetry in with cybernetics, quoting *Faust* in German, allusive, learned, reflective.

6   The people who put together those freshman anthologies are drawn to this sort of thing: It's in the tradition of the English essay and reflects rich learning and polished style. But it's easy to forget how difficult these essays can be and how developed a taste they require. When I was at Loyola, someone recommended I buy Jacques Barzun's *The Energies of Art,* a collection of "fifteen striking essays on art and culture." I remember starting one essay and stopping, adrift, two or three pages later. Then another, but no go. The words arose from a depth of knowledge and a developed perception and a wealth of received ways to talk about art and a seemingly endless reserve of allusions. I felt like a janitor at a gallery opening, silent, intimidated, little flecks of knowledge—Bagehot, Stendhal, baroque ideology—sticking to the fiber of my broom.

7   Marita's assignment assumed a number of things: an ability to slip into Bronowski's discussion, a reserve of personal experiences that the writer herself would perceive as creative, a knowledge of and facility with—confidence with, really—the kinds of stylistic moves you'd find in those *New Yorker* essays. And it did *not* assume that someone, by family culture, by gender, would be reluctant to engage the reading on its own terms. Marita was being asked to write in a cognitive and social vacuum. I'm sure the other students in her class had a rough time of it as well. Many competent adult writers would too. But the solution Marita used marked her as an outsider and almost tripped the legal switches of the university.

8 At twenty-eight, Lucia was beginning her second quarter at UCLA. There weren't many people here like her. She was older, had a family, had transferred in from a community college. She represented a population

that historically hadn't gained much entrance to places like this: the returning student, the single, working mother. She had a network of neighbors and relatives that provided child care. On this day, though, the cousin on tap had an appointment at Immigration, so Lucia brought her baby with her to her psychology tutorial. Her tutor had taken ill that morning, so rather than turn her away, the receptionist brought her in to me, for I had spoken with her before. Lucia held her baby through most of our session, the baby facing her, Lucia's leg moving rhythmically, continually—a soothing movement that rocked him into sleep.

9   Upon entrance to UCLA, Lucia declared a psychology major. She had completed all her preliminary requirements at her community college and now faced that same series of upper-division courses that I took when I abandoned graduate study in English some years before: Physiological Psychology, Learning, Perception . . . all that. She was currently enrolled in Abnormal Psychology, "the study of the dynamics and prevention of abnormal behavior." Her professor had begun the course with an intellectual curve ball. He required the class to read excerpts from Thomas Szasz's controversial *The Myth of Mental Illness,* a book that debunks the very notions underlying the traditional psychological study of abnormal behavior, a book that was proving very difficult for Lucia.

10   My previous encounter with Lucia had convinced me that she was an able student. She was conscientious about her studies—recopied notes, visited professors—and she enjoyed writing: she wrote poems in an old copy book and read popular novels, both in Spanish and English. But Szasz—Szasz was throwing her. She couldn't get through the twelve-and-a-half pages of introduction. I asked her to read some passages out loud and explain them to me as best she could. And as Lucia read and talked, it became clear to me that while she could, with some doing, pick her way through Szasz's sophisticated prose, certain elements of his argument, particular assumptions and allusions, were foreign to her—or, more precisely, a frame of mind or tradition or set of assumptions that was represented by a single word, phrase, or allusion was either unknown to her or clashed dramatically with frames of mind and traditions of her own.

11   Here are the first few lines of Szasz's introduction:

> Psychiatry is conventionally defined as a medical specialty concerned with the diagnosis and treatment of mental diseases. I submit that this definition, which is still widely accepted, places psychiatry in the company of alchemy and astrology and commits it to the category of pseudoscience. The reason for this is that there is no such thing as "mental illness."

One powerful reason Lucia had decided to major in psychology was that she wanted to help people like her brother, who had a psychotic break in his teens and had been in and out of hospitals since. She had lived with mental illness, had seen that look in her brother's eyes, felt drawn to help people whose mind had betrayed them. The assertion that there was no such thing as mental illness, that it was a myth, seemed incomprehensible to her. She had trouble even entertaining it as a hypothesis, and thus couldn't play out its resonances and implications in the pages that followed. Szasz's bold claim was a bone sticking in her assumptive craw.

12   Here's another passage alongside which she had placed a question mark:

> The conceptual scaffolding of medicine, however, rests on the principles of physics and chemistry, as indeed it should, for it has been, and continues to be, the task of medicine to study and if necessary to alter, the physiochemical structure and function of the human body. Yet the fact remains that human sign-using behavior does not lend itself to exploration and understanding in these terms. We thus remain shackled to the wrong conceptual framework and terminology.

To understand this passage, you need to have some orientation to the "semiotic" tenet that every human action potentially carries some kind of message, that everything we do can be read as a sign of more than itself. This has become an accepted notion in high-powered liberal studies, an inclination to see every action and object as a kind of language that requires interpretation. The notion and its implications—the conversation within which the phrase "sign-using" situates you—was foreign to Lucia. So it was difficult for her to see why Szasz was claiming that medicine was the "wrong conceptual framework" with which to study abnormal behavior.

13   Here's a third passage:

> Man thus creates a heavenly father and an imaginary replica of the protected childhood situation to replace the real or longed-for father and family. The differences between traditional religious doctrine, modern political historicism, and psychoanalytic orthodoxy thus lie mainly in the character of the "protectors": they are, respectively, God and the priests, the totalitarian leader and his apologists, and Freud and the psychoanalysts.
>
> While Freud criticized revealed religion for the patent infantilism that it is, he ignored the social characteristics of closed societies and the psychological characteristics of their loyal supporters. He thus failed to see the religious character of the movement he himself was creating.

14   Lucia's working-class Catholicism made it difficult for her to go along with, to intellectually toy with, the comparison of Freud to God, but there was another problem here too, not unlike the problem she had with the "sign-using" passage. It is a standard move in liberal studies to find religious analogues to nonreligious behaviors, structures, and institutions. Lucia could certainly "decode" and rephrase a sentence like: "He thus failed to see the religious character of the movement he himself was creating," but she didn't have the background to appreciate what happens to Freud and psychoanalysis the moment Szasz makes his comparison, wasn't familiar with the wealth of conclusions that would follow from the analogy.

15   And so it went with other key passages. Students like Lucia are often thought to be poor readers or to have impoverished vocabularies (though

Lucia speaks two languages); I've even heard students like her referred to as culturally illiterate (though she has absorbed two cultural heritages). It's true there were words Lucia didn't know *(alchemy, orthodoxy)* and sentences that took us two or three passes to untangle. But it seemed more fruitful to see Lucia's difficulties in understanding Szasz as having to do with her belief system and with her lack of familiarity with certain ongoing discussions in humanities and social science—with frames of mind, predispositions, and background knowledge. To help Lucia with her reading, then, I explained five or six central discussions that go on in liberal studies: the semiotic discussion, the sacred-profane discussion, the medical vs. social model discussion. While I did this, I was encouraging her to talk through opinions of her own that ran counter to these discussions. That was how she improved her reading of Szasz. The material the professor assigned that followed the introduction built systematically off it, so once Lucia was situated in that introduction, she had a framework to guide her through the long passages that followed, all of which elaborated those first twelve pages.

16   The baby pulled his face out of his mother's chest, yawned, squirmed, and turned to fix on me, wide-eyed. Lucia started packing up her books with a free hand. I had missed lunch. "Let's go," I said. "I'll walk out with you." Her movement distressed the baby, so Lucia soothed him with soft coos and clicks, stood up, and shifted him to her hip. We left Campbell Hall and headed southeast, me toward a sandwich, Lucia toward the buses that ran up and down Hilgard on UCLA's east boundary. It was a beautiful California day, and the jacarandas were in full purple bloom. Lucia talked about her baby's little discoveries, about a cousin who worried her, about her growing familiarity with this sprawling campus. "I'm beginning to know where things are," she said, pursing her lips. "You know, the other day some guy stopped me and asked *me* where Murphy Hall was . . . and I could tell him." She looked straight at me: "It felt pretty good!" We walked on like this, her dress hiked up where the baby rode her hip, her books in a bag slung over her shoulder, and I began to think about how many pieces had to fall into place each day in order for her to be a student: The baby couldn't wake up sick, no colic or rashes, the cousin or a neighbor had to be available to watch him, the three buses she took from East L.A. had to be on time—no accidents or breakdowns or strikes—for travel alone took up almost three hours of her school day. Only if all these pieces dropped in smooth alignment could her full attention shift to the complex and allusive prose of Thomas Szasz. "Man thus creates a heavenly father and an imaginary replica of the protected childhood situation to replace the real or longed-for father and family."

•   •   •

17   James had a different reaction to failure.

18   He sat in my office and repeated that he was doing okay, that he'd been studying hard and would pull his grades up on his finals. "I've got my study skills perfected, and I am punctual about visiting the library." He paused and looked at his legs, placed his two hands palms down on his thighs, and

then he pressed. "I will make it. My confidence was down before." James was on academic probation; he needed to pass all his courses or he would be what they called STD: subject to dismissal. "I've got the right attitude now. I took a motivation course over the break, and that helped me improve my study skills and get my priorities straight." He was looking right at me as he said all this: handsome, muscular, preppy. Dressed for success. Mechanical successfulness. I'm okay, you're okay. Jay Gatsby would have noted his poise and elocution. I sat there quietly listening, trying to decide what to do with his forced jock talk. I drifted a little, trying to conjure up the leader of James' "motivation seminar," the person delivering to him a few techniques and big promises: a way to skim a page or manage his time. James listened desperately and paid his money and went off with a positive attitude and his study skills perfected, emboldened with a set of gimmicks, holding a dream together with gum and string.

19   James's tutor suggested that he come see me because he was getting somewhere between a C and a D in his composition course and seemed increasingly unable to concentrate. His responses to the tutor's questions were getting vague and distracted. I asked James for his paper and could quickly see that he had spent time on it; it was typed and had been proofread. I read further and understood the C–; his essay missed the mark of the assignment, which required James to critically analyze a passage from John Berger's *Ways of Seeing.* What he did instead was summarize. This was something I had seen with students who lacked experience writing papers that required them to take an idea carefully apart. They approach the task in terms they can handle, retell the material to you, summarize it, demonstrate that, yes, they can understand the stuff, and here it is. Sometimes it is very hard to get them to see that summary is not adequate, for it had been adequate so many times before. What you have to do, then, is model step by step the kind of critical approach the paper requires. And that was what I started to do with James.

20   I asked him what he thought Berger's reason was for writing *Ways of Seeing,* and he gave me a pretty good answer. I asked another question, and for a brief while it seemed that he was with me. But then he stopped and said, "I should have gotten better than a C–. I think I deserve way higher than that." There is was. A brand. I said that I knew the grade was a disappointment, but if he'd stick with me he'd do better. He didn't say much more. He looked away. I had tacitly agreed with his teacher, so we were past discussing the paper: We were discussing his identity and his future. I work hard, he's really saying to me. I go to class. I read the book. I write the paper. Can't you see. I'm not a C–. Don't tell me I'm a C–. He was looking straight ahead past me at the wall. His hands were still on his legs.

◆ ◆ ◆

21   Students were coming to college with limited exposure to certain kinds of writing and reading and with conceptions and beliefs that were dissonant with those in the lower-division curriculum they encountered. And that

curriculum wasn't doing a lot to address their weaknesses or nurture their strengths. They needed practice writing academic essays; they needed opportunities to talk about their writing—and their reading; they needed people who could quickly determine what necessary background knowledge they lacked and supply it in comprehensible ways. What began troubling me about the policy documents and the crisis reports was that they focused too narrowly on test scores and tallies of error and other such measures. They lacked careful analysis of the students' histories and lacked, as well, analysis of the cognitive and social demands of the academic culture the students now faced. The work I was doing in the Tutorial Center, in the Writing Research Project, and in the Summer Program was guiding me toward a richer understanding of what it meant to be underprepared in the American research university. It seemed to me there were five overlapping problem areas—both cognitive and social—that could be used to explain the difficulties experienced by students like Marita and James and Lucia. These by no means applied equally to all the students whom I came to know, but taken together they represent, better than pie charts and histograms, what it means to be underprepared at a place like UCLA. Many young people come to the university able to summarize the events in a news story or write a personal response to a play or a movie or give back what a teacher said in a straightforward lecture. But they have considerable trouble with what has come to be called critical literacy: framing an argument or taking someone else's argument apart, systematically inspecting a document, an issue, or an event, synthesizing different points of view, applying a theory to disparate phenomena, and so on. The authors of the crisis reports got tremendously distressed about students' difficulty with such tasks, but it's important to remember that, traditionally, such abilities have only been developed in an elite: in priests, scholars, or a leisure class. Ours is the first society in history to expect so many of its people to be able to perform these very sophisticated literacy activities. And we fail to keep in mind how extraordinary it is to ask *all* our schools to conduct this kind of education—not just those schools with lots of money and exceptional teachers and small classes—but massive, sprawling schools, beleaguered schools, inner-city schools, overcrowded schools. It is a charge most of them simply are not equipped to fulfill, for our educational ideals far outstrip our economic and political priorities.

22   We forget, then, that by most historical—and current—standards, the vast majority of a research university's underprepared students would be considered competently literate. Though they fail to meet the demands made of them in their classes, they fail from a literate base. They are literate people straining at the boundaries of their ability, trying to move into the unfamiliar, to approximate a kind of writing they can't yet command. And as they try, they'll make all the blunders in word choice and sentence structure and discourse strategy that regularly get held up for ridicule, that I made when I was trying to write for my teachers at Loyola. There's a related

phenomenon, and we have research evidence of this: As writers move further away from familiar ways of expressing themselves, the strains on their cognitive and linguistic resources increase, and the number of mechanical and grammatical errors they make shoots up. Before we shake our heads at these errors, we should also consider the possibility that many such linguistic bungles are signs of growth, a stretching beyond what college freshmen can comfortably do with written language. In fact, we should *welcome* certain kinds of errors, make allowance for them in the curricula we develop, analyze rather than simply criticize them. Error marks the place where education begins.

23   Asked to produce something that is beyond them, writers might also fall back on strategies they already know. Asked to take a passage critically apart, they'll summarize it. We saw this with James, the young man distressed with his C−, but as with so much else in this book, the principle applies to more than just those labeled underprepared. I was personally reminded of it when I was writing my dissertation. My chairman was an educational research methodologist and statistician; my background straddled humanities and social science, but what I knew about writing tended to be shaped by literary models. When it came time to report on the procedures I was using in my study—the methods section of the dissertation—I wrote a detailed chronology of what I did and how I did it. I wanted to relay all the twists and turns of my investigation. About a week later I got it back covered with criticism. My chairman didn't want the vagaries of my investigative life; he wanted a compressed and systematic account. "What do you think this is," he wrote alongside one long, dancing stretch of narrative, *"Travels with Charley?"*

24 Associated with these difficulties with critical literacy are students' diverse orientations toward inquiry. It is a source of exasperation to many freshmen that the university is so predisposed to question past solutions, to seek counterexplanations—to continually turn something nice and clean and clear into a problem. English professor David Bartholomae recalls a teacher of his suggesting that, when stuck, student writers should try the following "machine": "While most readers of _____ have said _____, a close and careful reading shows that _____." The teacher's machine perfectly expresses the ethos of the university, a fundamental orientation toward inquiry. University professors have for so long been socialized into this critical stance, that they don't realize how unsettling it can be to students who don't share their unusual background.

25   There is Scott sitting in an Astronomy tutorial, his jaw set, responding to another student's question about a finite versus an infinite universe: "This is the kind of question," he says, "that you'll argue and argue about. It's stupid. No one wins. So why do it?" And there is Rene who can't get beyond the first few sentences of her essay for Speech. She has to write a critical response to an address of Ronald Reagan's. "You can't criticize the president," she

explains. "You've gotta support your president even if you don't agree with him." When students come from other cultures, this discordance can be even more pronounced. Our tutors continually encouraged their students to read actively, to ask why authors say what they say, what their claims are, what assumptions they make, where you, the reader, agree or disagree. Hun's tutor is explaining this to him, then has him try it, has him read aloud so she can guide him. He reads a few lines and stops short. After two more abortive trials, she pulls out of Hun the explanation that what gets written in books is set in tradition, and he is not learned enough to question the authority of the book.

26 Remember Andrea? She was the distressed young woman who was failing chemistry. Andrea could memorize facts and formulas but not use them to solve problems—and her inability was representative of a whole class of difficulties experienced by freshmen. What young people come to define as intellectual competence—what it means to know things and use them—is shaped by their schooling. And what many students experience year after year is the exchange of one body of facts for another—an inert transmission, the delivery and redelivery of segmented and self-contained dates and formulas—and thus it is no surprise that they develop a restricted sense of how intellectual work is conducted. They are given Ancient History one year and American History the next, and once they've displayed knowledge of the Fertile Crescent and cuneiform and Assyrian military campaigns, there is little need for them to remember the material, little further opportunity to incorporate it, little reason to use these textbook facts to engage historical problems. Next year it will be American History: a new textbook, new dates and documents and campaigns, new tests—but the same rewards, and the same reasons to forget. John Dewey saw the difficulty long ago: "Only in education, never in the life of the farmer, sailor, merchant, physician, or laboratory experimenter, does knowledge mean primarily a store of information aloof from doing."

27   Students like Andrea are caught in a terrible bind. They come to the university with limited experience in applying knowledge, puzzling over solutions, solving problems. Many of the lower-division courses they encounter—their "general education" or "breadth" requirements—will involve little writing or speaking or application, will rely on so-called objective tests that, with limited exception, stress the recall of material rather than the reasoned elaboration of it. But the gatekeeper courses—the courses that determine entrance to a major—they up the intellectual ante. Courses like Andrea's bête noire, Chemistry 11-A, are placed like land mines in the uneven terrain of the freshman year. The special nature of their demands is not made the focus of attention that it should be; that is, the courses are not taught explicitly and self-consciously as courses on how to think as a chemist or a psychologist or a literary critic. And there are few opportunities for students to develop such ability before they enroll in those courses. The faculty, for the most part, do

not provide freshmen with instruction on how to use knowledge creatively—and then penalize them when they cannot do so.

28 It is not unusual for students to come to the university with conceptualizations of disciplines that are out of sync with academic reality. Like the note taker in the lecture hall who opened this chapter, a lot of entering freshmen assume that sociology is something akin to social work, an applied study of social problems rather than an attempt to abstract a theory about social interaction and organization. Likewise, some think psychology will be a discussion of human motivation and counseling, what it is that makes people do what they do—and some coverage of ways to change what they do. It comes as a surprise that their textbook has only one chapter on personality and psychotherapy—and a half dozen pages on Freud. The rest is animal studies, computer models of thought, lots of neurophysiology. If they like to read novels, and they elect a literature course, they'll expect to talk about characters and motive and plot, but instead they're asked to situate the novel amid the historical forces that shaped it, to examine rhetorical and stylistic devices and search the prose for things that mean more than they seem to mean. Political science should be politics and government and current events—nuclear treaties, trade sanctions, and Iran-Contra scandal—but instead it's Marx and Weber and political economy and organizational and decision-making models. And so goes the litany of misdirection. This dissonance between the academy's and the students' definitions of disciplines makes it hard for students to get their bearings with material: to know what's important, to see how the pieces fit together, to follow an argument, to have a sense of what can be passed over lightly. Thus I would see notebooks that were filled—in frantic script—with everything the professor said or that were scant and fragmented, records of information without coherence.

29 The discourse of academics is marked by terms and expressions that represent an elaborate set of shared concepts and orientations: alienation, authoritarian personality, the social construction of the self, determinism, hegemony, equilibrium, intentionality, recursion, reinforcement, and so on. This language weaves through so many lectures and textbooks, is integral to so many learned discussions, that it's easy to forget what a foreign language it can be. Freshmen are often puzzled by the talk they hear in their classrooms, but what's important to note here is that their problem is not simply one of limited vocabulary. If we see the problem as knowing or not knowing a list or words, as some quick-fix remedies suggest, then we'll force glossaries on students and miss the complexity of the issue. Take, for example, *authoritarian personality*. The average university freshman will know what *personality* means and can figure out *authoritarian;* the difficulty will come from a lack of familiarity with the conceptual resonances that *authoritarian personality* has acquired in the discussions of sociologists and psychologists and political

scientists. Discussion . . . you could almost define a university education as an initiation into a variety of powerful ongoing discussions, an initiation that can occur only through the repeated use of a new language in the company of others. More than anything, this was the opportunity people like Father Albertson, my Shakespeare teacher at Loyola, provided to me. The more comfortable and skillful students become with this kind of influential talk, the more they will be included in further conversations and given access to further conceptual tools and resources—the acquisition of which virtually defines them as members of an intellectual community.

30   All students require such an opportunity. But those coming to the university with less-than-privileged educations, especially those from the lower classes, are particularly in need. They are less likely to have participated, in any extended way, in such discussions in the past. They won't have the confidence or the moves to enter it, and can begin to feel excluded, out of place, put off by a language they can't command. Their social marginality, then, is reinforced by discourse and, as happened to me during my first year at Loyola, they might well withdraw, retreat to silence.

31   This sense of linguistic exclusion can be complicated by various cultural differences. When I was growing up, I absorbed an entire belief system—with its own characteristic terms and expressions—from the worried conversations of my parents, from the things I heard and saw on South Vermont, from the priest's fiery tales. I thought that what happened to people was pre-ordained, that ability was a fixed thing, that there was one true religion. I had rigid notions about social roles, about the structure of society, about gender, about politics. There used to be a rickety vending machine at Manchester and Vermont that held a Socialist Workers newspaper. I'd walk by it and feel something alive and injurious: The paper was malevolent and should be destroyed. Imagine, then, the difficulty I had when, at the beginning of my senior year at Mercy High, Jack MacFarland tried to explain Marxism to us. How could I absorb the language of atheistic materialism and class struggle when it seemed so strange and pernicious? It wasn't just that Marxist terms-of-art were unfamiliar; they felt assaultive. What I did was revert to definitions of the social order more familiar to me, and Mr. MacFarland had to draw them out of me and have me talk about them and consider them alongside Marx's vision and terminology, examining points of conflict and points of possible convergence. It was only then that I could appropriate Marx's strange idiom.

32 Once you start to think about underprepared students in terms of these overlapping problem areas, all sorts of solutions present themselves. Students need more opportunities to write about what they're learning and guidance in the techniques and conventions of that writing—what I got from my mentors at Loyola. They need more opportunities to develop the writing strategies that are an intimate part of academic inquiry and what has come to be called critical literacy—comparing, synthesizing, analyzing—the sort of

thing I gave the veterans. They need opportunities to talk about what they're learning: to test their ideas, reveal their assumptions, talk through the places where new knowledge clashes with ingrained belief. They need a chance, too, to talk about the ways they may have felt excluded from all this in the past and may feel threatened by it in the present. They need the occasion to rise above the fragmented learning the lower-division curriculum encourages, a place within a course or outside it to hear about and reflect on the way a particular discipline conducts its inquiry: Why, for example, *do* so many psychologists who study thinking rely on computer modeling? Why is mathematics so much a part of economics? And they need to be let in on the secret talk, on the shared concepts and catchphrases of Western liberal learning.

33   There is nothing magical about this list of solutions. In fact, in many ways, it reflects the kind of education a privileged small number of American students have received for some time. The basic question our society must ask, then, is: How many or how few do we want to have this education? If students didn't get it before coming to college—and most have not—then what are we willing to do to give it to them now? Chip and I used to talk about our special programs as attempts to create an Honors College for the underprepared. People would smile as we spoke, but, as our students would have said, we were serious as a heart attack. The remedial programs we knew about did a disservice to their students by thinking of them as *remedial*. We wanted to try out another perspective and see what kind of program it would yield. What would happen if we thought of our students' needs and goals in light of the comprehensive and ambitious program structures more often reserved for the elite?

· · ·

34   Not too long ago I was speaking about curriculum at another university. It was a lunchtime speech, preceded by murmurs and clinking glassware, and I was about to leave my chair for the podium when a young woman walked up to me and asked me if I remembered her. She was vaguely familiar, a little lighter or a little heavier than someone I once knew, hair longer, shorter maybe—something. "I'm Concepción Baca," she said, extending her hand. "I was in the first summer program. I'm in graduate school here. I'm in Comparative Literature." She paused. "You're surprised, aren't you? I bet I'm the last person you expected to see here." Well, not the last. But I was surprised.

35   After my talk, Concepción and I sat down together. She had come, it turned out, because the director of Freshman Writing at this school had asked his teaching assistants to attend. He came over and joined us. Concepción, he said, was one of his best writing teachers. She was also doing excellent work in her graduate studies. Comparative Literature is a backbreaking degree—you must be proficient in the literature of three languages—and Concepción was getting close to the dissertation stage. "So, how'd you end up here?," I asked. "Well," she shrugged, "it's a long story. Did you know that

I dropped out of UCLA?" I didn't, and as she spoke, I heard an interesting and not unfamiliar story.

36   Concepción stayed at UCLA for almost two years, taking a range of courses, from history and psychology to English and linguistics. Her record was spotty: some A's, some C's, two incompletes that turned to F's because she failed to make them up. That put her on academic probation. In the middle of her sophomore year, she quit. "I never really got used to living away from home," she explained. "I never felt right about it." She had trouble deciding on a major. Her best grades were in Latin American Studies, American Immigrant History, and English. She had liked English in the summer program and elected three or four other English courses along the way. Her teachers said her writing was okay, told her she should work on it. But what would she do with an English major? Her parents were spending a lot of money on her. She missed them. What would she major in? How could she keep going to school when their money was so tight? She withdrew and went to work. Two years later, she entered a different University of California campus. She had made some money herself and had a lot of time to think about those two years at UCLA. She liked cultural history and English, and those interests led her to comparative literature. She blossomed. She graduated with very good grades and went on to graduate school.

37   People who work in tutoring centers and preparatory programs get used to spending intense bursts of time with their students. You get closely involved for a few weeks or a few months, and then you send them off. And you wonder. You know some won't make it. There's too much working against their success. They'll drift in and out of academic probation, their transcripts a listing of C's, C-minuses, a D or two, and then the fatal F that exits them. That was what happened to Andrea, the young woman who was having such a miserable time with chemistry, who I was afraid might hurt herself just to escape. She was longing to be premed when General Chemistry was insurmountable. There are some, though, who do make it. Even those you thought were doomed. There was Vincent, whose summer program teacher commented that his writing was "very poor," who was on academic probation for part of his freshman year, who kept showing up at the Tutorial Center to work on his writing, who finally had to withdraw but came back and cleared his record as a sophomore—and by the time he was a junior was getting B's, who earned an A-minus in Advanced Composition during his senior year. Vincent's parents were migrant workers in South Fresno. Neither had gone to high school. Vincent was now thinking about graduate school in urban planning. It can happen.

38   As I was driving home, I thought about Concepción. I thought about how long it sometimes takes to achieve a balance, how much of myself I saw in her, how easy it would have been to misperceive her as a freshman: scattershot course selection, incompletes, C's in introductory courses, probation—and finally withdrawal. She was listed, I'm sure, as one of the summer program's

failures. An attrition statistic. Concepción eventually found her way; many like her aren't as fortunate. Research universities are awful places for freshman to be adrift, to be searching, to be in need. Attrition may be a blessing, as many contend, for it naturally purges the university of those who don't belong, those who never should have come. There's a kind of harsh institutional truth to that, I suppose, but to embrace it, you'll have to limit your definition of achievement—blunt your sense of wonder. What you'll have to do, finally, is narrow your vision of the society you want to foster.

FOLLOW-UP ACTIVITIES

Discussing the Rhetoric

1. Note the details that Rose uses to describe Lucia. What do they tell you about her character? Why would Rose include a sentence like "Lucia held her baby through most of our session, the baby facing her, Lucia's leg moving rhythmically, continually—a soothing movement that rocked him into sleep," instead of simply reporting "Lucia was a good mother"?

2. Typically, we are led to believe that success in school is strictly a result of one's cognitive or intellectual endowments and efforts. Rose uses several examples to suggest that social factors play a part in a student's success. Who might disagree with Rose on this position? How does Rose set about convincing those who might not wish to acknowledge social factors?

3. At what point in the essay does Rose begin to use the voice of a scholar rather than a storyteller? Considering that he is writing for other college professors, how would you explain this change in tone?

Discussing the Conversation

1. Compose a sentence that summarizes Rose's position on the factors that hinder a student's success at the university.

2. Do you agree or disagree with the five overlapping problem areas that Rose uses to explain student difficulties? How do these areas compare with your experience at the university? What other problems might you name?

3. Compare what Rose says about "critical" inquiry to Newenhuyse's attitude toward criticism ("De-Constructive Criticism," p. xx). Do you think Newenhuyse would have the same problems with the academic view of criticism that Rose's students had? What does Rose add to your understanding of the academic meaning of the term?

4. Rose mentions another term that came up in the discussion of Newenhuyse's article—discourse. What does Rose add to your understanding of this term?

5. hooks and Rodriguez both describe their experiences as incoming Stanford students in ways similar to Rose's descriptions of his own experiences and the experiences of students he has known. Bloom, however, makes no mention of "marginalization," or feeling like a foreigner in the land of the university. What assumptions might you draw from each of these writer's descriptions of the university students' experience? Which stories seem most closely aligned with your own? What do you learn about yourself from reading the experiences of other students at the university?

6. Make a list of the suggestions that Rose offers to help students better succeed at the university. How might you use this list to improve your own university experience?

Joining the Conversation

1. How does your experience so far with university classes compare with the experiences of the students Rose describes? Do you find yourself empathizing with or discounting the argument Rose makes on behalf of these students? With that in mind, write an informal paper in which you explain how your university experiences (1) have led you to believe you can succeed or (2) have left you wondering about your abilities to succeed. Make recommendations of ways your writing instructor might help you learn the requirements of academic reading and writing.

2. Do you think that the students Rose describes are typical of other university students with whom you attend school? In what ways? What implications might your answer hold for those who make decisions about who to teach, what to teach, and how to teach? What recommendations would you make regarding admission policies, curricular choices, and use of teaching strategies in your classes? Would you agree with Rose?

3. The cognitive/social constructivist debate regarding fitness to succeed in school has long captivated Western educators and educational commentators. Some have argued that members of certain cultures are cognitively inferior and genetically predisposed to fail in school. Others have argued that the canonical curriculum privileges members of certain cultures at the expense of others on the basis of background preparation rather than cognitive ability. Interpretations of positions on this debate have sparked heated controversy and have been appropriated to make far-ranging decisions about educational curriculum and university admission policies. If you have read the Bloom selection, you are familiar with one viewpoint. Rose presents another. Write an informal paper in which you discuss your current view on the question of the academic curriculum. Do you think that a Great Books curriculum will best suit your educational needs and goals? Do you think courses that expose you to a wider range of literature might best suit your needs and goals? Do you think a more complex arrangement of choices about what to study at the university would be appropriate? Who do you think should choose? Why do you think so?

4. Marita was asked to "join the conversation" among scientists and artists about creativity, but felt that she didn't have the background to do so. Write an informal paper in which you describe a time when you felt yourself to be in the same position. How did you handle it? How would you handle it now?

INTRODUCTORY COMMENTS ON "KEEPING CLOSE TO HOME: CLASS AND EDUCATION" BY BELL HOOKS

Reading the Context

The selection that follows, "Keeping Close to Home: Class and Education" is a chapter excerpted from *Talking Back* (1989) by bell hooks, born Gloria Watkins. It is a book about coming of age and the difficult decisions that were a necessary part of it. In this selection, hooks describes herself as "a southern black girl from a working class background." The many concerns she raises and discusses have everything to do with her current place in the university: she was a professor of English at Yale University when she wrote this. In this selection, as well as in others, hooks writes that memories not only reflect, but more importantly politicize, difference. Because this message is so central to hooks, autobiography (one's history of identity) becomes a necessary ingredient in political writing. In this selection, autobiography is inextricably fused with contemporary issues of race, gender, and class. hooks' complex perspective joins with other voices, other identities past and present, who found pain and isolation to be irreducible counterparts to growing up in the dominant structures of contemporary North American society.

bell hooks has contributed to many popular and academic magazines. Recently, she has edited an anthology of contemporary African-American women writers entitled *GumboYaYa* (1995) and a critical study entitled *Art on My Mind: Visual Politics* (1995).

Reading the Rhetoric

Your language is part of your identity. It marks you as a member or nonmember of certain "discourse communities"—groups of people whose usage of language reflects their common interests. hooks observes how her allegiance to an academic discourse community estranged her from her home community. She contends that keeping close to the language of one's home identity is essential to every individual. According to hooks, attempts to assimilate or blend the values of both discourse communities together into one harmonious whole will only "undermine and destroy potential structures of opposition." These structures of opposition must be preserved and explored if we are to work toward understanding and representing communities.

hooks proposes a way of writing that combines a personal voice with the critical analysis of the academic community while maintaining the distinctiveness of both voices. She is aware that how she uses the discourses available to her is a rhetorical and political choice. As you read the essay, notice how hooks' choice of language seems to shift, depending on the community she is speaking from. Can you locate passages where hooks seems to be speaking predominantly from her home identity? From her academic identity? You'll also want to consider who hooks saw as her audience. Are you a member of this audience? Consider hooks' organizational choices. Which sections of the essay are more difficult to read? Which sections are easier to read?

Reading the Conversation

hooks claims that nonwhite, nonmiddle class groups can and must resist the ever-present pressure to assimilate with the majority. While reading hooks' essay, think about how the essay compares with the other essays and articles in this section. For example, how does Kent Kirkpatrick's portrayal of Judge Nomoto's home identity compare to hooks' portrayal of her own home identity? Which representation seems to be more politically motivated? Locate particular passages and terms to support your view. How do hooks' views differ from those of other writers in this part? Is there anyone she seems to agree with completely?

Keeping Close to Home:
Class and Education
bell hooks

1 We are both awake in the almost dark of 5 A.M. Everyone else is sound asleep. Mama asks the usual questions. Telling me to look around, make sure I have everything, scolding me because I am uncertain about the actual time the bus arrives. By 5:30 we are waiting outside the closed station. Alone together, we have a chance to really talk. Mama begins. Angry with her children, especially the ones who whisper behind her back, she says bitterly, "Your childhood could not have been that bad. You were fed and clothed. You did not have to do without—that's more than a lot of folks have and I just can't stand the way y'all go on." The hurt in her voice saddens me. I have always wanted

to protect mama from hurt, to ease her burdens. Now I am part of what troubles. Confronting me, she says accusingly, "It's not just the other children. You talk too much about the past. You don't just listen." And I do talk. Worse, I write about it.

2   Mama has always come to each of her children seeking different responses. With me she expresses the disappointment, hurt, and anger of betrayal: anger that her children are so critical, that we can't even have the sense to like the presents she sends. She says, "From now on there will be no presents. I'll just stick some money in a little envelope the way the rest of you do. Nobody wants criticism. Everybody can criticize me but I am supposed to say nothing." When I try to talk, my voice sounds like a twelve year old. When I try to talk, she speaks louder, interrupting me, even though she has said repeatedly, "Explain it to me, this talk about the past." I struggle to return to my thirty-five year old self so that she will know by the sound of my voice that we are two women talking together. It is only when I state firmly in my very adult voice, "Mama, you are not listening," that she becomes quiet. She waits. Now that I have her attention, I fear that my explanations will be lame, inadequate. "Mama," I begin, "people usually go to therapy because they feel hurt inside, because they have pain that will not stop, like a wound that continually breaks open, that does not heal. And often these hurts, that pain has to do with things that have happened in the past, sometimes in childhood, often in childhood, or things that we believe happened." She wants to know, "What hurts, what hurts are you talking about?" "Mom, I can't answer that. I can't speak for all of us, the hurts are different for everybody. But the point is you try to make the hurt better, to heal it, by understanding how it came to be. And I know you feel mad when we say something happened or hurt that you don't remember being that way, but the past isn't like that, we don't have the same memory of it. We remember things differently. You know that. And sometimes folk feel hurt about stuff and you just don't know or didn't realize it, and they need to talk about it. Surely you understand the need to talk about it."

3   Our conversation is interrupted by the sight of my uncle walking across the park toward us. We stop to watch him. He is on his way to work dressed in a familiar blue suit. They look alike, these two who rarely discuss the past. This interruption makes me think about life in a small town. You always see someone you know. Interruptions, intrusions are part of daily life. Privacy is difficult to maintain. We leave our private space in the car to greet him. After the hug and kiss he has given me every year since I was born, they talk about the day's funerals. In the distance the bus approaches. He walks away knowing that they will see each other later. Just before I board the bus I turn, staring into my mother's face. I am momentarily back in time, seeing myself eighteen years ago, at this same bus stop, staring into my mother's face, continually turning back, waving farewell as I returned to college—that experience which first took me away from our town, from family. Departing was as painful then as it is now. Each movement away

makes return harder. Each separation intensifies distance, both physical and emotional.

4   To a southern black girl from a working-class background who had never been on a city bus, who had never stepped on an escalator, who had never travelled by plane, leaving the comfortable confines of a small town Kentucky life to attend Stanford University was not just frightening; it was utterly painful. My parents had not been delighted that I had been accepted and adamantly opposed my going so far from home. At the time, I did not see their opposition as an expression of their fear that they would lose me forever. Like many working-class folks, they feared what college education might do to their children's minds even as they unenthusiastically acknowledged its importance. They did not understand why I could not attend a college nearby, an all-black college. To them, any college would do. I would graduate, become a school teacher, make a decent living and a good marriage. And even though they reluctantly and skeptically supported my educational endeavors, they also subjected them to constant harsh and bitter critique. It is difficult for me to talk about my parents and their impact on me because they have always felt wary, ambivalent, mistrusting of my intellectual aspirations even as they have been caring and supportive. I want to speak about these contradictions because sorting through them, seeking resolution and reconciliation has been important to me both as it affects my development as a writer, my effort to be fully self-realized, and my longing to remain close to the family and community that provided the groundwork for much of my thinking, writing, and being.

5   Studying at Stanford, I began to think seriously about class differences. To be materially underprivileged at a university where most folks (with the exception of workers) are materially privileged provokes such thought. Class differences were boundaries no one wanted to face or talk about. It was easier to downplay them, to act as though we were all from privileged backgrounds, to work around them, to confront them privately in the solitude of one's room, or to pretend that just being chosen to study at such an institution meant that those of us who did not come from privilege were already in transition toward privilege. To not long for such transition marked one as rebellious, an unlikely to succeed. It was a kind of treason not to believe that it was better to be identified with the world of material privilege than with the world of the working class, the poor. No wonder our working-class parents from poor backgrounds feared our entry into such a world, intuiting perhaps that we might learn to be ashamed of where we had come from, that we might never return home, or come back only to lord it over them.

6   Though I hung with students who were supposedly radical and chic, we did not discuss class. I talked to no one about the sources of my shame, how it hurt me to witness the contempt shown the brown-skinned Filipina maids who cleaned our rooms, or later my concern about the $100 a month I paid for a room off-campus which was more than half of what my parents paid for rent. I talked to no one about my efforts to save money, to send a little

something home. Yet these class realities separated me from fellow students. We were moving in different directions. I did not intend to forget my class background or alter my class allegiance. And even though I received an education designed to provide me with a bourgeois sensibility, passive acquiescence was not my only option. I knew that I could resist. I could rebel. I could shape the direction and focus of the various forms of knowledge available to me. Even though I sometimes envied and longed for greater material advantages (particularly at vacation times when I would be one of few if any students remaining in the dormitory because there was no money for travel), I did not share the sensibility and values of my peers. That was important—class was not just about money; it was about values which showed and determined behavior. While I often needed more money, I never needed a new set of beliefs and values. For example, I was profoundly shocked and disturbed when peers would talk about their parents without respect, or would even say that they hated their parents. This was especially troubling to me when it seemed that these parents were caring and concerned. It was often explained to me that such hatred was "healthy and normal." To my white, middle-class California roommate, I explained the way we were taught to value our parents and their care, to understand that they were not obligated to give us care. She would always shake her head, laughing all the while, and say, "Missy, you will learn that it's different here, that we think differently." She was right. Soon, I lived alone, like the one Mormon student who kept to himself as he made a concentrated effort to remain true to his religious beliefs and values. Later in graduate school I found that classmates believed "lower class" people had no beliefs and values. I was silent in such discussions, disgusted by their ignorance.

7   Carol Stack's anthropological study, *All Our Kin,* was one of the first books I read which confirmed my experiential understanding that within black culture (especially among the working class and poor, particularly in southern states), a value system emerged that was counter-hegemonic, that challenged notions of individualism and private property so important to the maintenance of white-supremacist, capitalist patriarchy. Black folk created in marginal spaces a world of community and collectivity where resources were shared. In the preface to *Feminist Theory: from margin to center,* I talked about how the point of difference, this marginality can be the space for the formation of an oppositional world view. That world view must be articulated, named if it is to provide a sustained blueprint for change. Unfortunately, there has existed no consistent framework for such naming. Consequently both the experience of this difference and documentation of it (when it occurs) gradually loses presence and meaning.

8   Much of what Stack documented about the "culture of poverty," for example, would not describe interactions among most black poor today irrespective of geographical setting. Since the black people she described did not acknowledge (if they recognized it in theoretical terms) the oppositional value of their world view, apparently seeing it more as a survival strategy

determined less by conscious efforts to oppose oppressive race and class biases than by circumstance, they did not attempt to establish a framework to
transmit their beliefs and values from generation to generation. When circumstances changed, values altered. Efforts to assimilate the values and beliefs of privileged white people, presented through media like television,
undermine and destroy potential structures of opposition.

9   Increasingly, young black people are encouraged by the dominant culture (and by those black people who internalize the values of this hegemony) to believe that assimilation is the only possible way to survive, to
succeed. Without the framework of an organized civil rights or black resistance struggle, individual and collective efforts at black liberation that focus
on the primacy of self-definition and self-determination often go unrecog-
nized. It is crucial that those among us who resist and rebel, who survive
and succeed, speak openly and honestly about our lives and the nature of
our personal struggles, the means by which we resolve and reconcile contradictions. This is no easy task. Within the educational institutions where we
learn to develop and strengthen our writing and analytical skills, we also
learn to think, write, and talk in a manner that shifts attention away from
personal experience. Yet if we are to reach our people and all people, if we
are to remain connected (especially those of us whose familial backgrounds
are poor and working-class), we must understand that the telling of one's
personal story provides a meaningful example, a way for folks to identify
and connect.

10   Combining personal with critical analysis and theoretical perspectives
can engage listeners who might otherwise feel estranged, alienated. To
speak simply with language that is accessible to as many folks as possible is
also important. Speaking about one's personal experience or speaking with
simple language is often considered by academics and/or intellectuals (irrespective of their political inclinations) to be a sign of intellectual weakness
or even anti-intellectualism. Lately, when I speak, I do not stand in place—
reading my paper, making little or no eye contact with audiences—but instead make eye contact, talk extemporaneously, digress, and address the
audience directly. I have been told that people assume I am not prepared,
that I am anti-intellectual, unprofessional (a concept that has everything to
do with class as it determines actions and behavior), or that I am reinforcing
the stereotype of black people as non-theoretical and gutsy.

11   Such criticism was raised recently by fellow feminist scholars after a talk
I gave at Northwestern University at a conference on "Gender, Culture, Politics" to an audience that was mainly students and academics. I deliberately
chose to speak in a very basic way, thinking especially about the few community folks who had come to hear me. Weeks later, KumKum Sangari, a fellow participant who shared with me what was said when I was no longer
present, and I engaged in quite rigorous critical dialogue about the way my
presentation had been perceived primarily by privileged white female
academics. She was concerned that I not mask my knowledge of theory, that

I not appear anti-intellectual. Her critique compelled me to articulate concerns that I am often silent about with colleagues. I spoke about class allegiance and revolutionary commitments, explaining that it was disturbing to me that intellectual radicals who speak about transforming society, ending the domination of race, sex, class, cannot break with behavior patterns that reinforce and perpetuate domination, or continue to use as their sole reference point how we might be or are perceived by those who dominate, whether or not we gain their acceptance and approval.

12   This is a primary contradiction which raises the issue of whether or not the academic setting is a place where one can be truly radical or subversive. Concurrently, the use of a language and style of presentation that alienates most folks who are not also academically trained reinforces the notion that the academic world is separate from real life, that everyday world where we constantly adjust our language and behavior to meet diverse needs. The academic setting is separate only when we work to make it so. It is a false dichotomy which suggests that academics and/or intellectuals can only speak to one another, that we cannot hope to speak with the masses. What is true is that we make choices, that we choose our audiences, that we choose voices to hear and voices to silence. If I do not speak in a language that can be understood, then there is little chance for dialogue. This issue of language and behavior is a central contradiction all radical intellectuals, particularly those who are members of oppressed groups, must continually confront and work to resolve. One of the clear and present dangers that exists when we move outside our class of origin, our collective ethnic experience, and enter hierarchical institutions which daily reinforce domination by race, sex, and class, is that we gradually assume a mindset similar to those who dominate and oppress, that we lose critical consciousness because it is not reinforced or affirmed by the environment. We must be ever vigilant. It is important that we know who we are speaking to, who we most want to hear us, who we most long to move, motivate, and touch with our words.

13   When I first came to New Haven to teach at Yale, I was truly surprised by the marked class divisions between black folks—students and professors— who identify with Yale and those black folks who work at Yale or in surrounding communities. Style of dress and self-presentation are most often the central markers of one's position. I soon learned that the black folks who spoke on the street were likely to be part of the black community and those who carefully shifted their glance were likely to be associated with Yale. Walking with a black female colleague one day, I spoke to practically every black person in sight (a gesture which reflects my upbringing), an action which disturbed my companion. Since I addressed black folk who were clearly not associated with Yale, she wanted to know whether or not I knew them. That was funny to me. "Of course not," I answered. Yet when I thought about it seriously, I realized that in a deep way, I knew them for they, and not my companion or most of my colleagues at Yale, resemble my family. Later that year, in a black women's support group I started for undergraduates,

students from poor backgrounds spoke about the shame they sometimes feel when faced with the reality of their connection to working-class and poor black people. One student confessed that her father is a street person, addicted to drugs, someone who begs from passersby. She, like other Yale students, turns away from street people often, sometimes showing anger or contempt; she hasn't wanted anyone to know that she was related to this kind of person. She struggles with this, wanting to find a way to acknowledge and affirm this reality, to claim this connection. The group asked me and one another what we [should] do to remain connected, to honor the bonds we have with working-class and poor people even as our class experience alters.

14   Maintaining connections with family and community across class boundaries demands more than just summary recall of where one's roots are, where one comes from. It requires knowing, naming, and being ever mindful of those aspects of one's past that have enabled and do enable one's self-development in the present, that sustain and support, that enrich. One must also honestly confront barriers that do exist, aspects of that past that do diminish. My parents' ambivalence about my love for reading led to intense conflict. They (especially my mother) would work to ensure that I had access to books, but would threaten to burn the books or throw them away if I did not conform to other expectations. Or they would insist that reading too much would drive me insane. Their ambivalence nurtured in me a like uncertainty about the value and significance of intellectual endeavor which took years for me to unlearn. While this aspect of our class reality was one that wounded and diminished, their vigilant insistence that being smart did not make me a "better" or "superior" person (which often got on my nerves because I think I wanted to have that sense that it did indeed set me apart, make me better) made a profound impression. From them I learned to value and respect various skills and talents folk might have, not just to value people who read books and talk about ideas. They and my grandparents might say about somebody, "Now he don't read nor write a lick, but he can tell a story," or as my grandmother would say, "call out the hell in words."

15   Empty romanticization of poor or working-class backgrounds undermines the possibility of true connection. Such connection is based on understanding difference in experience and perspective and working to mediate and negotiate these terrains. Language is a crucial issue for folk whose movement outside the boundaries of poor and working-class backgrounds changes the nature and direction of their speech. Coming to Stanford with my own version of a Kentucky accent, which I think of always as a strong sound quite different from Tennessee or Georgia speech, I learned to speak differently while maintaining the speech of my region, the sound of my family and community. This was of course much easier to keep up when I returned home to stay often. In recent years, I have endeavored to use various speaking styles in the classroom as a teacher and find it disconcerts those who feel that the use of a particular patois excludes them as listeners, even if there is translation into the usual acceptable mode of speech. Learning to

listen to different voices, hearing different speech challenges the notion that we must all assimilate—share a single, similar talk—in educational institutions. Language reflects the culture from which we emerge. To deny ourselves daily use of speech patterns that are common and familiar, that embody the unique and distinctive aspect of our self is one of the ways we become estranged and alienated from our past. It is important for us to have as many languages on hand as we can know or learn. It is important for those of us who are black, who speak in particular patois as well as standard English, to express ourselves in both ways.

16   Often I tell students from poor and working-class backgrounds that if you believe what you have learned and are learning in schools and universities separates you from your past, this is precisely what will happen. It is important to stand firm in the conviction that nothing can truly separate us from our pasts when we nurture and cherish that connection. An important strategy for maintaining contact is ongoing acknowledgement of the primacy of one's past, of one's background, affirming the reality that such bonds are not severed automatically solely because one enters a new environment and moves toward a different class experience.

17   Again, I do not wish to romanticize this effort, to dismiss the reality of conflict and contradiction. During my time at Stanford, I did go through a period of more than a year when I did not return home. That period was one where I felt that it was simply too difficult to mesh my profoundly disparate realities. Critical reflection about the choice I was making, particularly about why I felt a choice had to be made, pulled me through this difficult time. Luckily I recognized that the insistence on choosing between the world of family and community and the new world of privileged white people and privileged ways of knowing was imposed upon me by the outside. It is as though a mythical contract had been signed somewhere which demanded of us black folks that once we entered these spheres we would immediately give up all vestiges of our under-privileged past. It was my responsibility to formulate a way of being that would allow me to participate fully in my new environment while integrating and maintaining aspects of the old.

18   One of the most tragic manifestations of the pressure black people feel to assimilate is expressed in the internalization of racist perspectives. I was shocked and saddened when I first heard black professors at Stanford downgrade and express contempt for black students, expecting us to do poorly, refusing to establish nurturing bonds. At every university I have attended as a student or worked at as a teacher, I have heard similar attitudes expressed with little or no understanding of factors that might prevent brilliant black students from performing to their full capability. Within universities, there are few educational and social spaces where students who wish to affirm positive ties to ethnicity—to blackness, to working-class backgrounds—can receive affirmation and support. Ideologically, the message is clear—assimilation is the way to gain acceptance and approval from those in power.

19   Many white people enthusiastically supported Richard Rodriguez's vehement contention in his autobiography, *Hunger of Memory,* that attempts to maintain ties with his Chicano background impeded his progress, that he had to sever ties with community and kin to succeed at Stanford and in the larger world, that family language, in his case Spanish, had to be made secondary or discarded. If the terms of success as defined by the standards of ruling groups within white-supremacist, capitalist patriarchy are the only standards that exist, then assimilation is indeed necessary. But they are not. Even in the face of powerful structures of domination, it remains possible for each of us, especially those of us who are members of oppressed and/or exploited groups as well as those radical visionaries who may have race, class, and sex privilege, to define and determine alternative standards, to decide on the nature and extent of compromise. Standards by which one's success is measured, whether student or professor, are quite different from those of us who wish to resist reinforcing the domination of race, sex, and class, who work to maintain and strengthen our ties with the oppressed, with those who lack material privilege, with our families who are poor and working-class.

20   When I wrote my first book, *Ain't I a Woman: black women and feminism,* the issue of class and its relationship to who one's reading audience might be came up for me around my decision not to use footnotes, for which I have been sharply criticized. I told people that my concern was that footnotes set class boundaries for readers, determining who a book is for. I was shocked that many academic folks scoffed at this idea. I shared that I went into working-class black communities as well as talked with family and friends to survey whether or not they ever read books with footnotes and found that they did not. A few did not know what they were, but most folks saw them as indicating that a book was for college-educated people. These responses influenced my decision. When some of my more radical, college-educated friends freaked out about the absence of footnotes, I seriously questioned how we could ever imagine revolutionary transformation of society if such a small shift in direction could be viewed as threatening. Of course, many folks warned that the absence of footnotes would make the work less credible in academic circles. This information also highlighted the way in which class informs our choices. Certainly I did feel that choosing to use simple language, absence of footnotes, etc. would mean I was jeopardizing the possibility of being taken seriously in academic circles but then this was a political matter and a political decision. It utterly delights me that this has proven not to be the case and that the book is read by many academics as well as by people who are not college-educated.

21   Always our first response when we are motivated to conform or compromise within structures that reinforce domination must be to engage in critical reflection. Only by challenging ourselves to push against oppressive boundaries do we make the radical alternative possible, expanding the realm and scope of critical inquiry. Unless we share radical strategies, ways of

rethinking and revisioning with students, with kin and community, with a larger audience, we risk perpetuating the stereotype that we succeed because we are the exception, different from the rest of our people. Since I left home and entered college, I am often asked, usually by white people, if my sisters and brothers are also high achievers. At the root of this question is the longing for reinforcement of the belief in "the exception" which enables race, sex, and class biases to remain intact. I am careful to separate what it means to be exceptional from a notion of "the exception."

22   Frequently I hear smart black folks, from poor and working-class backgrounds, stressing their frustration that at times family and community do not recognize that they are exceptional. Absence of positive affirmation clearly diminishes the longing to excel in academic endeavors. Yet it is important to distinguish between the absence of basic positive affirmation and the longing for continued reinforcement that we are special. Usually liberal white folks will willingly offer continual reinforcement of us as exceptions—as special. This can be both patronizing and very seductive. Since we often work in situations where we are isolated from other black folks, we can easily begin to feel that encouragement from white people is the primary or only source of support and recognition. Given the internalization of racism, it is easy to view this support as more validating and legitimizing than similar support from black people. Still, nothing takes the place of being valued and appreciated by one's own, by one's family and community. We share a mutual and reciprocal responsibility for affirming one another's successes. Sometimes we have to talk to our folks about the fact that we need their ongoing support and affirmation, that it is unique and special to us. In some cases, we may never receive desired recognition and acknowledgement of specific achievements from kin. Rather than seeing this as a basis for estrangement, for severing connection, it is useful to explore other sources of nourishment and support.

23   I do not know that my mother's mother ever acknowledged my college education except to ask me once, "How can you live so far away from your people?" Yet she gave me sources of affirmation and nourishment, sharing the legacy of her quilt-making, of family history, of her incredible way with words. Recently, when our father retired after more than thirty years of work as a janitor, I wanted to pay tribute to this experience, to identify links between his work and my own as writer and teacher. Reflecting on our family past, I recalled ways that he had been an impressive example of diligence and hard work, approaching tasks with a seriousness of concentration I work to mirror and develop, with a discipline I struggle to maintain. Sharing these thoughts with him keeps us connected, nurtures our respect for each other, maintaining a space, however large or small, where we can talk.

24   Open, honest communication is the most important way we maintain relationships with kin and community as our class experience and backgrounds change. It is as vital as the sharing of resources. Often financial assistance is given in circumstances where there is no meaningful contact.

However helpful, this can also be an expression of estrangement and alienation. Communication between black folks from various experiences of material privilege was much easier when we were all in segregated communities
sharing common experiences in relation to social institutions. Without this
grounding, we must work to maintain ties, connection. We must assume
greater responsibility for making and maintaining contact, connections that
can shape our intellectual visions and inform our radical commitments.

25   The most powerful resource any of us can have as we study and teach in
university settings is full understanding and appreciation of the richness,
beauty, and primacy of our familial and community backgrounds. Maintaining awareness of class differences, nurturing ties with the poor and working-
class people who are our most intimate kin, our comrades in struggle,
transforms and enriches our intellectual experience. Education as the practice of freedom becomes not a force which fragments or separates, but one
that brings us closer, expanding our definitions of home and community.

FOLLOW-UP ACTIVITIES

Discussing the Rhetoric

1. What are the various groups that constitute hooks' audience? How does
the diversity of her intended audience complicate her rhetorical choices? Do
you consider yourself a member of hooks' audience? Why or why not?

2. Why does hooks begin with a story from her memory about her relationship with her mother? If this rhetorical choice is motivated by any of the political goals hooks discusses later in the essay, which ones?

3. hooks writes that it was her responsibility to find a way of being that
would always allow her full access into both environments—home and academic. How does hooks' organizational pattern illustrate this responsibility?

4. What rhetorical features does hooks use to create her position of authority with both her home and academic audiences?

Discussing the Conversation

1. Look up the word *assimilation*. Why do you think hooks resists assimilation?

2. What connections can you make between hooks' discussion of assimilation and the representation of Judge Nomoto in "Spandex Judge"?

3. In your estimation, would Elizabeth Cody Newenhuyse agree with hooks'
critique of assimilation? Locate passages in "De-Constructive Criticism" to
support your answer.

4. Would Mike Rose agree with hooks that our first response is always "to conform or compromise within structures that reinforce domination"? Recall Rose's discussion of his student, Marita.

5. How do you think hooks would respond to Bloom's representation of the student in "The Student and the University"? Locate passages in hooks' essay where she seems to be responding to Bloom's argument.

6. How do the appeals Bloom constructed differ from hooks' appeals? What do these differences suggest about the respective audiences?

7. What rhetorical strategies enable hooks to illustrate how difficult it is to persevere in the face of opposition? Which other writers in this Part take advantage of these strategies to make a similar point?

Joining the Conversation

1. In her conclusion, hooks claims that if we maintain ties to our home identities, we will enrich our intellectual experiences because our definitions of home and community will expand. Locate passages in the essay where hooks uses her personal experience to illustrate this claim. Write a short essay in which you consider how these passages illustrate the same idea differently. Which passage strikes you as most meaningful? Why do you think so? How does hooks' language choice affect your selection?

2. In an informal paper, recall a time when you felt as if you were conforming to or compromising your home identity. Have you ever challenged yourself by pushing against a boundary that seemed oppressive? How did these experiences make you feel?

INTRODUCTORY COMMENTS ON "STUDENTS' RIGHT TO THEIR OWN LANGUAGE"

Reading the Context

The following selection is a resolution passed by the College Conference on Composition and Communication (CCCC) in 1974 and ratified by the National Council of Teachers of English (NCTE), the CCCC's parent organization, the following year. The membership of both of these organizations consists of high school and college teachers of English and composition, though the CCCC focuses more specifically on college. Such organizations are important to professional discourse communities. Some, like the American Medical Association (the national professional organization for doctors), the American Bar Association (for lawyers), and the National Education Association (for school teachers of all subjects and all grade levels) are very well known. Others like the American Psychological Association and the American Society of Mechanical Engineers may be less familiar.

Professional organizations are important because they sponsor professional journals in which the members can publish their own research and read about the most recent work of their colleagues, and because they hold conferences in which the members can meet face-to-face to discuss their common issues. Some also publish statements of principle or policy as part of their responsibility to disseminate their professional knowledge to the public. For instance, the American Medical Association has published statements on the health hazards of smoking, on treating alcoholism as a disease rather than a moral weakness, and on treating violence as a medical problem as well as a criminal problem. The NCTE resolution is also a statement of principle based on the organization's expert knowledge.

Reading the Rhetoric

The rhetorical situation surrounding the publication of statements and resolutions passed by professional organizations is worth examining. What do you see as the purpose of such statements? Think also about the ethos and voice of such a resolution. What effect does a resolution that is published under the name of the American Medical Association or the National Council of Teachers of English have on the public? Although the organization is listed as the author of such statements, individuals or committees must compose them. What sort of *tone* (see the Appendix for definition) do you think the writers strive for? Why?

Reading the Conversation

"Students' Right to Their Own Language" was published in 1974, well before Richard Rodriguez, bell hooks, and Mary Louise Pratt (three of the writers included in this Part of the book) joined the written conversation about the relationship of formal education to students' home languages and identities. Moreover, the CCCC published a ten-page bibliography with its original statement to allow readers to catch up on the conversation upon which its view was based. If you would like to become more familiar with that conversation yourself, you might look up the CCCC's original statement and the explanation that accompanied it in the Fall 1774 Special Issue of the journal *College Composition and Communication.* As this book goes to press, the conversation still rages in the form "English Only" rules and laws proposed by various state legislatures and some members of Congress.

Students' Right to Their Own Language*
The National Council of Teachers of English

1 We affirm the students' right to their own patterns and varieties of language—the dialects of their nurture or whatever dialects in which they find their own identity and style. Language scholars long ago denied that the myth of a standard American dialect has any validity. The claim that any one dialect is unacceptable amounts to an attempt of one social group to exert its dominance over another. Such a claim leads to false advice for speakers and writers, and immoral advice for humans. A nation proud of its diverse heritage and its cultural and racial variety will preserve its heritage of dialects. We affirm strongly that teachers must have the experiences and training that will enable them to respect diversity and uphold the right of students to their own language.

NOTE

*A position statement adopted by the Conference on College Composition and Communication, an affiliate of the National Council of Teachers of English, April, 1974.

FOLLOW-UP ACTIVITIES

Discussing the Rhetoric

1. Who is the audience for this resolution? What is its purpose?

2. Think about the role English teachers have traditionally held as guardians of "proper" English. Which sentence of this statement addresses that role? How does it answer English teachers who may respond "But it's my job to eradicate nonstandard dialects"?

3. How would you describe the tone of this statement?

Discussing the Conversation

1. Locate recent newspaper articles or columns about groups advocating "English Only" rules and laws. If the articles quote proponents of the laws, compare their tone to that of the CCCC resolution.

2. Do you think Rodriguez agrees with the CCCC statement? When you read hooks and Pratt, consider where they would probably stand regarding this statement. Would they support it or oppose it?

3. Both sides of the "English Only" controversy base their views on certain American values. What values guided the CCCC in formulating its position? What values guide the "English Only" proponents?

Joining the Conversation

1. This is a collaborative writing exercise in which, working in small groups, you will role play the members of an organization that has decided to issue a public statement about a matter in which it has expertise. (You might be an association of high school coaches, members of the board of an environmental organization, student members of a committee redesigning your college's freshman literature requirement, or come up with your own group.) Your task is to decide what you want your statement of principle to advocate and then to write it in a short resolution form. The point of this exercise is to gain some experience working in a group to make rhetorical choices about wording and tone.

2. Using the first person "I" instead of "we," and substituting Rose, hooks, Rodriguez, or Bloom as the writer, rewrite the resolution in that writer's style. Then append a paragraph in which you reflect upon this assignment. Was it difficult? Did it seem inappropriate to use the style of any of these authors for this purpose? Did the rhetorical situation of such a resolution make some styles inappropriate? Did you find yourself writing a parody of the resolution? What effects does parody have on a reader?

INTRODUCTORY COMMENTS ON "THE ACHIEVEMENT OF DESIRE" BY RICHARD RODRIGUEZ

Reading the Context

Richard Rodriguez completed a doctorate in English Renaissance Literature at the University of California at Berkeley. He currently lives in San Francisco and is a lecturer, freelance writer, and educational consultant. He appears frequently on the *News Hour* with Jim Lehrer on public television, offering commentaries on controversial issues such as cultural awareness and diversity, as well as art criticism. "The Achievement of Desire" is excerpted from Rodriguez's autobiography, *Hunger of Memory* (1982). In this selection, Rodriguez surveys how his working class Mexican-American home culture made entering Anglo schools difficult. Rodriguez explores the tension between assimilating and resisting established academic conventions and discourse. As he retraces his identity, he argues that he had no choice but to move away from the conventions and language of his home environment in order to assimilate successfully into his academic environment. It is worth noting that Rodriguez's position generated much controversy, especially in the Hispanic community.

For Rodriguez, experiencing this separation of home and academic identities is a crucial part of a person's development. People who are not members of minority groups still must deal with the cultural tension between academic ways of thinking and their home belief systems.

Reading the Rhetoric

As you read, think about which rhetorical strategies Rodriguez uses to illustrate the cultural extremes of home and school environments. For example, can you locate passages in which Rodriguez seems to be speaking from one particular environment? Given the passages you've located, what audience do you think Rodriguez most desires to reach? Consider also Rodriguez' choice to tell his readers so much about his troubled home and school life. What does this tell you about his intended audience?

Rodriguez' choice of language builds an emotionally moving narrative. As you read, locate words, phrases, and passages that create Rodriguez' tone.

Rodriguez begins this chapter by citing sociologist Richard Hoggart's book *The Uses of Literacy* and explains how Hoggart's description of "the scholarship boy" helped him define his student identity. Consider why it's significant that Rodriguez begins in this way.

Reading the Conversation

The readings in this Part focus on how writers' identities are constructed by their cultural heritage and how that identity is expressed through their language. Which essays in Part One are stylistically similar to Rodriguez'? What makes them similar? Consider the essays by hooks, Rose, and Bloom. In what ways do these authors also acknowledge the force of home communities in shaping a student's identity?

The Achievement of Desire
Richard Rodriguez

I

1 At the end, in the British Museum (too distracted to finish my dissertation) for weeks I read, speed-read, books by modern educational theorists, only to find infrequent and slight mention of students like me. (Much more is written about the more typical case, the lower-class student who barely is helped by his schooling.) Then one day, leafing through Richard Hoggart's

The Uses of Literacy, I found, in his description of the scholarship boy, my-self. For the first time I realized that there were other students like me, and so I was able to frame the meaning of my academic success, its consequent price—the loss.

2   Hoggart's description is distinguished, at least initially, by deep under-standing. What he grasps very well is that the scholarship boy must move be-tween environments, his home and the classroom, which are at cultural extremes, opposed. With his family, the boy has the intense pleasure of inti-macy, the family's consolation in feeling public alienation. Lavish emotions texture home life. *Then,* at school, the instruction bids him to trust lonely rea-son primarily. Immediate needs set the pace of his parents' lives. From his mother and father the boy learns to trust spontaneity and nonrational ways of knowing. *Then,* at school, there is mental calm. Teachers emphasize the value of a reflectiveness that opens a space between thinking and immediate action.

3   Years of schooling must pass before the boy will be able to sketch the cultural differences in his day as abstractly as this. But he senses those dif-ferences early. Perhaps as early as the night he brings home an assignment from school and finds the house too noisy for study.

> He has to be more and more alone, if he is going to 'get on'. He will have, probably unconsciously, to oppose the ethos of the hearth, the intense gre-gariousness of the working-class family group. Since everything centres upon the living-room, there is unlikely to be a room of his own; the bed-rooms are cold and inhospitable, and to warm them or the front room, if there is one, would not only be expensive, but would require an imagina-tive leap—out of the tradition—which most families are not capable of making. There is a corner of the living-room table. On the other side Mother is ironing, the wireless is on, someone is singing a snatch of song or Father says intermittently whatever comes into his head. The boy has to cut himself off mentally, so as to do his homework, as well as he can.*

4   The next day, the lesson is as apparent at school. There are even rows of desks. Discussion is ordered. The boy must rehearse his thoughts and raise his hand before speaking out in a loud voice to an audience of classmates. And there is time enough, and silence, to think about ideas (big ideas) never considered at home by his parents.

5   Not for the working-class child alone is adjustment to the classroom dif-ficult. Good schooling requires that any student alter early childhood habits. But the working-class child is usually least prepared for the change. And, un-like many middle-class children, he goes home and sees in his parents a way of life not only different but starkly opposed to that of the classroom. (He en-ters the house and hears his parents talking in ways his teachers discourage.)

---

*All quotations in this chapter are from Richard Hoggart, *The Uses of Literacy* (London: Chatto and Windus, 1957), Chapter 10.

6   Without extraordinary determination and the great assistance of others—at home and at school—there is little chance for success. Typically most working-class children are barely changed by the classroom. The exception succeeds. The relative few become scholarship students. Of these, Richard Hoggart estimates, most manage a fairly graceful transition. Somehow they learn to live in the two very different worlds of their day. There are some others, however, those Hoggart pejoratively terms 'scholarship boys,' for whom success comes with special anxiety. Scholarship boy: good student, troubled son. The child is 'moderately endowed,' intellectually mediocre, Hoggart supposes—though it may be more pertinent to note the special qualities of temperament in the child. High-strung child. Brooding. Sensitive. Haunted by the knowledge that one *chooses* to become a student. (Education is not an inevitable or natural step in growing up.) Here is a child who cannot forget that his academic success distances him from a life he loved, even from his own memory of himself.

7   Initially, he wavers, balances allegiance. ('The boy is himself [until he reaches, say, the upper forms] very much of *both* the worlds of home and school. He is enormously obedient to the dictates of the world of school, but emotionally still strongly wants to continue as part of the family circle.') Gradually, necessarily, the balance is lost. The boy needs to spend more and more time studying, each night enclosing himself in the silence permitted and required by intense concentration. He takes his first step toward academic success, away from his family.

8   From the very first days, through the years following, it will be with his parents—the figures of lost authority, the persons toward whom he feels deepest love—that the change will be most powerfully measured. A separation will unravel between them. Advancing in his studies, the boy notices that his mother and father have not changed as much as he. Rather, when he sees them, they often remind him of the person he once was and the life he earlier shared with them. He realizes what some Romantics also know when they praise the working class for the capacity for human closeness, qualities of passion and spontaneity, that the rest of us experience in like measure only in the earliest part of our youth. For the Romantic, this doesn't make working-class life childish. Working-class life challenges precisely because it is an *adult* way of life.

9   The scholarship boy reaches a different conclusion. He cannot afford to admire his parents. (How could he and still pursue such a contrary life?) He permits himself embarrassment at their lack of education. And to evade nostalgia for the life he has lost, he concentrates on the benefits education will bestow upon him. He becomes especially ambitious. Without the support of old certainties and consolations, almost mechanically, he assumes the procedures and doctrines of the classroom. The kind of allegiance the young student might have given his mother and father only days earlier, he transfers to the teacher, the new figure of authority. '[The scholarship boy] tends to make a father-figure of his form-master,' Hoggart observes.

10   But Hoggart's calm prose only makes me recall the urgency with which I came to idolize my grammar school teachers. I began by imitating their accents, using their diction, trusting their every direction. The very first facts they dispensed, I grasped with awe. Any book they told me to read, I read—then waited for them to tell me which books I enjoyed. Their every casual opinion I came to adopt and to trumpet when I returned home. I stayed after school 'to help'—to get my teacher's undivided attention. It was the nun's encouragement that mattered most to me. (She understood exactly what—my parents never seemed to appraise so well—all my achievements entailed.) Memory gently caressed each word of praise bestowed in the classroom so that compliments teachers paid me years ago come quickly to mind even today.

11   The enthusiasm I felt in second-grade classes I flaunted before both my parents. The docile, obedient student came home a shrill and precocious son who insisted on correcting and teaching his parents with the remark: 'My teacher told us. . . .'

12   I intended to hurt my mother and father. I was still angry at them for having encouraged me toward classroom English. But gradually this anger was exhausted, replaced by guilt as school grew more and more attractive to me. I grew increasingly successful, a talkative student. My hand was raised in the classroom; I yearned to answer any question. At home, life was less noisy than it had been. (I spoke to classmates and teachers more often each day than to family members.) Quiet at home, I sat with my papers for hours each night. I never forgot that schooling had irretrievably changed my family's life. That knowledge, however, did not weaken ambition. Instead, it strengthened resolve. Those times I remembered the loss of my past with regret, I quickly reminded myself of all the things my teachers could give me. (They could make me an educated man.) I tightened my grip on pencil and books. I evaded nostalgia. Tried hard to forget. But one does not forget by trying to forget. One only remembers. I remembered too well that education had changed my family's life. I would not have become a scholarship boy had I not so often remembered.

13   Once she was sure that her children knew English, my mother would tell us, 'You should keep up your Spanish.' Voices playfully groaned in response. '¡Pochos!' my mother would tease. I listened silently.

14   After a while, I grew more calm at home. I developed tact. A fourth-grade student, I was no longer the show-off in front of my parents. I became a conventionally dutiful son, politely affectionate, cheerful enough, even—for reasons beyond choosing—my father's favorite. And much about my family life was easy then, comfortable, happy in the rhythm of our living together: hearing my father getting ready for work; eating the breakfast my mother had made me; looking up from a novel to hear my brother or one of my sisters playing with friends in the backyard; in winter, coming upon the house all lighted up after dark.

15   But withheld from my mother and father was any mention of what most mattered to me: the extraordinary experience of first-learning. Late after-

noon: In the midst of preparing dinner, my mother would come up behind me while I was trying to read. Her head just over mine, her breath warmly scented with food. 'What are you reading?' Or, 'Tell me all about your new courses.' I would barely respond, 'Just the usual things, nothing special.' (A half smile, then silence. Her head moving back in the silence. Silence! Instead of the flood of intimate sounds that had once flowed smoothly between us, there was this silence.) After dinner, I would rush to a bedroom with papers and books. As often as possible, I resisted parental pleas to 'save lights' by coming to the kitchen to work. I kept so much, so often, to myself. Sad. Enthusiastic. Troubled by the excitement of coming upon new ideas. Eager. Fascinated by the promising texture of a brand-new book. I hoarded the pleasures of learning. Alone for hours. Enthralled. Nervous. I rarely looked away from my books—or back on my memories. Nights when relatives visited and the front rooms were warmed by Spanish sounds, I slipped quietly out of the house.

16   It mattered that education was changing me. It never ceased to matter. My brother and sisters would giggle at our mother's mispronounced words. They'd correct her gently. My mother laughed girlishly one night, trying not to pronounce *sheep* as *ship*. From a distance I listened sullenly. From that distance, pretending not to notice on another occasion, I saw my father looking at the title pages of my library books. That was the scene on my mind when I walked home with a fourth-grade companion and heard him say that his parents read to him every night. (A strange-sounding book—*Winnie the Pooh.*) Immediately, I wanted to know, 'What is it like?' My companion, however, thought I wanted to know about the plot of the book. Another day, my mother surprised me by asking for a 'nice' book to read. 'Something not too hard you think I might like.' Carefully I chose one, Willa Cather's *My Ántonia*. But when, several weeks later, I happened to see it next to her bed unread except for the first few pages, I was furious and suddenly wanted to cry. I grabbed up the book and took it back to my room and placed it in its place, alphabetically on my shelf.

17   'Your parents must be very proud of you.' People began to say that to me about the time I was in sixth grade. To answer affirmatively, I'd smile. Shyly I'd smile, never betraying my sense of the irony: I was not proud of my mother and father. I was embarrassed by their lack of education. It was not that I ever thought they were stupid, though stupidly I took for granted their enormous native intelligence. Simply, what mattered to me was that they were not like my teachers.

18   But, 'Why didn't you tell us about the award?' my mother demanded, her frown weakened by pride. At the grammar school ceremony several weeks after, her eyes were brighter than the trophy I'd won. Pushing back the hair from my forehead, she whispered that I had 'shown' the *gringos*. A few minutes later, I heard my father speak to my teacher and felt ashamed of his labored, accented words. Then guilty for the shame. I felt such contrary

feelings. (There is no simple roadmap through the heart of the scholarship boy.) My teacher was so soft-spoken and her words were edged sharp and clean. I admired her until it seemed to me that she spoke too carefully. Sensing that she was condescending to them, I became nervous. Resentful. Protective. I tried to move my parents away. 'You both must be very proud of Richard,' the nun said. They responded quickly. (They were proud.) 'We are proud of all our children.' Then this afterthought: 'They sure didn't get their brains from us.' They all laughed. I smiled.

19 Tightening the irony into a knot was the knowledge that my parents were always behind me. They made success possible. They evened the path. They sent their children to parochial schools because the nuns 'teach better.' They paid a tuition they couldn't afford. They spoke English to us.

20   For their children my parents wanted chances they never had—an easier way. It saddened my mother to learn that some relatives forced their children to start working right after high school. To *her* children she would say, 'Get all the education you can.' In schooling she recognized the key to job advancement. And with the remark she remembered her past.

21   As a girl new to America my mother had been awarded a high school diploma by teachers too careless or busy to notice that she hardly spoke English. On her own, she determined to learn how to type. That skill got her jobs typing envelopes in letter shops, and it encouraged in her an optimism about the possibility of advancement. (Each morning when her sisters put on uniforms, she chose a bright-colored dress.) The years of young womanhood passed, and her typing speed increased. She also became an excellent speller of words she mispronounced. 'And I've never been to college,' she'd say, smiling, when her children asked her to spell words they were too lazy to look up in a dictionary.

22   Typing, however, was dead-end work. Finally frustrating. When her youngest child started high school, my mother got a full-time office job once again. (Her paycheck combined with my father's to make us—in fact—what we had already become in our imagination of ourselves—middle class.) She worked then for the (California) state government in numbered civil service positions secured by examinations. The old ambition of her youth was rekindled. During the lunch hour, she consulted bulletin boards for announcements of openings. One day she saw mention of something called an 'anti-poverty agency.' A typing job. A glamorous job, part of the governor's staff. 'A knowledge of Spanish required.' Without hesitation she applied and became nervous only when the job was suddenly hers.

23   'Everyone comes to work all dressed up,' she reported at night. And didn't need to say more than that her co-workers wouldn't let her answer the phones. She was only a typist, after all, albeit a very fast typist. And an excellent speller. One morning there was a letter to be sent to a Washington cabinet officer. On the dictating tape, a voice referred to urban guerrillas. My mother typed (the wrong word, correctly): 'gorillas.' The mistake horrified

the anti-poverty bureaucrats who shortly after arranged to have her returned to her previous position. She would go no further. So she willed her ambition to her children. 'Get all the education you can; with an education you can do anything.' (With a good education *she* could have done anything.)

24   When I was in high school, I admitted to my mother that I planned to become a teacher someday. That seemed to please her. But I never tried to explain that it was not the occupation of teaching I yearned for as much as it was something more elusive: I wanted to *be* like my teachers, to possess their knowledge, to assume their authority, their confidence, even to assume a teacher's persona.

25   In contrast to my mother, my father never verbally encouraged his children's academic success. Nor did he often praise us. My mother had to remind him to 'say something' to one of his children who scored some academic success. But whereas my mother saw in education the opportunity for job advancement, my father recognized that education provided an even more startling possibility: It could enable a person to escape from a life of mere labor.

26   In Mexico, orphaned when he was eight, my father left school to work as an 'apprentice' for an uncle. Twelve years later, he left Mexico in frustration and arrived in America. He had great expectations then of becoming an engineer. ('Work for my hands and my head.') He knew a Catholic priest who promised to get him money enough to study full time for a high school diploma. But the promises came to nothing. Instead there was a dark succession of warehouse, cannery, and factory jobs. After work he went to night school along with my mother. A year, two passed. Nothing much changed, except that fatigue worked its way into the bone; then everything changed. He didn't talk anymore of becoming an engineer. He stayed outside on the steps of the school while my mother went inside to learn typing and shorthand.

27   By the time I was born, my father worked at 'clean' jobs. For a time he was a janitor at a fancy department store. ('Easy work; the machines do it all.') Later he became a dental technician. ('Simple.') But by then he was pessimistic about the ultimate meaning of work and the possibility of ever escaping its claims. In some of my earliest memories of him, my father already seems aged by fatigue. (He has never really grown old like my mother.) From boyhood to manhood, I have remembered him in a single image: seated, asleep on the sofa, his head thrown back in a hideous corpselike grin, the evening newspaper spread out before him. 'But look at all you've accomplished,' his best friend said to him once. My father said nothing. Only smiled.

28   It was my father who laughed when I claimed to be tired by reading and writing. It was he who teased me for having soft hands. (He seemed to sense that some great achievement of leisure was implied by my papers and books.) It was my father who became angry while watching on television some woman at the Miss America contest tell the announcer that she was going to college. ('Majoring in fine arts.') 'College!' he snarled. He despised the trivialization of higher education, the inflated grades and cheapened

diplomas, the half education that so often passed as mass education in my generation.

29   It was my father again who wondered why I didn't display my awards on the wall of my bedroom. He said he liked to go to doctors' offices and see their certificates and degrees on the wall. ('Nice.') My citations from school got left in closets at home. The gleaming figure astride one of my trophies was broken, wingless, after hitting the ground. My medals were placed in a jar of loose change. And when I lost my high school diploma, my father found it as it was about to be thrown out with the trash. Without telling me, he put it away with his own things for safekeeping.

30 These memories slammed together at the instant of hearing that refrain familiar to all scholarship students: 'Your parents must be very proud. . . .' Yes, my parents were proud. I knew it. But my parents regarded my progress with more than mere pride. They endured my early precocious behavior—but with what private anger and humiliation? As their children got older and would come home to challenge ideas both of them held, they argued before submitting to the force of logic or superior factual evidence with the disclaimer, 'It's what we were taught in our time to believe.' These discussions ended abruptly, though my mother remembered them on other occasions when she complained that our 'big ideas' were going to our heads. More acute was her complaint that the family wasn't close anymore, like some others she knew. Why weren't we close, 'more in the Mexican style'? Everyone is so private, she added. And she mimicked the yes and no answers she got in reply to her questions. Why didn't we talk more? (My father never asked.) I never said.

31   I was the first in my family who asked to leave home when it came time to go to college. I had been admitted to Stanford, one hundred miles away. My departure would only make physically apparent the separation that had occurred long before. But it was going too far. In the months preceding my leaving, I heard the question my mother never asked except indirectly. In the hot kitchen, tired at the end of her workday, she demanded to know, 'Why aren't the colleges here in Sacramento good enough for you? They are for your brother and sister.' In the middle of a car ride, not turning to face me, she wondered, 'Why do you need to go so far away?' Late at night, ironing, she said with disgust, 'Why do you have to put us through this big expense? You know your scholarship will never cover it all.' But when September came there was a rush to get everything ready. In a bedroom that last night I packed the big brown valise, and my mother sat nearby sewing initials onto the clothes I would take. And she said no more about my leaving.

32   Months later, two weeks of Christmas vacation: The first hours home were the hardest. ('What's new?') My parents and I sat in the kitchen for a conversation. (But, lacking the same words to develop our sentences and to shape our interests, what was there to say? What could I tell them of the

term paper I had just finished on the 'universality of Shakespeare's appeal'?) I mentioned only small, obvious things: my dormitory life; weekend trips I had taken; random events. They responded with news of their own. (One was almost grateful for a family crisis about which there was much to discuss.) We tired to make our conversation seem like more than an interview.

FOLLOW-UP ACTIVITIES

Discussing the Rhetoric

1. Why do you think Rodriguez chose to locate himself in the British Museum at the beginning of this selection? Why would he open with a quotation from Hoggart's book *The Uses of Literacy?*

2. Does Rodriguez assimilate or resist academic conventions in this essay? Locate passages to support your views.

3. This essay is a reflective account of Rodriguez' increasing awareness of the precarious, or ever-changing, nature of an identity. The author traces his growth through the essay's five parts. Name these parts. How are the five parts connected?

4. Who is Rodriguez' audience? What evidence suggests this? Are you one of its members?

5. What strategies does Rodriguez use to establish his authority?

Discussing the Conversation

1. What does Rodriguez add to this Part's conversation? In particular, what passages from "The Achievement of Desire" speak to hooks' conclusion that education doesn't separate but brings us together, "expanding our definitions of home and community?"

2. Mike Rose uses the case study of a student named Marita to illustrate the point that students' home identities often clash with teachers' expectations. Rose claims that Marita found herself "adrift in a set of conventions she didn't fully understand." Can you locate passages in this essay where Rodriguez seems to echo Marita's dilemma?

3. How do Rodriguez' appeals differ from the appeals Allan Bloom constructs in "The Student and the University"? What does this difference say about how Rodriguez and Bloom view their audiences?

4. What factors does Rodriguez think are important to consider when negotiating one's home and student identities? Compare your answers with Kent Kirkpatrick's portrayal of Judge Nomoto, the "Spandex Judge." What are the differences, and how might you account for these differences? Considering how "popular" and "academic" writing differs will help you answer this question.

Joining the Conversation

1. Can you recall experiencing any academic situation similar to what Rodriguez describes? That is, have you ever been forced to weigh the differences of your home and academic environments? Write an informal paper in which you take your audience through your experience.

2. In "De-Constructive Criticism," Elizabeth Cody Newenhuyse warns her readers that they must work toward ridding themselves of the "nasty little imp" of a critical spirit. In contrast, Rodriguez seems to revel in self-reflective criticism. Think about the different ways that Newenhuyse and Rodriguez view criticism. Write an informal paper in which you discuss these views and explain what role, if any, criticism plays in your personal growth.

INTRODUCTORY COMMENTS ON "ARTS OF THE CONTACT ZONE" BY MARY LOUISE PRATT

Reading the Context

Mary Louise Pratt is one of the cofounders of a freshman culture program at Stanford University. This program supplemented traditional Western civilization courses with courses that expanded the range of languages, cultures, and texts traditionally covered.

However, Pratt is doing more than supplementing the Western history curriculum and reporting on her students' responses to it in this selection. She is also re-defining the meaning of culture. For Pratt, culture is not the production of a homogeneous body of people that share the same values and speak the same language. Culture more often is constituted by a struggle in which one group continuously incorporates, resists, or erases aspects of another group's linguistic, symbolic, and traditional heritage. This selection, among other things, looks specifically at one man's struggle to resist a more powerful group's conquest and examines those attempts in order to identify rhetorical strategies that any cultural group uses when encountering the influence of another. Pratt discusses the challenges a redefinition of culture creates in the concluding section of this selection. She notes that such changes in curriculum do not make students comfortable, but instead provide them with an expanded view that introduces and accommodates discomfort as well.

Pratt is the author or co-author of several books, including *Toward a Speech Act Theory of Literary Discourse* (1977), *Linguistics for Students of Literature* (1983), *Women, Culture, and Politics in Latin America* (1990), and *Imperial Eyes: Studies in Travel Writing and Transculturation* (1992).

Reading the Rhetoric

The audience for "Arts of the Contact Zone," originally delivered as a speech, was the members of the Modern Language Association (MLA). The MLA is comprised of professors of modern languages, including English. One of the functions of groups like the MLA is to advance the study of literature through producing research on sources and interpretations of literature. How do you imagine a typical speech in front of such a group would start? What risks does Pratt take in approaching her audience the way she does? Consider also what it says about Pratt's position within this community that she was invited to address them. Does she sound like she's a member or not? In what ways does she seem to share the group's goals and ethics? In what ways does she challenge them?

Take a minute before reading the selection to think about how you would start such a speech. What would you do to engage the attention and command the respect of such an audience? Then, as you read, mark passages or words that seem odd given Pratt's audience and think about how you would continue, and end her speech.

Reading the Conversation

Pratt's essay, "Arts of the Contact Zone," provides a segue from the first to the second Part of this text. Pratt echoes the arguments of authors like bell hooks, who claim that individuals can resist the colonizing efforts of a dominant culture. But she simultaneously depicts individuals as communally situated. For Pratt, and for writers such as Jane Tompkins and Stanley Fish, whom you will read later in this book, resistance comes in the form of one communal group defying the impositions of another group, rather than one individual defying assimilation into a culture. Meaning is socially, not individually, constructed.

Imagine Pratt in a conversation with other writers you have read so far. Would she agree with any of them? In what ways?

Arts of the Contact Zone
Mary Louise Pratt

1 Whenever the subject of literacy comes up, what often pops first into my mind is a conversation I overheard eight years ago between my son Sam and his best friend, Willie, aged six and seven, respectively: "Why don't you trade me Many Trails for Carl Yats . . . Yesits . . . Yastrum-scrum." "That's not how you say it, dummy, it's Carl Yes . . . Yes . . . oh, I don't know." Sam and Willie had just discovered baseball cards. Many Trails was their decoding, with the help of first-grade English phonics, of the name Manny Trillo. The name they were quite rightly stumped on was Carl Yastremski. That was the first time I remembered seeing them put their incipient literacy to their own use, and I was of course thrilled.

2   Sam and Willie learned a lot about phonics that year by trying to decipher surnames on baseball cards, and a lot about cities, states, heights, weights, places of birth, stages of life. In the years that followed, I watched Sam apply his arithmetic skills to working out batting averages and subtracting retirement years from rookie years; I watched him develop senses of patterning and order by arranging and rearranging his cards for hours on end, and aesthetic judgment by comparing different photos, different series, layouts, and color schemes. American geography and history took shape in his mind through baseball cards. Much of his social life revolved around trading them, and he learned about exchange, fairness, trust, the importance of processes as opposed to results, what it means to get cheated, taken advantage of, even robbed. Baseball cards were the medium of his economic life too. Nowhere better to learn the power and arbitrariness of money, the absolute divorce between use value and exchange value, notions of long- and short-term investment, the possibility of personal values that are independent of market values.

3   Baseball cards meant baseball card shows, where there was much to be learned about adult worlds as well. And baseball cards opened the door to baseball books, shelves and shelves of encyclopedias, magazines, histories, biographies, novels, books of jokes, anecdotes, cartoons, even poems. Sam learned the history of American racism and the struggle against it through baseball; he saw the depression and two world wars from behind home plate. He learned the meaning of commodified labor, what it means for one's body and talents to be owned and dispensed by another. He knows something about Japan, Taiwan, Cuba, and Central America and how men and boys do things there. Through the history and experience of baseball stadiums he thought about architecture, light, wind, topography, meteorology, the dynamics of public space. He learned the meaning of expertise, of knowing about something well enough that you can start a conversation with a stranger and feel sure of holding your own. Even with an adult—especially with an adult.

Throughout his preadolescent years, baseball history was Sam's luminous point of contact with grown-ups, his lifeline to caring. And, of course, all this time he was also playing baseball, struggling his way through the stages of the local Little League system, lucky enough to be a pretty good player, loving the game and coming to know deeply his strengths and weaknesses.

4   Literacy began for Sam with the newly pronounceable names on the picture cards and brought him what has been easily the broadest, most varied, most enduring, and most integrated experience of his thirteen-year life. Like many parents, I was delighted to see schooling give Sam the tools with which to find and open all these doors. At the same time I found it unforgivable that schooling itself gave him nothing remotely as meaningful to do, let alone anything that would actually take him beyond the referential, masculinist ethos of baseball and its lore.

5   However, I was not invited here to speak as a parent, nor as an expert on literacy. I was asked to speak as an MLA member working in the elite academy. In that capacity my contribution is undoubtedly supposed to be abstract, irrelevant, and anchored outside the real world. I wouldn't dream of disappointing anyone. I propose immediately to head back several centuries to a text that has a few points in common with baseball cards and raises thoughts about what Tony Sarmiento, in his comments to the conference, called new visions of literacy. In 1908 a Peruvianist named Richard Pietschmann was exploring in the Danish Royal Archive in Copenhagen and came across a manuscript. It was dated in the city of Cuzco in Peru, in the year 1613, some forty years after the final fall of the Inca empire to the Spanish and signed with an unmistakably Andean indigenous name: Felipe Guaman Poma de Ayala. Written in a mixture of Quechua and ungrammatical, expressive Spanish, the manuscript was a letter addressed by an unknown but apparently literate Andean to King Philip III of Spain. What stunned Pietschmann was that the letter was twelve hundred pages long. There were almost eight hundred pages of written text and four hundred of captioned line drawings. It was titled *The First New Chronicle and Good Government.* No one knew (or knows) how the manuscript got to the library in Copenhagen or how long it had been there. No one, it appeared, had ever bothered to read it or figured out how. Quechua was not thought of as a written language in 1908, nor Andean culture as a literate culture.

6   Pietschmann prepared a paper on his find, which he presented in London in 1912, a year after the rediscovery of Machu Picchu by Hiram Bingham. Reception, by an international congress of Americanists, was apparently confused. It took twenty-five years for a facsimile edition of the work to appear, in Paris. It was not till the late 1970s, as positivist reading habits gave way to interpretive studies and colonial elitisms to postcolonial pluralisms, that Western scholars found ways of reading Guaman Poma's *New Chronicle and Good Government* as the extraordinary intercultural tour de force that it was. The letter got there, only 350 years too late, a miracle and a terrible tragedy.

7   I propose to say a few more words about this erstwhile unreadable text, in order to lay out some thoughts about writing and literacy in what I like to call the *contact zones.* I use this term to refer to social spaces where cultures meet, clash, and grapple with each other, often in contexts of highly asymmetrical relations of power, such as colonialism, slavery, or their aftermaths as they are lived out in many parts of the world today. Eventually I will use the term to reconsider the models of community that many of us rely on in teaching and theorizing and that are under challenge today. But first a little more about Guaman Poma's giant letter to Philip III.

8   Insofar as anything is known about him at all, Guaman Poma exemplified the sociocultural complexities produced by conquest and empire. He was an indigenous Andean who claimed noble Inca descent and who had adopted (at least in some sense) Christianity. He may have worked in the Spanish colonial administration as an interpreter, scribe, or assistant to a Spanish tax collector—as a mediator, in short. He says he learned to write from his half brother, a mestizo whose Spanish father had given him access to religious education.

9   Guaman Poma's letter to the king is written in two languages (Spanish and Quechua) and two parts. The first is called the *Nueva corónica* 'New Chronicle.' The title is important. The chronicle of course was the main writing apparatus through which the Spanish represented their American conquests to themselves. It constituted one of the main official discourses. In writing a "new chronicle," Guaman Poma took over the official Spanish genre for his own ends. Those ends were, roughly, to construct a new picture of the world, a picture of a Christian world with Andean rather than European peoples at the center of it—Cuzco, not Jerusalem. In the *New Chronicle* Guaman Poma begins by rewriting the Christian history of the world from Adam and Eve (Figure 1), incorporating the Amerindians into it as offspring of one of the sons of Noah. He identifies five ages of Christian history that he links in parallel with the five ages of canonical Andean history—separate but equal trajectories that diverge with Noah and reintersect not with Columbus but with Saint Bartholomew, claimed to have preceded Columbus in the Americas. In a couple of hundred pages, Guaman Poma constructs a veritable encyclopedia of Inca and pre-Inca history, customs, laws, social forms, public offices, and dynastic leaders. The depictions resemble European manners and customs description, but also reproduce the meticulous detail with which knowledge in Inca society was stored on *quipus* and in the oral memories of elders.

10   Guaman Poma's *New Chronicle* is an instance of what I have proposed to call an *autoethnographic* text, by which I mean a text in which people undertake to describe themselves in ways that engage with representations others have made of them. Thus if ethnographic texts are those in which European metropolitan subjects represent to themselves their others (usually their conquered others), autoethnographic texts are representations that the so-defined others construct *in response to* or in dialogue with those texts.

Figure 1   Adam and Eve.

Autoethnographic texts are not, then, what are usually thought of as autochthonous forms of expression or self-representation (as the Andean *quipus* were). Rather they involve a selective collaboration with and appropriation of idioms of the metropolis or the conqueror. These are merged or infiltrated to varying degrees with indigenous idioms to create self-representations intended to intervene in metropolitan modes of understanding. Autoethnographic works are often addressed to both metropolitan audiences and the speaker's own community. Their reception is thus highly indeterminate. Such texts often constitute a marginalized group's point of entry into the dominant circuits of print culture. It is interesting to think, for example, of American slave autobiography in its autoethnographic dimensions, which in some respects distinguish it from Euramerican autobiographical tradition. The concept might help explain why some of the earliest published writing by Chicanas took the form of folkloric manners and customs sketches written in English and published in English-language newspapers or folklore magazines (see Treviño). Autoethnographic representation often involves concrete collaborations between people, as between literate ex-slaves and abolitionist intellectuals, or between Guaman Poma and the Inca elders who were his informants. Often, as in Guaman Poma, it involves more than one language. In recent decades autoethnography, critique, and resistance have reconnected with writing in a contemporary creation of the contact zone, the *testimonio.*

11   Guaman Poma's *New Chronicle* ends with a revisionist account of the Spanish conquest, which, he argues, should have been a peaceful encounter of equals with the potential for benefiting both, but for the mindless greed of the Spanish. He parodies Spanish history. Following contact with the Incas, he writes, "In all Castille, there was a great commotion. All day and at night in their dreams the Spaniards were saying 'Yndias, yndias, oro, plata, oro, plata del Piru'" ("Indies, Indies, gold, silver, gold, silver from Peru") (Figure 2). The Spanish, he writes, brought nothing of value to share with the Andeans, nothing "but armor and guns con la codicia de oro, plata, oro y plata, yndias, a las Yndias, Piru" ("with the lust for gold, silver, gold and silver, Indies, the Indies, Peru") (372). I quote these words as an example of a conquered subject using the conqueror's language to construct a parodic, oppositional representation

Figure 2   Conquista. Meeting of Spaniard and Inca. The Inca says in Quechua, "You eat this gold?" Spaniard replies in Spanish, "We eat this gold."

of the conqueror's own speech. Guaman Poma mirrors back to the Spanish (in their language, which is alien to him) an image of themselves that they often suppress and will therefore surely recognize. Such are the dynamics of language, writing, and representation in contact zones.

12   The second half of the epistle continues the critique. It is titled *Buen gobierno y justicia* 'Good Government and Justice' and combines a description of colonial society in the Andean region with a passionate denunciation of Spanish exploitation and abuse. (These, at the time he was writing, were decimating the population of the Andes at a genocidal rate. In fact, the potential loss of the labor force became a main cause for reform of the system.) Guaman Poma's most implacable hostility is invoked by the clergy, followed by the dreaded *corregidores,* or colonial overseers (Figure 3). He also praises good works, Christian habits, and just men where he finds them, and offers at length his views as to what constitutes "good government and justice." The Indies, he argues, should be administered through a collaboration of Inca and Spanish elites. The epistle ends with an imaginary question-and-answer session in which, in a reversal of hierarchy, the king is depicted asking Guaman

Figure 3   Corregidor de minas. Catalog of Spanish abuses of indigenous labor force.

Poma questions about how to reform the empire—a dialogue imagined across the many lines that divide the Andean scribe from the imperial monarch, and in which the subordinated subject single-handedly gives himself authority in the colonizer's language and verbal repertoire. In a way, it worked—this extraordinary text did get written—but in a way it did not, for the letter never reached its addressee.

13   To grasp the import of Guaman Poma's project, one needs to keep in mind that the Incas had no system of writing. Their huge empire is said to be the only known instance of a full-blown bureaucratic state society built and administered without writing. Guaman Poma constructs his text by appropriating and adapting pieces of the representational repertoire of the invaders. He does not simply imitate or reproduce it; he selects and adapts it along Andean lines to express (bilingually, mind you) Andean interests and aspirations. Ethnographers have used the term *transculturation* to describe processes whereby members of subordinated or marginal groups select and invent from materials transmitted by a dominant or metropolitan culture. The term, originally coined by Cuban sociologist Fernando Ortiz in the 1940s, aimed to replace overly reductive concepts of acculturation and assimilation used to characterize culture under conquest. While subordinate peoples do not usually control what emanates from the dominant culture, they do determine to varying extents what gets absorbed into their own and what it gets used for. Transculturation, like autoethnography, is a phenomenon of the contact zone.

14   As scholars have realized only relatively recently, the transcultural character of Guaman Poma's text is intricately apparent in its visual as well as its written component. The genre of the four hundred line drawings is European—there seems to have been no tradition of representational drawing among the Incas—but in their execution they deploy specifically Andean systems of spatial symbolism that express Andean values and aspirations.[1]

15   In figure 1, for instance, Adam is depicted on the left-hand side below the sun, while Eve is on the right-hand side below the moon, and slightly lower than Adam. The two are divided by the diagonal of Adam's digging stick. In Andean spatial symbolism, the diagonal descending from the sun marks the basic line of power and authority dividing upper from lower, male from female, dominant from subordinate. In figure 2, the Inca appears in the same position as Adam, with the Spaniard opposite, are the two at the same height. In figure 3, depicting Spanish abuses of power, the symbolic pattern is reversed. The Spaniard is in a high position indicating dominance, but on the "wrong" (right-hand) side. The diagonals of his lance and that of the servant doing the flogging mark of a line of illegitimate, though real, power. The Andean figures continue to occupy the left-hand side of the picture, but clearly as victims. Guaman Poma wrote that the Spanish conquest had produced "un mundo al reves" the world in reverse.

16   In sum, Guaman Poma's text is truly a product of the contact zone. If one thinks of cultures, or literatures, as discrete, coherently structured,

monolingual edifices, Guaman Poma's text, and indeed any autoethnographic world appears anomalous or chaotic—as it apparently did to the European scholars Pietschmann spoke to in 1912. If one does not think of cultures this way, then Guaman Poma's text is simply heterogeneous, as the Andean region views itself and remains today. Such a text is heterogeneous at the reception end as well as the production end: it will read very differently to people in different positions in the contact zone. Because it deploys European and Andean systems of meaning making, the letter necessarily means differently to bilingual Spanish-Quechua speakers and to monolingual speakers in either language; the drawings mean differently to monocultural readers, Spanish or Andean, and to bicultural readers responding to the Andean symbolic structures embodied in European genres.

17   In the Andes in the early 1600s there existed a literate public with considerable intercultural competence and degrees of bilingualism. Unfortunately, such a community did not exist in the Spanish court with which Guaman Poma was trying to make contact. It is interesting to note that in the same year Guaman Poma sent off his letter, a text by another Peruvian was adopted in official circles in Spain as the canonical Christian mediation between the Spanish conquest and Inca history. It was another huge encyclopedic work, titled the *Royal Commentaries of the Incas,* written, tellingly, by a mestizo, Inca Garcilaso de la Vega. Like the mestizo half brother who taught Guaman Poma to read and write, Inca Garcilaso was the son of an Inca princess and a Spanish official, and had lived in Spain since he was seventeen. Though he too spoke Quechua, his book is written in eloquent, standard Spanish, without illustrations. While Guaman Poma's life's work sat somewhere unread, the *Royal Commentaries* was edited and reedited in Spain and the New World, a mediation that coded the Andean past and present in ways thought unthreatening to colonial hierarchy.[2] The textual hierarchy persists: the *Royal Commentaries* today remains a staple item on PhD reading lists in Spanish, while the *New Chronicle and Good Government,* despite the ready availability of several fine editions, is not. However, though Guaman Poma's text did not reach its destination, the transcultural currents of expression it exemplifies continued to evolve in the Andes, as they still do, less in writing than in storytelling, ritual, song, dance-drama, painting and sculpture, dress, textile art, forms of governance, religious belief, and many other vernacular art forms. All express the effects of long-term contact and intractable, unequal conflict.

18   Autoethnography, transculturation, critique, collaboration, bilingualism, mediation, parody, denunciation, imaginary dialogue, vernacular expression—these are some of the literate arts of the contact zone. Miscomprehension, incomprehension, dead letters, unread masterpieces, absolute heterogeneity of meaning—these are some of the perils of writing in the contact zone. They all live among us today in the transnationalized metropolis of the United States and are becoming more widely visible, more pressing, and, like Guaman Poma's text, more decipherable to those who

once would have ignored them in defense of a stable, centered sense of knowledge and reality.

CONTACT AND COMMUNITY

19 The idea of the contact zone is intended in part to contrast with ideas of community that underlie much of the thinking about language, communication, and culture that gets done in the academy. A couple of years ago, thinking about the linguistic theories I knew, I tried to make sense of a utopian quality that often seemed to characterize social analyses of language by the academy. Languages were seen as living in "speech communities," and these tended to be theorized as discrete, self-defined, coherent entities, held together by a homogeneous competence or grammar shared identically and equally among all the members. This abstract idea of the speech community seemed to reflect, among other things, the utopian way modern nations conceive of themselves as what Benedict Anderson calls "imagined communities."[3] In a book of that title, Anderson observes that with the possible exception of what he calls "primordial villages," human communities exist as *imagined* entities in which people "will never know most of their fellow-members, meet them or even hear of them, yet in the minds of each lives the images of their communion." "Communities are distinguished," he goes on to say, "not by their falsity/genuineness, but by *the style in which they are imagined*" (15; emphasis mine). Anderson proposes three features that characterize the style in which the modern nation is imagined. First, it is imagined as *limited,* by "finite, if elastic, boundaries"; second, it is imagined as *sovereign;* and, third, it is imagined as *fraternal,* "a deep, horizontal comradeship" for which millions of people are prepared "not so much to kill as willingly to die" (15). As the image suggests, the nation-community is embodied metonymically in the finite, sovereign, fraternal figure of the citizen-soldier.

20   Anderson argues that European bourgeoisies were distinguished by their ability to "achieve solidarity on an essentially imagined basis" (74) on a scale far greater than that of elites of other times and places. Writing and literacy play a central role in this argument. Anderson maintains, as have others, that the main instrument that made bourgeois nation-building projects possible was print capitalism. The commercial circulation of books in the various European vernaculars, he argues, was what first created the invisible networks that would eventually constitute the literate elites and those they ruled as nations. (Estimates are that 180 million books were put into circulation in Europe between the years 1500 and 1600 alone.)

21   Now obviously this style of imagining of modern nations, as Anderson describes it, is strongly utopian, embodying values like equality, fraternity, liberty, which the societies often profess but systematically fail to realize. The prototype of the modern nation as imagined community was, it seemed to me, mirrored in ways people thought about language and the

speech community. Many commentators have pointed out how modern views of language as code and competence assume a unified and homogeneous social world in which language exists as a shared patrimony—as a device, precisely, for imagining community. An image of a universally shared literacy is also part of the picture. The prototypical manifestation of language is generally taken to be the speech of individual adult native speakers face-to-face (as in Saussure's famous diagram) in monolingual, even monodialectal situations—in short, the most homogeneous case linguistically and socially. The same goes for written communication. Now one could certainly imagine a theory that assumed different things—that argued, for instance, that the most revealing speech situation for understanding language was one involving a gathering of people each of whom spoke two languages and understood a third and held only one language in common with any of the others. It depends on what workings of language you want to see or want to see first, on what you choose to define as normative.

22   In keeping with autonomous, fraternal models of community, analyses of language use commonly assume that principles of cooperation and shared understanding are normally in effect. Descriptions of interactions between people in conversation, classrooms, medical and bureaucratic settings, readily take it for granted that the situation is governed by a single set of rules or norms shared by all participants. The analysis focuses then on how those rules produce or fail to produce an orderly, coherent exchange. Models involving games and moves are often used to describe interactions. Despite whatever conflicts or systematic social differences might be in play, it is assumed that all participants are engaged in the same game and that the game is the same for all players. Often it is. But of course it often is not, as, for example, when speakers are from different classes or cultures, or one party is exercising authority and another is submitting to it or questioning it. Last year one of my children moved to a new elementary school that had more open classrooms and more flexible curricula than the conventional school he started out in. A few days into the term, we asked him what it was like at the new school. "Well," he said "they're a lot nicer, and they have a lot less rules. But know *why* they're nicer?" "Why?" I asked. "So you'll obey all the rules they don't have," he replied. This is a very coherent analysis with considerable elegance and explanatory power, but probably not the one his teacher would have given.

23   When linguistic (or literate) interaction is described in terms of orderliness, games, moves, or scripts, usually only legitimate moves are actually named as part of the system, where legitimacy is defined from the point of view of the party in authority—regardless of what other parties might see themselves as doing. Teacher-pupil language, for example, tends to be described almost entirely from the point of view of the teacher and teaching, not from the point of view of pupils and pupiling (the world doesn't even exist, though the thing certainly does). If the classroom is analyzed as a social world unified and homogenized with respect to the teacher, whatever

students do other than what the teacher specifies is invisible or anomalous to the analysis. This can be true in practice as well. On several occasions my fourth grader, the one busy obeying all the rules they didn't have, was given writing assignments that took the form of answering a series of questions to build up a paragraph. These questions often asked him to identify with the interests of those with power over him—parents, teachers, doctors, public authorities. He invariably sought ways to resist or subvert these assignments. One assignment, for instance, calling for imagining "a helpful invention." The students were asked to write single-sentence responses to the following questions:

What kind of invention would help you?

How would it help you?

Why would you need it?

What would it look like?

Would other people be able to use it also?

What would be an invention to help your teacher?

What would be an invention to help your parents?

24 Manuel's reply read as follows:

A grate adventchin

Some inventchins are GRATE!!!!!!!!!!!! My inventchin would be a shot that would put every thing you learn at school in your brain. It would help me by letting me graduate right now!! I would need it because it would let me play with my friends, go on vacachin and, do fun a lot more. It would look like a regular shot. Ather peaple would use to. This inventchin would help my teacher parents get away from a lot of work. I think a shot like this would be GRATE!

Despite the spelling, the assignment received the usual star to indicate the task had been fulfilled in an acceptable way. No recognition was available, however, of the humor, the attempt to be critical or contestatory, to parody the structures of authority. On that score, Manuel's luck was only slightly better than Guaman Poma's. What is the place of unsolicited oppositional discourse, parody, resistance, critique in the imagined classroom community? Are teachers supposed to feel that their teaching has been most successful when they have eliminated such things and unified the social world, probably in their own image? Who wins when we do that? Who loses?

25   Such questions may be hypothetical, because in the United States in the 1990s, many teachers find themselves less and less able to do that even if they want to. The composition of the national collectivity is changing and so are the styles, as Anderson put it, in which it is being imagined. In the 1980s in many nation-states, imagined national syntheses that had retained hegemonic force began to dissolve. Internal social groups with histories and lifeways

different from the official ones began insisting on those histories and life-ways *as part of their citizenship,* as the very mode of their membership in the national collectivity. In their dialogues with dominant institutions, many groups began asserting a rhetoric of belonging that made demands beyond those of representation and basic rights granted from above. In universities we started to hear, "I don't just want you to let me be here, I want to belong here; this institution should belong to me as much as it does to anyone else." Institutions have responded with, among other things, rhetorics of diversity and multiculturalism whose import at this moment is up for grabs across the ideological spectrum.

26   These shifts are being lived out by everyone working in education today, and everyone is challenged by them in one way or another. Those of us committed to educational democracy are particularly challenged as that notion finds itself besieged on the public agenda. Many of those who govern us display, openly, their interest in a quiescent, ignorant, manipulable electorate. Even as an ideal, the concept of an enlightened citizenry seems to have disappeared from the national imagination. A couple of years ago the university where I work went through an intense and wrenching debate over a narrowly defined Western-culture requirement that had been instituted there in 1980. It kept boiling down to a debate over the ideas of national patrimony, cultural citizenship, and imagined community. In the end, the requirement was transformed into a much more broadly defined course called Cultures, Ideas, Values.[4] In the context of the change, a new course was designed that centered on the Americas and the multiple cultural histories (including European ones) that have intersected here. As you can imagine, the course attracted a very diverse student body. The classroom functioned not like a homogeneous community or a horizontal alliance but like a contact zone. Every single text we read stood in specific historical relationships to the students in the class, but the range and variety of historical relationships in play were enormous. Everybody had a stake in nearly everything we read, but the range and kind of stakes varied widely.

27   It was the most exciting teaching we had ever done, and also the hardest. We were struck, for example, at how anomalous the formal lecture became in a contact zone (who can forget Atahuallpa throwing down the Bible because it would not speak to him?). The lecturer's traditional (imagined) task—unifying the world in the class's eyes by means of a monologue that rings equally coherent, revealing, and true for all, forging an ad hoc community, homogeneous with respect to one's own words—this task became not only impossible but anomalous and unimaginable. Instead, one had to work in the knowledge that whatever one said was going to be systematically received in radically heterogeneous ways that we were neither able nor entitled to prescribe.

28   The very nature of the course put ideas and identities on the line. All the students in the class had the experience, for example, of hearing their culture discussed and objectified in ways that horrified them; all the students saw their roots traced back to legacies of both glory and shame; all the students

experienced face-to-face the ignorance and incomprehension, and occasionally the hostility, of others. In the absence of community values and the hope of synthesis, it was easy to forget the positives; the fact, for instance, that kinds of marginalization once taken for granted were gone. Virtually every student was having the experience of seeing the world described with him or her in it. Along with rage, incomprehension, and pain, there were exhilarating moments of wonder and revelation, mutual understanding, and new wisdom—the joys of the contact zone. The sufferings and revelations were, at different moments to be sure, experienced by every student. No one was excluded, and no one was safe.

29   The fact that no one was safe made all of us involved in the course appreciate the importance of what we came to call "safe houses." We used the term to refer to social and intellectual spaces where groups can constitute themselves as horizontal, homogeneous, sovereign communities with high degrees of trust, shared understandings, temporary protection from legacies of oppression. This is why, as we realized, multicultural curricula should not seek to replace ethnic or women's studies, for example. Where there are legacies of subordination, groups need places for healing and mutual recognition, safe houses in which to construct shared understandings, knowledges, claims on the world that they can then bring into the contact zone.

30   Meanwhile, our job in the Americas course remains to figure out how to make that crossroads the best site for learning that it can be. We are looking for the pedagogical arts of the contact zone. These will include, we are sure, exercises in storytelling and in identifying with the ideas, interests, histories, and attitudes of others; experiments in transculturation and collaborative work and in the arts of critique, parody, and comparison (including unseemly comparisons between elite and vernacular cultural forms); the redemption of the oral; ways for people to engage with suppressed aspects of history (including their own histories), ways to move *into and out of* rhetorics of authenticity; ground rules for communication across lines of difference and hierarchy that go beyond politeness but maintain mutual respect; a systematic approach to the all-important concept of *cultural mediation.* These arts were in play in every room at the extraordinary Pittsburgh conference on literacy. I learned a lot about them there, and I am thankful.

NOTES

1. For an introduction in English to these and other aspects of Guaman Poma's work, see Rolena Adorno. Adorno and Mercedes Lopez-Baralt pioneered the study of Andean symbolic systems in Guaman Poma.
2. It is far from clear that the *Royal Commentaries* was as benign as the Spanish seemed to assume. The book certainly played a role in maintaining the identity and aspirations of indigenous elites in the Andes. In the mid-eighteenth century, a

new edition of the *Royal Commentaries* was suppressed by Spanish authorities because its preface included a prophecy by Sir Walter Raleigh that the English would invade Peru and restore that Inca monarchy.

3. The discussion of community here is summarized from my essay "Linguistic Utopias."

4. For information about this program and the contents of courses taught in it, write Program in Cultures, Ideas, Values (CIV), Stanford Univ., Stanford, CA 94305.

WORKS CITED

Adorno, Rolena. *Guaman Poma de Ayala: Writing and Resistance in Colonial Peru.* Austin: U of Texas P, 1986.

Anderson, Benedict. *Imagined Communities: Reflections on the Origins and Spread of Nationalism.* London: Verso, 1984.

Garcilaso de la Vega, El Inca. *Royal Commentaries of the Incas.* 1613. Austin: U of Texas P, 1966.

Guaman Poma de Ayala, Felipe. *El primer nueva corónica y buen gobierno.* Manuscript. Ed. John Murra and Rolena Adorno. Mexico: Siglo XXI, 1980.

Pratt, Mary Louise. "Linguistic Utopias." *The Linguistics of Writing.* Ed. Nigel Fabb et al. Manchester: Manchester UP, 1987. 48-66.

Treviño, Gloria. "Cultural Ambivalence in Early Chicano Prose Fiction." Diss. Stanford U, 1985.

FOLLOW-UP ACTIVITIES

Discussing the Rhetoric

1. Pratt offers a long and detailed definition of the term "contact zones" as "social spaces where cultures meet, clash, grapple with each other, often in contexts of highly asymmetrical relations of power, such as colonialism, slavery or their aftermaths as they are lived out in many parts of the world today." Why is it important that Pratt defines her own meaning of the term "contact zone"?

2. As you read, you probably noticed that parts of Pratt's essay did not sound like a typical speech to a distinguished body of experts. Her language and organizational form are quite peculiar for the genre of formal, academic speeches. Considering her audience, what do you suppose Pratt hoped to accomplish by including examples, for instance, of her son's baseball interests?

3. How are the three sections of Pratt's essay related? In what ways does Pratt's synthesis of these three topics create a "contact zone" within the speech itself?

Discussing the Conversation

1. What connections can you make between Pratt's discussion of contact zones and the issues in contemporary education explored by Rose, hooks, and Rodriguez? In what ways is academic discourse a contact zone? What does it mean to you as a student that writing in college is more like writing in a contact zone than in a safe house?

2. How does Pratt's concept of "autoethnographic representations" enable hooks' assertion in "Keeping Close to Home: Class and Education" that home languages and values can be maintained in an academic setting? (This is a big question. You could, in fact, write a formal synthesis paper on this topic.)

3. In what ways could you read Rodriguez' quandary between home and school environments as anticipating Pratt's concept of a "contact zone"?

4. How does Pratt's view of the university as a contact zone differ from Bloom's representation of the university?

Joining the Conversation

1. Write an informal paper in which you consider Pratt's concepts in relation to your own life. What "contact zones" affect your life? Can you think of any discourse communities that function as a "safe house" for you?

2. In an informal paper, describe the relationship between Pratt's three sections. Why does she start with the story of her son's baseball endeavors and end with her Americas class, and why is the section on Guaman Poma in the middle?

3. Much of Pratt's essay concerns how power influences interpretation. The powerful group gets to say what's right and wrong. In an informal paper, expound on instances in our society that show underprivileged groups resisting this authoritative "stamp of truth."

4. Think of a group that represents a dominating influence in your life. Create an autoethnographic text to resist that group's efforts to dominate you. Remember that, in order for your text to be successful, you need to make the dominating group pay attention to it. Incorporate at least one of the "literate arts" that Pratt identifies in her discussion of Guaman Poma.

PART TWO

Conversations about Knowing

WHAT IS THE STUDY OF KNOWLEDGE?

How do your professors decide what knowledge you should have? What does it mean to "know" something? How is "knowledge" produced? What kind of evidence do people use to support claims that they have discovered new facts or knowledge? What does it mean to be a "scholar" or to "do" scholarship? How do a scholar's cultural identities affect her work in the academic world? These questions are the focus for people who consider the study of knowledge or *epistemology*. In this Part, you will have the opportunity to read some of the major discussions among scholars who study epistemology in the disciplines of the sciences, social sciences, and humanities. Why should freshmen college students read such arcane discussions? If you understand how your professors decide what knowledge is credible, you will also understand their expectations for student writing.

Let's talk about those expectations. One writer, Janet Giltrow, explains the relationship between professors' work and their expectations for students in this way:

> The most important distinction between school situations and university situations is that the latter are located in research institutions. While students may see themselves as learners rather than researchers, they nevertheless do their learning under the direction of people who are trained as researchers and who read and write research publications. The knowledge

students acquire is the kind of knowledge that comes from the techniques of inquiry developed by the various academic disciplines.

Giltrow, Janet. *Academic Writing*
Ontario: Broadview Press, 1995, p. 24

Because professors are also trained as researchers, they choose what you will learn on the basis of the research or knowledge-making that occurs in their discipline.

The purposes, formats, conventions, and language that are expected in student writing all evolve from the shared purposes and values of professors who are also researchers. If you learn how professors use writing strategies to convince their peers of the validity of their claims to new knowledge, you will learn by extension what type of writing they will value from you. In this Part, you will have opportunities to learn more about the methods used to conduct research and disseminate new findings. Because the readings are both difficult and subtle, you will have opportunities to read closely and think critically. The writing you do will introduce you to conventional academic expectations for student writing and provide opportunities to challenge those expectations.

HISTORICAL BACKGROUND AND OVERVIEW

Philosophers and historians who study "knowledge-making" have usually looked for basic truths that can serve as foundations upon which to build systematic explanations of the natural world. Foundationalists believe that there is only one reality, and logically enough, because there is only one reality, there is only one true way of describing it. Traditional foundationalist scientists believe that such "true" statements about reality can be made by means of closely observing the natural world and making generalizations from those observations—the scientific method.

As an example of how the scientific method operates, consider the following: In the classical experiments of behavioral psychology, mice were taught to find their way through a maze by receiving a reward of food at the end. Psychologists who conducted the experiments closely observed individual mice in order to generalize about the ways rewards (and punishments) affect learning. But they were not interested in the learning behavior of a particular mouse or even of mice as a species. They were interested in the generalizations they could make about learning, whether in mice or in "men." Scientists assume that accurate observations together with logical reasoning about those observations would produce valid knowledge about learning. This example gives a very simplified account of the scientific method. The first four readings discuss the processes of scientific or empirical knowledge-making in greater depth.

The scientific method has proved hugely successful. It has, for instance, produced vaccines, computer chips, and hybrid wheats. However, it is also through the methods of empirical science that people were first led to question the limits of empirical science. As new scientific discoveries exposed the inaccuracies of formerly "true" theories, those who study knowledge-making, epistemologists, began to ask whether the knowledge produced under even the most controlled conditions could be considered certain.

Epistemologists have recently turned their attention to the effects social relations may have on knowledge-making. Questioning the classical model of empirical science, which is based on the notion of a clear separation between the objective, material world being observed and the scientist doing the observation, epistemologists ask whether scientific research can ever be unaffected by influences from the world beyond the experiment. This perspective first gained prominence when Thomas Kuhn, a philosopher and historian of science, published *The Structure of Scientific Revolutions* (1962). Several of the authors in Part Two refer to Kuhn, who initiated the discussion about how scientific knowledge is affected by the social conditions surrounding research. These social conditions include, among others, the scientist's relations to his or her colleagues, the prestige and aims of the institutions for which he or she works, the values of the scientist's own discipline, and the sources of funding available to support the research. Ultimately, according to this view of scientific work, these social conditions affect what problems are studied and what ideas are accepted as true.

When you read and discussed the selections in Part One, you engaged issues of student identity and university expectations. This Part also deals with relationships between individuals and the university community, but focuses on the perspective of professors rather than students. By understanding how professors view their work, you will also better understand their expectations for your writing.

KNOWLEDGE CONSTRUCTION AND WRITING

Credible knowledge-makers consider the expectations of their professional peers when they do research and write about it. They select what findings to communicate and make decisions about how to convey them convincingly in light of the interests of their research community. In other words, they consider their rhetorical situation—how best to communicate their message to their intended audience. In this sense, even scientists use writing strategies rhetorically to persuade their audiences of the truth of their claims.

Assigning meaning to the readings in this part may prove to be a difficult analytical task because it requires that you enter a rich, ongoing conversation with which you may be unfamiliar. However, as you work through the readings, you will begin to understand the ways in which various systems of knowledge are founded, raised, decorated, dismantled, and restructured. When you are finished, you will have a clearer idea about life and learning at the university and about the expectations your professors have of you as a learner and writer.

CONVERSATIONS AMONG READINGS

The readings in this Part constitute a somewhat narrower conversation than those in the last section. They begin with E. D. Klemke and Bryan Magee's pieces, which describe knowledge-making in the sciences. Following these are several readings that consider knowledge as socially and culturally constructed. Kathryn Pyne Addelson's chapter, for example, represents the complexity of the scientist's position when viewed from a social and cultural perspective. In later readings in this Part, scholars from the disciplines of history and literature join with scientists to question knowledge-making processes. These writers revise the foundationalist model of truth and, by doing so, force us to examine our own willingness to accept others' truth claims.

If some people are becoming less willing to accept others' knowledge claims for the reasons you will encounter in these readings, then researcher/ writers must be more self-conscious about the strategies they use to persuade others. You will witness rhetorical strategies in the following readings that range from adherence to the form of the typical scientific report to open-ended narrative reflections and satire. Begin to look for writers' reasons for conforming to or transgressing conventional forms, and by extension, you will find out why professors sometimes expect rigid conformity in student writing and sometimes welcome transgressive alternative modes. You will also understand what is at stake for you in choosing either to conform to or to challenge academic conventions for writing.

INTRODUCTORY COMMENTS ON "SCIENCE AND NONSCIENCE: INTRODUCTION" BY E. D. KLEMKE, ROBERT HOLLINGER, AND A. DAVID KLINE

Reading the Context

This reading is excerpted from *Introductory Readings in the Philosophy of Science,* a philosophy of science textbook for beginning students. Such texts commonly have multiple authors or editors. E. D. Klemke's major areas of study were contemporary British and American philosophy, the philosophy of logic, and metaphysics. Hollinger and Kline, the other two editors, were colleagues of Klemke's in the Department of Philosophy at Iowa State University when this text was compiled.

This reading is included to introduce you to a conversation that has fascinated people since the earliest recorded philosophers began to question the natural world. There are a couple of ways to phrase the central question of the conversation. One is "How can we be sure of what we know?" Or one could ask, "By what standards do we judge our beliefs to be true?" The philosophical field of study that considers these questions is called "epistemology."

Throughout history, people have located their standards for judging the truth of a proposition in various frameworks. Among them are cultural traditions, or beliefs we hold because society approves of them. In ancient times, these would include traditions handed down orally in myths and legends; in more recent times, an example might be the beliefs encoded in the Constitution. Other frameworks include religious revelation (beliefs attested to by holy books or by specially chosen authorities like priests or lamas); poetic inspiration (the idea that inner truths expressed through poetry transcend the truths available in the material world); and, since the seventeenth century, the scientific method. We'll learn in the following readings that the scientific method relies on empirical observations and logical conclusions drawn from them. In fact, the scientific method currently so dominates thinking about how to judge the accuracy of new knowledge that it has become hegemonic, and all other methods are consistently denigrated as "mere" myth or superstition.

Reading the Rhetoric

You will notice that the format and organization of this reading are very different from those you have encountered in both popular writing and in most of the other readings in this book. This essay is an example of how some philosophers, especially philosophers of science and language, organize their writing to define precisely the terms in which they think. As you read, note both the tone of the writing and the division of the subject matter into various categories in order to define it. The essay seems to be a straightforward definition of science and the scientific method. However, you need to keep in mind that "straightforwardness" is a style achieved through language just as much as biased or emotional writing is achieved through language. Reading rhetorically will lead you to examine how language works to achieve the appearance of straightforwardness.

Reading the Conversation

The approach to scientific method described by Klemke and his co-editors exemplifies "logical positivism," or, as Herbert Feigl, whose ideas the editors build upon in this reading, preferred to call it, "logical empiricism." Positivism is a philosophical view that has been conventionally defined as "the purely disinterested scientific interpretation of experience." The modifier "disinterested" refers to the belief that objects exist in their own right regardless of human interests, as things wholly outside of, or wholly separate from, our minds.

Logical positivists hold that if we observe experience accurately and get the logical connections right, we will arrive at statements of truth. As one of the original members in the Vienna circle of Logical Positivists, Feigl was interested in the task of purifying philosophy. He believed that in order to purify it, one must sift out problems that are inexplicable on the basis of experience and logic, such as questions of moral choices. Such problems, claim logical positivists, should be investigated in the separate domain of metaphysics. The goal of logical positivists, as well as "neo-positivists" (contemporary philosophers from many disciplines who believe that logical positivism's methods remain the best approach to doing science) is to reinvestigate the implications of logical inquiry that undergird the way scientific work gets done. Later readings in Part Two will question the view that scientific work is actually conducted according to the principles of logical positivism.

Science and Nonscience: Introduction
E. D. Klemke, Robert Hollinger, and
A. David Kline

1 The major topics we shall discuss in this essay are: the aims of science; the criteria of science, or the criteria for distinguishing that which is scientific from that which is nonscientific; the question 'What is science?'; and the central issues of the readings which follow. But, first, let us begin by making some distinctions.

I. SOME DISTINCTIONS

2 Before turning to the topics above it will be helpful to consider some ways of classifying the various sciences. Among these, the following should be noted.

3   (1) Pure sciences versus applied sciences. It is widely held that we must distinguish: (A) science as a field of knowledge (or set of cognitive disciplines) from (B) the applications of science. It is common to refer to these as the pure and applied sciences. (A) Among the pure sciences we may distinguish: (a) the formal sciences, logic and mathematics; and (b) the factual or

empirical sciences. Among the latter we may also distinguish: (b1) the natural sciences, which include the physical sciences, physics, chemistry, and so on, and the life and behavioral sciences, such as biology and psychology; and (b2) the social sciences, such as sociology and economics. (B) The applied sciences include the technological sciences—such as engineering and aeronautics—medicine, agriculture, and so on.

4   It should be noted that there are at least two levels of application among the various sciences. There is, first, the application of the formal sciences to the pure, factual sciences. Since the factual sciences must have logical form and usually utilize some mathematics, such application is often held to be essential for the development of the pure factual sciences. Different from this is, second, the application of the factual sciences to the applied sciences. Here the findings of the pure, empirical sciences are applied (in a different sense of 'applied') to disciplines which fulfill various social, human purposes, such as building houses or roads and health care.

5   (2) Law-finding sciences versus fact-finding sciences. We recognize that such sciences as chemistry and physics attempt to discover universal laws which are applicable everywhere at all times, whereas such sciences as geography, history (if it is a science), and perhaps economics are concerned with local events. It is often said that the subject matter of the latter consists of particular facts, not general laws. As a result, there are some who wish to limit the term 'science' to the law-finding sciences. Upon the basis of the criteria of science (such as those which will be presented later, or others), we believe that we may say that both the law-finding disciplines and the fact-finding disciplines are capable of being sciences if those (or other) criteria are met. Furthermore, one might argue that there are no purely fact-finding sciences. If so, to speak of law-finding *versus* fact-finding may, in many cases, indicate an artificial disjunction.

6   (3) Natural sciences versus social sciences. Related to (2), we find that some would limit the giving of scientific status to the natural sciences alone. Sometimes the reason given is the distinction referred to above—that the natural sciences are primarily law-finding, whereas the social sciences are predominantly fact-finding. But sometimes the distinction is based on subject matter. Hence it is held by some that natural phenomena constitute the field of science but cultural phenomena constitute the field of scholarship and require understanding, *verstehen,* and empathy. But there are points at which the classification does not hold up. First, there are some predominantly fact finding natural sciences, such as geography, geology, and paleontology. And there are some law-finding social sciences, such as sociology and linguistics. Second, the distinction according to subject matter is not a clear-cut one. Hence we shall take a "liberal" view of science and allow the use of the term 'science' to apply to both the natural and the social sciences—with the recognition that there are some differences.

7   It is widely held that distinctions (2) and (3) do not hold up but that (1) is an acceptable distinction. However, as we shall see in the readings which

follow, some have even raised doubts about the significance of (1). Here, as always, we urge the reader to reflect upon these matters.

II. THE AIMS OF SCIENCE

8 Let us now turn to the question 'What are the aims of science?' Using the above distinction between pure (empirical) and applied science, we may then cite the following as some of the aims of science.

9   (1) The aims of applied science include: control, planning, technological progress; the utilization of the forces of nature for practical purposes. Obvious examples are: flood control, the construction of sturdier bridges, and the improvement of agriculture. Since this is all fairly obvious, no further elaboration is needed.

10   (2)   The aims of the pure, factual sciences may be considered from two standpoints. (a) Psychologically considered, the aims of the pure, empirical sciences are: the pursuit of knowledge; the attainment of truth (or the closest possible realization of truth); the satisfaction of using our intellectual powers to explain and predict accurately. Scientists, of course, derive enjoyment from rewards, prestige, and competing with others. But they often achieve a genuine inner gratification which goes with the search for truth. In some ways this is similar in quality to artistic satisfaction. It is seen, for example, in the enjoyment one derives from the solution of a difficult problem.

11   (b) Logically considered, the aims of the pure, factual sciences are often held to be: description, explanation, and prediction. (b1) Description includes giving an account of what we observe in certain contexts, the formulation of propositions which apply to (or correspond to) facts in the world. (b2) Explanation consists of accounting for the facts and regularities we observe. It involves asking and answering 'Why?' or 'How come?' This may be done by subsuming facts under laws and theories. (b3) Prediction is closely related to explanation. It consists in deriving propositions which refer to events which have not yet happened, the deducing of propositions from laws and theories and then seeing if they are true, and hence provide a testing of those laws and theories. (b4) We might also mention post- or retro-diction, the reconstruction of past events. This process is also inferential in character. Since these issues will be discussed in subsequent parts of this volume, we shall not elaborate upon them at this time. (See some of the readings in Part 1 and those in Parts 2, 3 and 4.) However, we might mention that, here again, there is not unanimity with regard to the aims characterized above. Once more we urge the reader to think about these (and other) issues.

III. THE CRITERIA OF SCIENCE

12 In this section we shall state and discuss one view with regard of what are the essential criteria of science, that is, those criteria which may be used for

at least two purposes: first, to distinguish science from commonsense knowledge (without claiming that the two are radically disjunctive—in some cases they may differ only in degree, not in kind); second, to distinguish that which is scientific, on the one hand, from that which is either nonscientific or unscientific, on the other—for example, to distinguish between theories which are genuinely scientific and those which are not. It has been maintained that any enterprise, discipline, or theory is scientific if it is characterized by or meets those criteria.

13   Before turning to the view which we have selected for consideration, let us consider an example. It is quite likely that most scientists and others who reflect upon science would hold that (say) Newton's theory of gravitation is scientific (even if it had to be modified), whereas (say) astrology is not scientific. Perhaps the reader would agree. But just what is it that allows us to rule in Newton's theory and to rule out astrology? In order to stimulate the reader's reflection, we shall consider one view of what the criteria for making such distinctions are. These criteria have been stated by Professor Herbert Feigl in various lectures. Our discussion of them corresponds fairly closely, but not entirely, to the discussion given by Professor Feigl. The five criteria are:

14   (1) Intersubjective testability. This refers to the possibility of being, in principle, capable of corroboration or "check-up" by anyone. Hence: *inter*-subjective. (Hence, private intuitions and so forth must be excluded.)

15   (2) Reliability. This refers to that which, when put to a test, turns out to be true, or at least to be that which we can most reasonably believe to be true. Testing is not enough. We want theories which, when tested, are found to be true.

16   (3) Definiteness and precision. This refers to the removal of vagueness and ambiguity. We seek, for example, concepts which are definite and delimited. We are often helped here by measurement techniques and so forth.

17   (4) Coherence or systematic character. This refers to the organizational aspect of a theory. A set of disconnected statements is not as fruitful as one which has systematic character. It also refers to the removal of, or being free from, contradictoriness.

18   (5) Comprehensiveness or scope. This refers to our effort to attain a continual increase in the completeness of our knowledge and also to our seeking theories which have maximum explanatory power—for example, to account for things which other theories do not account for.

19   Let us consider these criteria in greater detail.

20   (1) Intersubjective testability. (a) Testability. We have noted that in science we encounter various kinds of statements: descriptions, laws, theoretical explanations, and so on. These are put forth as knowledge-claims. We must (if possible) be able to tell whether evidence speaks for or against such knowledge claims. If the propositions which express those claims are not capable of tests, we cannot call those propositions true or false or even know how to go about establishing their truth or falsity. It should be noted that the criterion is one of *testability*, not *tested*. For example, at a given

point in time, 'There are mountains on the far side of the moon' was testable though not tested.

21   (b) Intersubjective. 'Intersubjectivity' is often employed as a synonym for 'objectivity.' And the latter term has various meanings. Some of these are: (i) A view or belief is said to be objective if it is not based on illusions, hallucinations, deceptions, and so on. (ii) Something is referred to as objective if it is not merely a state of mind but is really "out there" in the external world. (iii) We often use 'objective' to indicate the absence of bias and the presence of disinterestedness and dispassionateness. (iv) 'Objectivity' also refers to the possibility of verification by others, and hence excludes beliefs, which stem from private, unique, unrepeatable experiences. Science strives for objectivity in all of these senses. Hence Feigl takes 'intersubjective' to include all of them.

22   (c) Intersubjective testability. It is often held that (according to the view we are considering) in order for a proposition or theory to be judged scientific it must meet this first requirement. Indeed, many of the other criteria presuppose intersubjective testability. We cannot even begin to talk of reliability or precision unless this first criterion has been met.

23   (2) Reliability. Science is not merely interested in hypotheses which are intersubjectively testable. It is also interested in those which are true or at least have the greatest verisimilitude or likelihood of being true. Hence the need arises for the criterion of reliability. Whereas the first criterion stressed the possibility of finding assertions which are true *or* false, the second stresses the end result of that process. We judge a claim or body of knowledge to be reliable if it contains not merely propositions which are capable of being true *or* false but rather those which *are true* or which have the greatest verisimilitude. We find such propositions to be true (or false) by means of confirmation. Complete verification, and hence complete certainty, cannot be achieved in the factual sciences.

24   It should be noted that, first, the reliability of scientific assertions make them useful for prediction; second, although the assertions of many enterprises are testable (for example, those of astrology as much as those of astronomy), only some of them are reliable. And we reject some of them precisely because they are unreliable. The evidence is against them; we do not attain truth by means of them.

25   (3) Definiteness and precision. The terms 'definiteness' and 'precision' may be used in at least two related senses. First, they refer to the delimitation of our *concepts* and to the removal of ambiguity or vagueness. Second, they refer to a more rigid or exact formulation of laws. For example, 'It is more probable than not that X causes disease Y' is less desirable than 'The probability that X causes Y is 9.1.'

26   (4) Coherence or systematic character. In the sciences, we seek not merely disorganized or loosely related facts but a well-connected account of the facts. It has been held by many that we achieve this via what has been called the hypothetico-deductive procedure of science. This procedure

includes: (a) our beginning with a problem (which pertains to some realm of phenomena); (b) the formulation of hypotheses, laws, and theories by which to account for those phenomena or by which to resolve the problem; (c) the deriving (from (b)) of statements which refer to observable facts; (d) the testing of those deduced assertions to see if they hold up. Thus we seek an integrated, unified network, not merely a congeries of true statements.

27   But, of course, we also seek theories which are consistent, which are free from self-contradictions. The reason for insisting upon such coherence is obvious; hence there is no need for elaboration.

28   (5) Comprehensiveness or scope. The terms 'comprehensiveness' and 'scope' are also used in two senses, both of which are essential in science. First, a theory is said to be comprehensive if it possesses maximum explanatory power. Thus Newton's theory of gravitation was ranked high partly because it accounted not only for the laws of falling bodies but also for the revolution of the heavenly bodies and for the laws of tides. Second, by 'comprehensive' we often refer to the completeness of our knowledge. This of course does not mean finality. We do not think of the hypotheses of the empirical sciences as being certain for all time. Rather we must be ready to modify them or even, on occasion, to abandon them.

29   To summarize: According to the view we have presented, we judge a law, hypothesis, theory, or enterprise to be scientific if it meets all five of the above criteria. If it fails to meet all five, it is judged to be unscientific or at least nonscientific. To return to our earlier example, it seems clear that Newton's theory thus passes the test. Astrological theory or Greek mythology does not.

30   It should be noted that, in presenting Professor Feigl's criteria for the reader's consideration, we do not claim that they are correct or free from defects. Indeed, as we shall see in the readings which follow, many writers have rejected some (or all) of those criteria. The reader should once again attempt to seek an acceptable criterion or set of criteria, if such can be found.

FOLLOW-UP ACTIVITIES

Discussing the Rhetoric

1. Besides quoting a well-known philosopher of science, by what other means do the writers establish their credibility as authorities on the subject of science and the scientific method? What rhetorical choices about organization, sentence structure and diction lend to their credibility?

2. Compare the register "level of formality" of this piece to that of two or three others you have read in this text. You might consider Bloom's, Rose's or hooks' selections. Which readings does it most closely resemble? Is the register more or less consistent than in the other readings? What is the effect of the register on you as the reader?

3. Compare the authorial voice in this article to that in some of the others you have read so far. Do you feel that you know these authors in the same way you knew Rose or Pratt or hooks? How did the aims of those writers differ from the aims of Klemke and his colleagues? What rhetorical choices let you get to know some authors better than others? How do the discourse communities or audiences for whom the pieces are written differ? How do these factors explain the rhetorical choices you have identified?

Discussing the Conversation

1. Consider the following statements. Which ones would you characterize as scientific? Nonscientific? Why? This exercise should help you clarify your own assumptions about the differences between science and nonscience.

- Water boils at 212°F.
- Abortion is murder.
- The square of the hypotenuse is equal to the sum of the squares of the legs of the right triangle.
- Abused children are likely to become abusive parents.
- Chocolate is the best flavor of ice cream.
- Seventy-six percent of all released prisoners eventually return to prison.
- For every action, there is an equal and opposite reaction.
- According to a poll conducted on January 24 by CNN and Time/Warner, President Clinton's approval rating is 63 percent.

2. Klemke and his co-editors quote another philosopher of science, Herbert Feigl, who is one of the foremost thinkers in the area of positivistic science. However, the term "positivism" itself does not appear in this article. Look up "positivism" in a dictionary. What is the definition? How does the definition fit with this description of science? What does it imply that Klemke never uses the word "positivism" in this piece? Are there any other ways to do science besides those described by Klemke? Recall the discussion of the term *hegemony* in the introduction to Part One. Does it apply to the position of positivism in scientific thinking?

3. Think about high school classes that were described as "science" classes compared to those considered nonscience—history, English, physical education, chorus, for instance. How do they differ in subject matter? Methodology? Do any nonscience courses have scientific characteristics?

Joining the Conversation

1. Write an informal paper about a time when you were told something you didn't believe. What did you do to check or verify whether it was true? Would you describe your processes as scientific? Why or why not, in Klemke's terms? Were you satisfied that at the end you arrived at truth?

2. Write an informal paper about activities in which you normally participate that could be described as scientific. Why would you characterize them as scientific? Besides performing sciencelike processes of observation and generalizing (the inductive process), by what other means do you come to new knowledge? Do you think that the scientific method is the only path to true knowledge? If you think there are others, what are they? Why do you think they are valid?

3. Write an informal paper in which you compare the writing in this piece with your textbooks for other courses. Consider organizational patterns, sentence structure, diction and methods of explanation. What are the similarities? Differences? How would you explain the similarities and differences? In other words, how do audience and purpose affect the author's rhetorical choices?

INTRODUCTORY COMMENTS ON "FIRST AND SECOND THESIS" BY KARL POPPER

Reading the Context

Born in 1902 in Vienna, Sir Karl Popper is perhaps the pre-eminent philosopher of science of the twentieth century. Philosophy of science is a branch of philosophy that studies the logical and methodological principles behind scientific research. Popper is best known for having addressed an unresolved problem brought up two centuries earlier by another philosopher, David Hume, concerning the logic upon which scientific conclusions are based. You will be reading more about that problem in the articles to come. After completing his education at the University of Vienna, Popper left Austria before World War II. He served as professor of logic and the scientific method at the University of London from 1949 until his retirement in 1969. Throughout his career, he held guest lectureships at major universities around the world, including American universities such as Stanford, Harvard, the University of California-Berkeley, the University of Minnesota, Indiana University, Emory University, and Brandeis University.

His major publications in English include *The Open Society and Its Enemies,* (1945); *The Poverty of Historicism,* (1957); *The Logic of Scientific Discovery,* (1959); *Conjectures and Refutations,* (1963); *Objective Knowledge,* (1972); and *Unended Quest: An Intellectual Autobiography,* (1976).

Reading the Rhetoric

This is the second reading in the form of a short statement of principle that you have encountered in this text (the first was the NCTE's statement about the students' right to their own language). What are the advantages for the

author of publishing a short, pithy statement like this? What rhetorical constraints do authors of such statements have to keep in mind?

Reading the Conversation

As you read the selections in this section of the book, you need to keep in
mind that all professors in a university, not just those in the hard sciences,
are expected to be producers of knowledge. Professors in history, political
science, literature, sociology, animal husbandry, philosophy, and education,
as well as those in the hard sciences, do research. We begin this section with
Karl Popper's views about scientific methodology because the selections engage in a conversation about principles fundamental to the conduct of research for professors, and by extension, for students. Notice that Popper
states his two theses in antithetical terms. This organization is typical of the
binary logic that serves as the starting point of much of western thought.
How does the opposition serve as a starting point for Popper?

First and Second Thesis
Karl Popper

1 *First thesis:* We know a great deal. And we know not only many details of
doubtful intellectual interest but also things which are of considerable practical significance and, what is even more important, which provide us with
deep theoretical insight, and with a surprising understanding of the world.

2   *Second thesis:* Our ignorance is sobering and boundless. Indeed, it is
precisely the staggering progress of the natural sciences (to which my first
thesis alludes) which constantly opens our eyes anew to our ignorance, even
in the field of the natural sciences themselves. This gives a new twist to
the Socratic idea of ignorance. With each step forward, with each problem
which we solve, we not only discover new and unsolved problems, but we
also discover that where we believed that we were standing on firm and safe
ground, all things are, in truth, insecure and in a state of flux.

FOLLOW-UP ACTIVITIES

Discussing the Rhetoric

1. Who do you think Popper's intended audience is for this statement? Are
you one of its members? How do you know?

2. Except for private diaries or meditations, people write to convey their thoughts to others. If this is Popper's goal, do you think this short statement of two principles, or theses, was more or less successful in conveying Popper's ideas than a longer paper would be? In other words, what does the writer gain or lose by attempting such a short statement? You might want to return to this question after reading the following two pieces excerpted from a book explaining Popper's thinking.

Discussing the Conversation

1. We have included this reading as an introduction to a very big conversation about the limits of human knowledge and research methodology. In your own words, what is Popper's view of the possibilities and limitations of scientific knowledge? According to Popper, are human beings ever likely to have all the answers?

2. Do Klemke and his co-editors at any point take Popper's first or second thesis into account? If so, where? Locate passages from Klemke to support your answers.

3. If you do not consider yourself a member of Popper's audience, you have something in common with Mike Rose's student Lucia, who considered herself an outsider to the conversations of her professor and textbook. What are some of the ways you can respond to the situation of being on the outside of an academic conversation?

Joining the Conversation

1. Could you rewrite Popper's theses in the voices of writers from the first section of this text? Try it. For example, what if you were to rewrite the first thesis in Newenhuyse's voice? hooks' voice? How would changes in style reflect differences in worldviews and discursive communities?

INTRODUCTORY COMMENTS ON "SCIENTIFIC METHOD—THE TRADITIONAL VIEW AND POPPER'S VIEW" BY BRYAN MAGEE

Reading the Context

Bryan Magee (b. 1930) has been active in public as well as scholarly affairs throughout his life in his native England, as well as in the United States. He has lectured at a variety of American and British universities and published several books about the philosophy of science. But he has been equally active as an art, music, and cultural critic for the *Times,* the *Guardian,* and the BBC. For nine years, from 1974–1983, he served as a member of the British Parliament. His work shows an avid interest in connecting people to the life of aesthetics and the intellect.

Here are some important things to keep in mind as you read Bryan Magee's article. You will have no problem seeing that the terms *scientific law, induction,* and *falsifiable* are central to Magee's discussion of Popper. But an equally important phrase for Hume's and Popper's argument, though not itself a topic of discussion, is *logically entail.* That a statement is *logically entailed* means that it is an accurate statement by force of the logic, not because of the truth of the content. Take the series of propositions traditionally used to demonstrate how deductive logic works:

All men are mortal.

Socrates is a man.

Therefore Socrates is mortal.

The conclusion is *logically* entailed: because Socrates fits in the larger category "man" he, like all other members of that category, fits the category "mortal."

Here's the hitch. Let's change a word in the first statement:

All men are immortal.

Socrates is a man.

Therefore Socrates is immortal.

The conclusion "Socrates is immortal" is still *logically entailed* even though it is not true. Think about it. If we relied on the logic alone, rather than what we know the statements to mean, we would have to say that the final statement is a logical conclusion—Socrates, a man, still fits in the category of the adjective, immortal, that describes the category "man," even though the adjective is untrue. It is not the logic of the statement that is at fault, but its content.

Logicians call the group of propositions made up of a major premise (first statement), minor premise (second statement), and conclusion (third statement) a syllogism. If a syllogism is properly constructed, the conclusion is logically entailed by the first two premises. This is the classical pattern of *deductive* logic. It is also the starting point of Hume's problem, though his real concern is not with deductive logic, but with inductive logic. After you read this chapter, think about what Hume (as described by Magee) meant when he said that the conclusions reached through inductive reasoning are *not* logically entailed.

Reading the Rhetoric

The book from which these chapters were excerpted is an introduction to key ideas in the thinking of Karl Popper, a major figure in twentieth-century philosophy of science. It is written for educated laypeople and/or university students. As you read, consider Magee's relationship to his audience. What does he assume about the readers' background knowledge? To answer this, think about which terms he thinks he needs to explain, and which ones not. Think as well about the examples Magee uses. Do you think he is successful in reaching his intended audience? Why or why not?

Reading the Conversation

Like other readings in this text, consider Magee's chapters as participating in an ongoing conversation about a particular topic, in this case a central issue in the philosophy of science: how scientists can be certain of the "truth" of their findings. According to Magee, with whom did this conversation begin? What other voices does Magee privilege?

Scientific Method—The Traditional View and Popper's View
Bryan Magee

1   The word 'law' is ambiguous, and anyone who talks of a natural or scientific law being 'broken' is confusing the two main uses of the word. A law of society prescribes what we may or may not do. It can be broken—indeed, if we could not break it there would be no need to have it: society does not legislate against a citizen's being in two places at once. A law of nature, on the other hand, is not prescriptive but descriptive. It tells us what happens—for instance that water boils at 100° Centigrade. As such it purports to be nothing more than a statement of what—given certain initial conditions, such as that there is a body of water and that it is heated—occurs. It may be true or false, but it cannot be 'broken', for it is not a command; water is not being *ordered* to boil at 100° Centigrade. The pre-scientific belief that it was (by some god) is the reason for the unfortunate ambiguity; the laws of nature were thought to be commands of the gods. But nowadays no one would dispute that they are not prescriptions of any kind, to be 'kept' or 'obeyed' or 'broken', but explanatory statements of a general character which purport to be factual and must therefore be modified or abandoned if found to be inaccurate.

2   The search for natural laws has long been seen as the central task of science, at least since Newton. But the way scientists were supposed to proceed was first systematically described by Francis Bacon. Although his formulation has been much qualified, added to, refined and sophisticated since his day, something in the tradition he pioneered has been accepted by nearly all scientifically minded people since the seventeenth century. The scientist begins

by carrying out experiments whose aim is to make carefully controlled and meticulously measured observations at some point on the frontier between our knowledge and our ignorance. He systematically records his findings, perhaps publishes them, and in the course of time he and other workers in the field accumulate a lot of shared and reliable data. As this grows, general features begin to emerge, and individuals start to formulate general hypotheses—statements of a lawlike character which fit all the known facts and explain how they are causally related to each other. The individual scientist tries to confirm his hypothesis by finding evidence which will support it. If he succeeds in verifying it he has discovered another scientific law which will unlock more of the secrets of nature. The new seam is then worked—the new discovery is applied wherever it is thought it might yield fresh information. Thus the existing stock of scientific knowledge is added to, and the frontier of our ignorance pushed back. And the process begins again on the new frontier.

3   The method of basing general statements on accumulated observations of specific instances is known as *induction,* and is seen as the hallmark of science. In other words the use of the inductive method is seen as the criterion of demarcation between science and nonscience. Scientific statements, being based on observational and experimental evidence—based, in short, on the facts—are contrasted with statements of all other kinds, whether based on authority, or emotion, or tradition, or speculation, or prejudice, or habit, or any other foundation, as alone providing sure and certain knowledge. Science is the corpus of such knowledge, and the growth of science consists in the endless process of adding new certainties to the body of existing ones.

4   Some awkward questions about this were raised by Hume. He pointed out that no number of singular observation statements, however large, could logically entail an unrestrictedly general statement. If I observe that event A is attended by event B on one occasion, it does not logically follow that it will be attended by it on any other occasion. Nor would it follow from two such observations—nor from twenty, nor from two thousand. If it happens often enough, said Hume, I may come to expect that the next A will be attended by a B, but this is a fact of psychology, not of logic. The sun may have risen again after every past day of which we have knowledge, but this does not entail that it will rise tomorrow. If someone says: Ah yes, but we can in fact predict the precise time at which the sun will rise tomorrow from the established laws of physics, as applied to conditions as we have them at this moment', we can answer him twice over. First, the fact that the laws of physics have been found to hold good in the past does not logically entail that they will continue to hold good in the future. Second, the laws of physics are themselves general statements which are not logically entailed by the observed instances, however numerous, which are adduced in their support. So this attempt to justify induction begs the question by taking the validity of induction for granted. The whole of our science assumes the reg-

ularity of nature—assumes that the future will be like the past in all those respects in which natural laws are taken to operate—yet there is no way in which this assumption can be secured. It cannot be established by observation, since we cannot observe future events. And it cannot be established by logical argument, since from the fact that all past futures have resembled past pasts it does not follow that all future futures will resemble future pasts. The conclusion Hume himself came to was that although there is no way of demonstrating the validity of inductive procedures we are so constituted psychologically that we cannot help thinking in terms of them. And since they seem to work in practice we go along with them. This does mean, however, that scientific laws have no rationally secure foundation—neither in logic, nor in experience, since every scientific law, being unrestrictedly general, goes beyond both.

5   The problem of induction, which has been called 'Hume's problem', has baffled philosophers from his time to our own. C. D. Broad described it as the skeleton in the cupboard of philosophy. Bertrand Russell wrote in his *History of Western Philosophy* (pp. 699-700): 'Hume has proved that pure empiricism is not a sufficient basis for science. But if this one principle [induction] is admitted, everything else can proceed in accordance with the theory that all our knowledge is based on experience. It must be granted that this is a serious departure from pure empiricism, and that those who are not empiricists may ask why, if one departure is allowed, others are to be forbidden. These, however, are questions not directly raised by Hume's arguments. What these arguments prove—and I do not think the proof can be controverted—is, that induction is an independent logical principle, incapable of being inferred either from experience or from other logical principles, and that without this principle science is impossible.'

6   That the whole of science, of all things, should rest on foundations whose validity it is impossible to demonstrate has been found uniquely embarrassing. It has turned many empirical philosophers into sceptics, or irrationalists, or mystics. Some it has led to religion. Virtually all have felt bound to say, in effect: 'We have to admit that, strictly speaking, scientific laws cannot be proved and are therefore not certain. Even so, their degree of probability is raised by each confirming instance; and in addition to the whole of the known past every moment of the world's continuance brings countless billions of confirming instances—and never a single counterexample. So, if not certain, they are probable to the highest degree which it is possible to conceive; and in practice, if not in theory, this is indistinguishable from certainty.' Nearly all scientists, in so far as they reflect on the logical foundations of what they are doing, go along with this attitude. To them the overwhelmingly important thing is that science delivers the goods—it works, it produces a never-ending stream of useful results; and rather than go on banging their heads against the brick wall of an apparently insoluble logical problem they prefer to get on with doing more science and getting more results. The more philosophically reflective among them, however,

have been deeply troubled. For them, and for philosophers generally, induction has presented an unsolved problem at the very foundations of human knowledge, and until such time as it might be solved the whole of science, however intrinsically consistent and extrinsically useful, must be conceded to be somehow floating in mid air, unfixed to *terra firma.*

7 Popper's seminal achievement has been to offer an acceptable solution to the problem of induction. In doing this he has rejected the whole orthodox view of scientific method outlined so far in this chapter and replaced it with another. It is, of course, this that lies behind the quotations from Medawar, Eccles and Bondi on the first page of this book. And as might be expected of so fundamental an achievement it has proved fruitful beyond the confines of the problem that gave rise to it, and has led to the solution of other important problems.

8   Popper's solution begins by pointing to a logical asymmetry between verification and falsification. To express it in terms of the logic of statements: although no number of observation statements reporting observations of white swans allows us logically to derive the universal statement 'All swans are white', one single observation statement, reporting one single observation of a black swan, allows us logically to derive the statement 'Not all swans are white.' In this important logical sense empirical generalizations, though not verifiable, are falsifiable. This means that scientific laws are testable in spite of being unprovable; they can be tested by systematic attempts to refute them.

9   From the beginning Popper drew the distinction between the logic of this situation and the implied methodology. The logic is utterly simple: if a single black swan has been observed then it *cannot* be the case that all swans are white. In *logic,* therefore—that is, if we look at the relation between statements—a scientific law is conclusively falsifiable although it is not conclusively verifiable. *Methodologically* however, we are presented with a different case, for in practice it is always possible to doubt a statement; there may have been some error in the reported observation; the bird in question may have been wrongly identified; or we may decide, *because* it is black, not to categorize it as a swan but to call it something else. So it is always possible for us to refuse, without self-contradiction, to accept the validity of an observation statement. We could thus reject all falsifying experiences whatsoever. But since conclusive falsification is not attainable at the methodological level it is a mistake to ask for it. If we did, and meanwhile kept reinterpreting the evidence to maintain its agreement with our statements, our approach would have become absurdly unscientific. Popper therefore proposes, as an article of method, that we do not systematically evade refutation, whether by introducing *ad hoc* hypotheses, or *ad hoc* definitions, or by always refusing to accept the reliability of inconvenient experimental results, or by any other such device; and that we formulate our theories as unambiguously as we can, so as to expose them as clearly as

possible to refutation. On the other hand he also says we should not abandon our theories lightly, for this would involve too uncritical an attitude towards tests, and would mean that the theories themselves were not tested as rigorously as they should be. So although Popper is what might be called a naive falsificationist at the level of logic he is a highly critical falsificationist at the level of methodology. Much misunderstanding of his work has sprung from a failure to appreciate this distinction.

10   Let us now consider a practical example. Suppose we start by believing, as most of us are taught at school, that it is a scientific law that water boils at 100° Centigrade. No number of confirming instances will prove this, but we can nevertheless test it by searching for circumstances in which it does not hold. This alone challenges us to think of things which, so far as we know, no one else has hit on. If we are at all imaginative we shall soon discover that water does not boil at 100° Centigrade in closed vessels. So what we thought was a scientific law turns out not to be one. Now at this point we could take a wrong turning. We could salvage our original statement by narrowing its empirical content to 'Water boils at 100° Centigrade in open vessels.' And we could then look systematically for a refutation of our second statement. And if we were rather more imaginative than before we should find it at high altitudes; so that to salvage our second statement we would have to narrow *its* empirical content to 'Water boils at 100° Centigrade in open vessels at sea-level atmospheric pressure.' And we could then begin a systematic attempt to refute our third statement. And so on. In this way we might regard ourselves as pinning down ever more and more precisely our knowledge about the boiling point of water. But to proceed in this way, through a series of statements with vanishing empirical content, would be to miss the most important features of the situation. For when we discovered that water did not boil at 100° Centigrade in closed vessels we had our foot on the threshold of the most important kind of discovery of all, namely the discovery of a new problem: 'Why not?' We are challenged now to produce a hypothesis altogether richer than our original, simple statement, a hypothesis which explains both why water boils at 100° Centigrade in open vessels and also why it does not in closed ones; and the richer the hypothesis is the more it will tell us about the relationship between the two situations, and the more precisely it will enable us to calculate different boiling points. In other words we will now have a second formulation which has not less empirical content than our first but very considerably more. And we should proceed to look systematically for a refutation of *that*. And if, say, we were to find that although it gave us results in both open and closed vessels at sea-level atmospheric pressure it broke down at high altitudes we should have to search for a third hypothesis, richer still, which would explain why each of our first two hypotheses worked, up to the point it did, but then broke down at that point; and also enables us to account for the new situation as well. And then we should test *that*. From each of our successive formulations consequences would be derived which

went beyond the existing evidence; our theory, whether true or false, would tell us more about the world than we yet knew. And one of the ways in which we tested it would be by devising confrontations between its consequences and new observable experience; and if we discovered that some of the things it told us were not the case this would be a new discovery; it would add to our knowledge and it would start all over again the search for a better theory.

11   This, in a nutshell, is Popper's view of the way knowledge advances. There are several things to emphasize. If we had set out to 'verify' our original statement that water boils at 100° Centigrade by accumulating confirming instances of it we should have found no difficulty whatever in accumulating any number of confirming instances we liked, billions and billions of them. But this would not have proved the truth of the statement, nor would it (and this realization may come as something of a shock) have increased the probability of its being true. Worst of all, our accumulation of confirming instances would of itself never have given us reason to doubt, let alone replace, our original statement, and we should never have progressed beyond it. Our knowledge would not have grown as it has—unless in our search for confirming instances we accidentally hit upon a counter-instance. Such an accident would have been the best thing that could have happened to us. (It is in this sense that so many famous discoveries in science have been 'accidental'.) For the growth of our knowledge proceeds from problems and our attempts to solve them. These attempts involve the propounding of theories which, if they are to provide possible solutions at all, must go beyond our existing knowledge, and which therefore require a leap of the imagination. The bolder the theory the more it tells us, and also the more daring the act of imagination. (At the same time, though, the greater is the probability that what the theory tells us is wrong; and we should use rigorous tests to discover whether it is.) Most of the great revolutions in science have turned on theories of breathtaking audacity not only in respect of creative imagination but in the depth of insight involved, and the independence of mind, the unsecured adventurousness of thought, required.

12   We are now in a position to see why it is inherent in Popper's view that what we call our knowledge is of its nature provisional, and permanently so. At no stage are we able to prove that what we now 'know' is true, and it is always possible that it will turn out to be false. Indeed, it is an elementary fact about the intellectual history of mankind that most of what has been 'known' at one time or another has eventually turned out to be not the case. So it is a profound mistake to try to do what scientists and philosophers have almost always tried to do, namely prove the truth of a theory, or justify our belief in a theory, since this is to attempt the logically impossible. What we can do, however, and this is of the highest possible importance, is to justify our preference for one theory over another. In our successive examples about the boiling of water we were never able to show that our current theory was true, but we were at each stage able to

show that it was preferable to our preceding theory. This is the characteristic situation in any of the sciences at any given time. The popular notion that the sciences are bodies of established fact is entirely mistaken. Nothing in science is permanently established, nothing unalterable, and indeed science is quite clearly changing all the time, and not through the accretion of new certainties. If we are rational we shall always base our decisions and expectations on 'the best of our knowledge', as the popular phrase so rightly has it, and provisionally assume the 'truth' of that knowledge *for practical purposes,* because it is the least insecure foundation available; but we shall never lose sight of the fact that at any time experience may show it to be wrong and require us to revise it.

FOLLOW-UP ACTIVITIES

Discussing the Rhetoric

1. Do you see yourself as part of Magee's audience? How would you describe the audience he was writing for? What is his purpose?

2. Magee begins by clarifying the meaning of "law" as it is used in science. All scientists understand scientific laws as Magee defines them, but still, like Magee, generally refer to such statements as laws rather than "descriptions." What do scientists gain rhetorically by continuing to use the term "law"?

3. Philosophers typically use "hypothetical examples" to make their points. A hypothetical example is made up to illustrate a point. What hypothetical examples does Magee use? Which ideas do they help explain?

4. Magee never provides a definition of the phrase "logically entail." What strategies does he use instead to help readers understand the term?

5. What words would you use to describe the tone of Magee's chapter? Compare the tone to that of readings in Part One. Is it more or less formal? Examine Magee's diction and sentence structure to describe what makes the tone more or less formal.

Discussing the Conversation

1. Does Magee's description of the scientific method agree with Klemke's? Identify points of similarity and difference.

2. Why was Hume's point important to the continuing conversation about the philosophy of science? Why was it less important to working scientists?

3. What was Popper's contribution to the conversation? What does Popper's contribution suggest for how scientists should do their work?

4. Popper's second thesis ends with the statement "all things are, in truth, insecure and in a state of flux." Having read Magee's explanation of Popper's thinking, can you explain Popper's reasons for saying this?

5. How do you think Pratt or Bloom would define "truth?" Would they agree with each other? Would they agree with Popper?

Joining the Conversation

The issue discussed in this reading, the problem of induction and Popper's response to it, are very important to the philosophy of science as will become evident in the rest of the readings in Part Two. Do you also find them compelling? Write a reflective paper in which you account for your response to this issue. What aspects of your background help you to understand why you are or are not interested in such issues?

INTRODUCTORY COMMENTS ON "THE CRITERION OF DEMARCATION BETWEEN WHAT IS AND WHAT IS NOT SCIENCE" BY BRYAN MAGEE

Reading the Context

See the previous reading, "Scientific Method—The Traditional View and Popper's View," for background information on the author and conversation.

Reading the Rhetoric

This reading is from the second chapter of Magee's book on Sir Karl Popper's thinking. Consider how it extends, reworks, or re-presents ideas introduced in the first chapter. You might reconsider here the question asked about Popper's two statements of principle: What are the advantages or disadvantages to a short, succinct statement of central ideas as compared to a longer, more leisurely explanation? For what audience is the short statement likely to be more effective? The longer explanation?

Reading the Conversation

In this chapter Magee returns to the central question of the philosophy of science: What distinguishes science from nonscience? Watch for signs that Magee is participating in a larger conversation about this topic. What other voices does he bring into or acknowledge in the conversation?

As you read, also think about how Magee's explanation of the differences between science and nonscience differs from Klemke's and his co-editors'.

The Criterion of Demarcation between What Is and What Is Not Science
Bryan Magee

1   A sense of awe at science and the world it reveals is to be found even in Popper's writings on politics. In *The Poverty of Historicism* (p. 56) he says: 'Science is most significant as one of the greatest spiritual adventures that man has yet known.' This is like a form of the religious sense, though Popper is perhaps not what people usually mean by a religious man; for it is, after all, central to most religious beliefs that behind the world of appearances, the everyday world of common sense and ordinary human observation and experience, there is a reality of a different order which sustains that world and presents it to our senses. Now it is precisely such a reality that science reveals—a world of unobservable entities and invisible forces, waves, cells, particles, all interlockingly organized and structured down to a deeper level than anything we have yet been able to penetrate. Men presumably always have looked at flowers and been moved by their beauty and their smell: but only since the last century has it been possible to take a flower in your hand and know that you have between your fingers a complex association of organic compounds containing carbon, hydrogen, oxygen, nitrogen, phosphorus, and a great many other elements, in a complex structure of cells, all of which have evolved from a single cell; and to know something of the internal structure of these cells, and the processes by which they evolved, and the genetic processes by which this flower was begun, and will produce other flowers; to know in detail how the light from it is reflected to your eye; and to know details of those workings of your eye, and your nose, and your neurophysiological system, which enable you to see and smell and touch the flower. These inexhaustible and almost incredible realities which are all around us and within us are recent discoveries which are still being explored, while similar new discoveries continue to be made; and we have before us an endless vista of such new possibilities stretching into the future, all of it beyond man's wildest dreams until almost the age we ourselves are living in. Popper's ever-present and vivid sense of this, and of the fact that every discovery opens up new problems for us, informs his theoretical methodology. He knows that our ignorance grows with our knowledge, and that we shall therefore always have more questions than answers. He knows that interesting truth consists of quite staggeringly unlikely propositions, not to be even conjectured without a rare boldness of imagination. And he knows that such adventurous hypotheses are far more likely to be wrong than right, and can not be even provisionally accepted until we have made a serious attempt to find out what might be wrong with them. He knows that if, on the other hand, we reach for the most probable explanation every time

we come up against a problem it will always be that *ad hoc* explanation which goes least beyond existing evidence, and therefore gets us least far. Bolder theorizing, though it will get us further if proved right, is more likely to be proved wrong. But that is not to be feared. 'The wrong view of science betrays itself in the craving to be right.'[1]

2   The realization that this is so can have a liberating effect on the working scientist which Sir John Eccles has headily described. 'The erroneous belief that science eventually leads to the certainty of a definitive explanation carries with it the implication that it is a grave scientific misdemeanor to have published some hypothesis that eventually is falsified. As a consequence scientists have often been loath to admit the falsification of such an hypothesis, and their lives may be wasted in defending the no longer defensible. Whereas according to Popper, falsification in whole or in part is the anticipated fate of all hypotheses, and we should even rejoice in the falsification of an hypothesis that we have cherished as our brain-child. One is thereby relieved from fears and remorse, and science becomes an exhilarating adventure where imagination and vision lead to conceptual developments transcending in generality and range the experimental evidence. The precise formulation of these imaginative insights into hypotheses opens the way to the most rigorous testing by experiment, it being always anticipated that the hypothesis may be falsified and that it will be replaced in whole or in part by another hypothesis of greater explanatory power.'[2]

3   Not only working scientists may be liberated in this way. For all of us, in all our activities, the notions that we can do better only by finding out what can be improved and then improving it; and therefore that shortcomings are to be actively sought out, not concealed or passed over; and that critical comment from others, far from being resented, is an invaluable aid to be insisted on and welcomed, are liberating to a remarkable degree. It may be difficult to get people—conditioned to resent criticism and expect it to be resented, and therefore to keep silent about both their own mistakes and others'—to provide the criticisms on which improvement depends; but no one can possibly give us more service than by showing us what is wrong with what we think or do; and the bigger the fault, the bigger the improvement made possible by its revelation. The man who welcomes and acts on criticism will prize it almost above friendship: the man who fights it out of concern to maintain his position is clinging to non-growth. Anything like a widespread changeover in our society towards Popperian attitudes to criticism would constitute a revolution in social and interpersonal relationships—not to mention organizational practice, which we shall come to later.

4   But to return to the scientist: his critical search for better and better theories imposes high demands on any he is prepared to entertain. A theory must first of all provide a solution to a problem that interests us. But it must also be compatible with all known observations, and contain its predecessor theories as first approximations—though it must also contradict them at the

points where they failed, and account for their failure. (Herein, incidentally, lies the explanation of the continuity of science.) If in a given problem situation more than one theory is put forward which does all these things we have to try to decide between them. The fact that they are different may mean that from one of them it is possible to deduce testable propositions which are not deducible from the other; and this may make our preference empirically decidable. If other things remain equal our preference will always be, after tests, for the theory with the higher informative content, both because it has been better tested and because it tells us more: such a theory is better corroborated as well as more useful. 'By the degree of corroboration of a theory I mean a concise report evaluating the state (at a certain time *t*) of the critical discussion of a theory, with respect to the way it solves its problems; its degree of testability; the severity of tests it has undergone; and the way it has stood up to these tests. Corroboration (or degree of corroboration) is thus an evaluating *report of past performance.* Like preference, it is essentially comparative: in general, one can only say that the theory *A* has a higher (or lower) degree of corroboration than a competing theory *B,* in the light of the critical discussion, which includes testing, *up to some time t.*[3] So at any given time, among competing theories, it is the best corroborated theory with the highest informative content that gives the best results and is therefore, or should be, the prevailing one.

5   The point has been made that at any given time the overwhelming majority of scientists are not trying to overthrow the prevailing orthodoxy at all but are working happily within it. They are not innovating, and they seldom have to choose between competing theories: what they are doing is putting accepted theories to work. This is what has come to be known as 'normal science', from Thomas S. Kuhn's use of the phrase in *Structure of Scientific Revolutions* (second edition 1970). The point is a valid one, I think, but it is not a point against Popper. It is true that Popper's writings are somewhat loftily exclusive in their references to the pathbreaking geniuses of science, whose activities his theories most obviously fit. And it is also true that most scientists take for granted, in order to solve problems at a lower level theories, which only a few of their colleagues are questioning. But at that lower level their activities will be found to be open to the Popperian analysis, which is essentially a logic of problem solving. Popper has always been primarily concerned with discovery and innovation, and therefore with the testing of theories and the growth of knowledge: Kuhn is concerned with how the people who apply these theories and this knowledge go about their work. Popper has always been careful to make the distinction, drawn already in this book, between the logic of scientific activities and their psychology, sociology, and so forth: Kuhn's theory is in fact a sociological theory about the working activity of scientists in our society. It is not irreconcilable with Popperism, and what is more, Kuhn has modified it considerably in Popper's direction since he first put it forward. Readers who

want to pursue this question are referred to the symposium *Criticism and the Growth of Knowledge.*[4]

NOTES

1. The Logic of Scientific Discovery, p. 281.
2. J. C. Eccles: Facing Reality, p. 107.
3. Objective Knowledge, p. 18.
4. Ed. Lakatos and Musgrave, Cambridge University Press, 1970.

FOLLOW-UP ACTIVITIES

Discussing the Rhetoric

1. How does Magee demonstrate the importance of falsifiability to scientific work?

2. Did you notice that Magee uses the word "men" or "man" when referring to people in general? Why do you think you noticed/failed to notice?

3. Compare Magee's tone to Klemke's and his co-editors'. How does it differ? What stylistic features account for the differences? What do the differences in tone suggest about each writer's assumptions about the discourse communities for which they are writing?

4. What assumptions about his audience's background knowledge is Magee making when he brings Thomas Kuhn into the conversation in the last paragraph of this chapter? What does Magee's purpose seem to be in bringing up Kuhn?

Discussing the Conversation

1. According to Magee, what do religious and scientific beliefs have in common? Were you surprised that Magee would view the two kinds of beliefs as similar? What differences do you see between religious and scientific beliefs?

2. According to Magee, what does "criticism" mean to a scientist? Why is it important in the scientific community? How does this meaning differ from that which you first met in Newenhuyse's article "De-Constructive Criticism"? How do you account for the different uses of the term? (Consider the values of the community and its purposes for writing as you answer.)

3. What implications does science's demand for rigorous criticism have for your writing as a university student? Does this concern help explain the reasons for an instructor's comments like "be specific," "develop your ideas," and "where's your evidence?"

4. This article is about epistemology—how we decided what to count as truth. Summarize the characteristics of scientific research that Magee argues will lead to reliable theories. How do his emphases differ from Klemke's?

5. In the last paragraph, the conversation becomes focused to the point that Magee seems to be in dialogue with a particular individual, Thomas Kuhn. What is at issue in this discussion? The following readings in this text will continue the discussion of how scientists work to make knowledge.

Joining the Conversation

Karl Popper holds up a rigorous standard for scientists to meet. Write an informal paper in which you summarize that standard and then consider it from a psychological standpoint. Is it reasonable to expect scientists to look for ways to prove their own ideas wrong? What does a statement like "The man [sic] who welcomes and acts on criticism will prize it almost above friendship" suggest about a scientist's relationship to his or her work? What methods would you suggest to ensure accuracy in scientific work?

INTRODUCTORY COMMENTS ON "THE MAN OF PROFESSIONAL WISDOM" BY KATHRYN PYNE ADDELSON

Reading the Context

Like bell hooks, Kathryn Pyne Addelson grew up in a working class family and culture. First attending night school part-time while working to support her two daughters, and then attending college as a full-time student while working half-time, Addelson finally earned her bachelor's degree from Indiana University in 1961. She was awarded a graduate fellowship to study philosophy at Stanford and received her doctorate in 1968. Since then, she has worked both academically and politically to combat social hierarchies structured by gender, race, and especially class. She is currently a professor of philosophy at Smith College.

About this essay, Addelson says, "[It] speaks of the authority by which professionals make official definitions and preempt the meaning we may give to their actions and our own. . . . In the essay, I am particularly concerned with the contribution of professional authority to creating and maintaining hierarchies of class, gender, age, and race." (p. 9, *Impure Thoughts*) Although this article is about doing research, Addelson is more concerned as a philosopher with the ethics of social and professional relations among scientists than with the processes of scientific research. As you read, see if you can identify these varied relationships. You might begin by thinking about whom she means by "we" in her first sentence in the quotation above.

Reading the Rhetoric

This particular essay is about how scientific work is accomplished, but Addelson is not a specialist in the field of epistemology. You will notice that not only does she have a different perspective from Magee, she uses different language. The phrase "metaphysical commitments" is an example of the particular philosophical discourse in which Addelson is at home. As you read, find other terms that sound like "philosophers' talk." What strategies can you use to figure out what they mean? Why do philosophers use them?

Reading the Conversation

In this essay, Addelson acknowledges "metaphysical commitments." You may recall how positivists commonly view metaphysical approaches to the epistemics of science as contaminations. Addelson argues that metaphysics cannot be purged from science, claiming that philosophers of science have actually built the foundations of positivistic science on the metaphysical assumption that there is one reality and, hence, only one understanding of it. Thus, Addelson illustrates how metaphysical concerns are written into scientific ways of knowing. As you read, consider other ways Addelson seems to redefine the task of science that logical positivists have outlined.

Addelson picks up the conversation about knowledge-making where Magee leaves off and redirects it. Preview this reading by scanning the introduction (Part One, "Cognitive Authority and the Growth of Knowledge") and finding the statements that refer to or reflect Popper's views. Addelson also tells us more about Thomas Kuhn's contributions to the conversation about how scientific work is done. From this introduction, do you expect Addelson's arguments to align more closely with Popper's or with Kuhn's?

Note that we have omitted Section III of the essay, a long, demanding section with several examples. Although Section IV makes references to those examples, you will be able to understand Addelson's major points without them.

The Man of Professional Wisdom
Kathryn Pyne Addelson

I. COGNITIVE AUTHORITY AND THE GROWTH OF KNOWLEDGE

1 Most of us are introduced to scientific knowledge by our schoolteachers, in classrooms and laboratories, using textbooks and lab manuals as guides. As beginners, we believe that the goal of science is "the growth of knowledge

through new scientific discoveries" (Cole, 1979, 6n). We believe that the methods of science are the most rational that human kind has devised for investigating the world and that (practiced properly) they yield objective knowledge. It seems to us that because there is only one reality, there can be only one real truth and that science describes those facts. Our teachers and our texts affirm this authority of scientific specialists.

2   The authority of specialists in science is not per se an authority to command obedience from some group of people, or to make decisions on either public policy or private investment. Specialists have, rather, an epistemological or cognitive authority: We take their understanding of factual matters and the nature of the world within their sphere of expertise as knowledge, or as the definitive understanding. I don't mean that we suppose scientific specialists to be infallible. Quite the contrary. We believe scientific methods are rational because we believe that they require, and get, criticism of a most far-reaching sort. Science is supposed to be distinguished from religion, metaphysics, and superstition *because* its methods require criticism, test, falsifiability.

3   Our word "science" is ambiguous. Is it a body of knowledge, a method, or an activity? Until recently many Anglo-American philosophers of science ignored science as an activity and applied themselves to analyzing the structure of the body of knowledge, which they conceived narrowly as consisting of theories, laws, and statements of prediction. To a lesser degree, they spoke of "scientific method," conceived narrowly as a set of abstract canons. With such an emphasis, it is easy to assume that it is theory and method that give science its authority. It is easy to assume that researchers' cognitive authority derives from their use of an authoritative method, and that they are justified in exercising authority only within the narrow range of understanding contained in the theories and laws within their purview. Everyone knew, of course, that "scientific method" had been developed within a historical situation: but commitment to abstract canons led philosophers to put aside questions of how particular methods were developed, came to dominate, and (perhaps) were later criticized and rejected.[1] Everyone believed that it is an essential characteristic of scientific knowledge that it grows, and that new theories are suggested, tested, criticized, and developed. But the narrow focus on knowledge as theories and laws, and the emphasis on analyzing their abstract structure or the logical form of scientific explanation, led philosophers to neglect asking how one theory was historically chosen for development and test rather than another.[2] Most important, philosophers did not ask about the social arrangements through which methods and theories came to dominate or to wither away. Although the "rationality of science" is supposed to lie in the fact that scientific understanding is the most open to criticism of all understanding, a crucial area for criticism was ruled out of consideration: the social arrangements through which scientific understanding is developed and through which cognitive authority of the specialist is exercised.

4   Within the past twenty years, many scientists, historians, and philosophers have begun to move away from the abstract and absolutist conceptions

of theory and method. The work that has reached the widest audience is Thomas Kuhn's *The Structure of Scientific Revolutions* (1970). Two major changes in analytic emphasis show in his work. First, Kuhn focuses on science as an activity. Second, given this focus, he construes the content of scientific understanding to include not only theories and laws but also metaphysical commitments, exemplars, puzzles, anomalies, and various other features. Altering the focus to activity does lead one to ask some questions about rise and fall of methods and theories, and so Kuhn could make his famous distinction between the growth of knowledge in normal science and its growth in revolutionary science. However, he makes only the most limited inquiry into social arrangements in the practice of science. And, although he says that under revolutionary science proponents of the old and the new paradigms may engage in a power struggle, he does not explicitly consider cognitive authority.[3] Yet the power struggle in a period of revolutionary change is over which community of scientists will legitimately exercise cognitive authority, whose practices will define the normal science of the specialty and whose understanding will define the nature of the world that falls within their purview. To take cognitive authority seriously, one must ask seriously after its exercise, as embodied in social arrangements inside and outside science.

5   Within the activity of science in the United States today, researchers exercise cognitive authority in various ways.[4] One major way is within the specialties themselves. In accord with the norm of the "autonomy of science," researchers develop hypotheses and theories, discover laws, define problems and solutions, criticize and falsify beliefs, make scientific revolutions. They have the authority to do that on matters in their professional specialty: microbiologists have authority on questions of viruses and demographers, on questions of population changes, though within a specialty some have more power to exercise cognitive authority than others. Researchers have authority to revise the history of ideas in their field, so that each new text portrays the specialty as progressing by developing and preserving kernels of truth and rooting out error and superstition, up to the knowledge of the present.

6   Researchers also exercise cognitive authority outside their professions, for scientific specialists have an authority to define the true nature of the living and nonliving world around us. We are taught their scientific understanding in school. Public and private officials accept it to use in solving political, social, military, and manufacturing problems. The external authority follows the lines of the internal authority. Experts are hired and their texts adopted according to their credentials as specialists in the division of authority-by-specialty within science. But because, within specialties, some people have more power than others, many people never have a text adopted and most never serve as expert advisors.

7   If we admit Kuhn's claim that metaphysical commitments are an integral part of scientific activity, then we see that scientific authority to define the nature of the world is not limited to the laws and theories printed in boldface sentences in our textbooks. Metaphysical commitments are beliefs about the

nature of the living and nonliving things of our world and about their relations with us and with each other. In teaching us their scientific specialties, researchers simultaneously teach us these broader understandings. Speaking of Nobel Prize winners in physics from the time of Roentgen to Yukawa, Nicholas Rescher says, "The revolution wrought by these men in our understanding of nature was so massive that their names became household words throughout the scientifically literate world" (Rescher, 1978, 27). The Darwinian revolution, even more thoroughgoing, changed the metaphysics of a world designed by God in which all creatures were ordered in a great chain of being, to a world of natural selection. These scientific breakthroughs were not simply changes in laws, hypotheses, and theories. They were changes in scientists' understanding of the categories of reality, changes in the questions they asked, the problems they worked with, the solutions they found acceptable. After the revolution, the changed understanding defined "normal science."

8   I will use the notion of cognitive authority to argue that making scientific activity more rational requires that criticizing and testing social arrangements in science be as much a part of scientific method as criticizing and testing theories and experiments. In doing this, I will talk a little more about how cognitive authority is exercised within professional specialties (section II). To make my case, I assume (with Kuhn) that metaphysical commitments are an essential part of scientific understanding, and that greater rationality in science requires criticizing such commitments. I give a number of examples in section III [omitted here]. Section IV considers whether social arrangements within the sciences limit criticism of scientific understanding. I suggest that prestige hierarchies, power within and without the scientific professions, and the social positions of researchers themselves affect which group can exercise cognitive authority. Thus these features of social arrangements play a major role in determining which metaphysical commitments come to dominate, thus what counts as a legitimate scientific problem and solution. In the end, they affect how we all understand the nature of our world and our selves.

II. COGNITIVE AUTHORITY, AUTONOMY, AND CERTIFIED KNOWLEDGE

9 Philosophy of science texts, as well as the *New York Times,* talk of "science" and "scientific knowledge" as if there were one unified activity and one stock of information. But, as we all know, there are many scientific specialties, each with its own Ph.D. program. Members of each specialty or subspecialty certify and criticize their own opinions in their own journals and at their own professional meetings. Each specialist shows excellence by climbing the prestige ladder of the specialty.

10   Only some of the many people who work within a research specialty have epistemological authority within it. Barbara Reskin remarks, "The roles

of both student and technician are characterized by lower status and by a technical division of labor that allocates scientific creativity and decision making
to scientists and laboratory work to those assigned the role of technician or
student" (Reskin, 1978, 20).[5] The role division justifies assigning credit to the
chief investigator, but its most important effect is on communication. Technicians and students work on the chief investigator's problems in ways he or she
considers appropriate.[6] They rarely communicate with other researchers
through conferences or journal articles or by chatting over the WATS line. They
are not among the significant communicators of the specialty.

11   Researchers who *are* significant communicators set categories for classifying their subjects of study, and they define the meaning of what is taking
place. With the aid of physicists, chemists define what chemical substance
and interaction are. Microbiologists categorize viruses and molecules and explain the significance of electron microscopes. These are different from the
understandings we all have of the physical and chemical parts of our world
as we live in it. We choose honey by taste, smell, and color, not by chemical
composition, and we meet viruses in interactions we know as flus and colds.[7]

12   Scientific understandings appear in hypotheses, laws, and theories, but
they presuppose metaphysics and methodology. Thomas Kuhn mentions the
importance of metaphysics, using physical science in the seventeenth century as an example:

> [Among the] still not unchanging characteristics of science are the . . .
> quasi-metaphysical commitments that historical study so regularly displays.
> After about 1630, for example, and particularly after the appearance of
> Descartes' immensely influential scientific writings, most physical scien-
> tists assumed that the universe was composed of microscopic corpuscles
> and that all natural phenomena could be explained in terms of corpuscular
> shape, size, motion, and interaction. That nest of commitments proved to
> be both metaphysical and methodological. As methodological, it told them
> what ultimate laws and fundamental explanations must be like: laws must
> specify corpuscular motion and interaction, and explanation must reduce
> any given natural phenomenon to corpuscular action under laws. More im-
> portant still, the corpuscular conception of the universe told scientists
> what many of their research problems should be. (Kuhn, 1970, 41)

13   The seventeenth-century scientists also made metaphysical assumptions that most contemporary scientists share. They assumed that because
there is *one* reality, there can be only one correct understanding of it. That
metaphysical assumption, disguised as a point of logic, took root in Western
thought more than two millennia ago, when Parmenides said that being and
thinking are the same; that which exists and that which can be thought are
the same. From that maxim, he concluded that the reality that is the object
of knowledge, and not mere opinion, is one and unchanging. Differ though
they might about the nature of reality, both Plato and Aristotle shared the
metaphysical assumption that the object of scientific knowledge is the one,
essential, intelligible structure of the one reality. Contemporary scientists

share an analogous metaphysical assumption when they presuppose that reality is known through universal laws and predictions, which give the correct description of the world. All admit, of course, that in its present state, scientific knowledge is partial, suffering from inaccuracies, and so on. But, they say, this incompleteness and error is what is to be corrected by the scientific method. In principle the scientific enterprise is based on the metaphysical premises that because there is one reality, there must be one, correctly described truth. This premise is the foundation of the cognitive authority of scientific specialties. The specialist offers the correct understanding of reality while the lay person struggles in the relativity of mere opinion.

●   ●   ●

IV. COGNITIVE AUTHORITY AND POWER

14 In section II, I suggested that the conventional understandings of significant communicators in science are the definitive understandings of the nature of the world within their spheres of expertise. In section III, I suggested that metaphysical commitments are important to the growth of knowledge. In those sections, I spoke as though any researcher with the appropriate certificates of training could serve as a significant communicator, and the reader might think that if one group exercised greater cognitive authority it was on meritocratic or purely rational grounds. Their theories and commitments have been shown to withstand test and criticism better than those of their competitors. I believe it is a valuable feature of the scientific enterprise that rational criticism is a factor in determining which group exercises cognitive authority. However, social arrangements are factors as well, and to the degree that we refuse to acknowledge that fact, we limit criticism and cause scientific work to be less rational than it might be. In this section, I will indicate some social factors that may be relevant, and then I will close with an example of how scientific understanding has been improved by recent criticisms that did take social arrangements into account.

15   First, let me take up questions of prestige. The sciences differ in prestige, physics having more than economics, and both having more than educational psychology. Specialties in a science, too, differ in prestige, experimental having more than clinical psychology, for example. Prestige differences affect researchers' judgments on which metaphysical and methodological commitments are to be preferred. Carolyn Wood Sherif remarks on the "prestige hierarchy" in psychology in the 1950s:

> Each of the fields and specialties in psychology sought to improve its status by adopting (as well and as closely as stomachs permitted) the perspectives, theories, and methodologies as high on the hierarchy as possible. The way to "respectability" in this scheme has been the appearance of rigor and scientific inquiry, bolstered by highly restricted notions of what science is about. (Sherif, 1979, 98)

16 Many philosophers of science have not only taken prestige hierarchies to be irrelevant to scientific rationality, they have accepted the hierarchies themselves and in doing so have shared and justified "highly restricted notions of what science is about." This failing was blatant in the work of logical positivists and their followers, for they constructed their analysis of scientific method to accord with an idealization of what goes on in physics, and they discussed the "unity of science" in a way that gave physics star status.[8]

17   Within specialties, researchers differ in prestige, so that some have access to positions of power while others do not. Some teach in prestigious institutions and train the next generation of successful researchers. Researchers judge excellence in terms of their own understanding of their field, of which problems are important, of which methods are best suited to solving them. Researchers in positions of power can spread their understandings and their metaphysical commitments. Consider the primatology example in section III:

18   Because Robert Yerkes held influential positions, he was able to give an important backing to Clarence Ray Carpenter's career, helping Carpenter to compete successfully for the positions and funding needed to do his research. Haraway says of Carpenter, "From his education, funding, and social environment, there was little reason for Carpenter to reject the basic assumptions that identified reproduction and dominance based on sex with the fundamental organizing principles of a body politic" (Haraway, 1978, 30). Yerkes shared the "body politic" metaphysics. In helping Carpenter, he was helping to spread his own metaphysical commitments.

19   The question is not whether top scientists in most fields produce some very good work but rather the more important question of whether other good work, even work critical of the top scientists, is not taken seriously because its proponents are not members of the same powerful networks and so cannot exercise the same cognitive authority. The question is made particularly difficult because, by disregarding or downgrading competing research, the "top scientists" cut off the resources necessary for their competition to develop really good work. In most fields it is next to impossible to do research without free time, aid from research assistants, secretaries, craftsmen, custodians, and in many cases, access to equipment.

20   Some very influential philosophers of science have insisted that criticism is an essential part of scientific method, and that criticism requires that there be competing scientific theories. (See Popper, 1965; Feyerabend, 1970.) Accepting that as an abstract canon, one might philosophically point out that Yerkes should have encouraged more competition and (if one becomes particularly moralistic) that he should have been more careful about showing favoritism and bias. But it would be a mistake to describe Yerkes as showing favoritism and bias. As a matter of fact, he did much to set the practice of researchers investigating unpopular subjects and reaching unpopular results in the interests of scientific freedom and research in "pure science." But he made his judgments according to his own understanding of scientific research. Any researcher must do that. Researchers are also the judges of

which competing theories it makes sense to pursue or to encourage others to pursue. If this seems to result in bias, the way to correct it is not by blaming individual researchers for showing favoritism because they depart from some mythical set of abstract canons. The way to begin to correct it is to broaden rational criticism in science by requiring that both philosophers of science and scientists understand how prestige and power are factors in the way cognitive authority is exercised.

21   So far I have talked about influences on the exercises of cognitive authority with the scientific professions. Many people have observed that there are outside influences on scientific research-funding, for example. Given legally dominant understandings of capitalism in the United States, many people consider it proper for private business to fund research on problems that need solving for reasons of economic competition and expansion. Most of us considered it appropriate that public agencies in a democracy should fund research to help solve social problems of the moment (as do private philanthropic foundations for the most part). If we think of science as a stock of knowledge embodied in theories, then the problem of funding does not seem to be a problem having to do with rationality and criticism in science. Instead it may appear to be a question of political or other outside interference with the autonomy of the researchers, at worst preventing them from setting their own problems to investigate.[9] If we use the notion of cognitive authority, however, we may see that the question of funding indeed has to do with scientific rationality and with the content of our scientific understanding of the world.

22   Metaphysical commitments of a science tell scientists what many of their research problems should be (Kuhn, 1970, 41). As we saw from the Merton-Becker example, a difference in metaphysics may bring a difference in *what the problem is taken to be*. In that case, it was a difference between explaining why people rob banks and explaining how robbing banks comes to have the quality of being deviant (Debro, 1970, 167). Because problems investigated by a tradition are related to the metaphysical and methodological commitments of its researchers, some understandings of nature will have a better chance for support than others.[10] Those researchers will have a better opportunity to exercise cognitive authority and to help others of their metaphysical persuasion rise in the ranks. They will write the texts and serve as advisors and use their external authority to popularize their metaphysical outlook. So funding influences the content of science at a given historical moment, and it influences the way we all come to understand the world.

23   The influence goes beyond the question of which of a number of competing traditions are to be rewarded. Arlene Daniels traces some of the ramifications in discussing Allan Schnaiberg's remarks on obstacles to environmental research.

Schnaiberg shows us how unpopular socioenvironmental research is within establishment contexts. The science industries won't pay for it, the research foundations won't sanction it. Rewards in the academic market place depend on quick payoffs: accordingly, independent researchers there cannot wait for results that require large expenditures of time in unfunded research. (Daniels, 1979, 38-39)

This means not only that some existing metaphysical and methodological traditions will flourish while others are passed over. It means that potentially fruitful metaphysics and methods will not get a chance for development at all, because social arrangements in the scientific professions and the influence of funding work against it.

24   So far, I've suggested that social arrangements within the scientific professions, and between those professions and the larger society, involve factors relevant to the exercise of cognitive authority in the sciences and thus to the content of scientific understanding. Are the professional and social life experiences of researchers also relevant to their metaphysical commitments? This is an extremely interesting question because of the quite general assumption in the United States that there is a privileged definition of reality that scientists capture, a main assumption underlying the authority we give them. Feminists in nearly every scientific field have questioned that assumption.[11] I questioned it from an interactionist perspective in discussing Merton, above. Let me give two suggestive examples here.

25   The anthropologist Edwin Ardener suggests that because of their social experience, men and women conceptualize their societies and communities differently (Ardener, 1975a, 1975b). In most societies, men more frequently engage in political activities and public discourse and have the definitional problem of bounding their own society or community off from others. Models suited to the usual women's experience aren't the object of public discourse, so when circumstances call for it, women will use men's models, not their own.

26   Ethnographers tend to report the male models for three reasons, according to Ardener. They are more accessible to the researcher. Male models are the officially accepted ones in the ethnographer's home society. And they accord with the metaphysical and theoretical outlook of functionalism which, in the past, many ethnographers have held. Milton reports Ardener's claim this way: "Ethnographers, especially those who have adopted a functionalist approach, tend to be attracted to the bounded models of society, with which they are presented mainly by men and occasionally by women. These models accord well with functionalist theory and so tend to be presented as *the* models of society" (Milton, 1979, 48).

27   We need not accept Ardener's claims as gospel truth to realize that we *cannot* accept without test the empirical assumption that a specialist's social experience has no significant effect on his or her scientific understanding of the world.

28   Nor can we accept, without test, the empirical hypothesis that the long training and isolating, professional experience of scientific specialists has

no significant effect on their scientific understanding. The sociologist Vilhelm Aubert says,

> Members of society have, through their own planning and their own subsequent observations, verifications, and falsifications, built up a cognitive structure bearing some resemblances to a scientific theory. . . . But . . . social man behaves only in some, albeit important, areas in this purposive way. Any attempt, therefore, to stretch the predictability criterion beyond these areas—their limits are largely unknown—may result in a misrepresentation of the nature of human behavior. This danger is greatly increased by origin of most social scientists in cultures which heavily stress a utilitarian outlook, and by their belonging even to the subcultures within these, which are the main bearers of this ethos. A sociology produced by fisherman from northern Norway or by Andalusian peasants might have been fundamentally different. The leading social scientists are people with tenure and right of pension. (Aubert, 1965, 135)

The leading physicists, biologists, and philosophers of science are also people with tenure and right of pension. They live in societies marked by dominance of group over group. As specialists, they compete for positions at the top of their professional hierarchies that allow them to exercise cognitive authority more widely. Out of such cultural understandings and social orderings, it is no wonder that we get an emphasis on predictive law and an insistence that the currently popular theories of a specialty represent the one, true, authoritative description of the world. It is no wonder that our specialists continually present us with metaphysical descriptions of the work in terms of hierarchy, dominance, and competition. The wonder is that we get any development of our understanding at all.

29   But we do. Scientific understanding does seem to grow (in however ungainly a fashion), and our knowledge does seem to "advance" (however crabwise).

30   In our own century, scientific knowledge has often seemed to grow at the expense of wisdom. However, the corrective is not to dismiss science as hopelessly biased and wrongheaded and return to some kind of folk wisdom. We can't get along without science anymore. The corrective seems rather to ferret out all the irrationalities we can find in scientific activity and to expand our understanding of science and scientific rationality. To do this, we should acknowledge metaphysical commitments as part of the content of scientific understanding and thus open them to scrutiny and criticism by specialist and nonspecialist alike. Feminist criticism offers a very instructive example here. In the past twenty years, political feminists have given lay criticisms of much of our scientific metaphysics. Other feminists have gained specialist training and brought the lay criticisms to bear on technical theories within their fields.[12] This was possible because sexism is a political issue at the moment, and funding, journals, and other resources are available for this sort of research and criticism. I am suggesting that we

should institutionalize this form of criticism and make it an explicit part of "scientific method." We should also try using the notion of cognitive authority and expanding the range of the criteria of scientific rationality and criticism so that it includes social arrangements within the scientific professions.

31   If we expand the range of criticism, I believe that philosophers of science and scientists as well will find themselves advocating change in our social system. This would not result in a sudden illegitimate politicization of science or an opening of the floodgates of irrationality. Quite the contrary. Because they have cognitive authority, our scientists already *are* politicized. It is the *unexamined* exercise of cognitive authority within our present social arrangements that is most to be feared. Illegitimate politicization and rampant irrationality find their most fruitful soil when our activities are mystified and protected from criticism.

NOTES

Acknowledgments: Research for this paper was supported in part by a grant from the National Endowment for the Humanities and by the Mellon Foundation grant to the Smith College project on Women and Social Change. I am very grateful for criticism or advice I received from Howard Becker, Donna Haraway, Arlene Daniels, Sandra Harding, Vicky Spelman, Helen Longino, Kay Warren, Noretta Koertge, Arnold Feldman, and members of two seminars I taught in the Northwestern University sociology department, fall 1980. I have previously published work under the name Kathryn Pyne Parsons.

1. Instead, philosophers criticized one another's versions of the abstract canons. Positivist Rudolf Carnap was particularly painstaking at criticizing his own and other positivists' analyses of the structure of scientific theories. See, for example, Carnap, 1956. Karl Popper also devoted time and energy to criticizing the positivists. See, for example, Popper, 1965.
2. At the beginning of the "new wave" in philosophy of science, N. R. Hanson did ask after the choosing of new theories, but he did so by discussing the logic of discovery and the ways in which theories that groups of scientists develop are constrained by their patterns of conceptual organization rather than by asking after constraints in the social arrangements within which scientific understanding is developed and criticized. See Hanson, 1958.
3. It is there implicitly, however, particularly in his wonderful discussion of science texts.
4. Whether or not a group has authority regarding something depends on social arrangements in the society in which they form a group, thus my restriction to "the United States today." I should make more severe restrictions because there are subgroups in the USA, which don't grant "scientists" much authority. We do it through our public and major private educational systems, however.

5. One doesn't usually think of artisans as part of science, but one physicist said of his university's craftsmen, "The gadgets they produce for us are just crucial. The reason the work the department does is internationally competitive with major research centers all over the world is in part due to the capabilities of the people in the machine shop. Some of the research simply could not be done without them." *Contact,* August 1980, 8 (University of Massachusetts, Amherst, publication).

6. Within the hierarchical social relations of the research group, the chief investigator has authority to command obedience from technicians, students, secretaries, and the like. I am not concerned with that kind of authority in this chapter.

7. My remark about honey may still be true, but because of changes in the food industry consequent to the "growth of scientific knowledge," we are learning to choose foods by applying the chemist's categories to lists of ingredients on packages at the supermarket.

8. Some philosophers of science have insisted that the methods of the physical sciences are not suitable for historical sciences—see, for example, the whole *Verstehen* controversy (Collingwood 1946) as a classic source. For social sciences generally, see Winch (1958).

9. George H. Daniels suggests that the rise of the ideal of pure scientific research in the late-nineteenth century led to conflicts with democratic assumptions in "The Pure-Science Ideal and Democratic Culture," *Science* 156 (1976): 1699–1705. My discussion here displays the other side of the conflict.

10. I am not claiming here that stating a problem in a certain way ensures that you'll have a certain metaphysics, or even determines it in some unidirectional way. My point is about the ranges of theories and traditions available at a historical moment and which of them will receive encouragement and support.

11. See, for example, the essays in Millman and Kanter (1975), Sherman and Beck (1979), and Harding and Hintikka (1983).

12. Feminist criticism may seem more obviously politicized than, say, Yerkes's or Merton's or Becker's criticisms discussed above, but I think that is because feminists themselves insist on the political connections.

FOLLOW-UP ACTIVITIES

Discussing the Rhetoric

1. Who is Addelson's intended audience? What is her purpose?

2. Typical of the organization of academic writing is to begin with a summary of what others in the field think, followed by a statement something like "but I assert" in which the writer states her own view or thesis. Examine Addelson's third paragraph. Point out sentences that exemplify this pattern. In what ways does the fourth paragraph echo this pattern? Given that the central purpose of academic writing is to disseminate new knowledge, why would this pattern make an effective introduction?

3. A central issue Addelson addresses is what she calls "cognitive authority." Writers have a variety of tools at hand for defining terms—they can write a definition for it; they can give examples, both hypothetical and real; they can compare it to other similar terms. To define "cognitive authority," does Addelson use just one of these or several? Find places in the text that contribute to your understanding of "cognitive authority" and explain the techniques Addelson has used for definition.

4. Addelson also uses the phrase "metaphysical commitments" frequently. Besides defining the term on as "beliefs about the nature of living and non-living things of our world and about their relations with us and with each other," how else does she explain what the term means? What terms have you come across in previous readings that seem synonymous?

5. Note the final paragraph in Part One. What is its purpose? Have you encountered similar paragraphs in previous readings? Which readings?

6. One of the rhetorical obligations of writers is to catch their readers up on the larger conversation in which they are engaged. Addelson does this especially in Part Two, "Cognitive Authority, Autonomy, and Certified Knowledge." Summarize the conversation in your own words. What does it have in common with the conversation Magee was engaged in? Where does it diverge?

7. What voices does Addelson privilege as she recounts the larger conversation? Are they some of the same ones Magee privileges? Are some different? What changes in the story result from privileging different voices?

Discussing the Conversation

1. According to Addelson, how does a researcher's metaphysical commitments influence his/her scientific work? (In the readings following this one, such questions will become central.)

2. What social hierarchies does Addelson identify in the academic world? What privileges are available to those at the top of the academic hierarchy that are not available to people at the lower levels? (These issues, too, will figure in the following readings in this Part of the text.)

3. Addelson questions who gets to tell the stories in the academic world. How is this similar to Pratt's central concern about what happens in contact zones? Why does Addelson object to such hierarchies?

4. What is Addelson's solution to the problem of social hierarchies in scientific research? Compare her view of the value and uses of criticism to Magee's. How are they similar or different?

5. Do you think that Addelson questions the value of scientific knowledge? What, exactly, does she question?

Joining the Conversation

1. Although Addelson respects scientific work, she depicts it very differently from Magee or Klemke. Choose an idea or point of view of Addelson's that you find particularly surprising, intriguing or offensive. Write an informal paper in which you consider that view against your own background knowledge or assumptions about scientific work. Does her point of view support or challenge your previous assumptions? How do you respond to that point of view?

2. If you are planning a career in the sciences, write a reflective essay about how Addelson's view of scientific work complicates your assumptions about what it means to be a scientist.

INTRODUCTORY COMMENTS ON "STAR-SPANGLED SCANDAL" BY NICHOLAS WADE

Reading the Context

Nicholas Wade is the science and health editor of the *New York Times.* Prior to working for the *Times,* he was a reporter for *Science* magazine, based in Washington, D.C., and *k* magazine, published in London. He is a graduate of Cambridge University in England. Joining the *New York Times* as an editorial writer in 1982, Wade was promoted to Science and Health editor in 1990. In addition to writing articles for the *Times,* Wade has written several books, including *The Nobel Duel* about the competition between two biologists, Andrew Schally and Roger Guillemin, who finally shared the Nobel prize for their independent work in growth hormones, and *Betrayers of the Truth,* an analysis of intentional misrepresentation in science.

Reading the Rhetoric

This article was originally published in the *New York Times Magazine,* a supplement to the Sunday edition of the paper. You will notice conspicuous stylistic differences between this article and other pieces you have read in this text. As you read, think about the reasons for those differences. How do the audience and purpose of a *New York Times* feature article differ from those of previous selections?

Reading the Conversation

We include this article in part to demonstrate that discussions about how science is done extend beyond the small group of specialists in the philosophy and sociology of science. Written for readers of the *New York Times,* a diverse though perhaps somewhat more educated and affluent group than the average American, this piece addresses the very issues that Magee and Addelson discuss, the question of the extent to which Popperian notions of falsifiability actually operate in science. In their articles, Addelson and Keller systematically spell out the forces that they believe complicate Feigl's or Popper's notions about how pure science should work. What forces does Wade identify? What does he add to the conversation?

Star-Spangled Scandal
Nicholas Wade

1 Tired of Gossip from Buckingham Palace? Sick to the gills of the Simpson trial? I've got a real scandal for you. It doesn't have any sex, race or class, but you don't mind that, do you?

2   It's a scandal of the intellectual kind. You know, like iatrogenic disease or the Constitution's provisions for slavery. And it comes from the people we pay to explain the structure of the universe.

3   Once these cosmologists had a beautiful idea, called the Steady State Theory. It held that the universe was expanding yet stayed the same in all parts and directions because of the steady creation of hydrogen atoms to fill in the gaps. That's the way things always had been and always would be.

4   This graceful theory had an ugly sister, the notion that once there was nothing and out of this nothingness appeared a blob of immensely hot, dense stuff that has been ferociously expanding ever since.

5   The astronomer Fred Hoyle, a gallant defender of the fair Steady State, used to ridicule the ugly sister's inelegance and crude origins. For the universe to pop up tackily out of nowhere, as this notion held, just replaced one mystery with another. He likened it to a party girl jumping out of a birthday cake, and hoping to smother this flashy pyrotechnic folly with ridicule, he named it the Big Bang.

6   The Big Bang's defenders couldn't immediately think of any better name for their inamorata, and while they were dallying, a strange event forced them into a shotgun marriage: the discovery all around the universe of faint heat such as might be left over from an ancient explosion.

7   Astronomers and cosmologists have been wedded to the Big Bang for 30 years now. They are not universally happy in this crisis-racked union. There are many embarrassing things Big Bang can't explain. They are faithful only because there is no other theory with legs. "Most cosmologists would be delighted to abandon the standard model for something new to think about if

only the alternatives looked reasonably promising," P. J. E. Peebles of Princeton University wrote last year in his textbook, "Principles of Physical Cosmology."

8   With astronomers' eyes still roving, a delicious scandal has now flared up. It seems, would you believe it, that Big Bang has told a terrible lie about her age.

9   The details came out last month when astronomers using the Hubble space telescope were eyeing a specially beautiful galaxy in Virgo called M100. Up above the atmosphere, the telescope recorded the true brightness of certain stars in M100 and hence the real distance from here to Virgo. Given that yardstick, and the known speed of Virgo's advance, astronomers could at last fix with reasonable confidence the approximate date of the Big Bang. The birthday was eight billion years ago.

10   But the oldest known stars in the universe, as judged by the state of their stellar evolution, are known to be up to 16 billion years old. How could that be? The universe cannot be half the age of its oldest stars. The two strong measurements stand in the starkest contradiction.

11   Philosophers of science, like the late Karl Popper, enjoy saying that scientific theories cannot be proved, only falsified, and that scientists abandon a theory as soon as they stumble on a single contradiction. Little did Popper understand the psychology of scientists. People who have spent a lifetime constructing and defending a theory don't give it up because of a few mere counterexamples or contradictions. They furiously cut and patch and defend their precious intellectual creation to the bitter end.

12   Nor do scientists like to abandon a boat, however leaky it may be, until a new ship is in sight. Cosmologists have to stick with Big Bang. Divorce would cost them the three things they can truly explain about the universe—the fact of its expansion, the pivotal ratio of helium to hydrogen and the faint whispering of residual heat found in all quarters of the sky. So the revelation that Big Bang is very seriously under age may embarrass them but will in no way loosen their attachment. Instead, they are reaching for the cosmetics case. A measure of their desperation is that they favor a hazardous contrivance known as the Cosmological Constant.

13   The constant was invented by Einstein in 1917 to force his elegant general theory of relativity into describing a universe that was static, that being the fashionable expectation at the time. The constant embodied the ad hoc idea of a mysterious force that counteracts gravity. Just imagine Einstein's shock and chagrin on learning his unlovely constant was unnecessary when in 1929 Edwin P. Hubble showed the universe was not static but dynamically expanding. Meanwhile, others had found solutions of Einstein's field equations that described the universe without involving Star Trek-like anti-gravity machines.

14   Cosmologists are now resorting to Einstein's constant because it would imply that the universe expanded at first more slowly and then more quickly than thought. That scenario would allow the new measurement of

the universe's rate of expansion to be stretched into alignment with a much greater age. The adjustment is fully in the spirit of the astrophysicist Sir Arthur Eddington, who declared that, in astronomy, no experiment should be believed until confirmed by theory.

15   Cosmologists' lives were more comfortable when a flawed mirror blurred the Hubble telescope's vision. Now that it's fixed, the new instrument is seeing a universe quite unlike what they expected. The clash between observation and theory promises exciting times ahead in cosmology. How long will Big Bang believers be able to smooth over the age contradiction with a constant rescued from the trash can of history? How long can cosmology stay respectable when its practitioners have no idea what kind of matter makes up at least 90 percent of the universe? Cosmology, as the Russian physicist Lev Landau once observed, is often in error but never in doubt—a perfect recipe for embarrassments. You want real scandal, soap opera, stars in serious trouble? Nothing beats the cosmologists' cosmic strip.

FOLLOW-UP ACTIVITIES

Discussing the Rhetoric

1. Journalistic writers talk about "the hook"—the attention-getting device that "hooks" a reader into an article. What "hooks" can you find in this piece? Why are hooks necessary in journalistic writing? Do you think they are necessary in other kinds of writing?

2. What other stylistic characteristics differentiate this article from others you have read so far? Consider register (level of formality), length of paragraphs, length of sentences, and diction. What connections can you draw between a newspaper audience's expectations and the rhetorical choices you have identified?

3. Note Wade's metaphorical language in this article. Look particularly at the nouns and verbs used to describe the Big Bang and Steady State theories and scientists' relationship to them. What patterns do you notice?

4. What lines in this article tickle your funnybone? What are the advantages of humor as a rhetorical technique?

Discussing the Conversation

1. Consider Wade's metaphorical patterns in relation to claims that male scientists name nature as the passive, feminine other. What inferences can you draw?

2. Consider Wade's depiction of cosmologists' reactions to the new discoveries of the Hubble telescope in relation to Popper's advocacy of falsification as the best guarantee of rigorous science. What problems does Wade point out in Popper's program?

3. Consider scientists' belief in either the Big Bang theory or the Steady State theory as examples of metaphysical commitments in Addelson's terms. (Addelson defines metaphysical commitments as "beliefs about the nature of the living and nonliving things of our [universe] and about their relations with us and with each other.") According to Addelson, what effects do such commitments have on scientific work? Are they positive, negative or both? How do her views differ from Wade's perspective that for psychological reasons scientists are unlikely to work to falsify their views?

4. Recall that Nicholas Wade's position at the *New York Times* is Science and Health Editor. What does this title suggest about how the *New York Times* constructs the subject of "health?" What groups or discourse communities would argue against this construction? What consequences might result for these communities from the *Times* construction of "health" as a science?

Joining the Conversation

1. To get people to read his article, Wade must capture the attention of newspaper readers who may think that discoveries about deep space, unlike information about medical advances or crime statistics, have absolutely nothing to do with their personal lives. Write an informal paper about the rhetorical devices Wade uses to connect with his audience.

2. Write an informal paper about the relationships between technology and science. New questions about theories of the origin of the universe have emerged because of improved technology that allows us to see deeper into space. To think about ideas for this informal paper, consider the following: Can you cite other instances when improved technology preceded new knowledge? Several of the readings in this unit have argued that scientific work is influenced by nonobjective factors like people's convictions or their social arrangements. How would you say technology fits into the equation? Does it influence scientific findings? Is it an objective factor?

3. Write an informal paper in which you treat any of the topics mentioned so far in this text humorously. You might, for instance, examine the topic of the college curriculum, students' problems adjusting to the requirements of the university, or the conduct of scientific research.

INTRODUCTORY COMMENTS ON "A FEELING FOR THE ORGANISM" BY EVELYN FOX KELLER

Reading the Context

Evelyn Fox Keller graduated with a doctorate in theoretical physics from Harvard University and she has spent much of her career working as a "traditional" scientist. In addition to her work in theoretical physics, Keller has also published in the field of molecular biology. Although her work has received mixed reviews, several of her papers have become classics in their fields.

Keller troubles reviewers because she is at once an "insider" (a practicing scientist), and an "outsider" (a practicing feminist and theoretician). Her ambiguous place in the scientific community is reflected in her teaching positions. Keller taught at the University of California at Berkeley in the Rhetoric, Women's Studies, and History of Science departments. After that she accepted an appointment at MIT, where she now holds a full professorship in the Program of Science, Technology, and Society. Keller's aim is to conceptualize new ways of "doing" science. In *Reflections on Gender and Science* she describes her goal as the "reclamation, from within science, of science as a human instead of a masculine project."

This essay is the last chapter of Keller's first book titled *A Feeling for the Organism: The Life and Work of Barbara McClintock* (1983). Born in 1902, Barbara McClintock received a doctorate from Cornell when few women were studying science at all. She eventually received numerous prizes and accolades, including the Nobel Prize, for her work on genetic transposition. She was a scientist who viewed science as a connected and complicated whole, and although most of her theories are now considered "factual," the gradual acceptance of those theories by the scientific community was hard won.

Keller is also the author or co-author of *Reflections on Gender and Science* (1985), *Secrets of Life, Secrets of Death* (1992), *Body Politics* (1990), and *Keywords in Evolutionary Biology* (1992).

Reading the Rhetoric

Even though this biography of McClintock's life was published early in Keller's career, her audience is not limited to cytogeneticists, or even to other biologists. It is much broader. What rhetorical strategies in the text indicate Keller's attention to a broader audience? Given her position as both insider and outsider, why might she target a broad audience?

Although the book is a biography, Keller also makes numerous comments about McClintock's observations, interpreting them in light of her own theories. Do you think this strengthens or weakens Keller's credibility as a writer? What do Keller's purposes for writing this biography seem to be?

Reading the Conversation

Part Two focuses on some of the various views people have about knowledge. To some, knowledge is absolute. To others it is dependent on certain perspectives and subject to interpretation. Keller's article offers us a window into the diverse opinions on knowledge construction within science itself. Through McClintock, Keller highlights a "scientific methodology" considerably different from what you read about in Klemke's and Magee's essays. If a methodology is a set of procedures for establishing meaning or truth, in what ways is McClintock's methodology different from the standard scientific method outlined by Klemke? Which methodology is more comfortable to you? Why do you think this is?

A Feeling for the Organism
Evelyn Fox Keller

There are two equally dangerous extremes—to shut reason out, and to let nothing else in.

Pascal

1   If Barbara McClintock's story illustrates the fallibility of science, it also bears witness to the underlying health of the scientific enterprise. Her eventual vindication demonstrates the capacity of science to overcome its own characteristic kinds of myopia, reminding us that its limitations do not reinforce themselves indefinitely. Their own methodology allows, even obliges, scientists to continually reencounter phenomena even their best theories cannot accommodate. Or—to look at it from the other side—however severely communication between science and nature may be impeded by the preconceptions of a particular time, some channels always remain open; and, through them, nature finds ways of reasserting itself.

2   But the story of McClintock's contributions to biology has another, less accessible, aspect. What is it in an individual scientist's relation to nature that facilitates the kind of seeing that eventually leads to productive discourse? What enabled McClintock to see further and deeper into the mysteries of genetics than her colleagues?

3   Her answer is simple. Over and over again, she tells us one must have the time to look, the patience to "hear what the material has to say to you," the openness to "let it come to you." Above all, one must have "a feeling for the organism."

4   One must understand "how it grows, understand its parts, understand when something is going wrong with it. [An organism] isn't just a piece of plastic, it's something that is constantly being affected by the environment, constantly showing attributes or disabilities in its growth. You have to be aware of all of that. . . . You need to know those plants well enough so that if anything changes, . . . you [can] look at the plant and right away you know what this damage you see is from—something that scraped across it or something that bit it or something that the wind did." You need to have a feeling for every individual plant.

5   "No two plants are exactly alike. They're all different, and as a consequence, you have to know that difference," she explains. "I start with the
seedling, and I don't want to leave it. I don't feel I really know the story if I
don't watch the plant all the way along. So I know every plant in the field. I
know them intimately, and I find it a great pleasure to know them."

6   This intimate knowledge, made possible by years of close association
with the organism she studies, is a prerequisite for her extraordinary perspi-
cacity. "I have learned so much about the corn plant that when I see things,
I can interpret [them] right away." Both literally and figuratively, her "feeling for the organism" has extended her vision. At the same time, it has sustained her through a lifetime of lonely endeavor, unrelieved by the solace of
human intimacy or even by the embrace of her profession.

7   Good science cannot proceed without a deep emotional investment on
the part of the scientist. It is that emotional investment that provides the motivating force for the endless hours of intense, often grueling, labor. Einstein
wrote: ". . . what deep longing to understand even a faint reflexion of the
reason revealed in this world had to be alive in Kepler and Newton so that
they could in lonely work for many years disentangle the mechanism of ce-
lestial mechanics?"[1] But McClintock's feeling for the organism is not simply
a longing to behold the "reason revealed in this world." It is a longing to embrace the world in its very being, through reason and beyond.

8   For McClintock, reason—at least in the conventional sense of the
word—is not by itself adequate to describe the vast complexity—even mystery—of living forms. Organisms have a life and order of their own that scientists can only partially fathom. No models we invent can begin to do full
justice to the prodigious capacity of organisms to devise means for guaran-
teeing their own survival. On the contrary, "anything you can think of you
will find." In comparison with the ingenuity of nature, our scientific intelligence seems pallid.

9   For her, the discovery of transposition was above all a key to the complexity of genetic organization—an indicator of the subtlety with which cy-
toplasm, membranes, and DNA are integrated into a single structure. It is the
overall organization, or orchestration, that enables the organism to meet its
needs, whatever they might be, in ways that never cease to surprise us. That
capacity for surprise gives McClintock immense pleasure. She recalls, for example, the early post-World War II studies of the effect of radiation on
Drosophila: "It turned out that the flies that had been under constant radiation were more vigorous than those that were standard. Well, it was hilarious;
it was absolutely against everything that had been thought about earlier. I
thought it was terribly funny; I was utterly delighted. Our experience with
DDT has been similar. It was thought that insects could be readily killed off
with the spraying of DDT. But the insects began to thumb their noses at anything you tried to do to them."

10   Our surprise is a measure of our tendency to underestimate the flexibility of living organisms. The adaptability of plants tends to be especially un-
appreciated. "Animals can walk around, but plants have to stay still to do the

same things, with ingenious mechanisms. . . . Plants are extraordinary. For instance, . . . if you pinch a leaf of a plant you set off electric pulses. You can't touch a plant without setting off an electric pulse. . . . There is no question that plants have [all] kinds of sensitivities. They do a lot of responding to their environment. They can do almost anything you can think of. But just because they sit there, anybody walking down the road considers them just a plastic area to look at, [as if] they're not really alive."

11   An attentive observer knows better. At any time, for any plant, one who has sufficient patience and interest can see the myriad signs of life that a casual eye misses: "In the summertime, when you walk down the road, you'll see that the tulip leaves, if it's a little warm, turn themselves around so their backs are toward the sun. You can just see where the sun hits them and where the sun doesn't hit. . . . [Actually], within the restricted areas in which they live, they move around a great deal." These organisms "are fantastically beyond our wildest expectations."

12   For all of us, it is need and interest above all that induce the growth of our abilities; a motivated observer develops faculties that a casual spectator may never be aware of. Over the years, a special kind of sympathetic understanding grew in McClintock, heightening her powers of discernment, until finally, the objects of her study have become subjects in their own right; they claim from her a kind of attention that most of us experience only in relation to other persons. "Organism" is for her a code word—not simply a plant or animal ("Every component of the organism is as much of an organism as every other part")—but the name of a living form, of object-as-subject. With an uncharacteristic lapse into hyperbole, she adds: "Every time I walk on grass I feel sorry because I know the grass is screaming at me."

13   A bit of poetic license, perhaps, but McClintock is not a poet; she is a scientist. What marks her as such is her unwavering confidence in the underlying order of living forms, her use of the apparatus of science to gain access to that order, and her commitment to bringing back her insights into the shared language of science—even if doing so might require that language to change. The irregularities or surprises molecular biologists are now uncovering in the organization and behavior of DNA are not indications of a breakdown of order, but only of the inadequacies of our models in the face of the complexity of nature's actual order. Cells, and organisms, have an organization of their own in which nothing is random.

14   In short, McClintock shares with all other natural scientists the credo that nature is lawful, and the dedication to the task of articulating those laws. And she shares, with at least some, the additional awareness that reason and experiment, generally claimed to be the principal means of this pursuit, do not suffice. To quote Einstein again, ". . . only intuition, resting on sympathetic understanding, can lead to [these laws]; . . . the daily effort comes from no deliberate intention or program, but straight from the heart."[2]

15   A deep reverence for nature, a capacity for union with that which is to be known—these reflect a different image of science from that of a purely rational enterprise. Yet the two images have coexisted throughout history.

We are familiar with the idea that a form of mysticism—a commitment to the unity of experience, the oneness of nature, the fundamental mystery underlying the laws of nature—plays an essential role in the process of scientific discovery. Einstein called it "cosmic religiosity." In turn, the experience of creative insight reinforces these commitments, fostering a sense of the limitations of the scientific method, and an appreciation of other ways of knowing. In all of this, McClintock is no exception. What is exceptional is her forthrightness of expression—the pride she takes in holding, and voicing, attitudes that run counter to our more customary ideas about science. In her mind, what we call the scientific method cannot by itself give us "real understanding." "It gives us relationships which are useful, valid, and technically marvelous; however, they are not the truth." And it is by no means the only way of acquiring knowledge.

16   That there are valid ways of knowing other than those conventionally espoused by science is a conviction of long standing for McClintock. It derives from a lifetime of experiences that science tells us little about, experiences that she herself could no more set aside than she could discard the anomalous pattern on a single kernel of corn. Perhaps it is this fidelity to her own experience that allows her to be more open than most other scientists about her unconventional beliefs. Correspondingly, she is open to unorthodox views in others, whether she agrees with them or not. She recalls, for example, a lecture given in the late 1940s at Cold Spring Harbor by Dick Roberts, a physicist from the Carnegie Institution of Washington, on the subject of extrasensory perception. Although she herself was out of town at the time, when she heard about the hostile reaction of her colleagues, she was incensed: "If they were as ignorant of the subject as I was, they had no reason for complaining."

17   For years, she has maintained an interest in ways of learning other than those used in the West, and she made a particular effort to inform herself about the Tibetan Buddhists: "I was so startled by their method of training and by its results that I figured we were limiting ourselves by using what we call the scientific method."

18   Two kinds of Tibetan expertise interested her especially. One was the way the "running lamas" ran. These men were described as running for hours on end without sign of fatigue. It seemed to her exactly the same king of effortless floating she had secretly learned as a child.

19   She was equally impressed by the ability that some Tibetans had developed to regulate body temperature: "We are scientists, and we know nothing basically about controlling our body temperature. [But] the Tibetans learn to live with nothing but a tiny cotton jacket. They're out there cold winters and hot summers, and when they have been through the learning process, they have to take certain tests. One of the tests is to take a wet blanket, put it over them, and dry that blanket in the coldest weather. And they dry it."

20   How were they able to do these things? What would one need to do to acquire this sort of "knowledge"? She began to look at related phenomena that

were closer to home: "Hypnosis also had potentials that were quite extraordinary." She began to believe that not only one's temperature, but one's circulation, and many other bodily processes generally thought to be autonomous, could be brought under the influence of mind. She was convinced that the potential for mental control revealed in hypnosis experiments, and practiced by the Tibetans, was something that could be learned. "You can do it, it can be taught." And she set out to teach herself. Long before the word "biofeedback" was invented, McClintock experimented with ways to control her own temperature and blood flow, until, in time, she began to feel a sense of what it took.

21   But these interests were not popular. "I couldn't tell other people at the time because it was against the 'scientific method.' . . . We just hadn't touched on this kind of knowledge in our medical physiology, [and it is] very, very different from the knowledge we call the only way." What we label scientific knowledge is "lots of fun. You get lots of correlations, but you don't get the truth. . . . Things are much more marvelous than the scientific method allows us to conceive."

22   Our own method could tell us about some things, but not about others—for instance, she reflects, not about "the kinds of things that made it possible for me to be creative in an unknown way. *Why* do you know? Why were you so sure of something when you couldn't tell anyone else? You weren't sure in a boastful way; you were sure in what I call a completely internal way. . . . What you had to do was put it into their frame. Wherever it came in your frame, you had to work to put in into their frame. So you work with so-called scientific methods to put it into their frame *after* you know. Well, [the question is] *how* you know it. I had the idea that the Tibetans understood this *how* you know."

23   McClintock is not the only scientist who has looked to the East for correctives to the limitations of Western science. Her remarks on her relation to the phenomena she studies are especially reminiscent of the lessons many physicists have drawn from the discoveries of atomic physics. Erwin Schrödinger, for example, wrote: ". . . our science—Greek science—is based on objectification. . . . But I do believe that this is precisely the point where our present way of thinking does need to be amended, perhaps by a bit of blood-transfusion from Eastern thought."[3] Niels Bohr, the "father of quantum mechanics," was even more explicit on the subject. He wrote: "For a parallel to the lesson of atomic theory . . . [we must turn] to those kinds of epistemological problems with which already thinkers like the Buddha and Lao Tzu have been confronted, when trying to harmonize our position as spectators and actors in the great drama of existence."[4] Robert Oppenheimer held similar views: "The general notions about human understanding . . . which are illustrated by discoveries in atomic physics are not in the nature of being wholly unfamiliar, wholly unheard of, or new," he wrote. "Even in our culture they have a history, and in Buddhist and Hindu thought a more considerable and central place."[5] Indeed, as a result of a number of popular accounts published in the

last decade, the correspondences between modern physics and Eastern thought have come to seem commonplace.[6] But among biologists, these interests are not common. McClintock is right to see them, and herself, as oddities. And here, as elsewhere, she takes pride in being different. She is proud to call herself a "mystic."

24   Above all, she is proud of her ability to draw on these other ways of knowing in her work as a scientist. It is that which, to her, makes the life of science such a deeply satisfying one—even, at times, ecstatic. "What is ecstasy? I don't understand ecstasy, but I enjoy it. When I have it. Rare ecstasy."

25   Somehow, she doesn't know how, she has always had an "exceedingly strong feeling" for the oneness of things: "Basically, everything is one. There is no way in which you draw a line between things. What we [normally] do is to make these subdivisions, but they're not real. Our educational system is full of subdivisions that are artificial, that shouldn't be there. I think maybe poets—although I don't read poetry—have some understanding of this." The ultimate descriptive task, for both artists and scientists, is to "ensoul" what one sees, to attribute to it the life one shares with it; one learns by identification.[7]

26   Much has been written on this subject, but certain remarks of Phyllis Greenacre, a psychoanalyst who has devoted a lifetime to studying the dynamics of artistic creativity, come especially close to the crux of the issue that concerns us here. For Greenacre, the necessary condition for the flowering of great talent or genius is the development in the young child of what she calls a "love affair with the world."[8] Although she believes that a special range and intensity of sensory responsiveness may be innate in the potential artist, she also thinks that, under appropriate circumstances, this special sensitivity facilitates an early relationship with nature that resembles and may in fact substitute for the intimacy of a more conventional child's personal relationships. The forms and objects of nature provide what Greenacre calls "collective alternatives," drawing the child into a "collective love affair."

27   Greenacre's observations are intended to describe the childhood of the young artist, but they might just as readily depict McClintock's youth. By her own account, even as a child, McClintock neither had nor felt the need of emotional intimacy in any of her personal relationships. The world of nature provided for her the "collective alternatives" of Greenacre's artists; it became the principal focus of both her intellectual and her emotional energies. From reading the text of nature, McClintock reaps the kind of understanding and fulfillment that others acquire from personal intimacy. In short, her "feeling for the organism" is the mainspring of her creativity. It both promotes and is promoted by her access to the profound connectivity of all biological forms—of the cell, of the organism, of the ecosystem.

28   The flip side of the coin is her conviction that, without an awareness of the oneness of things, science can give us at most only nature-in-pieces; more often it gives us only pieces of nature. In McClintock's view, too restricted a reliance on scientific methodology invariably leads us into difficulty. "We've been spoiling the environment just dreadfully and thinking we were fine,

because we were using the techniques of science. Then it turns into technology, and it's slapping us back because we didn't think it through. We were making assumptions we had no right to make. From the point of view of how the whole thing actually worked, we knew how part of it worked. . . . We didn't even inquire, didn't even see how the rest was going on. All these other things were happening and we didn't see it."

29   She cites the tragedy of Love Canal as one example, the acidification of the Adirondacks Lakes as another. "We didn't think [things] through. . . . If you take the train up to New Haven . . . and the wind is from the southeast, you find all of the smog from New York is going right up to New Haven. . . . We're not thinking it through, just spewing it out. . . . Technology is fine, but the scientists and engineers only partially think through their problems. They solve certain aspects, but not the total, and as a consequence it is slapping us back in the face very hard."

30   Barbara McClintock belongs to a rare genre of scientist; on a short-term view of the mood and tenor of modern biological laboratories, hers is an endangered species. Recently, after a public seminar McClintock gave in the Biology Department at Harvard University, she met informally with a group of graduate and postdoctoral students. They were responsive to her exhortation that they "take the time and look," but they were also troubled. Where does one get the time to look and to think? They argued that the new technology of molecular biology is self-propelling. It doesn't leave time. There's always the next experiment, the next sequencing to do. The pace of current research seems to preclude such a contemplative stance. McClintock was sympathetic, but reminded them, as they talked, of the "hidden complexity" that continues to lurk in the most straightforward-seeming systems. She herself had been fortunate; she had worked with a slow technology, a slow organism. Even in the old days, corn had not been popular because one could never grow more than two crops a year. But after a while, she'd found that as slow as it was, two crops a year was too fast. If she was really to analyze all that there was to see, one crop was all she could handle.

31   There remain, of course, always a few biologists who are able to sustain the kind of "feeling for the organism" that was so productive—both scientifically and personally—for McClintock, but to some of them the difficulties of doing so seem to grow exponentially. One contemporary, who says of her own involvement in research, "If you want to really understand about a tumor, you've got to *be* a tumor," put it this way: "Everywhere in science the talk is of winners, patents, pressures, money, no money, the rat race, the lot; things that are so completely alien . . . that I no longer know whether I can be classified as a modern scientist or as an example of a beast on the way to extinction."[9]

32   McClintock takes a longer view. She is confident that nature is on the side of scientists like herself. For evidence, she points to the revolution now occurring in biology. In her view, conventional science fails to illuminate not only "how" you know, but also, and equally, "what" you know. McClintock

sees additional confirmation of the need to expand our conception of science in her own—and now others'—discoveries. The "molecular" revolution in biology was a triumph of the kind of science represented by classical physics. Now, the necessary next step seems to be the reincorporation of the naturalist's approach—an approach that does not press nature with leading questions but dwells patiently in the variety and complexity of organisms. The discovery of genetic liability and flexibility forces us to recognize the magnificent integration of cellular processes—kinds of integration that are "simply incredible to our old-style thinking." As she sees it, we are in the midst of a major revolution that "will reorganize the way we look at things, the way we do research." She adds, "And I can't wait. Because I think it's going to be marvelous, simply marvelous. We're going to have a completely new realization of the relationship of things to each other."

NOTES

1. Quoted in E. Broda, "Boltzman, Einstein, Natural Law and Evolution," *Comparative Biochemical Physiology* 67B (1980): 376.
2. Quoted in Banesh Hoffmann and Helen Dukes, *Albert Einstein, Creator and Rebel* (New York: New American Library, 1973), p. 222.
3. Schrödinger, *What Is Life?*, op. cit., p. 140.
4. Niels Bohr, *Atomic Physics and Human Knowledge* (New York: John Wiley & Sons, 1958), p. 33.
5. Robert J. Oppenheimer, *Science and the Common Understanding* (New York: Simon & Schuster, 1954), pp. 8-9.
6. See, for example, Fritz Capra, *The Tao of Physics* (Berkeley, Ca.: Shambhala, 1975), and Gary Zukov, *The Dancing Wu Li Masters* (New York: William Morrow, 1979).
7. The word "ensoul" is taken from Marion Milner, who wrote of her own endeavors as an artist: "I wanted to ensoul nature with what was really there." Marion Milner, *On Not Being Able to Paint* (New York: International Universities Press, 1957), p. 120.
8. Phyllis Greenacre, "The Childhood of the Artist: Libidinal Phase Development and Giftedness" (1957), reprinted in Phyllis Greenacre, *Emotional Growth: Psychoanalytic Studies of the Gifted and a Great Variety of Other Individuals* (New York: International Universities Press, 1971), p. 490.
9. June Goodfield, *An Imagined World: A Story of Scientific Discovery* (New York: Harper & Row, 1981), p. 213.

FOLLOW-UP ACTIVITIES

Discussing the Rhetoric

1. Earlier in the text we stated that Keller's audience is comprised of more than just scientists. What discourse communities (academic or nonacademic) are addressed by Keller? What words or phrases lead you to believe that?

2. Part of Keller's essay seems to be addressing the fate of a "woman in a man's world." Do you think this is her main point? If not, what do you think her main point is?

3. Do you think it is risky on Keller's part to talk about science as being guided by a "feeling"? Does it make her argument more or less persuasive, given her audience? What effect do you think words like "embrace" and "longing" have on her audience? Remember, your answers here could vary depending upon who you think the audience is.

4. In what ways does Keller's strange choice of words support and reflect her thesis?

Discussing the Conversation

1. On the basis of the information from high school or early college courses, describe in your own words what you consider the "scientific method" to be. Do you feel that, by using this methodology, a scientist could discover truth?

2. Klemke defines science as "objective," that is "the absence of bias and presence of disinterestedness and dispassionateness." Compare this to McClintock's view as conveyed by Keller: "One must have the time to look, the patience to 'hear what the material has to say to you,' the openness to 'let it come to you.' Above all, one must have 'a feeling for the organism.'" Are these two views of science hopelessly at odds? If so, which do you think would lead to better science? Or can the two be reconciled? If so, how?

3. Addelson notes that the legacy of seventeenth-century science includes an assumption of one reality, which entailed one correct way of understanding reality. How does Keller confound this metaphysical assumption?

4. Think about McClintock's metaphor of being open, in touch with one's surroundings. Do you think Popper would have agreed with McClintock's open philosophy? In what ways would he have disagreed?

5. In many ways, McClintock resisted the norms and methods of the scientific world of which she was a part, though she still sought to convey her views in the terms of the scientific community. In what ways does McClintock's ability to resist the "interpretive strategies" of the scientific community speak to Fish's assertion that interpretation is governed by communities?

Joining the Conversation

1. McClintock was a maverick. Write an informal paper in which you consider in what ways you see yourself as being a maverick in your academic career. What methodologies feel uncomfortable or "wrong" to you? Do you resist them? What are some of your own strategies of resistance?

2. Write an informal paper concerning how you feel about Keller's assertion that science has, up to this point, been a masculine endeavor that needs to become a human endeavor. Do you think science has been a masculine endeavor? If so, in what ways?

INTRODUCTORY COMMENTS ON "WHO SHOULD DO SCIENCE?" BY LONDA SCHIEBINGER

Reading the Context

Like many other contemporary writers and thinkers in departments of history and women's studies, Londa Schiebinger's goal is to make a practice of revisiting and interrogating historic sites where particularly privileged voices were chosen at the expense of other less privileged voices to wholly represent the knowledge-making enterprise. Eighteenth-century Europe, wherein scientific inquiry became synonymous with reason, provides Schiebinger with fertile ground. That is, those in control believed the methodologies of scientific inquiry represented human reason in its purest and most objective form. However, Schiebinger believes this Enlightenment legacy is mistaken. In *Nature's Body* (1993), from which this selection is excerpted, Schiebinger explores how notions of gender and race shaped the way European science was constructed in the eighteenth century. Of particular concern is the fact that perceptions of gender and race became significant principles for organizing nature, and thus helped to build the foundation of the scientific enterprise. Far from being neutral, these informing principles, she claims, "perpetuated a system in which those who might have brought new perspectives to the study of nature were barred from the enterprise at the outset, and the findings of science crafted in their absence were used to justify their continued exclusion" (Introduction, p. 7).

Reading the Rhetoric

According to Schiebinger, the question of "who should do science" took center-stage in eighteenth-century Europe, when the natural sciences gained power and prestige. In the chapter excerpted here, she limits this discussion to two aspects of the question: race and education. She hopes to compel her readers to consider the origins of traditional science's methodology.

What rhetorical strategies does Schiebinger use to get her readers to question traditional science's methodology? In particular, notice Schiebinger's use of evidence. What types of evidence does she most frequently use? Why? Given the evidence provided, is she able to convince you that the origins of traditional science are problematic? How well does she convince or fail to convince?

Look at Schiebinger's choice of vocabulary. Given her word choice, whom does she seem to be addressing? That is, how would you describe her intended audience? What assumptions does she make about her audience's background?

Reading the Conversation

Consider Schiebinger's chapter as participating in an ongoing conversation of which you are now a part. What does investigating the question of who should do science have in common with Keller's discussion of a "scientific methodology"? According to McClintock, "too restricted a reliance on scientific methodology invariably leads us into difficulty." Also, how do Addelson's concerns with "the contribution of professional authority to creating and maintaining hierarchies of class, gender, age, and race" compare to Schiebinger's inquiry into who has done science?

Who Should Do Science?
Londa Schiebinger

Ethiopians, Egyptians, Africans, Jews, Phoenicians, Persians, Assyrians, and Indians have invented many curious sciences, revealed the mysteries and secrets of Nature, put order into mathematics, observed the motions of the heavens, and introduced the worship of gods.

Ambroise Paré, *Les oeuvres,* 1575

1   In his controversial *Black Athena,* Martin Bernal argues that the celebration of Greece as the cradle of Western civilization began in the eighteenth century as an attempt to erase from historical consciousness Afroasiatic contributions to Western arts and sciences. Until that time, he argues, Greece had been seen merely as an outpost of Egyptian and Phoenician culture, a land civilized by colonizing Africans and Semites.[1] According to Bernal, the myth of a white dawn of Western civilization resulted from the upsurge in anti-Semitism and racism at the end of the eighteenth century.

2   Critics have charged (among other things) that Bernal's project to locate the origins of Western science in Africa is Eurocentric insofar as its primary goal is to claim for blacks a place in European science—charges we will investigate below.[2] Bernal has, however, identified a broad shift in historical consciousness that was important for the definition of European science. In the seventeenth and eighteenth centuries, men of Western science had commonly celebrated ancient Egypt along with Mesopotamia, Persia, and India as birthplaces of Europe's classical arts and sciences.[3] Galileo, coinventor of the telescope, believed that ancient peoples had employed similar devices to

map the heavens; Newton, too, at least in his early years, had a rather romantic and far-fetched admiration of the ancient Egyptians for their science and their philosophy.[4]

3   By the late eighteenth century, however, the notion of an Egyptian origin of science ran headlong into the growing consensus that people with black skin and sloping foreheads were incapable of abstract thought. William Lawrence framed the issue in stark terms in his lectures before the Royal College of Surgeons in 1819:

> Egypt was venerated, even by antiquity, as the birth-place of the arts. . . . With our present experience of the capacity of Negroes, and our knowledge of the state in which the whole race has remained for twenty centuries, can we deem it possible that they should have achieved such prodigies? that Homer, Lycurgus, Solon, Pythagoras, and Plato should have resorted to Egypt to study the sciences, religion, and laws, discovered and framed by men with black skin, woolly hair, and slanting forehead?[5]

Lawrence refused to believe that the Egyptians "now so devoted to slavery" could have created such grandeur in antiquity.

4   As the natural sciences gained power and prestige, the question of who was capable of engaging in science took on a new urgency. European men of science debated the intellectual abilities of men of various races and of women. Were women and blacks capable of abstract thought? And just who was black?

5   Inquiry into these questions took several forms in the eighteenth century, and in this chapter I look rather briefly at two aspects of this large history. First was the question of the race of those who invented the sciences. If Egyptians had, indeed, been among those who made important contributions to science, what did they look like? Were the ancient Egyptians, whose mummified remains had just been unwrapped as a consequence of Napoleon's invasion, black or white? Second was the question of whether women and black men could be educated. This era saw a number of "experiments" in education. A few European women and African men were admitted to universities in Germany in attempts to see if, "by proper cultivation," they could learn to excel in philosophy, poetry, medicine, and the natural sciences. And could a Madame du Châtelet, an Anton Amo, or a Phillis Wheatley enter the hallowed halls of Europe's academies of arts and sciences?

THE ORIGINS OF SCIENCE: BLACK OR WHITE?

6   The notion that Western science had its origins in Egypt, Mesopotamia, India, and Persia had foundations in the ancient theory of humors, according to which dry heat fostered wit and science, while damp cold cultivated bodily strength and a bellicose spirit. At the heart of the humoral tradition lay the teaching that terrestrial elements stood in a hierarchical relationship to one

another: things hot and dry were superior to things cold and moist. Predictably this accounted for the dominance of the hotter male over the colder woman. For thousands of years, men's superior heat had explained their social superiority. Less predictably, this theory seemed to hold dramatic implications for the ordering of the races. The intense heat of southern regions would seem to have proclaimed the victory of black over white. For this reason, Ambroise Paré, surgeon to the king of France, went so far as to suggest that peoples inhabiting the middle regions of the globe (that is, Greece and Rome) lacked the natural endowments required for the more "abstruse sciences."[6]

7   The theory of humors, however, was designed to explain the nature of provident government (and, for Galen, ultimately the success of the Roman empire), not the origin of science—which was not at issue in Europe before intellect and technical innovation became measures of personal worth and national strength.[7] In the case of race, *excess* heat was seen as a liability. Aristotle, in an effort to give pride of place to his own civilization, taught that those burned with immoderate heat (in Africa) or oppressed with excessive cold (in northern Europe) were intemperate, barbarous, and cruel. For him, superiority lay with the people of temperate regions who blended the wisdom of the south with the fortitude of the north.[8] As we have seen, it was within this region that Blumenbach located the origin of humankind.[9]

8   In the late eighteenth century, men of science, interested in uncovering a genealogy of science, set out to debunk what they considered to be the myth of a black origin of Western science. Physical anthropologists reduced the question of Egypt's contributions to the arts and sciences to the question of whether Egyptians were black or white. The answer seemed to them to lie beneath the cotton wrappings of mummies. Napoleon's foray into Egypt in the 1790s yielded a vast store of scientific spoils, including a large number of mummies which naturalists immediately transported to Paris, London, Göttingen, Leipzig, Kassel, and Gotha.[10] Blumenbach alone unwrapped six mummies and examined many others.[11] Sir Joseph Banks, Christoph Meiners, Samuel Thomas von Soemmerring, and Georges Cuvier studied mummy skulls along with paintings and carvings on sarcophagi, pottery, and murals, all in an attempt to determine whether these ancient people had the upturned noses and high foreheads of Caucasians, or the broad, flat noses and jutting chins of modern Africans.

9   Constantin-François Volney, in his influential *Voyage en Syrie et en Egypte,* was one of the few to say that the progenitors of modern science had been black. He identified the ancient Egyptians as the true physical (and therefore intellectual) ancestors of modern Africans, sharing with them a smoky yellow hue, flat noses, and large lips. He based his conclusion on his studies of the Sphinx, whose features he found distinctly negroid, and on Herodotus's depiction of the Egyptians as a people with black skin and curly hair. Despite the fact that he saw the ancient Egyptians as "true"—that is, black—Africans, Volney continued to attribute to them the origin of Europe's classical arts and science.

How astonishing it is to see the barbarism and ignorance of the present day Copts, descendants of the profound genius of the Egyptians and the brilliant spirit of Greece. [It is astonishing] to think that that race of black men, today our slaves and the objects of our contempt, is the same from which we received our arts, our sciences, and our very use of language.[12]

10   At the other extreme were the influential German classicists Johann Winckelmann and Christoph Meiners, along with the French naturalist Georges Cuvier, who denied that *any* Egyptians had ever been black. Winckelmann considered ancient Egyptians to be essentially of the same racial type as the Chinese (a view that Blumenbach took seriously enough to oppose vehemently), while Meiners considered them to be of the same stock as Hindus.[13] In his memoir on the Hottentot Venus, Cuvier emphatically declared that "no race of Negro produced that celebrated people who gave birth to the civilization of ancient Egypt, and from whom the whole world has inherited the principles of its laws, sciences, and perhaps also religion." Cuvier compared over fifty mummy skulls to the skulls of Europeans, Negroes, and Hottentots, and concluded that, whatever the hue of their skin, the ancient Egyptians belonged to "the same race of men as us, sharing with us a voluminous cranium and brain." Without exception, the "cruel law" of nature had "condemned to eternal inferiority those races with a depressed and compressed cranium."[14]

11   The British surgeon William Lawrence also argued that if the arts and sciences indeed had emanated from ancient Egypt, it was from those among them who were "Caucasian" (adopting Blumenbach's term). The few true Negroes were, then as now, their slaves. "To give the few Negroes the glory of all the discoveries and achievements of this first-civilized race, and overlook the more numerous individuals of different character would be in opposition to the invariable tenor of our experience respecting human nature."[15] For Lawrence, the vaulted Caucasian skull housed an expansive intellect dominating the instruments of sense and animal needs. It was fitting, he proclaimed, that this race should rule the world, holding in permanent subjection all other races. Edward Long, who believed that blacks constituted a separate and inferior species closely related to simians, simply remarked that Africans—both ancient and modern—were incapable of genius, and that those mechanical arts they might have produced they did in a "bungling and slovenly manner, perhaps not better than an orangutang."[16]

12   Most European naturalists took a more moderate view, suggesting that ancient Egypt had been a crossroads of commerce and cultural exchange, and that, as a result, its population had been mixed. Blumenbach, from his extensive investigations of mummies, distinguished among them three racial types: (1) the Ethiopian, with its prominent maxillae, turgid lips, broad, flat noses, and protruding eyeballs; (2) the Hindu, with its long, slender nose, long and thin eyelids, ears placed high on the head, and short and thin bodies (similar features, he argued, could also be seen painted on the sarcophagus of Captain Lethieullier's mummy in the British Museum); (3) a mixed type with features somewhere between the Caucasian and Ethiopian.[17]

13   While Blumenbach participated in debates over the racial features of the ancient Egyptians, he remained silent on the larger issue of whether Africans had contributed to the development of the world's arts and sciences. Unlike many of his colleagues, he did not consider the Africans of his day incapable of scientific pursuit. In his article "Concerning the Negro," he argued vigorously against those who believed that Africans stood far behind others in mental abilities. He argued further that if blacks were to be judged by their *nature*, they should be judged in their natural condition, not after having been brutalized by "white executioners" in a state of slavery.[18] James Prichard made a similar point, arguing that Europeans commonly drew conclusions about African intellectual capacities from skulls of enslaved populations which did not provide the most favorable specimens.

14   In the eighteenth century, as Europeans began colonizing and plundering Africa, they also attempted to claim part of its cultural heritage as their own. As noted above, questions about the origins of Western science have been revived in recent years by Bernal's *Black Athena*. The main contribution of Bernal's book has been to question why Europeans were so unwilling to grant an African ancestry to European science. Critics have pointed to problems with Bernal's formulations. Bernal tends toward Afrocentrism perhaps in claiming too much for Egypt in his attempt to refute histories claiming that science is an exclusively Greek invention owing little or nothing to earlier civilizations. More seriously, Bernal's project is Eurocentric in attempting to place Egypt within a Western genealogy. In this, Bernal leaves Western science as the culmination of intellectual and cultural achievement and perpetuates the project of valuing one kind of knowledge over all others.[19]

15   In the eighteenth century, attempts were also made to deny that women had ever contributed to the development of the arts and sciences.[20] As the prestige of science began to grow, history was rallied to lend legitimacy to European males' claims as sole heirs to its fortunes. (Indeed, some of the women stripped of cultural achievement—Isis, the mythical inventor of medicine, for example—were Egyptian.) In the middle of the eighteenth century, Voltaire baldly pronounced that "all the arts have been invented by man, not by woman." He did this by subscribing to a very narrow sense of what is art, namely, "things mechanical, gunpowder, printing, and the clock."[21] If we broaden Voltaire's list to include innovation in other areas he considered the principal occupations of the human species—"lodging, nourishment, and clothing"—he might have been led to evaluate women's contributions differently.

EIGHTEENTH-CENTURY EXPERIMENTS IN EDUCATION

16 As increasingly impressive collections of skulls were gathered to show that women and blacks lacked native intelligence, proponents of equality began collecting examples of learned women and Africans. In both instances the task was the same: to find the exceptional woman or black who had excelled

in science or scholarship in order to prove that they were capable of abstract thought. Environmentalists, denying that there was any fixed and obvious relationship between the mind and bodily structure, brought forth examples of learned women and blacks to prove their case.[22]

17   European literature on learned women is older than that on learned blacks. Giovanni Boccaccio's fourteenth-century *Claris mulieribus,* for example, presents short biographies of one hundred and four queens, some real, some mythical, of the ancient world. Encyclopedias such as these—the most common type of women's history in this period—documented the triumphs of the learned lady.[23] A similar literature, perhaps modeled on the lexicons of learned ladies, was developed for blacks. Blumenbach, who had a library entirely composed of books written by European-educated Africans, published a lexicon of learned black men and women in order to show that "in regard to their mental faculties and capacity, they are not inferior to the rest of the human race."[24] There was the African Freidig, well known in Vienna as a master of the viola and violin. Anton Wilhelm Amo, a native of Guinea (Ghana), received a doctorate from the University of Wittenberg in 1734, the first African to obtain that degree at any European university.[25] Jacobus Elisa Capitein, also from Guinea, studied theology at the University of Leyden, graduating in 1742. Phillis Wheatley, a servant to Mr. John Wheatley of Boston, was listed as the first African to publish neo-classical poetry in English.[26] There was also the unnamed "Negress of Yverdun," celebrated as the best midwife in the Italian part of Switzerland.[27] Blumenbach's essay demonstrating the intellectual capacities of Africans circulated widely among abolitionists for the next half century.[28]

18   In order to be recognized as equals, learned women or blacks generally had to excel in those arts and sciences recognized by the white male academy—fields such as classical music, astronomy, Latin, or mathematics. The experiments in education carried out in the eighteenth century required that women and blacks assimilate to European university culture.[29] Germany was, perhaps surprisingly, a pioneer among European countries in accepting the occasional European woman or African man for admission to university study. (There were, to my knowledge, no examples of university-educated African women. Phyllis Hazeley was an African woman educated in England in the mid-eighteenth century, but not at a university. Upon her return to her native Sierra Leone, she opened a school to teach reading, writing, arithmetic, and needlework.)[30] German universities were being revived at this time and new universities, including Halle (where Anton Amo matriculated in 1727 and Dorothea Erxleben received her M.D. in 1754) and Göttingen (where Dorothea Schlözer took her Ph.D. in 1787), were founded to foster the growth of Enlightenment ideas.[31] The circumstances surrounding these experiments were similar in several respects. In each case, the student was shepherded by an enlightened patriarch: Amo was sponsored by the Duke of Brunswick-Wolfenbüttel; Erxleben studied with her father and won special dispensation from Frederick the Great to study at Halle;

Schlözer took her degree in the faculty where her father served as a professor. Despite the success of these individuals, European universities generally remained closed to both European women and Africans of either sex until late in the nineteenth and sometimes even into the twentieth centuries.

19   There were also interesting differences in how European women and black men fared in academic life. The African man, Anton Amo, was publicly feted during his university years. He was chosen to lead the entire student body in a parade celebrating the visit of local royalty to the University of Wittenberg in 1733, where Amo was then studying.[32] Dorothea Schlözer, by contrast, was not allowed to attend her commencement exercises because her father thought it improper for her to take part in the public celebration. "Since I could not go into the church [where the degrees were awarded]," she wrote a friend, "I went to the library, where I could see and hear everything through a broken pane of glass."[33]

20   Despite their university educations, European women remained barred from the public realm of science and scholarship, while black men were, in rare instances, able to go on to limited professional work. Schlözer never intended for her Ph.D. to lead to any career but marriage; her doctorate served merely as another badge of honor for an already illustrious academic family. Erxleben's degree served to legitimate her medical practice (and shield her from prosecution by jealous local doctors). It should be pointed out, however, that her admission to the university rested on the legal decision that medicine was not a public office and that women should therefore not be barred from its practice.[34] The case of Amo was quite different. Having completed his doctoral degree at Wittenberg, he lectured at Halle for about eight years (from 1739 to 1747) and was then appointed a counsellor at the court of Frederick the Great in Berlin—public positions that never would have been accorded a woman. His education was similar to that of Schlözer; they were both well trained in languages, mathematics, philosophy, and the classics. Yet Amo's degree carried him into a kind of public employment not open to women.

21   Amo was not the only university-educated male of African descent to go on to public service. Edward Long reported the case of Francis Williams, a Jamaican boy, whom the Duke of Montagu educated in order to discover whether "by proper cultivation" a Negro might become as capable as a white person.[35] The Duke sent Williams first to grammar school in England and then to the University of Cambridge where he excelled in mathematics, poetry, and the classics (Figure 1). The Duke intended to continue his experiment by appointing Williams to a seat in the government of Jamaica, but he never managed to override the objections of the local English governor. Consequently, Williams went on to head a school for black boys. Long, who reported the story, belittled Williams's achievement, saying that the experiment might have been more significant had it been made using a native African. Long implied that Williams succeeded because he was not truly black. He also reported the failure of Williams's protégé (a young boy trained to be his successor at the school) who

Figure 1   Francis Williams at the University of Cambridge. Europeans celebrated Blacks who received European educations and assimilated into the White world. Courtesy of the National Library of Jamaica.

went mad, it was said, from too much learning. Long took this to prove that the "African head is not adapted by nature to such profound contemplations"; he also quoted with approval David Hume's judgment that Williams himself was like "a parrot who speaks a few words plainly."[36]

22   The most striking difference, however, between educated minority men and majority women in this period was their eligibility for membership in scientific academies. Europe's major scientific academies were founded in the seventeenth century—the Royal Society of London in 1660, the Parisian Académie Royale des Sciences (the most prestigious European academy of science) in 1666, the Akademie der Wissenschaften in Berlin in 1700. Despite the face that women, such as the German astronomer Maria Winkelmann or the French physicist Emilie du Châtelet, were trained and ready to take their places among the men of science, they were excluded from these academies for over two hundred years (women were first admitted to the Royal Society in 1945, to the Berlin Academy of Sciences in 1949, and to the Académie des Sciences in 1979).[37] One might imagine that racial prejudice would have proven as insurmountable a barrier to black men. And in many cases, it did. Francis Williams, for instance, was refused membership in the Royal Society because

of "his complexion," even though, as newspapers reported, he was "dressed like other gentlemen in a tye-wig [and] sword."[38] The expansive mood of the Enlightenment did make room for a few minority men. Moses da Costa became the first Jewish fellow of the Royal Society in 1736 (another Jewish fellow, Emanuel Mendes da Costa, was elected in 1747).[39]

23   The more remarkable case of a man of color elected to an eminent scientific body was that of Jean-Baptiste Lislet-Geoffroy, who became the first black member (albeit a corresponding member) of the Académie Royale des Sciences in Paris in 1786. Lislet was the son of Jean-Baptiste Geoffroy, a French engineer working on the Ile de France (Mauritius), and a black slave from the coast of Guinea whom his father freed in order to take her as his mistress (as allowed for in the *Code noir*). Because he was illegitimate, Lislet took the name of his place of birth, as was customary; his father did not lend him his name (Geoffroy) until Lislet was thirty-eight years old, seven years after he had been elected to the academy. Lislet-Geoffroy worked for the French government for most of his life, as head of the army corps of engineers, as a cartographer (he mapped the Ile de France, Réunion, and Madagascar), as a meteorologist, botanist, geologist, and astronomer.[40]

24   Lislet-Geoffroy's term as an academician was not without its troubles. Like other members of the Academy, he lost his title during the reorganization of 1793. But unlike most other members, he was not reinstated when the academy reopened. Several explanations have been given. Some said it was the difficulty of communications between France and its colonies that held up his reappointment until 1821; others said he was simply overlooked. Still others said that it was because of racial prejudice. Unable to travel to France because he had been denied a pension, Lislet-Geoffroy founded the *Société des Sciences et Arts de l'Ile de France* (today the *SociÇtÇ Royale des Arts et Sciences de Maurice*). It was reported that whites refused to join this academy because it was founded by a black.[41] Lislet's attempt to mix with the learned men of Europe did not open the doors of the Parisian academy to blacks. As of 1934, he was the only man of color ever to have been a member of the academy in Paris.[42]

25   This discussion is not intended to suggest that the advantage of being male outweighed the overwhelming disadvantages of being black in European society, but to show the deep confusion about gender and race among Europe's elites in this period. In some cases, being male did open the doors of public institutions to black men. But, in the eighteenth century, these men, like the learned European women, were curiosities educated at the pleasure of patrons. These exceptional individuals lived under constant scrutiny, always representatives of their race or sex, their positions tenuous and easily revoked. Anton Amo, for example, was publicly forced out of Germany after the death of his benefactor, the Duke of Brunswick. He returned to his homeland on the Gold Coast (then under Dutch rule), and nothing more was ever heard of him. Some say he died there in a slaver's prison.[43]

26   While black males seemed to fare modestly better than females in the newly established institutions of science, one should remember that propertied European women often ruled over men, especially men of African descent. In the frontispiece of his *Traité de la couleur de la peau humaine*, Claude-Nicolas Le Cat featured an upper-class European woman as the principal figure receiving an Ethiopian and American male (see Figure 2).[44] This scene, though presented in a scientific treatise, could have been taken from any number of New World plantations where elite European women ruled over black men. But the power these women held came to them via birth and inheritance—principles governing the Ancien Régime. To the extent that science, supposedly representing a new democracy of talent, required certificates such as university degrees for passage into the public realm, women were excluded.

27   As mentioned above, no woman of African descent ever attended a European university in the eighteenth century. In the late-eighteenth century, however, we have a fictional account (supposedly based on a true story) of a young woman educated in the Parisian salons, an intellectual setting that rivaled universities and academies in this era.[45] The account of Ourika, a young girl from Senegal, reveals the differing experiences of African men and women brought into Europe by enlightened elites. It also throws into sharp relief the fact that the experiences of women imported from Africa into Europe could be very different. Duchesse de Duras's *Ourika* (1824) created a stir—Parisians adopted Ourika's fashions and envied her color—at the same time that, in another part of Paris, spectators ogled Sarah Bartmann's "grotesque figure."

28   As the tale recounts, Ourika was rescued from a slave ship off the coast of Senegal by Le Chevalier de Beauvau, governor of that settlement, and brought to Paris at the age of two where she was cherished as a daughter by Madame de Beauvau, the governor's aunt. Ourika was given all the advantages of girls of her benefactress's rank and raised amidst the conversation of the most distinguished philosophers of the time in Madame de Beauvau's salon. There she learned music, art, English, Italian, and the elements of good taste. In this rarified atmosphere, she was completely unaware of what it meant to be a black woman in France.

29   The privileges of her acquired rank, however, could not save her from racial prejudice. One day, Ourika overheard her benefactress lamenting the fact that her charge had no prospects for marriage and was destined to be forever alone. When Ourika became aware of her color, she was struck with horror and disgusted with herself: "When my eyes fell upon my black hands I thought they were like those of an ape."[46] She wept to discover that she belonged to a proscribed race.

30   According to Duras's story, the French Revolution renewed Ourika's hope that, with the collapse of the Ancien Régime of rank, her personal merits would place her well in society. She did not aspire to become a public figure, as did some of the educated men of African descent living in Europe.

Figure 2   The three species of mankind, according to Claude-Nicolas Le Cat. The accompanying texts explains that this meeting takes place in America, as one can see by the exotic parrot, monkey, and pineapples. A French woman, the mistress of the house, dominates the scene; she is being served lemonade by her maid. These two women of diverse classes represent "the White or European nation." The black man standing behind her represents the Ethiopian nation. An American, dressed and armed, represents the whole of his nation. He has come to trade with the European woman and regards himself with astonishment in the mirror presented to him by the Negro. The purpose of Le Cat's illustration was to show that the physiognomy and color of faces are different in all parts of the world. Claude-Nicolas Le Cat, *Traité de la couleur de la peau humaine* (Amsterdam, 1765), frontispiece. (Sign.: Kx 10 850R.) By permission of the Staatsbibliothek zu Berlin—Preußischer Kulturbesitz.

Her aspirations were consonant with the new ideals of French womanhood: to find a place in the bosom of a family as a cherished wife and loving mother. But she was to be disappointed. In Europe, black men tended to marry white women. Certainly no French man of significant rank would marry a black woman, even one of high social standing or with a large dowry (after the 1760s the slightest trace of black blood barred one from the nobility). After 1778, it became illegal for a person of color to marry a native Frenchman or woman.[47] At the same time, she was too highly educated to marry according to the dictates of her racial rank, to wed a person of "inferior condition." In despair, Ourika longed to be sent to the colonies as a slave so that she would have a place to call home. She was, as Duras wrote, "a person without a nation, a stranger to the whole human race." During the Restoration, Ourika found salvation not in "equality, liberty, and fraternity," but in religion. God, she was assured, knew no distinction of color or race. Like the wild girl of Champagne who had no place in society or hope for marriage (see chapter 3), Ourika became a nun. As a Sister of Charity she became a mother to orphans, a child to the poor and aged, a sister to all in adversity.

31   Despite the brilliance of the individuals involved in these eighteenth-century experiments in education, both women and Africans were excluded (but for exceptional cases) from the power and prestige of public life. They were and remained unwelcome outsiders. The traditional exclusion of European women from centers of learning was reaffirmed in the eighteenth century while the exclusion of minority men from European universities and professions was formalized. In France in 1763 royal ordinance forbade any black or man of color, whether slave or free, to practice medicine or surgery in the colonies.[48] Before this time men of color had trained in surgery at Paris and elsewhere. Colonial universities were also closed to people of color. John Baptiste Philip, a man of African descent who earned a medical degree from the University of Edinburgh in 1815, complained of the racial prejudice of the medical board in his native Trinidad. White candidates were admitted after perfunctory examinations, Philip charged, while many well-qualified men of African descent were denied a license merely because of the color of their skin.[49]

32   The failure of academies and universities to open their doors to blacks and women on a regular basis is especially poignant, considering that they were the objects of intense study by anatomists and medical men in this period. Excluded from centers of learning, women and Africans could say little about their own nature, at least not in the idiom of modern science. What they did write on their own behalf was often lost. It is significant that Amo's dissertation, *De jure Maurorum in Europa,* on the rights of Africans in Europe (one of his earliest works) has been lost, while his writings on traditional philosophical questions—the art of philosophizing and the mind-body distinction, for example—have been preserved in university libraries and archives.[50]

NOTES

1. Bernal has argued further that the Greek achievement in arts and letters might best be seen as resulting from a felicitous mixing of native Europeans and colonizing Africans and Semites. Martin Bernal, *Black Athena: The Afroasiatic Roots of Classical Civilization* (New Brunswick: Rutgers University Press, 1987).

2. Heinrich von Staden, "Affinities and Elisions: Helen and Hellenocentrism," *Isis* 83 (1992): 578–595, especially 589. Both von Staden and G. E. R. Lloyd caution that looking for a single origin of Western science fails to appreciate the permeability of cultural boundaries, both ancient and modern. G. E. R. Lloyd, "Methods and Problems in the History of Ancient Science: The Greek Case," *Isis* 83 (1992): 564–577, especially 572. See also "The Challenge of Black Athena" special issue of *Arethusa* (1989).

3. See, for example, William Lawrence, *Lectures on Physiology, Zoology, and the Natural History of Man* (London, 1819), p. 340; Etienne Geoffroy Saint-Hilaire cited in Nicole et Jean Dhombres, *Naissance d'un pouvoir: Sciences et savants en France (1793–1824)* (Paris: Payot, 1989), p. 106. See also Diderot and d'Alembert's *Encyclopédie, ou Dictionnaire raisonné des sciences, des arts et des métiers* (Paris, 1751–1765), vol. 5, "Egyptiens." China was an ancient civilization favored by eighteenth-century physiocrats. The Freemasons were especially appreciative of Egyptian accomplishments.

4. Ivan Van Sertima, ed., *Blacks in Science: Ancient and Modern* (New Brunswick: Transaction Books, 1984), p. 13. Alexander von Humboldt addressed similar issues concerning pre-Colombian civilizations in the Americas. See Mary Louise Pratt, *Imperial Eyes: Travel Writing and Transculturation* (London: Routledge, 1992), p. 134.

5. Lawrence, *Lectures,* p. 340.

6. Ambroise Paré, *The Collected Works of Ambroise Paré,* trans. Thomas Johnson (1634; New York: Milford House, 1968), p. 20. Jean Bodin, the French political philosopher, also taught that the peoples of northern regions produced military power, the peoples of the southern regions produced science and religion, and the peoples of the temperate zone founded greatest empires (*The Six Books of a Commonweale,* trans. Richard Knolles [London, 1606], p. 550).

7. The influence of the theory of humors can be seen in Linnaeus's classification of humans, where he assigned a mode of governing to each race. Americans governed by customs, Europeans by laws, Asians by opinions, and Africans by caprice (Carl Linnaeus, *Systema naturae per regna tria naturae,* 10th ed. [Stockholm, 1758], p. 38).

8. Aristotle, *Politics,* VII, 6.

9. Georges-Louis Leclerc, comte de Buffon, *Histoire naturelle, générale et particulière* (Paris, 1749–1804), vol. 3, p. 528. Also Johann Winckelmann, *Reflections Concerning the Imitation of the Grecian Artists in Painting and Sculpture* (1755; Glasgow, 1766), p. 4.

10. Dhombres, *Naissance d'un pouvoir,* pp. 93–149.

11. Johann Blumenbach, "Observations on some Egyptian Mummies opened in London," *Philosophical Transactions of the Royal Society of London* 84 (1794): pt. 2, 177–195.

12. Constantin-François Volney, *Voyage en Syrie et en Egypte* (1787; Paris: Mouton & Co., 1959), pp. 62-64.

13. Christoph Meiners, "De veterum Aegyptiorum origine," *Commentationes Societatis Scientiarum Regiae Gottingensis* 10 (1791): 57-79; Winckelmann, cited in Blumenbach, "Observations on some Egyptian Mummies," p. 193.

14. Georges Cuvier, "Extrait d'observations faites sur le cadavre d'une femme connue à Paris et à Londres sous le nom de Vénus Hottentotte," *Mémoires du Muséum d'Histoire Naturelle* 3 (1817): 272-273.

15. Lawrence, *Lectures,* pp. 341-342.

16. Edward Long, *The History of Jamaica* (London, 1774), vol. 2, p. 355.

17. Blumenbach, "Observations on some Egyptian Mummies," pp. 177-195. Soemmerring also concluded that ancient Egypt had had a mixed population. Of the four mummy heads he examined, he described two as European and one as African (Samuel Thomas von Soemmerring, *Vom Baue des menschlichen Körpers* [Frankfurt, 1791-1796], vol. 1, p. 74).

18. Johann Blumenbach, *Beyträge zur Naturgeschichte* (Göttingen, 1790), pp. 85, 91.

19. Von Staden pointed out how historical selectivity has produced such a view. Heinrich von Staden, "Affinities and Elisions," p. 584. See also Francesca Rochberg, "Introduction" to special section on the Cultures of Ancient Science, ibid., pp. 547-553.

20. Londa Schiebinger, *The Mind Has No Sex? Women in the Origins of Modern Science* (Cambridge, Mass.: Harvard University Press, 1989), pp. 102-104.

21. François-Marie Arouet de Voltaire, *Dictionnaire philosophique* (1764; Amsterdam, 1789), vol. 5, p. 255.

22. Blumenbach, *On the Natural Varieties of Mankind,* p. 81. On African men and women, see Henry Louis Gates, Jr., *Figures in Black: Words, Signs, and the "Racial" Self* (New York: Oxford University Press, 1989), pp. 3-24.

23. We hear about Bettisia Gozzadini, who lectured in law at the University of Bologna in 1296. Novella d'Andrea replaced her deceased father as professor of canon law at the University of Bologna in the fourteenth century. In 1678, Elena Cornaro Piscopia became the first woman to receive the doctorate of philosophy at Padua. Maria Agnesi of Milan became well known for her work in differential and integral calculus. Laura Bassi taught physics at the University of Bologna for forty-eight years. Dorothea Erxleben became the first woman ever to receive a medical degree in Germany in 1754. See my *The Mind Has No Sex?* pp. 12-17, 250-257.

24. Johann Blumenbach, "Observations on the Bodily Conformation and Mental Capacity of the Negroes," *Philosophical Magazine* 3 (1799): 141-146, especially 145. This library was auctioned off in Göttingen in 1840.

25. On Amo, see *Antonius Guilielmus Amo, Afer aus Axim in Ghana: Dokumente, Autographe, Belege* (Halle: Martin Luther Universität, 1968); Burchard Brentjes, *Anton Wilhelm Amo: Der schwarze Philosoph in Halle* (Leipzig: Koehler & Amelang, 1976); also Blumenbach, "Observations on the Bodily Conformation and Mental Capacity of the Negroes"; Henri Grégoire, *De la littérature des nègres, ou Recherches sur leurs facultés intellectuelles, leurs qualités morales et leur littérature* (Paris, 1808), pp. 198-202; Paulin Hountondji, *African Philosophy: Myth and Reality,* trans. Henri Evans (London: Hutchinson University Library for Africa, 1983), chap. 5; and Gates, *Figures in Black,* pp. 11-12. Blumenbach's

information about Amo apparently came from the philosopher Hollmann who had instructed Amo in philosophy at Wittenberg (Bentjes, *Amo*, p. 72).

26. On Wheatley, see Gates's excellent discussion, *Figures in Black*, pp. 61-79.

27. Hans Debrunner identifies her as Pauline Hippolyte de Buisson (*Presence and Prestige: Africans in Europe* [Basil: Basler Afrika Bibliographen, 1979], p. 143).

28. Hans-Konrad Schmutz, "Friedrich Tiedemann und Johann Friedrich Blumen-bach: Anthropologie und Sklavenfrage," in *Die Natur des Menschen: Probleme der Physischen Anthropologie und Rassenkunde, (1750-1850)*, ed. Gunter Mann, Jost Benedum, and Werner Kümmel (Stuttgart: Gustav Fischer Verlag, 1990), p. 358.

29. There were also experiments in elementary- and secondary-school education: Wilberforce established a school for Africans at Clapham, near London; African children from Coesnon's college in Paris were examined by members of the French National Institute. Grégoire, *De la littérature des nègres*, pp. 176-177.

30. Folarin Shyllon, *Black People in Britain, 1555-1833* (Oxford: Oxford University Press, 1977), p. 48.

31. In addition to Amo, a Sultan Achmet from India matriculated at Halle in 1733 and Salomon Negri from Damascus in 1701 (*Antonius Guilielmus Amo*, p. 296).

32. Ibid., pp. 9-10.

33. Ibid., pp. 125 and 134.

34. Schiebinger, *Mind Has No Sex?* chap. 9.

35. Long, *History of Jamaica*, vol. 2, pp. 475-485.

36. David Hume, "Of National Characters," in *The Philosophical Works*, ed. Thomas Green and Thomas Grose (London, 1886), vol. 4, p. 252 n. 1.

37. The Berlin Academy was unusual in having women of high rank, such as Catherine the Great, as honorary members in the eighteenth and nineteenth centuries. The first woman to be elected for her scientific merit was Lise Meitner in 1949. Italian academies also admitted some women in the eighteenth century. Emilie du Châtelet, for example, who was denied membership in French scientific academies, was honored with membership in Italian academies.

38. An African of fortune and a friend of many well-known men of science, Williams was admitted to the meetings of the Royal Society and even proposed as a member (*Gentlemen's Magazine* 42 [1771]: 595). Blumenbach had a copy of this article among his papers (Cod. Ms. Blum IXb, B1.36, p. 48, Niedersächsische Staats- und Universitätsbibliothek, Göttingen).

39. I thank Mary Sampson, archivist at the Royal Society, for helping to clarify this matter.

40. M. Argo, "Notices nécrologiques," *Comptes Rendus* (1836): 96-101. Alfred Lacroix, "Notice historique sur les membres et correspondants de l'Académie des Sciences ayant travaillé dans les colonies françaises des Mascareignes et de Madagascar au XVIIIe siècle et au début du XIXe," *Mémoires de l'Académie des Sciences* 62 (17 December 1934): 82-85.

41. Grégoire, *De la littérature des nègres*, pp. 207-208.

42. Lacroix, "Notice historique sur les membres et correspondants de l'Académie des Sciences," p. 82. The Académie des Sciences in Paris was unable to tell me if any persons of African descent had become members since the 1930s.

43. Brentjes, *Anton Wilhelm Amo*, p. 71.

44. Claude-Nicolas Le Cat, *Traité de la couleur de la peau humaine* (Amsterdam, 1765).

45. Joan Landes, *Women and the Public Sphere in the Age of the French Revolution* (Ithaca: Cornell University Press, 1988), pp. 23–28; Schiebinger, *Mind Has No Sex?* pp. 30–32; and Dena Goodman, "Enlightenment Salons: The Convergence of Female and Philosophic Ambitions," *Eighteenth-Century Studies* 22 (1989): 329–350.

46. Claire de Durfort, duchesse de Duras, *Ourika,* ed. Claudine Herrmann (Paris: Des Femmes, 1979), p. 38.

47. David Geggus, "Racial Equality, Slavery, and Colonial Secession during the Constituent Assembly," *The American Historical Review* 94 (1989): 1290–1308, especially 1297.

48. Shelby McCloy, *The Negro in France* (Lexington: University of Kentucky Press, 1961), pp. 38–39.

49. Richard Sheridan, *Doctors and Slaves: A Medical and Demographic History of Slavery in the British West Indies, 1680-1834* (Cambridge: Cambridge University Press, 1985), pp. 49–50.

50. *De Jure Maurorum in Europa* (1729), discussed in *Wöchentliche Hallische Nachrichten* 12 (1729), reprinted in *Antonius Guilielmus Amo,* pp. 5-6. His standard works, *De humanae mentis apatheia* (Wittenberg, 1734), *Ideam distinctam* (Wittenberg, 1734), and *Tractatus de arte sobrie et accurate philosophandi* (Halle, 1738), sound familiar themes: What is sensation? Does the faculty of sense belong to mind? How do we acquire distinct ideas? See also Hountondji, *African Philosophy,* p. 111. The same was true of women's writings in this period; see my *Mind Has No Sex?* pp. 270–271.

FOLLOW-UP ACTIVITIES

Discussing the Rhetoric

1. Schiebinger begins this chapter by summarizing Martin Bernal's controversial thesis in his Book, *Black Athena.* According to Bernal, "the myth of a white dawn of Western civilization resulted from the upsurge in anti-Semitism and racism at the end of the eighteenth century." Why do you think Schiebinger chooses to begin the chapter with Bernal's thesis?

2. Besides Bernal, Schiebinger quotes many other writers. Are you familiar with them? Do you think her intended audience would be familiar with them? How do these other voices in the chapter help her represent her overall purpose?

3. This chapter is divided into three parts. How are the parts interrelated?

4. Did any of Schiebinger's language or examples offend you? If giving offense was part of the author's rhetorical strategy, what does she gain by it?

5. What kinds of evidence does Schiebinger use? Do any of her rhetorical strategies remind you of Rose? hooks? In what ways? What kind of appeal is she making?

Discussing the Conversation

1. Why does Schiebinger want to convince her readers that early European science privileged European males? What other authors in this text are concerned with the role one's cultural heritage plays in one's success?

2. According to Schiebinger, why does it matter that the voices of women and people of color were lost to early science? Compare Schiebinger's concerns to Mary Louise Pratt's about the loss of Guaman Poma's manuscript.

3. How would you describe how Schiebinger contributes to the larger conversation of knowledge-making? How does her perspective compare to those of Keller, Addelson, and Crews? How does her perspective differ?

4. Like bell hooks and Richard Rodriguez, Schiebinger spends time discussing the role of the exceptional person in scholarship. Are their concerns parallel, or do they diverge?

5. For Pratt, resistance to dominant ways of thinking is in part a rhetorical act. How does Schiebinger's effort to recuperate the history of excluded groups cooperate with Pratt's project? In what ways do their rhetorical strategies differ?

Joining the Conversation

1. Write an informal summary of Schiebinger's account of how the classification of physical traits by eighteenth-century natural scientists perpetuated "the project of valuing one kind of knowledge over another."

2. Does Schiebinger, in your estimation, ever provide an answer for the question posed in the chapter's title? Write an informal paper in which you first try to answer the title's question on the basis of Schiebinger's chapter and, second, address whether Schiebinger's chapter has caused you to revise your assumptions about how scientific knowledge is constructed.

3. Schiebinger concludes that despite the proven capabilities of women and Africans involved in eighteenth-century experiments in education, these groups remained outsiders, and such exclusion became a legacy we've inherited. Write an informal paper in which you consider the contemporary implications of Schiebinger's conclusion. You'll want to consider the following questions: Have you ever been an outsider? What strategies did you find yourself using to gain acceptance by that community? Were your attempts successful?

INTRODUCTORY COMMENTS ON "ANIMAL SEXUALITY" BY DAVID CREWS

Reading the Context

In the article, "Animal Sexuality," David Crews questions the legitimacy of a theory on the nature of sexuality known as the organizational concept, which asserts that an individual's chromosomes determine which sex hormones its gonads will produce, and that these hormones organize the development of male or female physical characteristics. Crews argues that this theory is based on too narrow a sampling—only a few warm-blooded species. If scientists are to generalize about the nature of sexual development, they must also examine reptiles and fish. His own research on cold-blooded species has shown that their sexual development is not necessarily determined by the chromosomes, but is often controlled by environmental factors instead.

David Crews is a professor of zoology and psychology specializing in reproductive biology at the University of Texas-Austin. He received his doctorate in biology from Rutgers University in 1973 and has been teaching at UT-Austin since 1982. The selection here is reprinted from an article published in *Scientific American,* which notes that Crews has explored the evolutionary roots of sexuality and the role of hormones in controlling sexual differentiation and behavior for many years. Crews' research has focused on sexuality among garter snakes, whiptail lizards, red-eared slider turtles, and leopard geckos.

Crews founded Reproductive Sciences, a biotechnology firm that is using a patented process of hormone-induced sex determination to assist in the breeding of rare birds. He also formed Reptile Conservation International, a nonprofit corporation that is using estrogen treatment selectively to build up female populations of endangered turtles in Mexico and South America.

Reading the Rhetoric

As a result of the research he has done with reptiles, David Crews wants the readers of his *Scientific American* article to think about the influences of social environments on determining characteristics of animal sexuality. To be convincing, Crews must set up a situation in which his readers will question the validity of an explanation of sexuality that is based strictly on genetics. As you read, look for rhetorical strategies that Crews uses to open the door for his readers to question the organizational concept of sexuality. Pay particular attention to Crews' use of evidence. How does he assemble evidence to support his position? Is he able to convince you that sex is not so much a matter of biology as of environmental influences? How well does he convince or fail to convince? How do you think Crews' zoology colleagues might react to his argument?

As you read, look in particular at Crews' choice of words. What words does he choose to present evidence that supports his position that sexuality is environmentally conditioned? Why might these words be convincing or unconvincing to readers of *Scientific American?* Do they convince you? What do you think other zoologists might think of Crews' use of terms like "gender bending" and "female mimic"? What nonscientific discourses do they remind you of? How do Crews' descriptions of characteristically female and characteristically male behaviors change over the course of the article?

Both Crews' choice of words and his use of evidence help to present his position to his readers. Think about how the words you choose and the evidence you collect help to formulate a position that is convincing to your readers.

Reading the Conversation

Crews is reporting generalizations from findings on animal sexuality that are based on years of laboratory and field research. How might Crews' discussion of the organizational concept of sexuality and his proposed evolutionary concept of sexuality fit with what Addelson or Schiebinger have to say about the gender-determining language of science? Based on his list of criteria, do you think that Klemke and his co-editors would argue that Crews is doing scientific research? How do you think Addelson, Keller, and Schiebinger might respond to Crews' choice of words and evidence?

Animal Sexuality
David Crews

Animals have evolved a range of mechanisms to determine whether an individual takes on masculine or feminine traits. Cross-species comparisons offer some surprising insights into the nature of sexuality.

1   One of the most fundamental characteristics of life is sexuality, the division into male and female. Sexual considerations influence the appearance, form, behavior and chemical makeup of nearly all multicellular organisms. Amazingly enough, scientists cannot conclusively say why sex exists. In recent years, however, animal studies have provided a great deal of information about the multifaceted components of sexuality. These studies reveal that many familiar aspects are less universal than once supposed. The work provides a new framework for understanding the relationship between males and females and a glimpse at how sex evolved.

Whiptail lizards engage in elaborate mating rituals even though some whiptail species consist of self-producing females only. Sexual behavior seems to be a deeply ingrained trait that serves biological functions other than just fertilization: for example, mounting induces asexual whiptails to lay more eggs.

2   Among vertebrate animals, sexuality is expressed in a number of ways. Males and females exhibit a wide variety of chemical, anatomic and behavioral disparities. The most obvious of the behavioral divergences lies in an animal's copulatory activity. In general, individuals having testes attempt insemination (male-typical behavior), whereas individuals having ovaries are receptive to being inseminated (female-typical behavior). Males and females often differ in other, less overt ways, such as level of activity, regulation of body weight, level of aggression and learning patterns. Some gender-specific actions are associated with, but not necessarily caused by, systematic dissimilarities in certain parts of the brain.

3   Over the past four decades, biologists have pieced together a master outline of the nature of sexuality, known as the organizational concept. Although it is not totally inclusive, the organizational concept broadly accounts for the structure of sexuality in humans and other mammals. A number of my colleagues and I are currently investigating how to apply the outline more generally to all vertebrate animals.

4   According to the organizational concept, an animal's sex—specifically, the nature of its gonads—is determined at the time of conception by the chromosomal constitution inherited from its parents. The gonads produce sex steroid hormones that circulate during the early stages of embryonic development; these hormones sculpt the individual's masculine or feminine features. Male sexual traits are instigated primarily by androgens, a class of hormones (including testosterone) produced in the testes. Individuals that

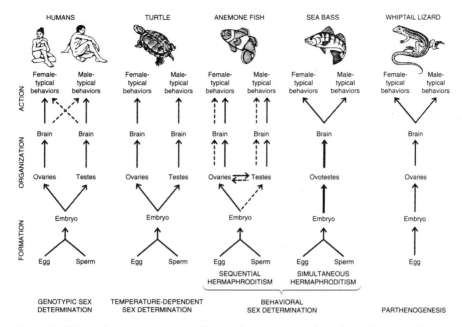

Sexual differentiation occurs in all vertebrate species but through several quite different mechanisms. In mammals, chromosomes inherited at the time of fertilization dictate whether an individual develops male or female sexual organs. In many reptiles, incubation temperature of the embryo controls an individual's sex. Hermaphroditic animals switch from male to female reproductive behavior, usually triggered by the individual's social environment. Simultaneous hermaphrodites can alternate gender repeatedly. Sequential hermaphrodites change once from male to female, or vice versa. Even parthenogenic species display male- and female-typical sexual behavior.

lack testes develop ovaries, which generate mostly female hormones called estrogens and progestins. In this scenario, the female is the neutral, or default, sex, whereas the male is the organized sex.

5   A key element of the organizational concept is the central role of sex steroid hormones. Modern understanding of the influence of such hormones on sexual differentiation began with the work of Frank R. Lillie of the University of Chicago. Early in this century, Lillie observed that when cows gave birth to twins of opposite sexes, the female twin was sterile and had masculine traits. Lillie, who was an embryologist by training, suggested that androgenic hormones secreted by the male twin in the womb imbued the female twin with some male traits. Scientists have since thoroughly corroborated Lillie's conjecture that the gonads in embryos secrete the hormones that cause males to differ from females.

6   Among mammals, an embryo starts out having a mass of primordial sexual tissue. Genetic signals determine whether that tissue develops into male

or female gonads. Subsequent hormonal triggers that act in the embryo control the sex of the genitalia. The testes of genetic males produce significant concentrations of androgens, which induce the formation of the vas deferens, a penis and a scrotum. In the absence of androgens, the embryo acquires female sexual organs: a uterus, a clitoris and vaginal labia.

7   Accumulating evidence from animal experiments suggests that many components of adult sexuality—not just the structure of the sexual organs—depend on the hormonal environment during fetal development. Some of the most persuasive support of this notion comes from studies of species that produce litters of many young from each pregnancy. During such pregnancies, the fetuses are arranged like peas in a pod inside the uterus. This grouping results in female and male fetuses residing next to one another in random order.

8   In such an environment, steroid hormones produced by one fetus's gonads could influence the developing neural and secondary and accessory sex structures in an adjacent fetus. Lynwood G. Clemens of Michigan State University discovered that the hormonal surroundings created by neighboring fetuses can profoundly affect adult sexuality in rats. Mertice Clark and Bennett G. Galef of McMaster University have recently observed a similar effect among gerbils.

9   Frederick S. vom Saal of the University of Missouri has conducted an especially thorough study of sexual development in mice. He found that female mice developing between two male mouse fetuses (known as 2M females) are exposed to higher concentrations of testosterone and lower concentrations of estrogen than are female fetuses that do not develop next to a male (OM females). After birth, 2M females evince a more masculine anatomy than do OM females. 2M females also take longer to reach puberty and have shorter and fewer reproductive cycles as adults. Finally, compared with OM females, 2M females are less attractive and less sexually arousing to males and are more aggressive toward other females.

10   The spotted hyena, a nocturnal African carnivore, offers another prime example of how fetal hormones can direct adult sexuality. Female hyenas exhibit many characteristics usually associated with male mammals. Adult female hyenas within a clan, or social group, are larger and heavier than the males; females dominate nearly all of the adult males in aggressive disputes and in access to food. Female spotted hyenas have normal-looking ovaries and internal genitalia, but their external genitalia have a strongly masculine morphology. They lack external vaginas, and their labia are fused, forming a scrotal sac complete with two bulging pads of fat that simulate testes. The large, erectile clitoris of a female spotted hyena closely resembles a male's penis. Much like many male animals, female spotted hyenas use their clitorises in greeting displays and in dominance interactions.

11   Stephen E. Glickman and Laurence G. Frank of the University of California at Berkeley recently deduced that this masculinization occurs in the womb as a consequence of the high levels of the chemical androstenedione

in the mother's bloodstream. Androstenedione is an inactive compound that can be converted into either estrogen or testosterone. In the placenta of a pregnant hyena, little of the androstenedione turns into estrogen, which leads to high levels of testosterone in the fetus. The abundant testosterone presumably causes the masculine traits of the female hyenas.

12   Evidently, some mechanism enables the hormonal environment of an embryo to influence that animal's adult sexual behavior. In 1959 Charles H. Phoenix, Robert W. Goy, Arnold A. Gerall and William C. Young, while working at the University of Kansas, proposed that steroid hormones secreted in mammalian embryos help to organize the sexuality of the brain. Subsequent research has shown that in vertebrates steroid hormones act directly on specific neurons that are linked together in circuits. These neural circuits seem to provide the impetus for behavioral differences between males and females.

13   Several recent discoveries greatly clarify the link between hormones, brain structure and sexual behavior. For instance, Pauline I. Yahr and her colleagues at the University of California at Irvine identified a nucleus in the gerbil brain that is present only in males. This nucleus lies embedded in an area that helps to control copulatory behavior in male gerbils. Female gerbils injected with androgen early in life develop this "male" nucleus and take on some male behavioral characteristics.

14   Certain species of small songbirds also manifest hormone-influenced brain structures that seem to correspond to gender roles in courtship. Male canaries begin to sing in the spring, when their androgen levels are high. The singing both establishes breeding territories and attracts females. Females respond to the song but do not sing themselves. Fernando Nottebohm of the Rockefeller University and others have determined that the contrasting behavior of male and female canaries and other sondbirds is matched by differences in the structures of their brains.

15   The workers find that singing is mediated by an interconnected series of brain nuclei that control the vocal organs. The song-control regions in the brains of female songbirds normally are much smaller than those in the brains of the males. Steroid hormones in songbird embryos determine which neurons survive and which die. The result is that the size and number of neurons, as well as the quantity of synapses, in the song-control nuclei are much greater in males than in females.

16   Nottebohm has shown that the song controlling brain nuclei vary in size seasonally, waxing and waning in conjunction with the flow of the reproductive cycle. By castrating male songbirds (to lower their androgen levels) or injecting them with androgen (to raise those levels), he and his colleagues have artificially re-created such seasonal changes in singing. In related work, female canaries given appropriate injections of androgen have been induced to sing [see "From Bird Song to Neurogenesis," by Fernando Nottebohm; *Scientific American*, February 1989].

17   A particularly exciting and controversial discovery of a link between sexual behavior and brain structure concerns homosexuality in humans. Simon

LeVay, then at the Salk Institute for Biological Studies in San Diego, has reported that the size of a nucleus in the anterior hypothalamus of homosexual men more closely resembles the comparable structure in women than that in heterosexual men. Dean H. Hamer and his colleagues at the National Institutes of Health claim to have found a region on the X chromosome that may contain a gene or genes for homosexuality. If so, the associated brain structure may be under direct genetic control. It is also possible, however, that the hormonal environment surrounding the fetus may partially or totally control the development of the brain nucleus.

18   These discoveries illustrate the inadequacy of stereotypical divisions of male or female. As the organizational concept makes clear, sexuality depends on subtle hormonal controls, not just on either-or genetic labeling. This finding applies to all the tissues associated with reproduction, including the circuits in the brain that underlie sexual behavior.

19   In most vertebrate species, adults usually exhibit mating behaviors characteristic of their own gonadal sex, known as homotypical sexual behaviors. Not infrequent, however, individuals also perform behavior patterns normally associated with the opposite sex, known as heterotypical behaviors. For example, females sometimes engage in mounting, and males sometimes solicit being mounted.

20   Such heterotypical sexual behaviors are a frequent and important part of the social biology of many species, especially among mammals. Female cows commonly mount other females, a practice that seems to help synchronize the reproductive cycles of the herd. In rhesus monkeys, mounting functions as an indicator of dominance and so maintains an orderly social hierarchy. Even though embryonic hormones direct neuronal development, it seems that the brain never completely loses the dual circuitry that permits both homotypical and heterotypical sexual behavior.

21   So far the organizational concept seems to offer a complete framework by which to understand animal sexuality. There is, however, a danger in making sweeping statements about its nature on the basis of observations of a very small number of species, all of them warm-blooded vertebrates, such as birds and mammals. To evaluate the resulting conclusions about sexuality, one must look at a far more comprehensive range of vertebrate species. Much of my own research has concentrated on determining how well the organizational concept applies to coldblooded reptiles and fish.

22   Such investigations are crucial for elaborating a more complete picture of animal sexuality. The kinds of sexual maturation and behavior found in any particular mammal or bird may reflect the unique adaptations of that species. Sexual traits that are shared by many different kinds of vertebrates, in contrast, presumably date from a more ancient evolutionary stage. Likewise, sexual behaviors (such as mounting) that appear in both males and females may predate more familiar, sex-specific mating activities. Only by knowing the evolutionary roots of sexuality will scientists be able to learn the rules that govern this omnipresent life process.

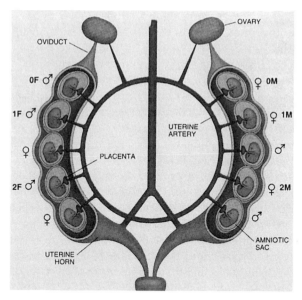

Hormonal environment in the uterus affects adult sexuality in mice, gerbils and rats. Female embryos surrounded by males on both sides (2M females) are exposed to higher levels of testosterone than those that do not develop next to a male (OM females). Mature 2M females have a masculinized anatomy; they are also more aggressive and less attractive to males than are OM females. The opposite feminizing effect is seen in males surrounded by females (2F males).

23   When viewed through a broadened perspective that embraces the full diversity of vertebrate animals, the organizational concept clearly fails. I see only one truly essential component of animal sexuality: the organizing effects of sex steroid hormones on the tissues that mediate reproduction. The mechanism that directs those effects varies considerably, however.

24   In the organizational concept, the sex chromosomes exert ultimate control over whether an animal develops into a male or a female. Yet many fish and reptiles lack sex chromosomes. These species depend on nongenetic triggers to guide sexual differentiation.

25   Among such species, an individual's gender usually depends on the environment it experiences. In some cases, the determining factor is the temperature at which the embryo develops (temperature-dependent sex determination). In other instances, the adult's social surroundings control its sex (behavior-dependent sex determination). Certain animal species even dispense with sexual differentiation and reproduce asexually, a process known as parthenogenesis. These nongenetic methods of sexual differentiation may be evolutionary precursors of the chromosomal control used in mammals.

26   Temperature-dependent sex determination was identified more than 25 years ago, when Madeline Charnier of the University of Dakar in Senegal

reported that the temperature at which rainbow lizard eggs are incubated governs that animal's sex ratio. In the late 1970s James J. Bull and Richard Vogt, then at the University of Wisconsin, conclusively demonstrated that temperature activates some as yet unknown sex-determining mechanism.

27   Scientists now know that temperature controls gender in many kinds of reptiles, including all crocodilians, many turtles and some lizards. Although all temperature-dependent reptiles lack sex chromosomes, their gender, once set, remains permanent throughout their life. In these species, sex determination occurs in the middle of embryological development, coinciding with the differentiation of the gonads.

28   Temperature regulation of sexuality takes place in an all-or-nothing fashion. Intermediate temperatures do not produce hermaphrodites; rather they result in a more evenly balanced sex ratio. This pattern indicates that temperature activates a biological switch that determines gonadal sex. I have studied this phenomenon in conjunction with Bull, Judith M. Bergeron of the University of Texas at Austin and Thane Wibbels, now at the University of Alabama at Birmingham. We found that temperature acts by modifying the distribution of enzymes and hormone receptors, including estrogen and androgen receptors, in the growing embryo.

29 In the leopard gecko, low and high incubation temperatures produce females, whereas intermediate temperatures yield males (different patterns prevail in other species). Working with Bull and William H. N. Gutzke, now at Memphis State University, I administered estrogen to gecko eggs early in development. The estrogen overrode the male-determining temperatures so that all of the young had ovaries.

30   At temperatures close to those that produce females, lower dosages of estrogen suffice to induce the formation of ovaries. Bergeron, Wibbels and I recently recognized that chemicals that inhibit the production of estrogens and androgens can prevent an embryo from developing the usual, temperature-controlled male or female gonads. It seems that sex hormones function as the physiological equivalent of incubation temperatures among species that utilize temperature sex determination.

31   The temperature at which leopard gecko eggs are incubated has a permanent imprint on adult sexuality. Alan Tousignant, a graduate student of mine, and I found that females from eggs incubated at relatively cool temperatures mature faster than those that develop at warmer, predominantly male-producing temperatures. Deborah Flores, another graduate student, and I determined that female geckos from male-biased incubation temperatures are less attractive to males than are females from female-biased temperatures.

32   Both male and female leopard geckos are more aggressive if they experienced high temperatures during incubation and are more submissive if they experienced low temperatures. Further, females that incubated at male-biased temperatures develop pubic glands having patent pores similar to those found in males; females that developed at female-biased temperatures have smaller

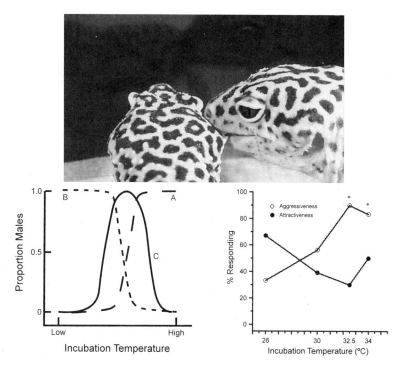

Incubation temperature of embryos determines the sex ratio in many kinds of reptiles. Depending on the species, the embryos develop into males predominantly at low, intermediate or high temperatures (above, bottom left). Among female leopard geckos, warmer incubation temperatures (up to 32.5 degrees Celsius) engender heightened aggressiveness and reduced attractiveness to males (above, bottom right). The photograph shows normal courtship among leopard geckos.

glands and closed pores. In general, the circulating concentrations of androgens in adult females are lower than those in adult males. But the androgen levels in females form male-biased temperatures are higher, and estrogen levels lower, than in those that developed at female-biased temperatures. It seems that adult behavior and sexual chemistry reflect an individual's early, temperature-modulated hormonal environment.

33   Temperature-dependent sex determination may be an evolutionary precursor to the genetic control of gender found in mammals. If so, relics of temperature-sensitive behavior might survive in some higher vertebrates. Several workers, including Evelyn Satinoff of the University of Illinois and Christiana L. Williams of Hunter College, report that modifying the temperature drastically influences the behavior of rat pups. This finding hints that even in mammals temperature changes may modulate the organizing effects of steroid hormones. Perhaps the fairly constant body temperatures of warm blooded animals mask a surviving mechanism whereby temperature can affect the sexual differentiation of the fetus.

34 Among temperature-dependent species, sex remains fixed once it is set. But species that experience behavior-dependent sex determination, the other main form of nongenetic control of gender stray even further from the organizational concept and from genetically determined sex. In most cases, these animals are hermaphrodites—that is, individuals that possess both male and female gonads. The social environment controls whether an individual takes on a male or female reproductive role; in other words, sensory stimuli rather than chromosomes direct sexual differentiation. Even so, hermaphroditic species share many chemical and behavioral characteristics with warm-blooded vertebrates.

35   Some behavior-dependent species of fish are sequential hermaphrodites. These creatures change from one sex to another during their lifetime but express only one gonadal sex at any given time. Orange and white anemone fish are born male and later develop into females. Certain coral reef fish in the Pacific Ocean and in the Caribbean Sea follow the opposite course, starting out female and becoming male. The timing of the sex change depends on a social trigger, such as the disappearance of a dominant male or female. Other fish species are simultaneously hermaphroditic, meaning they possess a gonad containing both ovarian and testicular tissue. Interestingly, individuals of these species almost never fertilize their own eggs. Instead they continue to mate, perhaps so as to retain the advantages of genetic diversity provided by sexual reproduction. Eric A. Fischer, then at the University of Washington, showed that mating pairs of hermaphroditic butter hamlet alternate between male and female behavioral roles during successive matings. The sex expressed by an individual fish depends on its social surroundings.

36   How do sequentially hermaphroditic fish accomplish their gender switch? Such species may change from male to female sexual behavior within minutes after witnessing an appropriate change in the number or social structure of the surrounding fish. That rapid transformation must result from signals originating in the brain. Neural connections between the hypothalamus and the gonads exist in all vertebrates. Leo S. Demski of New College of the University of South Florida observed that electrical stimulation in the hypothalamus region of the brain of the hermaphroditic sea bass can induce the release of eggs or sperm. Perhaps in sequential hermaphrodites these nerves alter the hormonal environment within the gonad; the hormones, in turn, carry the ultimate responsibility for executing changes in sexuality. Less obvious kinds of brain-controlled changes in sexuality may occur in other animals.

37   Parthenogenesis, or self-cloning, offers yet another alternative to genetically determined reproductive roles. The species that perform this kind of replication consist of females only. One might think that self-cloning species would have no need of any noticeable form of sexual behavior, yet such is not the case. Species of whiptail lizards that reproduce by parthenogenesis exhibit identical mating behavior to related species that engage in conventional sex, except that each individual alternatives between male and female behavior. I have determined that this behavior is controlled by hormones,

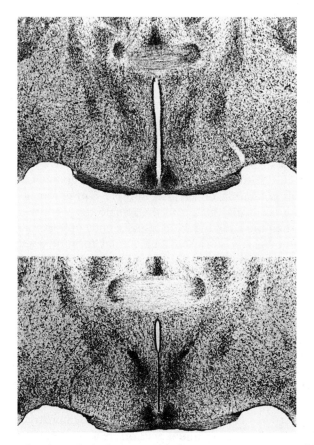

Brain structure has been linked to sexual behavior in many species. These images show neural differences in the preoptic region of female (top) and male (bottom) gerbil brains. That region is involved in the control of masculine copulatory behavior and scent marking, behaviors influenced by androgenic hormones. Females given androgens early in life develop masculine brain structures.

much as it is in related, sexual species of whiptails. The persistence of sexual behavior even in an all-female species indicates that such activity is not just a vestigial trait but one that serves an important biological function [see "Courtship in Unisexual Lizards: A Model for Brain Evolution," by David Crews; *Scientific American,* December, 1987]. Among whiptail lizards, sexual interactions cause the animals to lay many more eggs than they would if they were alone.

38   My studies of animal sexuality have convinced me that coordinated, complementary, male and female behaviors are crucial for healthy reproduction, even in single-sex species. It is noteworthy that in certain conventional male-and-female species, members of one sex may turn such coordination to

their advantage by imitating members of the opposite sex. Such activity may be thought of as another nongenetic form of sexual differentiation.

39   The bluegill sunfish engages in an intriguing form of such gender bending. Wallace Dominey, while at Cornell University, and Mart R. Gross, now at the University of Toronto, independently discerned that male bluegill sunfish exist in three different forms. Large, colorful males court females and defend their territories. A second kind of male—often known as a "sneaker"—becomes sexually mature at a much younger age and smaller size. These small males live on the periphery of a bigger male's territory and clandestinely mate with females while the dominant male is otherwise occupied.

40   Sneaker males mature into a third kind of male, one that assumes the behavior and drab coloration of a female sunfish. These female mimics intervene between a territorial male and the female he is courting. The female mimic, rather than the courting male, usually ends up fertilizing the eggs.

41   Male red-sided garter snakes enact a similar form of sexual mimicry. At times of peak sexual activity, males congregate around females, forming a so-called mating ball. Robert T. Mason, a former graduate student of mine now at Oregon State University, examined many such balls. He found that in 16 percent of the balls, the snake being courted by the males was in fact a disguised male, which we call a she-male. She-males have testes that produce normal sperm, and they court and mate with females. But in addition to exhibiting male-typical behaviors, she-males produce the same attractiveness pheromone as do adult females. In the mating ball, this second source of the pheromone confuses the more prevalent conventional males, giving the she-male a decided mating advantage.

42   Numerous studies of lower vertebrates clearly demonstrate that the organizational concept we have outlined here offers an incomplete picture of animal sexuality. I propose that a slightly broader view could encompass all vertebrates. I look beyond the kind of genetically determined sexuality encompassed in the organizational concept toward a more comprehensive, evolutionary view of sexuality. That view builds on the notion that males most certainly evolved only after the evolution of the first self-replicating (and hence female) organisms.

43   In the organizational concept the female is the default sex and the male the organized sex, imposed on the female by the action of hormones. In my alternative scenario, the female is the ancestral sex and the male the derived sex. Consider hermaphroditic fishes. Douglas Y. Shapiro of Eastern Michigan University has found that fish species that are born male and become female nevertheless pass through a modified ovarian stage before developing testes. To me, such observations suggest that males may be more like females than females are like males.

44   Given that every male must contain evolutionary traces of femaleness, biologists might be well served to focus less on the differences between the sexes and more in terms of the similarities. A logical place to concentrate

Sexual behavior does not always cleave neatly into male and female categories. Female spotted hyenas, such as this one with a cub (left), have many male behavioral and physical attributes, including a penislike clitoris used in greeting displays. Pairs of hermaphroditic butter hamlet (right) repeatedly trade gender roles during mating.

that search would be the sex hormones that are ubiquitous among vertebrates. Some research directed along these lines is in fact paying off. Endocrinologists have found evidence that estrogen and progesterone, both usually associated only with female sexual behavior, may function actively in the sexuality of both genders. In some species, testosterone is converted to estrogen in the brain; in those species, estrogen activates both copulatory behavior in males and sexual receptivity in females. In songbirds, estrogen originates primarily in the brain, implying that its presence transcends gender boundaries and hinting at the existence of brain-controlled sexuality in some higher vertebrates.

45 Progesterone is generally thought to inhibit sexual activity in males; it even has been used as a form of chemical castration in felony rape convictions. Most researchers therefore have assumed that progesterone has no place in normal male sexuality. Male rats and humans, however, show a pronounced daily rhythm in progesterone secretion; peak progesterone levels occur at the onset of night, when copulatory behavior most often occurs. Diane Witt of the National Institute of Mental Health, Larry Young, one of my graduate students, and I recently observed that physiological dosages of progesterone can induce castrated male rats to resume mounting. Moreover, injections of RU 486, a hormone that chemically nullifies progesterone, reduces sexual behavior in intact male rats. Like estrogen, progesterone seems to be both a female and a male hormone—an evolutionary relic extending beyond the confines of the organizational concept. Further investigation of the similarities of males and females may turn up additional instances of "female"

aspects of sexuality that might be more correctly viewed as "ancestral." Such work may yield more clues about the mode of action and evolutionary origins of sex steroid hormones. It may also illuminate connections between the mechanisms by which temperature, brain function and genetics determine gender. In this way, researchers will achieve a deeper and richer understanding of the essential nature of sex.

FURTHER READING

Functional Associations in Behavioral Endocrinology. David Crews in *Masculinity/Femininity: Basic Perspectives.* Edited by J. M. Reinisch, L. A. Rosenblum and S. A. Sanders. Oxford University Press, 1987.

Behavioral Endocrinology. Jill B. Becker, S. Marc Breedlove and David Crews. MIT Press, 1992.

The Organizational Concept and Vertebrates Without Sex Chromosomes. David Crews in *Brain, Behavior and Evolution,* Vol. 42, Nos. 4-5, pages 202-214; October 1993.

The Differences Between the Sexes. Edited by R. V. Short and E. Balaban. Cambridge University Press (in press).

FOLLOW-UP ACTIVITIES

Discussing the Rhetoric

1. What one sentence in the text describes Crews' position on the factors that determine animal sexuality?

2. How might Crews present his position if he were writing for a journal read mostly by other zoologists instead of for the readers of *Scientific American?* Do you think he might use the same words and evidence to convince other zoologists?

3. Note the narrative parts that tell a story of the research in Crews' article. How do they affect the tone of the article? Would you expect to find these parts in an article written for a strictly professional audience? Why would they be acceptable in *Scientific American?*

4. How would you describe Crews' tone when he presents the organizational view of sexuality? Were you surprised when he informs the reader that he disagrees with it? What are the rhetorical advantages of describing the organizational concept with such neutral terms?

5. In the organizational concept the female is the default sex and the male the organized sex, imposed on the female by the action of hormones. In Crews' alternative scenario, the female is the ancestral sex and the male the derived sex. Did Crews convince you? Why or why not?

Discussing the Conversation

1. Unlike other authors in this section who are writing about how scientific knowledge is constructed and written, Crews is reporting findings of actual scientific studies. In what ways might Crews respond to Jane Tompkins' claim that there are no facts or that truth is a matter of perspective? What inferences might you draw about Crews' foundation work to save rare birds and prevent the extinction of endangered South American reptiles in relation to his other work? How might his research to promote an evolutionary view of sexuality that sees females as the ancestral sex and males as the derived sex support a conservation position? Do you see any evidence in this article of environmental conservationism?

2. Barbara McClintock was also a biologist. How do you think she would have responded to the work that Crews is doing? Would she endorse the gender and sexuality issues that Crews raises?

3. Does Crews' way of doing science or his methodology differ from Feigl's way as outlined in Klemke's essay? If so, are the differences significant? In what ways?

Joining the Conversation

1. Findings from animal research are often extrapolated to humans. Write an informal paper in which you consider whether Crews' alternative scenario of sex determination can be directly applied to human development. Explain how reversing the standard narrative, "female is the default sex and male is the organized sex," changes views of human femaleness and maleness.

2. The nature versus nurture debate has long captured Western attention. Many scholars have argued about whether humans are products of their social environments or their genetic biology. Interpretations of positions on this debate have been appropriated to make far-ranging social policy decisions. For example, tracking students into certain levels of classes in school based on their IQ derives from a position that assumes that humans are products of their genetic biology. Write an informal paper in which you discuss your position on sexuality characteristics. Do you think that sex and gender are products of nature or of nurture? Or do you see a more complex arrangement of effects? How do you think Crews might argue? Why do you think so?

3. Several authors have indicated that one's historical position influences what and how findings are recorded. Write an informal paper in which you discuss why Crews' alternative position might be more or less accepted today than one hundred years ago. Discuss historical events that influence your position. If necessary, use Schiebinger and Tompkins for reference.

INTRODUCTORY COMMENTS ON "DISCOVERING THE CLAY FEET OF SCIENCE" BY JOYCE APPLEBY, LYNN HUNT, AND MARGARET JACOB

Reading the Context

This essay is a chapter from a book entitled *Telling the Truth About History* (1993) that examines the research methods of historians. Like scientists, historians are committed to searching for truth, and like scientists, they attempt to make true statements on the basis of empirical evidence. In this chapter, these historians apply empirical methods adopted from the sciences to the study of the history of science itself with somewhat ironic results. Led to question popular assumptions about how scientific work is accomplished, they in turn must question historical methods as well.

Reading the Rhetoric

It is important that the authors represent a collective effort by projecting a unified voice. This is the second selection you have read by multiple authors. Klemke, Hollinger, and Kline also faced the problem of achieving a consistent tone and style. Do the writers manage to maintain a unified voice? How do the collective voices of the two pieces differ from each other? Do you feel that selections like these with multiple writers seem more or less authoritative than pieces written by single authors? Why?

Reading the Conversation

In the introduction to this book, the authors say they hope to "provide general readers, history students, and professional historians with some sense of the debates currently raging about history's relationship to scientific truth, objectivity, postmodernism, and the politics of identity." Because the authors provide background to the conversation about the history of science and the larger issue of knowledge-making that Popper, Magee, Addelson, Keller, and Schiebinger also address, your instructor may assign this article earlier in your work on this Part.

The first sentence of this reading, "Of all the certainties inherited from the eighteenth and nineteenth centuries, the heroic model of science has proved to be the most enduring," seems to continue, even restate, Schiebinger's conclusion. As you read, consider other ways in which Schiebinger's question, "Who should do science?" supplements Appleby, Hunt, and Jacob's discussion of the "heroic model of science." You will also want to think about how these authors challenge Klemke's science/nonscience distinction.

Discovering the Clay Feet of Science
Joyce Appleby, Lynn Hunt, and Margaret Jacob

1   Of all the certainties inherited from the eighteenth and nineteenth centuries, the heroic model of science has proved to be the most enduring. Even radicals and skeptics considered science an essential tool in the dismantling of old absolutisms. Throughout most of this century, American historians in the Progressive tradition, from Beard and his followers to the new social historians of the 1960s, found an ally in pure science. With methods they labeled scientific, the twentieth-century reformers of the American historical consciousness shattered old icons about the nation. The result has been the creation of competing, multicultural visions of the American past.

2   Understandably, those with a liberal or reformist persuasion recoiled at dismantling the model of science which had served them so well. For a long time the intellectual and material benefits derived from science appeared so unmitigated by bad side effects, unintended consequences, or environmentally dangerous applications that the heroic model of value-free science seemed the only way to guarantee the certainty of knowledge about the human condition, past or present. Then, rather suddenly, the reticence to criticize it vanished. In the postwar era the heroic model of science came undone.

3   In the history of Western science, as in much else, Hiroshima marked a major and frightening turning point. In the decades that followed, nuclear science, cloaked in the mantle of disinterest and neutrality, served the interests of all Cold Warriors while the nuclear scientists and bomb-builders worked for any government that needed them. To no one's surprise, at the end of the Cold War some nuclear scientists and technologists faced with imminent unemployment seemed capable of taking their skills to any tyrant or potentate, or simply to the highest bidder. As military goals came increasingly to shape the contours of postwar science and technology, people became anxious about the uses to which the new technology might actually be put.[1] To the fear of nuclear war was added concern about environmental damage. In this menacing setting, the notion of value-free science, ready to be taken up by whatever government or cause, seemed not just amoral but potentially immoral.

4   Cold War anxieties and disillusionment with the heroic image of science encouraged historians and philosophers to interrogate scientists and their practices. Immediately after World War II, historians of science, many of whom had seen war service, resumed their investigations with the encouragement of the scientists. But the history of science now took on a new mission. Some of its promoters had also been at the very center of the American wartime effort to build the nuclear bomb. With the end of the war the

question became who would control nuclear technology. In 1945 many feared that if nuclear science and technology were not brought under firm civilian control, the power of the military might undermine democracy, scientific freedom, and international stability. Among the four or five most important American administrators of the American wartime nuclear program was the chemist and president of Harvard, James B. Conant. With various liberal allies he joined a national campaign to promote the civilian control of nuclear power. Scientists like Conant did not want to see postwar nuclear policy set secretly by the military; they also wanted to foster international cooperation and arms control. Within the framework of these prescriptions, a citizenry knowledgeable about science through its history would become indispensable supporters of Conant's cause.

5   From the podium provided by the presidency of Harvard University, Conant made the case for civilian control and scientific freedom along with a revitalized study of the history of science. Science had to be made accessible if it was to be understood. Its traditions and rational procedures had to be appreciated by laymen, whose task in a democracy was to exert firm civilian control over all matters in domestic and foreign policy. Recognizing that much of twentieth-century science was so complicated as to be daunting, Conant urged that science be taught to nonspecialists through its history. He called for the creation of whole new disciplines to study science and to teach about its centuries of achievement to a new postwar generation of American undergraduates.

6   Led by the Harvard initiative, the history, sociology, and philosophy of science emerged after 1945 as distinct disciplines with new departments established at a number of major universities. At Harvard, historical case studies were used in courses about science in order to illustrate its extraordinary progress. In other universities, history departments once content to teach nothing but political, diplomatic, and military history hired their token historian of science. In the 1970s the history of technology also emerged as a distinct discipline.

7   At the heart of Conant's vision for the history of science lay value-free, progressive science. That model prevailed in most history of science courses right into the 1960s. In the previous decade, John U. Nef, a leading historian of industrialization, explained that Western science alone could be distinguished "from all science of the past . . . [by] the rigour with which the scientists have confined themselves in their inquiries . . . to the objective analysis and examination of matter, space, time and motion." For Nef the freedom of the human spirit "was the principal power behind the scientific revolution."[2] His contemporary the Cambridge University historian Herbert Butterfield insisted that the history of science should be the bridge between the arts and the sciences. In 1948 he offered a series of general lectures about the Scientific Revolution to students at Cambridge and assured them that "since the rise of Christianity their is no landmark in history that is worthy to be compared with this." He also believed that living in the postwar

era gave the historian a unique understanding of the historical importance of science in Western culture since the eighteenth century. To this day Butterfield's lectures remain the most readable general introduction to the Scientific Revolution that has been written in English.[3]

8   But by the 1970s everything Conant, Butterfield, and their generation had in mind when they urged that science be taught through its history had unraveled. Instead of illustrating the wonders of scientific rationality and objectivity—the obstacles met and conquered by the heroes of science—a new history of science challenged the heroic model. Some suspected that rather than making students more knowledgeable about the West's most distinctive cultural achievements, Conant and his allies had unwittingly created a sinister Trojan horse concealing irreverent critics. Once released, they would trample irresponsibly through the academic groves and damage the reputation of the science in which Conant's generation had so fervently believed.

THE KUHNIAN TROJAN HORSE

9 Ironically, it was one of Conant's followers at Harvard, Thomas S. Kuhn, who brought the horse into the center of public controversy. A teacher in the new history of science curriculum there, Kuhn developed a thesis that relied upon social factors to help explain the origins of scientific revolutions. In *The Structure of Scientific Revolutions,* published in 1962 and prefaced by a statement from Conant, Kuhn argued that each scientific field is organized around an overarching, or paradigmatic, theory. In normal, everyday science the social networks and community experiences of scientists in laboratories and professional associations help reinforce the dominant paradigm. Sealed off in their working enclaves, scientists routinely try to explain away any anomalies that their research might turn up. Only when forced by mounting evidence to confront these anomalies will some scientists—they are always rare—make a sudden mental shift which permits them to break with normal science. This is how scientific revolutions occur. The paradigm shift, from one theory to another, permits scientists to break away from the assumptions taken for granted in old theory governing everyday normal science. Again according to Kuhn, social factors keep scientists tied to normal science, while theory shifts let them escape.

10   Nothing in this account seems either sinister or suggestive of a Trojan horse.[4] But when it first appeared, Kuhn's book was blamed for introducing the notion of social conditioning into the way in which scientists routinely proceed, and thus conceivably into the way they break with existing paradigms. In retrospect, it is possible to see Kuhn's book as a sign of the times, an example of the growing effort, originally encouraged by Conant and others, to understand the nature of scientific knowledge because it had become increasingly and disturbingly important.

11   Notice what Kuhn's book did and did not say. In the Kuhnian model, scientists most of the time are sequestered, not only from rival theories, but also away from larger social, economic, and political interests. In that situation and under the guiding influence of their paradigm, they routinely do normal science. Only a dramatic, theoretical innovation, the now famous paradigm shift, will shake them loose from their theoretical moorings and permit the emergence of new, revolutionary science. Kuhn did not say that these shifts occur in opposition to the methods of science or without regard for empirical work.

12   Kuhn did not intend to open the door to relativism. His model remained true to essentially realist assumptions about the relationship between what the scientist can know and how scientific laws mirror nature. For the classic philosophical realist, it is possible to imagine a tight, uncomplicated fit between the language of science and nature. In the Kuhnian model the paradigm shifts permit the scientist to adjust the angle from which the mirror is fixed on nature. The emphasis on paradigm shifts leaves the impression that at moments the mirrors can get a little fogged over by habits and clubbiness; but, in the Kuhnian model, science works because it corresponds to what is in nature, *more or less.* In contrast to a naive version of human knowing which conceives of the mind as a blank slate upon which sense date drawn from nature write, Kuhn saw the mind organized by theories, reinforced by social conventions. Kuhn did not believe, however, that the disclosure of the workings of theories or social conventions invalidated the scientific enterprise. It just made it a little more human.[5]

13   No amount of realism saved Kuhn from being blamed almost immediately for the rising skepticism about science. For even mentioning the social, he was accused of rendering the once objective into the hopelessly subjective. Because he said that scientific change is frequently the result of paradigm shifts made by small groups of scientists, critics said he made it seem that the "adoption of a new scientific theory is an intuitive or mystical affair, a matter for psychological description," rather than a matter of evidence and logic, pure and simple.[6] In the last thirty years *The Structure of Scientific Revolutions* has been translated into many languages and has sold over 750,000 copies worldwide. Kuhn's sociological vision of science became synonymous with retreat from the heroic model of scientists with their special purchase on truth. That retreat was, however, neither swift nor steady. Before it occurred, one final philosophical barrier had to be breached.

14   In the eyes of Kuhn's generation, the generation that fought and won World War II, heroic science had seemed both philosophically correct and morally necessary. Even the threat of nuclear destruction could not shake their conviction that science and its history provided, as Conant put it, "the basis for a better discussion of the ways in which rational methods may be applied to the study and solution of human problems."[7] As to what might be concluded from the history of twentieth-century nuclear science once the story got to the nuclear bomb, Conant assured Americans that its destructive power

might just be "the price we pay for health and comfort and aids to learning in this scientific age."[8] Believing that science laid the foundations for progress and rationality in the West, Conant and his generation of historians and scientists were not about to sacrifice it on the altar of social explanations. As Western scientists had done ever since Descartes, believers in heroic science grouped behind the barrier provided by philosophy. They were convinced that the social represented the irrational, and that only the mantle provided by logic and reason, philosophically understood, would save science from contamination.

THE PHILOSOPHICAL ARMOR OF HEROIC SCIENCE

15 Historians and scientists of the generation of Conant and Butterfield institutionalized the history of science in American universities because they believed that its history, as they understood it, underwrote the Enlightenment's vision of science. They also possessed a powerful moral armor in academic philosophy as it was taught from the 1940s onward. Its positive approach to science stressed that science, alone among the various forms of human inquiry, worked because of an inherent rationality. At the core of science lay logical rules upon which a few of the early geniuses of science had first managed to stumble. Right into the 1980s, in some quarters of public and academic opinion the legend of science had it that "successive generations of scientists have filled in more and more parts of the Complete True Story of the World."[9] It had been that simple and that positive.

16 The roots of a positive philosophy of science go back to Comte and the early nineteenth century, but more immediately to Vienna during the 1920s. There, one of the most influential philosophers of science in this century, Karl Popper, first published on the logic of scientific discovery. Forced to flee Austria and Germany in the 1930s because of Nazi persecution, Popper and his philosophical associates went to major English-speaking universities on both sides of the Atlantic. From those institutional bases their positive vision of how science works influenced historians, many of whom had been combatants against the evil that Popper and his colleagues had fled.

17 Buoyed by Popper and his associates, the latter sometimes called logical positivists, these philosophers taught that only a positive—and we would argue an essentially ahistorical—understanding of science could reinforce the barrier of reason in a century where reason had been in short supply.[10] Popper emphasized that cooperation among disinterested scientists makes for objective knowledge. If it cannot be falsified, this knowledge is true forever. In Popper's telling, the job of the philosopher was to understand how the game of science is played, how the scientist probes "into the unknown reality behind the appearances, and [is] anxious to learn from mistakes."[11] Allied to science, the philosopher explicates the philosophical logic working in it. The logic of science is distinctive, and the discipline provided by

scientific experimentation and mathematical reasoning rivets the mind on nature. The positive, unrelenting logic of science, the armor that girds Western truth-seeking, stands as the model for the methods of all other disciplines.

18   Popper's faith in the logic of science had been forged amid a bitter reality. Throughout much of this century the assault on rationality has been associated, quite rightly, with totalitarian political systems. Popper and his fellow refugees from Nazism saw its irrationalities as further support for their belief in the intimate link between the neutrality of science and the possibility of rational thought and action. Only the Nazis, they believed, had sought to manipulate science, and they of course were the great enemies of both reason and objectivity. The point was not lost on British and American intellectuals of the 1940s. They had watched with horror as fascism took hold in the heart of scientifically advanced industrial countries. Suddenly the Western enterprise with its commitment to scientific rationality seemed fragile at best. Added to its fragility came the threat posed by Soviet communism. Both before and after the war, the emergence of communism and Nazism provided very good reasons for preserving every aspect of the Enlightenment legacy. The generation that fought against totalitarianism and won World War II needed heroic science. Because those of that generation knew that totalitarianism was inherently immoral and its premises irrational, they naturally believed that science in totalitarian societies could not be rational.

19   The generation of Conant, Butterfield, and Nef viewed science through lenses that had been focused by Popper and his followers. Some of these philosophers believed that the methods of science and in particular its search for the laws of nature could be transferred to the social sciences and to the study of history. Historians should look for the laws of historical development. As late as the 1960s, students in American graduate schools of history were asked to read articles about the nature of history's "covering laws." That no historian had ever been able to find a single historical law that worked universally left the logical positivists unmoved.[12] Generally, and perhaps mercifully, most of them ignored history, regarding it as irrelevant to the task of explicating philosophically the rationality and neutrality of science. Their enterprise recalls the agenda set by those positivists of the nineteenth century, Comte and his followers. They too had named science—pure, simple, unadulterated—the last, positive stage of human inquiry.

20   Into the 1970s, Karl Popper was still arguing that the purpose of his philosophy of science had been to justify the rationality of science and to counter intellectual and moral relativism, which he saw as the main philosophical malady of the time. Popper worried about the renewed danger of relativism revived by Kuhn's book and the implications drawn from it by a rising generation of social historians. Of course, Popper had always thought that historical arguments would lead to relativism, and here it was back again, alive and well (even if hiding in the Trojan horse) in the work of Thomas Kuhn.

21   Popper took the highest ground he could find against a social reading of science by appealing to metaphysics. Imagine the contempt in his voice when he said: "I do not regard methodology as an empirical discipline, to be tested, perhaps by the facts of the history of science."[13] So much for the social history of science, at least as far as Popper and his followers were concerned. Instead Popper wrapped science in a mantle he described as metaphysical realism. Scientific method rested on the rules of logic, on the testing of theories, not simply upon fact-gathering. The relative success or failure of any empirically focused exploration of natural phenomena did not determine the rationality of science.

22   When Popper invoked metaphysical realism, he was trying to move the terrain right out from under the fact of the new social history of science. But he also wanted to be sophisticated and cautious about the way he mounted his philosophical rescue operation. As seen in the earlier discussion of heroic science, philosophical realism lies at the heart of its claim to represent nature exactly in its laws. When the scientist speaks, whatever the vernacular, his words are really about the eternally true, or the eternally unfalsifiable in Popper's important modification. Unlike all previous science, which barely deserves the name, true science depends upon the mirrors that the scientist flashes on the world.

23   But as Popper well knew, there are dangers in a naive version of the realist argument. What if accepted, everyday science gets it wrong and is overthrown by new, better science? Was Ptolemy doing bad science, or no science at all, when he postulated the earth in the center of the universe, an error which Copernicus and his followers caught only centuries later? Does progress in science render nonscientific everything that went before the latest discovery? To argue that science *is* nature in the sense that its laws correspond to what is actually going on in nature opens up as many philosophical problems as it seeks to close down.

24   Popper argued instead that the realism of science lies not in a naive correspondence between the empirically tested world and the mind of the scientist, but in the rules of logic, in falsification and verification. He preferred the term "metaphysical realism," because it suggested a model of science evolving by its own internal logic—a logic that transcends history—and leaves open the question of just how tight the fit need be between the laws and the there out there. Placed in opposition to the social history of science, metaphysical realism claims that there are "purely scientific revolutions that are not connected with *ideological* revolutions." In Popperian logic, ideology equals impurity, and both equal the illogical, and hence neither has anything to do with the actual thought processes of the scientist. Popper tried to save the scientific baby by taking it out of the historical water altogether before the skeptical social historians could come along and drown it in historicity. By contrast, we will argue that scientific revolutions are also ideological revolutions but that the ideological dimension does not undermine the validity of the scientific breakthrough. Science can be historically and socially framed and still be true.

THE GENERATION OF THE 1960s

25 Right up to the 1960s the understanding of science taught in American universities had stayed close to the triumphant story told by Andrew Dickson White at Cornell in the 1890s. The history of science had been written by men with strong backgrounds in science and little training in historical methods. In the history of medicine up to the 1960s the situation was similarly skewed toward doctors who also practiced history. Then a new generation of young women and men came to White's Cornell from the big East Coast cities, from parochial and public schools, from parents who had seen war service as ordinary soldiers, sometimes in segregated units, or who had immigrated from Eastern and Western Europe in this century. To their skepticism about elite culture was added the moral turmoil induced by the Vietnam War and the civil rights movement. Professionalization accompanied democratization. In perhaps the final irony of all, science fell under the gaze of science-inspired historical methods wielded by a new generation more interested in writing true history than in preserving the truth of science.

26   In nearly every field the new social history described in Chapter 4 challenged and dethroned the inherited intellectual absolutisms. When the same thing happened in the history of science, an icon of Western culture was undermined. The challenge ignited a war, what we will call, in honor of the terminology used at the time, the War between the Internalists and the Externalists. The so-called Internalists took an essentially Popperian position with regard to science. Its historical development occurred as the result of empirical work and the unfolding of the rules of logic. Basically the history of science had nothing to do with the social. The heroes of science got put up on their pedestals because they were true heroes, smarter and more creative than everyone else.

27   Under the influence of social history, a new generation of so-called Externalist historians of science looked for the larger interests and values at work within communities of scientists. The Externalist position—the term misleadingly predetermines what is inside and what must therefore be outside—vastly extended the definition of the social. Whereas Kuhn confined it to networks of scientists, the generation of the 1960s made it the universe beyond the laboratory or university. With the battle cry "social context," the Externalists took up arms against the Internalists. The war was waged, not surprisingly, around the pedestals of the scientific heroes.

28   Born under the shadow of the bomb, the generation of the 1960s took a very different approach to science from that of most of its predecessors, Kuhn included. Like the Progressive historians of an earlier era, they developed new methods and asked new questions in an effort to understand the role of interests and ideologies in the making of science. Given the strength of social history by the 1960s, the history of science, not surprisingly, took a turn toward the social, now broadly defined. In centuries where most men and more women were neither literate nor leisured, it was relatively easy to find the scientists among elites, sharing their social outlook and political

interests. Looking in private letters and diaries, social historians of science found the heroes of science immersed in the power relations of their time, willing to adopt or abandon theories for many complex, and not always disinterested, reasons. The new social historians sought to understand scientists in relation to governments, churches, religious beliefs, political ideologies, even with regard to their gender identities and their material assets and property.

29   In the expanded social understanding of science associated with the Externalists, the interests, values, linguistic conventions, even pride and greed of scientists shaped their understanding of nature. In effect, the definition of what should be considered internal to science changed dramatically. The heroes of science tumbled off their pedestals, their statuesque feet upon closer inspection seemed more clay than marble. Perhaps Popper had been right after all. If those mirrors in the heads of the heroes and founders of Western science could be shown to have been made by society, surely all of human knowledge could be revealed as socially constructed. The position was paradoxically a remake of the older realist, mirrors-in-the-head version of the scientific mind common among the positivists. The positivists and Internalists said that the scientists had mirrors always trained on nature; the extreme Externalists said that if so, those mirrors were the products of society. Thus trapped in the thicket of linguistic conventions, modern science succeeds only by using words like "nature" and "society" in ways that are entirely the result of linguistic moves made by seventeenth-century scientists like Boyle and Newton. They invented the modern meaning of "nature," and thereby tailor-made for themselves a world which they and their successors could in turn investigate.

30   Such a dramatic paradigm shift in the way historians understood science now requires inspection. The generation of Conant, Butterfield, and Nef would have been horrified by the gap that has opened between the few remaining defenders of heroic science and the social historians of science. Among Conant's generation, the great teachers of the postwar history of science, Henry Guerlac, I. B. Cohen, and Richard Westfall, never imagined that their discipline could even remotely challenge the truth and status of science. In the 1950s they began programs to train the next generation to study science historically. But once again, history intervened and a process we have described as the democratization of higher education began in earnest. By the time their programs were well established an explosion had occurred in the demand for college teachers and hence in the number of graduate students seeking higher degrees. Once trained and placed in the academy, the rising generation of historians turned to the heroes.

REEVALUATING THE HEROES: NEWTON AND DARWIN

31 Beginning in the 1960s, historians of science began to put the great icons of heroic science back into their social context. Not surprisingly, they look remarkably different when placed under a broad, social lens. The seventeenth-century English scientist Robert Boyle turned out to have formulated

his law of gases while deeply involved in political and religious issues.[14] Worse still, his contemporary Isaac Newton was discovered in his laboratory practicing alchemy—nothing is as external to heroic science as magic— while a century and a half later Charles Darwin put together the theory of natural selection with one eye on the impoverished classes. The history that produced these findings was never what Conant, or even Kuhn, had in mind. It was close, however, to fulfilling Popper's fear that the study of ideology at work in the mind of scientists would lead to philosophical relativism. Could science still be true when it resulted from such a messy, seemingly irrational process of thought?

32   Venturing into seventeenth-century England to discover the social lair inhabited by the great geniuses of science can be a formidable excursion. Concepts like "matter theory" or definitions of pantheism do not readily spring to mind. Even defining an Anglican, never mind a Leveller or a Digger, taxes the historical memory. Yet those were household words to the age when Newton lived. If you want to understand someone born in 1642, there is no escaping a brief journey into baroque metaphysics and religious sectarianism. Broaching the new social history of science requires some general history. Consolation may be found in knowing that after Newton, Darwin cannot be too far away.

33   Once, Westerners had a tidy picture of Newton, the rationalist. It seemed that nothing would ever destroy it, but in the 1930s new evidence about Isaac Newton, who had died two hundred years before in 1727, surfaced in the form of thousands of unpublished manuscripts. When they came up for auction in 1936 at Sotheby's in London, many were discovered to be of a decidedly "unscientific" character. Few bidders could be found for the hundreds of theological and alchemical manuscripts in the collection. At bargain prices, they dispersed to every corner of the globe, some probably lost forever. It was only in the 1960s with the professionalization of the history of science that anyone bothered to take a serious look at Newton's private writings. What historians found turned out to weaken further the model of science beloved by the logical positivists and their many followers. New evidence sometimes gives rise to anomalies, for both historians and scientists.

34   Reexamining the writings, both published and unpublished, of the titan of the Enlightenment revealed an Isaac Newton radically at odds with the secular hero. Newton can now be shown to have rejected certain philosophical positions not simply because the science they supported was wrong, but also, and perhaps primarily, because he believed that those positions would lead to atheism. Good seventeenth-century Protestant that he was, Newton rejected Descartes's theory of matter because it led to the denial of God's activity in the universe, and hence in Newton's mind to atheism. The Cartesian universe worked because it was completely filled: bodies moved by constantly colliding with each other; all motion resulted from the mechanical push-pull interaction between bodies, whether large or minuscule like an ether; no spiritual agency was necessary.[15]

35   Newton's unpublished writings, now housed in libraries from California to Israel, show him to be horrified by the religious implication of the filled

Cartesian universe. To him Descartes's universe appeared not only self-regulated but also self-perpetuating, and hence godless.

36   The new socially focused scholarship on Newton saw religious values at work in his rejection of Descartes, and the new scholarship also revealed Newton's fascination with alchemy. The question loomed large: had Newton, one of the founders of modern science, in fact reneged on the central commitment of the new science, to pursue nature through experiment and not through magical shortcuts? Did Newton sacrifice science on the altar of his religious convictions? If historians frame the questions in ways that reflect their definitions of what science must be like, refusing to suspend belief in those definitions, then even Newton fails the test.

37   Religiosity approached historically held the key to explaining how Newton understood nature and science. Because of his belief in the supreme power and authority of God, as expressed through spiritual agents and immaterial forces at work in the universe, Newton was able to escape the trap set by magic on one side—seen as fostering a kind of atheism because it made nature and magicians into forces independent from the deity—and on the other move beyond the prevailing science of his day, the Cartesian model. Newton postulated a universe with empty space dominated by spiritual forces: God, angels, "active principles," even Christ. Space became, to use his metaphor, the sensorium of God wherein He established contact with His creation. In Newton's view, the matter of the universe was dead, "brute and stupid," moved only by immaterial forces. With this model, Newton could abandon contact action between bodies as the key to motion in the Cartesian universe. He could also devote a good portion of his working life to alchemical experiments. To him they revealed the presence of invisible forces derived from an all-powerful creator. Whether Newton was studying planets or minuscule portions of chemical substances, he sought to demonstrate definitively God's creative force and continuing power.

38   Without the religious element in his life, Newton could not have articulated the law of universal gravitation. Newton's social universe, as it worked into his science, lay just as much in the chapel of Trinity College, Cambridge, as it did in his laboratory. Religious conviction enabled him to conceptualize universal gravitation. Divinely implanted, gravitation operates as a force in a universe composed of planets at motion in a vacuum. The physical truth of the mathematical law could finally be possible for Newton because of his religious and metaphysical convictions.

•   •   •

39   Newton's idea of the absolute, eternal truth of every aspect of his science followed from his belief in his God and his concomitant fear of atheism. With God in place, Newton knew there could be order in the universe, possibly also in society. There could also be absolute Truth which existed in a higher spiritual realm into which the world offered only occasional moments of insight. The kind of transcendent truth that Newton believed his science to possess, and that he bequeathed to the Enlightenment,

started with a transference. He transferred divine authority to the laws of science. Three centuries after the first major revolution in the West it is possible to see the origins of the modern belief in the transcendence of scientific rationality in those distant seventeenth-century struggles to maintain the transcendence of the deity, to assert the supremacy of orthodox Christianity over heresy and disorder.

•   •   •

40   Their religious and philosophical roots buried in his private papers, Newton's laws bequeathed to the Enlightenment an understanding of nature as mathematical, ordered, and harmonious. With the assistance of some of Newton's closest associates, the *Principia* was also used against the atheists, to argue that God had designed the Newtonian universe. But gradually and ironically, the immediacy of Newton's God faded out of the Newtonian universe, and deism became the commonplace creed of many an educated person in eighteenth-century Europe. The invisible hand of the ordering deity became increasingly remote, and in the nineteenth century under the impact of Darwin's writings it became irrelevant.

•   •   •

41   Darwin's wide familiarity with economics and social theory through the writings of Adam Smith, Auguste Comte, and especially Thomas Malthus facilitated his development of an explanation for what he had seen on his exploratory 5-year voyage. A generation earlier in his *Essay on Population* (1798), Malthus had formulated a law of population development which stated that while the food supply increases arithmetically, as one plus one, people increase exponentially, two times two. To curtail the growth of the masses and thus to obviate the necessity for this struggle, Malthus recommended sexual abstinence, particularly for the lower orders, whom he regarded as almost a separate race. The Malthusian perspective reinforced policies toward the poor being advocated by middle-class reformers. They would make the poor work and force them to compete, rather than remain tied to the charity of their betters. Many of these same liberal reformers were also freethinkers, eager to reform science, to make it less subservient to Christian doctrine and the influence of the clergy. It too should stand on its own, not shackled by the tyranny of dogma.

42   As a liberal Whig with industrialists in his family, Darwin sympathized with the reforming impulse. His recent biographers describe his circle as a place where "politics, science and literature were all of a piece."[16] Reform suggested that the present was better than the past, that in effect the superior drove out the inferior. In addition, the idea that struggle was at the heart of the development of a species, the Malthusian vision of population survival of the strongest with containment of the weakest by plague and famine, set Darwin to thinking. Before him lay the evidence he collected of fossils and birds which suggested that species had replaced other species, or

that in certain geographical conditions only species with certain characteristics survived.

43   The fossil evidence came from his years of travel, and with it uppermost in his mind Darwin sat in his London study reading among scientists as well as theorists of market society. Perhaps the constant pressure for survival experienced by variants within an animal or human population wedged them into certain niches from which they might perish or develop. Out of the variants new species would emerge. Perhaps species are not fixed after all, simply God-given. Did he not live in a society where the poor were manifestly weaker, struggling to survive? Did it not appear that the obviously superior Europeans, heady from technological and imperial pursuits, had evolved because of certain characteristics that made it seem ridiculous now in the present that they would ever again fear barbarians?[17] Did it not seem that the reform movements of the 1830s signaled the evolving progress and improvement of society and government? These were questions alive in Darwin's intellectual circle but also in the larger society.

44   Darwin needed the social ideas of Malthus and others, for without them he could not have formulated the explanatory and theoretical mechanism of natural selection. Randomness—the random mutations of species—could work toward their survival or extinction, and it lay at the heart of Darwin's model. But randomness was incompatible with any belief in the divine oversight of fixed species or with a moment for special human creation. Newton's God could not have permitted the natural world seen by Darwin. Darwin needed a different metaphysics, his slowly, even painfully, acquired and very privately held atheism and materialism. Now with access to Darwin's diaries listen to him say, almost offhandedly to himself, "It is an argument for materialism, that cold water brings on suddenly in [the] head, a frame of mind, analogous to those feelings which may be considered as truly spiritual." Hardly the sentiments of a Christian, or even of a theist. Almost incredulous, Darwin wondered to himself if it wasn't "a little remarkable that the fixed laws of nature should be 'universally' thought to be the *will* of a superior being."[18] Newton would have been horrified if he had ever peered into the heart of Charles Darwin.

45   The social attitudes of an imperial and market-oriented society in which continuous reform seemed possible were woven through Darwin's science. On one hand Darwin the materialist could conceptualize human equality—simply the equality of all atoms—randomly selected; the inheritance of acquired characteristics was incompatible with random selection. But Darwin the British gentleman could also effortlessly imagine that moral superiority, a characteristic so fortuitously acquired by Westerners, particularly by men, might even be inherited: "the low morality of savages . . . their insufficient power of reasoning . . . weak power of self-command . . . this power has not been strengthened through long-continued, perhaps inherited habit, instruction and religion."[19] Darwin's racial and sexual views permeated his discussion of the origin of species and especially of

the descent of man. His contemporaries were shocked by the notion that human beings had evolved from the primates. Now many people are shocked by his racism.

• • •

TRUTH WITHOUT THE HEROES

46 The social history of science suggests that people create knowledge in time and space. Such truths do not permit access to the transcendent realm that Newton believed his science could reveal. This limitation constrains science, making it neither very heroic nor grand, but leaving it both rational and powerful. Indeed, unheroic truths even have their philosophical advocates. Since the early nineteenth century and the writings of the German philosopher Hegel, Westerners have been able to articulate a human situation in which truths occur in history, in which forms of knowledge are invented by human beings trapped in time, deeply influenced by the social and natural worlds around them.

47 Historicizing science has rendered it the work of human beings; it becomes truth-seeking and truth-finding without the possibility of transcendence. Despite what Newton, and even Hegel believed, there can be no dwelling among the gods. But Popper also got it wrong when he thought that historicity makes relativism inevitable. It is possible to have scientific revolutions influenced by both technical problems *and* ideologies. The one need not exclude the other, now or in the past.

48 Historians of science sometimes get the defenders of science very mad because they think that historical reconstruction suggests the futility of believing that science can produce a workable, practical truth. They assume that the social historians are the new relativists who would deny the possibility of articulating laws reasonably true to nature. They wrongly presume that historians embrace what can be called, somewhat ironically, an absolute, as opposed to a methodological, relativism. The method of relativism draws upon Descartes's prescription "I imitated the skeptics who doubt only for doubting's sake . . . in order to find rock or clay."[20] Skepticism, or relativism, by this method becomes a means toward the end of finding a more workable truth. In other words, to do the history of science, the historian begins with a willing suspension of belief. If you presume that Newton was simply right, it becomes harder to ask what he thought he was doing and why he did it. Historically situating any body of knowledge, including science, is how historians go about the job of discovering, describing, and explaining the past. But did not the methods of science help shape the practices of modern historians? Some might say that in the course of applying their critical methods, especially to the truth claims of science, modern historians have become an ungrateful lot.

49 The charge of ingratitude should not be dismissed lightly. Watching the assault mounted in this century against truth and the search for objectivity by various forms of totalitarianism, some people have concluded that putting

history back into science will undermine its truth and the achievements of its practitioners. But it is not necessary for the historian to endorse that conclusion in order to see the larger issue. Given the status and achievements of modern science, its relativizing would be the ultimate goal in any project to destabilize the search for truths or the endorsement of objectivity. Because the study of history, as well as the entire enterprise of Western learning, has been tied to science since the Enlightenment, the demise of heroic science has implications for all historians. Denying the possibility of truth produces a relativism that makes it impossible to choose between ethical systems. And since the demise of Newton's God, epistemological and moral relativisms are always a possibility; indeed, they are even once again fashionable.

50   But relativism need not be the only option. Just because science, like everything else, has a history does not mean the end of truth. It does mean that the nineteenth-century philosophers attributed far too much to its power, and then in the process tried to make history be like it. In the nineteenth-century sense, there is no scientific history, nor is there even scientific science. But it is possible to know some things more rather than less truly. In their respective realms, both history and science seek to do that. Given the issues about truth and relativism that have been raised late in this century, historians cannot pretend that it is business as usual. It is essential to rethink the understanding of truth and objectivity. Faced with what is known about the interaction of the social and the scientific, philosophers of science are groping their way through the thicket, and so, too, must historians and scientists.

51   Philosophers can offer historians some help in the debate about relativism. Most of them have moved beyond the positivist/social constructionist dichotomy. Their approach to the problem of truth-seeking is relevant to any discipline coming to terms with the social, gendered, temporal, and linguistic nature of human knowledge and with the concomitant challenge of relativism. Historically informed philosophers argue, for instance, that the social nature of scientific work is part of its essence, not simply the aftermath of too much conference-attending. In other words, the social is essential to scientific truth-seeking. "Scientific knowledge cannot be reduced to the knowledge of an individual and cannot be understood in terms of processes in principle individualistic, such as the simple additive accumulation of the individual's knowledges."[21] Social perspectives such as these do not seek to deny the existence of truths hard won by reasoned inquiry and contestation (even if the struggle appears to be largely private, resembling Newton's dialogue with Descartes). Rather they point toward renewed understandings of objectivity, of how reason works in complex ways. They imply that the objective does not simply reside within each individual, but rather is achieved by criticism, contention, and exchange. Without the social process of science—cumulative, contested, and hence at moments ideological—there is no science as it has come to be known since the seventeenth century. Criticism fosters objectivity and thereby enhances reasoned inquiry. Objectivity is not a stance arrived at by sheer willpower, nor is it the way most people, most of

the time, make their daily inquiries. Instead it is the result of the clash of social interests, ideologies, and social conventions within the framework of object-oriented and disciplined knowledge-seeking. Encouragement to continue seeking comes from truths discovered in time, a temporal process preserved by memory and history for all time.

52   An argument emphasizing the social character of scientific research points directly toward the history of democratic practices and institutions in the West. The emergence of a relatively free social space for discussion and contention depended upon the creation of civil society. Still other aspects of the Enlightenment's legacy are germane. Hermeneutics, the art of interpreting the world through its texts, applies to both scientific and historical truth-seeking. There is a hermeneutics within science. Scientists give meaning to objects; they too are bound by linguistic conventions, by discourse. Even experimental and experiential knowledge has to be expressed by languages which can embody theoretical presuppositions and social values. "Facts," before they can be discussed, must be named.[22] Such arguments should not undercut the ability to say meaningfully true things about the world. Regardless of language and human linguistic conventions, nature, whether in the form of planets or microbes, would still be real, out there and behaving in predictable ways, even if there were no way of saying so.[23] Colliding with a moving object repeatedly could, however, only illicit a growl and never the law of inertia.

53   From this philosophical perspective the scientist's language, or the historian's language, becomes actively involved in the knowledge created. When Newton used the word "matter" he had to have in his mind an entity without life or will before he could have conceived of a separate dynamic, gravitational force in the universe. And the words "force" and "universe" and "God" all had to have meanings distinctive to his mind and hence to his time. This does not mean, however, that no longer believing as Newton did that matter is "brute and stupid," twentieth-century people cannot understand or refine the law of universal gravitation. Or take Darwin. When he saw the evidence for species that had perished he could imagine random survival partly because of the harsh circumstances of survival he witnessed in the social world that nurtured him so comfortably. Neither historical insight undercuts the truth of evolutionary biology or Newtonian mechanics; both offer a historical perspective on the hermeneutics through which truths were discovered. Truths hard won by human beings, however mired in time and language, can make for consoling allies. In the darkest moments of this century they have kept many people from despair. Historicizing any moment need not, should not, sacrifice the truths people discovered in it. Indeed, historicizing entails imitating their quest, searching for other kinds of knowledge, for historical knowledge.

54   Precisely as a consequence of that search, the absolutist, heroic science bequeathed to the twentieth century by the true believers of previous centuries came under fire. In the postwar era, given the role played by science and technology in war-making, the very nature of science had to be dissected and reevaluated. No body of knowledge of such power, no group of men (or

women) with such command of resources—some kept secret from public inspection—could be allowed to go unexamined and unchallenged. The icon of heroic science found its iconoclasts. Yet not despite but because of all that is now known about the unheroic, deeply social nature of scientific truth-seeking, science still stands at the center of the enterprise of knowing. A democratic society with roots in the Enlightenment depends upon the positioning of science, upon the affirmation it gives to the human ability to reason independently and successfully about objects outside the mind, while recognizing the social and ideological dimension of all knowledge.

NOTES

1. Ann Markusen, Peter Hall, Scott Campbell, and Sabina Deitrick, *The Rise of the Gun Belt: The Military Remapping of Industrial America* (New York, 1991), p. 3. And for prescriptions, Ann Markusen, "Dismantling the Cold War Economy," *World Policy Journal,* Summer 1992, pp. 389-99. See also Arnold Thackray, ed., *Science After '40* (Chicago, 1992) and Stuart W. Leslie, *American Science and the Cold War* (New York, 1992).
2. John U. Nef, *Cultural Foundations of Industrial Civilization* (Cambridge, England, 1958), pp. 23, 64.
3. Herbert Butterfield, *The Origins of Modern Science 1300-1800* (New York, 1957), p. 201.
4. The following essay offers a similar analysis of what Kuhn said: Steve Fuller, "Being There with Thomas Kuhn: A Parable for Postmodern Times," *History and Theory,* 31 (1992): 241-75.
5. We owe our emphasis here to Ruth Bloch.
6. Israel Scheffler, *Science and Subjectivity* (New York, 1967), p. 18.
7. James B. Conant, *On Understanding Science: An Historical Approach* (New Haven, 1947), pp. xii-xiii.
8. Ibid., p. 5.
9. Written with irony by Philip Kitcher, *The Advancement of Science: Science without Legend, Objectivity without Illusions* (New York, 1993), p. 3.
10. In the interest of brevity we have necessarily elided the differences between Popper and many logical positivists. We take Popper as the emblematic figure because of his enduring interest in the questions that concern us here; cf. Robert Proctor, *Value-Free Science? Purity and Power in Modern Knowledge* (Cambridge, Mass., 1991), pp. 209-12.
11. Karl P. Popper, *Realism and the Aim of Science* (Totowa, N.J., 1983), p. xxv. Much of this was written in the 1950s, but publication was delayed into the 1980s.
12. In saying there are no universal laws of history, we do not seek to deny the possibility of there being patterns of cause and effect that may even on occasion be replicable. For covering laws, see C. G. Hempel, "The Function of General Laws in History," *Journal of Philosophy,* 39 (1942): 35-48; and for a discussion of Hempel's position, see Louis O. Mink, *Historical Understanding,* eds. Brian Fay, Eugene O. Golob, and Richard T. Vann (Ithaca, N.Y., 1987).
13. Popper, *Realism,* p. xxv.

14. James R. Jacob, *Robert Boyle and the English Revolution* (New York, 1977).

15. See A. Rupert Hall and Marie Boas Hall, trans. and eds., *Unpublished Scientific Paper of Isaac Newton* (Cambridge, 1962), pp. 142–43.

16. Adrian Desmond and James Moore, *Darwin* (New York, 1991), p. 216, quoting Herschel. The quotation about his delight is on p. 140 and comes from a letter Darwin wrote to a friend. The mention of the "gradual birth and death of species" comes from his notes taken on the *Beagle* and refers to his reading of Lyell (p. 159).

17. David R. Oldroyd, "How Did Darwin Arrive at His Theory? The Secondary Literature to 1982," *History of Science,* 22 (1984): 325–74; on the barbarians, see Charles Darwin, *The Descent of Man, and Selection in Relation to Sex,* vol. 1 (London, 1871), p. 239.

18. Paul H. Barrett, Peter J. Gautrey, Sandra Herbert, et al., eds., *Charles Darwin's Notebooks, 1836-1844. Geology, Transmutation of Species, Metaphysical Enquiries* (Ithaca, N.Y., 1987), pp. 524, 535. Both excerpts were written in 1838.

19. Darwin, *Descent of Man,* vol. 1, pp. 225, 97.

20. René Descartes, *Discourse on Method and The Meditations* (New York, 1968), p. 50.

21. Helen E. Longino, *Science as Social Knowledge: Values and Objectivity in Scientific Inquiry* (Princeton, N.J., 1990), p. 231.

22. Joseph Rouse, *Knowledge and Power: Toward a Political Philosophy of Science* (Ithaca, N.Y., 1987), p. 47.

23. See Charles S. Peirce, "Critical Review of Berkeley's Idealism," in *Values in a Universe of Chance: Selected Writings of Charles S. Peirce,* ed. Philip P. Wiener (New York, 1958), p. 84.

FOLLOW-UP ACTIVITIES

Discussing the Rhetoric

1. Who do you think is the authors' intended audience for this reading? Are you one of its members? How do you know?

2. Although the authors have many purposes in this long essay, what is their overall purpose? Is it stated explicitly, or is it implied?

3. Identify at least three significant rhetorical strategies the authors use to substantiate their thesis.

4. Where does the voice in this piece sound like a textbook? Where does it sound like researchers arguing for the acceptance of their vision of the "truth"? What can you conclude about the rhetorical and stylistic differences between the situation of writing a textbook for students and writing up research results for colleagues?

Discussing the Conversation

1. What do these authors contribute to Part Two's conversation about the value of the discipline of the history of science?

2. Note the attention to metaphysical commitments in the piece. Where else have you encountered this focus? How do Appleby and her co-authors' views compare to other writers'?

3. What new questions arise in this essay regarding how knowledge is made and how it should be made? That is, how do the authors go beyond, for example, Schiebinger's perspective?

4. In section 3 of this reading, the authors retrace Sir Karl Popper's "positive approach to science." They conclude that "Popper tried to save the scientific baby by taking it out of the historical water altogether before the skeptical social historians could come along and drown it in historicity." This inference concurs with other authors who have tried to illustrate the dangers of separating the activities of science from culture, or history. Recall who those authors are, and locate passages in their readings which support this point of view.

5. The authors go into great detail re-evaluating two heroes of science: Newton and Darwin. In what way do these re-evaluations serve to further support the thesis of this reading? Keller's thesis? Schiebinger's thesis?

Joining the Conversation

After reviewing the last section of the reading, "Truth Without Heroes," write an informal paper in which you respond to the following questions:

- According to the authors, is historical objectivity possible?
- Recall a time in childhood when a hero you had was contested. How did you respond? Did you defend your beliefs? Or did you give up your hero?

INTRODUCTORY COMMENTS ON "INDIANS: TEXTUALISM, MORALITY, AND THE PROBLEM OF HISTORY" BY JANE TOMPKINS

Reading the Context

This selection, originally published in *Critical Inquiry* (1986), may seem to be about history, but it also concerns the more general issue of academic research. Looking to unsettle and reformulate the methods historians use to tell tales, Jane Tompkins also examines how academics in general produce and justify knowledge claims. She performs this work by writing a "rhetorical analysis," much like the rhetorical analysis writing assignment described in Part Four of this text, in which she examines the contexts of some examples of historical writing. The content of the historical treaties she cites become meaningful to Tompkins only within the context of their historical and cultural moment. But, as she discovers, those contexts are difficult to interpret.

Tompkins is not primarily a historian; she is also a literary critic and English professor. As a result, her work focuses on literary practices and the cultural work they perform. One of the methodologies literary critics frequently employ is called "hermeneutics." You might recall the term from "Discovering the Clay Feet of Science" by Appleby, Hunt, and Jacob. This term is commonly defined as "interpretive understanding." Originally, hermeneutics was a method used to interpret biblical texts. It was used to establish meanings of texts in their own terms, as well as taking the text's meanings for contemporary readers into account. Expanded beyond analysis of literary texts, hermeneutics is now more commonly viewed as applicable to all events and situations that can be subjected to interpretation. Moreover, the concept of hermeneutics is frequently set in opposition to the concept of positivism by many critical theorists. Both concepts have been historically employed as epistemic methods, or methods for gathering knowledge. Like many literary theorists, Tompkins uses hermeneutical, or interpretative methods in this selection to challenge positivistic ways of knowing.

Tompkins received her undergraduate degree from Bryn Mawr College (1961) and her masters (1962) and doctorate (1966) from Yale University. Her numerous writings include four books and many essays for professional journals.

Reading the Rhetoric

Considering that Tompkins is writing about the problems of constructing knowledge within academia, her essay is a surprising mix of personal stories, anecdotes, and examples. Much of her essay is spent trying to convince her readers that there is a problem with how history is currently recorded and read. If, as she concludes in the essay, individual perspectives can "alter" or maybe even "create" knowledge, it is important that Tompkins reflect on her own historical moment. In effect, she examines how her own understandings, beliefs, cultural ties, and education influence her telling of history. Notice how her rhetorical choices reinforce her challenges to naive positivistic assumptions about the availability of truth to careful observers.

As you read, pay attention to how Tompkins divides her essay into a problem/solution structure. Think about whom she is trying to convince. Notice how much of her essay is devoted to documenting the problem and how much is spent suggesting a solution. Why would she spend a greater proportion on one rather than the other?

You will probably encounter some unfamiliar words while reading Tompkins. Pay careful attention to how Tompkins defines the terms she uses. How does her language identify her as a member of certain academic (or discourse) communities?

Reading the Conversation

Since Tompkins argues that one's personal situation affects one's interpretation of reality, it is interesting to note that in 1982, four years before she published this essay, Jane Tompkins married Stanley Fish. Compare Fish's theory of "interpretive communities" with Tompkins' theory of perspectivism. Does one provide a foundation for the other? Does one challenge, support, or build upon the ideas introduced in the other?

All of the essays in Part Two deal with factors that affect our "construction" or "understanding" of the world around us. As you read, think about what methods Tompkins uses to decide what's "true." Compare her methodology to the scientific method, as it's represented by E. D. Klemke in "Science and Nonscience."

Indians: Textualism, Morality, and the Problem of History
Jane Tompkins

1 When I was growing up in New York City, my parents used to take me to an event in Inwood Park at which Indians—real American Indians dressed in feathers and blankets—could be seen and touched by children like me. This event was always a disappointment. It was more fun to imagine that you *were* an Indian in one of the caves in Inwood Park than to shake the hand of an old man in a headdress who was not overwhelmed at the opportunity of meeting you. After staring at the Indians for a while, we would take a walk in the woods where the caves were, and once I asked my mother if the remains of a fire I had seen in one of them might have been left by the original inhabitants. After that, wandering up some stone steps cut into the side of the hill, I imagined I was a princess in a rude castle. My Indians, like my princesses, were creatures totally of the imagination, and I did not care to have any real exemplars interfering with what I already knew.

2 I already knew about Indians from having read about them in school. Over and over we were told the story of how Peter Minuit had bought Manhattan Island from the Indians for twenty-four dollars' worth of glass beads. And it was a story we didn't mind hearing because it gave us the rare pleasure of having someone to feel superior to, since the poor Indians had not known (as we eight-year-olds did) how valuable a piece of property Manhattan Island would become. Generally, much was made of the Indian

presence in Manhattan: a poem in one of our readers began: "Where we walk to school today/ Indian children used to play," and we were encouraged to write poetry on this topic ourselves. So I had a fairly rich relationship with Indians before I ever met the unprepossessing people in Inwood Park. I felt that I had a lot in common with them. They, too, liked animals (they were often named after animals); they, too, made mistakes—they liked the brightly colored trinkets of little value that the white men were always offering them; they were handsome, warlike, and brave and had led an exciting, romantic life in the forest long ago, a life such as I dreamed of leading myself. I felt lucky to be living in one of the places where they had definitely been. Never mind where they were or what they were doing now.

3   My story stands for the relationship most non-Indians have to the people who first populated this continent, a relationship characterized by narcissistic fantasies of freedom and adventure, of a life lived closer to nature and to spirit than the life we lead now. As Vine Deloria, Jr., has pointed out, the American Indian Movement in the early seventies couldn't get people to pay attention to what was happening to Indians who were alive in the present, so powerful was this country's infatuation with people who wore loincloths, lived in tepees, and roamed the plains and forests long ago.[1] The present essay, like these fantasies, doesn't have much to do with actual Indians, though its subject matter is the histories of European-Indian relations in seventeenth-century New England. In a sense, my encounter with Indians as an adult doing "research" replicates the childhood one, for while I started out to learn about Indians, I ended up preoccupied with a problem of my own.

4   This essay enacts a particular instance of the challenge poststructuralism poses to the study of history. In simpler language, it concerns the difference that point of view makes when people are giving accounts of events, whether at first or second hand. The problem is that if all accounts of events are determined through and through by the observer's frame of reference, then one will never know, in any given case what really happened.

5   I encountered this problem in concrete terms while preparing to teach a course in colonial American literature. I'd set out to learn what I could about the Puritans' relations with American Indians. All I wanted was a general idea of what had happened between the English settlers and the natives in seventeenth-century New England; poststructuralism and its dilemmas were the furthest thing from my mind. I began, more or less automatically, with Perry Miller, who hardly mentions the Indians at all, then proceeded to the work of historians who had dealt exclusively with the European-Indian encounter. At first, it was a question of deciding which of these authors to believe, for it quickly became apparent that there was no unanimity on the subject. As I read on, however, I discovered that the problem was more complicated than deciding whose version of events was correct. Some of the conflicting accounts were not simply contradictory, they were completely incommensurable, in that their assumptions about what counted as a valid approach to the subject, and what the subject itself was, diverged in fundamental ways. Faced with an

array of mutually irreconcilable points of view, points of view which determined what was being discussed as well as the terms of the discussion, I decided to turn to primary sources for clarification, only to discover that the primary sources reproduced the problem all over again. I found myself, in other words, in an epistemological quandary, not only unable to decide among conflicting versions of events but also unable to believe that any such decision could, in principle, be made. It was a moral quandary as well. Knowledge of what really happened when the Europeans and the Indians first met seemed particularly important, since the result of that encounter was virtual genocide. This was the kind of past "mistake" which, presumably, we studied history in order to avoid repeating. If studying history couldn't put us in touch with actual events and their causes, then what was to prevent such atrocities from happening again?

6   For a while, I remained at this impasse. But through analyzing the process by which I had reached it, I eventually arrived at an understanding which seemed to offer a way out. This essay records the concrete experience of meeting and solving the difficulty I have just described (as an abstract problem, I thought I had solved it long ago). My purpose is not to throw new light on antifoundationalist epistemology—the solution I reached is not a new one—but to dramatize and expose the troubles antifoundationalism gets you into when you meet it, so to speak, in the road.

7   My research began with Perry Miller. Early in the preface to *Errand into the Wilderness,* while explaining how he came to write his history of the New England mind, Miller writes a sentence that stopped me dead. He says that what fascinated him as a young man about his country's history was "the massive narrative of the movement of European culture into the vacant wilderness of America."[2] "Vacant?" Miller, writing in 1956, doesn't pause over the word "vacant," but to people who read his preface thirty years later, the word is shocking. In what circumstances could someone proposing to write a history of colonial New England *not* take account of the Indian presence there?

8   The rest of Miller's preface supplies an answer to this question, if one takes the trouble to piece together its details. Miller explains that as a young man, jealous of older compatriots who had had the luck to fight in World War I, he had gone to Africa in search of adventure. "The adventures that Africa afforded," he writes, "were tawdry enough, but it became the setting for a sudden epiphany" (p. vii). "It was given to me," he writes, "disconsolate on the edge of a jungle of central Africa, to have thrust upon me the mission of expounding what I took to be the innermost propulsion of the United States, while supervising, in that barbaric tropic, the unloading of drums of case oil flowing out of the inexhaustible wilderness of America" (p. viii). Miller's picture of himself on the banks of the Congo furnishes a key to the kind of history he will write and to his mental image of a vacant wilderness: it explains why it was just there, under precisely these conditions, that he should have had his epiphany.

9   The fuel drums stand, in Millers mind, for the popular misconception of what this country is about. They are "tangible symbols of [America's] appalling power," a power that everyone but Miller takes for the ultimate reality (p. ix). To Miller, "the mind of man is the basic factor in human history," and he will plead, all unaccommodated as he is among the fuel drums, for the intellect—the intellect for which his fellow historians, with their chapters on "stoves and bathtubs, or tax laws," "the Wilmot Proviso" and "the chain store," "have so little respect" (p. viii, ix). His preface seethes with a hatred of the merely physical and mechanical, and this hatred, which is really a form of moral outrage, explains not only the contempt with which he mentions the stoves and bathtubs but also the nature of his experience in Africa and its relationship to the "massive narrative" he will write.

10   Miller's experiences in Africa are "tawdry," his tropic is barbaric because the jungle he stands on the edge of means nothing to him, no more, indeed something less, than the case oil. It is the nothingness of Africa that precipitates his vision. It is the barbarity of the "dark continent," the obvious (but superficial) parallelism between the jungle at Matadi and America's "vacant wilderness" that releases in Miller the desire to define and vindicate his country's cultural identity. To the young Miller, colonial Africa and colonial America are—but for the history he will bring to light—mirror images of one another. And what he fails to see in the one landscape is the same thing he overlooks in the other: the human beings who people it. As Miller stood with his back to the jungle, thinking about the role of mind in human history, his failure to see that the land into which European culture had moved was not vacant but already occupied by a varied and numerous population, is of a piece with his failure, in his portrait of himself at Matadi, to notice *who* was carrying the fuel drums he was supervising the unloading of.

11   The point is crucial because it suggests that what is invisible to the historian in his own historical moment remains invisible when he turns his gaze to the past. It isn't that Miller didn't "see" the black men, in a literal sense, any more than it's the case that when he looked back he didn't "see" the Indians, in the sense of not realizing they were there. Rather, it's that neither the Indians nor the blacks *counted* for him, in a fundamental way. The way in which Indians can be seen but not counted is illustrated by an entry in Governor John Winthrop's journal, three hundred years before, when he recorded that there had been a great storm with high winds "yet through God's great mercy it did not hurt, but only killed one Indian with the fall of a tree."[3] The juxtaposition suggests that Miller shared with Winthrop a certain colonial point of view, a point of view from which Indians, though present, do not finally matter.

12   A book entitled *New England Frontier: Puritans and Indians, 1620-1675,* written by Alden Vaughan and published in 1965, promised to rectify Miller's omission. In the outpouring of work on the European-Indian encounter that began in the early sixties, this book is the first major landmark, and to a neophyte it seems definitive. Vaughan acknowledges the absence of Indian sources and emphasizes his use of materials which catch the

Puritans "off guard."[4] His announced conclusion that "the New England Puritans followed a remarkably humane, considerate, and just policy in their dealings with the Indians" seems supported by the scope, documentation, and methodicalness of his project (*NEF,* p. vii). The author's fair-mindedness and equanimity seem everywhere apparent, so that when he asserts "the history of interracial relations from the arrival of the Pilgrims to the outbreak of King Philip's War is a credit to the integrity of both peoples," one is positively reassured (*NEF,* p. viii).

13   But these impressions do not survive an admission that comes late in the book, when, in the course of explaining why works like Helen Hunt Jackson's *Century of Dishonor* had spread misconceptions about Puritan treatment of the Indians, Vaughan finally lays his own cards on the table.

> The root of the misunderstanding [about Puritans and Indians] . . . lie[s] in a failure to recognize the nature of the two societies that met in seventeenth-century New England. One was unified, visionary, disciplined, and dynamic. The other was divided, self-satisfied, undisciplined, and static. It would be unreasonable to expect that such societies could live side by side indefinitely with no penetration of the more fragmented and passive by the more consolidated and active. What resulted, then, was not—as many have held—a clash of dissimilar ways of life, but rather the expansion of one into the areas in which the other was lacking. [*NEF,* p. 323]

From our present vantage point, these remarks seem culturally biased to an incredible degree, not to mention inaccurate: was Puritan society unified? If so, how does one account for its internal dissensions and obsessive need to cast out deviants? Is "unity" necessarily a positive culture trait? From what standpoint can one say that American Indians were neither disciplined nor visionary, when both these characteristics loom so large in the ethnographies? Is it an accident that ways of describing cultural strength and weakness coincide with gender stereotypes active/passive, and so on? Why is one culture said to "penetrate" the other? Why is the "other" described in terms of "lack"?

14   Vaughan's fundamental categories of apprehension and judgment will not withstand even the most cursory inspection. For what looked like even-handedness when he was writing *New England Frontier* does not look that way anymore. In his introduction to *New Directions in American Intellectual History,* John Higham writes that by the end of the sixties

> the entire conceptual foundation on which [this sort of work] rested [had] crumbled away. . . . Simultaneously, in sociology, anthropology, and history, two working assumptions . . . came under withering attack: first, the assumption that societies tend to be integrated, and second, that a shared culture maintains that integration. . . . By the late 1960s all claims issued in the name of an "American mind" . . . were subject to drastic skepticism.[5]

"Clearly," Higham continues, "the sociocultural upheaval of the sixties created the occasion" for this reaction.[6] Vaughan's book, it seemed, could only have been written before the events of the sixties had sensitized scholars to questions of race and ethnicity. It came as no surprise, therefore, that ten years later there appeared a study of European-Indian relations which reflected the new awareness of social issues the sixties had engendered. And it offered an entirely different picture of the European-Indian encounter.

15   Francis Jennings's *The Invasion of America* (1975) rips wide open the idea that the Puritans were humane and considerate in their dealings with the Indians. In Jennings's account, even more massively documented than Vaughan's, the early settlers lied to the Indians, stole from them, murdered them, scalped them, captured them, tortured them, raped them, sold them into slavery, confiscated their land, destroyed their crops, burned their homes, scattered their possessions, gave them alcohol, undermined their systems of belief, and infected them with diseases that wiped out ninety percent of their numbers within the first hundred years after contact.[7]

16   Jennings mounts an all-out attack on the essential decency of the Puritan leadership and their apologists in the twentieth century. The Pequot War, which previous historians had described as an attempt on the part of Massachusetts Bay to protect itself from the fiercest of the New England tribes, becomes, in Jennings's painstakingly researched account, a deliberate war of extermination, waged by whites against Indians. It starts with trumped-up charges, is carried on through a series of increasingly bloody reprisals, and ends in the massacre of scores of Indian men, women, and children, all so that Massachusetts Bay could gain political and economic control of the southern Connecticut Valley. When one reads this and then turns over the page and sees a reproduction of the Bay Colony seal, which depicts an Indian from whose mouth issue the words "Come over and help us," the effect is shattering.[8]

17   But even so powerful an argument as Jennings's did not remain unshaken by subsequent work. Reading on, I discovered that if the events of the sixties had revolutionized the study of European-Indian relations, the events of the seventies produced yet another transformation. The American Indian Movement, and in particular the founding of the Native American Rights Fund in 1971 to finance Indian litigation, and a court decision in 1975 which gave the tribes the right to seek redress for past injustices in federal court, created a climate within which historians began to focus on the Indians themselves. "Almost simultaneously," writes James Axtell, "frontier and colonial historians began to discover the necessity of considering the American natives as real determinants of history and the utility of ethnohistory as a way of ensuring parity of focus and impartiality of judgment."[9] In Miller, Indians had been simply beneath notice; in Vaughan, they belonged to an inferior culture; and in Jennings, they were the more or less innocent prey of power-hungry whites. But in the most original and provocative of the ethnohistories, Calvin Martin's *Keepers of the Game,* Indians became complicated, purposeful human beings, whose lives were spiritually motivated to a high degree.[10] Their relationship to the animals they hunted, to the natural environment, and to the whites with whom they traded became intelligible

within a system of beliefs that formed the basis for an entirely new perspective on the European-Indian encounter.

18   Within the broader question of why European contact had such a devastating effect on the Indians, Martin's specific aim is to determine why Indians participated in the fur trade which ultimately led them to the brink of annihilation. The standard answer to this question had always been that once the Indian was introduced to European guns, copper kettles, woolen blankets, and the like, he literally couldn't keep his hands off them. In order to acquire these coveted items, he decimated the animal populations on which his survival depended. In short, the Indian's motivation in participating in the fur trade was assumed to be the same as the white European's—a desire to accumulate material goods. In direct opposition to this thesis, Martin argues that the reason why Indians ruthlessly exploited their own resources had nothing to do with supply and demand, but stemmed rather from a breakdown of the cosmic worldview that tied them to the game they killed in a spiritual relationship of parity and mutual obligation.

19   The hunt, according to Martin, was conceived not primarily as a physical activity but as a spiritual quest, in which the spirit of the hunter must overmaster the spirit of the game animal before the kill can take place. The animal, in effect, *allows* itself to be found and killed, once the hunter has mastered its spirit. The hunter prepared himself through rituals of fasting, sweating, or dreaming which revealed the identity of his prey and where he can find it. The physical act of killing is the least important element in the process. Once the animal is killed, eaten, and its parts used for clothing or implements, its remains must be disposed of in ritually prescribed fashion, or the game boss, the "keeper" of that species, will not permit more animals to be killed. The relationship between Indians and animals, then, is contractual; each side must hold up its end of the bargain, or no further transactions can occur.

20   What happened, according to Martin, was that as a result of diseases introduced into the animal population by Europeans, the game suddenly disappeared, began to act in inexplicable ways, or sickened and died in plain view, and communicated their diseases to the Indians. The Indians, consequently, believed that their compact with the animals had been broken and that the keepers of the game, the tutelary spirits of each animal species whom they had been so careful to propitiate, had betrayed them. And when missionization, wars with the Europeans, and displacement from their tribal lands had further weakened Indian society and its belief structure, the Indians, no longer restrained by religious sanctions, in effect, turned on the animals in a holy war of revenge.

21   Whether or not Martin's specific claim about the "holy war" was correct, his analysis made it clear to me that, given the Indians' understanding of economic, religious, and physical processes, an Indian account of what transpired when the European settlers arrived here would look nothing like our own. Their (potential, unwritten) history of the conflict could bear only

a marginal resemblance to Eurocentric views. I began to think that the key
to understanding European-Indian relations was to see them as an encounter
between wholly disparate cultures, and that therefore either defending or attacking the colonists was beside the point since, given the cultural disparity
between the two groups, conflict was inevitable and in large part a product
of mutual misunderstanding.

22   But three years after Martin's book appeared, Shepard Krech III edited a
collection of seven essays called *Indians, Animals, and the Fur Trade,* attacking Martin's entire project. Here the authors argued that we don't need
an ideological or religious explanation for the fur trade. As Charles Hudson
writes,

> The Southeastern Indians slaughtered deer (and were prompted to enslave
> and kill each other) because of their position on the outer fringes of an ex-
> panding modern worldsystem. . . . In the modern world-system there is a
> core region which establishes *economic* relations with its colonial periph-
> ery. . . . If the Indians would not produce commodities, they were on the
> road to cultural extinction. . . . To maximize his chances for survival, an
> eighteenth-century Southeastern Indian had to. . . . live in the interior, out
> of range of European cattle, forestry, and agriculture. . . . He had to pro-
> duce a commodity which was valuable enough to earn him some protec-
> tion from English slavers.[11]

Though we are talking here about Southeastern Indians, rather than the sub-
arctic and Northeastern tribes Martin studied, what really accounts for these
divergent explanations of why Indians slaughtered the game are the assumptions that underlie them. Martin believes that the Indians acted on the basis of
perceptions made available to them by their own cosmology; that is, he explains their behavior as the Indians themselves would have explained it (insofar as he can), using a logic and a set of values that are not Eurocentric but
derived from within Amerindian culture. Hudson, on the other hand, insists
that the Indians' own beliefs are irrelevant to an explanation of how they
acted, which can only be understood, as far as he is concerned, in the terms of
a Western materialist economic and political analysis. Martin and Hudson, in
short, don't agree on what counts as an explanation, and this disagreement
sheds light on the preceding accounts as well. From this standpoint, we can
see that Vaughan, who thought that the Puritans were superior to the Indians,
and Jennings, who thought the reverse, are both, like Hudson, using Eurocentric criteria of description and evaluation. While all three critics (Vaughan,
Jennings, and Hudson) acknowledge that Indians and Europeans behave differently from one another, the behavior differs, as it were, within the order of
the same: all three assume, though only Hudson makes the assumption explicit, that an understanding of relations between the Europeans and the Indians must be elaborated in European terms. In Martin's analysis, however,
what we have are not only two different sets of behavior but two incommensurable ways of describing and assigning meaning to events. This difference

at the level of explanation calls into question the possibility of obtaining any theory-independent account of interaction between Indians and Europeans.

23   At this point, dismayed and confused by the wildly divergent views of colonial history the twentieth-century historians had provided, I decided to look at some primary materials. I thought, perhaps, if I looked at some first-hand accounts and at some scholars looking at those accounts, it would be possible to decide which experts were right and which were wrong by comparing their views with the evidence. Captivity narratives seemed a good place to begin, since it was logical to suppose that the records left by whites who had been captured by Indians would furnish the sort of firsthand information I wanted.

24   I began with two fascinating essays based on these materials written by the ethnohistorian James Axtell, "The White Indians of Colonial America" and "The Scholastic Philosophy of the Wilderness."[12] These essays suggest that it would have been a privilege to be captured by North American Indians and taken off to Canada to dwell in a wigwam for the rest of one's life. Axtell's reconstruction of the process by which Indians taught European captives to feel comfortable in the wilderness, first taking their shoes away and giving them moccasins, carrying the children on their backs, sharing the scanty food supply equally, ceremonially cleansing them of their old identities, giving them Indian clothes and jewelry, assiduously teaching them the Indian language, finally adopting them into their families, and even visiting them after many years if, as sometimes happened, they were restored to white society—all of this creates a compelling portrait of Indian culture and helps to explain the extraordinary attraction that Indian culture apparently exercised over Europeans.

25   But, as I had by now come to expect, this beguiling portrait of the Indians' superior humanity is called into question by other writings on Indian captivity—for example, Norman Heard's *White into Red,* whose summation of the comparative treatment of captive children east and west of the Mississippi seems to contradict some of Axtell's conclusions:

> The treatment of captive children seems to have been similar in initial stages. . . . Most children were treated brutally at the time of capture. Babies and toddlers usually were killed immediately and other small children would be dispatched during the rapid retreat to the Indian villages if they cried, failed to keep the pace, or otherwise indicated a lack of fortitude needed to become a worthy member of the tribe. Upon reaching the village, the child might face such ordeals as running the gauntlet or dancing in the center of a throng of threatening Indians. The prisoner might be so seriously injured at this time that he would no longer be acceptable for adoption.[13]

One account which Heard reprints is particularly arresting. A young girl captured by the Comanches who had not been adopted into a family but used as a slave had been peculiarly mistreated. When they wanted to wake

her up the family she belonged to would take a burning brand from the fire
and touch it to her nose. When she was returned to her parents, the flesh of
her nose was completely burned away, exposing the bone.[14]

26   Since the pictures drawn by Heard and Axtell were in certain respects irreconcilable, it made sense to turn to a firsthand account to see how the Indians treated their captives in a particular instance. Mary Rowlandson's
"The Soveraignty and Goodness of God," published in Boston around 1680,
suggested itself because it was so widely read and had set the pattern for
later narratives. Rowlandson interprets her captivity as God's punishment
on her for failing to keep the Sabbath properly on several occasions. She sees
everything that happens to her as a sign from God. When the Indians are
kind to her, she attributes her good fortune to divine Providence; when they
are cruel, she blames her captors. But beyond the question of how Rowlandson interprets events is the question of what she saw in the first place and
what she considered worth reporting. The following passage, with its
abrupt shifts of focus and peculiar emphases, makes it hard to see her testimony as evidence of anything other than the Puritan point of view:

> Then my heart began to fail: and I fell weeping, which was the first time to
> my remembrance, that I wept before them. Although I had met with so
> much Affliction, and my heart was many times ready to break, yet could I
> not shed one tear in their sight: but rather had been all this while in a
> maze, and like one astonished: but not I may say as. Psal. 137.1. *By the
> Rivers of Babylon, there we sate down; yea, we wept when we remem-
> bered Zion.* There one of them asked me, why I wept, I could hardly tell
> what to say: yet I answered, they would kill me: No, said he, none will hurt
> you. Then came one of them and gave me two spoon-fulls of Meal to com-
> fort me, and another gave me half a pint of Pease: which was more worth
> than many Bushels at another time. Then I went to see King Philip, he bade
> me come in and sit down, and asked me whether I woold smoke it (a usual
> Complement nowadayes among Saints and Sinners) but this no way suited
> me. For though I had formerly used Tobacco, yet I had left it ever since I
> was first taken. It seems to be a Bait, the Devil layes to make men loose
> their precious time: I remember with shame, how formerly, when I had
> taken two or three pipes, I was presently ready for another, such a be-
> witching thing it is: But I thank God, he has now given me power over it:
> surely there are many who may be better imployed than to ly sucking a
> stinking Tobacco-pipe.[15]

Anyone who has ever tried to give up smoking has to sympathize with Rowlandson, but it is nonetheless remarkable, first, that a passage which begins
with her weeping openly in front of her captors, and comparing herself to Israel in Babylon, should end with her railing against the vice of tobacco; and,
second, that it has not a word to say about King Philip, the leader of the Indians who captured her and mastermind of the campaign that devastated the
white population of the English colonies. The fact that Rowlandson has just
been introduced to the chief of chiefs makes hardly any impression on her at

all. What excites her is a moral issue which was being hotly debated in the seventeenth century: to smoke or not to smoke (Puritans frowned on it, apparently, because it wasted time and presented a fire hazard). What seem to us the peculiar emphases in Rowlandson's relation are not the result of her having *screened out* evidence she couldn't handle, but of her way of constructing the world. She saw what her seventeenth-century English Separatist background made visible. It is when one realizes that the biases of twentieth-century historians like Vaughan or Axtell cannot be corrected for simply by consulting the primary materials, since the primary materials are constructed according to their authors' biases, that one begins to envy Miller his vision at Matadi. Not for what he didn't see—the Indian and the black—but for his epistemological confidence.

27   Since captivity narratives made a poor source of evidence for the nature of European-Indian relations in early New England because they were so relentlessly pietistic, my hope was that a better source of evidence might be writings designed simply to tell Englishmen what the American natives were like. These authors could be presumed to be less severely biased, since they hadn't seen their loved ones killed by Indians or been made to endure the hardships of captivity, and because they weren't writing propaganda calculated to prove that God had delivered his chosen people from the hands of Satan's emissaries.

28   The problem was that these texts were written with aims no less specific than those of the captivity narratives, though the aims were of a different sort. Here is a passage from William Wood's *New England's Prospect,* published in London in 1634.

> To enter into a serious discourse concerning the natural conditions of these Indians might procure admiration from the people of any civilized nations, in regard of their civility and good natures. . . . These Indians are of affable, courteous and well disposed natures, ready to communicate the best of their wealth to the mutual good of one another: . . . so . . . perspicuous is their love . . . that they are as willing to part with a mite in poverty as treasure in plenty. . . . If it were possible to recount the courtesies they have showed the English, since their first arrival in those parts, it would not only steady belief, that they are a loving people, but also win the love of those that never saw them, and wipe off that needless fear that is too deeply rooted in the conceits of many who think them envious and of such rancorous and inhumane dispositions, that they will one day make an end of their English inmates.[16]

However, in a pamphlet published twenty-one years earlier, Alexander Whitaker of Virginia has this to say of the natives:

> These naked slaves . . . serve the divell for feare, after a most base manner, sacrificing sometimes (as I have heere heard) their own Children to him. . . . They live naked in bodie, as if their shame of their sinne deserved no covenng: Their names are as naked as their bodie: They esteem it a virtue to lie, deceive and steale as their master the divell teacheth to them.[17]

According to Robert Berkhofer in *The White Man's Indian,* these divergent reports can be explained by looking at the authors' motives. A favorable report like Wood's, intended to encourage new emigrants to America, naturally represented Indians as loving and courteous, civilized and generous, in order to allay the fears of prospective colonists. Whitaker, on the other hand, a minister who wishes to convince his readers that the Indians are in need of conversion, paints them as benighted agents of the devil. Berkhofer's commentary constantly implies that white men were to blame for having represented the Indians in the image of their own desires and needs.[18] But the evidence supplied by Rowlandson's narrative, and by the accounts left by early reporters such as Wood and Whitaker, suggests something rather different. Though it is probably true that in certain cases Europeans did consciously tamper with the evidence, in most cases there is no reason to suppose that they did not record faithfully what they saw. And what they saw was not an illusion, was not determined by selfish motives in any narrow sense, but was there by virtue of a way of seeing which they could no more consciously manipulate than they could choose not to have been born. At this point, it seemed to me, the ethnocentric bias of the firsthand observers invited an investigation of the cultural situation they spoke from. Karen Kupperman's *Settling with the Indians* (1980) supplied just such an analysis.

29   Kupperman argues that Englishmen inevitably looked at Indians in exactly the same way that they looked at other Englishmen. For instance, if they looked down on Indians and saw them as people to be exploited, it was not because of racial prejudice or antique notions about savagery, it was because they looked down on ordinary English men and women and saw them as subjects for exploitation as well.[19] According to Kupperman, what concerned these writers most when they described the Indians were the insignia of social class, of rank, and of prestige. Indian faces are virtually never described in the earliest accounts, but clothes and hairstyles, tattoos and jewelry, posture and skin color are. "Early modern Englishmen believed that people can create their own identity, and that therefore one communicates to the world through signals such as dress and other forms of decoration who one is, what group or category one belongs to."[20]

30   Kupperman's book marks a watershed in writings on European-Indian relations, for it reverses the strategy employed by Martin two years before. Whereas Martin had performed an ethnographic analysis of Indian cosmology in order to explain, from within, the Indians' motives for engaging in the fur trade, Kupperman performs an ethnographic study of seventeenth-century England in order to explain, from within, what motivated Englishmen's behavior. The sympathy and understanding that Martin, Axtell, and others extend to the Indians are extended in Kupperman's work to the English themselves. Rather than giving an account of "what happened" between Indians and Europeans, like Martin, she reconstructs the worldview that gave the experience of one group its content. With her study, scholarship on European-Indian relations comes full circle.

31   It may well seem to you at this point that, given the tremendous variation among the historical accounts, I had no choice but to end in relativism. If the experience of encountering conflicting versions of the "same" events suggests anything certain it is that the attitude a historian takes up in relation to a given event, the way in which he or she judges and even describes "it"—and the "it" has to go in quotation marks because, depending on the perspective, that event either did or did not occur—this stance, these judgments and descriptions are a function of the historian's position in relation to the subject. Miller, standing on the banks of the Congo, couldn't see the black men he was supervising because of his background, his assumptions, values, experiences, goals. Jennings, intent on exposing the distortions introduced into the historical record by Vaughan and his predecessors stretching all the way back to Winthrop, couldn't see that Winthrop and his peers were not racists but only Englishmen who looked at other cultures in the way their own culture had taught them to see one another. The historian can never escape the limitations of his or her own position in history and so inevitably gives an account that is an extension of the circumstances from which it springs. But it seems to me that when one is confronted with this particular succession of stories, cultural and historical relativism is not a position that one can comfortably assume. The phenomena to which these histories testify—conquest, massacre, and genocide, on the one hand; torture, slavery, and murder on the other—cry out for judgment. When faced with claims and counterclaims of this magnitude one feels obligated to reach an understanding of what actually did occur. The dilemma posed by the study of European-Indian relations in early America is that the highly charged nature of the materials demands a moral decisiveness which the succession of conflicting accounts effectively precludes. That is the dilemma I found myself in at the end of this course of reading, and which I eventually came to resolve as follows.

32   After a while it began to seem to me that there was something wrong with the way I had formulated the problem. The statement that the materials on European-Indian relations were so highly charged that they demanded moral judgment, but that the judgment couldn't be made because all possible descriptions of what happened were biased, seemed to contain an internal contradiction. The statement implied that in order to make a moral judgment about something, you have to know something else first—namely, the facts of the case you're being called upon to judge. My complaint was that their perspectival nature would disqualify any facts I might encounter and that therefore I couldn't judge. But to say as I did that the materials I had read were "highly charged" and therefore demanded judgment suggests both that I was reacting to something real—to some facts—and that I had judged them. Perhaps I wasn't so much in the lurch morally or epistemologically as I had thought. If you—or I—react with horror to the story of the girl captured and enslaved by Comanches who touched a firebrand to her nose every time they wanted to wake her up, it's because we read this as a story about cruelty and

suffering, and not as a story about the conventions of prisoner exchange or the economics of Comanche life. The seeing of the story as a cause for alarm rather than as a droll anecdote or a piece of curious information is evidence of values we already hold, of judgments already made, of facts already perceived as facts.

33   My problem presupposed that I couldn't judge because I didn't know what the facts were. All I had, or could have, was a series of different perspectives, and so nothing that would count as an authoritative source on which moral judgments could be based. But, as I have just shown, I did judge, and that is because, as I now think, I did have some facts. I seemed to accept as facts that ninety percent of the native American population of New England died after the first hundred years of contact, that tribes in eastern Canada and the northeastern United States had a compact with the game they killed, that Comanches had subjected a captive girl to casual cruelty, that King Philip smoked a pipe and so on. It was only where different versions of the same event came into conflict that I doubted the text was a record of something real. And even then, there was no question about certain major catastrophes. I believed that four hundred Pequots were killed near Saybrook, that Winthrop was the Governor of the Massachusetts Bay Colony when it happened, and so on. My sense that certain events, such as the Pequot War, did occur in no way reflected the indecisiveness that overtook me when I tried to choose among the various historical versions. In fact, the need I felt to make up my mind was impelled by the conviction that certain things *had* happened that shouldn't have happened. Hence it was never the case that "what happened" was completely unknowable or unavailable. It's rather that in the process of reading so many different approaches to the same phenomenon I became aware of the difference in the attitudes that informed these approaches. This awareness of the interests motivating each version cast suspicion over everything, in retrospect, and I ended by claiming that there was nothing I could know. This, I now see, was never really the case. But how did it happen?

34   Someone else, confronted with the same materials, could have decided that one of these historical accounts was correct. Still another person might have decided that more evidence was needed in order to decide among them. Why did I conclude that none of the accounts was accurate because they were all produced from some particular angle of vision? Presumably there was something in my background that enabled me to see the problem in this way. That something, very likely, was poststructuralist theory. I let my discovery that Vaughan was a product of the fifties, Jennings of the sixties, Rowlandson of a Puritan worldview, and so on lead me to the conclusion that all facts are theory dependent because that conclusion was already a thinkable one for me. My inability to come up with a true account was not the product of being situated nowhere; it was the product of certitude that existed *somewhere else,* namely, in contemporary literary theory. Hence, the level at which my indecision came into play was a function of particular

beliefs I held. I was never in a position of epistemological indeterminacy, I was never *en abyme*. The idea that all accounts are perspectival seemed to me a superior standpoint from which to view all the versions of "what happened," and to regard with sympathetic condescension any person so old-fashioned and benighted as to believe that there really was some way of arriving at the truth. But this skeptical standpoint was just as firm as any other. The fact that it was also seriously disabling—it prevented me from coming to any conclusion about what I had read—did not render it any less definite.

35   At this point something is beginning to show itself that has up to now been hidden. The notion that all facts are only facts within a perspective has the effect of emptying statements of their content. Once I had Miller and Vaughan and Jennings, Martin and Hudson, Axtell and Heard, Rowlandson and Wood and Whitaker, and Kupperman; I had Europeans and Indians, ships and canoes, wigwams and log cabins, bows and arrows and muskets, wigs and tattoos, whiskey and corn, rivers and forts, treaties and battles, fire and blood—and then suddenly all I had was a metastatement about perspectives. The effect of bringing perspectivism to bear on history was to wipe out completely the subject matter of history. And it follows that bringing perspectivism to bear in this way on any subject matter would have a similar effect; everything is wiped out and you are left with nothing but a single idea—perspectivism itself.

36   But—and it is a crucial but—all this is true only if you believe that there is an alternative. As long as you think that there are or should be facts that exist outside of any perspective, then the notion that facts are perspectival will have this disappearing effect on whatever it touches. But if you are convinced that the alternative does not exist, that there really are no facts except as they are embedded in some particular way of seeing the world, then the argument that a set of facts derives from some particular worldview is no longer an argument against that set of facts. If all facts share this characteristic, to say that any one fact is perspectival doesn't change its factual nature in the slightest. It merely reiterates it.

37   This doesn't mean that you have to accept just anybody's facts. You can show that what someone else asserts to be a fact is false. But it does mean that you can't argue that someone else's facts are not facts *because they are only the product of a perspective,* since this will be true of the facts that you perceive as well. What this means then is that arguments about "what happened" have to proceed much as they did before post-structuralism broke in with all its talk about language-based reality and culturally produced knowledge. Reasons must be given, evidence adduced, authorities cited, analogies drawn. Being aware that all facts are motivated, believing that people are always operating inside some particular interpretive framework or other is a pertinent argument when what is under discussion is the way beliefs are grounded. But it doesn't give one any leverage on the facts of a particular case.[21]

38   What this means for the problem I've been addressing is that I must piece together the story of European-Indian relations as best I can, believing this version up to a point, that version not at all, another almost entirely, according to what seems reasonable and plausible, given everything else that I know. And this, as I've shown, is what I was already doing in the back of my mind without realizing it, because there was nothing else I *could* do. If the accounts don't fit together neatly, that is not a reason for rejecting them all in favor of a metadiscourse about epistemology: on the contrary, one encounters contradictory facts and divergent points of view in practically every phase of life, from deciding whom to marry to choosing the right brand of cat food, and one decides as best one can given the evidence available. It is only the nature of the academic situation which makes it appear that one can linger on the threshold of decision in the name of an epistemological principle. What has really happened in such a case is that the subject of debate has changed from the question of what happened in a particular instance to the question of how knowledge is arrived at. The absence of pressure to decide what happened creates the possibility for this change of venue.

39   The change of venue, however, is itself an action taken. In diverting attention from the original problem and placing it where Miller did, on "the mind of man," it once again ignores what happened and still is happening to American Indians. The moral problem that confronts me now is not that I can never have any facts to go on, but that the work I do is not directed toward solving the kinds of problems that studying the history of European-Indian relations has awakened me to.

NOTES

1. See Vine Deloria, Jr., *God Is Red* (New York, 1973), pp. 39–56.
2. Perry Miller, *Errand into the Wilderness* (Cambridge, Mass., 1964), p. vii; all further references will be included in the text.
3. This passage from John Winthrop's *Journal* is excerpted by Perry Miller in his anthology *The American Puritans: Their Prose and Poetry* (Garden City, N.Y., 1956), p. 43. In his headnote to the selections from the *Journal,* Miller speaks of Winthrop's "characteristic objectivity" (p. 37).
4. Alden T. Vaughan, *New England Frontier: Puritans and Indians, 1620–1675* (Boston, 1965). pp. vi–vii; all further references to this work, abbreviated *NEF,* will be included in the text.
5. John Higham, intro. to *New Directions in American Intellectual History,* ed. Higham and Paul K. Conkin (Baltimore, 1979), p. xii.
6. Ibid.
7. See Francis Jennings, *The Invasion of America: Indians, Colonialism, and the Cant of Conquest* (New York, 1975), pp. 3–31. Jennings writes: "The so-called settlement of America was a resettlement, reoccupation of a land made waste by the diseases and demoralization introduced by the newcomers. Although the

source data pertaining to populations have never been compiled, one careful scholar, Henry F. Dobyns, has provided a relatively conservative and meticulously reasoned estimate conforming to the known effects of conquest catastrophe. Dobyns has calculated a total aboriginal population for the western hemisphere within the range of 90 to 112 million, of which 10 to 12 million lived north of the Rio Grande" (p. 30).

8. Jennings, fig. 7, p. 229; and see pp. 186–229.
9. James Axtell, *The European and the Indian: Essays in the Ethnohistory of Colonial North America* (Oxford, 1981), p. viii.
10. See Calvin Martin, *Keepers of the Game: Indian-Animal Relationships and the Fur Trade* (Berkeley and Los Angeles, 1978).
11. See the essay by Charles Hudson in *Indians, Animals, and the Fur Trade: A Critique of "Keepers of the Game,"* ed. Shepard Krech III (Athens, Ga., 1981), pp. 167–169.
12. See Axtell, "The White Indians of Colonial America" and "The Scholastic Philosophy of the Wildnerness." *The European and the Indian,* pp. 168–206 and 131–167.
13. J. Norman Heard, *White into Red: A Study of the Assimilation of White Persons Captured by Indians* (Metuchen, N.J., 1973), p. 97.
14. See ibid., p. 98.
15. Mary Rowlandson, "The Soveraignty and Goodness of God, Together with the Faithfulness of His Promises Displayed: Being a Narrative of the Captivity and Restauration of Mrs. Mary Rowlandson (1676)," in *Held Captive by Indians: Selected Narratives, 1642–1836,* ed. Richard VanDerBeets (Knoxville, Tenn., 1973), pp. 57–58.
16. William Wood, *New England's Prospect,* ed. Vaughan (Amherst, Mass., 1977), pp. 88–89.
17. Alexander Whitaker, *Goode Newes from Virginia (1613),* quoted in Robert F. Berkhofer, Jr., *The White Man's Indian: Images of the American Indian from Columbus to the Present* (New York, 1978), p. 19.
18. See, for example, Berkhofer's discussion of the passages he quotes from Whitaker (*The White Man's Indian,* pp. 19, 20).
19. See Karen Ordahl Kupperman, *Settling with the Indians: The Meeting of English and Indian Cultures in America, 1580–1640* (Totowa, N.J., 1980), pp. 3, 4.
20. Ibid., p. 35.
21. The position I've been outlining is a version of neopragmatism. For an exposition, see *Against Theory: Literary Studies and the New Pragmatism,* ed. W. J. T. Mitchell (Chicago, 1985).

FOLLOW-UP ACTIVITIES

Discussing the Rhetoric

1. Whose viewpoint does Tompkins say she represents? Who do you think her intended audience is? Do you think most of her readers will identify with her or feel estranged?

2. As with some of the other essays you've read, Tompkins begins with a personal example. Do you see any common threads in the aims or purposes of the writers who have used personal stories? How does Tompkins' use of personal stories tie in with her overall purpose?

3. Tompkins includes many historical accounts from both first-hand and second-hand sources. However, Tompkins never includes accounts written by Native Americans about their own experience. How might Native American accounts change Tompkins' essay? Why do you think she might have chosen not to include these accounts?

4. Which of the viewpoints presented most closely resembles your own? How is your viewpoint of "Indians" different from any portrayed in Tompkins' text? According to Tompkins, will we ever know whose viewpoint is the "right" one?

Discussing the Conversation

1. In "The Man of Professional Wisdom," Kathryn Pyne Addelson introduces the concept that "cognitive authority" affects the growth of knowledge by limiting the authorization of knowledge to certain individuals. If truth is a matter of perspective, as Tompkins claims, what role does "cognitive authority" play in determining whose perspective becomes historical truth?

2. Do you think Evelyn Fox Keller would agree with Tompkins that there are no facts? What implication does this assertion have for a scientist?

3. In "Scientific Method: The Traditional View and Popper's View," Bryan Magee writes:

> The popular notion that the sciences are bodies of established fact is entirely mistaken. Nothing in science is permanently established, nothing unalterable, and indeed science is quite clearly changing all the time, and not through the accretion of new certainties. If we are rational we shall always base our decisions and expectations on 'the best of our knowledge,' as the popular phrase so rightly has it, and provisionally assume the 'truth' of that knowledge for practical purposes, because it is the least insecure foundation available; but we shall never lose sight of the fact that at anytime experience may show it to be wrong and require us to change it.

How is this advice similar and/or dissimilar to the following quote from Tompkins?

> What this [the loss of certainty] means then is that arguments about "what happened" have to proceed much as they did before poststructuralism broke in with all its talk about language-based reality and culturally produced knowledge. Reasons must be given, evidence adduced, authorities cited, analogies drawn.

To answer this question, think about who gets to decide which evidence counts, which authorities are cited, and which reasons are considered valid.

4. How does Tompkins extend Schiebinger's views about the importance of the inclusion of nondominant voices in the making of knowledge?

Joining the Conversation

1. Tompkins claims that a historian's own "historical moment" influences what and how events are recorded. On a piece of paper, draw a time-line, starting with the 1950s and extending into the 1990s. Under each decade, write the name(s) of the historians that wrote during that period. Then describe briefly under each historians' name their view of American Indians. Last, write any information you can find in Tompkins' text, or that you know from other sources, about the political situation of that time. What connections can you make between the historians' interpretations and the politics of their time?

2. In a paragraph, describe your perception of American Indians when you were about twelve. Then describe your perceptions now. Have they changed? To what do you attribute the change? If you are an American Indian, include what social sources influenced your perception of yourself and your people then and now.

INTRODUCTORY COMMENTS ON "HOW TO RECOGNIZE A POEM WHEN YOU SEE ONE" BY STANLEY FISH

Reading the Context

Stanley Fish is a literary critic and theoretician who has taught at Duke University since 1984. He received his masters (1960) and doctorate (1962) from Yale University. Even with this traditional training, Fish endorses two somewhat untraditional ideas. The first idea is that the meaning of a text is not actually in the printed words, but more in the experience of the reader trying to make sense of those words. This notion is commonly referred to as reader-response criticism. Reader-response criticism focuses, not on any "objective reality," but on the experiences of readers.

The second idea Fish endorses in his writings is that readers do not create meaning in a vacuum. The means (or strategies) they use to create meaning are influenced by their surroundings: intellectual discussions of the time, social position, cultural backgrounds, previously held beliefs, and so on. These surroundings are what Fish refers to as "interpretive communities."

The essay "How to Recognize a Poem When You See One" comes from a collection of essays published in a book titled *Is There a Text in This Class? The Authority of Interpretive Communities* (1980). Stanley Fish is also the author of several other books and articles and is an active participant in both written and oral conversations about academic work.

Reading the Rhetoric

This essay was written as Fish was shifting his focus from the practice of reading to literary theory. In the book, Fish addresses his fellow literary critics and attempts to persuade them that, although meaning is produced by a reader's unconscious interpretive decisions, these decisions are regulated by the standards and beliefs of discourse communities. Discourse communities limit what a text can mean. Fish wants other literary theorists to question how their own interpretations are structured by the "literary theory community." As you read, look for rhetorical techniques Fish uses to persuade his literary audience of his argument.

When this book was published, Fish was already an established name in the field of literary criticism and was being included in collections and encyclopedias of literary theorists. This acceptance among scholars gave him the freedom to question literary theory and its approach to finding truth. What can you see in Fish's "playful" language that demonstrates he is already an accepted member of the community he's addressing?

Reading the Conversation

In Part Two, you learned that authors' opinions about how knowledge is made differ. Authors like David Crews and E. D. Klemke assert that the truth is out there in the natural world and people can discover it through empirical research. Other authors, like Appleby and her colleagues, Schiebinger, Tompkins, and Keller focus more on how social, historical, and political surroundings effect interpretation. As you read, consider how Fish, who is clearly a member of the second group, accords with or differs from other members of the second group.

How to Recognize a
Poem When You See One
Stanley Fish

1 Last time I sketched out an argument by which meanings are the property neither of fixed and stable texts nor of free and independent readers but of interpretive communities that are responsible both for the shape of a reader's activities and for the texts those activities produce. In this lecture I propose

to extend that argument so as to account not only for the meanings a poem might be said to have but for the fact of its being recognized as a poem in the first place. And once again I would like to begin with an anecdote.

2   In the summer of 1971 I was teaching two courses under the joint auspices of the Linguistic Institute of America and the English Department of the State University of New York at Buffalo. I taught these courses in the morning and in the same room. At 9:30 I would meet a group of students who were interested in the relationship between linguistics and literary criticism. Our nominal subject was stylistics but our concerns were finally theoretical and extended to the presuppositions and assumptions which underlie both linguistic and literary practice. At 11:00 these students were replaced by another group whose concerns were exclusively literary and were in fact confined to English religious poetry of the seventeenth century. These students had been learning how to identify Christian symbols and how to recognize typological patterns and how to move from the observation of these symbols and patterns to the specification of a poetic intention that was usually didactic or homiletic. On the day I am thinking about, the only connection between the two classes was an assignment given to the first which was still on the blackboard at the beginning of the second. It read:

Jacobs-Rosenbaum

Levin

Thorne

Hayes

Ohman (?)

3   I am sure that many of you will already have recognized the names on this list, but for the sake of the record, allow me to identify them. Roderick Jacobs and Peter Rosenbaum are two linguists who have coauthored a number of textbooks and co-edited a number of anthologies. Samuel Levin is a linguist who was one of the first to apply the operations of transformational grammar to literary texts. J. P. Thorne is a linguist at Edinburgh who, like Levin, was attempting to extend the rules of transformational grammar to the notorious irregularities of poetic language. Curtis Hayes is a linguist who was then using transformational grammar in order to establish an objective basis for his intuitive impression that the language of Gibbon's *Rise and Fall of the Roman Empire* is more complex than the language of Hemingway's novels. And Richard Ohmann is the literary critic who, more than any other, was responsible for introducing the vocabulary of transformational grammar to the literary community. Ohmann's name was spelled as you see it here because I could not remember whether it contained one or two n's. In other words, the question mark in parenthesis signified nothing more than a faulty memory and a desire on my part to appear scrupulous. The fact that the names appeared in a list that was arranged vertically, and that Levin, Thorne, and Hayes formed a column that was more or less centered in relation to the paired names of Jacobs and Rosenbaum, was similarly accidental and was evidence only of a certain compulsiveness if, indeed, it was evidence of anything at all.

4   In the time between the two classes I made only one change. I drew a frame around the assignment and wrote on the top of that frame "p. 43." When the members of the second class filed in I told them that what they saw on the blackboard was a religious poem of the kind they had been studying and I asked them to interpret it. Immediately they began to perform in a manner that, for reasons which will become clear, was more or less predictable. The first student to speak pointed out that the poem was probably a hieroglyph, although he was not sure whether it was in the shape of a cross or an altar. This question was set aside as the other students, following his lead, began to concentrate on individual words, interrupting each other with suggestions that came so quickly that they seemed spontaneous. The first line of the poem (the very order of events assumed the already constituted status of the object) received the most attention: Jacobs was explicated as a reference to Jacob's ladder, traditionally allegorized as a figure for the Christian ascent to heaven. In this poem, however, or so my students told me, the means of ascent is not a ladder but a tree, a rose tree or rosenbaum. This was seen to be an obvious reference to the Virgin Mary who was often characterized as a rose without thorns, itself an emblem of the immaculate conception. At this point the poem appeared to the students to be operating in the familiar manner of an iconographic riddle. It at once posed the question, "How is it that a man can climb to heaven by means of a rose tree?" and directed the reader to the inevitable answer: by the fruit of that tree, the fruit of Mary's womb, Jesus. Once this interpretation was established it received support from, and conferred significance on, the word "thorne," which could only be an allusion to the crown of thorns, a symbol of the trial suffered by Jesus and of the price he paid to save us all. It was only a short step (really no step at all) from this insight to the recognition of Levin as a double reference, first to the tribe of Levi, of whose priestly function Christ was the fulfillment, and second to the unleavened bread carried by the children of Israel on their exodus from Egypt, the place of sin, and in response to the call of Moses, perhaps the most familiar of the old testament types of Christ. The final word of the poem was given at least three complementary readings: it could be "omen," especially since so much of the poem is concerned with foreshadowing and prophecy; it could be Oh Man, since it is man's story as it intersects with the divine plan that is the poem's subject; and it could, of course, be simply "amen," the proper conclusion to a poem celebrating the love and mercy shown by a God who gave his only begotten son so that we may live.

5   In addition to specifying significances for the words of the poem and relating those significances to one another, the students began to discern larger structural patterns. It was noted that of the six names in the poem three—Jacobs, Rosenbaum, and Levin—are Hebrew, two—Thorne and Hayes—are Christian, and one—Ohman—is ambiguous, the ambiguity being marked in the poem itself (as the phrase goes) by the question mark in parenthesis. This division was seen as a reflection of the basic distinction between the old dispensation and the new, the law of sin and the law of love. That

distinction, however, is blurred and finally dissolved by the typological perspective which invests the old testament events and heroes with new testament meanings. The structure of the poem, my students concluded, is therefore a double one, establishing and undermining its basic pattern (Hebrew vs. Christian) at the same time. In this context there is finally no pressure to resolve the ambiguity of Ohman since the two possible readings—the name is Hebrew, the name is Christian—are both authorized by the reconciling presence in the poem of Jesus Christ. Finally, I must report that one student took to counting letters and found, to no one's surprise, that the most prominent letters in the poem were S, O, N.

6   Some of you will have noticed that I have not yet said anything about Hayes. This is because of all the words in the poem it proved the most recalcitrant to interpretation, a fact not without consequence, but one which I will set aside for the moment since I am less interested in the details of the exercise than in the ability of my students to perform it. What is the source of that ability? How is it that they were able to do what they did? What is it that they did? These questions are important because they bear directly on a question often asked in literary theory, What are the distinguishing features of literary language? Or, to put the matter more colloquially, How do you recognize a poem when you see one? The commonsense answer, to which many literary critics and linguists are committed, is that the act of recognition is triggered by the observable presence of distinguishing features. This is, you know a poem when you see one because its language displays the characteristics that you know to be proper to poems. This, however, is a model that quite obviously does not fit the present example. My students did not proceed from the noting of distinguishing features to the recognition that they were confronted by a poem; rather, it was the act of recognition that came first—they knew in advance that they were dealing with a poem—and the distinguishing features then followed.

7   In other words, acts of recognition, rather than being triggered by formal characteristics, are their source. It is not that the presence of poetic qualities compels a certain kind of attention but that the paying of a certain kind of attention results in the emergence of poetic qualities. As soon as my students were aware that it was poetry they were seeing, they began to look with poetry-seeing eyes, that is, with eyes that saw everything in relation to the properties they knew poems to possess. They knew, for example (because they were told by their teachers), that poems are (or are supposed to be) more densely and intricately organized than ordinary communications; and that knowledge translated itself into a willingness—one might even says a determination—to see connections between one word and another and between every word and the poem's central insight. Moreover, the assumption that there *is* a central insight is itself poetry-specific, and presided over its own realization. Having assumed that the collection of words before them was unified by an informing purpose (because unifying purposes are what poems have), my students proceeded to find one and to formulate it. It was

in the light of that purpose (now assumed) that significances for the individual words began to suggest themselves, significances which then fleshed out the assumption that had generated them in the first place. Thus the meanings of the words and the interpretation in which those words were seen to be embedded emerged together, as a consequence of the operations my students began to perform once they were told that this was a poem.

8   It was almost as if they were following a recipe—if it's a poem do this, if it's a poem, see it that way—and indeed definitions of poetry *are* recipes, for by directing readers as to what to look for in a poem, they instruct them in ways of looking that will produce what they expect to see. If your definition of poetry tells you that the language of poetry is complex, you will scrutinize the language of something identified as a poem in such a way as to bring out the complexity you know to be "there." You will, for example, be on the look-out for latent ambiguities; you will attend to the presence of alliterative and consonantal patterns (there will always be some), and you will try to make something of them (you will always succeed); you will search for meanings that subvert, or exist in a tension with the meanings that first present themselves; and if these operations fail to produce the anticipated complexity, you will even propose a significance for the words that are *not* there, because, as everyone knows, everything about a poem, including its omissions, is significant. Nor, as you do these things, will you have any sense of performing in a willful manner, for you will only be doing what you learned to do in the course of becoming a skilled reader of poetry. Skilled reading is usually thought to be a matter of discerning what is there, but if the example of my students can be generalized, it is a matter of knowing how to *produce* what can thereafter be said to be there. Interpretation is not the art of construing but the art of constructing. Interpreters do not decode poems; they make them.

9   To many, this will be a distressing conclusion, and there are a number of arguments that could be mounted in order to forestall it. One might point out that the circumstances of my students' performance were special. After all, they had been concerned exclusively with religious poetry for some weeks, and therefore would be uniquely vulnerable to the deception I had practiced on them and uniquely equipped to impose religious themes and patterns on words innocent of either. I must report, however, that I have duplicated this experiment any number of times at nine or ten universities in three countries, and the results were always the same, even when the participants know from the beginning that what they are looking at was originally an assignment. Of course this very fact could itself be turned into an objection: doesn't the reproducibility of the exercise prove that there is something about these words that leads everyone to perform in the same way? Isn't it just a happy accident that names like Thorne and Jacobs have counterparts or near counterparts in biblical names and symbols? And wouldn't my students have been unable to do what they did if the assignment I gave to the first class had been made up of different names? The answer to all of these questions is no. Given a firm belief that they were

confronted by a religious poem, my students would have been able to turn any list of names into the kind of poem we have before us now, because they would have read the names within the assumption that they were informed with Christian significances. (This is nothing more than a literary analogue to Augustine's rule of faith.) You can test this assertion by replacing Jacobs-Rosenbaum, Levin, Thorne, Hayes, and Ohman with names drawn from the faculty of Kenyon College—Temple, Jordan, Seymour, Daniels, Star, Church. I will not exhaust my time or your patience by performing a full-dress analysis, which would involve, of course, the relation between those who saw the River Jordan and those who saw *more* by seeing the Star of Bethlehem, thus fulfilling the prophecy by which the temple of Jerusalem was replaced by the inner temple or church built up in the heart of every Christian. Suffice it to say that it could easily be done (you can take the poem home and do it yourself) and that the shape of its doing would be constrained not by the names but by the interpretive assumptions that gave them a significance even before they were seen. This would be true even if there were no names on the list, if the paper or blackboard were blank; the blankness would present no problem to the interpreter, who would immediately see in it the void out of which God created the earth, or the abyss into which unregenerate sinners fall, or, in the best of all possible poems, both.

10   Even so, one might reply, all you've done is demonstrate how an interpretation, if it is prosecuted with sufficient vigor, can impose itself on material which has its own proper shape. Basically, at the ground level, in the first place, when all is said and done, "Jacobs-Rosenbaum Levin Thorne Hayes Ohman(?)" is an assignment; it is only a trick that allows you to transform it into a poem, and when the effects of the trick have worn off, it will return to its natural form and be seen as an assignment once again. This is a powerful argument because it seems at once to give interpretation its due (as an act of the will) and to maintain the independence of that on which interpretation works. It allows us, in short, to preserve our commonsense intuition that interpretation must be interpretation of *something*. Unfortunately, the argument will not hold because the assignment we all see is no less the product of interpretation than the poem into which it was turned. That is, it requires just as much work, and work of the same kind, to see this as an assignment as it does to see it as a poem. If this seems counterintuitive, it is only because the work required to see it as an assignment is work we have already done, in the course of acquiring the huge amount of background knowledge that enables you and me to function in the academic world. In order to know what an assignment is, that is, in order to know what to do with something identified as an assignment, you must first know what a class is (know that it isn't an economic grouping) and know that classes meet at specified times for so many weeks, and that one's performance in a class is largely a matter of performing between classes.

11   Think for a moment of how you would explain this last to someone who did not already know it. "Well," you might say, "a class is a group situation in which a number of people are instructed by an informed person in

a particular subject." (Of course the notion of "subject" will itself require ex-
plication.) "An assignment is something you do when you're not in class."
"Oh, I see," your interlocutor might respond, "an assignment is something
you do to take your mind off what you've been doing in class." "No, an assignment is a part of a class." "But how can that be if you only do it when the
class is not meeting?" Now it would be possible, finally, to answer that question, but only by enlarging the horizons of your explanation to include the
very concept of a university, what it is one might be doing there, why one
might be doing it instead of doing a thousand other things, and so on. For
most of us these matters do not require explanation, and indeed, it is hard for
us to imagine someone for whom they do; but that is because our tacit knowledge of what it means to move around in academic life was acquired so gradually and so long ago that it doesn't seem like knowledge at all (and therefore
something someone else might *not* know) but a part of the world. You might
think that when you're on campus (a phrase that itself requires volumes) that
you are simply walking around on the two legs God gave you; but your walking is informed by an internalized awareness of institutional goals and practices, of norms of behavior, of lists of do's and don't's, of invisible lines and
the dangers of crossing them; and, as a result, you see everything as *already*
organized in relation to those same goals and practices. It would never occur
to you, for example, to wonder if the people pouring out of that building are
fleeing from a fire; you *know* that they are exiting from a class (what could
be more obvious?) and you know that because your perception of their action
occurs within a knowledge of what people in a university could possibly be
doing and the reasons they could have for doing it (going to the next class,
going back to the dorm, meeting someone in the student union). It is within
that same knowledge that an assignment becomes intelligible so that it appears to you immediately as an obligation, as a set of directions, as something
with parts, some of which may be more significant than others. That is, it is a
proper question to ask of an assignment whether some of its parts might be
omitted or slighted, whereas readers of poetry know that no part of a poem
can be slighted (the rule is "everything counts") and they do not rest until
every part has been given a significance.

12   In a way this amounts to no more than saying what everyone already
knows: poems and assignments are different, but my point is that the differences are a result of the different interpretive operations we perform and not
of something inherent in one or the other. An assignment no more compels
its own recognition than does a poem; rather, as in the case of a poem, the
shape of an assignment emerges when someone looks at something identified
as one with assignment-seeing eyes, that is, with eyes which are capable of
seeing the words as already embedded within the institutional structure that
makes it possible for assignments to have a sense. The ability to see, and
therefore to make, an assignment is no less a learned ability than the ability to
see, and therefore to make, a poem. Both are constructed artifacts, the products and not the producers of interpretation, and while the differences be-

tween them are real, they are interpretive and do not have their source in some bedrock level of objectivity.

13   Of course one might want to argue that there is a bedrock level at which these names constitute neither an assignment or a poem but are merely a list. But that argument too falls because a list is no more a natural object—one that wears its meaning on its face and can be recognized by anyone—than an assignment or a poem. In order to see a list, one must already be equipped with the concepts of seriality, hierarchy, subordination, and so on, and while these are by no mean esoteric concepts and seem available to almost everyone, they are nonetheless learned, and if there were someone who had not learned them, he or she would not be able to see a list. The next recourse is to descend still lower (in the direction of atoms) and to claim objectivity for letters, paper, graphite, black marks on white spaces, and so on; but these entities too have palpability and shape only because of the assumption of some or other system of intelligibility, and they are therefore just as available to a deconstructive dissolution as are poems, assignments, and lists.

14   The conclusion, therefore, is that all objects are made and not found, and that they are made by the interpretive strategies we set in motion. This does not, however, commit me to subjectivity because the means by which they are made are social and conventional. That is, the "you" who does the interpretative work that puts poems and assignments and lists into the world is a communal you and not an isolated individual. No one of us wakes up in the morning and (in French fashion) reinvents poetry or thinks up a new educational system or decides to reject seriality in favor of some other, wholly original, form of organization. We do not do these things because we could not do them, because the mental operations we can perform are limited by the institutions in which we are *already* embedded. These institutions precede us, and it is only by inhabiting them, or being inhabited by them, that we have access to the public and conventional senses they make. Thus while it is true to say that we create poetry (and assignments and lists), we create it through interpretive strategies that are finally not our own but have their source in a publicly available system of intelligibility. Insofar as the system (in this case a literary system) constrains us, it also fashions us, furnishing us with categories of understanding, with which we in turn fashion the entities to which we can then point. In short, to the list of made or constructed objects we must add ourselves, for we no less than the poems and assignments we see are the products of social and cultural patterns of thought.

15   To put the matter in this way is to see that the opposition between objectivity and subjectivity is a false one because neither exists in the pure form that would give the opposition its point. This is precisely illustrated by my anecdote in which we do *not* have free-standing readers in a relationship of perceptual adequacy or inadequacy to an equally free-standing text. Rather, we have readers whose consciousnesses are constituted by a set of conventional notions which when put into operation constitute in

turn a conventional, and conventionally seen, object. My students could do what they did, and do it in unison, because as members of a literary community they knew what a poem was (their knowledge was public), and that knowledge led them to look in such a way as to populate the landscape with what they knew to be poems.

16   Of course poems are not the only objects that are constituted in unison by shared ways of seeing. Every object or event that becomes available within an institutional setting can be so characterized. I am thinking, for example, of something that happened in my classroom just the other day. While I was in the course of vigorously making a point, one of my students, William Newlin by name, was just as vigorously waving his hand. When I asked the other members of the class what it was that Mr. Newlin was doing, they all answered that he was seeking permission to speak. I then asked them how they knew that. The immediate reply was that it was obvious; what else could he be thought to be doing? The meaning of his gesture, in other words, was right there on its surface, available for reading by anyone who had the eyes to see. That meaning, however, would not have been available to someone without any knowledge of what was involved in being a student. Such a person might have thought that Mr. Newlin was pointing to the fluorescent lights hanging from the ceiling, or calling our attention to some object that was about to fall ("the sky is falling," "the sky is falling"). And if the someone in question were a child of elementary or middle-school age, Mr. Newlin might well have been seen as seeking permission not to speak but to go to the bathroom, an interpretation or reading that would never occur to a student at Johns Hopkins or any other institution of "higher learning" (and how would we explain to the uninitiated the meaning of *that* phrase).

17   The point is the one I have made so many times before: it is neither the case that the significance of Mr. Newlin's gesture is imprinted on its surface where it need only be read off, or that the construction put on the gesture by everyone in the room was individual and idiosyncratic. Rather, the source of our interpretive unanimity was a structure of interests and understood goals, a structure whose categories so filled our individual consciousnesses that they were rendered as one, immediately investing phenomena with the significance they *must* have, given the already-in-place assumptions about what someone could possibly be intending (by word or gesture) in a classroom. By seeing Mr. Newlin's raised hand with a single shaping eye, we were demonstrating what Harvey Sacks has characterized as "the fine power of a culture. It does not, so to speak, merely fill brains in roughly the same way, it fills them so that they are alike in fine detail."[1] The occasion of Sack's observation was the ability of his hearers to understand a sequence of two sentences—"The baby cried. The mommy picked it up."—exactly as he did (assuming, for example that "the 'mommy' who picks up the 'baby' is the mommy of that baby"), despite the fact that alternative ways of understanding were demonstrably possible. That is, the mommy of the second sentence could well have been the mommy of some other baby, and it need not even

have been a baby that this "floating" mommy was picking up. One is tempted to say that in the absence of a specific context we are authorized to take the words literally, which is what Sacks's hearers do; but as Sacks observes, it is within the assumption of a context—one so deeply assumed that we are unaware of it—that the words acquire what seems to be their literal meaning. There is nothing *in the words* that tells Sacks and his hearers how to relate the mommy and the baby of this story, just as there is nothing *in the form* of Mr. Newlin's gesture that tells his fellow students how to determine its significance. In both cases the determination (of relation and significance) is the work of categories of organization—the family, being a student—that are from the very first giving shape and value to what is heard and seen.

18   Indeed, these categories are the very shape of seeing itself, in that we are not to imagine a perceptual ground more basic than the one they afford. That is, we are not to imagine a moment when my students "simply see" a physical configuration of atoms and *then* assign that configuration a significance, according to the situation they happen to be in. To be in the situation (this or any other) is to "see" with the eyes of its interests, its goals, its understood practices, values, and norms, and so to be conferring significance *by* seeing, not after it. The categories of my students' vision are the categories by which they understand themselves to be functioning as students (what Sacks might term "doing studenting"), and objects will appear to them in forms related to that way of functioning rather than in some objective or preinterpretive form. (This is true even when an object is seen as not related, since nonrelation is not a pure but a differential category—the specification of something by enumerating what it is not; in short, nonrelation is merely one form of relation, and its perception is always situation-specific.)

19   Of course, if someone who was not functioning as a student was to walk into my classroom, he might very well see Mr. Newlin's raised hand (and "raised hand" is already an interpretation-laden description) in some other way, as evidence of a disease, as the salute of a political follower, as a muscle-improving exercise, as an attempt to kill flies; but he would always see it in *some* way, and never as purely physical data waiting for his interpretation. And, moreover, the way of seeing, whatever it was, would never be individual or idiosyncratic, since its source would always be the institutional structure of which the "see-er" was an extending agent. This is what Sacks means when he says that a culture fills brains "so that they are alike in fine detail"; it fills them so that no one's interpretive acts are exclusively his own but fall to him by virtue of his position in some socially organized environment and are therefore always shared and public. It follows, then, that the fear of solipsism, of the imposition by the unconstrained self of its own prejudices, is unfounded because the self does not exist apart from the communal or conventional categories of thought that enable its operations (of thinking, seeing, reading). Once one realizes that the conceptions that fill consciousness, including any conception of its own status, are culturally derived, the

very notion of an unconstrained self, of a consciousness wholly and danger-
ously free, becomes incomprehensible.

20   But without the notion of the unconstrained self, the arguments of
Hirsch, Abrams, and the other proponents of objective interpretation are de-
prived of their urgency. They are afraid that in the absence of the controls afforded by a normative system of meanings, the self will simply substitute its
own meanings for the meanings (usually identified with the intentions of the
author) that texts bring with them, the meanings that texts *"have"*; however,
if the self is conceived of not as an independent entity but as a social construct whose operations are delimited by the systems of intelligibility that inform it, then the meanings it confers on texts are not its own but have their
source in the interpretive community (or communities) of which it is a function. Moreover, these meanings will be neither subjective nor objective, at
least in the terms assumed by those who argue within the traditional framework: they will not be objective because they will always have been the product of a point of view rather than having been simply "read off"; and they
will not be subjective because that point of view will always be social or institutional. Or by the same reasoning one could say that they are *both* subjective and objective: they are subjective because they inhere in a particular
point of view and are therefore not universal; and they are objective because
the point of view that delivers them is public and conventional rather than individual or unique.

21   To put the matter in either way is to see how unhelpful the terms "subjective" and "objective" finally are. Rather than facilitating inquiry, they
close it down, by deciding in advance what shape inquiry can possibly take.
Specifically, they assume, without being aware that it is an assumption and
therefore open to challenge, the very distinction I have been putting into
question, the distinction between interpreters and the objects they interpret. That distinction in turn assumes that interpreters and their objects are
two different kinds of *a*contextual entities, and within these twin assumptions the issue can only be one of control: will texts be allowed to constrain
their own interpretation or will irresponsible interpreters be allowed to obscure and overwhelm texts. In the spectacle that ensues, the spectacle of
Anglo-American critical controversy, texts and selves fight it out in the persons of their respective champions, Abrams, Hirsch, Reichert, Graff on the
one hand, Holland, Bleich, Slatoff, and in some characterizations of him)
Barthes on the other. But if selves are constituted by the ways of thinking
and seeing that inhere in social organizations, and if these constituted selves
in turn constitute texts according to these same ways, then there can be no
adversary relationship between text and self because they are the necessarily related products of the same cognitive possibilities. A text cannot be
overwhelmed by an irresponsible reader and one need not worry about pro-
tecting the purity of a text from a reader's idiosyncrasies. It is only the distinction between subject and object that gives rise to these urgencies, and
once the distinction is blurred they simply fall away. One can respond with

a cheerful yes to the question "Do readers make meanings?" and commit oneself to very little because it would be equally true to say that meanings, in the form of culturally derived interpretive categories, make readers.

22   Indeed, many things look rather different once the subject–object dichotomy is eliminated as the assumed framework within which critical discussion occurs. Problems disappear, not because they have been solved but because they are shown never to have been problems in the first place. Abrams, for example, wonders how, in the absence of a normative system of stable meanings, two people could ever agree on the interpretation of a work or even of a sentence; but the difficulty is only a difficulty if the two (or more) people are thought of as isolated individuals whose agreement must be compelled by something external to them. (There is something of the police state in Abrams's vision, complete with posted rules and boundaries, watchdogs to enforce them, procedures for identifying their violators as criminals.) But if the understandings of the people in question are informed by the same notions of what counts as a fact, of what is central, peripheral, and worthy of being noticed—in short, by the same interpretive principles—then agreement between them will be assured, and its source will not be a text that enforces its own perception but a way of perceiving that results in the emergence to those who share it (or those whom it shares) of the same text. That text might be a poem, as it was in the case of those who first "saw" "Jacobs-Rosenbaum Levin Hayes Thorne Ohman(?)," or a hand, as it is every day in a thousand classrooms; but whatever it is, the shape and meaning it appears immediately to have will be the "ongoing accomplishment"[2] of those who agree to produce it.

NOTES

1. "On the Analysability of Stories by Children," in *Ethnomethodology*, ed. Roy Turner (Baltimore: Penguin, 1974), p. 218.
2. A phrase used by the ethnomethodologists to characterize the interpretive activities that create and maintain the features of everyday life. See, for example, Don H. Zimmerman, "Fact as a Practical Accomplishment," in *Ethnomethodology*, pp. 128–143.

FOLLOW-UP ACTIVITIES

Discussing the Rhetoric

1. What is Fish's purpose in writing this essay? What does he want his audience to believe about knowledge-making?

2. Consider the title, "How to Recognize a Poem When You See One." What tone does this title set for the entire essay?

3. Does the author play a prominent role or a background role in the essay? What rhetorical features help you answer this? How does his positioning of himself within the essay affect what he has to say?

4. Would you consider Fish's language to be casual or formal? How do you think his language influenced you as you read the essay? Did it alienate you? Did it make his ideas easier to understand? Did it play any role in convincing you that his argument was wrong or right?

5. What role do you think the anecdotes play? What proportion of the essay is devoted to telling classroom stories and how much is theorizing? Why is the proportion important?

6. How is the essay organized? Is the heavy theory right at the beginning of the essay, in the middle, or at the end? Why? How is this similar or different from other essays included in this text?

Discussing the Conversation

1. In what ways does Evelyn Fox Keller's essay function as a bridge from the other scientific essays to the essays like this one, written by historians and literary critics?

2. Although Keller and Fish never directly engage gender issues in their essays, both authors agree that individuals are constructed by social patterns. What implications do both essays offer for gender studies? Would Crews agree or disagree with these implications?

3. Tompkins' article "Indians" focuses on the ways writers' perspectives alter how historical events are recorded. What would Fish say is the foundation of individual perspectives?

4. Fish argues that meaning is constructed by the interpretive strategies of communities. What differing views do the articles you've read in Part Two assert? For example, do you think Crews believes that there is a true nature of sexuality, or is it a matter of perspective? Does Magee believe we can find truth if we use the right method? What about Popper?

Joining the Conversation

1. What would Fish say determines, or at least influences, what you see as good or bad, right or wrong? Do you agree with him? Write an informal paper in which you discuss your views of how moral/ethical values are formed.

2. Make a list of rules that influence how you interpret "truth" for at least two of the communities to which you belong. You might consider, for instance, your religious community, your circle of close friends, your school community, or your work community. Write an informal paper in which you describe the rules in each community and trace how they change from community to community.

INTRODUCTORY COMMENTS ON "TERMINISTIC SCREENS" BY KENNETH BURKE

Reading the Context

Kenneth Burke (1897–1993) was an intellectual who never finished college, although he taught at various universities and published several books over a long, productive career. Though known primarily as a literary critic and rhetorician, he has been difficult to identify with a single discipline. His writings range broadly to encompass questions at issue in a wide variety of fields including philosophy, psychology, sociology, communications, linguistics, and history. He began to write during the Great Depression of the 1930s and continued throughout World War II, the McCarthy era of the 1950s, the social unrest of the 1960s, and beyond. Throughout this time, he was concerned with the interrelationships between real world events, systems of belief, language, and human motivation.

Reading the Rhetoric

Burke might be considered a "typical" academic writer (in spite of his atypical education) in that he makes heavy demands on the reader. His vocabulary is difficult, his sentence structure complex, his references sometimes arcane, and he expects the reader to be somewhat familiar with his own previous writing. These are all clearly rhetorical choices; Burke assumes an academic audience—that is, educated readers who are willing to exert the same kind of intellectual effort that Burke expended to formulate the ideas.

Note that this article is structured like traditional academic writing. The first two paragraphs are especially important. It is here that he makes a crucial distinction upon which the remainder of his argument rests: the distinction between his view of language (which he labels "dramatistic") and the view he opposes (labeled "scientistic"). Overall, his organization loosely follows the structure of classical argument: introduction (including the thesis), confirmation (points in support of the writer's view), refutation (arguments against the opponents' point of view), and conclusion. Think about why Burke might have chosen to write in such a traditional academic style and format.

Reading the Conversation

Originally a chapter in a book titled *Language and Symbolic Action* (1966), the piece reprinted here predates most of the selections in this anthology. However, you will see that Burke's discussion of "terministic screens" seems to be engaged with the very questions that will become central to writers publishing in the next three decades. One of the reasons Burke is still studied attentively is that people keep rediscovering that he had valuable insights long ago about contemporary problems. The issue of Part Two that Burke addresses most directly is whether language is an objective or neutral tool, as scientists would like to believe (what Burke refers to as "scientistic" language), or whether language itself actively shapes observations. Burke views language as a kind of human action, using the term "dramatistic" to emphasize its active character. You will recognize that this is another take on issue of language and objectivity discussed by Fish and Pratt, among others.

Terministic Screens
Kenneth Burke

I. DIRECTING THE ATTENTION

1 We might begin by stressing the distinction between a "scientistic" and a "dramatistic" approach to the nature of language. A "scientistic" approach begins with questions of *naming,* or *definition.* Or the power of language to define and describe may be viewed as derivative; and its essential function may be treated as attitudinal or hortatory: attitudinal as with expressions of complaint, fear, gratitude, and such; hortatory as with commands or requests, or, in general, an instrument developed through its use in the social processes of cooperation and competition. I say "developed"; I do *not* say "originating." The ultimate *origins* of language seem to me as mysterious as the origins of the universe itself. One must view it, I feel, simply as the "given." But once an animal comes into being that does happen to have this particular aptitude, the various tribal idioms are unquestionably *developed* by their use as instruments in the tribe's way of living (the practical role of symbolism in what the anthropologist, Malinowski, has called "context of situation"). Such considerations are involved in what I mean by the "dramatistic," stressing language as an aspect of "action," that is, as "symbolic action."

2   The two approaches, the "scientistic" and the "dramatistic" (language as definition, and language as act) are by no means mutually exclusive. Since both approaches have their proper uses, the distinction is not being introduced invidiously. Definition itself is a symbolic act, just as my proposing of this very distinction is a symbolic act. But though at this moment of beginning, the overlap is considerable, later the two roads diverge considerably, and direct our attention to quite different kinds of observation. The quickest way to indicate the differences of direction might be by this formula: The "scientistic" approach builds the edifice of language with primary stress upon a proposition such as "It *is,* or it *is not.*" The "dramatistic" approach puts the primary stress upon such hortatory expressions as comes quite obvious, since the scientistic approach culminates in the kinds of

speculation we associate with symbolic logic, while the dramatistic culminates in the kinds of speculation that find their handiest material in stories,
plays, poems, the rhetoric of oratory and advertising, mythologies, theolo-
gies, and philosophies after the classic model.

3   The dramatistic view of language, in terms of "symbolic action," is exercised about the necessarily *suasive* nature of even the most unemotional scientific nomenclatures. And we shall proceed along those lines; thus:

4   Even if any given terminology is a *reflection* of reality, by its very nature
as a terminology it must be a *selection* of reality; and to this extent it must
function also as a *deflection* of reality.

• • •

5   Here the kind of deflection I have in mind concerns simply the fact that
any nomenclature necessarily directs the attention into some channels rather
than others. In one sense, this likelihood is painfully obvious. A textbook on
physics, for instance, turns the *at*tention in a different direction from a textbook on law or psychology. But some implications of this terministic incentive are not so obvious.

6   When I speak of "terministic screens," I have particularly in mind some
photographs I once saw. They were *different* photographs of the *same* objects, the difference being that they were made with different color filters.
Here something so "factual" as a photograph revealed notable distinctions in
texture, and even in form, depending upon which color filter was used for
the documentary description of the event being recorded in school. In each
case, we might say, the "same" dream will be subjected to a different color
filter, with corresponding differences in the nature of the event as perceived,
recorded, and interpreted. (It is a commonplace that patients soon learn to
have the kind of dreams best suited to the terms favored by their analysts.)

II. OBSERVATIONS IMPLICIT IN TERMS

7 We have now moved things one step further along. Not only does the nature
of our terms affect the nature of our observations, in the sense that the terms
direct the *at*tention to one field rather than to another. Also, *many of the
"observations" are but implications of the particular terminology in terms
of which the observations are made.* In brief, much that we take as observations about "reality" may be but the spinning out of possibilities implicit in
our particular choice of terms.

• • •

8   By its very thoroughness theology [has] a formula that we can adapt, for
purely secular purposes of analysis. I have in mind the injunction, at once
pious and methodological, "Believe, that you may understand *(crede, ut in-
telligas)*." In its theological application, this formula served to define the relation between faith and reason. That is, if one begins with "faith," which

must be taken on authority, one can work out a rationale based on this faith. But the faith must "precede" the rationale.

• • •

9   In my book, *The Rhetoric of Religion,* I have proposed that the word "logology" might be applied in a special way to this issue. By "logology," as so conceived, I would mean the systematic study of theological terms, not from the standpoint of their truth or falsity as statements about the supernatural, but purely for the light they might throw upon the *forms* of language. That is, the tactics involved in the theologian's "words about God" might be studied as "words about words" (by using as a methodological bridge the opening sentence in the Gospel of John: "In the beginning was the Word, and the Word was with God, and the Word was God").

10   "Logology" would be a purely empirical study of symbolic action. Not being a theologian, I would have no grounds to discuss the truth of falsity of theological doctrines as such. But I do feel entitled to discuss them with regard to their nature merely as language. And it is my claim that the injunction, "Believe, that you may understand," has a fundamental application to the purely secular problem of "terministic screens."

11   The "logological," or "terministic" counterpart of "Believe" in the formula would be: *Pick some particular nomenclature, some one terministic screen.* And for "That you may understand," the counterpart would be: *"That you may proceed to track down the kinds of observation implicit in the terminology you have chosen, whether your choice of terms was deliberate or spontaneous."*

III. EXAMPLES

12 I can best state the case by giving some illustrations. But first let me ask you to reconsider a passage from Chapter One which presents the matter in the most general sense:

> . . .can we bring ourselves to realize just how overwhelmingly much of what we mean by "reality" has been built up for us through nothing but our symbol systems? Take away our books, and what little do we know about history, biography, even something so "down to earth" as the relative position of seas and continents? What is our "reality" for today (beyond the paper-thin line of our own particular lives) but all this clutter of symbols about the past, combined with whatever things we know mainly through maps, magazines, newspapers, and the like about the present? In school, as they go from class to class, students turn from one idiom to another. The various courses in the curriculum are in effect but so many different terminologies. And however important to us is the tiny sliver of reality each of us has experienced firsthand, the whole overall "picture" is but a construct of our symbol systems. To meditate on this fact until one sees its full implications is much like peering over the edge of things into an ultimate abyss. And doubtless that's one

reason why, though man is typically the symbol-using animal, he clings to a kind of naïve verbal realism that refuses to let him realize the full extent of the role played by symbolicity in his notions of reality.

13   I hope the passage can serve at least somewhat to suggest how fantastically much of our "Reality" could not exist for us, were it not for our profound and inveterate involvement in symbol systems. Our presence in a room is immediate, but the room's relation to our country as a nation, and beyond that, to international relations and cosmic relations, dissolves into a web of ideas and images that reach through our senses only insofar as the symbol systems that report on them are heard or seen. To mistake this vast tangle of ideas for immediate experience is much more fallacious than to accept a dream as an immediate experience. For a dream really is an immediate experience, but the information that we receive about today's events throughout the world most decidedly is *not*.

14   But let us consider some examples of terministic screens, in a more specific sense. The child psychologist, John Bowlby, writes a subtle and perceptive paper on "The Nature of the Child's Ties to Its Mother." He observes what he calls "five instinctual responses" of infants, which he lists as: crying, smiling, sucking, clinging, following. Surely no one would deny that such responses are there to see. But at the same time, we might recall the observations of the behaviorist, John B. Watson. He, too, found things that were there to see. For instance, by careful scientific study, he discovered sure ways to make babies cry in fright or shriek with rage.

15   In contrast with Watson's terminology of observation regarding the nature of infantile reflexes, note that Bowlby adopted a much more *social* point of view. His terms were explicitly designed to study infantile responses that involved the mother in a reciprocal relationship to the child.

16   At the time I read Bowlby's paper, I happened to be doing a monograph on "Verbal Action in St. Augustine's *Confessions*." I was struck by the fact that Augustine's terms for the behavior of infants closely paralleled Bowlby's. Three were definitely the same: crying, smiling, sucking. Although he doesn't mention clinging as a particularly notable term with regard to infancy, as the result of Bowlby's list I noticed, as I might otherwise not have, that he frequently used the corresponding Latin term *(inhaerere)* regarding his attachment to the Lord. "Following" was not explicitly worked out, as an infantile response, though Augustine does refer to God as his leader. And I began wondering what might be done with Spinoza's *Ethics* in this connection, whether his persistent concern with what necessarily "follows" what in Nature could have been in part a metaphysician's transformation of a personal motive strong in childhood. Be that as it may, I was struck by the fact that Augustine made one strategically important addition to Bowlby's list: rest. Once you mention it, you realize that it is very definitely an instinctual response of the sort that Bowlby was concerned with, since it involves a social relation between mother and child. In Augustine's scheme, of course, it also allowed for a transformation from resting as an infant to hopes of ultimately "resting in God."

17   Our point is: All three terminologies (Watson's, Bowlby's, Augustine's) directed the attention differently, and thus led to a correspondingly different quality of observations. In brief, "behavior" isn't something that you need but observe; even something so "objectively there" as behavior must be observed through one or another kind of *terministic screen,* that directs the attention in keeping with its nature.

18   Basically, there are two kinds of terms: terms that put things together, and terms that take things apart. Otherwise put, A can feel himself identified with B, or he can think of himself as disassociated from B. Carried into mathematics, some systems stress the principle of continuity, some the principle of discontinuity, or particles. And since all laboratory instruments of measurement and observation are devices invented by the symbol-using animal, they too necessarily give interpretations in terms of either continuity or discontinuity. Hence, physicists forever keep finding that some sub-sub-sub-sub-aspect of nature can be again subdivided; whereupon it's only a question of time until they discover that some new cut merges moments previously considered distinct—and so on. Knowing nothing much about physics except the terministic fact that any observation of a physicist must necessarily be stated within the resources and embarrassments of man-made terminologies, I would still dare risk the proposition that Socrates' basic point about dialectic will continue to prevail; namely, there is composition, and there is division.

19   Often this shows up as a distinction between terministic screens positing differences of *degree* and those based on differences of *kind.* For instance, Darwin sees only a difference of degree between man and other animals. But the theologian sees a difference in kind. That is, where Darwin views man as *continuous* with other animals, the theologian would stress the principle of *discontinuity* in this regard. But the theologian's screen also posits a certain kind of *continuity* between man and God that is not ascribed to the relation between God and other animals.

20   The logological screen finds itself in a peculiar position here. It holds that, even on the purely secular level, Darwin overstated his case. And as a consequence, in his stress upon the principle of *continuity* between man and the other animals, he unduly slighted the evidence for *discontinuity* here. For he assumed that the principle of discontinuity between man and other animals was necessarily identical with a theological view of man.

21   Such need not be the case at all. Darwin says astonishingly little about man's special aptitudes as a symbol-user. His terministic screen so stressed the principle of continuity here that he could view the principle of discontinuity only as a case of human self-flattery. Yet, logology would point out: We can distinguish man from other animals without necessarily being over-haughty. For what other animals have yellow journalism, corrupt politics, pornography, stock market manipulators, plans for waging thermonuclear, chemical, and bacteriological war? I think we can consider ourselves different in kind from the other animals, without necessarily being overproud of our distinction. We don't need theology, but merely the evidence of our

characteristic sociopolitical disorders, to make it apparent that man, the typically symbol-using animal, is alas! something special.

IV. FURTHER EXAMPLES

22 Where are we, then?

23   We *must* use terministic screens, since we can't say anything without the use of terms; whatever terms we use, they necessarily constitute a corresponding kind of screen; and any such screen necessarily directs the attention to one field rather than another. Within that field there can be different screens, each with its ways of directing the attention and shaping the range of observations implicit in the given terminology. All terminologies must implicitly or explicitly embody choices between the principle of continuity and the principle of discontinuity.

24   [An]other variant of this point about continuity and discontinuity should be mentioned. Note how it operates in political affairs: During a national election, the situation places great stress upon a *division* between the citizens. But often such divisiveness (or discontinuity) can be healed when the warring factions join in a common cause against an alien enemy (the division elsewhere thus serving to reestablish the principle of continuity at home). It should be apparent how either situation sets up the conditions for its particular kind of scapegoat, as a device that unifies all those who share the same enemy.

·   ·   ·

25   One more point will end this part of our discussion. Recently I read a paper in which one sociologist accused other sociologists of "oversocializing" their terms for the discussion of human motives. (The article, "The Oversocialized Conception of Man in Modern Sociology," by Dennis H. Wrong, appears in the April 1961 issue of the *American Sociological Review.*)

26   This controversy brings us to a variant of the terministic situation I discussed in distinguishing between terms for Poetics in particular and terms for Language in General. But the author's thesis really has a much wider application than he claims for it. To the extent that all scientific terminologies, by their very role in specialized disciplines, are designed to focus attention upon one or another particular field of observation, would it not be technically impossible for any such specialized terminology to supply an adequate definition for the discussion of *man in general?* Each might serve to throw light upon one or another aspect of human motives. But the definition of man in general would be formally possible only to a *philosophic* terminology of motives (insofar as philosophy is the proper field for thoughts on man in general). Any definition of man in terms of specialized scientific nomenclatures would necessarily be "over-socialized," or "over-biologized," or "over-psychologized," or "over-physicized," or "over-poetized," and so on, depending upon which specialized terministic screen was being stretched to cover not just its

own special field but a more comprehensive area. Or, if we try to correct the excesses of *one terminology,* by borrowing from several, what strictly *scientific* canon (in the modern sense of scientific specialization) could we adduce as sanction? Would not such an eclectic recipe itself involve a generalized philosophy of some sort?

V. OUR ATTEMPTS TO AVOID MERE RELATIVISM

27 And now where are we? Must we merely resign ourselves to an endless catalogue of terministic screens, each of which can be valued for the light it throws upon the human animal, yet none of which can be considered central? In one sense, yes. For, strictly speaking, there will be as many different world views in human history as there are people. *(Tot homines, tot sententiae.)* We can safely take it for granted that no one's "personal equations" are quite identical with anyone else's. In the unwritten cosmic constitution that lies behind all man-made Constitutions, it is decreed by the nature of things that each man is "necessarily free" to be his own tyrant, inexorably imposing upon himself the peculiar combination of insights associated with his peculiar combination of experiences.

28   At the other extreme, each of us shares with all other members of our kind (the often-inhuman human species) the fatal fact that, however the situation came to be, all members of our species conceive of reality somewhat roundabout, through various *media* of symbolism. Any such medium will be, as you prefer, either a way of "dividing" us from the "immediate" (thereby setting up a kind of "alienation" at the very start of our emergence from infancy into that state of articulacy somewhat misleadingly called the "age of reason"); or it can be viewed as a paradoxical way of "uniting" us with things on a "higher level of awareness," or some such. (Here again, we encounter our principles of continuity and discontinuity.)

29   Whether such proneness to symbolic activity be viewed as a privilege or a calamity (or as something of both), it is a distinguishing characteristic of the human animal in general. Hence it can properly serve as the basis of a general, or philosophic definition of this animal. From this terministic beginning, this intuitive grounding of a position, many observations "necessarily follow." But are we not here "necessarily" caught in our own net? Must we not concede that a screen built on this basis is just one more screen; and that it can at best be permitted to take its place along with all the others? Can we claim for it special favors?

30   If I, or any one person, or even one particular philosophic school, had invented it, such doubts would be quite justified. But if we pause to look at it quizzically, I think we shall see that it is grounded in a kind of "collective revelation," from away back. This "collective revelation" involves the pragmatic recognition of a distinction between persons and things. I say "pragmatic" recognition, because often the distinction has not been *formally*

recognized. And all the more so because, if an object is closely associated with some person whom we know intimately, it can readily become infused with the identity of that person.

31   Reverting now to our original term, "dramatistic," I would offer this basic proposition for your consideration: Despite the evidences of primitive animism (that endows many sheer things with "souls") and the opposite modes of contemporary behaviorism (designed to study people as mere things), we do make a pragmatic distinction between the "actions" of "persons" and the sheer "motions" of "things." The slashing of the waves against the beach, or the endless cycle of births and deaths in biologic organisms would be examples of sheer motion. Yet we, the typically symbol-using animal, cannot relate to one another sheerly as things in motion. Even the behaviorist, who studies man in terms of his laboratory experiments, must treat his colleagues as *persons,* rather than purely and simply as automata responding to stimuli.

32   I should make it clear: I am not pronouncing on the metaphysics of this controversy. Maybe we are but things in motion. I don't have to haggle about that possibility. I need but point out that, whether or not we are just things in motion, we think of one another (and especially of those with whom we are intimate) as *persons.* And the difference between a thing and a person is that the one merely *moves* whereas the other *acts.* For the sake of the argument, I'm even willing to grant that the distinction between *things moving* and *persons acting* is but an illusion. All I would claim is that, illusion or not, the human race cannot possibly get along with itself on the basis of any other intuition. The human animal, as we know it, *emerges into personality* by first mastering whatever tribal speech happens to be its particular symbolic environment.

33   We could not here list even summarily the main aspects of the Dramatistic screen without launching into a whole new project. For present purposes, I must only say enough to indicate my grounds for contending that a Dramatistic screen does possess the philosophic character adapted to the discussion of man in general, as distinct from the kinds of insight afforded by the application of special scientific terminologies.

34   In behalf of my claim that the "dramatistic screen" is sanctioned by a "collective revelation" of long standing, suffice it to recall such key terms as *tao, karma, dike, energeia, hodos, actus*—all of them words for *action* (to which we might well add *Islam,* as the name for a submission *attitude* with its obviously active possibilities). The Bible starts with God's act, by creative fiat. Contemporary sociological theories of "role-taking" fit into the same general scheme. Terms like "transactions," "exchange," "competition," "cooperation," are but more specific terms for "action." And there are countless words for specific acts: give, take, run, think, etc. The contemporary concern with "game theories" is obviously a subdivision of the same term. Add the gloomy thought that such speculative playfulness now is usually concerned with "war games." But in any case, the concept of such games must

involve, in however fragmentary a fashion, the picture of persons acting under stress. And even when the "game" hypothetically reduces most of the players to terms of mere pawns, we can feel sure in advance that, if the "game" does not make proper allowance for the "human equation," the conclusions when tested will prove wrong.

35   But the thought should admonish us. Often it is true that people can be feasibly reduced to terms of sheer motion. About fifty years ago, I was suddenly *startled* into thinking when (encountering experience purely "symbolwise," purely via the news) I read of the first German attacks against a Belgian fortress in World War I. The point was simply this: The approach to the fortress was known to be mined. And the mines had to be exploded. So wave after wave of human flesh was sent forward, as conditioned cattle, to get blown up, until all the mines had been touched off. Then the next wave, or the next two or three waves thereafter, could take the fort. Granted, that comes pretty close to sheer motion, doubtless conceived in the best war-game tradition.

36   Basically, the Dramatistic screen involves a methodic tracking down of the implications in the idea of symbolic action, and of man as the kind of being that is particularly distinguished by an aptitude for such action. To quote from Webster's *Third New International Dictionary,* which has officially recognized "Dramatism" in my sense of the term, as treated schematically in my *Grammar of Motives,* it is "A technique of analysis of language and thought as basically modes of action rather than as means of conveying information." I would but note that such an "Ism" can also function as a philosophy of human relations. The main consideration to keep in mind, for present purposes, is that two quite different but equally justifiable positions are implicit in this approach to specifically human motivation.

FOLLOW-UP ACTIVITIES

Discussing the Rhetoric

1. Who does Burke's intended audience seem to be? Do you include yourself among the members of this audience? Why or why not?

2. Note that Burke uses an analogy together with an example to define "terministic screens." Do you think his analogy is effective? Why do you think Burke settled on the words "terministic" and "screen" to name his concept? What are the advantages of using analogies to explain a concept?

3. Where else does Burke use an analogy to explain his ideas? What point does he make through the use of the analogy?

4. In what ways is this selection rhetorically similar to Pratt's "Arts of the Contact Zone"? to Fish's "How to Recognize a Poem When You See One"? How does it differ? Given that the audiences for all three selections are academics, how would you explain the differences in rhetorical choices the authors make?

Discussing the Conversation

1. Which of the writers you have read so far seem to have a "scientistic" view of language? Explain why you think their view is scientistic.

2. What similarities do you see between Burke's and Keller's (or McClintock's) ideas about the effects of viewpoint on observations? Though they seem to agree on some specifics, how do their central interests diverge?

3. What similarities do you see between Burke's and Addelson's views about the possibility of neutral observation? How do they differ in their explanations of why researcher's views are never neutral?

4. How are Burke's and Fish's views similar? In what ways do their focuses differ?

Joining the Conversation

1. At the beginning of Part III: "Examples," Burke says, "However important to us is the tiny sliver of reality each of us has experienced firsthand, the whole overall 'picture' is but a construct of our symbol systems. To meditate on this fact until one sees its full implications is much like peering over the edge of things into an ultimate abyss." In an informal paper, explain what the first sentence of this quotation means to you. Then meditate on its implications for awhile, and write about your meditations.

2. Keller, Addelson, Appleby and her colleagues, Fish, Tompkins, Pratt, and Burke all argue that observations are never neutral. Pick three of these writers and compare their views, considering not only how they are different or similar, but also how one may exemplify, elaborate, or build upon the ideas of another. You will be writing an informal version of the formal synthesis assignment in Part Four of this text.

3. If an election campaign is in process as you are studying this course, examine the campaign ads and speeches for ways in which language is used to divide or unify people. What factions does the language create? What groups are set in opposition to each other? Are any "common enemies" proposed against which the campaigners try to unite a majority? What do you think is the effect of such attempts at division or unity on a nation's social cohesion? Write an informal paper in which you relate Burke's approach to issues of unity and discontinuity.

PART THREE

Conversations about Writing

Have you ever overheard your name dropped in a conversation in which you were not a part? What was your response? Did you hurry out of earshot? Did you edge closer to the group so you could hear what was being said about you? Did you burst into the conversation and good-naturedly invite yourself to participate? Did you clear your throat or try to make yourself noticed and let the others know you were standing there listening? What did you do with the information you overheard? Did you try to forget that you ever heard it? Did you confront the speakers with their rudeness? Did you decide to cut off contact with the thoughtless traitors? Did you find yourself basking in the warmth of unexpected praise? Did you tuck the information away and scheme to use it strategically at the perfect time?

In Part Three, we invite you to eavesdrop on several discussions in which you are the topic of conversation. You will "hear" researchers and teachers of college composition "talking" about what student writers do and about what they ought to be taught to succeed as college writers.

They describe the ways that students struggle in learning to read and write appropriately at the college level and explain what students need to learn to do to be successful college writers. They discuss student mistakes and student progress. They talk to each other to understand the best ways to help their students learn how to negotiate the varying terrain of college writing.

BACKGROUND AND OVERVIEW

English composition has been taught at the university level since 1874 when the first freshman writing class was instituted at Harvard University. Scholars who study writing practices and teaching are known as compositionists. To understand writers, writing practices, and the best ways to teach academic writing to college students, compositionists draw from many disciplines: rhetoric, philosophy, psychology, history, sociology, literary studies, linguistics, communication, cultural studies, computer science, and educational studies.

Some composition research examines the history of writing instruction; writers' invention practices, forms of expression, and ways of making meaning; or the roles that audiences play in text production. Other research may examine the influences of culture on writing processes, the specific rhetorical and linguistic features of written text, the evolution of genre conventions, or the varied uses for writing within different discourse communities. Compositionists study a wide array of issues so that they can make recommendations both about writing in many disciplines and about the best ways to teach writing to students who must write in a number of disciplinary areas to succeed as college students.

As you have seen in this collection, academics do not all write alike. Each discipline has its own conventions for writing and writers choose to write within or to transgress them for various reasons. You have seen writers doing both—writing within and transgressing—in the selections in this text. Compositionists attempt to reveal the strategies academic writers use, describe the conventions managing various disciplinary writing, and investigate the complexities of intersections between the writer's audience, purpose, and rhetorical choices. They do this primarily so that they can teach students what is at stake in either learning to conform to the conventions or in resisting them.

In his essay, "Inventing the University," which appears in this part, compositionist David Bartholomae observes the activities a student needs to engage in to learn to write within academic conventions as follows:

> Every time a student sits down to write for us, he has to invent the university for the occasion—invent the university, that is, or a branch of it, like History or Anthropology or Economics or English. He has to learn to speak our language, to speak as we do, to try on the peculiar ways of knowing, selecting, evaluating, reporting, concluding, and arguing that define the discourse of our community. Or perhaps I should say the various discourses of our community, since it is in the nature of a liberal arts education that a student, after a year or two, must learn to try on a variety of voices and interpretive schemes—to write, for example, as a literary critic one day and an experimental psychologist the next, to work within fields where the rules governing the presentation of examples or the development of an argument are both distinct and even to a professional, mysterious. (p. x)

CONVERSATIONS BETWEEN READINGS

The readings in this part constitute a conversation in a single discipline, Composition Studies. The Part begins with Bartholomae's article, "Inventing the University," in which he discusses "commonplaces" in terms of student writing. He shows how these accepted notions and forms determine a system of interpretation for readers and writers and describes successful student writing as being able to write within and against that system.

The selections following Bartholomae examine the reading and writing processes of several college students. The excerpt from a book by Linda Flower, Victoria Stein, John Ackerman, Margaret Kantz, Kathleen McCormack, and Wayne Peck examines the developing processes of students learning to write. Flower and her colleagues take a detailed look at the ways freshman writers interpret and negotiate a writing assignment. They note that students can interpret a writing task in a variety of ways and that these interpretations can affect their success as a writer. In the next reading, Karen Spear identifies problems in peer response groups commonly experienced by students in composition courses. You may be able to chart a more successful collaborative course by reading about the conflicts and confusion over sharing writing that are described in this excerpt from the author's comprehensive work, *Sharing Writing*. The next selection, "Learning to Read Biology: One Student's Rhetorical Development in College" by Christine Haas, provides you an opportunity to learn how to read a long research study as well as the chance to read about one student's progress toward negotiating academic discourse. The following article by Mariolina Salvatori discusses the role reading plays in the composition classroom. She indicates how students' reading strategies may direct their writing decisions, using literary examples to demonstrate her points.

Following these readings is a piece by Jim Corder, "Argument as Emergence, Rhetoric as Love," which brings the issue of home identities full circle by returning to the ways one's history and beliefs influence the writing one does. Corder provides an opportunity to revisit the tenuous nature of the negotiation of ideas and positions.

READING AND WRITING OBJECTIVES

In Part One, you began to recognize the ways that home identities influence the development of one's student or academic identity. In Part Two, you learned about the rhetorical nature of writing and knowledge construction in the university and its relation to professors' expectations for your writing. You have also learned and practiced the expectations for typical student writing forms or genres throughout. We have two primary reading and writing goals for Part Three. The first is to make visible the otherwise invisible reading and writing strategies and processes that writers like you have learned in order to produce successful writing in college. The second goal is to offer you a wider range of processes and strategies from which to choose as you develop your own academic writing identity. As you see what others have done, you are better able to adopt additional strategies to use in your academic endeavors. We invite you to listen to the conversations about you, unravel the mystery, and strategize your plan for success. Join in the conversations as you discuss your developing plans for writing with your peers and your professors. Add your own views about how best to accomplish college writing as a developing student writer. Think about what you might have to discuss with compositionists about learning to write at the university. Jump in when you're ready.

INTRODUCTORY COMMENTS ON "INVENTING THE UNIVERSITY" BY DAVID BARTHOLOMAE

Reading the Context

David Bartholomae has been influential in constructing a view of writing instruction that suggests that student difficulties with college writing stem, not from the texts they read or from the skills they bring with them to the text, but from their interpretation of what it means to read and write in an academic context. This view encompasses how students read, mark texts, interact with instructors, engage in classroom interactions, interpret individual writing assignments, and more.

"Inventing the University" comes from Bartholomae's book *When a Writer Can't Write* (1985). He also co-authored *Facts, Artifacts, and Counterfacts: Reading and Writing in Theory and Practice.*

Reading the Rhetoric

In this essay, Bartholomae addresses other writing teachers, so it is written about, not to, beginning college writers. Here is an opportunity to be a "fly on the wall" and see what writing professionals say about you. Pay attention to the words Bartholomae chooses when describing beginning writers. If terms (or the way he's using those terms) are new to you, use the surrounding text to help you figure out a probable meaning.

Bartholomae's essay represents a voice in an ongoing conversation among compositionists about the difficulties beginning writers face when they enter the university. The essay suggests that one of the differences between beginning and experienced writers is that the experienced ones can "imagine how a reader will respond to a text and can transform or restructure what they have to say around a goal shared with the reader." Given what you now know about Bartholomae's audience, what do you think is the goal that Bartholomae and his readers share?

Reading the Conversation

Many of Bartholomae's readers have responded in print to the issues he raises in this essay, such as his view that students must assimilate to academic discourse. Some of those readers' voices are heard in other readings in Part Three. Peter Elbow, especially, has taken issue with Bartholomae's contention that student writing must be constructed by academic conventions rather than be the expression of the writer's personal voice. It might be helpful to use Bartholomae's essay as a starting point and to imagine that other writers in this part are responding to him in various ways. Highlighting parts of this essay that seem novel, interesting, provoking, or otherwise meaningful to you will help you be conscious of issues that come up in other readings.

Inventing the University[1]
David Bartholomae

Education may well be, as of right, the instrument whereby every individual, in a society like our own, can gain access to any kind of discourse. But we well know that in its distribution, in what it permits and in what it prevents, it follows the well-trodden battle-lines of social conflict. Every educational system is a political means of maintaining or of modifying the appropriation of discourse, with the knowledge and the powers it carries with it.

Foucault, "The Discourse on Language" (227)

1 Every time a student sits down to write for us, he has to invent the university for the occasion—invent the university, that is, or a branch of it, like History or Anthropology or Economics or English. He has to learn to speak our language, to speak as we do, to try on the peculiar ways of knowing, selecting, evaluating, reporting, concluding, and arguing that define the discourse of our community. Or perhaps I should say the *various* discourses of our community, since it is in the nature of a liberal arts education that a student, after the first year or two, must learn to try on a variety of voices and interpretive schemes—to write, for example, as a literary critic one day and an experimental psychologist the next, to work within fields where the rules governing the presentation of examples or the development of an argument are both distinct and, even to a professional, mysterious.

2   The students have to appropriate (or be appropriated by) a specialized discourse, and they have to do this as though they were easily and comfortably one with their audience, as though they were members of the academy,

or historians or anthropologists or economists; they have to invent the university by assembling and mimicking its language, finding some compromise between idiosyncrasy, a personal history, and the requirements of convention, the history of a discipline. They must learn to speak our language. Or they must dare to speak it, or to carry off the bluff, since speaking and writing will most certainly be required long before the skill is "learned." And this, understandably, causes problems.

3   Let me look quickly at an example. Here is an essay written by a college freshman, a basic writer:

> In the past time I thought that an incident was creative was when I had to make a clay model of the earth, but not of the classical or your everyday model of the earth which consists of the two cores, the mantle and the crust. I thought of these things in a dimension of which it would be unique, but easy to comprehend. Of course, your materials to work with were basic and limited at the same time, but thought help to put this limit into a right attitude or frame of mind to work with the clay. In the beginning of the clay model, I had to research and learn the different dimensions of the earth (in magnitude, quantity, state of matter, etc.). After this, I learned how to put this into the clay and come up with something different than any other person in my class at the time. In my opinion, color coordination and shape was the key to my creativity of the clay model of the earth.

> Creativity is the venture of the mind at work with the mechanics relay to the limbs from the cranium, which stores and triggers this action. It can be a burst of energy released at a precise time a thought is being transmitted. This can cause a frenzy of the human body, but it depends of the characteristics of the individual and how they can relay the message clearly enough through mechanics of the body to us as an observer. Then we must determine if it is creative or a learned process varied by the individuals thought process. Creativity is indeed a tool which has to exist, or our world will not succeed into the future and progress like it should.

4   I am continually impressed by the patience and good will of our students. This student was writing a placement essay during freshman orientation. (The problem set to him was, "Describe a time when you did something you felt to be creative. Then, on the basis of the incident you have described, go on to draw some general conclusions about 'creativity'.") He knew that university faculty would be reading and evaluating his essay, and so he wrote for them.

5   In some ways it is a remarkable performance. He is trying on the discourse even though he doesn't have the knowledge that makes the discourse more than a routine, a set of conventional rituals and gestures. And he does this, I think, even though he knows he doesn't have the knowledge that makes the discourse more than a routine. He defines himself as a researcher working systematically, and not as a kid in a high school class: "I though of these things in a dimension of . . ."; "had to research and learn the different dimensions of the earth (in magnitude, quantity, state of matter, etc.)." He

moves quickly into a specialized language (his approximation of our jargon) and draws both a general, textbook-like conclusion ("Creativity is the venture of the mind at work . . .") and a resounding peroration ("Creativity is indeed a tool which has to exist, or our world will not succeed into the future and progress like it should.") The writer has even, with that "indeed" and with the qualifications and the parenthetical expressions of the opening paragraphs, picked up the rhythm of our prose. And through it all he speaks with an impressive air of authority.

6   There is an elaborate but, I will argue, a necessary and enabling fiction at work here as the student dramatizes his experience in a "setting"—the setting required by the discourse—where he can speak to us as a companion, a fellow researcher. As I read the essay, there is only one moment when the fiction is broken, when we are addressed differently. The student says, "Of course, your materials to work with were basic and limited at the same time, but thought help to put this limit into a right attitude or frame of mind to work with the clay." At this point, I think, we become students and he the teacher, giving us a lesson (as in, "You take your pencil in your right hand and put your paper in front of you."). This is, however, one of the most characteristic slips of basic writers. It is very hard for them to take on the role—the voice, the person—of an authority whose authority is rooted in scholarship, analysis, or research. They slip, then, into the more immediately available and realizable voice of authority, the voice of a teacher giving a lesson or the voice of a parent lecturing at the dinner table. They offer advice or homilies rather than "academic" conclusions. There is a similar break in the final paragraph, where the conclusion that pushes for a definition ("Creativity is the venture of the mind at work with the mechanics relay to the limbs from the cranium . . .") is replaced by a conclusion which speaks in the voice of an Elder ("Creativity is indeed a tool which has to exist or our world will not succeed into the future and progress like it should.").

7   It is not uncommon then, to find such breaks in the concluding sections of essays written by basic writers. Here is the concluding section of an essay written by a student about his work as a mechanic. He had been asked to generalize about "work" after reviewing an on-the-job experience or incident that "stuck in his mind" as somehow significant.

> How could two repairmen miss a leak? Lack of pride? No incentive? Lazy? I don't know.

At this point the writer is in a perfect position to speculate to move from the problem to an analysis of the problem. Here is how the paragraph continues however (and notice the change in pronoun reference):

> From this point on I take *my* time do it right and don't let customers get under your skin. If they have a complaint tell them to call your boss and he'll be more than glad to handle it. Most important worry about yourself and keep a clear eye on everyone for there's always someone trying to take advantage of you anytime and anyplace.

We get neither a technical discussion nor an "academic" discussion but a Lesson on Life.[2] This is the language he uses to address the general question, "How could two repairmen miss a leak?" The other brand of conclusion, the more academic one, would have required him to speak of his experience in our terms; it would, that is, have required a special vocabulary, a special system of presentation and an interpretive scheme (or a set of commonplaces) he could use to identify and talk about the mystery of human error. The writer certainly had access to the range of acceptable commonplaces for such an explanation: "lack of pride," "no incentive," "lazy." Each would dictate its own set of phrases, examples, and conclusions, and we, his teachers, would know how to write out each argument, just as we would know how to write out more specialized arguments of our own. A "common-place," then, is a culturally or institutionally authorized concept or statement that carries with it its own necessary elaboration. We all use commonplaces to orient ourselves in the world; they provide a point of reference and a set of "prearticulated" explanations that are readily available to organize and interpret experience. The phrase "lack of pride" carries with it its own account for the repairman's error just as, at another point in time, a reference to "original sin" would provide an explanation, or just as, in a certain university classroom, a reference to "alienation" would enable a writer to continue and complete the discussion. While there is a way in which these terms are interchangeable, they are not all permissible. A student in a composition class would most likely be turned away from a discussion of original sin. Commonplaces are the "controlling ideas" of our composition textbooks, textbooks that not only insist upon a set form for expository writing but a set view of public life.[3]

8   When the student above says, "I don't know," he is saying then, that he has nothing to say. He is saying that he is not in a position to carry on this discussion. And so we are addressed as apprentices rather than as teachers or scholars. To speak to us as a person of status or privilege, the writer can either speak to us in our terms—in the privileged language of university discourse—or, in default (or in defiance), he can speak to us as though we were children, offering us the wisdom of experience.

9   I think it is possible to say that the language of the "Clay Model" paper has come *through* the writer and not from the writer. The writer has located himself (he has located the self that is represented by the I on the page) in a context that is, finally, beyond him, not his own and not available to his immediate procedures for inventing and arranging text. I would not, that is, call this essay an example of "writer-based" prose. I would not say that it is egocentric or that it represents the "interior monologue of a writer thinking and talking to himself" (Flower 63). It is, rather, the record of a writer who has lost himself in the discourse of his readers. There is a context beyond the reader that is not the world but a way of talking about the world, a way of talking that determines the use of examples, the possible conclusions, the acceptable commonplaces, and the key words of an essay on the construction of a

clay model of the earth. This writer has entered the discourse without successfully approximating it.

10   Linda Flower has argued that the difficulty inexperienced writers have with writing can be understood as a difficulty in negotiating the transition between writer-based and reader-based prose. Expert writers, in other words, can better imagine how a reader will respond to a text and can transform or restructure what they have to say around a goal shared with a reader. Teaching students to revise for readers, then, will better prepare them to write initially with a reader in mind. The success of this pedagogy depends upon the degree to which a writer can imagine and conform to a readers' goals. The difficulty of this act of imagination, and the burden of such conformity, are so much at the heart of the problem that a teacher must pause and take stock before offering revision as a solution. Students like the student who wrote the "Clay Model" paper are not so much trapped in a private language as they are shut out—from one of the privileged languages of public life, a language they are aware of but cannot control.

11   Our students, I've said, have to appropriate (or be appropriated by) a specialized discourse, and they have to do this as though they were easily or comfortably one with their audience. If you look at the situation this way, suddenly the problem of audience awareness becomes enormously complicated. One of the common assumptions of both composition research and composition teaching is that at some "stage" in the process of composing an essay a writer's ideas or his motives must be tailored to the needs and expectations of his audience. A writer has to "build bridges" between his point of view and his readers. He has to anticipate and acknowledge his readers' assumptions and biases. He must begin with "common points of departure" before introducing new or controversial arguments. There is a version of the pastoral at work here. It is assumed that a person of low status (like a shepherd) can speak to a person of power (like a courtier), but only (at least so far as the language is concerned) if he is not a shepherd at all, but actually a member of the court out in the fields in disguise.

12   Writers who can successfully manipulate an audience (or, to use a less pointed language, writers who can accommodate their motives to their readers' expectations) are writers who can both imagine and write from a position of privilege. They must, that is, see themselves within a privileged discourse, one that already includes and excludes groups of readers. They must be either equal to or more powerful than those they would address. The writing, then, must somehow transform the political and social relationships between basic writing students and their teachers.

13   If my students are going to write for me by knowing who I am—and if this means more than knowing my prejudices, psyching me out—it means knowing what I know; it means having the knowledge of a professor of English. They have, then, to know what I know and how I know what I know (the interpretive schemes that define the way I would work out the problems I set for them); they have to learn to write what I would write, or to offer up

some approximation of that discourse. The problem of audience awareness, then, is a problem of power and finesse. It cannot be addressed, as it is in most classroom exercises, by giving students privilege and denying the situation of the classroom, by having students write to an outsider, someone excluded from their privileged circle: "Write about 'To His Coy Mistress,' not for your teacher, but for the students in your class": "Describe Pittsburgh to someone who has never been there"; "Explain to a high school senior how best to prepare for college"; "Describe baseball to a Martian."

14   Exercises such as these allow students to imagine the needs and goals of a reader and they bring those needs and goals forward as a dominant constraint in the construction of an essay. And they argue, implicitly, what is generally true about writing—that it is an act of aggression disguised as an act of charity. What they fail to address is the central problem of academic writing, where students may assume the right of speaking to someone who knows Pittsburgh or "To His Coy Mistress" better than they do, a reader for whom the general commonplaces and the readily available utterances about a subject are inadequate. It should be clear that when I say that I know Pittsburgh better than my basic writing students I am talking about a way of knowing that is also a way of writing. There may be much that they know that I don't know, but in the setting of the university classroom I have a way of talking about the town that is "better" (and for arbitrary reasons) than theirs.

15   I think that all writers, in order to write, must imagine for themselves the privilege of being "insiders"—that is, of being both inside an established and powerful discourse, and of being granted a special right to speak. And I think that right to speak is seldom conferred upon us—upon any of us, teachers or students—by virtue of the fact that we have invented or discovered an original idea. Leading students to believe that they are responsible for something new or original, unless they understand what those words mean with regard to writing, is a dangerous and counterproductive practice. We do have the right to expect students to be active and engaged, but that is more a matter of being continually and stylistically working against the inevitable presence of conventional language; it is not a matter of inventing a language that is new.

16   When students are writing for a teacher, writing becomes more problematic than it is for the students who are describing baseball to a Martian. The students, in effect, have to assume privilege without having any. And since students assume privilege by locating themselves within the discourse of a particular community—within a set of specifically acceptable gestures and commonplaces—learning at least as it is defined in the liberal arts curriculum, becomes more a matter of imitation or parody than a matter of invention and discovery.

17   What our beginning students need to learn is to extend themselves into the commonplaces, set phrases, rituals, gestures, habits of mind, tricks of persuasion, obligatory conclusions, and necessary connections that determine the "what might be said" and constitute knowledge within the various

branches of our academic community. The course of instruction that would make this possible would be based on a sequence of illustrated assignments and would allow for successive approximations of academic or "disciplinary" discourse. Students will not take on our peculiar ways of reading, writing, speaking, and thinking all at once. Nor will the command of a subject like sociology, at least as that command is represented by the successful completion of a multiple choice exam, enable students to write sociology. Our colleges and universities, by and large, have failed to involve basic writing students in scholarly projects, projects that would allow them to act as though they were colleagues in an academic enterprise. Much of the written work students do is test-taking, report or summary, work that places them outside the working discourse of the academic community, where they are expected to admire and report on what we do, rather than inside that discourse, where they can do its work and participate in a common enterprise.[4] This is a failure of teachers and curriculum designers who, even if they speak of writing as a mode of learning, all too often represent writing as a "tool" to be used by an (hopefully) educated mind.

18   Pat Bizzell is one of the most important scholars writing now on basic writers and on the special requirements of academic discourse.[5] In a recent essay, "Cognition, Convention and Certainty: What We Need to Know About Writing," she argues that the problem of basic writers might be

> better understood in terms of their unfamiliarity with the academic discourse community, combined, perhaps, with such limited experience outside their native discourse communities that they are unaware that there is such a thing as a discourse community with conventions to be mastered. What is underdeveloped is their knowledge both of the ways experience is constituted and interpreted in the academic discourse community and of the fact that all discourse communities constitute and interpret experience. (230)

19   One response to the problems of basic writers, then, would be to determine just what the community's conventions are, so that those conventions can be written out, "demystified," and taught in our classrooms. Teachers, as a result, could be more precise and helpful when they ask students to "think," "argue," "describe," or "define." Another response would be to examine the essays written by basic writers—their approximations of academic discourse—to determine more clearly where the problems lie. If we look at their writing, and we look at it in the context of other student writing, we can better see the points of discord when students try to write their way into the university.

20   The purpose of the remainder of this paper will be to examine some of the most striking and characteristic problems as they are presented in the expository essays of basic writers. I will be concerned, then, with university discourse in its most generalized form—that is, as represented by introductory courses—and not with the special conventions required by advanced

work in the various disciplines. And I will be concerned with the difficult, and often violent, accommodations that occur when students locate themselves in a discourse that is not "naturally" or immediately theirs.

21   I have reviewed 500 essays written in response to the "creativity" question used during one of our placement exams. (The essay cited at the opening of this paper was one of that group.) Some of the essays were written by basic writers (or, more properly, those essays led readers to identify the writers as "basic writers"); some were written by students who "passed" (who were granted immediate access to the community of writers at the university). As I read these essays, I was looking to determine the stylistic resources that enabled writers to locate themselves within an "academic" discourse. My bias as a reader should be clear by now. I was not looking to see how the writer might represent the skills demanded by a neutral language (a language whose key features were paragraphs, topic sentences, transitions and the like—features of a clear and orderly mind). I was looking to see what happened when a writer entered into a language to locate himself (a textual self) and his subject, and I was looking to see how, once entered, that language made or unmade a writer.

22   Here is one essay. Its writer was classified as a basic writer. Since the essay is relatively free of sentence level errors, that decision must have been rooted in some perceived failure of the discourse itself.

> I am very interested in music, and I try to be creative in my interpretation of music. While in high school, I was a member of a jazz ensemble. The members of the ensemble were given chances to improvise and be creative in various songs. I feel that this was a great experience for me, as well as the other members. I was proud to know that I could use my imagination and feelings to create music other than what was written.

> Creativity to me, means being free to express yourself in a way that is unique to you, not having to conform to certain rules and guidelines. Music is only one of the many areas in which people are given opportunities to show their creativity. Sculpting, carving, building, art, and acting are just a few more areas where people can show their creativity.

> Through my music I conveyed feelings and thoughts which were important to me. Music was my means of showing creativity. In whatever form creativity takes, whether it be music, art, or science, it is an important aspect of our lives because it enables us to be individuals.

23   Notice, in this essay, the key gesture, one that appears in all but a few of the essays I read. The student defines as his own that which is a commonplace. "Creativity, *to me,* means being free to express yourself in a way that is unique to you, not having to conform to certain rules and guidelines." This act of appropriation constitutes his authority; it constitutes his authority as a writer and not just as a musician (that is, as someone with a story to tell). There were many essays in the set that told only a story, where the writer's established presence was as a musician or a skier or someone who painted

designs on a van, but not as a person removed from that experience interpreting it, treating it as a metaphor for something else (creativity). Unless those stories were long, detailed, and very well told (unless the writer was doing more than saying, "I am a skier or a musician or a van-painter"), those writers were all given low ratings.

24   Notice also that the writer of the jazz paper locates himself and his experience in relation to the commonplace (creativity is unique expression: it is not having to conform to rules or guidelines) regardless of whether it is true or not. Anyone who improvises "knows" that improvisation follows rules and guidelines. It is the power of the commonplace (its truth as a recognizable and, the writer believes, as a final statement) that justifies the example and completes the essay. The example, in other words, has value because it stands within the field of the commonplace. It is not the occasion for what one might call an "objective" analysis or a "close" reading. It could also be said that the essay stops with the articulation of the commonplace. The following sections speak only to the power of that statement. The reference to "sculpting, carving, building, art, and acting" attests to the universality of the commonplace (and it attests to the writer's nervousness with the status he has appropriated for himself—he is saying, "Now, I'm not only the one here who's done something unique."). The commonplace stands by itself. For this writer, it does not need to be elaborated. By virtue of having written it, he has completed the essay and established the contract by which we may be spoken to as equals: "In whatever form creativity takes, whether it be music, art, or science, it is an important aspect of our lives because it enables us to be individuals." (For me to break that contract, to argue that *my* life is not represented in that essay, is one way for me to begin as a teacher with that student in that essay.)

25   I said that the writer of the jazz paper offered up a commonplace regardless of whether it was "true" or not, and this, I said, was an example of the power of a commonplace to determine the meaning of an example. A commonplace determines a system of interpretation that can be used to "place" an example within a standard system of belief. You can see a similar process at work in this essay.

> During the football season, the team was supposed to wear the same type of cleats and the same type socks. I figured that I would change this a little by wearing my white shoes instead of black and to cover up the team socks with a pair of my own white ones. I thought that this looked better than what we were wearing, and I told a few of the other people on the team to change too. They agreed that it did look better and they changed their combination to go along with mine. After the game people came up to us and said that it looked very good the way we wore our socks, and they wanted to know why we changed from the rest of the team.
>
> I feel that creativity comes from when a person lets his imagination come up with ideas and he is not afraid to express them. Once you create something to do it will be original and unique because it came about from your

own imagination and if any one else tries to copy it, it won't be the same because you thought of it first from your own ideas.

26   This is not an elegant paper, but it seems seamless, tidy. If the paper on the clay model of the earth showed an ill-fit between the writer and his project, here the discourse seems natural, smooth. You could reproduce this paper and hand it out to a class, and it would take a lot of prompting before the students sensed something fishy and one of the more aggressive ones might say, "Sure he came up with the idea of wearing white shoes and white socks. Him and Billy White-shoes Johnson. Come on. He copied the very thing he said was his own idea, 'original and unique.'"

27   The "I" of this text, the "I" who "figured," "thought," and "felt" is located in a conventional rhetoric of the self that turns imagination into origination (I made it), that argues an ethic of production (I made it and it is mine), and that argues a tight scheme of intention (I made it because I decided to make it). The rhetoric seems invisible because it is so common. This "I" (the maker) is also located in a version of history that dominates classroom accounts of history. It is an example of the "Great Man" theory, where history is rolling along—the English novel is dominated by a central, intrusive narrative presence: America is in the throes of a great depression; during football season the team was supposed to wear the same kind of cleats and socks—until a figure appears, one who can shape history—Henry James, FDR, the writer of the football paper—and everything is changed. In the argument of the football paper, "I figured," "I thought," "I told," "They agreed," and, as a consequence, "I feel that creativity *comes from when* a person lets his imagination come up with ideas and he is not afraid to express them." The story of appropriation becomes a narrative of courage and conquest. The writer was able to write that story when he was able to imagine himself in that discourse. Getting him out of it will be difficult matter indeed.

28   There are ways, I think, that a writer can shape history in the very act of writing. Some students are able to enter into a discourse, but, by stylistic maneuvers, to take possession of it at the same time. They don't originate a discourse, but they locate themselves within it aggressively, self-consciously.

29   Here is one particularly successful essay. Notice the specialized vocabulary, but also the way in which the text continually refers to its own language and to the language of others.

> Throughout my life, I have been interested and intrigued by music. My mother has often told me of the times, before I went to school, when I would "conduct" the orchestra on her records. I continued to listen to music and eventually started to play the guitar and the clarinet. Finally, at about the age of twelve, I started to sit down and to try to write songs. Even though my instrumental skills were far from my own high standards, I would spend much of my spare time during the day with a guitar around my neck, trying to produce a piece of music.
>
> Each of these sessions, as I remember them, had a rather set format. I would sit in my bedroom, strumming different combinations of the five or

six chords I could play, until I heard a series which sounded particularly good to me. After this, I set the music to a suitable rhythm, (usually dependent on my mood at the time), and ran through the tune until I could play it fairly easily. Only after this section was complete did I go on to writing lyrics, which generally followed along the lines of the current popular songs on the radio.

At the time of the writing, I felt that my songs were, in themselves, an original creation of my own: that is, I, alone, made them. However, I now see that, in this sense of the word, I was not creative. The songs themselves seem to be an oversimplified form of the music I listened to at the time. In a more fitting sense, however, I was being creative. Since I did not purposely copy my favorite songs, I was, effectively, originating my songs from my own "process of creativity." To achieve my goal, I needed what a composer would call "inspiration" for my piece. In this case the inspiration was the current hit on the radio. Perhaps with my present point of view, I feel that I used too much "inspiration" in my songs, but, at that time, I did not.

Creativity, therefore, is a process which, in my case, involved a certain series of "small creations" if you like. As well, it is something, the appreciation of which varies with one's point of view, that point of view being set by the person's experience, tastes, and his own personal view of creativity. The less experienced tend to allow for less originality, while the more experienced demand real originality to classify something a "creation." Either way, a term as abstract as this is perfectly correct, and open to interpretation.

30   This writer is consistently and dramatically conscious of herself forming something to say out of what has been said and out of what she has been saying in the act of writing this paper. "Creativity" begins, in this paper, as "original creation." What she thought was "creativity," however, she now calls "imitation" and, as she says, "in this sense of the word" she was not "creative." In another sense, however, she says that she was creative since she didn't purposefully copy the songs but used them as "inspiration."

31   The writing in this piece (that is, the work of the writer within the essay) goes on in spite of, or against, the language that keeps pressing to give another name to her experience as a song writer and to bring the discussion to closure. (Think of the quick closure of the football shoes paper in comparison.) Its style is difficult, highly qualified. It relies on quotation marks and parody to set the language and attitudes that belong to the discourse (or the discourses) it would reject, that it would not take as its own proper location.[6]

32   In the papers I've examined in this essay, the writers have shown a varied awareness of the codes—or the competing codes—that operate within a discourse. To speak with authority student writers have not only to speak in another's voice but through another's "code"; and they not only have to do this, they have to speak in the voice and through the codes of those of us with power and wisdom; and they not only have to do this, they have to do it before they know what they are doing, before they have a project to participate

in and before, at least in terms of our disciplines, they have anything to say. Our students may be able to enter into a conventional discourse and speak, not as themselves, but through the voice of the community. The university, however, is the place where "common" wisdom is only of negative value; it is something to work against. The movement toward a more specialized discourse begins (or perhaps, best begins) when a student can both define a position of privilege, a position that sets him against a "common" discourse, and when he can work self-consciously, critically, against not only the "common" code but his own.

33   The stages of development that I've suggested are not necessarily marked by corresponding levels in the type or frequency of error, at least not by the type or frequency of sentence level errors. I am arguing, then, that a basic writer is not necessarily a writer who makes a lot of mistakes. In fact, one of the problems with curricula designed to aid basic writers is that they too often begin with the assumption that the key distinguishing feature of a basic writer is the presence of sentence level error. Students are placed in courses because their placement essays show a high frequency of such errors and those courses are designed with the goal of making those errors go away. This approach to the problems of the basic writer ignores the degree to which error is not a constant feature but a marker in the development of a writer. Students who can write reasonably correct narratives may fall to pieces when faced with more unfamiliar assignments. More importantly, however, such courses fail to serve the rest of the curriculum. On every campus there is a significant number of college freshman who require a course to introduce them to the kinds of writing that are required for a university education. Some of these students can write correct sentences and some cannot, but as a group they lack the facility other freshmen possess when they are faced with an academic writing task.

34   The "White Shoes" essay, for example, shows fewer sentence level errors than the "Clay Model" paper. This may well be due to the fact, however, that the writer of that paper stayed well within the safety of familiar territory. He kept himself out of trouble by doing what he could easily do. The tortuous syntax of the more advanced papers on my list is a syntax that represents a writer's struggle with a difficult and unfamiliar language, and it is a syntax that can quickly lead an inexperienced writer into trouble. The syntax and punctuation of the "Composing Songs" essay, for example, shows the effort that is required when a writer works against the pressure of conventional discourse. If the prose is inelegant (although I'll confess I admire those dense sentences), it is still correct. This writer has a command of the linguistic and stylistic resources (the highly embedded sentences, the use of parentheses and quotation marks) required to complete the act of writing. It is easy to imagine the possible pitfalls for a writer, working without this facility.

35   There was no camera trained on the "Clay Model" writer while he was writing, and I have no protocol of what was going through his mind, but it is possible to speculate that the syntactic difficulties of sentences like the

following are the result of an attempt to use an unusual vocabulary and to extend his sentences beyond the boundaries that would be "normal" in his speech or writing:

> In past time I thought that an incident was creative was when I had to make a clay model of the earth, but not of the classical or your everyday model of the earth which consists of the two cores, the mantle and the crust. I thought of these things in a dimension of which it would be unique, but easy to comprehend.

There is reason to believe, that is, that the problem is with this kind of sentence, in this context. If the problem of the last sentence is a problem of holding together these units—"I thought," "dimension," "unique," and "easy to comprehend"—then the linguistic problem is not a simple matter of sentence construction.

36   I am arguing, then, that such sentences fall apart not because the writer lacks the necessary syntax to glue the pieces together but because he lacks the full statement within which these key words are already operating. While writing, and in the thrust of his need to complete the sentence, he has the key words but not the utterance. (And to recover the utterance, I suspect, he will need to do more than revise the sentence.) The invisible conventions, the prepared phrases remain too distant for the statement to be completed. The writer must get inside of a discourse he can only partially imagine. The act of constructing a sentence, then, becomes something like an act of transcription, where the voice on the tape unexpectedly fades away and becomes inaudible.

37   Mina Shaughnessy speaks of the advanced writer as a writer with a more facile but still incomplete possession of this prior discourse. In the case of the advanced writer, the evidence of a problem is the presence of dissonant, redundant, or imprecise language, as in a sentence such as this: "No education can be total, it must be continuous." Such a student Shaughnessy says, could be said to hear the "melody of formal English" while still unable to make precise or exact distinctions. And, she says, the pre-packaging feature of language, the possibility of taking over phrases and whole sentences without much thought about them, threatens the writer now as before. The writer, as we have said, inherits the language out of which he must fabricate his own messages. He is therefore in a constant tangle with the language, obliged to recognize its public, communal nature, and yet driven to invent out of this language his own statements (19).

38   For the unskilled writer, the problem is different in degree and not in kind. The inexperienced writer is left with a more fragmentary record of the comings and goings of academic discourse. Or, as I said above, he often has the key words without the complete statements within which they are already operating.

39   It may very well be that some students will need to learn to crudely mimic the "distinctive register" of academic discourse before they are

prepared to actually and legitimately do the work of the discourse, and before they are sophisticated enough with the refinements of tone and gesture to do it with grace or elegance. To say this, however, is to say that our students must be our students. Their initial progress will be marked by their abilities to take on the role of privilege, by their abilities to establish authority. From this point of view, the student who wrote about constructing the clay model of the earth is better prepared for his education than the student who wrote about playing football in white shoes, even though the "White Shoes" paper was relatively error-free and the "Clay Model" paper was not. It will be hard to pry the writer of the "White Shoes" paper loose from the tidy, pat discourse that allows him to dispose of the question of creativity in such a quick and efficient manner. He will have to be convinced that it is better to write sentences he might not so easily control, and he will have to be convinced that it is better to write muddier and more confusing prose (in order that it may sound like ours), and this will be harder than convincing the "Clay Model" writer to continue what he has begun.[7]

NOTES

1. This article represents an abridged version of a chapter in *When A Writer Can't Write: Studies in Writer's Block and Other Composing Problems.* Ed. Mike Rose. New York: The Guilford Press, 1985.

    David Bartholomae is Associate Professor of English and Director of Composition at the University of Pittsburgh. He has served on the executive committees of CCCC, WPA, and the College Section of NCTE. He has just been elected Assistant Chair of CCCC. He has written extensively on basic writing and basic writers. © Journal of Basic Writing, Vol. 5 No. 1 1986.

2. David Olson has made a similar observation about school-related problems of language learning in younger children. Here is his conclusion: "Hence, depending upon whether children assumed language was primarily suitable for making assertions and conjectures or primarily for making direct or indirect commands, they will either find school texts easy or difficult" (107).

3. For Aristotle there were both general and specific commonplaces. A speaker, says Aristotle, has a "stock of arguments to which he may turn for a particular need."

> If he knows the topic (regions, places, lines of argument)—and a skilled speaker will know them—he will know where to find what he wants for a special case. The general topics, or commonplaces, are regions containing arguments that are common to all branches of knowledge. . . . But there are also special topics (regions, places, loci) in which one looks for arguments appertaining to particular branches of knowledge, special sciences, such as ethics or politics. (154–155)

And, he says, "The topics or places, then, may be indifferently thought of as in the science that is concerned, or in the mind of the speaker." But the question of location is "indifferent" *only* if the mind of the speaker is in line with set opinion, general assumption. For the speaker (or writer) who is not situated so comfortably in the privileged public realm, this is indeed not an indifferent matter at all. If he does not have the commonplace at hand, he will not, in Aristotle's terms, know where to go at all.

4. See especially Bartholomae and Rose for articles on curricula designed to move students into university discourse. The movement to extend writing "across the curriculum" is evidence of a general concern for locating students within the work of the university: see especially Bizzell and Maimon et al. For longer works directed specifically at basic writing, see Ponsot and Dean, and Shaughnessy. For a book describing a course for more advanced students, see Coles.

5. See especially Bizzell, and Bizzell and Herzberg. My debt to Bizzell's work should be evident everywhere in this essay.

6. In support of my argument that this is the kind of writing that does the work of the academy, let me offer the following excerpt from a recent essay by Wayne Booth ("The Company We Keep: Self-Making in Imaginative Art, Old and New"):

> I can remember making up songs of my own, no doubt borrowed from favorites like "Hello, Central, Give Me Heaven," "You Can't Holler Down My Rain Barrel," and one about the ancient story of a sweet little "babe in the woods" who lay down and died with her brother.
>
> I asked my mother, in a burst of creative egotism, why nobody ever learned to sing my songs, since after all I was more than willing to learn theirs. I can't remember her answer, and I can barely remember snatches of two of "my" songs. But I can remember dozens of theirs, and when I sing them, even now, I sometimes feel again the emotions, and see the images, that they aroused then. Thus who I am now the very shape of my soul—was to a surprising degree molded by the works of "art" that came my way.
>
> I set "art" in quotation marks, because much that I experienced in those early books and songs would not be classed as art according to most definitions, but for the purposes of appraising the effects of "art" on "life" or "culture," and especially for the purposes of thinking about the effects of the "media" we surely must include every kind of artificial experience that we provide for one another. . . .
>
> In this sense of the word, all of us are from the earliest years fed a steady diet of art . . . (58–59).

While there are similarities in the paraphrasable content of Booth's arguments and my student's, what I am interested in is each writer's method. Both appropriate terms from a common discourse about (art and inspiration) in order to push against an established way of talking (about tradition and the individual). This effort of opposition clears a space for each writer's argument and enables the writers to establish their own "sense" of the key words in the discourse.

7. Preparation of this manuscript was supported by the Learning Research and Development Center of the University of Pittsburgh, which is supported in part by the National Institute of Education. I am grateful also to Mike Rose, who pushed and pulled at this paper at a time when it needed it.

WORKS CITED

Aristotle. *The Rhetoric of Aristotle.* Trans. I. Cooper. Englewood Cliffs, NJ: Prentice, 1932.

Bartholomae, David. "Teaching Basic Writing: An Alternative to Basic skills." Journal of Basic Writing 2(1979) 85–109.

_____ "Writing Assignments: Where Writing Begins." Forum. Ed. P. P. Stock. Montclair, NJ: Boynton/Cook, 1983. 300–312.

Bartholomae, David and Anthony Petrosky. *Facts, Artifacts and Counterfacts: A Basic Reading and Writing Course for the College Curriculum.* Montclair, NJ: Boynton/Cook, forthcoming.

Bizzell, Patricia. "The Ethos of Academic Discourse." *College Composition and Communication* 29(1978): 351–55.

_____ "Cognition, Convention and Certainty: What We Need to Know About." Pre/Text 3(1982): 213–244.

_____ "College Composition: Initiation Into the Academic Discourse Communities." Curriculum Inquiry 12(1982): 191–207.

Bizzell, Patricia and Bruce Herzberg. "'Inherent' Ideology, 'Universal' History, 'Empirical' Evidence, and 'Context-Free' Writing: Some Problems with E. D. Hirsch's *The Philosophy of Composition.*" *Modern Language Notes* 95(1980): 1181–1202.

Booth, Wayne. "The Company We Keep: Self-Making in Imaginative Art, Old and New." *The Pushcart Prize, VIII: Best of the Small Presses,* Ed. Bill Henderson. Wainscott, NY: Pushcart, 1983. 57–95.

Coles, William E., Jr. *The Plural I.* New York: Holt, 1978.

Flower, Linda S. "Revising Writer-Based Prose." *Journal of Basic Writing* 3(1981): 62–74.

Foucault, Michel. *The Archaeology of Knowledge.* Trans. A. M. Sheridan Smith. New York: Harper, 1972.

Maimon, Elaine P., G.L. Belcher, G.W. Hearn, B.F. Nodine, and F.X. O'Connor. *Writing in the Arts and Sciences.* Cambridge, MA: Winthrop, 1981.

Olson, David R. "Writing: The Divorce of the Author From the Text." *Exploring Speaking-Writing Relationships: Connections and Contrasts.* Eds. B. Kroll and R. Vann. Urbana, IL: NCTE, 1981.

Ponsot, Marie and Rosemary Deen. *Beat Not the Poor Desk.* Montclair, NJ: Boynton/Cook, 1982.

Rose, Mike. "Remedial Writing Courses: A Critique and a Proposal." *College English* 45(1983): 109–128.

_____. *When a Writer Can't Write: Studies in Writer's Block and Other Composing Problems.* New York: Guilford, 1985.

Shaughnessy, Mina. *Errors and Expectations.* New York: Oxford UP, 1977.

FOLLOW-UP ACTIVITIES

Discussing the Rhetoric

1. Try to summarize Bartholomae's main point in one sentence.

2. Bartholomae encloses many terms in quotation marks. Can you see any consistent reasons for his use of quotation marks when not quoting another writer?

3. The background information reveals that David Bartholomae is an accepted expert in the field of composition and basic writing. Do you feel that Bartholomae's tone and writing style position him as a leader or expert, or do they position him as just another voice in the crowd? How does this positioning affect his authority?

4. Would you consider Bartholomae's argument to be strictly logical, strictly emotional, or a mixture? Supply at least two quotations from the essay that support your answer.

5. Look at what you marked in your text while reading this essay. Which did you mark more frequently, Bartholomae's actual writing or student examples? When you did mark student examples, was it to highlight an interesting idea or to critique the writing? When you marked Bartholomae, what were you highlighting? Did you ever critique his writing? Why or why not?

6. If you had to write a research paper on the subject "Teaching College Students How to Write," what hints can you find in this essay (including the notes printed at the end) that could guide your research? Whose views and ideas do you think are privileged in this conversation?

Discussing the Conversation

1. What does it mean to you to have to "invent the university" every time you sit down to write a paper?

2. Based on your answer to the above question, do you think Bartholomae believes knowledge is socially constructed? How does your answer take into account Bartholomae's introductory quote from Foucault?

3. Bartholomae writes that students "have to appropriate (or be appropriated by) a specialized discourse." Do you think Rose, hooks, or Rodriguez would agree or disagree with Bartholomae? Would these writers' responses differ from each other? How?

4. What does Bartholomae's term "commonplaces" add to our discussion of disciplines as on-going conversations?

Joining the Conversation

1. Have you ever felt that you were "bluffing," faking an ease with academic language that you didn't feel because, as Bartholomae puts it, "speaking and writing will most certainly be required long before the skill is 'learned'"? Write an informal paper in which you describe an experience when you bluffed your way through a writing assignment or essay test. Is there anything that you've learned in this class about academic discourse that would have helped you then? If so, write about it.

2. Bartholomae suggests that student writing is less "a matter of invention and discovery" and more a matter of "imitation or parody." Does this remind you of Pratt's language? Write an informal paper in which you consider what it means that you may be expected to imitate or parody academic writing rather than write in your "own" voice. (If you recall Pratt's discussion of the arts of the contact zone, you may find complex things to say and ways to say it as you write your paper.)

INTRODUCTORY COMMENTS ON LINDA FLOWER'S PREFACE AND INTRODUCTION TO "READING TO WRITE: EXPLORING A COGNITIVE AND SOCIAL PROCESS"

Reading the Context

A professor of rhetoric at Carnegie Mellon University, Linda Flower is credited with identifying ways in which writing processes relate to thinking processes. Flower is co-director of The Center for the Study of Writing at Berkeley and Carnegie Mellon, and is often mentioned as one of the founders of the field of composition. Although the selection excerpted here was written by Flower, the entire book was a collaborative effort including many of Flower's former graduate students. These graduate students have themselves gone on to become professors in the fields of composition and rhetoric.

This selection explores a small piece of the larger conversation represented in this part—how to teach students to write for college. In academic writing, territory is generally marked by defining and solving a particular problem or by supplying a piece of a puzzle that was missing. Look for and mark passages that identify for you what territory within the landscape of teaching student writing Flower has mapped as her own.

Reading the Rhetoric

This selection is the preface and the introductory pages of a much longer study. Because it's only a piece, you'll be introduced to the purpose and goals of the study, but you won't be to read the results. This provides an opportunity for you to consider what authors include in a preface or an introduction. From reading just this much, see if you can identify some underlying assumptions about student writing and how Flower thinks it should be taught. Look for how Flower coaxes her readers into spending their time to read a long study. Does she summarize the entire study? Does she list its goals? Does she define a problem that the study will attempt to solve? In other words, what is a reader going to know after reading this study that he or she didn't know before?

As short as this excerpt is, Flower draws other voices into this conversation. What rhetorical technique(s) does she use to summon these other voices? Once you've determined that, think about how her choice of technique influences her ethos.

Reading the Conversation

Flower is writing about students who feel that they don't understand the assignment and don't know what the professor is "looking for." As you read, look for the cause that Flower claims is the root of this problem. Do you think Bartholomae would agree with her?

Think back to the Rose selection in Part One. As you read, consider which of Rose's five problem areas Flower addresses here and whether she adds anything new to Rose's discussion. Listen for echoes of other writers from Part One as well.

Reading to Write: Exploring a Cognitive and Social Process
Linda Flower

PREFACE

So I'm just gonna—I don't care, I'm just going to interpret them the only way I can interpret them. . . . Let's just put what the authors agreed on. *Authors agree*—We'll just—If at least two of them concur, we'll say they agree. *Authors in general agree that* . . . But then they don't agree— There's nothing you can say about this. . . .

Can I leave it at that. . . . Oh give me a break, I don't know what I'm doing. I'm only a freshman. I have no idea what to do.

Darlene, a first-semester freshman

1 Darlene's college assignment asked for synthesis and interpretation. The paper she turned in—a short, simplistic review of material from her

sources—failed to meet her own expectations and her readers'. And yet, a chance to look at the process behind this unsophisticated product revealed serious thinking, a complicated, if confused, decision process, and a trail of unused abilities and discarded ideas—an active encounter with academic discourse that her teacher would never see.

2   The study presented here takes an unusually comprehensive look at one critical point of entry into academic performance. It shows a group of freshmen in the transition into the academic discourse of college, looking at the ways in which they interpret and negotiate an assignment that calls for reading-to-write. On such tasks, students are reading to create a *text* of their own, trying to integrate information from sources with *ideas* of their own, and attempting to do so under the guidance of a *purpose* they must themselves create. Because these reading-to-write tasks ask students to integrate reading, writing, and rhetorical purpose, they open a door to critical literacy. Yet this same interaction often makes reading-to-write a difficult process for students to learn and to manage.

3   To provide a rounded picture of cognition in this academic context, the study examines these students' thinking processes from a number of perspectives, drawing on their think-aloud protocols of writing and revising, on interviews with and self-analyses by the students, and on comparisons of teachers' and students' perceptions of texts the students wrote. It attempts to place these observations within a broader contextual analysis of the situation as students saw it and the social and cultural assumptions about schooling they brought with them.

4   What this study reveals are some radical differences in how individual students represent an academic writing task to themselves—differences teachers might interpret simply as an indication of a student's ability rather than his or her interpretation of the task. Students were often unaware that such alternative representations existed or that they might hold such significance. Some images of the task, for instance, were dominated by the goals of comprehension, summary, and simple response, and offered little or no place for critical response, original synthesis, or interpretation for a rhetorical purpose.

5   The reading-to-write task students imagined for themselves also had a direct effect on performance: it affected the goals they set, the strategies they used, and the ways they solved problems during composing. And it led to differences in teachers' evaluations of the texts—although, this study suggests, these evaluations may confuse the conventions of organization (e.g., use of topic sentences) with the writer's control of ideas. When students began to examine their options and attempt the more demanding task of interpreting for a purpose, certain students, whom we called the Intenders, showed important changes in their writing and thinking process. These changes, however, were not evident in the text nor apparent to teachers. Finally, this study showed how students' images of the task were rooted in the students'

histories, the context of schooling, and cultural assumptions about writing they brought to college.

6   It is not surprising that some of the images students bring with them are at odds with the expectations they encounter at a university. However, when the expectations for "college-level" discourse are presented in oblique and indirect ways, the transition students face may be a *masked* transition. That is, the task has changed, but for a number of reasons, the magnitude and real nature of this change may not be apparent to students, even as they fail to meet the university's expectations.

7   One of the key implications of this study is that reading-to-write is a task with more faces and a process with more demands than we have realized. We see students thinking hard and doing smart things, even when they misgauge their goals or their written text fails to meet certain standards. This close survey of the cognitive and social landscape of reading-to-write in a college class gives one added respect for the students in this transition and for the complexity and sophistication of the "freshman" task as they face it.

8   Our heartfelt thanks go to our colleagues John R. Hayes, Karen A. Schriver, Nancy Spivey, Tom Huckin, Christina Haas, Lorraine Higgins, Stuart Greene, Jennie Nelson, Tim Flower, Stephen Witte, Mike Rose, Gerald Rutledge, and Kathy R. Meinzer.

L.F.

Pittsburgh
May 1989

THE ROLE OF TASK REPRESENTATION IN READING-TO-WRITE

9 Academic papers are typically written in the context of a rich rhetorical situation that includes not only the conventions of academic discourse, but the expectations of the instructor, the context of the course, and the terms of the assignment. These requirements can seem so self-evident we are surprised when once again twenty students in a class interpret the same "standard" college writing assignment in strikingly different ways. This chapter is about that act of interpretation. Task representation is an interpretive process that translates the rhetorical situation—as the writer reads it—into the act of composing. As such, it is the major bridge linking the public context of writing with the private process of an individual writer. Therefore, let me introduce this process by sketching three public contexts in which students' task representations make a difference.

10   In the first context, the freshman composition instructors at my school were in a weekly seminar meeting, trying to understand and diagnose some

of the student strategies behind the papers we were reading from the problem analysis assignment. Finding, defining, and analyzing a problem, as we saw the task, was an occasion to struggle with a significant personal or public issue—a problem of the sort that resisted pat answers and called for the extra scrutiny writing allows. In the paper at hand, a young woman had written a polished, coherent essay on the problem posed by a "rainy day" with its awful train of decisions about choosing the right clothes and the dilemma of skipping puddles to class—a mildly clever, discouraging paper. It was not the sort of analysis we had in mind. In the freshman literature course that same week the instructors had spent a class session talking with students about how the response statements due Monday would allow, even demand, students to go beyond the summaries they had written in high school. A response statement, the instructors had discussed, asked students to record and then examine their own response. The first papers were turned in with students claiming they had indeed done this analysis. Fifty percent were plot summaries. Meanwhile, over the bridge at the University of Pittsburgh was a third context we can reconstruct from David Bartholomae's (1985) discussion of a student's freshman placement essay. The reader on the placement committee had come to that point in the essay that would make or break it as acceptable academic discourse—that would place this student in or out of basic writing: "At this point the [student] writer is in a perfect position to speculate, to move from the problem to an analysis of the problem, however. . . . We get neither a technical discussion nor an 'academic' discussion but a Lesson on Life" (p. 137). In failing to make that expected move to analysis, the student had just become a basic writer in the eyes of an institution.

11   Why, we want to ask, are these students doing what seems to be the "wrong task" in the eyes of their readers, especially on these short assignments to which a grade or even placement is attached? Is it because they are unmotivated, despite the serious looks that suggest they, too, are disappointed if not perplexed by our response? Is standard "academic discourse" a new phenomenon to *all* of these students? Is the assignment not clear, even explicit? If our task involves reading to write, is it that they just have not thought about the assigned readings deeply enough to have something to say? Somehow these answers do not do justice to the real effort made by both students and teachers.

12   The phenomenon repeats itself in classes outside of English. Teachers ask students to attempt some "standard" form of disciplinary discourse because they want to expand the students' repertoire by teaching a particular way of thinking and writing. Yet the class members seem to be doing a variety of different assignments. Some of these variations are welcome inventions; but others suggest that the student is still confused about what academic discourse calls for. Writing about the problem of a rainy day probably seemed as trivial to the student who did it as it did to the instructor. The purposes of college were not being served for anyone. When writing goes

awry in this way, it is as though there were a band of writers each marching to a different drummer in the good faith that he or she was "doing what the assignment called for."

13   This study looks at one way we might help students to understand and manage the special demands of academic discourse. Part of the problem, we propose, may not lie in the student's ability or even knowledge of the discourse per se, but in the way that student has construed the task. If this is true, students are likely to have many abilities they could use if they prompted themselves to do so. This chapter suggests that we may want to look at *task representation* not as a single, simple decision, but as an extended interpretive process that weaves itself throughout composing. The task, as students represent it to themselves, is the one they perform, but that representation is subject to many influences and may evolve in surprising ways during writing. This process of task representation, we suggest, may be far more involved, unpredictable, and powerful than we have supposed.

14   This problem of interpretation can be partly described in terms of the implicit requirements of academic discourse students are expected to infer. For instance, if we tell students they need only look into their hearts and write from experience, are we assuming the "personal essay" *our field has in mind* is simply a natural genre the student would discover by consulting those private wellsprings? Pat Bizzell and Bruce Herzberg (1986) have criticized this assumption in textbooks that purport to teach "good" writing when, in fact, they aim to teach a genre-specific form of good writing that has quite explicit, if unarticulated rules. Kathleen McCormick's (1985) critique of a naive use of "response statements" makes a similar point. Response statements, as she describes them, are not pure, untrammeled "responses" to a text. Rather, they are a specialized form of discourse in which students are expected to *use* their personal response to examine their own reading process and assumptions about texts. Charles Bazerman (1981) argues that the discourse conventions of the various disciplines pose a similar problem in writing across the curriculum. The task of student writers is to enter the ongoing intellectual conversation of an established community.

15   Writing is a move in a discourse game with rules, an action in an intellectual and interpersonal context. Nevertheless, the process of interpreting a task—imagining the action that is called for—is sometimes equated with merely "following an assignment" and, as such, is relegated to remedial workshops on study skills. Teachers want to deal with heady intellectual processes, not with helping students ferret out "what the teacher wants," so they leave it to students to interpret assignments, even though the instructions may be long, imaginative, and complex. Indeed, many teachers hold it as a badge of merit that they refuse to tell the students "what they want" in the desire to foster independent thought. Yet there is sometimes a fine line between maintaining this proper reticence and creating a guessing game in which students who know how to succeed in school do, while those who do not are expected to infer the rules of the game on their own.

16   We find ourselves in a perplexing position. The genres we hold to be self-evident are not that way to everybody. As Mina Shaughnessy (1977) has suggested, we seem to be urging some students, who do not know the "rituals and ways of winning arguments in academia, . . . into the lion's den of academic disputation with no more than an honest face for protection" (p. 319). But this is not merely a problem of underprepared students. As we become more aware of the interpretive processes of readers and the multiple faces of academic discourse across disciplines, we must face the fact that students do interpret, and often misinterpret, the college writing tasks they set out to do. If, indeed, the process of task representation plays the significant role I am suggesting, our problem is even more interesting. As a field we have almost nothing to say to students or each other about *how* writers represent tasks during composing and about the *features* of alternative representations students bring to any standard task.

FOLLOW-UP ACTIVITIES

Discussing the Rhetoric

1. Is Flower addressing composition teachers or is her audience larger? Select two quotes that support your conclusion.

2. Why do you think Flower begins her preface with a quotation from a student? What purpose does this quotation have? How does she use it? To develop? To support? To introduce?

3. Does Flower quote or make reference to any other "writing experts"? Who? Have you heard any of those names before? How could you use a list of names like this when researching a topic?

4. Flower places many terms and phrases in italics, bold print, or quotation marks. Do these changes in text mean the same thing or different things? Did they influence how you read the text, what you paid attention to?

5. Can you identify a thesis statement in this reading? Is it located in the first sentence? The first paragraph? The end of the preface? The end of the introduction? If you were writing a preface and an introduction to a study, where would you put the thesis? Why?

Discussing the Conversation

1. What opinion do you think Flower has of student writers? What quotations from the text support your conclusion?

2. Have any of your writing assignments in this course fit Flower's description of a reading-to-write assignment? Does Flower offer any insights about such assignments that might have been helpful to you as a student writer? If so, what were they?

3. Flower discusses the importance of a "rhetorical context." Now that you have completed much of this course, with its emphasis on rhetorical issues, do you feel that you know what they mean when they use this word? Think about how different your current response is from what it might have been at the beginning of the course.

4. Flower quotes Bartholomae's essay "Inventing the University." If you have already read Bartholomae's essay, do you remember what point Bartholomae was originally making? How does it help you understand the conversation when you realize that you have read more than one piece of it, heard more than one voice?

Joining the Conversation

In an informal paper, first summarize what the problem was with the "rainy day" paper, then describe a time when you feel you interpreted a writing assignment differently than the professor intended. Conclude with your opinion as to whether the misunderstanding resulted from how the professor worded the assignment, how carefully you read the assignment, your lack of knowledge about academic expectations, or the effects of your frame of reference and background experiences on your interpretation. Before you write, think about which of these causes contribute to what Flower terms a "task representation."

INTRODUCTORY COMMENTS ON "WRITING FOR TEACHERS" BY PETER ELBOW

Reading the Context

This selection is excerpted from a chapter in Peter Elbow's text *Writing with Power* (1981). Elbow is fascinated with the difference between what he calls "natural communication," (simply explaining "what you understand to someone who doesn't understand it"), and writing for teachers. According to Elbow, the "natural direction of communication," in which the audience is present, is too frequently frustrated by teachers who ask for written assignments without providing for their students any working idea of who the audience is or should be. Moreover, Elbow asserts that the concept of audience must be more deeply considered if students are to learn how to write effective arguments.

In the course of the selection, Elbow challenges students as well as teachers in order to "empower" both. Elbow's choice of criticizing both communities is significant—such a choice goes against the more common-place assumption that the community of teachers is above criticism. Elbow suggests students can understand ambiguous writing assignments by opening a dialogue with their teachers. He then grounds his advice by listing "concrete suggestions" students can use to get the most out of the teacher-student relationship. Such a list provides tangible ways for students to improve their writing situations, as well as for teachers to improve their response techniques.

It is also interesting to note that in his introduction to *Writing with Power,* Elbow writes:

> A note on gender. In some chapters I call people "he" and in others I call them "she." I do so because I believe that "he" refers to men more than it does to women, despite the convention that says it can refer equally to both sexes. Of course the ideal pronoun arrangement would not distract any of a reader's attention away from the main message of the sentence—as I fear mine sometimes does. But I can't imagine a really ideal arrangement until we finish the process of relinquishing cultural habits of male primacy.

Reading the Rhetoric

Unlike other writers in this Part, Elbow addresses his book to students as well as teachers. His mission in this selection is to equip both groups with certain rhetorical tools. For both, awareness of the rhetorical concepts of purpose and audience are indispensable. As you read, try to identify the rhetorical strategies Elbow suggests to empower you. Think about which strategies seem particularly effective to you and why. Also think about Elbow's ethos. Why do you suppose he tells us so much about his experience? How does his personal account help to support his purpose? Finally, you'll want to consider who Elbow's audience is. Does he seem to be speaking to a particular group?

Reading the Conversation

Consider the other writers in this part and think about how they might respond to Elbow. Which other writers rely on rhetorical strategies similar to Elbow's? Who shares his purposes? Is Elbow's characterization of the student writer similar to Bartholomae's? Salvatori's? Flower's? Does it differ in any significant ways? Particularly, how does Elbow's characterization of the relationships between the student and the teacher or the student and academic writing differ from Bartholomae's?

Writing for Teachers
Peter Elbow

1 When you write for a teacher you are usually swimming against the stream of natural communication. The natural direction of communication is to explain what you understand to someone who doesn't understand it. But in writing an essay for a teacher your task is usually to explain what you are still engaged in trying to understand to someone who understands it better. You seldom feel you are writing because *you* want to tell someone something. More often you feel you are being examined as to whether you can say well what *he* wants you to say. Even if you are invited to write on a subject you know better than the teacher, the teacher's knowledge turns out to be the standard for judging whether you really do know it. There's nothing wrong with this as a testing or evaluative relationship, but it's peculiar as a communicative or audience relationship.

2 The result of this wrong-way communication is a pervasive weakness that infects much student writing—and persists in many people's writing for the rest of their lives: a faint aura of questioning which lurks behind assertions. The student writes "This is so and that is so," but somehow between the lines he is also saying, "Is this so? Will you buy that?"

3 If it is a story or poem rather than an essay you are writing, it's hard to feel that you are doing what is most natural for someone writing a story or poem, that is, trying to give pleasure or enlightenment. It feels as though your task is to *satisfy* or *get criticism* from a teacher who must read from 25 to 50 such pieces in one sitting. Instead of *giving* the reader something with a definite gesture, hand thrust firmly outward, students usually hand in their stories or poems with a bent and hoping arm. Instead of a statement—"Here is something for you, here is a piece of me, take it"—the student often implies a question: "Is this ok? I hope I didn't do something wrong?" It's striking how often students actually say those words to you as they give you their papers: "I hope this is what you wanted?"

4 This subliminal question mark lurks in the writing even of some very skilled students, but skilled students more often risk a different infection. A student who wants to be a good student cannot be content just to satisfy teachers. He must write a paper that will wake the teacher up and give him some relief when he is groggy from reading those twenty-five to fifty papers on the same topic. Such students must do something different, striking, unique with the same old ingredients. The school setting has rewarded generation after generation of good students *not* for saying clearly what is important and what they want to convey, but for doing some kind of better cartwheel or handstand. Good students often write not to communicate but to impress. Over and over again I have seen good students

knocked off balance when they get out of school and try to write for an audience other than teachers and discover how unsuccessful those shenani-
gans are which used to win good grades. Real readers are different from
teachers.

5 But that's the point. Teachers are not the real audience. You don't write *to*
teachers, you write for them. You can feel the difference vividly if you write
a regular essay assigned by your teacher and then go on to write something
directly *to* him: write him a letter asking him to change your grade or to contribute money to your political campaign. You will find these writing tasks
refreshing and satisfying compared to regular assignments—even if harder.
It's a relief to put words down on paper for the sake of *results*—not just for
the sake of getting a *judgment.* "Getting an A is results," you may say, but see
how you feel if you write your teacher for a contribution and get an "A" instead of a check. The grade or comment says "good persuasion," but you
know your words failed if there is no check in the envelope.

6   As teachers we come closest, perhaps, to being the real audience when
we ask you to write an essay that persuades us on some issue. But in most
cases there is something make-believe about the task, given our conditions
as readers. If as a teacher I am reading a stack of papers all on the same topic
I know I can't use completely realistic standards and only give a good grade
to papers that actually change my mind. That would be unfair—too hard—
especially since I probably know more about the topic than the student. I
give good grades and comments to papers which seem "well argued" but
which don't happen to budge my position at all. (And some papers, of
course, are trying to persuade me of what I already believe. How can I measure success there?) For the most part then my feedback is not really a measure of how much change the words actually produce in me but rather my
guess about how much change they *would* produce on some (ill-defined) hypothetical reader. Occasionally a teacher says, "Your job is actually to
change *my* mind," and really carries through—but more often he says, "Your
job is to write as though you were trying to change my mind." Those two
words, "as though," turn up often in writing assignments.

7   If you do write directly *to* your teacher on a persuasive or informative
essay he will usually feel something wrong. If, for example, you write "I
disagree with what you said last week in class about why Hamlet delays so
long. Here are some difficulties with your readings of the play . . . ," the
teacher will probably say, "You are not supposed to write a letter to me,
you are supposed to write an essay." In short there is usually something fictional about the transaction between reader and writer in most school
writing—a mismatch between what's actually going on between student
and teacher and what's allegedly going on between "the writer" and "the
reader": the student pretends to explain something to someone who
doesn't understand it; the teacher pretends to be this general reader reading for enlightenment.

8   (In most exams, by the way, the relationship between writer and reader more nearly matches the actual human transaction between parties. The teacher/reader is saying fairly openly, "Tell me what you know about the Incas—about why Hamlet delays—so I can see if you know what I think you should know," and the student/writer is saying just as openly, "I'm going to explain to you what you already know in order to show you that I know it, too.")

9   Pretending, in itself, is not a problem. All children are good at it and if a college student is not he needs to learn again. "Write to the Longshoremen's Union about manual versus desk labor," "Write to the third-grade student council about how to deal with bullies in the playground," "Write to Robert Redford about how he could best handle this scene from *Hamlet*." I doubt that there would be much problem with engaging in the fiction of writing to those audiences and then handing in your paper to an entirely different sort of reader, namely your teacher. Perhaps there's not enough pretending in school and college essay writing.

10   Or at least the problem lies in the slipperiness of a situation in which students must simultaneously pretend and not pretend when they write to the audience for most school and college writing: the general reader. This "general reader" is a tricky character. Teachers seldom define explicitly who he is, but common practice in the educational and academic world is based on the assumption that he is a creature blessed by intelligence, a certain amount of education ("general"), and an open mind. Someone much more reasonable and *general* than those longshoremen or third graders or even Robert Redford; someone, in short, much more like—guess who?—the teacher. Except this reader is general, not particular like the teacher, and is not meant to be an authority on the topic or someone in a position of authority over the writer.

11   In short, the audience situation is confusing because of the tricky combination of make believe and no make believe. The student is writing *for* a teacher and *to* a general reader. But this general reader does not exist. He is a construct. He is not a particular person like the teacher who reads the words. And yet one of the main things about him is that he reads in a peculiar way in which no one else but teachers read; not because he has a special interest or allegiance or commitment to the subject—not from a position of engagement in the world—but because he seeks a kind of disinterested enlightenment or disembodied pleasure. As a construct, the general reader is 100 percent audience, 0 percent person.

12   Yet none of these tricky audience issues tend to be raised for discussion. It's no wonder then that students have only a vague, fuzzy or shifting sense of their audience and write in a vague, fuzzy, or shifting voice. (That's also the kind of voice, by the way, that people often use when they write in a bureaucracy. The problem is the same: you are writing to an audience that seems unreal and ambiguous. School essays could serve as good practice for writing in bureaucracies if teachers spent more time talking about problems and solutions of dealing with "unreal audiences.")

13   Because of this slippery way in which the "general reader" is both like and unlike the teacher, teachers, too, are often unclear in their own minds as they comment on a student's paper whether they are saying "This doesn't work for *me*—given my knowledge of the topic, my position on it, and my situation in the world," or "I don't believe this would work for a general reader who doesn't already understand what you are trying to explain or doesn't already have his mind made up on the topic." It's hard to argue well or learn about argument when you are unsure who your audience is and what its position on the topic is likely to be.

14   And yet it could be an advantage rather than a problem that teachers are not the real audience. After all, what could be better than having a coach who is different from your real audience but whose job is to help you achieve success with that real audience? The problem is that most student writing never does go to a real audience. Writing for your teacher is like playing your violin for your violin teacher. It is a great help in learning to play the violin, but it is not the goal. The goal—and thus the reason for getting the teacher's help in the first place—is to play for yourself or for your friends or for a wider audience. Of course your violin teacher is, in a sense, a *good* audience. He listens carefully and thinks all the time about you and your technique. Your real audience doesn't do that because they are busy doing the one thing your teacher cannot do: they are listening for the enjoyment of hearing you and the music.

15   Writing for a teacher is like hitting the ball to your tennis coach. It should teach you a lot and it may be great fun, *but it is practice or exercise rather than the real thing.* It's a means toward improving your performance at the real thing—whether the real thing is success in professional competition or fun in casual tennis. But whereas very few play their musical instrument only for their teacher or hit balls only to their coach—or at least if they do they usually realize they are leaving out the goal for which the teaching is designed—most students in school and college write only for teachers and take the situation for granted.

16   It's true that teachers prepare their students for other teachers, but that is as though tennis coaches kept their students moving up the line, volleying with one coach after another, till everyone got so used to the process that finally no one ever bothered to ask the obvious question any more: "Hey coach, when do I actually get to play a game of tennis?"

17   When you write for a teacher he won't stay put on the other side of the net or across the dueling ground. When you make a really good shot and wipe the sweat from your forehead and look over to see him sprawled full length on the court unable to reach the ball—or when you put down your smoking pistol and walk over to see him flat on his back with a neat red hole in his brow—all of a sudden you hear someone say, "Nice shot," and there he is over on the sidelines, unharmed, unsweaty, unruffled. Next time you don't try so hard.

18 But students couldn't take it if teachers played for real instead of just practice. Students only dare get in the ring with their teachers because they know the teachers will pull their punches. Yet every now and then the student does get knocked flat on his back—even though the teacher didn't mean to. Students discover they get knocked down more when they try their hardest. All but the born fighters learn to hold back—to do less than their best—when they spar with teachers.

19 This odd state of affairs has serious consequences for learning to write. For one thing, it's hard to put your heart in your work when you never get the excitement and satisfaction of a real performance for a real audience. You may get *anxious* when you write for a teacher, but you don't get the satisfaction that goes with a real performance, the satisfaction of knowing that you can actually affect your reader with your words. Occasionally, of course, teachers *are* informed, persuaded, or entertained by student writing, but the conditions under which teachers read are the worst possible conditions for being informed, persuaded, or informed.

20 It is no bed of roses for teachers either. As a teacher I am a slave reader. I must read every piece to the end. I must say to every student those magic words that every writer wants to hear, "I couldn't put your writing down," only I say it through clenched teeth. Even if some of the writing is enjoyable, I can't really read for enjoyment when I'm not free to stop reading. I can't just sit back and be enlightened or entertained, I must look for weaknesses and mistakes.

21 Inevitably I improve. But students don't improve with me. That is, each year I get better at finding weaknesses and mistakes, but each new batch of students is just as unskilled as last year's batch. Thus, every year I find more mistakes and weaknesses per page. (How could I not believe that students get worse every year?) And yet I cannot do what every real reader can do, namely, say "The hell with you" or "That makes me furious, I want to punch you in the nose," and throw it in the trash. I must continue on to the end and then try to write a comment that will be helpful. And I mustn't express to the student the annoyance that I feel—sometimes the fury. Is it surprising if these feelings sometimes get through anyway? Or that I am not always as helpful and supportive as I ought to be toward these creatures who cause me weekly agony?

22 In short, teachers cannot easily give their real reactions to the writing of their students because their real reactions are usually too critical and sometimes unprintable. They know that their students cannot handle or benefit from a mirror which shows so devastatingly every single weakness and mistake. Therefore since teachers cannot communicate to students what it actually feels like to read these words, and since there is no one else who reads these words, the student *never* gets the experience of learning what actually happens to a real reader reading his words. He gets only the conclusions of a skilled cataloguer of weaknesses and (one hopes) strengths.

23   As a result of all this the student's job is both too easy and too hard. It's too easy in that the student knows his reader will keep on reading to the end, no matter how bad the writing is. The student never has that frustrating but healthy sense of a reader on the other end of the line making minute by minute decisions about whether to keep on reading or put it down. Nothing really gives you the strength you need for revising but that feeling of trying to keep a reader from hanging up on you; that feeling of having only one thin thread connecting you and the reader. Once that filament breaks, you have lost your reader for ever back to the wide sea—or at least until you manage to hook him again with some combination of luck and good bait.

24   And yet writing for teachers is at the same time too hard. For there is a price you must pay for having a reader who never stops reading your words. He never really takes your words seriously as messages intended genuinely for him.

25   In what is the trickiest audience situation of all, then, it is easiest not to think very much about audience—about whom your words are intended for and what you want those words to do. And not thinking about audience is one of the best ways to block improvement in writing. Most people keep up their school habit of not thinking enough about audience even after they leave school or college—unless they write a lot for real audiences and also get lots of accurate feedback from these audiences about what their words actually did. Most people just struggle along as they are writing something in an effort to make it "good writing in general" instead of thinking carefully or precisely about "good for what effect on what reader."

26   Teachers, too, drift into ignoring audience. It is unhelpful, for example, to give assignments—as most teachers do and indeed I realize I tend to do—without specifying clearly who the audience is and what effect the words are supposed to have on it. Are these words meant to inform? To inform whom? How much prior knowledge do they have? To persuade? To persuade whom? How much do we know about their position on the issue? To give pleasure? To whom? What kind of reading do they like?

27   It is also unhelpful to evaluate and give feedback to student writing about its quality *in general*. It is meaningless, really, to try to tell a student how successful his writing is in general without saying how successful it is at achieving a certain effect on a certain audience. The only way you can give feedback on "quality in general" is by doing what teachers have historically tended to do: concentrate mostly on the conventions of writing as a medium, namely, spelling, grammar, footnotes, and paragraphing, and ignoring the question of how well it would work on what kinds of readers. It's not that the conventions of writing as a medium are unimportant or easy to learn. Quite the contrary. They are *too* hard and onerous to learn if you try to learn them by themselves—as mere push-ups—without the incentive of actually trying to use them in real communication to real readers.

ADVICE IF YOU ARE CURRENTLY
WRITING FOR TEACHERS

28 It can be a great gift to have a writing teacher—to have the services of a coach watching you play, suggesting exercises, and giving you feedback and advice. But you will miss most of this benefit unless you learn to take a certain amount of control of your situation and use your teacher as a service, a helper, an ally—not fight him as an adversary or go limp. Here are some concrete suggestions for getting the most out of teachers.

29   ■ Don't just hit balls to your coach, find someone to play tennis with. Give your papers to a friend to read—first for sharing, later for feedback. Get together with a small sharing or feedback group. If you give your writing only to teachers you get into a terrible rut of caring too much about your writing in one way—as an ordeal—and not caring enough about it in another way—as a message that matters to real human beings.

30   Once you start giving your words to someone in addition to a teacher you will feel an immediate relief: new perspective, new energy. Even if you *hate* the assignment you now have an interesting challenge: taking your *friend* seriously enough to find something worth saying about that topic or to find a way of writing that gives pleasure. Both tasks, while difficult, turn out to be feasible and enormously rewarding.

31   ■ Work out alternative assignments with your teacher so that it will be easier and more natural to give your writing to others. If you make it clear to your teacher that you are really serious about your writing and if you accept the fact that he probably has a serious agenda of skills and techniques for his assignments, you can usually work out some alternatives:

> *Something quite close to the assignment.* Simply ask if you can write about the topic exactly as given but in the form of a letter or personal essay to a friend, or a memo or article to some other audience you would enjoy addressing.

> *Significant variation.* If you are supposed to write about some aspect of *Hamlet,* ask if you can write something you could submit to a literary magazine or to the arts section of a newspaper: something about *Hamlet* and some other play, novel, or movie that provides an interesting comparison—and promise to treat prominently that aspect of the play the teacher wanted you to treat. If you are supposed to write a history paper about a period in the relatively recent past, see if you can write it in terms of what it was like then for your ancestors and make it a piece of family history. If you are assigned a piece of persuasion on a topic of no concern to you, perhaps you could choose an entirely different topic where you have a real audience but where the *kind* of persuasion demanded is exactly the same as in the teacher's assignment. You may find the teacher more amenable if you ask him what skills or issues he is trying to emphasize in his assignment and then agree to emphasize them in your alternative assignment. For example, he may want you to document everything you say about

Hamlet with quotations from the text; or to deal particularly with imagery; or to highlight economic conditions in the period of history you write about. You can do these things in your alternative assignments.

Something completely different. Something you need to write or want to write such as a short story, a memo, a letter of application, a political pamphlet, a letter to the editor. Emphasize the fact that you'll work at least as hard or even harder on it than you would on his assignment—and learn a lot about writing. Make sure, however, that you aren't just trying to do exactly the same kind of writing over and over again (for instance, nothing but science fiction stories about the future) since the teacher will probably feel, legitimately, that you won't be practicing the range of skills he's trying to stress.

32   ■ Ask teachers to specify clearly the audience and purpose for any writing assignment they give. It helps most if these audiences are actual people or groups even if the writing is not in fact delivered to them. And there is always a useful real audience available to whom writing can easily be delivered: other members of the class.

33   ■ Ask teachers to give some class time to discussing this issue of audience and if possible to bring in some outside readers—other teachers, magazine or newspaper editors, public relations officers of a business—to describe frankly their specific reactions to actual pieces of writing.

34   ■ You need to master the traditional genre of writing essays for that tricky general reader. But ask the teacher to explain more clearly who he thinks this general reader is and to sponsor some discussion of the matter. What level of knowledge should you assume a general reader has about the topic? What point of view should you assume this reader has about the issue? There is an easy way to remove this slippery issue from the realm of the hypothetical and that is to ask your teacher to specify for every essay assignment a particular magazine or journal in which it should be published. Then the readership and editorial policy of this publication can be discussed and people can look at some of the pieces that it actually publishes. (Remember of course that it may help you to do all your raw writing to a different, more comfortable audience, or no audience at all, and wait till revising to make your words fit the general reader or the readership of this publication.)

35   ■ Ask your teacher to assign pieces of writing where he is, indeed, the direct and real audience: pieces of writing designed to affect him in particular. If he is trying to persuade his own child to do something or trying to decide which brand of whatsis to buy, students could write genuine advice to him. Ask him to think of theoretical or political or practical issues where he cannot make up his mind. Also issues where he already feels strongly one way or the other. Since he is the real audience, he can give accurate feedback on how the writing worked and didn't work on him.

36   ■ Ask your teacher to grade and comment on your paper not just as to its quality in general but as to how he thinks it will work on the particular

hypothetical audience. This change in feedback will come naturally if you have already persuaded him to specify audience and purpose more clearly—or worked out alternative assignments where you specify your own audience and purpose. And this change, interestingly, will usually lead him to do something else very helpful, namely to tell some of his own particular reactions—speaking as himself rather than as "representative reader." It will become easier for him to say things like "This would probably work on Robert Redford but it bothers me because . . ." or "I found this section particularly interesting but I don't think it will make sense to your third-grade readers."

37   ▪ Almost all these suggestions involve asking for more and clearer feedback than your teacher usually gives. Find ways to make it easier for him to give it. For example, try attaching a sheet of paper to your writing with some questions on it that will permit him to say more in fewer words. On the next page is an example that can easily be varied.

38   If he didn't specify audience and purpose, you will have to say what your audience and purpose are on that sheet of paper.

39   See the next section on feedback for other questions to ask of a reader.

40   Offer a cassette (and cassette player) with your paper so he can speak his comment without writing. You'll get a much more human comment and learn more about how your writing affected him. (This is probably feasible only if he reads papers in his office. You can't ask him to carry a cassette player home.) Don't ask for conferences on every paper. That takes too much time.

41   ▪ Ask your teacher to point out at least one thing you did well on each paper. If possible, one thing that's better than last time. (If they have too many students, however, you can't expect them to remember your last paper.) When teachers read huge stacks of papers they often drift into doing nothing but finding weaknesses. The goal of this request is not just to spare your feelings (though if you are too hurt you will learn poorly). Knowledge of what you did well is actually more potent in helping you improve your writing than knowledge of what you did poorly. If your teacher shows you what you did well, or even sort-of-well, you can do it again, more often, and even expand on it, because you already have the feeling for how to do it. You need only improve a behavior you already possess and learn to use it in more contexts. And as you learn to get your strengths into more of your writing you naturally tend to get rid of some of the other weaknesses. But if your teacher only tells you what you did wrong you may not be able to fix it no matter how clearly he explains the problem: he's asking for behavior you've never produced before.

42   For example, if you have consistently terrible organization and occasional powerful sentences, you may well improve your organization more quickly by trying to expand that gift for strong sentences than by working on organization. For some reason you have a serious blind spot or lack of feeling for organization, and it seldom does much good in such cases for someone to shout at you "pay more attention to organization." *You* have to

Please put a straight line alongside passages and underneath phrases that you like or that work for *you* as a reader; and a wiggly line alongside passages and underneath phrases that annoy or don't work for you.

Please write a brief comment here about the one matter that most affected your reading.

For the *intended audience,* which section(s) or aspect(s) of this piece do you think will work or be most successful? Why?

What do you think will fail or backfire on the intended audience? Why?

Here are some aspects of my writing that I especially want feedback on:

	strong	*adequate*	*weak*
• paragraphing	☐	☐	☐
• convincing argument	☐	☐	☐
• convincing evidence	☐	☐	☐
• liveliness of language or humaness of tone	☐	☐	☐
• punctuation	☐	☐	☐

What is the quickest simplest change I could make that would create the biggest improvement?

What one thing do you think I should try to work on or think about in my next piece of writing?

develop that feeling for organization, and often you can't do so until you improve enough *other* aspects of your writing that your imagination can finally work on organization.

43   ■ To get the most help from a teacher you need him as your ally and helper rather than as your enemy. You will go a long way toward that goal if you can get him to specify the audience for the writing assignments and then to grade them and give you feedback in terms of how he thinks your writing would succeed with that audience. This makes your teacher into a kind of coach helping you aim words at some third party. But there's a lot more you can do to overcome the structural features of school and college which make teachers into opponents and policemen (a role most teachers would like to get out of). Pretend, for instance, that in reacting and commenting on your paper, your teacher is a *friend* doing you a *favor*—not an employee doing a duty. (He certainly is doing you a favor if he does it well.) Think of the specific things you would do for your friend if you were asking a favor:

> You would probably make your paper neat and easy to read. I get mad at students when their papers are messy. I begin to feel them as the enemy.

> You would probably get your paper to him at a convenient time. I resent students who turn in papers late. It usually makes my life harder, and even when it doesn't, it makes me feel I have to be on guard against them.

> You would probably proofread and correct carefully to get rid of all the mistakes you can. When I get a paper full of mistakes I know the student could have removed, I immediately feel like *not helping* him. I feel he's treating me as a servant who is supposed to pick his smelly socks off the floor when he could just as well do it himself.

> You would probably make sure to stick to the assignment. When I come to a paper that avoids or drifts away from the assignment, I instinctively feel, "Uh oh, here's someone trying to get away with something. I'd better be on guard." I start relating to him as the enemy. (Usually, by the way, you *can* find a way to include almost anything that interests you, even if it seems quite distant, as long as you think carefully about how to make it *part* of something that does address the assignment squarely.) You can probably add to my list of suggestions for helping make your teacher into your ally rather than your adversary.

44   ■ None of those suggestions entails doing any *more* writing than what is already assigned to you by the teacher: merely giving that writing to other people and adjusting the transaction between you and the teacher. But the most powerful thing you can do to increase what you get from teachers is to write *more.* Not just because quantity helps—though that is probably the main fact about writing—but because you learn most from teachers if your writing for them is a *supplement* to other writing you are doing. Try to think of writing for teachers as sneaking off for a little help on the side, getting in some volleying with the coach between your real

games of tennis. Writing more means working more, but the amount of writing your teachers ask for will suddenly seem small once you stop treating assignments as ordeals and scary performances for the enemy and start treating them like mere practice games or chances for feedback from an ally on a nearly final draft.

45   Once you can write more you can look to them for what they *can* give and look elsewhere for what they cannot. Teachers are good for giving criticism because they read papers in piles of 25 or 50. Take that criticism and use it. They are good at making you write when you don't feel like it, simply because they have authority. Instead of resenting this, try appreciating it and internalizing from it what may be the most important skill of all: the ability to write when you are in the wrong mood. They are *not* good at telling you what your writing feels like to a real human being, at taking your words seriously as messages directed to them, at praising you, or perhaps even at noticing you. Get these things elsewhere. They are easier to find than what a teacher has to offer.

FOLLOW-UP ACTIVITIES

Discussing the Rhetoric

1. Who do you think is Elbow's primary audience?

2. How do you think Elbow's concept of his audience affects his style? Consider not just sentence structure and diction, but figurative language as well. How does Elbow's style differ from that of other writers included in this Part? How does figurative language help Elbow appeal to his audience?

3. What does Elbow's figurative language suggest about his view of students? Is it close to Allan Bloom's view? Mike Rose's? Bartholomae's? What other indicators in the reading suggest how Elbow characterizes students?

4. What is Elbow's main point? Can you summarize it in one sentence?

5. What appeals does Elbow use to construct his argument? An appeal to logic? Emotion? A mixture of the two? Choose three passages from the selection to support your answer.

6. Elbow writes that student writers who want to do more than merely satisfy their teachers "must do something different, striking, unique with the same old ingredients" of what makes a good essay. Does Elbow do anything striking or unique to make this essay an exciting piece of writing? If so, indicate a few passages where he does. What rhetorical strategies does he use to strike his readers in these passages?

7. What examples best illustrate how important the concept of audience awareness is to Elbow?

Discussing the Conversation

1. How should the students and teachers described in this selection "invent the university" through their writing and reading, according to Elbow? Would their inventions differ from Bartholomae's students' inventions? How so?

2. Like so many other writers collected in this text, Elbow writes from a teacher's perspective. How does his perspective as teacher differ from the perspectives we get from Mike Rose in Part One? From Mary Louise Pratt in Part Two? From Mariolina Salvatori in this part? You'll want to think about each writer's ethos as you formulate your responses.

3. Do you think Elbow would subscribe to Pratt's concept of "contact zone"? Why or why not?

4. Which other writers in this part of the text are concerned with problems that result from attempting to write for a "general reader"? (Other writers' concerns might be explicitly or implicitly voiced.)

5. Elbow suggests that sharing your writing with a friend for feedback is a good idea because you stand to gain a new perspective. Karen Spear discusses many problems students face when they share their writing, and proposes solutions to those problems. In your estimation, does Spear's account problematize Elbow's suggestion? In what ways?

6. What is Elbow's opinion of student writers? How does his opinion differ from Linda Flower's view of student writers? Locate quotations from both writers to illustrate the similarities and differences.

7. Elbow finds the concept of "general reader" highly problematic. Would Stanley Fish? How about bell hooks? What passages from their essays tell you they would or wouldn't?

Joining the Conversation

1. You could read Elbow's criticisms of the gulf that frequently exists between students and teachers in terms of Jim Corder's assumption that "people tend to dichotomize or divide the world and the people in it into two categories: self and other." In terms of Elbow's criticisms, does thinking deeply about audience help to create what Pratt calls a "contact zone" (a space where clashing views can be negotiated) between self and other, or writer and reader? How so? Respond in an informal paper.

2. Elbow finds a conflict between writing for a "general reader" and turning your writing into a particular teacher for evaluation. Have you ever experienced this conflict with your writing? Attempt to trace your conflict in an informal paper.

3. Elbow enjoys using gaming metaphors (such as comparing writing to tennis and fishing) in his writing. In an informal paper, think about why Elbow might choose these metaphors to construct his argument. What qualities might the notion of games have in common with Elbow's agenda? Do you think Bartholomae might agree with Elbow's metaphoric illustrations?

INTRODUCTORY COMMENTS ON "CONFLICT AND CONFUSION OVER SHARING WRITING" BY KAREN SPEAR

Reading the Context

Karen Spear is interested in the peculiar dynamics of peer response groups in a writing classroom. She brings to that interest a background in literature, writing, and psychology. Spear has a masters in psychology and a doctorate in American Studies, and is currently the dean of Arts and Sciences at Fort Lewis College in Durango, CO.

This reading is a chapter excerpted from her book, *Sharing Writing*. The book is about Spear's attempt to uncover possible solutions for the problems students face when they get together to critique each other's work. Because this essay comes from a much larger work, you will not read Spear's entire argument or learn all her strategies for making group work successful; you will, however, be introduced to many of the problems. Then you can brainstorm with your peers how you might solve problems in your own group work.

Reading the Rhetoric

Although Spear addresses other writing instructors, not students, the essay includes a transcription of direct student quotations. As you read, think about what strategies Spear uses to introduce these student voices. What purposes do they serve in (1) establishing a tone, and (2) creating a credible ethos for Spear? As she explains their "meaning," think about whether you agree with Spear's interpretation of what's going on in the group.

Consider carefully what Spear's goal might be. What ideas is she trying to get other writing professors to accept? What does she want students to do differently?

Reading the Conversation

As you read, mark passages or phrases in your text where you notice Spear responding to or commenting on a topic that other writers in this book address. Topics may be quite general or they may be more specific. Spear might not use the same words as others to discuss the topic, but look for more subtle connections. Does she create new terms to define something that has already been introduced by another writer? Does she explore an area of a conversation that hasn't been explored in other essays? Does she refute another writer's thesis? Does she provide evidence that you could use to support another writer's claims? These are some of the ways that writers interact when continuing written conversations.

Conflict and Confusion Over Sharing Writing
Karen Spear

1   When we picture students working collaboratively on writing, we envision stimulating, thoughtful exchanges among peers, something like our own conferences with students—but better. In removing the potentially intimidating influence of The Teacher, we imagine ourselves unleashing students' pent-up talents and allowing them to blossom in this freer atmosphere. So we carefully teach students to brainstorm ideas, and we prepare questions and devise checklists to guide their revising and editing. Then, expecting anything from minor improvement to miracles, we turn the class over to response groups.

2   And what do we often find? Students wandering indecisively through each other's drafts, making a comment here, questioning a sentence there, but by and large failing to emulate the purposeful give-and-take that more experienced writers engage in so regularly. Some benefits do crop up—an ambiguous sentence is identified, a grammatical or spelling error is corrected. However, the substantive stuff—exploring purpose, discovering new insights, developing ideas, challenging assumptions—remains unaccomplished.

3   To bring about our vision of collaborative groups, we need first to see more clearly their actual dynamics, discouraging as they sometimes can be. This chapter and the next two chapters explore peer interaction through information garnered from transcripts, interviews, and observations. The analysis shows how students perceive and carry out the tasks of sharing ideas and reviewing and editing each other's writing. Their interaction suggests five interrelated problems, which I treat as themes, that weave their way throughout the book:

1. confused expectations about the group's purpose and the individual's role in it
2. inability to read group members' texts analytically
3. misperceptions about the nature of revision and of writing as a process

  4. failure to work collaboratively with group members
  5. failure to monitor and maintain group activity.

If we can first understand the nature and causes of these problems, we can more readily anticipate how to structure groups for more effective interaction and more successful writing.

4   What follows is a segment of a transcript from a sophomore-level composition class composed mostly of juniors and seniors at Michigan State University.[1] The four students in the group had read and commented on each other's papers prior to this session, using a revision guide provided by the instructor and, presumably, modeling their responses on the whole-class revision sessions held throughout the term. Here, they are reviewing each other's essays before preparing a revision to be turned in several days later. The problems these students are having occur among students of all ages; the interaction here is quite typical. Many themes run through this transcript, but I have tried to highlight the most salient ones.

> BRENT: Want to do my paper? Really tell me—give me some good criticism on it.
>
> *The writer illustrates the assumption common among students that responding to a paper means criticizing it.*
>
> It really reeked, I—in my opinion.
>
> CARRIE: I thought it was a good paper—it held my attention.
>
> SHERRIE: Mmm.
>
> BRENT: It's true.
>
> CARRIE: It's like—reading it, you know. I was wondering if something good was going to happen to you, 'cause you kept saying—especially when the coach said "*even* Sweitzer can go out there and make better than a mediocre showing."
>
> *Readers immediately deviate from reading the text to inquiring about the story and the person behind it.*
>
> BRENT: That *really* happened.
>
> SHERRIE: I would've fallen on my face.
>
> BRENT: Yeah—I kept my cool pretty good. It was a really hard time in my life. But I really didn't—I really didn't say in the paper what I really wanted to say: it wasn't because I was so short so much as because I wasn't a, a schoolboard member's son. . . . I wasn't a schoolboard member's son, I wasn't a teacher's son.
>
> CARRIE: (Her comment is unintelligible.)
>
> BRENT: Yeah—this was a real small town—there was really a lot of hypocrites, you know.

SHERRIE: How small was it?

BRENT: 16,000.

SHERRIE: The high school was pretty small then.

CARRIE: What I thought you should've done was—in this one, I didn't know if you were um, really confident about going out there, or were you still nervous—you know—when you tried out for the second one—you see what I'm talking about?—when you tried out when you um, were in Michigan. You know.

Group begins to offer advice telling the writer what he should do rather than focusing on their own difficulties in understanding the text as it is.

BRENT: Yeah.

CARRIE: I know you said you aimed to do it in style—but were you still nervous?—were you scared at all, still?

The use of questions helps to probe and clarify meaning, but the group has trouble staying with the question.

BRENT: Yeah (Carrie: Yeah), I could've said that—of course, it was three in the morning (they both laugh)—I really didn't care at that point.

CARRIE: Well, it's all good stuff.

BRENT: As far as grammatical and things like that.

The group shows its ambivalence about being "critical"; they prefer safe, objective commentary.

JIM: It was good. But like I felt that you should have told, added more to the paper, more toward the ending, what happened that senior year, you know, how you felt. I feel I was cut short.

BRENT: (Laughs) Good line!

JIM: 'Cause you know, the coach said you were great—but what happened after that—the rest of the year?

CARRIE: Yeah—it'd be nice to hear the rest of it.

BRENT: You're right—go on with it.

CARRIE: It's just that . . .

BRENT: I didn't think that, though, was directly related to the whole idea of the paper—me being castigated for my height.

CARRIE: Yeah, yeah. Go on with it. I liked this, um, analogy—the ups and downs (little chuckle).

JIM: Yeah.

CARRIE: "The ups and down I was looking for."

BRENT: I originally used the word "indigenous" in there but it sounded too "flowery"—you know, "the ups and downs as indigenous characteristics."

JIM: Wh-where do you come up with these *words?* Are you an English major?

BRENT: No, I used to write a lot 'n; I—I don't know.

SHERRIE: With me, my vocabulary's about this big—I can never think of, you know, a word that . . .

CARRIE: The town in Michigan was bigger?

SHERRIE: Yeah, how big was it?

BRENT: OK, it's Highland, Michigan but—it's smaller, a lot smaller, but it's metro Detroit, which makes it part of the big megalopolis, so it didn't have that kind of down-home attitude. If you were good, you got to play. I did go on and . . .

CARRIE: Very interesting. (They laugh.)

BRENT: How about the, you know—what else d'you have written down there?—"lousy?"

The writer tries to recall the group to the task . . .

CARRIE: Um—no,—I was just going by—let me . . .

BRENT: Transitions and . . .

CARRIE: I like what you said about your goals. I can never set goals. You set one goal early in life—I have never set a goal in my life . . .

SHERRIE: And you went through with it—it was a good paper because of that . . .

CARRIE: If someone would've done that to me, I probably. . . . Something like that would've put me down just far enough that I wouldn't, I wouldn't have the guts to go in and try again—I'd be afraid to be put down again. You deserve a lot of credit for that.

. . . but Carrie's comment pulls them away from the text again and back to the larger context of the story.

BRENT: I was—I was hesitant to take them up on their suggestion because of that—the humiliation of it all (Carrie: Mm-hmm). I was sick to death of it.

SHERRIE: How long?

BRENT: How long?

SHERRIE: Like were you in school?

BRENT: It was my senior year.

SHERRIE: It was your senior year?

BRENT: Yeah.

CARRIE: Yeah—you should put that down.

JIM: And when your coach told you . . .

BRENT: Right—that was my junior year.

JIM: What—that the coach cut you down.

BRENT: Right.

JIM: And then between your junior and senior year you moved?

BRENT: Yeah.

JIM: Who was your paper aimed at?

The group recognizes the question of audience for the first time but fails to consider it specifically.

BRENT: Uh—I'd love to shove it in the face of my coach in Ohio (said very slowly and deliberately). (Chuckles)

CARRIE: Send him a copy!—Um, no—I thought it as aimed at almost anyone.

CARRIE: Really, 'cause anybody could get something out of it.

At this point the group begins to drift aimlessly in their conversation about Brent's experience on the high school basketball team. Their questions and comments on how Brent must have felt have no connection with Brent's draft until Sherrie suggests that readers might need more information. When they periodically return to the draft, they give Brent fragmentary advice on how to fix specific things but never really consider the draft as a whole.

BRENT: Anything else?

CARRIE: When I first started reading that part, "I aimed to do it in style," I didn't know if you made it til the end of the paper—'cause you said, "First a 20-footer." I didn't know if you made the 20-footer or not, you know what I mean?

Readers continue to offer vague suggestions but the group fails to develop, test, or apply them.

BRENT: Oh, yeah, OK.

CARRIE: You know? I thought, "Uh-oh." (Chuckles)

BRENT: I thought it was really vague there too, after I reread it.

CARRIE: You had high hopes.

BRENT: I thought it—you guys might think what I meant by that was "I aimed to do it in style, and first a 20-footer"—like this was my plan. (Chuckles)

Brent show his understanding of the response group as an audience for his work, but they don't know how to respond as readers of an in-process piece of writing.

CARRIE: Yeah, that's—see, that's what I thought.

BRENT: Then I read it again, and I thought, that couldn't possibly be my plan. (They both chuckle briefly.) I don't know—I don't know if that was vague or not—it seemed vague to me.

(Pause)

BRENT: Feel free—feel free to cut me to ribbons—'cause I won't learn anything unless you do.

(Pause)

Brent's implicit definition of criticism as a destructive act is apparently shared by his peers. Despite his invitation, no one really wants to engage in such an unpleasant process.

JIM: What'd you mean by "I never had the opportunity to encounter the kind of ups and downs that I was looking for"?

Jim interprets Brent's request for criticism as an instruction to challenge the writing at the sentence level, primarily to achieve greater clarity. The group still focuses on what the writer intended more than on what the readers experienced.

BRENT: Basketball. It was a direct analogy to basketball.

JIM: Well, I know—I could understand that, but you go, "Curiously enough, the ups and downs that I am alluding to are not the pros and cons of everyday life, but"—I don't know—it seems kind of . . .

BRENT: Redundant, maybe?

JIM: No—

BRENT: ". . . can certainly have its ups and downs. But unfortunately for me, I never"—ah, the first part was just, life in a small town—people can be really rude.

CARRIE: Maybe you should've said something about that—

Carrie's interruption prevents (saves?) Jim and Brent from exploring Jim's question.

'cause I don't think—

BRENT: But that has nothing to do with the paper.

CARRIE: Well, but it—you—it was because it was a small town, wasn't it? That—well, no, because then Highland was a small town too.

BRENT: Yeah.

CARRIE: Yeah, maybe you should've put something about the atmosphere at your school.

Readers appropriate the writer's text by giving vague advice on how to fix the writing rather than asking questions and identifying their own responses.

BRENT: Yeah.

JIM: Why was it that way, or why do you think it was that way?

BRENT: Yeah.

CARRIE: That might take away from the paper too.

BRENT: I want to keep on track, with the height thing.

Brent is not fully willing to entertain his reader's suggestions. His protestations about keeping on track may also be subliminally related to the texture of the discussion as a whole.

CARRIE: Yeah.

BRENT: I didn't want to get off on tangents, that's too easy to do.

SHERRIE: Your senior year.

BRENT: Yeah—I was short and fast.

SHERRIE: Oh, really?

BRENT: So we won games.

JIM: Maybe add on to the end—or just say how you . . . maybe not. Let's see what she says. (A reference to the instructor.)

BRENT: Yeah, I didn't know whether to go on or not. Flip it.

CARRIE: Mmmm.

JIM: That's life. We'd better move on.

The group abandons its task by deferring to a higher authority. They have not been able to reach closure on any of the ideas that arose in discussion, and they dismiss their own authority as readers in deference to the teacher's "right answers."

TO SHARE OR NOT TO SHARE—THE BASIC DILEMMA

5 Brent's opening comment represents most students' fundamental ambivalence over exposing their work to peers. "Want to do my paper?" he asks, much as if it will amount to something like an autopsy or the dissecting of a frog. "Really give me some good criticism on it," and later, in a comment that defines what he means by "criticism": "Feel free, feel free to cut me to

ribbons." His initial self-deprecation, "It really reeked," serves not only to invite his partners' responses but also to shield himself from potentially cutting criticism by reducing the importance of the paper in his own eyes.

6   Understandably, writers want help and advice, but they don't want to look foolish. They feel at home with peers but often admit that they doubt their peers' ability to help with revisions. Further, they accept the concept of revision but often remain convinced that *their* drafts are essentially finished. This ambivalence about the task and their peers' role in it is largely justified. Peers' natural reluctance to, as they see it, "criticize" or "evaluate" each other's work along with the rather strong cues they receive from teachers to do just that combine with their own self-doubts about their ability to make responsible judgments regarding others' work. As a result, students in writing groups tend to keep discussion safe, objective, and non-threatening.

7   As this session on Brent's essay indicates, readers typically begin by reassuring the writer that the piece is basically OK, primarily because the topic was "interesting." Carrie says, "I thought it was a good paper—it held my attention." Later, when the group reviews Jim's paper, Brent begins, "This was a really good paper, I really enjoyed it—kept me on the edge of my seat." In another group, the first reader says, "It's another good story . . . you're really good at description."

8   Though readers recognize the value of balancing praise with criticism, they implicitly set up a false either-or dilemma. They construe feedback as either positive or negative, praise or blame. With feedback so defined, they choose the safer option of keeping the discussion primarily non-critical. In fact, members of one very successful brainstorming group insisted to me that when it came to reviewing texts, discussing the ideas as they were presented in the paper was simply not an appropriate task—either for students or, implicitly, for teachers.[2] "A paper," explained one member, "has to stand on its own and you shouldn't have to defend or explain it. Besides," she added, "I don't know enough to *evaluate* other people's work." The dichotomy students create effectively rules out much of what we put them in groups to do. Critical generalities and social niceties supplant analysis and even description, since these activities seem to involve "picking things apart." Once you have excluded description, analysis, criticism, and evaluation, there's not much left to do in talking about a text.

9   Even when writers recognize substantial shortcomings in their own work and ask for help, groups tend to avoid the request, usually by simply ignoring it. In another group, such a request for help, vaguely phrased as it is, serves to end the group's discussion of the writer's paper:

> I don't know, it's kinda hard that part. I mean especially at this paragraph. 'Cause it's such a shapeless . . . it's so hard to explain exactly what it is, you know. The words . . . I just didn't know what to do. I really didn't.

Carol says, "Um," Carl sidesteps the question by calling for further comments, and they move on to review another student's paper. Linda's helplessness here recalls Brent's unresolved questions at the end of his group's review when he says, "Flip it," and decides to wait for the teacher's more authoritative commentary on his final revision.

10   Responses like these teach students that their peers have little of real worth to offer, causing the group as a whole to turn to safer, simpler tasks. What should also be clear, however, it that writers seem unable to ask questions in concrete ways and are therefore unable to help the group focus on their concerns. Meanwhile, readers lack knowledge of how to answer questions and, more importantly, how to use the group to find the answer. These matters will be considered in later chapters.

THE PRESERVATION OF HARMONY

11 Writers' apologies and readers' reassurances stem from a need to preserve harmony within the group. According to the self-reports of a group of freshman writers whom I observed and interviewed over a year's time, the need to establish and maintain harmony (and thus to avoid any vestige of conflict) became the group's primary goal, although it was never expressed as such. Consequently, they avoided focusing on potentially problematic issues; not until much later did they recognize their avoidance strategies. During group meetings, members maintained the paradox of appearing to respond while ducking the real issues. They affirmed writers as individuals while neatly avoiding the words and sentences that comprised their texts.

12   Thus, their presupposition about the task, combined with their limited interaction skills and their need to preserve harmony within the group, put them in direct conflict with the teacher's expectations that they should help each other think through and rethink their drafts. Students don't initially accept or perhaps understand writing as this kind of process. They have almost always experienced texts as completed rather than emerging products. So, no matter how dissatisfied they may be with their work, it is essentially finished when they come to a response group. Instead students perceive their task as mostly minor tinkering. Groups face the doublesided problem of quelling disharmony among themselves and resisting the intrusions of a teacher whose expectations vary so dramatically from their own.

THE SANCTITY OF OPINIONS

13 The reasons behind students' resistance to participating in the process of writing are too varied, complex, and interconnected to wholly account for. But one reason became abundantly clear in Lawson, Holt, and Newell's study that explored freshman attitudes toward questions of personal value and academic standards of evaluation. Interview data revealed that a majority of freshmen believed that challenging, questioning, and especially evaluating

students' opinions and beliefs, particularly once they are solidified in writing, is inappropriate both for teachers and students. One student's comment is representative:

> When they send back comments, a lot of papers are based on values and stuff that are a lot of your own opinions, and I have a hard time seeing how they could grade some of your own opinions. Writing style, maybe, technique, or mispelled words, maybe, they could grade on that, but for instance I got a paper back about a week ago. I got a C+ on it and I don't think there were any mispelled words and I doubt there were any sentence problems or paragraph problems, but for some reason he or she [the professor] just didn't match with my ideas.[3]

Facts, they felt, are subject to error and correction because there are right and wrong answers, but since "values and stuff" are personal matters, evaluating them (and all this implies) is merely a reflection of subjective bias and has no place in peer reviews of writing, a preconception for many students that puts them considerably at odds with their teachers' views of writing and peer review.

14   Thus, the logic of their behavior in groups is consistent with the suppositions about writing that is in any way connected with opinion. This attitude casts a very wide net indeed because, as William Perry found in his research on undergraduates' cognitive development, the ability to distinguish valid from invalid opinions, good ones from bad, seems to develop rather slowly.[4] In the meantime, students' emotional needs on the one hand and linguistic and cognitive abilities on the other are pitted against teachers' expectations and assumptions about the outcomes of group work.

A COMPREHENSIVE FRAMEWORK FOR UNDERSTANDING AND DEVELOPING GROUP BEHAVIOR

15 Developing successful peer response groups depends on understanding the causes of students' behavior before we can influence the behavior itself. Research into the composing process has begun to do that for writing. Much the same approach needs to be taken to diagnose group behavior. The two have much in common.

16   Both writing and peer interaction are improved when learners achieve insight into their behavior—its origins, consequences, and relationships with other experiences. The transcript just presented shows that the group has almost no understanding of why they are having the problems they are either in writing or sharing that writing. In fact, the group seems blissfully unaware of any problems at all. On the other hand, when writers—or groups—are able to perceive strengths and weaknesses in their interaction, as well as the reasons for them, their experience changes from a loose collection of unrelated phenomena to a thematically coherent web in which events are meaningfully connected.

17   In writing, we call this web *coherence* and seek to teach it by teaching such formal conventions as thesis statements, topic sentences, transitions, introductions and conclusions, and such rhetorical necessities as audience and purpose. In groups, the same web is defined by differentiating what are called *task functions* from *maintenance functions*—the group task as distinct from how the group goes about achieving it—and group members must learn to attend to the maintenance level of their interaction because it weaves together and gives meaning and purpose to the task.

18   Task functions ride on maintenance functions like telephone conversations on telephone wires: destroy the wire and you destroy the message. The same can be said about writing when it exists as a string of facts, ideas, or observations but lacks the thematic or purposive strand that organizes and holds together all the elements. Like writing, group interaction suffers when members fail to realize the complexity of the medium, becoming absorbed solely in the group task or content.

19   Group tasks have to do with the groups' immediate need: in peer response groups, sharing and responding to each other's ideas and drafts. Specifically, this involves defining problems, understanding intentions, expressing reactions, proposing alternatives, seeking clarification, asking questions. Underlying these issues, however, and directly influencing them, is the group's self-awareness in carrying out tasks. The ability to step back from the immediate problem to examine group procedures, note evasions or abrupt changes of subject, encourage participation, express feelings, integrate various points of view, summarize, devise alternative approaches—these are the ways in which a group fulfills its tasks. When groups bog down, it is frequently because members assume they have exhausted the task when it's more likely that they haven't developed a strategy for dealing with it. The same might be said about impasses in writing.

20   Freud's classic analogy of the iceberg is useful here in clarifying this business about functions. Maintenance functions, mostly invisible, provide a foundation for the more visible tasks. How the group goes about its tasks, the group's processes, occupies a larger mass than the tasks themselves, or the group's product. Much the same relationship between product and process in groups carries over to the relationship between content, or ideas, and how they are generated in writing. Exploring the relationships among ideas is probably the most significant source of content available to writers. For example, common to many current techniques of invention (brainstorming, free association, clustering, tagmemics) is a process of recombining old information to produce new ideas. A predominant concern in groups with either task or content leads to overemphasis on outcomes at the expense of the processes that make the outcomes possible.

21   The issue isn't solely that mature group interaction causes better writing, although in the long run it does, but that in the larger context of writing as a vehicle for learning and thinking, group interaction complements writing by stimulating thinking. If we are concerned with improving written products

by improving the processes that generate them, then developing students' interaction skills along with other composing skills comes down to realizing more fully all the implications of writing as a thinking and learning process.

NOTES

1. I am indebted to Professor Mary Francine Danis of Our Lady of the Lake College, San Antonio, Texas for sharing this and other transcripts with me. They were collected for her doctoral dissertation at Michigan State University, "Peer Response Groups in a College Writing Workshop: Students' Suggestions for Revising Compositions," *DAI* 41 (1981).
   To ensure as objective an analysis as possible, I've relied heavily on transcripts of students with whom I'm unacquainted. Throughout the book, I supplement my analysis of these transcripts with my own observations of peer response groups drawn principally from visits to discussion groups of the hundred students who participated in the Utah Plan, described in note #2 below. I visited these groups weekly for one term, then monthly throughout the rest of the school year. I followed one group (which is described in Chapter 4) with particular attention; in addition to observing this group, I interviewed the group as a whole twice and individual members frequently. Groups in my own writing classes have also been an important source of instruction.
2. The group participated in a two-year experimental liberal education program at the University of Utah. A study of this program provided valuable insights into the development of freshman attitudes toward their college experiences, cognitive styles, and values [Jane M. Lawson, Ladd A. Holt, and L. Jackson Newell, "The Utah Plan: College Freshmen in an Experimental Liberal Studies Program" *Journal of General Education* 35 (1983), pp. 136–153.]
3. Reported in "The Utah Plan: College Freshman in an Experimental Liberal Studies Program," p. 17.
4. William Perry, *Forms of Intellectual and Ethical Development in the College Years: A Scheme* (New York: Holt, Rinehart and Winston, 1968), Chapter 5.

FOLLOW-UP ACTIVITIES

Discussing the Rhetoric

1. What voices, besides her own and her students, does Spear bring into the conversation? How does she use these voices? To elaborate on a point? To support her ideas? To represent a dissenting view?

2. How would you characterize Spear's tone? Is it casual, professional, friendly, serious, reproachful, or something else altogether? What does her tone suggest about her attitude toward this topic?

3. How has Spear structured her essay? What does she start with, what does she move to next, and how does she end?

4. Spear creates and defines two new terms in this essay: "task functions" and "maintenance functions." Why do you think she creates new terms instead of expressing her ideas in terms that already exist?

Discussing the Conversation

1. Who is the "we" of Spear's first sentence? Had you thought previously about teachers' views of writing conferences? What did you learn about teachers from eavesdropping on this conversation?

2. Peer work can be compared to the group efforts required to produce a manufactured item, like a video game or a car. If a peer's rough draft were the raw materials, what steps would your group need to go through to create a product from this material? What does Spear call this process?

3. Do you think Spear addresses the same audience Bartholomae does in "Inventing the University?" Select two quotations from each essay that you feel support your conclusion.

4. Spear suggests that "reader expectations" should guide a peer group, rather than the story line or the author's intentions. What do you think Spear means by that phrase? Do you think Bartholomae would agree or disagree with her? How would Pratt respond?

5. How well do you think Spear interpreted students' reactions to response groups?

6. The common connotation is that criticism is negative. The conflict between the common connotation and its positive value in academic work comes to a head in Brent and his group's struggle to revise his paper. With your current understanding of criticism as it is practiced academically, how could you help Brent and his group to make better use of their peer group session?

Joining the Conversation

1. Reflect on your experiences in peer discussion groups in this class. Have they been helpful? If Spear had asked you to write a chapter for her book on peer group interactions from a student's perspective, what would you have included in the chapter? Write your version of the chapter. (This may be a good opportunity for parody or satire!)

2. In an informal paper, explain your definition of the word "critical" and describe experiences in your life that you feel shaped your definition.

INTRODUCTORY COMMENTS ON EXCERPTS FROM "LEARNING TO READ BIOLOGY: ONE STUDENT'S RHETORICAL DEVELOPMENT IN COLLEGE" BY CHRISTINA HAAS

Reading the Context

This essay is from an academic journal titled *Written Communication,* published for professors of composition, English, and communications. Christina Haas is assistant professor of English at Penn State University, where she teaches undergraduate and graduate courses in writing and rhetoric and directs the Writing Internship Program. She has published many articles on computers and the process of writing. Her first book is titled *The Materiality of Literacy: Studies of Technology, Culture, and Thinking.*

In this essay, Haas provides us with a longitudinal study, or one conducted over a relatively long period of time, usually several years. Such studies are common in the disciplines of the social sciences. Haas examines the reading processes and practices of one college student, Eliza, through eight semesters of undergraduate education. Specifically, the study traces the development of Eliza's beliefs about literate activity, her representations of the nature of texts, and her understanding of the relationship between knowledge and written discourse within her discipline.

Haas begins the essay by situating her longitudinal study in the larger context of academic rhetoric. According to Haas, becoming literate in the university means learning "the patterns of knowing about, and behaving toward, texts within a disciplinary field." In the course of this essay, Haas considers the growth of one student's understanding of these issues throughout her college career. She argues that rhetorical issues cannot be neglected when writing for the sciences, so a rhetorical understanding of the human or social enterprise of science is necessary. By examining scientists in their contexts as writers, we can move from the belief in scientific texts as autonomous or timeless to the view that scientific texts are manifestations of scientific action and, perhaps more importantly, records of human choices.

Reading the Rhetoric

Haas lists the elements of rhetorical awareness as thinking about authors, readers, motives, and contexts. As you read, try to note as much information as you can about each category. Who is Haas' audience? Are you a member? How does identifying Haas' audience help you to recognize her motives? Also—why does she use a longitudinal study format—a format that is common in the disciplines of social sciences and education, but uncommon for English professors?

Like most academic writers, Haas reiterates her most important ideas throughout the seven sections of her longitudinal study. After identifying her claims in the introduction, attempt to trace them through the essay. For example, where does she choose to repeat the key idea of "complexity" and the act of reading?

Reading the Conversation

Haas and Salvatori have many concerns in common. In "Conversations with Texts: Reading and Writing in the Teaching of Composition" Salvatori examines the interconnected activities of reading and writing in order to show how this interconnectedness allows different readers to construct different meanings. This point is important to Haas as well. Haas' study of Eliza's development as a reader in the university seems to illustrate Salvatori's desire to highlight the art of questioning the text. As you read, see if you can locate passages in which Haas seems to be conversant with Salvatori.

Note too that Christina Haas is one of the colleagues thanked by Linda Flower in her preface. It is often the case that written conversations in a discipline are in fact extensions of oral conversations among the same people.

Learning to Read Biology: One Student's Rhetorical Development in College
Christina Haas

1 *At the college level, to become literate* is in many ways to learn the patterns of knowing about, and behaving toward, texts within a disciplinary field (Bartholomae, 1985; Berkenkotter, Huckin, & Ackerman, 1988; Bizzell, 1982; Geisler, 1990; Herrington, 1985, 1992). Scholars from a wide variety of subject areas have acknowledged that within their disciplines, texts are best

Author's Note: I would like to thank John Buck, Davida Charney, Stephen Doheny-Farina, Rosa Eberly, Cheryl Geisler, Rich Haswell, David Kaufer, Marty Nystrand, Nancy Penrose, Jack Selzer, and Sandra Stotsky for provocative conversations which helped me think more clearly about many of the issues addressed here. Carrie Rose Haas of the Chemistry Department of the University of Washington, John Lowe of the Chemistry Department at Penn State, and Andy Stephenson of the Biology Department at Penn State provided technical assistance. My deepest debt is to Eliza, who opened her educational life to me for 4 years. Watching her grow in confidence, intellect, and ability was an exciting and humbling experience. Some of the data collection was supported by a grant to C. M. Neuwirth, J. R. Hayes, and C. Haas from the Fund for the Improvement of Post Secondary Education; the Information Technology Center at Carnegie Mellon University also provided partial support. A version of this article was given at a Writing Special-Interest-Group session at the 1992 American Educational Research Association meeting in San Francisco.

seen not as static, autonomous entities but as forms of dynamic rhetorical action: Authors create texts and readers read texts in a complex of social relationships, motivated by goals sanctioned (or not) by the surrounding culture, to achieve purposes that are always in the broadest sense persuasive. Disciplinary texts, like all texts, are intensely situated, rife with purpose and motive, anchored in myriad ways to the individuals and the cultures that produce them. This is true not only for texts within the humanities and softer social sciences (e.g., see Belsey, 1980; Fish, 1980; Tompkins, 1980, in literary theory; Geertz, 1983, in anthropology; Grice, 1975; Nystrand, 1986, in linguistics; Brown, Collins, & Duguid, 1989; Mishler, 1979, in psychology) but also those within "harder" disciplines such as economics (McCloskey, 1985), physics (Bazerman, 1988), and—more to my purposes here—the life sciences (Gould, 1993; Latour, 1987; Latour & Woolgar, 1979; Myers, 1985, 1991; Selzer, 1993).

2   Bruno Latour (1987; Latour & Woolgar, 1979), in particular, has been concerned with understanding how scientific facts (codified and reproduced as written texts) come to be seen as freed of the circumstances of their production. His work, along with others' (Bazerman, 1988; Gilbert & Mulkay, 1984; Myers, 1985), has shown scientific activity, and its resultant facts and theory—presented in the form of written texts—to be highly rhetorical and scientists themselves to be motivated and committed agents in this enterprise.[1] A great number of studies of science have focused on discourse—conversations and lab notes as well as conference presentations and formal articles—as both the means of scientific activity and the best way to study the scientific enterprise (e.g., Blakeslee, 1992; Gragson & Selzer, 1990; Herndl, Fennell, & Miller, 1991; Winsor, 1989). In short, much of the real work of science is the creation and dissemination of texts, broadly conceived. In addition, other studies of scientific discourse (Fahnestock, 1986; Gilbert & Mulkay, 1984) have suggested that scientists adjust the strength of their claims depending on the audience: Texts meant for scientific insiders hedge and qualify claims, while texts for lay persons and other outsiders strip out such qualifiers, making claims seem more certain and less open to question. Experts within scientific domains, then, draw upon rich representations of discourse as a social and rhetorical act, what Geisler (1991) has called socially configured mental models, as they create and interpret texts and as they judge the validity and usefulness of the information within them.

LEARNING ABOUT LITERATE ACTIVITY
IN THE SCIENCES

3 One of the things students of science must become privy to, as part of their disciplinary education, is this rhetorical, contingent nature of written scientific discourse. Science educators at every level have been concerned with fostering students' cognizance of the contexts, conduct, and purposes of

science as well as its factual content (Fensham, 1985; Mitman, Mergendoller, Marchman, & Packer, 1987; National Academy of Sciences, 1989). Mitman et al. (1987) have defined the components of "scientific literacy" as not only the mastery of scientific facts and concepts, but an understanding of "the evolving contributions of individual scientists and groups of scientists, . . . the social communities and historical settings in which scientists work" (p. 630) and the place of science within "the broader contexts of human endeavor" (p. 612). In general, these educators have argued that in order to understand, use, and judge scientific content—and, of course, scientific content remains of vital importance to science educators—students need a metaunderstanding of the motives of science and scientists and the history of scientific concepts. That is, a rhetorical understanding of the human enterprise of science, as well as the texts that constitute and reflect that enterprise should be bound to the learning of scientific facts.

4   The educational task of helping students recognize the human nature of scientific activity and rhetorical nature of scientific texts may be part of a larger problem in academic literacy for students: a "myth" of autonomous texts that seems to operate in academic settings at every level. This myth has been well described—and well critiqued—in other contexts by Nystrand (1987), Cazden (1989), Brandt (1990), and Farr (1993). In general, the belief in autonomous texts views written academic texts as discrete, highly explicit, even "timeless" entities functioning without contextual support from author, reader, or culture. Research studies by Applebee (1984), Geisler (1990), Haas and Flower (1988), Hynds (1989), Nelson (1990), and Vipond and Hunt (1984), among others, have suggested that beginning college students approach academic tasks as if they believe that texts are autonomous and context free. Treating texts as if they are autonomous may be facilitated both by features of academic discourse itself (see Farr, 1993, for a review of linguistic research on academic discourse) and by a culture of schooling that encourages students to see texts primarily as repositories of factual information (Goodlad, 1984). Certainly a number of school reading and writing tasks—in college as well as high school—seem to be predicated on the doctrine of the autonomous text: strict new critical readings of literary works; tests that ask students to recall and reiterate informational content only; textbooks that always seem to be written by nobody and everybody, as if the information embodied in them was beyond human composition, and beyond human question.[2] The educational problem, then, is this: Entering college students may hold an arhetorical or asituational theory of written discourse, a representation or model of discourse that precludes seeing text as motivated activity and authors as purposeful agents, when in fact discourse theorists and scientific educators agree that students would benefit from a more rhetorical model.

5   Do students' views of academic discourse change over the course of their college careers? Studies of development in the college years such as those by Perry (1970) and by Belenky, Clinchy, Goldberger, and Tarule (1986) have not specifically addressed issues of reading and writing, although I will return in

my discussion to their relevance for the case I present here. In an ambitious and extensive set of studies, Haswell (1988a, 1988b, 1991) looked at growth in writing competence through college but did not explicitly address how students view texts or how disciplinary training and literacy instruction interact. This article, then, provides an initial exploration of one student's developing rhetorical understanding of texts. It details a longitudinal study, an extended 4-year examination of one student as she progressed during college, focusing primarily on how the student's views of, and interactions with, disciplinary texts changed through her postsecondary education. Although Eliza (a pseudonym) may have tacitly subscribed to the doctrine of autonomous texts early in her college career, by the time she left college she had come to a greater awareness of the rhetorical, contingent nature of both the activities and discourses she participated in within her chosen field, biology.

6   In order to track Eliza's developing notions of text, I focused primarily on her reading processes and practices, and on the various texts she read, rather than on her writing processes and products. This was done for several reasons. First, studying Eliza's reading allowed me to examine her interactions with a greater number of texts, since she read many more texts than she wrote through the 4 years. She also read many more types of texts—textbooks, research reports, articles, proposals, lab notes, data sheets—than she wrote, especially in her biology and chemistry courses. In addition, I hypothesized that in her reading practices, Eliza might demonstrate more rhetorical sophistication than she would in her writing, where many more production skills must be managed (Scardamalia, Bereiter, & Goelman, 1982). Indeed, in discussions of her reading, Eliza showed a level of awareness of the activity and agents of discourse that seldom was obvious in the texts she wrote. Finally, while a great number of recent studies (Berkenkotter et al., 1988; Herrington, 1985, 1992; McCarthy, 1987; McCarthy & Fishman, 1991; Nelson, 1990) have examined students' writing in academic disciplines, few have expressly looked at how students read specialized texts within the disciplines.

RHETORICAL READING

7 Before discussing Eliza's case in detail, it is important to examine more closely the application of rhetorical theories of discourse to actual literate practice: how might we expect contextually rich social theories of discourse to play themselves out in the real-time practices and processes of actual readers? The beginnings of an answer to this question can be found in recent work in three separate but related disciplines—social psychology, linguistics, and rhetoric. In each of these fields, theoretical accounts of the pragmatics of social situation have been developed, motivated by questions such as "What is the nature of social situations, including discourse?" and "How are situations represented cognitively by individuals?" Three theories can serve as representatives of recent work in each field: Argyle, Furnham,

and Graham (1981) in social psychology, Van Dijk (1987) in linguistics, and Bitzer (1968) and his critics and correctors in rhetoric (Biesecker, 1989; Jamieson, 1973; Vatz, 1973). While these theorists have different foci, all three theories are concerned with the nature of social, communicative acts and how individuals participate in and understand those acts.

8   Drawing together common elements of these theories, I postulate a model or representation of discourse situations, a *rhetorical frame,* that helps readers account for the motives underlying textual acts and their outcomes. Elements of the rhetorical frame include participants, their relationships and motives, and several layers of context. For instance, when readers approach a discourse situation, they presumably have some knowledge or representation of the participants, including the identity, knowledge, and background of author and intended readers. While van Dijk (1987) and Argyle et al. (1981) did not differentiate between the persons involved in the discourse situation, rhetorical theorists (e.g., Bitzer, 1968; Vatz, 1973) named them as rhetor, or speaker, and audience. Readers may also know of, or postulate, a certain kind of relationship between the participants, what Argyle et al. (1981) labeled the participants' "roles and status." As examples of status, the reader and author may share (or not) a number of assumptions, or one participant may be in a position of greater power. Of the rhetoricians, Biesecker (1989) was the most directly concerned with social relationships. Also useful to the reader is some representation of the motives of the participants—why the author wrote the piece, why she or he chose the form that was chosen, why she or he used a particular structure or chose certain words. Van Dijk (1987), with his cognitive emphasis, was especially concerned with motivation and with the purposes, plans, and goals that are driven by motives.

9   Undergirding the settings of discourse participants are several layers of context: A text is an utterance, part of an intertextual context consisting of closely and distantly related texts, or what Jamieson (1973) called antecedent rhetorical forms. A text may draw upon, extend, or refute a myriad of other texts, whether those texts are directly cited or not. Knowing something about this complex of related texts will certainly aid a reader's interpretation. A text may also be supported by situational, cultural, and historical contexts. Argyle et al. (1981) and van Dijk (1987) treated context mostly in terms of setting, but Bitzer (1968) (and, following him, Biesecker, 1989) went further in identifying systems of belief, traditions, and cultural attitudes as constraints which shape and determine discourse. Knowledge of contexts will aid a reader's interpretation, and indeed, knowing something about cultural and historical contexts can reveal a great deal about discourse participants, and vice versa.

10   Acknowledging or attempting to understand these elements of discourse—constructing a rhetorical frame which includes authors, readers, motives, relationships, and contexts—is what I call the process of rhetorical reading. Although every text has an author, a context, and active readers, many texts are constructed in ways that downplay, hide, or strip away the

rhetorical frame. Rhetorical reading—that is, recognizing the rhetorical frame that surrounds a text, or constructing one in spite of conventions which attempt to obscure it—is often crucial for understanding argument and other sophisticated forms of discourse. Indeed, information about discourse situations—including representations of authorship, authorial intention, and intertextuality—has been identified as an aid to successful interpretation in previous research (Beach, Appleman, & Dorsey, 1990; Geisler, 1990; Haas & Flower, 1988; Huckin & Flower, 1991; Tierney, LaZansky, Raphael, & Cohen, 1987; Vipond & Hunt, 1984).

11   What does the process of rhetorical reading look like? Examples drawn from previous studies of readers reading both experimental and naturalistic texts, and thinking aloud as they did so (Haas, 1991, 1993; Haas & Flower, 1988), show some readers thinking about and using rhetorical elements of discourse, while others do not. For instance, one example of a rhetorical reader (from Haas & Flower, 1988) was an engineering graduate student reading a text, the source and author of which were not identified, in the experimental session. (The text was actually a psychology textbook preface.) During his reading, he assigned the author both a gender, "this guy," and a profession, "he's some kind of scientist." The reader also tried to account for the author's motives: "This guy is crying out for" a new kind of science. Later, the reader hypothesized a source for the text, at one point speculating that it came from a scholarly psychology journal and noting that the article "wouldn't work for the man-in-the-street."

12   Another rhetorical reader (from Haas, 1991) was a junior history major reading a more "naturalistic" text, a section of a book-length, policy-oriented historical analysis assigned in an elective history course. While reading aloud, this reader identified characteristics of the authors, noting that the text was written by "two men" who are "good writers." According to the reader, these authors wanted to encourage policymakers—the intended reader she constructs (based on her reading of the book itself and of prefatory material)—to think about faulty historical analogies. Further, she placed the text, its authors, and readers in a historical context (dealing with Korea after the Korean War).

13   Each of these readers moved beyond an "autonomous" text and tried to account for a number of situational or rhetorical elements—author, authorial intent, reader identity, and historical, cultural, and situational context—to "frame" or support the discourse. In short, these readers were not content simply to extract information or to accept the arguments of an autonomous text. Other readers, however, seemed to treat the text as more of an autonomous, context-less object. The protocols of these readers were characterized by the absence of the kinds of rhetorically based comments we saw above. In the face of confusion about the texts they were reading, these readers returned to the text itself, rereading sections of the text and making comments like, "I don't understand why he's saying that. Better reread it." Of course, rereading is often an appropriate and useful strategy for understanding difficult texts. My

point here is that some readers seemed to rely overly on this strategy, invoking it again and again. They attempted to understand the text not by moving out from it to a rhetorical context, but by moving in, focusing ever more closely on the text as an object.

THE STUDY

14 This longitudinal case study used a variety of methods and data sources to track Eliza's developing rhetorical understanding of scientific texts and other scientific acts. Specifically, I wanted to explore these questions: Does Eliza believe that academic texts are autonomous, or does she recognize the rhetorical nature of scientific action and scientific texts? Do these beliefs change as she moves through 4 years of college science instruction?

The Subject/Participant

15 Eliza was 1 of a group of 6 randomly selected case study participants that I began to track in their freshman year at a private research university. Eliza grew up in a middle-class family in a large eastern city and attended a large parochial high school near her home. She was the youngest of four children and had a large extended family, with aunts, uncles, and cousins living nearby. Her parents' education ended with high school, as did her two older sisters', while Eliza and her brother completed college. Eliza reported that her parents were "very proud, very supportive" of her during college,[3] both financially and emotionally. Her postsecondary education was partially financed by federal grants and through work-study awards.

16   Eliza graduated 14th out of a class of 450 from her high school, where she was in the upper tracks in English, math, and science. Eliza said she was "brainy" in high school, but "not a bookworm—more like the class nerd." She felt her high school education was "as good as any," and she was especially full of praise for the math program there—"Sister Elise could teach anyone mathematics." The math club won citywide competitions for 3 straight years while Eliza was in high school. The curriculum for science classes—1-year-long course for each of 4 years—consisted mostly of lectures and textbook reading, with a minimal amount of lab work. Students were evaluated almost exclusively through objective tests in these science courses.

17   Eliza came to college interested in biology and later considered the possibility of pursuing a double major in biology and chemistry before finally deciding (late in her sophomore year) to focus exclusively on biology. As a freshman, she said she was majoring in biology "because I'm pretty good at it," but by the time she graduated, her interest in the subject was much deeper and more committed. During her senior year, she made comments like, "I'm learning to be a scientist," or "I'm going to be a scientist," or even, "I am a scientist." College-level reading and writing were time consuming

for Eliza, as for many of her classmates, but she worked hard at both and was determined to do well. Her final college grade point average was about 3.0.

Setting

18 The study took place from August 1986, 1 week after Eliza arrived at college, to April 1990, a few weeks before she graduated with a BS in biology. The setting was a private research university in a medium-sized eastern city. About 6,500 students, one third of whom are graduate students, attend the university, which is predominately White. Males outnumber females by a ratio of about 3 to 1 among undergraduates.

19   Interviews took place in my office in a computer development center where I was a part-time consultant. Because Eliza did not identify me with any department from which she was taking classes, I believe she felt free to give honest and detailed descriptions of her teachers, assignments, and course work, and her feelings about them. At the same time, as Patton (1980) has suggested, I wanted Eliza to see me as someone who "spoke her language," that is, as someone who had at least a passing knowledge of the subjects in which she was interested. For the first three semesters, I could use course notes and background knowledge from my own upper-division undergraduate courses in biology to keep informed. Later, I relied on a colleague in chemistry (who had an undergraduate degree in biology) and on some outside reading to help me attain a cursory knowledge of some of the topics Eliza was addressing in reading, writing, and lab work assigned in biology.

Data Sources

20 Qualitative case study methods were used to track Eliza through her 4 years of college, and attempts were made to triangulate data sources. Figure 1 shows types and amounts of data collected. Interviews (several each year) were supplemented with the examination of artifacts (texts written and read for classes), reading/writing logs kept by Eliza (freshman and sophomore years), observations by the researcher of classes and reading sessions, and the collection of several read-and-think-aloud protocols (junior and senior years). As is often the case with qualitative research, data sources and methods evolved as the study progressed (see Goetz & LeCompte, 1984, especially chapter 5, Data Collection Strategies). For example, reading/writing logs were discontinued after the sophomore year because Eliza indicated that they were taking an inordinate amount of her study time to complete. At this point, read-and-think-aloud protocols were added (they were used in the junior and senior years only) as an alternative data source that could furnish some of the same kinds of information as the logs. In addition, I terminated my concurrent interviews with Eliza's teachers when she indicated that my talking to her teachers made her uncomfortable. (I did talk with some of these teachers later.)

Type of Data	Amount (and Unit of Measure)
Freshman year	
Three interviews	−6 hours; 2,428 words*
One interview with each teacher	45 minutes; not transcribed
Reading sessions observed	30 minutes total
Reading/writing logs, 2 classes	14 log pages
Texts written for one class	30 pages
Sample texts read for two classes	[examined and returned]
Sophomore year	
Four interviews	−7 hours; 3,345 words*
Reading session observed	20 minutes
Reading/writing logs, 8 classes	30 log pages
Texts written for two classes	39 pages (including figures)
Sample texts read for two classes	[examined and returned]
Junior year	
Two interviews	−5 hours; 2,925 words*
Texts written for two classes	[examined and returned]
Sample texts read for eight classes	[examined and returned]
Two read-and-think-aloud protocols	−30 minutes each
Senior year	
Two interviews	−4 hours; 4,250 words*
Texts written for two classes	[examined and returned]
Sample texts read for three classes	[examined and returned]
Two read-and-think-aloud protocols	−30 minutes each

*Excluding interviewer questions

Figure 1   Data sources for each year.

21   *Interviews.* Following Perry (1970) and Belenky et al. (1986), the most important data source for the study was a series of 11 extended, minimally structured interviews with Eliza, a total of more than 21 hours over the course of 4 years. I often went into interviews with a loose script, but I also allowed interviews to develop naturally, with ample time for clarification and follow-up.

22   Many of the interviews also included discourse-based questions. Eliza brought materials she was reading (and sometimes writing) for her classes to the interviews, and I asked her to tell me about the reading she was engaged with at that point. She often illustrated her points about the texts by explicitly pointing to the texts or parts of them: "See, these three are all related because they deal with tyrosine phosphorylation." At no point did I query Eliza directly about authors, their intentions, or contextual variables. What I learned about Eliza's thinking about these rhetorical elements arose in the natural course of her telling me about the texts she was reading and writing or about the classes. To elicit as much detail as possible, I sometimes prompted her to continue with neutral queries like, "What else?" or "Oh, really?" and "Can you

say more about that?" All interviews were audiotaped and later transcribed. I also took notes during all interviews.

23   *Reading/writing logs.* During the freshman and sophomore years, Eliza kept reading/writing logs of her activities in selected classes, two in freshman year and eight in sophomore year. I did not ask Eliza to write a discursive narrative via journal entries in the logs. Rather, using specially prepared log sheets, she kept track of dates and times of reading and writing, wrote a short characterization of the assignment (completed only in an initial entry about an assignment or when her thinking about the assignment was revised), provided a brief description of goals for the session, made a detailed list of the activities she engaged in during each session, and noted any problems or frustrations she encountered while working.[4] A sample set of entries from a sophomore reading/writing log is shown in Figure 2.

24   *Read-and-think-aloud protocols.* A total of four read-and-think-aloud protocols were collected during Eliza's junior and senior years. During the junior year, one of the texts Eliza read aloud was an experimental text used in a previous study (Haas & Flower, 1988); the other text in the junior year and both texts read during the senior year were "naturally occurring" texts that Eliza was reading in the course of her studies, rather than texts I assigned her to read. For these latter three read-aloud sessions, I asked Eliza to choose a text she planned to read but had not read yet. In each case, she selected a published article that she was assigned to read for a biology class. Protocols lasted approximately 30 minutes each; during this time, Eliza read about half of each article.

25   The experimental text was partitioned into segments (from one to five sentences each) with the question, "How do you interpret the text now?" presented between segments (see Haas & Flower, 1988, for further details about this experimental text). For the naturally occurring texts, I asked Eliza (before she began reading) to stop every paragraph or so and answer the question, "How do you interpret the text now?," which was typed on a card and put on the table in front of her. Because the expert scientists studied by Bazerman (1985) and by Charney (1993) often previewed, skimmed, and skipped parts of the articles they read, I told Eliza to read the articles as she normally would: "Feel free to skim, or skip around, or whatever you would like." In each case, however, she read the text linearly. Eliza was allowed to practice the think-aloud procedure on an unrelated text before each session began. Each session was tape-recorded and later transcribed for analysis.

26   *Observation of reading sessions.* During the freshman and sophomore years, I observed Eliza reading texts silently. These observation sessions usually followed interviews. During Eliza's junior and senior years, observation sessions were not a separate data source, but were collapsed into the read-and-think-aloud protocols (i.e., I observed her from across the room and took notes on her reading aloud during the protocols).

Date/Time	Assignment	Goals	Activities	Problems
11/26/87	Cell biology research paper*			
4:00		Read articles and decide if they're relevant to my paper; relatively easy.	Starting to read first article. Taking notes on index cards—writing down experiments and some facts.	
4:37				Tired; 5 minute break
4:50			Starting first article again.	Hard to understand—lots of technical words.
5:20			Finish first article.	
5:25			Found second article much shorter. Taking notes like before.	
6:00			Finish second article (not as complex).	

*Capitalization of initial word in each entry added in some cases.

Figure 2   Example of reading/writing log entries from Eliza's sophomore year.

LONGITUDINAL NARRATIVE

27 In order to examine—and do justice to—the richness of Eliza's undergraduate educational experience, I constructed a longitudinal narrative drawing on qualitative analysis of data from the sources described above.

Analysis

28 In constructing the narrative, I used the transcripts of the 11 interviews, Eliza's reading/writing logs, the writing sessions I observed that involved reading, and the read-and-think-aloud protocols. I focused on these aspects of Eliza's reading: (a) the reading tasks she was given or assumed and her stated goals for these reading tasks; (b) her practices and processes of reading; and (c) her views of discourse and knowledge.

29 *Reading tasks and goals.* Information about Eliza's reading tasks and goals were drawn from three sources: the interviews, the reading/writing logs, and the read-and-think-aloud protocols. From those segments of the interviews in which Eliza was discussing specific texts, I identified comments about reading tasks (including both class reading assignments and other tasks Eliza assumed on her own). These included such comments as, "I have to read about a hundred pages a night," "We have this stuff on tests," and "I'm reading this to get an idea of how to set up my own report." I also identified reading goals, which were often tied to means of evaluation, as in "I need to read this really carefully, because he's going to be picky about the details." In addition, I used stated goals from Eliza's reading/writing logs (e.g., "Get a general knowledge of my topic"). Finally, task-level goals (e.g., "I better get this for the test") were identified in the read-and-think-aloud protocols.

30 *Reading practices.* Observations of reading/writing sessions, interview transcripts, reading/writing logs, and read-and-think-aloud protocols were analyzed to characterize Eliza's reading practices during each of the 4 years. During observed writing sessions and during the protocols, I took notes on how Eliza interacted with the texts she read. These activities included linear reading, skimming, skipping, outlining, highlighting, and note making. I identified segments of the interviews in which Eliza discussed her approach to or interactions with specific texts (e.g., "I reread the intro several times" and "I looked first at the figures and legends") as well as those segments in which she discussed her search and note-taking strategies for research papers (e.g., "I just looked up some sources from the back of the textbook and took notes on three of the articles"). In the reading/writing logs, I identified instances in which Eliza described reading practices and activities (e.g., "took more notes on article," "skimmed first part," and "reread the methods section").

31 *Views of discourse and knowledge.* While the analysis of reading tasks and goals and reading practices was fairly straightforward, identifying and characterizing Eliza's views of discourse and knowledge was more

complicated; therefore, a second reader assisted in this phase of the analysis. The interview transcripts were the primary data source for identifying and characterizing Eliza's views of discourse and knowledge and the analysis proceeded as follows: First, working closely with the interview transcripts, we used analytic induction (Goetz & LeCompte, 1984) to identify seven kinds of statements that could reveal something about Eliza's views of discourse. These were instances in which Eliza was discussing (a) the nature of reading and writing generally; (b) characteristics of specific texts; (c) characteristics of authors, either generally or specifically; (d) explicit mention of the nature of knowing and learning; (e) specific mention of her own knowing or learning; (f) task-level goals for reading specific texts; or (g) reading tasks she was assigned or assumed on her own.

32   I was not interested in these seven categories per se (i.e., I did not compare types of statements). Rather, the scheme was used as a tool to help identify relevant segments of the interviews. Using this scheme, we identified 81 interview segments, 72 of which we agreed revealed something about Eliza's views of discourse and/or knowledge.

33   The second reader and I then determined that 30 of the 72 previously identified segments included some mention of one or more rhetorical elements—writer identity and purpose; intended or actual reader and motivation; and intertextual, situational, historical, and cultural context. Throughout this analysis, it was important to use the context surrounding segments (including interviewer questions and previous discussions) to determine whether a given segment could be used to infer Eliza's discourse views.

Results

34 As Table 1 shows, the number of interview segments identified as revealing something about Eliza's views of discourse were similar in freshman and sophomore years (10 and 13 respectively); in the junior and senior years, the number about doubled, to 24 and 25. The number of these identified segments that dealt with rhetorical concerns was 2 in the freshman year, 1 in

Year	Total Interview Segments Identified as Revealing Views of Discourse	Number of Identified Segments Dealing with Rhetorical Concerns	Proportion of Identified Segments Dealing with Rhetorical Concerns
Freshman	10	2	.20
Sophomore	13	1	.07
Junior	24	13	.53
Senior	25	14	.56
Total	72	30	—

Table 1   Interview Segments Revealing Views of Discourse and Rhetorical Concerns

the sophomore year. This number is markedly greater in the junior and senior years—13 and 14 respectively. And the proportions of segments dealing
with rhetorical concerns to total segments show a similar trend, with proportions of over 50% in the junior and senior years.

35   The following narrative traces Eliza's interactions with and learning
about texts through 4 years of college. For each of her 4 college years, I
discuss first the kinds of reading tasks in which Eliza engages, drawing
primarily on interviews and reading/writing logs. Next I describe Eliza's
reading processes and practices, drawing from the read-and-think-aloud
protocols, my observations of reading sessions, reading/writing logs, and
interviews. The narratives for each year conclude with a longer section,
which examines how Eliza's conceptions of the rhetorical nature of discourse and the contingent nature of scientific facts developed. Interviews
(particularly the segments identified as revealing views of discourse) were
the primary data source for these sections, and they were supplemented
with data from reading/writing logs, read-and-think-aloud protocols, and
teacher interviews.

36   *Eliza as a freshman: "The book says."* As a freshman, Eliza's academic
work focused almost exclusively on preparing for tests in her biology, chemistry, and math courses. She also wrote a fairly extensive synthesis of various
authors' positions papers in her English class. Her processes consisted of
mostly linear reading of textbooks and, for the English class, essays. If she
had trouble comprehending, her strategy was usually to reread, and she
made extensive use of a highlighter, sometimes marking whole paragraphs
with it. She also often took notes, usually verbatim, from her reading. According to statements made in interviews or entries in her reading/writing
logs, Eliza's goals for most of her reading were "to learn it," "to understand
it," or even "to memorize it." Understanding the book or what "the book
says" was paramount at this point in Eliza's college career. Eliza viewed her
role as a reader as one of extracting and retaining information, a not unsavvy
approach, given the ways that she was held accountable for the reading.

37   Two pairs of concepts developed by Belenky et al. (1986) are useful in
further examining Eliza's developing theories of knowledge. The notions of
received knowledge and procedural knowledge and of separate knowing and
connected knowing emerged at various points as Eliza's education progressed. As a freshman, Eliza's epistemological theory seemed to be one of
received knowledge, and her role was receiver of that knowledge. Her goals
were to learn or understand or memorize what "the book says," or "figure
out what he [the author] is really saying." Tellingly, she described how her
English teacher would have to accept the claims of her paper if "I can prove
it in writing from the book." The book here was the ultimate authority—
through which one received knowledge and by which one's own contributions were judged.

38   *Reading as a sophomore: Eliza encounters the research paper.* During
her sophomore year, Eliza's reading tasks and reading practices, and the

means by which she was evaluated, remained essentially the same. The one major change in her reading, from her point of view at least, was that there was simply a lot more of it. It was Eliza's and her classmates' impression that the department and the college attempted to "scare people away" with the amount of work that was required in the courses that Eliza took during this year. She continued to have hundreds of pages of textbook reading every week, frequent exams, and little discussion in her classes. Eliza did have more lab courses during this year than during the previous one, but these labs required little reading.

39   Eliza's reading practices showed an increased attention to the procedures of knowing. According to Belenky et al. (1986), procedural knowers are "absorbed in the business of acquiring and applying procedures of obtaining . . . knowledge" (p. 95). As a sophomore, Eliza seemed to view learning as the application of certain procedures: Reading was always done with highlighter in hand, for instance, and her notes (usually almost verbatim) were labeled and organized.

40   One interesting development during Eliza's sophomore year was the research paper assigned in her cell biology course. The instructor gave the students little direction on the project, assigning a research paper that was to be five or six pages long. In Eliza's words, "We're supposed to pick a topic that interests us, and then just go more in depth with it, go in research books and just write about it." The topic was selected from a list of cell structures provided by the instructor. The paper was also to include a section on experimental methods, but this section involved little reading and Eliza seemed to spend little time on it. According to Eliza, the goal was to write "a paper that tells what's known about our topic," and she did not attempt to develop a thesis or controlling idea, nor did she even see a need for one (cf. Stotsky, 1991).

41   The following excerpt shows the almost casual way that Eliza treated this assignment:

> I just took brief little notes, like types of drugs, or something about the experiment. And basically just sat down later on and just wrote the paper from there. I figure it was the next night. [Consults reading/writing log in front of her.] Yeah. Basically that's what everybody did, they waited—they just went and read the articles the night before, and got in groups or something and wrote it, you know, to help each other out.

42   Eliza's strategy for the research paper resembled what Nelson (1990) identified as a "low investment" strategy in students performing similar tasks: She waited until the last minute and then relied on a minimum number of sources, sources selected mainly because they were easy to locate and convenient. But my knowledge of Eliza even at this early point in her college career led me to believe that she was in fact quite committed and "invested" in her education, her field of study, and her future as a biologist. She approached classes with a real seriousness, and she spent a great deal of time and effort

preparing for tests in her chemistry and cell biology and genetics courses. I believe Eliza's limited, even cavalier, approach to the research paper assignment was due to the fact that it simply did not occur to her that reading articles and writing a research paper had much at all to do with her goal of becoming a biologist. Tasks like her chemistry lab or genetics exams, or even her math homework, were obviously tied in her mind to the work of biologists, and for these kinds of tasks Eliza had a very high investment approach. Writing a research paper may have seemed to her an exercise that was quite unconnected to the real work of science.

43   Eliza seemed to view her own research paper and the articles she read as unconnected to the field of biology as she construed it: autonomous information embodied in textbooks, which she was required to learn. This notion is supported by the almost complete lack of reference in her interviews and logs to rhetorical or contextual elements surrounding the texts she read. The attention to authors, which surfaced during her reading for her English class in her freshman year, had disappeared. There was no evidence that she viewed any of the texts she read as the product of an individual author's motives or actions. Nor did she exhibit any cognizance of the texts she read as historically or culturally situated. Even the citation lists in the articles she read were used primarily as a convenient way to find other articles, not as an intertextual system tying separate texts together.

44   During her sophomore year, Eliza still seemed happy with her arhetorical, asituational approach to reading texts that she viewed primarily as autonomous. Certainly, it was an approach that was well rewarded. She got a good grade on her research paper, and she did well on exams in all of her classes. If Eliza operated without a rhetorical frame for much of her reading and writing during her sophomore year, there was nothing in her school environment to signal weakness or problems with that approach.

45   *Eliza's junior year: Seeing authors as scientists.* One important change in Eliza's life this year was her new work study job. Beginning this year, Eliza took a work study job growing protein mutants in a lab run by one of her professors. Eliza's direct supervisor in this work, a graduate student named Shelly, became an important mentor for her during the junior year and on into the senior year. She described the work this way:

> It [the lab job] gives me a lot of individual attention because I work side by side with Shelly, who's a graduate student in the lab, and like she's—well they gave me a project and when I need help or have problems, she guides me through it. Like an apprentice, I guess. . . . I like it better [than classes] because it's more difficult. Well, not more difficult, exactly, but like nobody knows the end result, like [they would] in my bio lab.

46   As a reader, Eliza this year seemed much more sophisticated. In contrast to the methodical, linear reading she engaged in earlier, Eliza now exhibited a range of reading strategies—skimming, reading selectively, moving back and forth through texts, reading for different purposes at different times. In

this way, she was beginning to look like the practicing scientists whose reading Bazerman (1985) and Charney (1993) have studied. She also read some texts not solely to glean information but to learn about conventions and structures: "I'm reading this to get an idea of how to set up my own report." She also made a distinction now between "just textbook reading" and reading journal articles, and she predicted (probably accurately) that "in grad school, all I'll read will be journal articles."

47   The academic tasks that Eliza faced still included a number of exams, although her classes tended to be smaller and some of these exams were what she called "essay exams," which meant that students answered questions in short paragraphs rather than through one word responses or multiple choice. Eliza also had a research paper to do this year in her virology class. But the assignment itself, or Eliza's representation of it, was more specific and complex and connected the research paper to the larger situational and cultural context of virology research. Rather than a goal of "prepar[ing] a general knowledge" of her topic, as in the sophomore year, Eliza's goal was now to "find out what people are doing" with a particular virus, look at "where the technology is going in the future," and to "think up some experiments" to do with the vaccinia (cowpox) virus. Implicit here was the notion that her work on the vaccinia virus would be tied to the work of others, via her text.

48   In both her reading for this particular research paper and her reading more generally, Eliza exhibited a much greater awareness of the contexts surrounding the texts she read. This was reflected in the greater number of interview segments that dealt with rhetorical concerns (see Table 1). Her first-year attention to authors reemerged in the interviews during the junior year, but in a much more complex way. Whereas the authors she talked about as a freshman were writers only, the authors she talked about now were writers, certainly, but also scientists. She attributed motives to these authors, seeing them as making choices as researchers—"so they're using this as a prototype for the manipulation"—or as agents in an uncertain enterprise— "they're saying they're not sure if this is how it replicates" and "they don't know too much about the actual microbiology of the virus." She showed a cognizance of the activity of the field of virology, claiming that a particularly well-investigated virus is "like a beaten horse—they've studied it so much." When she encountered an article reporting what was to her a particularly esoteric and specialized kind of research, she asked somewhat sardonically, "What kind of people *do* research on this?" Now, texts were not autonomous objects, but manifestations of scientific action and human choices.

49   At this point, Eliza was also beginning to recognize a historical, situational context surrounding and supporting the texts she read. In one interview, she went on at great length about how she selected articles to read: "First, of course, I see if the titles are relevant . . . but some of them, like from 1979, well, 1979 isn't that far back, but they weren't sure then if what they were seeing was true." Later, she claimed that "some of them were really old, like in the 70s," and were "getting me nowhere," so "I set a limit of

like, maybe, 1980 to the present." In general, by her junior year, Eliza had a much more fleshed out representation of authors—authors as writers and as scientists, authors with motives and within circumstances—than did she earlier. And texts, the claims they make, and their truth value, were now seen as the product of a particular, historical time.

50   *Reading contingent science as a senior: Increasing sensitivity to context.* The academic tasks she was required to complete had changed somewhat by Eliza's senior year. She had exams now in only two of her courses, and other assignments included critical presentations of research articles and critiques of others' interpretations of similar articles. She had extensive writing assignments based on reading in two of her classes, but now she did not call these research papers; rather, they were a review article and a model proposal.

51   Eliza's reading processes and practices also continued to grow in complexity. She now spent a great deal of time and effort going over figures and tables in texts she read, offering by way of explanation: "This is important. Most professors can read just by looking at figures and their legends." She also exhibited a greater awareness of the intertextual nature of discourse; texts were not isolated, but linked. She still used citations to uncover relevant articles, but rather than skimming the citation lists as she did the year before, she now examined how particular sets of articles used and represented the claims of their sources (cf. Latour, 1987), and she claimed that one can often "tell by the title if they build on one another." The claims of another set of articles "are all related, indirectly," she said.

52   Eliza's attention to the rhetorical elements of discourse—authors, readers, motives, contexts—also exhibited increased sophistication in her senior year. For Eliza, as a senior, not all of an author's claims were equal. While the results section may have been solid, the claims of a discussion may have been more contingent, as illustrated in the following example, where Eliza demonstrated her understanding of scientists' uncertainty and their commitment to theory despite insufficient data and where she used a metaphorical term (handwaving) for how this uncertainty is manifest in written discourse:

> ELIZA: There's a lot of handwaving in the discussion.
>
> CH: What's that?
>
> ELIZA: Handwaving? They're not sure of their theory. They sort of have data which suggest it. But they can't come out and say that . . . You don't know what's happening first. Is it binding here first? Is it binding to an active enzyme? You're not sure.
>
> CH: Do you think they're not sure?
>
> ELIZA: Yes. I'm sure they're not sure.

53   Eliza also had specific representations of different kinds of authors. Authors who write journal articles were active scientists, "the people who

actually did the study," while authors of textbooks tended to be more senior with a great deal of experience: "even older than my boss [an associate professor who runs the lab where she works], because he's been around a long time but he's not qualified to do a textbook yet." Textbooks and journal articles were also seen in a certain historical context. Eliza recognized that one reads these texts with an eye toward this temporal aspect of their composition. She said, "By the time a textbook is written it's out of date. To really learn the stuff, you have to read the journals." This was a far different approach to text than the one she demonstrated as a freshman, when one simply memorized as best one could "what the book says."

54   Eliza's work with Shelly in the lab may also have contributed to her awareness of the social and rhetorical dimensions of discourse. This is suggested by the way she discussed her writing in conjunction with this work. She was concerned that readers of her lab journal be able to use the information there: "It [her writing] is important because somebody who comes when I leave is going to want to work with my mutants and they are going to want to understand how it works, how it grows." She was also beginning to understand how discourse fits into the larger culture of scientific research, recognizing how her own writing will help her make a place for herself within that culture. Regardless of her skill as an immunologist, she believed, without writing, "I'd never get my point across. I'd never get a grant. I'd never have any money, so forget it. I'd be out of luck." A text was now seen not as a storehouse of information but as a way to pursue one's scientific agenda; without it, the scientist is isolated, unable to do her work, "out of luck."

55   Despite her obviously greater sophistication, Eliza, as a senior, still exhibited a certain tension in the way she talked about texts and the way she talked about facts and knowledge. Like the scientists studied by Gilbert and Mulkay (1984), Eliza seemed to move back and forth between two repertoires, the first a foundationalist view of texts, demonstrated by comments like the following from a senior-year interview: "The teacher will nail us if we're not perfectly factual," an example that suggests as well that Eliza's professor was concerned with students factual understanding of course material. At other times, Eliza voiced a more contingent view of the texts she read, noting "handwaving" in the discussion of an article or mentioning that researchers may have been confused or mistaken in plotting their results.

56   Eliza also described her connections to the mutants that were the object of her research, connections that Harding (1986) identified as one of the traits of feminist science. Eliza said she knows "what it [the mutant] likes to grow on, what it hates to grow on. . . . It really is like the baby that you have to watch out for." Eliza here echoed the now-famous anecdote of geneticist Barbara McClintock, describing herself as "part of the system . . . right down there with [the chromosomes]," and the chomosomes themselves as her "friends" (cited in Keller, 1983).

Discussion of the Narrative

57 Through her 4 years of college, Eliza's theory of discourse changed in important ways. Early in her college career, the bulk of the texts she read for school were seen as sources of information, and her job as a reader was primarily to extract this information for use in tests or reports. For the most part, both texts and the information they contain seemed unconnected to the authors or the circumstances that produced them. Not that Eliza was unable to understand the concept of author or authorial claims: in the reading of essays for her English class, she became somewhat conversant with these notions. An English curriculum which stressed authorial conversations and encouraged students' graphic representations of authors' interactions may have contributed to Eliza's understanding of discourse during the freshman year. But, in the sophomore year, when the "scaffolding" (Applebee, 1984) provided by Eliza's English class and instructor were withdrawn, she again seemed content to view texts as autonomous. As evidenced by her approach to the research paper in her sophomore year, Eliza seemed to view reading and writing as unconnected to the scientific work for which she was preparing herself. Rather, at this point, reading and writing were seen as the work of school, not the work of science.

58   Beginning in her junior year, we begin to see important changes in Eliza's views of discourse: She exhibited a growing cognizance of texts (and the science they report) as the result of human agency. Similarly, her representations of discourse seem to have expanded to include a notion of texts as accomplishing scientific and rhetorical action, fulfilling purposes and motives, as well as presenting facts and information. Her recognition of the rhetorical nature of discourse was somewhat uneven, of course: Sometimes she talked as if science and scientific texts were purely factual, set in stone; other times, she saw them as more contingent. By her senior year she often viewed texts as multiply connected—to authors and scientists, to other readers, and to historical circumstances—and even demonstrated some understanding of her own connections both to scientific texts (and, by implication, to their authors) and to the objects of her own research.

GENERAL DISCUSSION

59 We have seen how Eliza developed as a reader in a number of ways through her 4 years of college. Her reading practices became more sophisticated as she moved away from the linear reading and verbatim-note taking strategies of her freshman year to the skimming, selective reading, and in-depth attention to tables and legends in the senior year. Her goals for reading changed as well. In the freshman year she was primarily concerned with "figuring out what the book says"—understanding and memorizing scientific concepts. As a senior, Eliza was trying to find or make a place for herself within

an academic community, and she used reading to help her reach that goal—although reading continued to function, as it had throughout her college career, as a way to become conversant with scientific concepts. Arguably, the most important change in Eliza's reading of texts, however, was in her growing awareness of the rhetorical frame supporting written discourse—including a representation of authors as active, motivated agents and a cognizance of the historical, situational, and intertextual contexts supporting both readers and writers. As a senior reading the texts of her major field, Eliza resembled expert readers in her attention to rhetorical concerns. To my mind, this change constituted the beginnings of a new theory of discourse for Eliza. She began to see texts as accomplishing scientific action as well as embodying scientific knowledge: She recognized that behind scientific texts are human authors with motives, authors who are also interested, but sometimes uncertain, scientists; she started to see that scientific facts are contingent and historically bound. The changes in Eliza's use of verbs to talk about texts and authors and the growing presence of human agents in her interview discourse suggest, as well, that important changes were going on in Eliza's view of the scientific enterprise. Possibly most importantly, Eliza began to see her own role as not simply learning the facts but of negotiating meaning—that is, doing her work—amidst the many voices of her discipline.

CONCLUDING COMMENTS

60 This study offers a detailed, fine-grained look at one student's development over time, something we could not see in a study designed to address similar questions with groups of students of different ages. Another of the real benefits of this kind of research—longitudinal, in-depth case study—is that it allows a richer picture of an individual. Multiple data sources enrich our view of Eliza and her learning, and observing her over time cautions us against making generalizations about her abilities or her thinking. Because many of Eliza's teachers knew her for only a semester or possibly a year, they may have had limited knowledge of her long-term educational and career goals and of her history as a learner. Indeed, it is interesting to contemplate how different our views of students might be, and how our teaching might differ as well, if we were able to learn about our students over a period of years rather than weeks.

61   As I suggested in the opening paragraphs of this article, we are beginning to understand a great deal about expert literate practice in a number of domains, both within and beyond the academy (Bazerman & Paradis, 1991; Geisler, in press; Nelson, Megill, & McCloskey, 1987; Simons, 1990). Our students, however, may not approach academic reading and writing with the same theories that disciplinary insiders do about how discourse works. We need to know more about the kinds of theories of discourse that students hold when they arrive in college, and how these theories are reinforced or

challenged by the instruction they receive across the university. And, if students do approach academic texts as autonomous rather than rhetorically and socially configured, it may be because such theories have served them well in a culture of schooling that emphasizes the retention of information. As I have suggested, one of the tasks of disciplinary education at the postsecondary level may be to help students move beyond theories of texts as autonomous to richer, more complex rhetorical theories of discourse. We need to know more, as well, about the complex of social, institutional, and cognitive factors that support this kind of learning, because to be literate involves not only attaining the skills to perform complex acts of reading and writing, but developing the rhetorical knowledge to understand and use the myriad contexts surrounding, supporting, and linking texts. Longitudinal studies provide one rewarding way to read students' stories of rhetorical development, reminding us that the stories of students' learning are not simple ones, and neither will be the theories that account for those stories.

NOTES

1. Scholars of the rhetoric of science are not in complete agreement about the precise relationship between science and rhetoric, however. A range of positions—from "science *uses* rhetoric" to "science *is* rhetoric"—are possible. See Simons (1990) for an overview of some of these controversies.
2. My comments here should not be construed as an indictment of teachers—within the sciences or elsewhere—or of secondary schools in general. As we shall see later, Eliza was in many ways very well-served by her previous science education. My claim (and it is not original) is that the myth of the autonomous text grows out of an entire *culture* of schooling, illustrated most powerfully for me by Goodlad's (1984) book *A Place Called School*. For a variety of reasons, many of them discussed by Goodlad, this culture often strips human context and rhetorical motive away from the learning of facts and concepts.
3. Currently, Eliza is less than 2 years away from a PhD in biology, conducting immune-system research in cell biology and coauthoring papers with her major professor. Her family continues to be supportive, says Eliza: "I'll be the first doctor—well, Ph.D.—in the family!"
4. For writing sessions, Eliza also noted whether she used a computer or pen and paper for composing. This data was used for a separate study (see Haas, 1989).

REFERENCES

Applebee, A. N. (1984). *Contexts for learning to write.* Norwood, NJ: Ablex.
Argyle, M., Furnham, A., & Graham, J. A. (1981). *Social situations.* London: Cambridge University Press.
Austin, J. L. (1962). *How to do things with words.* Oxford: Clarendon Press.
Bartholomae, D. (1985). Inventing the university. In M. Rose (Ed.), *When a writer can't write* (pp. 134-165). New York: Guilford.

Bazerman, C. (1985). Physicists reading physics: Schema-laden purposes and purpose-laden schema. *Written Communication, 2*, 3–23.

Bazerman, C. (1988). *Shaping written knowledge: The genre and activity of the experimental article in science.* Madison: University of Wisconsin Press.

Bazerman, C., & Paradis, J. (Eds.). (1991). *Textual dynamics of the professions.* Madison: University of Wisconsin Press.

Beach, R., Appleman, D., & Dorsey, S. (1990). Adolescents' use of intertextual links to understand literature. In R. Beach & S. Hynds (Eds.), *Developing discourse practices in adolescence and adulthood* (pp. 224–245). Norwood, NJ: Ablex.

Belenky, M. F., Clinchy, B. M., Goldberger, N. R., & Tarule, J. M. (1986). *Women's ways of knowing.* New York: Basic Books.

Belsey, C. (1980). *Critical practice.* London: Methuen.

Bereiter, C., & Scardamalia, M. (1987). *The psychology of written composition.* Hillsdale, NJ: Lawrence Erlbaum.

Berkenkotter, C., Huckin, T., & Ackerman, J. (1988). Conversation, conventions, and the writer. *Research in the Teaching of English, 22*, 9–44.

Biesecker, B. A. (1989). Rethinking the rhetorical situation from within the thematic of difference. *Philosophy and Rhetoric, 22*, 110–130.

Bitzer, L. F. (1968). The rhetorical situation. *Philosophy and Rhetoric, 1*, 1–14.

Bizzell, P. (1982). College composition: Initiation into the academic discourse community. *Curriculum Inquiry, 12*, 191–207.

Bizzell, P. (1984). William Perry and liberal education. *College English, 46*, 447–454.

Blakeslee, A. M. (1992). *Inventing scientific discourse: Dimensions of rhetorical knowledge in physics.* Unpublished doctoral dissertation, Carnegie Mellon University, Pittsburgh.

Brandt, D. (1990). *Literacy as involvement: The acts of writers, readers, and texts.* Carbondale: Southern Illinois University Press.

Brown, J. S., Collins, A., & Duguid, P. (1989). Situated cognition and the culture of learning. *Educational Researcher, 18*, 32–42.

Cazden, C. (1989). The myth of autonomous text. In D. M. Topping, D. C. Crowell, & V. N. Kobayashi (Eds.), *Thinking Across Cultures: Third International Conference on Thinking* (pp. 109–122). Hillsdale, NJ: Lawrence Erlbaum.

Charney, D. (1993). A study in rhetorical reading: How evolutionists read "The spandrels of San Marco." In J. Selzer (Ed.), *Understanding scientific prose* (pp. 203–231). Madison: University of Wisconsin Press.

Chase, W. G., & Simon, H. A. (1973). Perception in chess. *Cognitive Psychology, 4*, 55–81.

Fahnestock, J. (1986). The rhetorical life of scientific facts. *Written Communication, 3*, 275–296.

Farr, M. (1993). Essayist literacy and other verbal performances. *Written Communication, 8*, 4–38.

Fensham, P. J. (1985). Science for all: A reflective essay. *Journal of Curriculum Studies, 17*, 415–435.

Fish, S. (1980). *Is there a text in this class? The authority of interpretive communities.* Cambridge, MA: Harvard University Press.

Geertz, C. (1983). *Local knowledge: Further essays in interpretive anthropology.* New York: Basic Books.

Geisler, C. (1990). The artful conversation: Characterizing the development of advanced literacy. In R. Beach & S. Hynds (Eds.), *Developing discourse practices in adolescence and adulthood* (pp. 93–109). Norwood, NJ: Ablex.

Geisler, C. (1991). Toward a sociocognitive model of literacy: Constructing mental models in a philosophical conversation. In C. Bazerman & J. Paradis (Eds.), *Textual dynamics and the professions* (pp. 171–190). Madison: University of Wisconsin Press.

Geisler, C. (in press). *Academic literacy and the nature of expertise.* Hillsdale, NJ: Lawrence Erlbaum.

Gilbert, G. N., & Mulkay, M. (1984). *Opening Pandora's box: A sociological analysis of scientists' discourse.* Cambridge: Cambridge University Press.

Goetz, J. P., & LeCompte, M. D. (1984). *Ethnography and qualitative design in educational research.* Orlando, FL: Academic Press.

Goodlad, J. I. (1984). *A place called school: Prospects for the future.* New York: McGraw-Hill.

Gould, S. J. (1993). Fulfilling the spandrels of world and mind. In J. Selzer (Ed.), *Understanding scientific prose* (pp. 310–336). Madison: University of Wisconsin Press.

Gragson, G., & Selzer, J. (1990). Fictionalizing the readers of scholarly articles in biology. *Written Communication, 7,* 25–58.

Grice, H. P. (1975). Logic and conversation. In P. Cole & J. Morgan (Eds.), *Syntax and semantics. Vol. 3. Speech acts* (pp. 41–58). New York: Academic Press.

Haas, C. (1989). "Seeing it on the screen isn't really seeing it": Computer writers' reading problems. In G. E. Hawisher & C. L. Selfe (Eds.), *Critical perspectives on computers and composition instruction* (pp. 16–29). New York: Teachers College Press.

Haas, C. (1991, March). *Learning to read in college: Case studies of college readers in history and biology.* Paper presented at the Conference on College Composition and Communication, Boston.

Haas, C. (1993). Beyond just the facts: Reading and writing as rhetorical action. In A. Penrose & B. Sitko (Eds.), *Hearing ourselves think: Cognitive research in the college writing classroom* (pp. 19–32). New York: Oxford University Press.

Haas, C., & Flower, L. (1988). Rhetorical reading strategies and the construction of meaning. *College Composition and Communication, 39,* 167–183.

Harding, S. (1986). *The science question in feminism.* Ithaca, NY: Cornell University Press.

Haswell, R. H. (1988a). Dark shadows: The fate of writers at the bottom. *College Composition and Communication, 39,* 303–315.

Haswell, R. H. (1988b). Error and change in college student writing. *Written Communication, 5,* 479–499.

Haswell, R. H. (1991). *Gaining ground in college writing: Tales of development and interpretation.* Dallas: SMU Press.

Herndl, C. G., Fennell, B. A., & Miller, C. R. (1991). Understanding failures in organizational discourse. In C. Bazerman & J. Paradis (Eds.), *Textual dynamics and the professions* (pp. 279–304). Madison: University of Wisconsin Press.

Herrington, A. (1985). Writing in academic settings: A study of the contexts for writing in two college chemical engineering courses. *Research in the Teaching of English, 19,* 331–359.

Herrington, A. (1992). Composing one's self in a discipline. In M. Secor & D. Charney (Eds.), *Constructing rhetorical education* (pp. 91-115). Carbondale: Southern Illinois University Press.

Huckin, T., & Flower, L. (1991). Reading for points and purposes. *Journal of Advanced Composition, 11,* 347-362.

Hynds, S. (1989). Bringing life to literature and literature to life. *Research in the Teaching of English, 23,* 30-61.

Jamieson, K. H. (1973). Generic constraints and the rhetorical situation. *Philosophy and Rhetoric, 6,* 162-170.

Kaufer, D. S., Geisler, C., & Neuwirth, C. M. (1989). *Arguing from sources: Exploring issues through reading and writing.* San Diego: Harcourt Brace Jovanovich.

Keller, E. F. (1983). *A feeling for the organism.* San Francisco: Freeman.

Latour, B. (1987). *Science in action.* Cambridge: Harvard University Press.

Latour, B., & Woolgar, S. (1979). *Laboratory life: The social construction of scientific facts.* Beverly Hills, CA: Sage.

McCarthy, L. P. (1987). A stranger in strange lands: A college student writing across the curriculum. *Research in the Teaching of English, 21,* 233-265.

McCarthy, L. P., & Fishman, S. (1991). Boundary conversations: Conflicting ways of knowing in philosophy and interdisciplinary research. *Research in the Teaching of English, 25,* 419-468.

McCloskey, D. N. (1985). *The rhetoric of economics.* Madison: University of Wisconsin Press.

Mishler, E. G. (1979). Meaning in context: Is there any other kind? *Harvard Educational Review, 49,* 1-19.

Mitman, A. L., Mergendoller, J. R., Marchman, V. A., & Packer, M. J. (1987). Instruction addressing the components of scientific literacy and its relation to student outcomes. *American Educational Research Journal, 24,* 611-633.

Myers, G. (1985). The social construction of two biologists' proposals. *Written Communication, 2,* 219-245.

Myers, G. (1991). Stories and style in two molecular biology review articles. In C. Bazerman & J. Paradis (Eds.), *Textual dynamics and the professions* (pp. 45-75). Madison: University of Wisconsin Press.

National Academy of Sciences. (1989). *On being a scientist.* Washington, DC: National Academy of Sciences Press.

Nelson, J. (1990). This was an easy assignment: How students interpret academic writing tasks. *Research in the Teaching of English, 24,* 362-396.

Nelson, J. S., Megill, A., & McCloskey, D. N. (1987). *The rhetoric of the human sciences.* Madison: University of Wisconsin Press.

Nystrand, M. (1986). *The study of written communication: Studies in reciprocity between writers and readers.* New York: Academic Press.

Nystrand, M. (1987). The role of context in written communication. In R. Horowitz & J. Samuals (Eds.), *Comprehending oral and written language* (pp. 197-212). New York: Academic Press.

Patton, M. Q. (1980). *Qualitative evaluation methods.* Beverly Hills, CA: Sage.

Penrose, A. M., & Fennell, B. A. (1992, April). *Agency and proof in scientific prose.* Paper presented at the annual meeting of the American Educational Research Association, San Francisco.

Perry, W. G., Jr. (1970). *Forms of intellectual and ethical development in the college years: A scheme.* New York: Holt, Rinehart & Winston.

Rich, A. (1979). Toward a woman-centered university. In *On lies, secrets, and silence* (pp. 125–155). New York: Norton.

Rorty, R. (1979). *Philosophy and the mirror of nature.* Princeton, NJ: Princeton University Press.

Scardamalia, M., Bereiter, C., & Goelman, H. (1982). The role of production factors in writing ability. In M. Nystrand (Ed.), *What writers know* (pp. 173–210). New York: Academic Press.

Scribner, S., & Cole, M. (1981). *The psychology of literacy.* Cambridge, MA: Harvard University Press.

Searle, J. (1979). *Speech acts.* Cambridge: Cambridge University Press.

Selzer, J. (1993). Introduction. In J. Selzer (Ed.), *Understanding scientific prose.* Madison: University of Wisconsin Press.

Simons, H. W. (1990). The rhetoric of inquiry as an intellectual movement. In H. Simons (Ed.), *The rhetorical turn: Invention and persuasion in the conduct of inquiry* (pp. 1–34). Chicago: University of Chicago Press.

Stotsky, S. (1991). On developing independent critical thinking: What we can learn from studies of the research process. *Written Communication, 8,* 193–212.

Tierney, R. J., LaZansky, J., Raphael, T., & Cohen, P. (1987). Authors' intentions and readers' interpretations. In R. Tierney, P. L. Anders, & J. Mitchell (Eds.), *Understanding readers' understanding* (pp. 205–226). Hillsdale, NJ: Lawrence Erlbaum.

Tompkins, J. P. (1980). *Reader-response criticism: From formalism to post-structuralism.* Baltimore: Johns Hopkins.

van Dijk, T. (1987). Episodic models in discourse processing. In R. Horowitz & J. Samuals (Eds.), *Comprehending oral and written language* (pp. 161–196). New York: Academic Press.

Vatz, R. E. (1973). The myth of the rhetorical situation. *Philosophy and Rhetoric, 6,* 154–161.

Vipond, D., & Hunt, R. A. (1984). Point-driven understanding: Pragmatic and cognitive dimensions of literary reading. *Poetics, 13,* 261–277.

Winsor, D. A. (1989). An engineer's writing and the corporate construction of knowledge. *Written Communication, 6,* 270–285.

FOLLOW-UP ACTIVITIES

Discussing the Rhetoric

1. Haas positions herself among many scholarly names in the first section of the study. How does this affect her authority?

2. What is Haas' purpose in writing this longitudinal study? Where does she introduce her purpose?

3. Recall that it is typical of academic writers to cite other writers to review the written conversation thus far and to point out a gap in the knowledge that this writer's research will fill. Point out where Haas makes these moves.

4. Why does Haas claim it is necessary to construct a rhetorical frame with which to write? What are the motives behind Haas' doing so?

5. How is the essay organized? Which parts present the most difficulty? What choices by the author make those parts more difficult?

6. At least seven pages of this essay are devoted to research methods (and the excerpt here was condensed from the original). What rhetorical purpose does such detailed attention to methods serve?

7. In order to protect their subjects' privacy, social scientists never use their subjects' real names when they write up their research. Can you think of any reasons Haas might have chosen "Eliza" as the pseudonym for her subject?

8. How does Haas construct her essay to appeal to both professors of English and of the scientific disciplines? Does she seem to be speaking to one of these audiences more frequently than the other? Locate passages in the essay to support your view.

Discussing the Conversation

1. Haas argues that as rhetorical awareness grows, complexity grows. What is the value of this observation for students? What other writers in this part would agree with Haas?

2. Linda Flower believes that students' images of assignments, or tasks, "are rooted in the students' histories, the context of schooling, and cultural assumptions about writing." Although Haas focuses more on Eliza's reading process than her writing process, how does Eliza's reading development compare with Flower's view? Finally, how does this comparison justify Salvatori's claim that reading and writing are interconnected?

3. In Part Two, the idea that scientists are constructed by social patterns that inform the way they write scientific essays and reports was discussed. Recall some of the writers who explored this notion. How do those writers seem to be in conversation with Haas? For example, Haas reports that Eliza identifies with the traits of feminist science, a notion explored by Evelyn Fox Keller. Haas also says that scientific facts are not context-free. What other writers are concerned with this observation?

4. You may have picked up echoes of Burke's theories about discourse and rhetoric in some of the terms Haas uses. In what ways does Haas deploy Burke's theories in her discussion of the concrete circumstances of scientific writing?

Joining the Conversation

1. Have you had trouble figuring out what your professors expected for writing assignments in your university courses so far? If so, write an informal paper in which you describe such an experience. Then consider how the readings in Part Three, especially Haas' essay, can help you figure out what the professor is looking for.

2. Haas writes that a rhetorical frame helps readers discover an author's motives and the outcome of those motives. In an informal paper, construct a rhetorical frame by considering Haas' audience and purpose. Then review each section of Haas' study, locating passages where Haas' motives seem especially apparent.

3. Like Linda Flower, Haas is interested in trying to understand students' active encounters with the specialized languages in the disciplines of the university. Both writers draw inferences about how students think after observing students' processes. But whereas Flower examines the thinking processes of a group of students, Haas traces one student's development. In a one-page response paper, consider whose approach seems more reliable. To begin, you'll want to refer to each author's context or discourse communities, then consider why you answered like you did.

4. Write an informal paper in which you consider how you can apply what Eliza learned about rhetoric in biology to your own academic writing.

INTRODUCTORY COMMENTS ON "CONVERSATIONS WITH TEXTS: READING IN THE TEACHING OF COMPOSITION" BY MARIOLINA SALVATORI

Reading the Context

Mariolina Salvatori is associate professor of English at the University of Pittsburgh, where she teaches undergraduate and graduate courses in the composition and literature programs. She has written on twentieth-century Italian literature, literary perceptions of aging, and the immigrant experience. In her work on composition, she has continued to investigate the relationships between reading and writing, literature and composition, theory and practice. In this essay, Salvatori explores the role reading should play in writing classes. This essay illustrates how increasingly important it has become for many scholars to rethink the ways we converse with texts, as well as the consequences of these conversations. In this essay, Salvatori centers her investigation upon what she calls the "interconnectedness between reading and writing." According to Salvatori, the act of reading is a process of engaging in a conversation in which one partner is the text, and the other the interpreter of that text. When we acknowledge this relationship with reading in a critical fashion, we are left with a desire to generate critical questions, and these critical questions will provide us with insights into how different readers construct different meanings.

For Salvatori, thinking about *how* we think, rather than *what* we think and *why*, should be our focus as readers and writers. This process of reflection has historically preoccupied many theorists and philosophers. For example, in *Hegel's Dialectic: Five Hermeneutical Studies* the German philosopher Hans-Georg Gadamer claims that only by pointing to the way we actually experience language, or think about how we think, can we refute the commonplace that any science can be all-inclusive, autonomous, and timeless. That is, by examining the experiences that shape our concept of language, we can hope to recognize patterns of knowledge-making. According to Gadamer and Salvatori, it is by way of this fundamental recognition that we learn the art of posing questions—questions that will sustain and expand the important conversations of our time.

In this essay originally published in *College English,* an academic journal read by professors of English, composition, communications, and education, you will discover how important this notion about the relationship between language and knowledge is to Salvatori, not only as a scholar in the profession of English, but as a teacher. She devotes the last section of this essay to retelling experiences she has had with students in the classroom, showing us the joys and pains that result from putting her theories into practice.

Reading the Rhetoric

This is a difficult essay to read. But as Salvatori says, rather than opting for "simplifying solutions" in teaching reading and writing, we should opt for making the complexity of issues visible. In your estimation, what makes this essay so difficult to read? Consider the specialized language of her profession—Salvatori's style is informed by her discipline, which expects a certain way of writing. As you read, note the terms and concepts that seem especially difficult.

Also, consider how Salvatori's notion of the interconnectedness of reading and writing provide us with an attempt to find a way of effectively teaching reading and writing. For example, how does the opening epigraph in which Hans-Georg Gadamer ponders the value of the "art of dialectic" inform the way Salvatori structures her essay? That is, where do you see Salvatori practicing the art of asking questions in her writing? In what ways does the essay seem conversational? Who is participating in this conversation? What different conversations are taking place in this essay?

Your instructor may decide that the first half of this essay, devoted to the theoretical background of Salvatori's practices, is too esoteric to be useful to you, and assign you to start at the section "Teaching the Interconnectedness of Reading and Writing." If this is the case, do you notice any differences between the structure of the first paragraphs you read and the paragraphs written as introductions to previous articles?

Reading the Conversation

The essays in this part focus on how writing differs depending on the discipline, or context, in which we write. At the same time, Salvatori stresses

how important it is to reconsider what concepts inform the way we generally view the acts of reading and writing. A text's argument can function as
a "fulcrum," in Salvatori's terms, or a "contact zone," in Pratt's terms, brin-
ing reader and text together. Salvatori believes that if we can recognize the
value of situating ourselves within this contact zone where the art of questioning is practiced, then we will become responsible readers and writers.

Recall David Bartholomae's essay, "Inventing the University." Bartholomae writes that the student must assume the role of a participant in academic conversations. That is, the student must learn to speak the language,
by learning a specialized discourse, in order to enter the conversation of a
discipline. Bartholomae underscores the difficulty in asking this of students, while emphasizing that it is necessary. Salvatori adds to the complexity of Bartholomae's claim by introducing a historical context and three
interconnected questions in the body of her essay. As you progress through
Salvatori's essay, think about how Salvatori's analysis of these three questions extends Bartholomae's concerns.

Conversations with Texts: Reading in the Teaching of Composition
Mariolina Salvatori

The art of dialectic is not the art of being able to win every argument. . . .
Dialectic, as the art of asking questions, proves itself only because the person who knows how to ask questions is able to persist in his questioning. . . . The art of questioning . . . i.e. the art of thinking . . . is called
'dialectic,' for it is the art of conducting a real conversation. . . . To conduct a conversation means to allow oneself to be conducted by the object
to which the partners in the conversation are directed. It requires that one
does not try to out-argue the other person, but that one really considers
the weight of the other's position . . .

Hans-Georg Gadamer, *Truth and Method* (330)

1 Here Gadamer is writing about face-to-face conversations; but he does so in
order to articulate the rules and the workings of other inaudible conversations, those that readers make happen as they read. Gadamer theorizes reading as a "hermeneutical conversation with a text"—a conversation that can
only begin and be sustained if and when the reader/interlocutor reconstructs
and critically engages the "question," or the argument, that the text itself
might have been occasioned by or be an answer to. He writes, "Texts . . . have
to be *understood,* and that means that one partner in the hermeneutical

conversation, the text, is expressed only through the other partner, the interpreter" (349; emphasis added). This view of reading enables us to imagine a text's argument not as a position to be won and defended by one interlocutor at the expense of another, but rather as a "topic" about which interlocutors generate critical questions that enable them to reflect on the meaning of knowledge and on different processes of knowledge formation. Thus a text's argument can function as a fulcrum that brings parties (reader and text) together. But for this to happen a reader must accept and carry out the tremendous responsibility of giving a voice, and therefore a sort of life, to the text's argument. Although Gadamer does not point it out explicitly, a corollary to the reader's responsibility is the writer's responsibility, the responsibility of writing a text that asks (rather than answers) questions, that proposes (rather than imposes) arguments, and that therefore makes a conversation possible. And although Gadamer's subjects are expert readers and writers, what he has to offer those of us who teach as yet inexperienced readers and writers is, I believe, very valuable. Gadamer's emphasis on the reader's responsibility, for example, makes me think of the tremendous and delicate responsibility I have as reader of my students' arguments. But it also makes me think of the corollary to my responsibility, a student's responsibility to write argument in ways that allow a reader to converse with it. To teach students to assume and to exercise this responsibility is indeed very difficult. Nevertheless, I will suggest, they can learn to exercise this sophisticated practice of writing in the process of learning to understand and to appreciate the effects of writing on themselves as readers.

2   What follows is an argument on behalf of the theoretical and practical appropriateness of using "reading" as a means of teaching "writing." The word "argument" has multiple resonances here: my essay enters an ongoing argument or debate about the place of reading in the composition classroom (see for instance Gary Tate's and Erika Lindemann's recent essays in *College English*), and the arguments of texts are at the same time central to the particular understanding of reading and of teaching reading that I propose.

HISTORICAL CONTEXT

3 In 1974, in *Teaching Composing: A Guide to Teaching Writing as a Self-Creating Process,* William E. Coles argued against the use of reading in the composition classroom. He wrote:

> So we decided to get rid of everything that teachers and students alike are tempted to look at writing from behind or through or under. The anthology went; so did the standard plays, novels, poems. (2)

4   I remember, when I read these lines for the first time in the early 1980s, how struck I was by what seemed a peculiar and arbitrary decision. In 1992, in the process of composing a paper to be delivered at the Conference on

College Composition and Communication, I returned to Coles's text and for reasons that have to do with the kind of work I had done in the interim—mainly, my historical research in pedagogy, and my work with hermeneutics and the phenomenology of reading—I was able to read and to respond to this passage differently. In that paper (of which this essay is a revision) I myself returned to a subject that, though central to my intellectual formation as a compositionist, and central to my undergraduate and graduate teaching, I had not written about for some time. The paper was my attempt to understand which theoretical and institutional forces had led first to the separation and subsequently to the integration of the activities of reading and writing in the composition classroom. Focusing on the juncture of the theoretical and the institutional gave me a vantage point from which I was able to conjecture and to reconstruct the "argument" that had led Coles to make what had seemed to me such an iconoclastic gesture. This time, rather than judging Coles's statement as a blanket and arbitrary indictment of the presence of "reading" in composition classrooms, I began to see in his gesture a specific denunciation of what reading had been reduced to within *the teaching of composition* (but also within the teaching of literature, which problematically was and remains the model for much of the teaching of reading done in composition classrooms). I began to see that what Coles was indicting was a particularly enervated, atrophied kind of reading. A reading immobilized within textbooks, and reduced therein to sets of disparate simplifying practices that, separated from the various theories that motivate them, turn into meaningless and arbitrary exercises: reading for "the main idea," for "plot," for "argument," for "point of view," for "meaning," for "message"—interchangeably and without knowing what for. Or reading texts, especially literary texts, as inscrutable and unquestionable "models" of style or rhetorical strategies. Or as "blueprints" for linguistic theories, or political programs, or philosophies of language. I began to see, *through* Coles, the effects of practices that restrain students and teachers from asking questions of a text other than the ones the textbooks have already "gridded." I began to see, *with* Coles, why the kind of writing that these texts and their "facilitating" questions would foster could be nothing but "canned" or "theme" writing. This I understood to be the "problem" of reading that Coles was attacking, and for which he proposed, as a "pharmakon," getting rid of anthologies, plays, novels, poems, and replacing them with the text of the assignments and of the writing that students did in response to them.

5   Considering the position of composition in the academy in 1974, both inside and outside departments of English; considering the available work force of teachers of composition at the time; considering that the services of composition were in growing demand; considering the perceived need for compositionists to define their discipline on their own terms—considering all this, Coles's apparently "disciplinarian" act can be read, perhaps, as a stern act of self-discipline. That act, set in motion by a confluence of institutional needs, theoretical positions, and programmatic divisions, had a lasting influence.

Moreover, in complex ways, it encouraged or catalyzed other compositionists' felt need for a theory and practice of the reading-writing relation that would include the teacher's reading of student writing.

6   In the 1980s, Coles's move was challenged by some compositionists who shared his concern for student writing as the center of attention in the composition classroom. Rather than turning away from reading, however, these compositionists turned *to* theories of reading that seemed to offer fresh perspectives.

7   A 1985 essay by John Clifford and John Schilb, "Composition Theory and Literary Theory," reviewed the work of literary theorists who made it possible to imagine the teaching of literature and composition, reading and writing, as interconnected disciplines. Clifford and Schilb assessed the influence of reader-response poststructuralist theories and rhetoric and examined the work of those compositionists and literary critics who, they argued, offered ways of thinking about reading and writing that would elide programmatic and disciplinary separations (to name a few: Susan Miller, Richard Lanham, Ross Winterowd, Wayne Booth, Nancy Comley and Robert Scholes, and Terry Eagleton). Though remarkably different from one another, these theorists share a concern with *acts* rather than *facts* of reading (Ray). Instead of being seen as an intrusion onto the field of composition, or a pretext for paying attention to something other than students' writing, as in the thinking of the 1970s, reading, re-seen in the 1980s through new theories and practices, was now appealed to as a means of "bridging the gap" between the two activities and disciplines, a way of paying attention to reading and writing *differently*. But, I wish to argue, to set the two arguments side by side is to realize what either position may in debate unwittingly end up obscuring: that "the question of reading in the teaching of composition" is not merely the question of whether reading should or should not be used in the composition classroom. The issue is *what kind of reading* gets to be theorized and practiced. (Even if it were true that certain aspects of reading would always remain mysterious, teachers would still need to attend most closely to those aspects of reading which are not cloaked but can be made visible.) This issue cannot be critically and reflexively engaged apart from the following interconnected questions: (1) Which theories of reading are better suited to teaching reading and writing as interconnected activities? (2) What is the theoretical justification for privileging that interconnectedness? (3) How can one teach that interconnectedness?

THEORIES OF READING AND WRITING AS INTERCONNECTED ACTIVITIES

8 Not all theories of reading are suited to uncovering and enacting the interconnectedness of reading and writing. Among those least suited to doing so are those that construct writers as visionary shapers of meanings, and their

works as venerable repositories for those meanings (such theories generally discourage or consider inappropriate a reader's critical response to a text, particularly the response of an inexperienced reader); theories that construct as mysterious and magical the complicated processes of thinking on which writing imposes provisional order and stability (I am thinking here of critics/theorists as different as Benedetto Croce and Georges Poulet); and theories with unquestioned and unquestionable interpretive frames reducing texts to various thesis statements—cultural, political, religious, and so on. What I find objectionable in these theories is that they make it possible to cover over the processes by which knowledge and understanding are produced. By making it impossible to recapture and learn from the complex processes that have given a written text its particular shape, these theories, in different ways and for different reasons, simultaneously glorify reading and proclaim its unteachability. In classrooms where these theories of reading are unreflexively performed *for* students, where reading materials are used as mere pretexts for writing exercises, a *student's* reading of those materials may become *secondary* in at least two ways: it may become less important than the writing it produces; it may be constructed as needing to rely on a series of simplifying practices generated by somebody else. Such uses of reading as a means of teaching writing can indeed be arbitrary, questionable, even counterproductive.

9   In contrast with these notions about reading are theories that posit the possibility and the advantages of exploring the complex processes by which "reading" gives a voice to an otherwise mute "writing"; theories that turn texts and readers into "interlocutors" of each other; theories that interrogate rather than mystify the "naturalness," the mystery, and the interpretive "framing" both of the reading and of the writing processes. Such theories make it possible to claim not only that reading can be taught, but also that it can be taught as an opportunity to investigate knowledge-producing practices. Rather than divining a text's meaning or making a text subservient to preestablished significations, such theories construct reading as an activity by means of which readers can engage texts responsibly and critically. *Responsibly,* that is, in ways that as far as possible make *those* texts speak, rather than speak *for* them or make them speak *through* other texts. And *critically*—in ways, that is, that demand that readers articulate a reflexive critique both of the argument they attribute to those texts and of the argument they compose as they respond to those texts. (Among theorists of reading who, in different ways, provide such possibilities are Hans-Georg Gadamer, Wolfgang Iser, M. M. Bakhtin, and Paul de Man.) However, it does not follow that these theories automatically and necessarily lead to their own rigorous enactment.

10   Two of the texts that in the 1980s advocated a programmatic and theoretical rapprochement of reading and writing and their attendant domains of expertise and performance—literature and composition—demonstrate what I would call a perplexing inattentiveness to moving from theorizing

the interconnectedness of reading and writing to making it visible and teaching it. The texts are *Composition and Literature: Bridging the Gap,* edited by Winifred Bryan Horner, and *Writing and Reading Differently,* edited by Douglas Atkins and Michael Johnson. With a few notable exceptions (the essays by Sharon Crowley, Barbara Johnson, and Jasper Neel in *Writing and Reading Differently*), in these volumes reading and writing as interconnected activities are constructed as something that teachers do either *to* and *for* their students or for themselves and equally enlightened others—rather than something teachers do *with* their students to open up the areas of investigation that this particular focus makes possible. The interconnectedness of reading and writing (that virtual, provisional interaction between two extremely complex, invisible, imperceptible processes that can nevertheless be used to test and to foreground each other's moves) tends to be constructed as something either obvious or authorized by such an illustrious tradition—from Plato to Derrida—as not to require much explanation or articulation.

11   The advantages for the teaching of writing that this understanding of reading promises are ultimately invalidated. Teaching the reading/writing interconnection becomes another kind of hermetic performance, one that hides rather than reveals the processes of cognition that should be the subject of investigation and reflection. Paradoxically, these two texts end up reconfiguring the very situation that Coles was trying to avoid—approaching students' writing, and reading, "from behind or through or under" something else. Perhaps, though, what I perceive as a regrettable shortcoming of otherwise praiseworthy projects can serve an important function: it can remind us that although certain theories of reading *are* more conducive than others to teaching reading and writing as interconnected activities, to foreground and to teach—rather than just to understand—that interconnectedness is a highly constructed, unnatural, obtrusive activity—one that requires a particular kind of training that historically our educational systems and traditions have neither made available nor valorized.

THEORETICAL JUSTIFICATIONS FOR FOCUSING ON THE INTERCONNECTEDNESS OF READING AND WRITING

12 I wish to suggest at least two justifications for privileging this interconnectedness. First, insofar as reading is a form of thinking (Gadamer calls it "an analogue for thinking"), written accounts of it, however approximate, can provide us with valuable insights into the ways we think. Second, learning to recapture in one's writing that imperceptible moment when our reading of a text began to attribute to it—began to produce—a particular "meaning" makes it possible to consider what leads us to adopt and to deploy certain interpretive practices. In other words, although the processes that constitute our reading and writing are essentially invisible, those processes are, in principle, accessible to analysis, scrutiny, and reflection. "The ways we

think" need neither be kept shrouded in mystery, nor be reduced, in the interest of demystifying the reading process, to a bunch of technical, predictive, or authoritarian formulas. The possibility of gaining access to these processes by no means implies that they can be completely controlled or contained. Nor should they be. But through such access one might learn to account for, however approximately, and to understand, however imperfectly, how certain meanings, certain stories, certain explanations, certain interpretive frames come to be composed or adopted. Expert readers and writers have developed a kind of introspective reading that allows them to decide—as they read and as they write—when to pursue, when to revise, when to abandon a line of argument, and when to start afresh. They have devised a method of reading that, in Coleridge's words, functions as "a way or path of transit" that allows their minds "to classify" and "to appropriate" the events, the images, the thoughts they think as they read. Part of the challenge confronting us as teachers is to learn how to make it possible—within the time and institutional constraints that bind us—for students to learn to perform this kind of introspective reading. To think about reading and the teaching of reading in these terms—to think of reading, that is, as an analogue for thinking about one's own and others' thinking, about how one's thinking ignites and is ignited by the thoughts of others, justifies the presence of reading in composition classrooms not as a pretext but as a context for writing.

TEACHING THE INTERCONNECTEDNESS
OF READING AND WRITING

13 It is one thing to say that, even to articulate how, reading and writing are interconnected (as most of the authors featured in *Bridging the Gap* and *Writing and Reading Differently* do); and it is another to imagine and to develop teaching practices that both enact and benefit from that interconnectedness. This approach to teaching, one that requires teachers' and students' relentless attention and reflexivity, is difficult both to initiate and to sustain. Over the years, as a teacher of both composition and literature, I have learned to deploy certain teaching strategies that simultaneously enable and force me and my students to reflect on the moves we make as readers, writers, and thinkers. I do not consider these strategies as mere applications or implementations of somebody else's theories, and as I proceed to describe some of them I do not offer them as such. Nor—an important caveat—can these strategies be lifted out of the theoretical framework I have articulated here and seen as transportable tips or prescriptions; like all strategies, they make sense, that is, are plausible and justifiable, only within the particular approach to teaching that my understanding of "the act of reading" and its connections with writing calls for. I think of these strategies as means a teacher has of exposing (that is, of making visible as well as making available

to reflection and critique—her own and others') the *nexus* between the theory she espouses and the practices that theory demands.

14   To foreground and to exploit the interconnectedness of reading and writing, I make a point of framing reading and writing activities (formal assignments, in-class writings, journals) that ask students first to write their response to a text, second to construct a reflective commentary on the moves they made as readers and the possible reasons for them, and third to formulate an assessment of the particular text their reading produced (an adaptation of Ann E. Berthoff's double-entry journal). By means of this triadic (and recursive) sequence, I try to teach readers to become conscious of their mental moves, to see what such moves produce, and to learn to revise or to complicate those moves as they return to them in light of their newly constructed awareness of what those moves did or did not make possible. This "frame" is my attempt to imagine strategies that enact what Gadamer sees as the three pivotal and interconnected phases of reading—*erkennen, wiedererkennen,* and *herauserkennen.* It is important to note that this frame is not a "grid." Insofar as readers bring their own "presuppositions of knowledge" to the texts they read, the situations they find themselves in, and the experiences they live, and insofar as those presuppositions of knowledge will differ from one person to another, readers' readings of a text will vary.

15   Initially, my assignments generate considerable resistance on the part of students, mainly because they are not accustomed to performing this kind of introspective reading. When I ask of a point they made, "what made you think that?" or "how did you come to that conclusion?" they often hear reproach in my questions, in spite of my repeated efforts to explain my rationale for this approach. Occasionally students do readily learn to hear my questions as I intend them. But often they don't, and in this case I try to be extremely sensitive to any clues they offer that might make it possible for me to develop a strategy that answers the need of the moment. Here is an example.

16   Several years ago, one of the first times I taught Charlotte Perkins Gilman's "The Yellow Wall-Paper," I was temporarily silenced by a female student's defense of "the doctor." She was very articulate about all that the doctor had said and done, and she had come to the conclusion that the text made an argument for men's (as opposed to women's) inclination for science (medicine), and for what women had to lose when they did not abide by men's counsel. As I tried to collect myself enough to formulate a question that might make her reflect on what she had just said and why, the book in front of her caught my attention. It was highlighted, rather sparsely. I picked it up, flipped through it, and in a rare moment of extraordinary clarity I noticed that what she had marked in the text, what she had chosen to pay attention to, was everything in the text that had to do with "the doctor." She had paid little or not attention to anything else. I asked to be shown how other students had marked the text. Many had left it untouched (their reasons varied from not wanting to mark their books so that they could sell them to assuming that putting pen to page would interrupt their concentration, arrest their speed).

Others had highlighted it, some methodically, others erratically. What became evident to me was that "making a mark" on a text (Bartholomae and Petrosky) was a way of reading they had been taught *not* to perform. (A historical antecedent for my attempt to read the marks on the page as traces of a method could be found in the Renaissance "adversaria" [see Sherman].)

17   The rest of the period was spent first discussing the marks in the text as indicating what a reader chooses to be attentive to as she or he reads a text and then focusing on three representative samples: one by the student who mainly paid attention to the character of the doctor; one by a student who chose to focus on the narrator; and one by a student who, after an initial rather random system of marking the text, focused on the various characters' responses to the wallpaper. That class made it possible for me to turn a rather mechanical "study habit"—the highlighting of a text—into a strategy, one that can make "visible" the number and the intricacy of strands in a text's argument that a reader (or an interlocutor) pays attention to, and that can show how the selection, connection, and weaving of those strands affects the structuring of the argument a reader constructs. Like any strategy, this is not effective by itself. It is a tool to be used at the appropriate moment, more as a commentary on an incipient awareness of what it means to read an argument than as a means of instructing a reader how to pay attention to somebody else's argument.

18   A less local strategy, one less contingent on a particular context, is the assignment of what I call the "difficulty paper." (My article "Towards a Hermeneutics of Difficulty" articulates a theoretical framework for such an assignment; note also that Dave Bartholomae and Anthony Petrosky have developed a sequence of assignments around the generative force of difficulty.) Before we discuss a text collectively, I ask students to write a detailed one-page description of any difficulty the text they have been assigned to read might have posed for them. I photocopy what I consider a representative paper and distribute it for class discussion. Then, what I try to do is guide the discussion toward an assessment of the kind of reading that names a particular feature of a text as "difficult." Does difficulty arise because a reader's expectations blind her to a text's clues? Or because the method of reading a reader is accustomed to performing will not work with this particular text? Is it exacerbated when inexperienced readers assume that difficulties are an indictment of their abilities rather than characteristic features of a text? I have repeatedly relied on this kind of assignment, not as a means to expose my students' inadequacies, but as a reflexive strategy that eventually allows them to recognize that what they perceive as "difficult" is a feature of the text demanding to be critically engaged rather than ignored. What is remarkable about this approach is that students' descriptions of difficulties almost inevitably identify a crucial feature of the text they are reading and contain *in nuce* the interpretive move necessary to handle them. They might say for example that they had "difficulty" with a text because it

presented different and irreconcilable positions on an issue—their "difficulty" being in fact an accurate assessment of that text's argument.

19   The focus on difficulty can also be profitably used as a means of directing students' attention to the assignments by means of which many teachers suggest a possible reading of a text. Students can be asked to reflect on the kind of argument that the assignment's frame invites readers to construct about the text—and the kinds of arguments that it simultaneously close off. Thus the focus will be not only on the difficulty of doing justice to a complex text, but also on the difficulty of adequately representing the complexity of one's response to a complex text. This exercise can help foster habits of rigorous attention to one's reading of others' positions and to one's representations of them; and it can teach students (and remind teachers) to read assignments as more than sets of injunctions.

20   There are many ways of encouraging students to practice recursive and self-monitoring readings, and they will vary according to context, the rapport that teachers can establish with their students, the configuration of the group, the "feel" of the classroom . . . I am partial to those that can contribute to making what is imperceptible—thinking—at least dimly perceptible. Let's assume, for example, that a student writer has begun to compose a reading of a text (whether in response to an assignment, or to the "difficulty paper" instructions, or as a response of his own) that the teacher thinks might benefit from a second, more attentive reading. Perhaps the student has produced a hasty generalization or an inaccurate conclusion or an overbearingly biased and unexamined pre-understanding that made her oblivious to a text's argument. To ask that student to account for the steps she took to compose that reading, to ask her to actually *mark* which places in the text she "hooked up with" and which she merely scanned, can yield a dramatic visualization of how much of a text's argument can be erased because of preestablished conclusions or inattentiveness to the construction of that argument. Another way of putting students in a position to see the limits and the possibilities of how they choose to structure an argument is to set up a comparative analysis of two or three different papers. Focusing on the papers' introductory moves as simultaneously points of entry into a text (reading) and tentative beginnings for the arguments they will formulate (writing) helps to illuminate what difference it makes to begin a discussion of a text *there* rather than *elsewhere,* or to begin, say, with a question rather than an evaluative comment. It also helps teachers avoid interventions that focus on mistakes, on deficiencies, on what's wrong with this or that way of thinking.

21   The strategies I have cursorily described here represent some of the ways I choose to participate in and respond to my students' reading/thinking/writing activities. What is significant about these strategies is that they function simultaneously as heuristic devices for students (through them they learn how to perform certain reflexive moves) and as constant

reminders to me that as a teacher I must demonstrate in my reading of my students' words the responsiveness and the responsibility with which I expect them to engage texts. (This does not mean that I am always successful in doing so.) It is also significant that these strategies deliberately foreground "moments of reading" to show how these determine the writing students produce, and that they privilege places that can serve as points of critical reflection on the connection between reading and writing.

COUNTERING OBJECTIONS

22 I want now to turn to two of the most frequently articulated academic objections to the theory and practice of reading/writing interconnectedness I have outlined. I find these objections compelling and challenging, so much so that I keep returning to them to assess how they can help me understand better the assumptions about reading that subtend them. Insofar as for the past ten years these objections have consistently complicated and forced me to reexamine my positions on reading, on writing, on teaching, on education, I cannot exclude them from an argument of which they are such an integral part.

23   Using the names of the programs in my department whose theoretical orientations these objections could be said to represent, I will call them the "creative writing" and the "cultural studies" positions. What follows is a composite sketch of these objections that I have gleaned from three graduate courses I teach—the "Seminar in the Teaching of Composition," "Literacy and Pedagogy," and "Reception Theories." These courses lend themselves extremely well to engaging the issue of the intellectual and programmatic division of which the question of reading in the teaching of composition is both a cause and a consequence.

24   In the name of (a version of) "creativity" that is constructed as *being,* and *needing to remain,* beyond analysis, some of the representatives of the "creative writing" position articulate their opposition to the rigorous introspection that the interconnectedness of reading and writing requires. When as a group we grope for ways of describing not only *what* happens when we read, but also *how* it is that we tend to construct one and not another critical response to a text, some of the graduate students who align themselves with the "creative writing" position seem willing to engage the first but not the second line of inquiry. Their descriptions of reading are often magical, mysterious. They recollect, lyrically and convincingly, scenes of instruction within which—as children or adolescents—they taught themselves to read, with passion and imagination as their motives and guides. In response to questions about the context that favored their auto-didacticism, some will describe households replete with books and talk about books—a kind of oasis of family discourse that "naturally" fostered a love of reading and writing. Others, however, will describe settings that are exactly the opposite, within

which they performed a sort of heroic, individually willed—and therefore "natural" in quite a different sense of the word—form of self-education.

25   My aim in interrogating these moving accounts is not to devalue them or discredit their veracity, but to point out that these notions of reading may lead to approaches to teaching that are potentially elitist and exclusionary. (I develop this argument in "Pedagogy and the Academy," and more fully in *Pedagogy: Disturbing History*.) What happens when students show little cultural, emotional, or intellectual predisposition for this mystical love of reading? What kinds of responses will they write to a text they did not *love* reading? How can a teacher teach her students to perform a kind of reading that she has herself learned to perform mysteriously and magically? It is significant, I think, that when some of the readers who describe their reading processes as dream-like or intuitive are asked to read back those processes so as to gain insight into their habitual cognitive strategies, they often declare their suspicion of a process they name "critical dissecting."

26   The "cultural studies" position, on the other hand, objects to the focus on critical self-reflexivity as "nostalgic, reactionary, humanistic," and ultimately an ineffective educational practice. Such a focus, it is claimed, on the one hand can foster the illusion of human beings as independent, self-relying subjectivities; on the other hand, it can disseminate a pernicious account of knowledge-formation, one that exploits self-reflexivity, or a focus on method, as a tactic of avoidance, derailment, deflection. A teacher's commitment to enacting ways of reading that make it both possible and necessary for readers to reflect on and to be critically aware of how arguments—their own and others'—are constructed becomes within this critique a structured avoidance of more substantial issues. According to this critique, to focus, for example, on *how* John Edgar Wideman in "Our Time," or Alice Walker in "In Search of Our Mothers' Gardens," or Gloria Steinem in "Ruth's Song (Because She Could Not Sing It)" construct their narratives, is potentially a way of avoiding the ideological issues of race, class, and gender.

27   Insofar as it does not reduce "critical reflexivity" to an intentionally depoliticizing attention to form, the cultural studies position provides a salutary warning. Insofar as it does not reduce it to a version of necrophilia, the creative writing position on critical self-reflexivity as a potential blockage to action—creative or political—is compelling. But why is it that at their most oppositional, these and other critiques of self-reflexivity are predicated on a construction that turns it into an unnecessary, arbitrary, or stultifying practice?

28   What is so disturbing and uncomfortable about critical reflexivity? Why do the critical questioning and the introspective analysis it requires generate such suspicion and anxiety? How are we to read these responses? Do they indicate that the project of teaching reading and writing as interconnected activities is unreasonable, utopian, oblivious to the material circumstances within which it is to be carried out? Should we decide, as Coles did in the 1970s, that it might be opportune to scale down this

project of reading in the composition classroom from reading the inter-connectedness of reading and writing to the reading of the assignments and student papers? (What does this suggest about teachers' and students' ability to engage this task?) Does my critique of the ways most "integra-tionists" in the 1980s carried out the project of eliding the schism between reading and writing, literature and composition, confirm the wisdom of Coles's solution?

29   I see how it might be possible to answer all these questions in the affir-mative. And I become despondent. My current historical work in pedagogy, work that I undertook to understand what as a foreigner I found puzzling and disturbing, namely the separation of reading from writing, the proliferation of specialized programs within departments, the reduction of pedagogy from a philosophical science to a repertoire of "tips for teaching," shows that our educational system has consistently opted for simplifying solutions every time it has been confronted with the inherent and inescapable complexity of educational issues. What I find disturbing is that decisions often made for teachers, without the participation of teachers, are subsequently read as in-dictments of teachers' inadequate intellectual and professional preparation. (One of the most frequently voiced reservations to my project is that "it is too difficult" to carry it out without sacrificing writing to reading.) We cannot afford not to come to terms with the consequences of these streamlining in-terventions. We need to acknowledge that, for reasons whose complexity we cannot deny but that we can certainly call into question, our scheme of edu-cation has consistently and repeatedly skirted the responsibility of nurturing one of the most fundamental human activities—critical self-reflexivity.

30   Every time I teach reading and writing as interconnected activities, I begin by declaring, by making visible, my teaching strategies and by expos-ing their rationale. And yet every time it is a struggle for students to see this approach to teaching not as a cynical tendency to tear apart and to discredit the ways they read and write, as an exercise in dissection, or as a paralyzing threat, but rather, the way it is meant, as an attempt at promoting engage-ment in the kind of self-reflection and self-awareness that they are so often expected to demonstrate but are so seldom given an opportunity to learn.

31   In *On Literacy*, Robert Pattison argues that the project of developing the critical mind requires "another kind of training not generally available in the American scheme of education" (176). I agree with him, and I believe that we can and must find ways of providing that kind of training even within in-stitutional environments that are opposed to it. Let me suggest that teaching reading and writing as interconnected activities, teaching students how to perform critically, and self-reflexively, those recuperative acts by means of which they can conjecture an argument and can establish a responsible crit-ical dialogue with it, as well with the text they compose in response to it, might be an approach appropriate to developing the critical mind—an ap-proach that might mark the difference between students' participating in their own education and their being passively led through it.

WORKS CITED

Atkins, Douglas G., and Michael L. Johnson, eds. *Writing and Reading Differently: Deconstruction and the Teaching of Composition and Literature.* Lawrence, KS: U of Kansas P, 1985.

Bakhtin, M. M. *The Dialogic Imagination: Four Essays by M. M. Bakhtin.* Ed. Michael Holquist. Trans. Caryl Emerson and Michael Holquist. Austin: U of Texas P, 1981.

Bartholomae, David, and Anthony Petrosky. *Ways of Reading: An Anthology for Writers.* 2d ed. Boston: Bedford Books, 1990.

Clifford, John, and John Schilb. "Composition Theory and Literary Theory." *Perspectives on Research and Scholarship in Composition.* Ed. Ben W. McClelland and Timothy R. Donovan. New York: Modern Language Association, 1985.

Coleridge, Samuel Taylor. "On Method." *The Portable Coleridge.* Ed. I. A. Richards. New York: Viking, 1950.

Coles, William E. *Teaching Composing: A Guide to Teaching Writing as a Self-Creating Process.* Rochelle Park, NY: Hayden, 1974.

De Man, Paul. *Blindness and Insight: Essays in the Rhetoric of Contemporary Criticism.* Minneapolis: U of Minnesota P, 1983.

Gadamer, Hans-Georg. *Truth and Method.* New York: Continuum, 1975.

_____. *Philosophical Hermeneutics.* Trans. and ed. David E. Linge. Berkeley: U of California P, 1976.

Horner, Winifred Bryan, ed. *Composition and Literature: Bridging the Gap.* Chicago: U of Chicago P, 1983.

Iser, Wolfgang. *The Art of Reading: A Theory of Aesthetic Response.* Baltimore: Johns Hopkins UP, 1978.

_____. *The Fictive and the Imaginary: Charting Literary Anthropology.* Baltimore: Johns Hopkins UP, 1993.

Lindemann, Erika. "Freshman Composition: No Place for Literature." *College English* 55 (March 1993): 311–16.

_____. "Three Views of English 101:" *College English* 57 (March 1995): 287–302.

Pattison, Robert. *On Literacy: The Politics of the Word From Homer to the Age of Rock.* New York: Oxford UP, 1982.

Salvatori, Mariolina. "Towards a Hermeneutics of Difficulty." *Audits of Meaning: A Festschrift in Honor of Ann E. Berthoff.* Ed. Louise Z. Smith. Portsmouth, NH: Boynton/Cook, 1988.

_____. "Pedagogy and the Academy: 'The Divine Skill of the Born Teacher's Instincts.'" *Pedagogy in the Age of Politics: Writing and Reading (in) the Academy.* Ed. Patricia A. Sullivan and Donna J. Qualley. Urbana: NCTE, 1994.

_____. *Pedagogy: Disturbing History.* Pittsburgh: U of Pittsburgh P, forthcoming.

Ray, William. *Literary Meaning: From Phenomenology to Deconstruction.* New York: Basil Blackwell, 1984.

Sherman, William. *John Dee: The Politics of Reading and Writing in the English Renaissance.* Amherst: U of Massachusetts P, 1995.

Tate, Gary. "A Place for Literature in Freshman Composition." *College English* 55 (March 1993): 317–21.

_____. "Notes on the Dying of a Conversation." *College English* 57 (March 1995): 303–309.

FOLLOW-UP ACTIVITIES

Discussing the Rhetoric

1. How does citing the German philosopher Hans-Georg Gadamer help Salvatori outline her purpose? What does Salvatori's reliance on Gadamer tell us about the context, or discourse community, from which she is speaking?

2. The intended audience for this essay is English literature and composition professors. What academic conventions peculiar to this community did you notice in this essay? List them.

3. What parts of the essay were most difficult for you to read and understand? How do you account for the difficulty? You might consider your familiarity with Salvatori's theoretical background, her sentence structure, her vocabulary. What parts were easier for you to understand? Why?

4. What types of evidence does Salvatori use to construct her essay? Does she rely on one kind of evidence more than the others? Why do you think she relies on these types of evidence?

5. In Salvatori's estimation, which theory of reading should be used by teachers? How does Salvatori convince her audience that this theory of reading is the most satisfactory?

6. How much space does Salvatori devote to a discussion of theoretical background in the essay? To a discussion of practice? What do these allotments suggest about the topic of the essay?

Discussing the Conversation

1. In general, what does Salvatori add to this section's conversation? What passages seem to extend the complexity of Bartholomae's observation that students must learn to approximate the specialized discourse of the university?

2. According to Salvatori, a reader must accept the "tremendous responsibility of giving a voice" to any text's argument. Ultimately, students and teachers must share this responsibility. Salvatori believes instilling this responsibility is a difficult, but rewarding, process. What does Salvatori's idea of responsibility have in common with Pratt's concept of "contact zone"? In what other ways do you see Salvatori and Pratt conversing?

3. In the section entitled "Historical Context," Salvatori wonders what theoretical and institutional forces shaped her as a teacher and scholar. Which other authors in this text devote sections of their essays to this exploration? Which authors don't? How do these personalized histories add to each author's inquiry?

4. Compare your reading and text marking strategies with other members of your class. What strategies do you use to mark a text? What strategies do you discover among your classmates that you'd like to adopt?

Joining the Conversation

1. Salvatori writes that before asking her students to discuss a text in class, she asks them to write a detailed one-page description of any difficulties the text might have posed. Try this assignment yourself, referring to Salvatori's text. In an informal paper, discuss particular features of Salvatori's essay that you find difficult.

2. In an informal paper, recall a time in your student career when you decided the difficulty of reading a text for a particular discipline was too great. Can you recall what created the frustration? Do you think Salvatori's explanation of the interconnectedness of reading and writing will clarify or complicate your future experiences with reading and writing about texts? Support your response by locating passages that illustrate how you feel, then discuss why these passages make you feel either frustrated, enlightened, or something in between.

INTRODUCTORY COMMENTS ON "ARGUMENT AS EMERGENCE, RHETORIC AS LOVE" BY JIM W. CORDER

Reading the Context

In this selection, from a book entitled *Professing the New Rhetorics: A Sourcebook* (1994), Corder claims that a rhetorical approach provides the tools necessary to narrate our identities, a task fundamental to becoming an author. For Corder, it is important to realize that everyone is an author—individuals who in their writing and speaking are always striving to construct meaningful narratives. Our written and spoken language is part of how we define who we are. This attention to personal identities brings Corder's discussion of rhetoric out of a strictly academic realm into the vast expanse of interpersonal contact and, at the same time, brings this book's conversation full circle, to a connection with the rhetoric of identity formation that was Part One's central topic.

Corder's essay assumes that his readers are familiar with the theory that people tend to divide the world and the people in it into two categories: self and other. Whatever feels comfortable, familiar, and nonthreatening fits in the self category. Whatever seems "different" from one's norm, threatening, or contrary to current patterns and beliefs is corralled as "other." In this essay, Corder struggles with learning how to define a self while still staying open to and tolerant of whatever is designated as "other." Corder therefore describes narratives of identity formation as "open-ended"—always open to revision. Remaining open to revising our living narratives means that what we say will always be incomplete. As such, we cannot at any time establish a "timeless" or finished narrative of our existence. Corder's hope is that, as we encounter contending narratives (the life stories of others who are constructing their lives through their own rhetorical choices), we will take the time to listen and possibly revise.

The Appendix: Rhetorical Terms for Readers and Writers introduces the word "argument" as a rhetorical term. Corder's essay examines how our struggles to define ourselves through language have shaped our notion of argument. According to Corder, because we cannot escape the inevitable contact with "the other," we have no ethical choice but to reconsider, even redefine, our approach to argument. For Corder, appending the philosophical notion of "love" to the rhetoric that shapes argument enables us to work toward "creating a world full of space and time that will hold our diversities." When we expand our consciousness of rhetorical choices, we become not just arguers, but arguments, that create enough linguistic space to accommodate the other.

Reading the Rhetoric

Corder seems to be addressing an interdisciplinary audience. While reading this selection, think about whom he is trying to persuade. That is, how might you describe Corder's intended audience? The reading is divided into ten parts. Why do you suppose Corder chose this structure? As you read, take time to summarize the main ideas in each part. Also, think about Corder's tone. How does it differ from, for instance, Salvatori's? Spear's? Bartholomae's? How does his tone affect his ethos? How does it affect his relationship with his readers?

Reading the Conversation

Like the other readings in this part, this selection focuses on the rhetorical choices writers make when constructing arguments in certain contexts or disciplines. At first, Corder's tone might not seem to have a lot in common with that of the other writers, but the concerns he raises are similar. For example, Salvatori wants her audience to reconsider what informs the interconnected acts of reading and writing. According to Salvatori, a text's argument should function like a "fulcrum," bringing reader and text together. Similarly, Corder calls for a broad-based understanding of the concept of argument, in order to create a space in which different points of view can be heard, and valued. Can you think of other concerns Corder shares with other writers in this part?

Argument as Emergence,
Rhetoric as Love
Jim W. Corder

1 The editors think it appropriate to have Jim Corder, given his particular ethos, speak in his own voice.

> I was born in West Texas, in Jayton, a small town of some 600 souls. That doesn't include Mr. Boone Bilberry. He drank a little, sometimes turned fuzzy around the edges, and the Baptists said he didn't have a soul to count. Since, I have traveled the length and breadth of Kent County and Stonewall County, with occasional fearful expeditions elsewhere. I did graduate work at the University of Oklahoma, took the PhD in 1958, and came to Texas Christian University, where I have been since, though it's sometimes hard to tell, for I sometimes vanish before my very eyes. I have been chair of the English department, dean of the College of Arts and Sciences, and associate vice-chancellor, but I returned full-time to the English department some years ago. They told me that if I plugged away I would eventually get steady work.
>
> I came to the study of rhetoric late, as many my age did, having concentrated in graduate school on Restoration and eighteenth-century English literature. I taught Dryden and Pope and Johnson (or like to imagine that I did) long before I thought about rhetoric. More or less self-taught, therefore poorly taught, I think that much of my learning in rhetoric has been erratic and sporadic, unsystematic and inadequate. Sometimes, I not only don't know, I don't even suspect. I like to think about and around and once in a while through rhetoric, but I don't think of myself as a rhetorician. I'd rather be called by my name, if I'm to be called at all. I have committed papers and even composition textbooks with the word rhetoric in their titles, as if I knew and were composing a rhetoric. I'm no longer much interested in such enterprises, unless I can at the same time think about and understand a little the rhetoric I'm already in whenever I say or write anything about rhetoric. Since I can't fix either myself or rhetoric, I'd rather think about two or three small rhetorics, remembering to take the word as plural, trying to understand, for example, the consequences for rhetoric if one think of all speakers as remnants or leftovers, or trying to understand the consequences for rhetoric if one decides, momentarily say, that all rhetoric is nostalgic, resonant with regret and loss, or trying to understand how one might make a rhetoric yonder on the other side of regret and loss.

1

2 In a recent review in *The New York Times Book Review,* A. G. Mojtabai said, "We are all authors. Adding here, deleting there, we people the world with our needs: with friends, lovers, ciphers, enemies, villains—and heroes"

(March 3, 1985, 7). All authors, to be sure, we are more particularly narrators, historians, tale-tellers. Going through experience, hooking some version of it to ourselves, accumulating what we know as evidence and insight, ignoring what does not look like evidence and insight to us, finding some pieces of life that become life for us, failing to find others, or choosing not to look, each of us creates the narrative that he or she is. We tell our lives and live our tales, enjoying where we can, tolerating what we must, turning away to re-tell, or sinking into madness and disorder if we cannot make (or re-make) our tale into a narrative we can live in. Each of us forms conceptions of the world, its institutions, its public, private, wide, or local histories, and each of us is the narrative that shows our living in and through the conceptions that are always being formed as the tales of our lives take their shape. In this history-making, as E. L. Doctorow says, "there is no fiction or non-fiction as we commonly understand the distinction" ("False Documents," *American Review* 26 [1977]: 215–32). There is only our making, sometimes by design, sometimes not. None of us lives without a history; each of us is a narrative. We're always standing some place in our lives, and there is always a tale of how we came to stand there, though few of us have marked carefully the dimensions of the place where we are or kept time with the tale of how we came to be there.

3   The catch is that, though we are all fiction-makers/historians, we are seldom all that good at the work. Sometimes we can't find all that's needed to make the narrative we want of ourselves, though we still make our narrative. Sometimes we don't see enough. Sometimes we find enough and see enough and still tell it wrong. Sometimes we fail to judge either the events within our narrative or the people, places, things, and ideas that might enter our narrative. Sometimes we judge dogmatically, even ignorantly, holding only to standards that we have already accepted or established. We see only what our eyes will let us see at a given moment, but eventually make a narrative of ourselves that we can enjoy, tolerate, or at least not have to think about too much. Every so often, we will see something we have not seen before, and then we have to nudge, poke, and re-make our narrative, or we decide we can either ignore the thing seen or whittle it to shape the narrative we already have. We are always seeing, hearing, thinking, living, and saying the fiction that we and our times make possible and tolerable, a fiction that is the history we can assent to at a given time. But not only can we not always be good narrators/historians, we also cannot be thorough at the work. We never quite get the narrative all said: we're always making a fiction/history that always has to be re-made, unless we are so bound by dogma, arrogance, and ignorance that we cannot see a new artifact, hear a new opinion, or enter a new experience in our narrative.

4   When I say that we make the fictions that are our lives, I mean to identify a human activity, not a foolish or evil one. History as fiction may become evil, of course, if we refuse to see any history except the one we've already accepted or if we try to force that history upon others. At any rate,

making the fiction of our lives—not at all the same as discovering a way to present an objective, externally verifiable history, which is not possible, anywhere—is not by nature limited, valueless, ignorant, despicable, or "merely subjective." It is human. It is what we do and are, even if we think we are doing and being something else. Even if we imagine that we are learning what can be known "out there," some truths that are fixed and forever, we are after all creating our narratives "in here," ourselves always agents for what can be known. We are always, as the rhetorician might say, inventing the narratives that are our lives.

5   As I have already suggested, we are always standing somewhere in our narratives when we speak to others or to ourselves. When we use language, some choices have already been made and others must be made. Our narratives, which include our pasts, accompany us and exist in our statements and exercise their influence whether or not we are aware of the influence. Before we speak, we have lived; when we speak, we must continually choose because our mouths will not say two words simultaneously. Whether consciously or not, we always station ourselves somewhere in our narratives when we use language. This means that invention always occurs. The process of invention may occur in a conscious, deliberate way, but it will occur, even if at some subterranean level. Any statement carries its history with it. We may speak without knowing all of our narratives, but the history is there. If the history of a statement someone else makes isn't apparent to us as hearers, then we have to go and find it. If we are talking to someone and that person says something we don't understand, or something that offends us, or something we cannot easily agree to, then we have to start searching that person's history until we begin to understand what led him or her to speak just so. Sometimes we do less well: if the history isn't there for us, we don't learn it, but instead make it up to suit ourselves. If we learn or make up another's narrative so that it becomes part of our narrative, then we can live in some peace with the other. If the other's narrative will not enter our own, then something else happens, to which I'll return in a moment.

6   While the language that lets us invent our narratives and be human is a great gift, its capacities will not extend infinitely. Language comes out of us a word at a time; we cannot get all said at once. We open ourselves as we can to insight and experience and say what we can, but what we say will invariably be incomplete. Two words cannot occupy the same space at the same time; two messages cannot fully occupy the same space at the same time. Language enforces a closure: we must say one thing or the other; we choose, and make our narrative. To be sure, having lived, thought, and spoken, we can open ourselves again to insight and experience and evidence and try to say it all again. But what will come out will be the fiction we can make at the time. We cannot make all that was and is and shall be into an is of the moment's speaking. Whatever we can get into our heads we will make into the narratives that will be our truths unless we learn again.

2

7   Each of us is a narrative. A good part of the time we can live comfortably adjacent to or across the way from other narratives. Our narratives can be congruent with other narratives, or untouched by other narratives. But sometimes another narrative impinges upon ours, or thunders around and down into our narratives. We can't build this other into our narratives without harm to the tales we have been telling. This other is a narrative in another world; it is disruptive, shocking, initially at least incomprehensible, and, as Carl Rogers has shown us, threatening.

8   *When this happens, our narratives become indeed what they are perpetually becoming—arguments.* The choosing we do to make our narratives (whether or not we are aware of the nature of our choosing) also makes our narratives into arguments. The narratives we tell (ourselves) create and define the worlds in which we hold our beliefs. Our narratives are the evidence we have of ourselves and of our convictions. Argument, then, is not something we *make* outside ourselves; argument is what we are. Each of us is an argument. We always live in, through, around, over, and under argument. All the choices we've made, accidentally or on purpose, in creating our histories/narratives have also made us arguments, or, I should go on to say, sets of congruent arguments, or in some instances, sets of conflicting arguments.

3

9   Each of us is an argument, evidenced by our narrative. What happens, then, if the narrative of another crushes up against our own—disruptive, shocking, incomprehensible, threatening, suddenly showing us into a narrative not our own? What happens if a narrative not our own reveals to us that our own narrative was wanting all along, though it is the only evidence of our identity? What happens if the merest glimpse into another narrative sends us lurching, stunned by its differentness, either alarmed that such differentness could exist or astonished to see that our own narrative might have been or might yet be radically otherwise than it is? Do we hold our narratives? Keep telling the story we have been telling? At all costs?

10   We react, of course, in many different ways. Sometimes we turn away from other narratives. Sometimes we teach ourselves not to know that there are other narratives. Sometimes—probably all too seldom—we encounter another narrative and learn to change our own. Sometimes we lose our plot, and our convictions as well; since our convictions belong to our narratives, any strong interference with our narrative or sapping of its way of being will also interrupt or sap our convictions. Sometimes we go to war. Sometimes we sink into madness, totally unable to manage what our wit or judgment has shown us—a contending narrative that has force to it and charm and appeal and perhaps justice and beauty as well, a narrative compelling us to attention

and toward belief that we cannot ultimately give, a contending narrative that shakes and cracks all foundations and promises to alter our identity, a narrative that would educate us to be wholly other than what we are. Any narrative exists in time; any narrative is made of the past, the present, and the future. We cannot without potential harm shift from the past of one narrative into the present and future of another, or from the past and present of one narrative into the future of another, or from the future we are narrating into a past that is not readily ours. How can we take that one chance I mentioned just now and learn to change when change is to be cherished? How can we expect another to change when we are ourselves that other's contending narrative?

4

11 Let there be no mistake: a contending narrative, that is, an argument of genuine consequence because it confronts one life with another is a threat, whether it is another's narrative become argument impinging upon or thundering into ours, or our own, impinging upon the other's. A contending narrative, I'd suggest, is a threat more consequential than Carl Rogers has shown us. In *On Becoming a Person* (Boston: Houghton Mifflin Company, 1961), Rogers proposes that "significant learning . . . takes place when five conditions are met":

- When the client perceives himself as faced by a serious problem;
- When the therapist is a congruent person in the relationship, able to *be* the person he *is;*
- When the therapist feels an unconditional positive regard for the client;
- When the therapist experiences an accurate emphatic understanding of the client's private world and communicates this;
- When the client to some degree experiences the therapist's congruence, acceptance, and empathy.

Rogers had earlier applied his thinking more directly to rhetoric, announcing his belief that *a sense of threat usually blocks successful communication.* As he put it, "the major barrier to mutual interpersonal communication is our very natural tendency to judge, to evaluate, to approve or disapprove, the statement of the other person" ("Communication: Its Blocking and Its Facilitation," paper delivered at Northwestern University's Centennial Conference on Communication, Oct. 11, 1951, reprinted in Richard E. Young, Alton L. Becker, and Kenneth L. Pike, *Rhetoric: Discovery and Change* [New York: Harcourt, Brace, and World, 1979], 284–89). If we refrain from evaluating and instead "listen with understanding," according to Rogers, we will "see the expressed idea and attitude from the other person's point of view . . . sense how it feels to him . . . achieve his frame of reference in regard to the thing he is talking about" (285). When we are immersed in the attitudes, ideas, and beliefs of the other person, we "will find the emotion going out of the discussion, the differences being reduced, and those differences which remain being of a rational and understandable sort" (286).

12   Such insights have been enormously valuable in recent years. Some (Maxine Hairston, for example) believe that Rogers' work has brought a new dimension of rhetoric after all these centuries, changing our way of thinking about argument. Others believe that Rogers' views are assumed by Aristotle, as Andrea Lunsford put it, to be "the foundation which is necessary before successful argumentation begins" ("Aristotelian vs. Rogerian Argument: A Reassessment," *College Composition and Communication* [May, 1979]: 146–51). Lunsford singles out two texts that propose methods of organizing Rogerian argument. Young, Becker, and Pike (283) suggest the following method:

First: An introduction to the problem and a demonstration that the opponent's position is understood.

Second: A statement of the contexts in which the opponent's position may be valid.

Third: A statement of the writer's position, including the contexts in which it is valid.

Fourth: A statement of how the opponent's position would benefit if he were to adopt elements of the writer's position.

In *A Contemporary Rhetoric* (Boston: Houghton Mifflin and Co., 1974, 210–11), Maxine Hairston presents another Rogerian pattern:

1. A brief, objectively phrased statement of the issue.
2. A complete and impartially worded summary of your audience's opinions on the issue, demonstrating that you have made an honest effort to understand how they feel and why they feel that way. It would be useful to mention the values that underlie these opinions.
3. An objective statement of your opinions on the issue, along with your reasons for feeling as you do. Here again it would be useful to give the values on which you base your opinions.
4. An analysis of what your opinions have in common.
5. A proposal for resolving the issue in a way that injures neither party.

13   Such insights added to those of Carl Rogers, I'll say again, have been highly valuable. They lead to patterns of argument that may even work, part of the time, in some settings. But they won't do. They do not, I believe, face the flushed, feverish, quaky, shaky, angry, scared, hurt, shocked, disappointed, alarmed, outraged, even terrified condition that a person comes to when his

or her narrative is opposed by a genuinely contending narrative. Then it is one life or another, perhaps this life or none.

14   I want to pause a little to suggest some of the reasons that I think Rogers and others who have applied his work have not gone far enough, though this is not the place for a full critique, even if I could give it. First, we should remember, Rogers is talking about the therapist-client relationship, and much of what he says rises from that context. Since it takes two to tango, and since at least one of the participants in this context is already intent upon *not* being an adversary, then conflict may be resolved and mutual communication may ensue. The therapist-client relationship, I'd suggest, even at its prickliest, is simply not going to produce the stress and pain that can occur when contending narratives meet. It is by its nature more amenable to discussion and resolution, and the rules of conditions I cited earlier are, at any rate, *game* rules, as my colleague, Professor James Baumlin, has pointed out. In the passage I cited earlier, Rogers is talking about a client who already has a need (he or she is faced by a serious problem), and the therapist is already a congruent person in the relationship. Rogers proposes for the therapist an "unconditional positive regard," but straight away recommends that all take emotion out of discussions and reduce differences. If one holds another in "unconditional positive regard," that regard, I believe, includes both emotions and differences. They cannot be reduced, though their force may be diminished for a moment; such energy is always conserved. If emotions do go out of the discussion—and I don't think they do—it is only after time and care. What each must face in contention before emotions and differences dwindle is something in the other altogether more startling: a horror, a wrong, a dishonesty (as each sees the other), a shock, an outrage, or perhaps a beauty too startling and stunning to see. As for the texts that propose patterns of Rogerian arguments, I'd say that the recommended designs are altogether commendable and will sometimes work, so long as the argument isn't crucial to the nature of the narratives involved. Where arguments entail identity, the presentation of "a statement of how the opponent's position would benefit if he were to adopt elements of the writer's position" is about as efficacious as storming Hell with a bucket of water or trying to hide the glories of Heaven with a torn curtain. If I cannot accept the identity of the other, his kindness in offering me benefits will be of no avail. As for offering a "proposal for resolving the issue in a way that injures neither party," I'd say that in the arguments that grip us most tightly, we *do* injure the other, or the other injures us, or we seem about to injure each other, except we take the tenderest, strongest care. Paul Bator ("Aristotelian and Rogerian Argument," *College Composition and Communication* [Dec., 1980]: 427–32) acknowledges that Rogerian strategy works most effectively when students "encounter non-adversary writing situations." "Under the Rogerian schema," he continues, "students can be encouraged to view their writing as a communicative first step—one designed to build bridges and win over minds—

rather than being prompted to view the essay only as a finished product serving as an ultimate weapon for conversion."

15   I am suggesting that the arguments most significant to us are just where threat occurs and continues, just where emotions and differences do not get calmly talked away, just where we are plunged into that flushed, feverish, quaky, shaky, angry, scared, hurt, shocked, disappointed, alarmed, outraged, even terrified condition I spoke of a little earlier. Then what do we do?

5

16 To make the kind of contention or opposition I am trying to discuss a little clearer, I should add another term. I have been talking about contending narratives, or identities. Let me now add what I hope has been suggested all along: let us suppose that in this contention each narrator is entirely *steadfast,* wholly intent upon preserving the nature and movement of his or her narrative, earnest and zealous to keep its identity. I think we have not fully considered what happens in argument when the arguers are steadfast.

17   If Ms. Smith is steadfast in conviction and is outfitted with what she takes to be good evidence and sound reasoning, that means that she is living a narrative that is congruent with her expectations and satisfying to her needs. But if she speaks to Mr. Jones, who is at opposites and equally steadfast, who is his own satisfying narrative, then it's likely that Ms. Smith's evidence will not look like evidence to Mr. Jones, and Ms. Smith's reasoning will not look like reasoning. Evidence and reason are evidence and reason only if one lives in the narrative that creates and regards them.

18   That seems to picture a near-hopeless prospect.

19   Sometimes it is, at least for long periods of time. Sometimes we don't resolve oppositions, but must either remain apart or live as adversaries with the other. But the prospect doesn't have to be hopeless, at least not permanently.

20   What can change it? What can free us from the apparent hopelessness of steadfast arguments opposing each other? I have to start with a simple answer and hope that I can gradually give it the texture and capacity it needs: we have *to see* each other, *to know* each other, *to be present to* each other, *to embrace* each other.

21   What makes that possible? We have to change the way we talk about argument and conceive of argument.

6

22 I'm not ready to go on yet. I want to try to place my interest in argument, and perhaps I can do that by comparing my interest to those of Carl Rogers, to whom I am clearly much indebted. Rogers extrapolates from therapist-client relationships to public communication relationships. The base from

which he works (the therapist-client relationship) gives him a setting in which civil understanding is a goal to be reached through mutual communication transactions. He does recognize the potentially threatening effect of alien insights and ideas. Young, Becker, and Pike show that the Rogerian strategy "rests on the assumption that a man holds to his beliefs about who he is and what the world is like because other beliefs threaten his identity and integrity" (7). In the Rogerian view, as Paul Bator puts it, carefully reasoned arguments "may be totally ineffectual when employed in a rhetorical situation where the audience feels its beliefs or values are being threatened. No amount of reasoned argument will prompt the audience to consider the speaker's point of view if the audience senses that its opinions are somehow being 'explained away'" (428). Followers of Rogers see in Aristotle's *Rhetoric* an antagonistic speaker-audience relationship; they do not find this in Rogers, for, as Bator says, "Generation and control of audience expectation do not attract Rogers" (428). As I have already suggested, given the therapist-client relationship he starts from, Rogers is appropriately enough interested in rhetorical contexts that do not involve advocacy. As Rogers says, "If I can listen to what [the other person] can tell me, if I can understand how it seems to him, if I can see its personal meaning for him, if I can sense the emotional flavor which it has for him, then I will be releasing potent forces of change in him" (285–86). Since he is customarily talking about a mutual communication transaction, Rogers is often as concerned with the audience as with the speaker. A speaker, Bator says, "must be willing to achieve the frame of reference of the listener even if the values or views held by the other are antithetical to the speaker's personal code of ethics. A necessary correlate of acceptance (of the other's view) is understanding, an understanding which implies that the listener accepts the views of the speaker without knowing cognitively what will result. Such understanding, in turn, encourages the speaker to explore untried avenues of exchange" (428). Looking for the therapist-client relationship, Rogers sees the therapist/communicator as an understanding audience. He expects that the therapist-as-audience will not only accept, but also understand the feelings and thoughts of the client-as-speaker. When the therapist understands the feelings and thoughts that seem so horrible or weak or sentimental or bizarre to the client, when the therapist understands and accepts the client, then the therapist frees the client to explore deep experience freely. As each understands and accepts the other, then they may move toward the truth.

23   This, I would gladly agree, is the way we ought to argue, each accepting, understanding, and helping the other. However, I think the significant arguments that crowd us into each other are somewhat less kindly composed. I want to get to the place where we are threatened and where the setting doesn't seem to give us opportunity to reduce threat and to enter a mutual search for congruence and regard. I want to get to the place where we are advocates of contending narratives (with their accompanying feelings and thoughts), where we are adversaries, each seeming to propose the repudiation

or annihilation of what the other lives, values, and is, where we are beyond being adversaries in that strange kind of argument we seldom attend to, where one offers the other a rightness so demanding, a beauty so stunning, a grace so fearful as to call the hearer to forgo one identity for a startling new one.

7

24 What can free us from the apparent hopelessness of steadfast arguments contending with each other, of narratives come bluntly up against each other? Can the text of one narrative become the text of another narrative without sacrifice? If there is to be hope, we have to see each other, to know each other, to be present to each other, to embrace each other.

25   What makes that possible? I don't know. We can start toward these capacities by changing the way we talk about argument and conceive of argument.

26   It may be helpful, before I go on, if I try to explain a little more fully the kind of occasion I mean to refer to, the kind of setting in which contention generates that flushed, feverish, quaky, shaky, angry, scared, hurt, shocked, disappointed, alarmed, outraged, even terrified condition I have mentioned. Of course I cannot imagine, let alone explain or describe, all the oppositions that can occur. Perhaps I can by illustration at least suggest the kind of occasion that I want to talk about. I mean such occasions as these: let two people confront each other, each holding views antithetical to the sacred values and images of the other, one an extreme advocate of the current Pro-Life movement, the other an extreme advocate of the current movement to leave free choice open to women in the matter of abortion, each a mockery of the other; let two parties confront each other, zealous advocates of one contending that farmers must learn to stand on their own without government support, and zealous advocates of the other contending that the government, by withdrawing support, will literally kill farmers; let two tribes go to war for ancient reasons not entirely explicable to themselves or to outsiders, each a denial of the other, as in various current Middle East crises; let two nations confront each other in what sometimes appears to be a shocked and total inability to understand or even to recognize each other, as in continuing conflicts between the United States and Russia, wherever these conflicts happen to be located, whether in East Germany or in Nicaragua; let a beautiful Jewish woman encounter an aged captain of guards for Dachau; let some man confront an affirmation of life he has not been able to achieve; let an honest woman encounter cruel dishonesty; let a man encounter a narrative so beautiful but different that he cannot look; let two quite different narratives converge in conflict inside the head of a single lonely man or woman.

27   Given such occasions, what do we do in argument? Can we hope for happy resolution? I don't know. I do think the risk in argument is greater than we have learned from Aristotle or Rogers. What can we do, then?

28   We can start, as I suggested earlier, by changing the way we talk about argument.

29   As we presently understand, talk about, and teach argument, it is, whatever our intentions, *display* and *presentation.* We entice with an exordium and lay in a background. We present a proposition. We display our proofs, our evidence. We show that we can handle and if need be refute opposing views. We offer our conclusion. That is display and presentation. The same thing is true of proposed plans for Rogerian argument, as in the passages I cited earlier from Young, Becker, and Pike and from Maxine Hairston.

30   But argument is not something *to present* or *to display.* It is something *to be.* It is what we *are,* as I suggested earlier.

31   We are the argument over against another. Another is the argument over against us. We live in, through, around, and against arguments. To display or to present them is to pretend a disengagement that we cannot actually achieve and probably should not want to achieve. Argument is not display or presentation, for our engagement in it, or identity with it, will out. When argument is taken as display or presentation, then it eventually becomes a matter of my poster against yours, with the prize to the slickest performance.

32   If we are to hope for ourselves and to value all others, *we must learn that argument is emergence.*

8

33 Argument is emergence toward the other. That requires a readiness to testify to an identity that is always emerging, a willingness to dramatize one's narrative in progress before the other; it calls for an untiring stretch toward the other, a reach toward enfolding the other. It is a risky relevation of the self, for the arguer is asking for an acknowledgement of his or her identity, is asking for witness from the other. In argument, the arguer must plunge on alone, with no assurance of welcome from the other, with no assurance whatever of unconditional positive regard from the other. In argument, the arguer must, with no assurance, go out, inviting the other to enter a world that the arguer tries to make commodious, inviting the other to emerge as well, but with no assurance of kind or even thoughtful response. How does this happen? Better, how can it happen?

34   It can happen if we learn to love before we disagree. Usually, it's the other way around: if we learn to love, it is only after silence or conflict or both. In ancient times, I was in the United States Army. I spent the better part of 1951 and 1952 in Germany. In those years, American troops were still officially regarded as an Occupation Force, with certain privileges extended, such as free transportation. One service provided was a kind of rental agency in many large cities. On pass or on leave, one could go to this agency and be directed to a room for rent (very cheap) in a private home.

Since I was stationed only ten or twelve miles away, I often went to Heidelberg when I had just a weekend pass or a three-day pass. On one such occasion I went to Heidelberg, stopped in at the agency, and got directions to a room that was available. I found the address, a large brownstone just a block off the main street, met the matron of the house, and was taken to a small bedroom on the third floor that would be mine for a couple of days. I left shortly thereafter to go places and do things, paying no particular attention to the room except to notice it was clean and neat. The next morning was clear and bright and cool; I opened the windows and finally began to see the room. A picture on one wall startled me, more, stunned me.

35   On the kitchen wall in my parents' home in Texas there was a picture of my older brother, taken while he was in what was known as the Air Corps in World War II. It was a posed shot of the sort that I suppose most airmen had taken at one time or another to send home to the folks. In the picture, my brother is wearing the airman's favorite of that time, a leather jacket with knit cuffs and a knit band about the waist. He is wearing the old-fashioned leather cap with ear flaps and goggles, and there is a white scarf around his neck, one end tossed over his shoulder. Behind him there is a Consolidated-Vultee B-24.

36   The picture on the wall in the bedroom in Heidelberg showed a young man wearing a leather jacket with knit cuffs and a knit band about the waist. He wore an old-fashioned leather cap with ear flaps and goggles, and there is a white scarf around his neck, one end tossed over his shoulder. Behind him there was an airplane; it was a Focke-Wulfe 190. He might have been my brother. After a while, I guess I realized that he *was* my brother.

37   The television news on March 7, 1985, showed a memorial service at Remagen, Germany, marking the fortieth anniversary of the American troops' capture of the Remagen bridge, which let them cross the Rhine. No major world leaders were there, but veterans from both sides had come to look and take notice of the day. American and German veterans who had fought there wept and hugged each other and shook hands.

38   In the mid-fifties, another group of veterans met, to commemorate the fortieth anniversary of the end of battle at Verdun, that hellish landscape where over a million men died to gain or to preserve two or three miles of scrubby country, where no birds sang. They shook hands; they embraced; they wept; they sang an old song that begins, "Ich hatte ein kamaraden."

39   After a while, the hated dead can be mourned, and the old enemy can be embraced.

40   In these instances, we waited to love (or at least to accept) until long after silence and grim conflict. (I've not lost my head altogether: some conflicts will not be resolved in time and love—there's always that captain of guards from Dachau.) Often, we don't learn to love (or at least to accept) at all. All precedents and examples notwithstanding, I'll stand insist that argument—that rhetoric itself—must begin, proceed, and end in love.

9

41 But how is this to happen? How will we argue, or teach argument taken in this way? I don't know, but I'll chance some suggestions.

42   a. The arguer has to go alone. When argument has gone beyond attempts made by the arguer and by the other to accept and understand, when those early exploratory steps toward mutual communication are over, or when all of these stages have been bypassed altogether—as they often will be—then the arguer is alone, with no assurance at all that the other or any audience will be kindly disposed. When argument comes to advocacy or to adversarial confrontation, the mutuality that Rogers describes will probably not occur. At the point of advocacy, most particularly at the crisis point in adversarial relationships, the burden is on the maker of the argument as he or she is making the argument. At the moment of heat (which may last twenty seconds or twenty years and which may be feverish and scary), the arguer in all likelihood will not know whether or not the other, the audience, will choose to take the role of the well-disposed listener or the kindly therapist. The arguer, alone, must see in the reverence owed to the other, discover and offer all grace that he or she can muster, and, most especially, extend every liberty possible to the other. The arguer must hold the other wholly in mind and yet cherish his or her own identity. *Then,* perhaps, the arguer and the other may be able to break into mutuality.

43   b. The arguer must at once hold his or her identity and give it to the other, learning to live—and argue—provisionally. In "Supporting History Is a Woman—What Then?" (*The American Scholar,* Autumn, 1984), Gertrude Himmelfarb remarks:

> Whatever "truth or validity" adheres to history . . . does not derive, as the conventional historian might assume, from an "objective" world, a world of past events waiting to be discovered and reconstructed by the historian. For there is no objective world, no historical events independent of the experience of the historian, no events or facts which are not also ideas.

We must keep learning as speakers/narrators/arguers (and as hearers). We can learn to dispense with what we imagined was absolute truth and to pursue the reality of things only partially knowable. We can learn to keep adding pieces of knowledge here, to keep rearranging pieces over yonder, to keep standing back and turning to see how things look elsewhere. We can learn that our narrative/argument doesn't exist except as it is composed and that the "act of composition can never end," as Doctorow has said.

44   c. As I have just suggested, we arguers can learn to abandon authoritative positions. They cannot be achieved, at any rate, except as in arrogance, ignorance, and dogma we convince ourselves that we have reached authority. We should not want to achieve an authoritative position, anyway. An authoritative position is a prison both to us and to any audience.

45   d. We arguers can learn the lessons that rhetoric itself wants to teach us. By its nature, invention asks us to open ourselves to the richness of creation, to plumb its depths, search its expanses, and track its chronologies. But the moment we speak (or write), we are no longer open; we have chosen, whether deliberately or not, and so have closed ourselves off from some possibilities. Invention wants openness; structure and style demand closure. We are asked to be perpetually open and always closing. If we stay open, we cannot speak or act; if we stand closed, we have succumbed to dogma and rigidity. Each utterance may deplete the inventive possibilities if a speaker falls into arrogance, ignorance, or dogma. But each utterance, if the speaker having spoken opens again, may also nurture and replenish the speaker's inventive world and enable him or her to reach out around the other. Beyond any speaker's bound inventive world lies another: there lie the riches of creation, the great, unbounded possible universe of invention. All time is there, past, present, and future. The natural and the supernatural are there. All creation is there, ground and source for invention. The knowledge we have is formed out of the plentitude of creation, which is all before us, but must be sought again and again through the cycling process of rhetoric, closing to speak, opening again to invent again. In an unlimited universe of meaning, we can never foreclose on interpretation and argument. Invention is a name for a great miracle—the attempt to unbind time, to loosen the capacities of time and space into our speaking. This copiousness is eternally there, a plentitude for all. Piaget remarked that the more an infant sees and hears, the more he or she wants to see and hear. Just this is what the cycling of rhetoric offers us: opening to invention, closing to speak, opening again to a richer invention. Utterances may thus be elevated, may grow to hold both arguer and other.

46   e. We still need to study. There is much about argument that we still have not learned, or that we have not acknowledged. If we are accurate in our evaluation of what happens in conflict, I think we will have to concede that most of what happens is bad. If we know that accurately, we'll be a step farther than we were toward knowing how to deal with contention and the hurts that rise from conflict and argument. We have not at any time in our public or personal histories known consistently how to deal with conflicts, especially when each side or party or view arises normally according to its own variety of thought—and there is no arguer who does not believe that his or her view is a just consequence of normal thought and need. In discourse and behavior, our ways of resolving conflicts have typically been limited and unsatisfactory. When opposing views, each issuing by its own normal processes from its own inventive world, come together in conflict because each wants the same time and space, we usually have only a few ways of handling the conflict:

1. one view prevails, the other subsides;
2. advocates of the two views compromise;

3. the need for action prompts arbitrary selection of one of the two views, even if both are appealing and attractive;
4. we are paralyzed, unable to choose;
5. we go to war; or
6. occasionally, the advocates of one side learn gladly from those of the other and gladly lay down their own views in favor of the other.

To be sure, there are other patterns for resolving conflicts that I haven't had wit enough to recognize; I'd reckon, however, that most are unrewarding to some or all. Once a view emerges—that is, once an inventive process has become structure and style—it cannot wholly subside, as in (1), though it must seem to do so; required by force or expediency to subside, it does not subside but persists underground, festering. Compromise, as in (2), is likely to leave parts of both views hidden away and festering. Deliberate choice between two appealing views, as in (3), leaves the unchosen to grow and compete underground, generating a cynicism that undercuts the chosen argument. Paralysis, as in (4), clearly gives no view gain, though each remains, eating away at the paralyzed agent. War, physical or psychological, is plainly not an appropriate human resolution. In most of these instances there is a thwarted or misplaced or submerged narrative, a normality that may grow wild because it is thwarted, misplaced, or submerged. We have not learned how to let competing normalities live together in the same time and space. We're not sure, we frail humans, that it is possible.

47   f. The arguer must go alone, unaided by any world of thought, value, and belief except the one that he or she composes in the process of arguing, unassisted by the other because the other is over in a different place, being realized in a different narrative. In my mind, this means that the burden of argument is upon the *ethos* of the arguer. *Ethos,* of course, is a term still poorly understood. Among others, Bator objects to any concentration upon *ethos* because it seems to be "related primarily to adversary situations calling for argumentative strategies designed to persuade others," because "the speaker may be concerned particularly with enhancing her own image or character rather than addressing the issue at hand" (428). Ideally, Bator believes, the subject or problem "is viewed within the audience's framework of values, not simply from the writer's assumptions or premises. The *ethos* of the writer is not the main focus of attention, nor is it the primary means of appeal" (431). This view omits considering the likelihood that *ethos* occurs in various ways; the term does not require to be defined as it has formerly been defined. A genuinely provocative and evocative *ethos* does, in fact, hold the audience wholly in mind, does view matters both as the arguer sees them and as others see them. The self-authenticating language of such an *ethos* issues an invitation into a commodious universe. Argument is partial; when a speaker argues a proposition or develops a theme or makes an assertion, he or she has knowingly or not chosen one proposition, one theme, one assertion from all available. When we speak, we stand

somewhere, and our standing place makes both known and silent claims upon us. We make truth, if at all, out of what is incomplete or partial. Language is a closure, but the generative *ethos* I am trying to identify uses language to shove back the restraints of closure, to make a commodious universe, to stretch words out beyond our private universe.

48   g. We must pile time into argumentative discourse. Earlier, I suggested that in our most grievous and disturbing conflicts, we need time to accept, to understand, to love the other. At crisis points in adversarial relationships, we do not, however, have time; we are already in opposition and confrontation. Since we don't have time, *we must rescue time by putting it into our discourses and holding it there,* learning to speak and write not argumentative displays and presentations, *but arguments full of the anecdotal, personal, and cultural reflections that will make us plain to all others,* thoughtful histories and narratives that *reveal us as we're reaching for the others.* The world, of course, doesn't want time in its discourses. The world wants the quick memo, the rapid-fire electronic mail service; the world wants speed, efficiency, and economy of motion, all goals that, when reached, have given the world less than it wanted or needed. We must teach the world to want otherwise, to want time for care.

10

49 Rhetoric is love, and it must speak a commodious language, creating a *world full of space and time that will hold our diversities.* Most failures of communication result from some willful or inadvertent but unloving violation of the space and time we and others live in, and most of our speaking is tribal talk. But there is more to us than that. We can learn to speak a commodious language, and we can learn to hear a commodious language.

FOLLOW-UP ACTIVITIES

Discussing the Rhetoric

1. What is Corder's purpose? Refer to specific passages to provide evidence for your view.

2. What voices does Corder cite? How do these voices support his purpose? You might devote special attention to section 6.

3. How would you describe Corder's tone? In your estimation, does it sound like the professional tone of other writers in this part? Why do you think he chose this tone to develop his topic?

4. How does Corder construct his ethos in the reading? Does this sort of ethos carry more, less, or about the same amount of authority than the other writers in this part? Why?

5. In the concluding section, Corder writes that "most of our speaking is tribal talk." What does he mean by this?

6. Why did Corder divide this reading into ten sections? Does this rhetorical choice enhance your understanding of the issues? How so?

Discussing the Conversation

1. The writers in this part of the book discuss the importance of a rhetorical context. What does Corder add to this ongoing conversation?

2. Locate passages in which Corder illustrates Haas' observation that as rhetorical awareness grows, complexity grows. What terms does Corder introduce to illustrate the complexity of rhetoric? List them. How do these terms inform Haas' study?

3. According to Corder, "each of us is an argument." What does he mean by this? How does his explanation extend this part's conversation? You might recall Salvatori's or Bartholomae's introductions as well as Burke's theory that language is symbolic action.

4. In the first part of this essay, Corder states that "if we learn or make up another's narrative so that it becomes part of our narrative, then we can live in some peace with the other." In Part 3, Corder wonders "what happens if a narrative not our own reveals to us what our own narrative was wanting all along, though it is the only evidence of our identity"? Which other writers in this book share concerns that revolve around these two quotes? Consider in particular how hooks, Rodriguez, Pratt, and Keller might elaborate upon, or provide evidence for, Corder's statements.

5. What commonalities do you see between Corder's and Burke's views about self and other?

Joining the Conversation

1. In an informal paper, respond to Corder's concluding comments in section 10. According to Corder, "rhetoric is love." Why is it significant to learn to speak, as well as hear, a "commodious language"? According to Corder, what problems will result if rhetoric cannot learn to speak such a language?

2. In section 4, Corder elaborates on the term "contending narrative." He writes that a contending narrative is "an argument of genuine consequence because it confronts one life with another" and this is "a threat." Write an informal paper in which you recall participating in an argument of genuine consequence that made you feel threatened. (Did any of the arguments in the readings in the first or second part of this text feel threatening to you?)

First, think about what made the argument threatening: Was it the beliefs of the other impinging on yours? The rhetorical choices the other used to present his or her position? At what stage of the argument did you feel most threatened? Why? Second, consider the following questions: Were you able to resolve the argument? Did you hold to your narrative, or alter it after considering the others'? If neither, how did you resolve or fail to resolve the argument?

PART FOUR

Formal Writing Assignments

The writing assignments in this Part provide instruction and practice for some of the most familiar forms of student writing in college. They are designed to prepare you for writing in various college classes across the disciplines. The assignments include summary, rhetorical analysis, review, synthesis, annotated bibliography, researched argument, and self-reflection essay.

For each of the assignments, we have included detailed instructions that describe the typical expectations and conventions for these forms of writing. In fact, we refer to them as *formal* assignments because they describe in detail the typical *forms* such writing takes. We have also listed some representative types of college assignments in which you would be expected to use each form of writing.

Each formal assignment includes several parts intended to facilitate the writing process. It begins with a definition of the form and an explanation of the purpose for which it is usually assigned. It includes a checklist of typical expectations for the form or guidelines for composing. In addition, it lists peer review questions designed for the particular form to help you provide constructive criticism for your peers' and your own drafts. Finally, student models with discussion questions are included to give you an example of and means for constructively criticizing ways other students have interpreted these forms.

We give you explicit instructions to clarify the typical purposes for which each assignment is made and the typical standards of evaluation. By doing so, we wish to provide you with instructional support, but we do not intend to suggest that these guidelines comprise the single "right" way to approach assignments. As we have emphasized throughout the anthology, all writers make choices about language, type of appeals, kind of argument, selection and types of evidence, and arrangement of ideas according to their specific rhetorical situation, the audience, and the purpose for which they write. We do not want these guidelines to be interpreted as rigid standards or formulas that you can apply every time you are assigned to write in these forms. At the same time, we want you to have enough information to make informed rhetorical decisions.

We invite you not to take these guidelines at simple face value, but to converse with these instructions and expectations in order that you might join, continue, or transgress these forms of writing in ways that best fit your rhetorical situation(s).

We expect your instructors to select any or all of these assignments at their discretion, depending on their judgment of your needs for practice. Your instructor may choose to substitute the writing suggestions at the end of each reading for all of these formally developed assignments or may intermix those more informal assignments with these.

SUMMARY ASSIGNMENT

What Is Summary?

A summary attempts to capture the important turns of argument of a written source. Writers of summaries are expected, as objectively as possible, to present another writer's views. A straight summary should not include the summary writer's opinions.

Purpose of the Assignment

The need for summarizing appears in a variety of contexts. You may find that you will want to write a summary for yourself as a way to remember something you have read or heard. Additionally, you may be asked by a professor to write a summary that will demonstrate that you have read and understood a text. In your university work, you will most often have to incorporate summarizing as a starting point on your way to something else. You might first have to summarize before you can analyze a writer's ideas or before you can use a writer's ideas (with proper acknowledgment, of course) to support a position you wish to take. You also have to summarize other writers' ideas before you can evaluate them. In the latter cases, you will often find yourself thinking of the writer's work and your own in a dialogical relationship: you present a summary of the writer's view as responsibly as possible and then in some way, you respond to it stating your own views. In many of the assignments that you do in your college work, you will probably find that you are using the skills of summary in one or more of these ways.

Writing a Summary

Because of the many ways in which you might find it useful to use the techniques of summary throughout your college work, we suggest that you practice the basic technique of summarizing by writing this summary as though you were doing it as evidence of having read and understood a source. Your instructor will ask you to summarize one of the selections in this text. You can assume that your audience is a professor who has read the essay and is assigning the summary to check for your understanding.

CHECKLIST

The following criteria are a checklist for you to consider as you write. Most summaries attend to the following issues. As the writer, you must realize that your professor's purposes or your own purposes for writing the summary may cause variations in the particular standards your summary needs to meet. A good summary usually includes the following:

An Opening Sentence That Contains

- Name of author.
- Title of piece.
- Place and date of publication.
- Main point.

Additional Information

- The major subpoint or major turns in the writer's argument.
- The writer's ideas in paraphrase. Quotations are generally not used.
- Transitions that articulate clearly the relationship among the writer's ideas.

A good summary will probably NOT include the following:

- Minor points or evidence.
- Your own opinion or evaluation of the reading.

Your instructor may ask that you provide an evaluation or opinion of the information that you are summarizing. In this case, your summary moves into the realm of a review. It is prudent to listen carefully to what your instructor is asking for and to ask questions to clarify what you should do to complete the requirements of the assignment. However, if you meet the criteria that have been provided here, you will find that you have written a piece that fulfills the most common expectations for summarizing.

PEER RESPONSE QUESTIONS FOR SUMMARY ASSIGNMENT

Name of Student Writer _____

Name of Student Responder _____

1. Is the name of author, title of piece, place, and date of publication and main point in the first sentence of the summary, or close to it? If not, what is missing?

2. Do you agree that the writer has included the major subpoints or major turns in the author's argument? If not, what has he or she omitted that should be included? Do you think the writer has included any information that does not belong in a summary? Describe your rationale for inclusions or omissions.

3. Does the summary writer use transitions that clearly articulate the relationships among the author's ideas? Make margin notations on your copy of the summary to indicate places where transitions need to be clarified.

4. Are the author's ideas well paraphrased (accurate, but using the summary writer's words and phrases rather than the authors)? Are quotations used rarely, and when used, used for an obvious reason (to emphasize an idea, or because the author's phrase is particularly well-put)? Circle sentences or phrases on your copy of the summary that repeat too closely the author's wording or phraseology.

5. Does the summary fairly represent the author's points and omit the summary writer's views? If not, which statements are inaccurate, unfair or biased?

STUDENT MODEL OF A SUMMARY

The writer of this summary has chosen to organize her paper similarly to the structure of the text being summarized. The introduction identifies the text and publication information being summarized and paraphrases the author's main point. The writer identifies the author's main subpoints and explains the relationships among the author's ideas. The writer concludes the summary by reiterating the author's thesis.

Points for Discussion

1. Notice how the writer gets all the pertinent information in the introductory paragraph. Identify the writer's thesis sentence and the author's thesis. Are they in the same sentence?

2. How do you know what the writer is going to write about after reading the first paragraph?

3. What strategies does the writer use for letting you know that the points she or he is making are the points the author made?

4. Can you identify how the writer's organization of the summary mimics the author's organization of the selection?

5. One strategy that seems to work in writing summaries is to write one sentence that paraphrases the author's thesis or topic idea for every section or paragraph in the text. If you link your paraphrased sentences together, you have the beginnings of a summary of the author's main points written in your own words. Try this on the text you are planning to summarize. Think about the ways you will need to demonstrate the relationships that the author is making among those ideas. Develop transitions that help the reader to understand those relationships and you should have a good first draft of a summary.

Rhetorical Analysis
of Allan Bloom's "Liberal Education"

In "Liberal Education" an excerpt from Allan Bloom's 1987 book The Closing of the American Mind, Bloom deals with the condition of today's liberal arts schools. He argues that the specialization or "careerism" of today's colleges and universities is a poor choice for educating students to become enlightened to the "big ideas," ideas that will enrich and civilize their mind and help them fulfill their potential. A better approach relies on the use of the "great books," these "great books" provide classic texts for students to study and question.

Allan Bloom outlines many problem's with todays Liberal Arts Education. Bloom's relies on the belief that college is one of the most important times for students, between the wasted years of high school and the treachery of the professional world. Unfortunately for Bloom, what is happening in colleges today is the specialization or "careerism" of universities. Specialization routes students to a particular field or discipline, preparing them for ~~there~~ their future positions in the work force.

In Bloom's mind students get "short changed" with this specialization. Universities do not have enough material to teach students, so they send them on specialized tracks. Bloom comments that this specialization wastes students' time and money. Professors are also too ~~concerned~~ considered with their specialities to spend the time it takes to teach students properly.

Allan Bloom offers three alternative solutions, two of which he sees as unacceptable. Cores and combination courses are ineffective and are not truly liberal education. The only effective solution is the one that is least used,this solution involves the "great books." Bloom argues that when the "great books" are taught students are "excited and satisfied". (35)

There is great objection to the use of the great books, both the natural and social sciences do not want to incorporate them into their curriculum. The humanities are also wary of the great books approach. Yet Allan Bloom concludes that it is the only effective way to teach a beneficial and productive liberal arts curriculum.

RHETORICAL ANALYSIS ASSIGNMENT

What Is Analysis?

Professors will often ask you to write an analysis. When you analyze, you take apart the main components of an idea, object, text, or activity. Then you evaluate the parts in light of a selected theoretical framework. In fact, your theoretical framework will usually tell you what parts to look for. For example, you might be asked to analyze the position a writer takes in light of a particular economic or political theory in your Western Civics class. Or you may be asked to analyze the findings of an experiment demonstrated by your biology professor on the basis of an environmental or a viral theory. Whatever the task, the job of analysis generally asks that you take apart the components of a whole and explain them on the basis of a particular point of view.

Purpose of the Assignment

The purpose of asking you to write a rhetorical analysis is twofold: first, to practice analytical thinking as a cognitive activity, and second, to provide an opportunity for you to develop your knowledge of rhetoric as an analytical tool. A rhetorical analysis differs from a summary in that it assumes an understanding of the main points of the piece, but analyzes how the writer has constructed the piece to convince the audience that his or her points are valid and believable.

What Is a Rhetorical Analysis?

A rhetorical analysis explains how a piece of writing has been produced. Think about the rhetorical devices that the writer has used in this particular piece about which you are writing. (You will find an explanation of various rhetorical devices in the "Appendix: Rhetorical Terms for Readers and Writers," p. 439.) To do the analysis, the first step is to read the piece very carefully. As you read, you might identify and analyze how the writer represents his or her identity in the piece. This will give you some clues about how the writer constructs his or her ethos as credible to the audience. Then work on observing and describing how the writer employs the various rhetorical strategies with which you are now familiar to persuade the audience. Some contextual issues to consider as you read include:

- The writer's purpose.
- The intended audience or discourse community.
- The genre.

Some rhetorical strategies that you might consider (these are not mutually exclusive categories; you may need to consider one category in relation to another) include:

- Writer's use of appeals.

  Ethos. (How does the writer project an authoritative stance?)

  Pathos. (What techniques does the writer use to appeal to the readers' emotions?)

  Logos. (What techniques does the writer use to appeal to the readers' rationality?)
- Organization of the information.
- Selection and omission of information.
- Privileging and/or excluding various positions or voices.
- Kinds and use of evidence.
- Style.

See the "Appendix: Rhetorical Terms for Readers and Writers" for a detailed discussion of these concepts.

Organizing Your Analysis

The following structural suggestions are not the only way to proceed. Your professor might give you additional structural advice. We include these suggestions as a generic aid that you might find helpful.

Introduction

Begin your paper with an introduction, probably one paragraph of several sentences that do the following:

- Place your writing in a larger conversation (in this case, about writers' use of rhetorical strategies to accomplish their purposes).
- Introduce the article you plan to analyze. Name the writer, title of the piece, publication date, where the piece originally appeared.
- Identify the discourse community in which the writing participates and the audience for whom the writing is intended.
- Describe the writer's purpose. To do this, you might answer the following questions for yourself before you write: What does the writer want to achieve within this community with this writing? What does she or he want these particular people to think and/or do?
- Identify the rhetorical strategies that you have decided to discuss and indicate, in general terms, how they function to promote the author's purpose in relation to the intended audience.

Body

Each paragraph in the body of the paper generally consists of its own topic sentence and unified focus. For the purpose of this analysis, consider writing one paragraph on each of the rhetorical strategies you mentioned in the introduction. Useful strategies for developing these paragraphs include:

- Define the rhetorical strategy.
- Quote or paraphrase examples that illustate the writer's use of the strategy (two or three examples are probably sufficient).
- Explain how or why the example illustrates the strategy and how the strategy contributes to the writer's purpose.

You may find that you need several paragraphs to explain a single strategy, especially if you have several examples of the strategy. Just be sure that your transition at the beginning of a new paragraph makes it clear that you are still discussing the same strategy.

Conclusion

The purpose of the conclusion is to summarize briefly the main points of the analysis and to explain the significance of your analysis. Questions for considering the significance of this topic include:

- Do the rhetorical strategies that you discuss construct (or fail to construct) a persuasive argument for you? Do you think they were successful for the writer's intended audience?
- Can you generalize about the role of rhetorical strategies in producing persuasive writing?

An alternative or second rhetorical analysis assignment: Your instructor might assign a comparative analysis of the rhetorical strategies used in two different readings. For this assignment, you would compare how the writers' rhetorical choices differ in light of their audience, their relationship to their audience, and their purposes. This assignment provides practice in the additional conceptual problem of organizing a complex comparison.

Recommended Readings

Like the summary, the rhetorical analysis can be used effectively with any of the readings in the text. However, two aims are eminently demonstrable by the readings in this text—to recognize the rhetoric of traditional academic writing, and to recognize strategies that challenge traditional conventions. For the former, the readings by Klemke et al.; Addelson, Schiebinger, Appleby et al.; Haas, Burke, and Bartholomae are illustrative. For the latter, hooks, Pratt, and Tompkins exemplify transgressive attempts, while Rose blurs the personal and academic. One might also select the articles by Newenhuyse, Kirkpatrick, or Wade to contrast the strategies of popular writing with academic writing.

PEER RESPONSE QUESTIONS FOR RHETORICAL ANALYSIS ASSIGNMENT

Name of Student Writer _____

Name of Student Responder _____

1. Does the essay begin with an introductory paragraph of 4 to 6 sentences?

   a. Does the opening paragraph contain contextual information? That is, does the opening paragraph indicate that the conversation in which this paper is taking place is about writers' uses of rhetorical strategies to accomplish their purposes?

   b. Does the opening paragraph contain information about the article the writer will use to exemplify uses of rhetorical strategies?

   c. Does this paragraph include the name of the author, title of the article, publication date, and publication where the article originally appeared?

   d. Does it name the community(ies) out of which and for which the author has constructed this account?

   e. Does it state the author's purpose—what he or she wants to achieve within these communities? What does he or she want these particular people to think and/or do?

   f. Does the introduction name the rhetorical techniques or strategies that the paper will be discussing and give some indication of how these strategies function in relation to the text's audience and purpose?

   g. If the introductory paragraph lacks any of these components, explain what is missing.

   Comments:

2. Does the essay incorporate the terminology that we have been using in class to describe and discuss rhetorical contexts and strategies? Give some examples:

3. Read each paragraph separately. Does each paragraph focus on the rhetorical strategies mentioned in the introduction? That is, does the topic sentence of each paragraph indicate which strategy the paragraph will discuss? Is the paragraph developed by:

- Defining the strategy?
- Giving examples of it from the essay under analysis (2 to 3 of each strategy)?
- Explaining why the example illustrates the strategy the student writer claims it does, and explaining how the strategy contributes to the author's purpose?

4. If the writer used a section of more than one paragraph to explain a particular strategy, does he or she make it clear which paragraphs concern the same strategy and at what point the subject changes to a new strategy?

5. Does the essay use coherent transitions between sections, paragraphs, and sentences? Underline on your photocopy at least one particularly good transitional phrase or sentence. Write "transition?" in the margin if a transition is unclear or omitted.

6. Does the paper end with a conclusion of 1 or 2 paragraphs, explaining the significance of the analysis? Does it return to the opening conversation and consider the importance of understanding writing from a rhetorical perspective?

7. Does the paper observe the conventions of college discourse (i.e., correct spelling, grammar, sentence structure, punctuation)? Indicate errors in the margins of the photocopy.

8. What general comments can you make to help the writer successfully revise this essay?

STUDENT MODELS OF A RHETORICAL ANALYSIS

The writers of these papers have both chosen to rely on the structural organization provided in the assignment guidelines. You may notice that the first paragraph of each paper introduces the text the writer will examine, summarizes the main points of the text, states the author's purpose and audience, and introduces the rhetorical strategies that the writer will analyze in the paper. The body of the paper is organized by the order in which the writer names the strategies in the introduction. Each section of the body of the paper begins with a sentence that identifies the use of the rhetorical strategy that will be analyzed in that section. The writer then gives textual examples of the strategy in use and explains how the text and strategy affects the reader. In the conclusions of these papers, the writers briefly summarize the author's use of rhetorical strategies and make a claim about the resulting significance and persuasiveness of the author's point.

Points for Discussion

1. Identify the sentences in the introduction that summarize the author's main points, state the author's audience and purpose, and introduce the rhetorical strategies that the writer will analyze in the paper.

2. How do the writers of these papers signal the reader to let her or him know what the topic of discussion will be in the text that follows?

3. Notice the writers' use of evidence. How did the writers use evidence to support the points they are trying to make? Is the evidence credible? Why or why not?

4. In the conclusion of the papers, find the statements in which the writers analyze the significance or quality of the authors' arguments. Have the writers convinced you? Why or why not?

5. Identify the strengths of these papers. What are the writers doing well?

6. What suggestions might you give these writers for improving the papers?

7. Do a brief rhetorical analysis of the student models. What rhetorical strategies do the writers of the student papers incorporate into their rhetorical analyses? What effect does the use of these strategies have on you as a reader?

8. After analyzing the model papers, make an outline for your paper, or write yourself a memo in which you identify the points you will make in your paper. Identify the textual evidence you will use to make your points of analysis. Write a statement of significance that explains the degree to which you have been persuaded by the text. Use these as stepping stones in writing your first draft.

Rhetorical Analysis
of Allan Bloom's "Liberal Education" *(article titles in quotes/books either italicized or underlined)*

Allan Bloom's article "*Liberal Education*" is from his book <u>The Closing of the American Mind.</u> In this article Bloom strongly opinionates current liberal education to be of meager worth to college students *not a word* because programs do not emphasize the Great Books as indepthly as needed. According to Bloom these classic texts are essential for the educational process of a college student. In addressing this issue, his purpose is to convince individuals who share his opinion *One does not "convince" someone "into" doing something, but "to" do something* into making the Great Books prominent in liberal education. To achieve this purpose he incorporates the strategies of evidence, intensification and downplay, and passionate language.

By using evidence as a rhetorical strategy Bloom supports his claim that students are not being properly educated. The first type of evidence used by Bloom is an example of the liberal education program at Cornell University. He states that Cornell's primary objective "was to *these should be brackets* rush them (high school students) through to the start of their careers." *no italics* By doing this it effectively narrowed its liberal education program into a "sop given to desolate humanists in the form of money to fund seminars that these young careerists could take on their way through the College of Arts and Sciences." Bloom states that by doing this Cornell provided structure without content and failed to teach the students any valuable knowledge. Rather than encouraging insight and exploration Cornell "kept them busy enough to avoid thinking about the nothingness of their endeavor." By employing this example of administrators debilitating liberal education programs and injuring students potential for higher ✓ consciousness, Bloom engages the reader's emotions and insists that current programs must be changed.

In order to clarify his ideas to the reader Bloom uses analogies as his second form of evidence. In one analogy he compares liberal education and colleges to "the condition of churches as opposed to, say, hospitals." He states that although colleges and hospitals have a specific function "nobody is quite certain of what the religious institutions are supposed to do anymore." Because of this lack of definite purpose

2

churches have "the exploitation of quacks" and "the valiant efforts of persons of particular gravity." Bloom then compares the lack of purpose in churches to liberal education stating that "in liberal education, too, the worst and the best fight it out." By using this technique the reader can easily visualize Bloom's argument that without a specific function liberal education programs, like churches, are saturated with "fakers vs. authentics" and sophists vs. "philosophers," proving to the reader that a specific program involving the Great Books must be instigated.

good argument [margin note]

—um—this means "provoke" or "incite"—perhaps you mean implemented." [margin note]

Bloom utilizes anecdotes as his final evidence to provide a humorous atmosphere while maintaining the reader's interest and conveying a specific theme. In one anecdote Bloom writes about a student at the University of Chicago who "spoke in his paper of Mr. Aristotle, unaware that he was not a contemporary." While this seems preposterous to the reader familiar with Aristotle it shows that "only an American could have the naive profundity to take Aristotle as living thought." This shows the lack of experience of American students with the historically great minds that shaped their culture. Bloom insists that students have the desire and capacity to learn truth and passion from great men like Aristotle, but they haven't realized this because of their lack of a good liberal education.

Another rhetorical strategy Bloom uses in order to convince the reader that students are not receiving an adequate liberal education is intensification and downplay. He intensifies the necessity of the Great Books in a good education. This is evident when Bloom begins the article by emphasizing the necessary growth of a student undergoing a college education. He states that "in this short time he must learn that there is a great world beyond the little one he knows, experience the exhilaration of it and digest enough of it to sustain himself in the intellectual deserts he is destined to traverse." Bloom enhances the benefits of a college career as opposed to the negative aspects of normal life, giving education an important purpose and meaning. He then uses intensification to emphasize that through the Great Books a liberal education can give students this knowledge of the great world they have yet to discover. To further magnify the Great Books he not only states

3

that they are "the only serious solution" to current liberal education problems, but they also provide a base for student-to-student relationships. He describes the Great Books as "a fund of shared experiences and thoughts on which to ground their friendships with each other." This intensification magnifies Bloom's point that not only are the Great Books essential for a source of higher meaning, but also for student interactions.

Bloom then goes on to downplay any positive aspects of existing liberal education programs and their tenets in order to convince the reader of the necessity of a change. He conveys an incessant critical tone about current liberal education programs by describing them as being disorganized and having a "lack of vision." They hold "no official guidance, no university wide agreement about what he (*the student*) should study." To Bloom this results directly from the fact that university administrators don't give enough attention to liberal education programs. He describes professors as "specialists concerned only with their own fields," not as instructors trying to educate students. To Bloom even the attempts universities have made to modify their liberal education programs are futile. He portrays them as "various kinds of fancy packaging," stating that the universities are making a useless effort to teach what was already there. Bloom then cements his negativity towards current programs by taking another viewpoint describing how the students feel. Because of the lack of organization he states that the student finds a "bewildering variety of courses" creating confusion about what they should study. Bloom summarizes this by stating, "the net effect of the student's encounter with the college catalogue is bewilderment and very often demoralization." By using downplay as a strategy Bloom encourages the reader to perceive current liberal education as inept and nugatory.

Similar to the use of intensification Bloom utilizes passionate language as a rhetorical strategy in order to emotionally convey his feelings about liberal education to the reader. In order to emphasize his point Bloom will dramatize his opinions and use emotionally charged

4

words. In the first paragraph Bloom dramatizes a students opportunity to learn in the four years he spends at a university by stating "he must do this, that is, if he is to have any hope of a higher life." Conveying the attitude that receiving an adequate college education is the only opportunity individuals will ever have to improve their lives. Later in the article Bloom uses an example of dramatization when he depicts the problems with liberal education as "an intellectual crisis of the greatest magnitude, which constitutes the crisis of our civilization." This embellished account maintains that above all else the main crisis facing modern civilization is our existing liberal education. Although these statements are dramatic they force the reader to reconsider his opinion on the importance of liberal education.

this does not function as a complete sentence

In addition to dramatization, Bloom harshly depicts existing liberal education and its tenets to effectively convey the pathetic appeal. He uses emotionally charged words like "intellectual wasteland" and "dreary professional training" to describe existence outside of college. This makes the reader feel like the only stimulating aspect of life lies in a college education. He goes on to describe college professors as having a "strong element of specialist's jealousy and narrowness" towards the Great Books in order to enhance the readers emotions against current administrators. By using this technique of loaded language Bloom forces the reader to either accept or reject his point of view. Accomplishing Bloom's purpose of convincing those individuals who share his view into making the Great Books more prominent in Liberal Education.

this is another dependent clause

The use of irony is another way Bloom uses language as a tool to emphasize the necessity of a good liberal education. By stating the complete opposite of his intended purpose Bloom further emphasizes his main point. One example of this is that although Bloom insists that students need to spend less time specializing and more time in liberal education he states "better to give up on liberal education and get on with a specialty in which there is at least a prescribed curriculum and a prospective career." Because this is a direct contradiction of Bloom's

5

main point the reader understands the irony in Blooms statement and understands that it only promotes his argument. √

By incorporating the strategies of evidence, intensification and downplay, and passionate language Bloom successfully convinces the reader that colleges need to instigate a liberal education program emphasizing the Great Books. To do this he uses evidence in the form of examples, analogies, and anecdotes to support his claim that students are not being properly educated. He then goes on to intensify the potential of a good liberal education and downplay any positive aspects of current liberal education. In order to accomplish his purpose Bloom appeals to the reader's emotions by utilizing passionate language in the form of dramatization and irony. Overall, these strategies assert Bloom's thesis that the Great Books must be made a prominent involvement in liberal education.

good conclusion

wrong word

Michael—
You've constructed a very thorough & persuasive argument, with good use of textual evidence. The writing seems to strengthen as you go. Beware your tendency to make up words, as seen in the opening paragraph. Grammatically, the only consistent problems I can identify are:
1. Occasional use of dependent clauses as sentences—note the ones I've marked & look up why they cannot function independently—
2. Failure to include apostrophes to signify possessives. I've circled the places where these are missing.

Overall, well done—excellently constructed.

Rhetorical Analysis of Richard Rodriguez's
"The Achievement of Desire"

In his essay, "The Achievement of Desire," Richard Rodriguez narrates the course of his educational career. He begins by titling himself as a "scholarship boy," which he defines as being a student of meager resources, coming from a predominately uneducated family, who battles to break the bindings of mediocrity, and become an educated man. Rodriguez tells of the shame, and the internal struggle that the scholarship boy feels *towards* his uneducated parents. According to Rodriguez, the scholarship boy will inevitably diminish his relationships with his family, and will gradually forget his social, economic, and racial background, and will become a new educated individual. Using emotional appeal, Rodriguez proves his thesis by incorporating three rhetorical strategies: *lc* evidence, first person narrative, and comparison and contrast.

In an effort to establish the fact that he truly is a scholarship boy, Rodriguez presents various definitions and requirements of a scholarship boy, and contrasts himself relative to those definitions. He uses the expert testimony of Richard Hoggart, author of <u>The Uses of Literacy</u>, to establish a clear definition of a scholarship boy, which will be made evident throughout the paper. Rodriguez frequently refers back to Hoggart, to maintain credibility for various statements. For example, *g* Rodriquez makes the statement that: "The kind of allegiance the young ✓ student (scholarship boy) might have given his mother and father only days earlier, he transfers to the teacher, the new figure of authority." Following that sentence, Rodriguez quotes Hoggart saying, "The scholarship boy tends to make a father-figure out of his foremaster." By comparing a description of himself, to the expert testimony of Hoggart, Rodriguez is able to convince his reader that he is a scholarship boy.

Along with expert testimony, Rodriguez also uses personal examples and stories. In the following example, he relates a personal *e* experiance to show how he, a scholarship boy, had to withdraw from his family in order to become educated: "After dinner, I would rush to a bedroom with papers and books. As often as possible, I resisted parental pleas to 'save lights' by coming to the kitchen to work. I kept so much, so often, to myself. . . . I hoarded the pleasures of learning.

If you're going to use such a long quote, it needs to be set off & indented

2

Alone for hours . . . I rarely looked away from my books—or back on my memories. . . . Nights when relatives visited and the front rooms were warmed by Spanish sounds, I slipped quietly out of the house." With this excerpt, Rodriguez tells his reader that his yearning for knowledge, and his desire to become educated, inevitably forced him to withdraw from his family. Not only does he withdraw from his family, but he hints that he even withdraws from his ethnicity when he says: "Nights when relatives visited and the front rooms were warmed by Spanish sounds, I slipped quietly out of the house." Rodriguez uses these examples to first inform his reader about the behavior of a scholarship boy, and second, to prove that he is a scholarship boy.

With the fact that he is a scholarship boy already established, Rodriguez strategically uses his own voice in the first person narrative form to exploit the internal struggles, and to outline the expected course of the scholarship boy. Using his own voice, Rodriguez acts as his own expert witness, because the stories are his own personal experiences. One example in which Rodreguez uses his own voice to portray the internal struggle of the "scholarship boy" is as follows: "The enthusiasm I felt in second-grade classes I flaunted before both my parents. The docile, obedient student came home a shrill and precocious son who insisted on correcting and teaching his parents with the remark: 'My teacher told us. . . .' I intended to hurt my mother and father. I was still angry at them for having encouraged me toward classroom English. But gradually this anger was exhausted, replaced by guilt as school grew more and more attractive to me." Using first person narrative to relate this childhood experience, Rodriguez successfully illustrates the internal struggles that he, a scholarship boy, went through as he fulfilled his ever-increasing desire to obtain knowledge.

Rodriguez uses first person narrative to his advantage, when outlining the expected course of the scholarship boy. He says: ". . . he is enormously obedient to the dictates of the world of school, but emotionally still strongly wants to continue as part of the family circle."

3

Rodriguez then illustrates the huge attitudinal change that will eventually take place saying: ". . . I wanted to be like my teachers, to possess their knowledge, to assume their authority, their confidence, even to assume a teacher's persona . . ." Using these contrasting statements, Rodriguez shows how the scholarship boy begins his education with great respect and admiration for (him) family and parents. As he progresses in his education that respect is gradually transferred to his teachers, due to their profound influence upon him, the scholarship boy. With the aid of first person narrative, Rodriguez is able to make this crucial contrast, *good* which illustrates the emotional separation that took place between he and his family, and the new found respect that he had gained for his teachers.

The most prevalent and successful strategy Rodriguez uses is comparison and contrast. Rodriguez uses this strategy throughout his *good* essay, often in combination with other strategies. He compares and *point here* contrasts several subjects such as the scholarship boy and his parents, parents and school, and family and school. Rodriguez uses these comparisons to show how the scholarship boy will inevitably diminish his relationships with his parents and family as he pursues his educational goals. Early in his essay, Rodriguez compares the scholarship boy with his father, when he quotes Hoggart saying: ". . . or father says intermittently whatever comes into his head . . . ". Comparatively Rodriguez then says (speaking of the scholarship boy): "the boy must rehearse his thoughts and raise his hand before speaking out loud. . . .". *reverse* Rodriguez portrays the father to be a non-thinking, sporadic, disoriented, person, who says "whatever comes to his head." In contrast, Rodriguez portrays the scholarship boy as being well mannered, meditative, and patient. With these excerpts, Rodriguez shows his reader how the scholarship boy, and his father are very different. The boy is cultured and sophisticated, while the father is lacking in both areas. Rodriguez is illustrating the diminishing relationship between father and scholarship boy. Rodriguez also compares school, to the scholarship boys parents. He degrades the scholastic boys parents saying: "From his mother and father the boy

4

learns to trust spontaneity and non-rational ways of knowing. Then, at school, there is mental calm. Teachers emphasize the value of a reflectiveness that opens a space between thinking and immediate action." With this statement, Rodriguez continues to illustrate the diminishing relationships between scholarship boy and his parents.

Later on in the essay, Rodriguez makes an interesting comparison. He compares his parents (utilizing first person narrative) with his school teachers. He share the experience that people would often congratulate him saying ". . . your parents must be very proud of you. . . . " Exemplifying the struggle between the "scholarship boy" and his parents, he would shyly smile while thinking, "I was not proud of my mother and father. . . . Simply, what mattered to me was that they were not my teachers." This last statement epitomizes the phenomena that as he becomes more educated, the "scholarship boy" moves away from his parents and extends his admiration to his teachers, those who educated him.

add space

Writing in first person narrative, and in combination with emotional appeal, Richard Rodriguez uses evidence, and comparison and contrast to prove that the scholarship boy will inevitably diminish his relationship with his family, and will gradually forget his social, economic, and racial background, in his plight to become a new educated individual. Due to the scholarship boy's education, he will no longer relate with his predominately uneducated family, thus the bonds of their relationships will be forever broken. Rodriguez believes that this, however, is the price that must be made to break the mold of mediocrity, and to become a part of that elite educated society that the scholarship boy so painfully desires.

use a different phrase for variety

www—"quest"?

very nice conclusion

Greg

Your argument is excellent, and quotations are well selected & explained. You make some especially keen insights— Your proofreading seems to be going better, but I'm still circling spelling errors, omissions of apostrophes, etc. Go over your final draft a few times to catch these.

Good work—

REVIEW ASSIGNMENT

What Is a Review?

Perhaps you have read book, movie, travel, or restaurant reviews in your local newspaper or have seen them on TV. You may find that one of your professors asks you to use techniques similar to these types of reviews to review something that you have read, heard, seen, or participated in for one of your classes. A review is a critique that summarizes and evaluates a text, a film, a demonstration, a discussion, or, as you have probably concluded, any of a wide array of things and experiences. You may be asked by a professor to write a review as evidence of having read, understood, and evaluated the content of a text. But, as with summary, you might often incorporate the techniques of review as a starting point on your way to something else: to analyzing a writer's ideas, to using another writer's ideas (with proper acknowledgment) in building your own argument, or as the basis for evaluating the writer's ideas. Again, as with the summary, you can think of the writer's work and your own in a dialogical relationship: you present the writer's view objectively and then in some way respond to it.

Purpose of the Assignment

For this assignment, you may consider reviewing a selection you have read in *Conversations*. You begin a review much as you would a summary by explaining the writer's main points to your reader. A review differs from a summary in that it assesses the value of the selection under review on the basis of explicitly stated criteria. Some writers choose to summarize first and evaluate later. Other writers choose to weave evaluative remarks throughout their review.

CHECKLIST FOR WRITING A REVIEW

A good review of a written selection will incorporate the following:

- Name of the author, title of the piece, publisher, and date of publication and main point of the selection either in the first sentence of the review or close to it.
- Paraphrases of the major subpoints or major turns in the author's argument.
- Identification of the criteria used to judge the value of the content.
- Evaluation based on the stated criteria.
- Transitions that clearly articulate the relationships among the paper's ideas.
- A conclusion that reiterates the reviewer's major points about the piece under review.
- Matters of mechanical correctness that conform to standard edited American English.

PEER RESPONSE QUESTIONS FOR REVIEW ASSIGNMENT

Name of Student Writer _____

Name of Student Responder _____

1. Does the introductory paragraph include the name of the author, title, publisher, and date of publication of the piece under review?

2. Does the first paragraph give a sense of the purpose and central idea of the piece under review?

3. Does the first paragraph foreshadow the student writer's judgment of the piece?

4. In the body of the review, does the student writer provide enough summary information about the piece under review so that you can judge whether you would agree or disagree with the student writer's evaluation?

5. In the body of the review, does the student writer identify the criteria upon which he or she is basing the evaluation of the piece?

6. Are the student writer's judgments based on the stated criteria?

7. Does the student writer use transitions effectively to clarify the relations between the summary information, criteria for evaluation, and the student writer's judgments?

8. Does the conclusion reiterate the student writer's major points about the piece under review?

9. Does the writing generally conform to the standards of correctness of edited American English?

STUDENT MODELS OF REVIEW ASSIGNMENT

These student essays do not review an article from *Conversations,* but instead review a supplementary text. The first reviewer weaves her evaluation of the book throughout the review, whereas the second reviewer summarizes the main points of the book and then evaluates it. In both cases, the reviewers evaluate the book on the basis of their own experience and on the credibility of their methods for determining their findings. They review the authors' points within the framework of explicitly stated criteria for evaluation.

Points for Discussion

1. The first paragraph of these reviews look much like the first paragraphs of a summary. Identify the evaluative remarks that the writer incorporates into the review and explain why you would not find that type of statement in a summary.

2. The writers of the reviews do more than say that they "like" or "don't like" what the authors have to say, although they both indicate their judgment of the authors' points. What strategies do the writers use to indicate the criteria on which they are basing their evaluation of the authors' claims?

3. Do the writers give you enough information so that you can also pass evaluative judgment? Are you inclined to agree or disagree with the reviewers' evaluations? What additional information might you need before you could pass judgment?

4. Have the writers given you enough information from which to determine whether you might or might not want to read the book for yourself? What strategies did the writers rely upon to accomplish this?

5. If you are asked to write a review, you will first need to summarize the main points of the "text" you are asked to review. You might try the paraphrasing strategy suggested for writing a summary; however, you would also want to make evaluative remarks or ask questions of the author or performer/performance as you read and write. You will need to know the criteria on which you should base your judgment. Are you to judge the credibility of the evidence given in support of a particular point or are you to judge the humorous nature of the "text" or are you to judge the quality of engagement you experience or something else altogether? Once you know how you are supposed to evaluate, you can go ahead and begin to summarize and evaluate in order to write a review. Write a draft in which you summarize first and then add your evaluation. After you have read your first draft to a group of your peers, rewrite the draft weaving your evaluation throughout the text. Compare different reviews written by others. Which do you prefer? Why?

Review of Dorothy C. Holland and
Margaret A. Eisenhart's <u>Educated in Romance</u>

In their book, <u>Educated in Romance,</u> Dorothy C. Holland and
Margaret A. Eisenhart describe the educational and social systems
encountered by various groups of black and white women who were
attending one of two universities in the "American South," and how these
systems effected their goals of professionalism in the future. They kept
track of romantic situations, grades, their growth as learners and workers,
and everyday happenings. Although I found the book quite interesting, and
almost frightening, the parts I couldn't relate to I didn't really agree with.

excellent

The events that these women analyzed ranged form small,
everyday last minute choices, to personal relationships and intimate
feelings. They compare how the experiences differ from schools in the
United States, Britain, and Australia. Romance and attractiveness begin
to be seen on a cultural level, where some cultures raise people to
believe that romance is a critical part in being a women, while others
put less stress on it. The results were disheartening because "for a
majority of women, their developing interpretations of schoolwork,
together with their unrewarding and disappointing academic experiences
and the availability—not to mention the pressure—of the peer culture,
led to a marginalization of or a failure to develop their ideas of
themselves as having careers in the future." These women all started
out with a determination to be independent economically, and
throughout the book, the various factors tear away at their determination
until it is finally gone, and they turn to romance to fill the empty spot. I
found this very interesting, but I also found it to be annoying. This
analysis was done on a handful of women, and I find it hard to believe
that a majority of women are like this. I can't relate to these women
because I would never give up my future for someone else, because if I
couldn't be independent, I wouldn't be in control of myself.

In the end, the discontents the women voiced were generally with
men, instead of the university. They had a constant wondering of what
they might have seen, given their original goals, and now having a less
than acceptable outcome. Again, this book was fulfilling to read, but only
had a few women to support their ideas, which made it less credible.

Review of <u>Educated in Romance</u>

In 1990 Dorothy C. Holland and Margret A. Eisenhart published the book <u>Educated in Romance: Women, Achievement, and College Culture.</u> The book contains results of their ethnographic study that followed the lives of twenty-three women attending two southern universities and reveals startling evidence about young women and the pressure from their peer cultures to become involved in romantic relationships. Through personal interviews and observations of the selected women, academic strategies, college experiences, personal and group priorities and values, and responses to the systems of male privilege, were revealed and then related to critical educational and feminist issues.

The original purpose of the study was to find out how women chose and formed a commitment to a major and a future career with the hopes of uncovering why so few American college women were going into the high-paying traditionally male-dominated fields of math and science. The results of the study were so powerful that they disclosed a focus of many young women on romance and male relationships as well as their paths into traditional female positions in society.

Holland and Eisenhart's ethnographic, or cultural, study was conducted in the 1980's and followed the paths of twenty-three women attending Bradford University and Southern University. Their study plan, methods, results and evidence are substantial and credible. Yet despite this fact, I feel that their results are limited and outdated due to the changes in modern society.

Holland and Eisenhart's study purpose, design, and method are all clearly outlined and defined in the text. There is no ambiguity about what the study procedure entailed or how the results were obtained. Since a large portion of their study involved interviews, numerous quotes were incorporated throughout the text to cite specific examples and thus provide concrete support for their reasoning. For example, this quote was included to illustrate the women's created connection between physical attractiveness and prestige, "I am going to lose weight and [grow] out my hair so that I will be all beautiful this summer . . . When we did anything with the guys, we always asked them, 'what do you like in girls?' " Holland and Eisenhart also strengthen the credibility

2

of their study by citing other researchers that have produced similar results to theirs. For instance:

> Like Fordham and Ogbe's black students in an urban high school (1986), who responded variously to the student culture, the women in our study variously accepted pieces or parts of the prevailing peer culture and tried to live out the scripts as best they could.

This reference to other study results that correspond with theirs help to make the results of their study more reliable and credible and thus more convincing.

Despite their solid study design and credible results, a flaw that can be found in their study is that it is limited to the time period in which it was conducted and is presently outdated. This study was done about 15 years ago and although the results are startling and interesting, they do not correspond with what is occurring in society today. As a female *I don't think so* college student, typical of the subjects that were used for Holland's and Eisenhart's study, my priorities, believes, values, and focus do not correspond remotely with that of their subjects. For example, unlike their subjects, my prestige or that of other peers does not evolve from physical attractiveness, and I feel that in contrast to their findings, college women of the 1990's are not focused on men and romantic relationships but rather academic achievement and the pursuit of a career. This fact could be connected with the high tuition of present day institutions of higher education. The tuition of the two colleges where their study was conducted was not disclosed but, I feel that most women who are presently paying $20,000 to $25,000 per year would not be interested in majoring in "men" like the women of their study. Thus although their results may be accurate of the 1980's I feel that their value is limited in today's society due to the significant changes that have taken place.

Holland's and Eisenhart's book Educated in Romance: Women, Achievement, and College Culture is based on a credible and comprehensible study with strong evidence and believable results. However despite this fact, I feel that it is outdated and the attitudes and values of the women in their study are extremely uncharacteristic of most young women enrolled in institutions of higher education today.

SYNTHESIS ASSIGNMENT

What Is a Synthesis?

Synthesis is perhaps one of the more common techniques that you can expect to use in college writing. Professors often assign this type of paper so that you can demonstrate your understanding of multiple perspectives on a given issue as well as its context. Synthesis requires that you begin to make connections among ideas, texts, theories, activities, to name just a few of the possible range of options. A synthesis depends on a thoughtful and compelling thesis and entails selectively combining information from several sources into a coherent discussion. Synthesis makes use of both the summarizing and analytical techniques, which you practiced in the Summary and Rhetorical Analysis assignments.

For example, you might be asked in your Harlem Renaissance poetry class to synthesize the poets' use of rhyme and meter in three poems to determine effect on poetic tone and meaning. Or you may be asked in your Environmental Ecology class to synthesize the methodological decisions made by three groups of environmental researchers in three similar studies of toxic waste contamination at landfill sites to make recommendations for future investigations. To complete either of these assignments, you would first need to summarize the main points and then analyze the required components (e.g., rhyme and meter for effect; methodological decisions for future investigations) before you could synthesize, or make connections, among the components.

Purpose of the Assignment

To practice the skills of written synthesis, this assignment asks you to begin to make connections between texts and examine ways in which various texts participate in ongoing academic discussions. You will be identifying, analyzing and then explaining how you surmise that two or more authors in *Conversations* are "talking" to each other about a similar theme or topic. In other words, you will first need to consider what the authors are saying to each other, and second, how your views come to terms with the conversation. Then you will write a paper that connects these perspectives around a meaningful thesis.

This essay differs from the rhetorical analysis assignment in several respects. Your role in the rhetorical analysis was primarily that of a critical reader. The present assignment requires you to interact with the texts at a different level. Your role in the synthesis essay is to participate critically in the discussion. You are not expected to be as knowledgeable or conversant as the writers you select, but you can contribute by exploring their respective approaches. It may be helpful to think of your role as that of a discussant, and your paper as a conversation about the topic you will choose to address.

How Do I Get Started?

As you plan your synthesis paper, keep in mind classroom discussions on relationships among the various readings you will be using as sources.

When thinking about a topic, consider the following questions:

- What similarities, differences, and/or connections do you see among these writers' audiences, subject matter, points of view, and purposes?
- What main point is each writer trying to make?
- What other issues or topics of debate concern the writers?
- What general ideology or philosophical base, understanding, worldview, or metaphysical commitment grounds the position of each writer?

Select one issue of particular interest to you and think about how various writers engage it. You will need to begin by going through each selection that you will use and marking all the references to your theme. Then you can think about the relationships among those references.

Usually, you will have to infer the relationships, though sometimes you will find that writers explicitly address each other. Your goal is not only to analyze relationships among ideas but to contribute some insights of your own to the discussion.

The following categories should help you understand how the different authorial positions you're dealing with relate to each other.

Similar Opinions: Two writers' agreement with each other's opinions, each one validating what the other said.

Contrasting Opinions: Sometimes writers flat out disagree with each other on a particular point, or one writer illuminates problems with the other writer's view.

Expansion: One writer might elaborate the ideas of another in a variety of ways. For example, one writer might provide additional examples of something that another said; or one writer might agree with another, yet extend the discussion in a slightly different direction; or one might fill in gaps that another neglected to address.

Causal Connections: Sometimes one writer will name causes of a phenomenon mentioned by another or further develop potential (or real) consequences of another writer's position.

In all of these possible relationships, the point is first to recognize when authors are talking about approximately the same topic and then to examine the nuances in the ways they address it.

How Might I Organize the Synthesis Paper?

Your instructor may give you specific instructions regarding page length and number of articles and/or authors you will need to include in your paper. After you have closely reviewed what your chosen readings said about your topic, you will probably want to begin by writing a tentative introduction in terms of the significant thematic issue you have chosen. In the introduction, you will need to contextualize your topic in the larger discussion in which it participates and to state your own thesis.

Once you have come up with a tentative thesis, you may begin to outline subpoints that explain the relationships you have found among the ways various authors treat your topic. Remember as you develop your working notes or outline into full paragraphs that every time you interpret something an author said, you need to support your interpretation with quotations from the author's own words. In this way, your paragraphs will develop with your own interpretations supported by the author's words. This becomes the body of your paper. You should organize these paragraphs so that each subsequent idea builds on what you have said previously.

By the time you get to your conclusion, you should have demonstrated why your thesis claimed what it did. In your conclusion then, you can emphasize the strongest points you have made throughout your paper in support of your own thesis. In this way, you are becoming a participant in a written conversation with the authors whose ideas you are considering.

Recommended Readings

Authors in the following groups share concern about the same or similar issues, though they may take very different positions on them. It's important to remember that categorizing writers according to their shared concerns is not the same as grouping them on the basis of agreement. They may share the same concerns but disagree on how to deal with them.

These groupings are merely suggestions. Because the textbook is organized to exemplify the conversational character of writing, nearly any grouping would evoke productive discussions. However, here are some combinations grouped to elicit provocative discussions when the views of the authors are examined and compared:

Bloom, Rose and hooks

Bloom, hooks, and Pratt

Rodriguez, hooks and Pratt

Klemke et al., Magee, and Wade

Wade, Addelson, Tompkins

Magee, Addelson, and Fish

Addelson, Fish, and Burke

Pratt, Tompkins and Fish

Klemke et al., Appleby et al., and Tompkins

Magee, Keller, and Fish

Magee, Fish, and Burke

Shiebinger, Keller, and Klemke

Pratt, Shiebinger and Tompkins

Pratt, Bartholomae, and Haas

Appleby et al., Haas, and Bartholomae

Pratt, Haas, and hooks

Corder, Burke and Salvatori

PEER RESPONSE QUESTIONS FOR
SYNTHESIS ASSIGNMENT

Name of Student Writer _____

Name of Student Responder _____

1. Is there enough background information in the introduction to give the reader a context for understanding the theme or topic of the paper? Does the writer have a clear thesis statement in the introduction? Underline the thesis statement. If you are unsure about the thesis, write what you think it should be.

2. Can you identify the subpoints the writer makes to explain the relationships among the author's ideas? If not, what has he or she omitted that should be included or explained? If there is information included that seems peripheral to the writer's points, explain why you think the writer should omit that information.

3. Does the writer provide adequate evidence to support the points he or she is trying to make? Are you persuaded by the writer's points? If not, what does the writer need to do to persuade you?

4. Is the paper organized so that one point builds on another? Is there logical flow from one idea to the next? Has the writer used transitions that help the reader to see the connections and relationships the writer is making among his or her points? If not, what is missing and how might the writer create a coherent paper?

5. Does the writer's conclusion reflect the points the writer has been making throughout the paper? Does the writer explain the significance of the conclusion? If not, what could the writer do to create a logical and persuasive conclusion?

STUDENT MODELS OF SYNTHESIS ASSIGNMENT

Each of the writers of these papers introduce the theme they will address with a personal anecdote, or brief narration of a pertinent personal experience that illustrates the point they will be making in their paper. Other possible strategies for introducing a theme are summarizing background information relevant to the topic; relaying a current event that has relevance to the topic at issue; asking a question that the reader will seek to answer as she or he reads the paper; or giving an historical account that illustrates the point. Whatever strategy a writer selects, the purpose of the opening paragraphs in a synthesis is to introduce the reader to the topic the paper will address and to explain the thesis of the paper to the reader.

The points and subpoints of the paper develop in support of the thesis claim made in the introduction. The writer of the first paper argues that "studying the same ideas one way will prove to be an impediment on our quest for knowledge." The writer of the second paper argues that "Reality constantly changes, because truth varies depending on the perspective of the individual." The body of the papers are organized around the subpoints the writers make in support of their thesis. They use evidence from their reading to illustrate their claims. Each writer demonstrates the relationships and connections among the points of their thesis by summarizing and analyzing the textual points made by the authors they have read. The focus of the paper is the relationships and connections between these points themselves, and not the points made by other authors. The work of others is used to bolster the points the student writers are making in their papers. Both writers use examples from three or four other writers. In their conclusions, the writers focus on reexamining the significance of their thesis claim. They wrap things up by returning to the anecdotal information they gave in the introduction.

The writers are able to enter into the conversation of others, who presumably have more authority and privilege to speak on these issues than the students themselves, by finding ways to connect personally to the theme or topic they will address. In this manner, they find something unique and interesting to add to the ongoing conversation. You can do this by making your own connections with the questions at issue in the readings you have completed in class.

Points for Discussion

1. Identify the thesis sentence and the writer's subpoints made in support of the thesis. How does the writer introduce each of the subpoints and tie them together? What transitional strategies does the writer use? What signals of ordination and correlation of points does the writer make for the reader?

2. Notice the ways in which the writer incorporates evidence into the paper. Where do the examples from the readings appear in the sections of the paper? In the paragraphs? What effect does this organization have in persuading the reader of the validity of the points the writer makes?

3. What rhetorical strategies does the writer use to illustrate her or his analysis of the textual examples? How does the use of these strategies help the reader to understand and to be persuaded either for or against the writer's points?

4. Notice the organization of the conclusion. How does the writer summarize the points and bring the reader to contemplate the significance and persuasiveness of the topic at issue in the paper? Are you convinced by the writer's synthesis? Why or why not?

5. Underline the sentence in each paragraph that you think is the topic sentence of the paragraph. Read those sentences aloud with a partner. Do the points seem to follow logically from one to the next? What does the writer do to make the paper flow logically? What might the writer do better to improve the logical flow or coherence of the paper?

6. Notice the writer's word choice, or diction. How would you characterize the writer's choice of words? In what ways do you think the writer has written a text that fits and/or fails to fit your "commonplace" assumptions about academic discourse?

7. Write some questions that intrigue you as a result of the readings you have completed for the synthesis paper. Think about how you might take a position of interest to you if you were to respond to those questions in your synthesis paper. Write a possible thesis sentence for your paper and a potential introduction. Read it to a group of your peers. What is their response? What authors are addressing this issue? What points have they made that support or refute your position? Mark some possible places in the text that could provide you with evidence to support or refute your point. Think about how to incorporate these sources into your paper. Write an outline or semantic map to guide the writing of your first draft.

Synthesis

In early August of 1995, two months after high school graduation and after the University sent me a course catalog along with its class schedule, I was left to ponder on my first collegiate decision—what classes should I take for my first term in college? What I wanted from my college experience was a liberal education that provokes thought and would make me a better, more capable, and intellectual person. After taking everything into consideration including the fact that I wanted to start my college career with good grades, one of the classes I chose was "Introduction to the Philosophy of Religion."

Well, to my dismay, Philosophy of Religion was not an easy course. In fact, it was my hardest course and was particularly difficult. What made it difficult was the context. Back in Hawaii where I received all of my of my schooling, not much emphasis in english was on the Great Books and their authors. As a result, I was very underprepared and at a disadvantage to everyone else in my class where they did have previous experiences with the Canon. I can recall on the second day of lecture the professor asked who in the class has not heard of Descartes or some other name and I was the only one that raised my hand. True, it is possible that I was not the only ignorant student but only had the most courage to admit I was unacquainted with the subject, but that is insignificant. What is important is the fact that I had no previous knowledge of the Canon. Which leads to a bigger question concerning the liberal education in college. Many educators have debated over whether or not administrators in college are taking liberal education down the wrong path. Their claim is that it is time to move away from diversity and return to the basics, or in this case the study of the Great Books.

After a quarter of Philosophy where all of the reading were by such authors as Kant, Aquinas, and Descartes, I am puzzled by what a return to the Great Books would do since I don't believe I benefited much from that class. Sure, I learned a few names and a few important theological arguments but what Allan Bloom and other apologist of the Great Books method believed that students like I would go through a intellectual enlightenment has not materialized. The returning to the

2

Great Books would be reverting back to the ways of the white old boys club thereby excluding many students including females, minorities, and the poor. In the end, studying the same ideas one way will prove to be ✓✓ an impediment on our quest for knowledge.

   With no legitimate liberal education, students grow up with only a single-minded point of view. In his essay article "Liberal Education," Allan Bloom sees the culprit as specialization. This problem of specialization is students enter college ready to pursue their intended major without taking time to learn how to think (Bloom 32). Specialization trains people to think in one particular way resulting in a one-tracked mind. Bloom believes this leads to unenlightenment and his solution is the Great Books method which involves reading books Bloom and others alike would deem necessary for life. Bloom contradicts ✓✓ himself in his essay when he fails to understand his reading of the Great Books is similar to going the specialization route. Like specialization, reading primarily the Great Books leads to the closing of the mind as we deprive ourselves from new ideas while studying only old ones.

   In studying the Great Books, the message presented to students ✓✓ is that all other cultures are worthless and studying other works would be irrelevant. Revolutionary thinker Mike Rose in his essay "The Politics of Remediation" illustrates with describing one of the problems he sees in education—what people would consider being educated. Rose presents a case where a student is able to speak multiple languages but considered incapable and uneducated (Rose 18). There are students coming from two cultures are considered culturally illiterate (Rose 18). The problem Rose sees with studying the Great Books is its "linguistic exclusion" (Rose 22). It excludes people from different backgrounds. There are many students with different background and cultures that haven't had much exposure to the Great Books. Rose sees the studying multiculturalism is important as we try to diversify our education. Students not sharing similar backgrounds and from different cultures are taught there is only one way to think and only one set of ideas that ✓✓ should be absolutely right and unimpeachable. What professors fail to

3

realize is this is what prevents us from obtaining new found knowledge. Teaching students to think in one robotic, mechanical way oppresses new ideas. When we are forced to think in one particular fashion, the final product is the same ideas learned and we remain in a phase of unenlightenment.

The difference between Rose and Bloom is Bloom believes we must revert to the studies of the Great Books. The Canon, Bloom believes, is key to enlightenment. "Wherever the Great Books make up a central part of the curriculum, the students are excited and satisfied, feel they are doing something that is independent and fulfilling, getting something from the university they cannot get elsewhere" (Bloom 35). The Great Books help the students gain a respect for studying and the gaining of knowledge. Bloom contends that this will open the minds of the students, encouraging them to learn new ideas.

Rose, on the other hand, would believe the Great Books is exactly what causes unenlightenment. The studying of the Great Books closes our minds to new ideas. It excludes a new way of thinking shutting down another way to obtain knowledge. Our insistence on holding old ideas as the absolute truths insures that new knowledge, regardless if ~~they~~ holds any validity or not, go undiscussed, unmentioned resulting in another venue of thinking shut down. This could insure the potential knowledge we were about to obtain is delayed or even squandered at the uncompromising views of tradition. We are no longer in a world of independent cultures. Globally, different people are linked and dependent on each other. In our changing world, we must change and adapt or be left behind. The ideals of the Great Books no longer has any *I'd quarrel with this—no relevance at all* pertinence to our world. Anthony Platt in his essay "Beyond the Canon, With Great Difficulty" is relieved to see that "once again, the university is at the center of ideological controversy" (Platt 23). This is where change should start. We must determine whether or not we are taught in a way that is designed to make us think and see things in one particular way that is not necessarily correct and discourages new ways of thinking as it oppresses challenging viewpoints instead of encouraging new ideas.

4

Another way we impede on our quest for new knowledge is to do things the old-fashioned, never-to-be-impeached ways of yesteryears. The article entitled "A World of Difference" by Evelyn Keller is a biography about Barbara McClintock who Keller describes as a "maverick and a visionary" (Keller 97). These accolades were prompted by McClintock, in her approach to the study of genetics, who would not study the old-fashion *fashioned* way. The traditional method requires scientist, to formulate a hypothesis and research ways to validate their predictions while labeling conflicting evidence as aberrations and exceptions to <u>their</u> rule. McClintock's method would warrant nature to dictate the results and would try to discover the reasons for the so-called aberrations and exceptions. "The focus on classes and numbers, McClintock believes, encourages researchers to overlook difference" (Keller 100). Scientists, in the opinion of McClintock, in the process miss "what is going on" (Keller 100). The accepted practice of labeling things "aberrations" and "exceptions" has impeded on our knowledge-making by not permitting other point of view of science like how McClintock approaches research. Like Rose, Keller would believe the potential knowledge we would obtain from McClintock is delayed due to fact that McClintock's research did not follow the traditional scientific method.

Keller and Bloom both agree that having certain expectations before an event closes minds. Keller believes hypothesizing will shut our minds to what is present because we only look for things validating our claims. Bloom would believe that students coming into college with *good connections* career expectations and goals in mind are excluded from a liberal education that helps students treasure education. Bloom believes <u>than</u> *that* within these students, learning is secondary to the primary concern of prerequisites for majors that restricts students form expanding their horizons and the mind of these students result in "intellectual wastelands" because they are not intellectually enlightened.

On the other hand, Keller and Bloom would disagree with the solution to combat unenlightenment. The Great Books is to Bloom as DNA is <u>not</u> to Keller. There are differences between the argument Keller

5

and Bloom present$ to readers about traditional views. Bloom view⌣ the "only serious solution" to liberal education (is̄) the Great Books method which restricts students from reading writings from authors that Bloom and other educators like him would see as liberal and outrageous. This prevents students from learning new ideas and even learning outdated ideas. Keller uses the example of DNA, a concept most of science would hold high and mighty, to prove why we shouldn't be restricted from reading literature outside of the norm. DNA, Keller views, claims too much. DNA does not apply to everything: DNA concludes more information than it is able to prove. The problem with the relationship between scientists and the concept of DNA is scientists refuse to accept the ~~flaws~~ *limitation* of DNA. There has been evidence able to set a cloud of doubt over the idea of DNA. The problem Keller sees is despite the contradicting information discovered able to dismiss DNA, science has been unwilling to dismiss it as false.

Reading the works of these authors enables to see a correlation √ √ between the Great Books and the refusal to allow any data researched outside the traditional method of research developed probably by white men. Rose sees the studying of the Great Books as closing our minds to new ideas while only studying old ones. Keller believes researchers like McClintock would be scoffed at because their methods are radical. The data they produce from their research are almost refused because most scientists are insistent that there should only be one absolute, faultless, unblemished way of doing things. Should we dismiss McClintock's work as worthless even as it holds validity and truth just because it did not follow traditional techniques?

We have just seen why a complete return to the Great Books and doing things in only one way would have negative consequences. It closes our minds to new ideas and deprives us from knowledge we would have obtained had we been accepting to a new approach. Also, even as it is proven to have flaws we are unwilling to dismiss their ideas in search for new ones. The return to the basics is not a definite solution to our problem. There is no clear cut solution to

6

unenlightenment but what is necessary is we must keep on learning, keep our minds open to new ideas.

This quarter, I took chemistry and trigonometry. Again, I felt like I was being subjected to just learning old ideas and not doing anything worthwhile. Bloom is right. Students like me are more preoccupied with prerequisites to our majors than taking time to learn and be educated. *nice concl.* But studying the Great Books and their authors have not proven to me to be anything enlightening. What the university needs is a vague sense of requirements that would be a guideline to help students gain an appreciation for learning the classics as well as the contemporary. As we open our minds, only then will we be enlightened.

—*excellent connections between diff. authors ideas*
-*good transitions*
-*good use of own voice*

7

Work Cited

Bloom, Allan. "Liberal Education." <u>Contact Zone.</u> USA: Harcourt Brace &
    Company, 1995.

Keller, Evelyn Fox. "A World of Difference." <u>Contact Zone.</u> USA: Harcourt
    Brace & Company, 1995.

Pratt, Mary Louise. "Arts of the Contact Zone." <u>Contact Zone.</u> USA:
    Harcourt Brace & Company, 1995.

Rose, Mike. "The Politics of Remediation." <u>Contact Zone.</u> USA: Harcourt
    Brace & Company, 1995.

The Changing of Reality

Synthesis

"What! Thomas Jefferson owned slaves!" My seventh grade history class thought our teacher was crazy. To us Thomas Jefferson was one of the greatest men in our country's history. He helped write the Declaration of Independence. Every student in my classroom knew that the Declaration of Independence stated, "We hold these truths to be self evident, that all men are created equal, that they are endowed by their creator with certain unalienable rights." How could Jefferson own slaves while writing this document?

↑
*very
effective
intro*
↓

With our youthful lack of experience we couldn't understand the stark contradiction between Jefferson's writings and actions. This quandary began a series of observations that made us realize how impressions influence beliefs. Jefferson believed it when he wrote that "all men are created equal" but more practically, he meant "all [white, land-owning, Anglo-Saxon, over twenty-one year old] men are created equal." The fact that this didn't include American-Indians, women, Bond-Servants, and Afro-Americans allowed the freedom of owning slaves, and (in the other cases) discrimination and exploitation within the bounds of the Declaration of Independence. This may have been true in 1787 when Jefferson shared the prevailing view of most Americans, *but* the phrase "all men are created equal" has an entirely different application today. While my classmates assumed that all great Americans think as they do, the truth is that each interpretation forms its own reality in each era. Neither our interpretation of the Declaration of Independence nor Thomas Jefferson's is more accurate. Reality constantly changes, because truth varies depending on the perspective of the individual.

Where do we develop our perspective of reality? A commonly accepted answer to this question lies in the development of "the scientific method." A clear understanding of scientific method is necessary because it shows how scientific laws are developed. Bryan Magee explains this method in his article "Scientific Method—The Traditional View and Popper's View." He divides the procedure of scientific method into four parts. The first part is that "The scientist begins by carrying out experiments whose aim is to make carefully

2

controlled and meticulously measured observations at some point on the frontier between our knowledge and our ignorance"(73). Secondly, after these observations are carefully recorded the scientist will then share his information with other scientists in his field. Magee then describes the third step in the process, "As this grows, general features begin to emerge, and individuals start to formulate general hypotheses—statements of a law like character which fit all the known facts and explain how they are casually related to each other"(73). Last of all, the individual scientist will gather supporting evidence in an effort to verify his hypothesis. If this last step works, according to the scientific method the scientist has confirmed his discovery of another scientific law.

Magee's procedure is regularly followed by scientists, and directly informs our reality. It enables us to develop technology, like how to build faster cars and modern medicine, but does the scientific method give us truth? How do we know with certainty the next time we go to drive our car that it will even start, or that when we get our blood pressure checked that it will be accurate? Just because a car has started every morning for the past ten years doesn't prove that it will start tomorrow, or the fact that a blood pressure machine has been accurate your entire life doesn't prove that it won't make a mistake the next time you use it.

According to Magee, "the fact that the laws of physics have been found to hold good in the past does not logically entail that they will continue to hold good in the future"(pg. 74). Scientific method is based on extremely predictable observations but those observations are not constant; they can and often do change. While the atom was considered the smallest particle forty years ago, it is now known that atoms are composed of even smaller particles called quarks, and even the quark is currently believed to consist of smaller constituents. With the development of the atomic bomb, it was clear that the atom affected every human being. Imagine if scientists equally understood the quark; what life altering discoveries lurk there. As science changes so does our

3

reality. If scientists determined that chalk causes skin cancer, how many teachers would continue to use the chalkboard?

While changes in scientific discovery affect our reality, so do prevailing cultural views. Emphasis on cultural context is demonstrated in the manner in which we interpret events and activities. Jane Tompkins illustrates this in her article, "'Indians': Textualism, Morality, And The Problem Of History." While teaching a history class she sought information on the background of American Indians in New England. She researched several books written by prominent historians, about New England. She found that the more books she researched, the more they differed, and sometimes they directly contradicted each other. Although the historians utilized essentially the same facts, their interpretation of those facts varied largely depending on the time in which they wrote their account.

To portray the influence of cultural context among historians, Tompkins referenced three accounts of early New England written by historians over three decades. The first account, authored in 1956, failed to make any mention at all about the indigenous population. Tompkins quotes this author describing New England as a "vacant wilderness"(128).

The second author wrote in the 1960s. In his account, he mentions Native Indians, but in a negative light, and blames them for conflicts with European settlers. In one instance, according to Tompkins, the author describes the Indians as "divided, self-satisfied, undisciplined, and static"(130).

The final account was written in 1975. Here the author interprets New England history in a manner contradictory from the first two accounts. He does this by including the Indians and instead of blaming them for any problems that occurred, describes them as intelligent and civilized. In fact, the third author portrays the Indians as being free of any of the stereotypical misconceptions, and he blames the European settlers for the problems which occurred between the two cultures.

4

√   Because of the era in which these historians wrote their accounts, their reality varied greatly. In the 1950s little or no attention was given to American Indians. Tompkins reasons that the first author knew of Native Americans, but failed to recognize them. The author simply felt that Indians were not important for his historical account.

This reality is reinterpreted by the second author who, according to Tompkins, wrote just before "the events of the sixties had sensitized scholars to questions of race and ethnicity"(130). Because of the prevailing views when the second account was written, the author saw Indians as inferior and described them negatively, blaming them for problems which occurred with European settlers.

Lastly, in the late sixties the study of European-Indian relations changed drastically and revolutionized prevailing views of Indian culture. Accordingly, the third account emphasizes an understanding of the Indian's actions and portrays them in a positive, humane light. Although each historian likely had access to the same facts, their views directly mirrored the prevailing reality of their time. thus proving that the prevailing reality of the time in which we live affects our interpretation and explanation of events.

Like cultural context, the interpretative strategies we use likewise effects our perspective and interpretation of events. Scientists and historians assume complete separation between their interpretations and the events being interpreted. The interpretative strategies they set ok in motion greatly determine which events they interpret. Stanley Fish illustrates this concept in his article, "How To Recognize A Poem When You See One." Fish, a professor of English at the State University of New York, illustrates this by conducting an experiment in his interpretive poetry class. One day he outlined five author's names used as an assignment for another class, and told his students that they were a seventeenth-century poem. He then asked his class to interpret the five word poem. Although the names were not written as a poem, the students gave it the attention of one, and discerned all the characteristics apparent as if it had been a genuine poem. This occurred

5

because when the students believed that the assignment they saw on the board was a poem, it became one.

The example presented by Fish indicates that the type of attention we given an object directly determines how we interpret it. The students in his poetry class had been taught how to interpret a poem and when they were told it was a poem they interpreted it as one. On the other hand, if they had been told it was an assignment, they viewed *would have* it as an assignment.   *subjective mood*

Fish asserts that every individual has been taught a pre-set format on how to view certain facts, and based on our previous experience we determine that they have a specific meaning. This is illustrated by Fish when he was teaching a lesson and one of his students vigorously raised their hand. Before addressing the student Fish asked his class what this student was doing. As anyone familiar with education would expect, the class replied that he was "seeking permission to speak"(146). As Fish expected, the reason the class assumed the student was raising his hand to ask a question was because they had a pre-conceived notion of the meaning of the action. In fact, they had become so accustomed to this action that they couldn't think of any other reason for a student to raise his hand. The students asked Fish, "what else could he be thought of doing"(146)? They assumed the reason was obvious. However, suppose that someone without any previous knowledge had seen the same event. What would this individual think the raised hand meant? They might assume the *He* student was pointing at the ceiling, or doing stretching exercises, or maybe even swatting at a fly. The individual's interpretation could be completely different since they didn't have a pre-conceived notion. *he*

Like the class automatically assuming that the student was raising his hand to speak, our interpretations are preconditioned. We create our reality by the interpretive strategies we set in motion. When the scientist and historian paid the facts they observed a certain type of attention, this attention resulted in the emergence of specific qualities. Through the scientific method the scientist created his own hypothesis

6

and used experiments to prove its truthfulness until it became a scientific law. This law was not waiting for a individual scientist to discover it, but instead was imagined, experimented upon, and finally defined by a scientist using the scientific method. In the same fashion historians all had the same facts to determine their opinions, but each choose to emphasize certain events and downplay others creating different interpretations of what happened. The class which was told that an assignment was a poem interpreted it as one and gave it all the characteristics that can be found in a genuine poem. In truth, every individual does not decode their meaning, they make it.

By comparing scientific laws, historian's accounts, and the interpretive strategies developed by an individual, reality is shown to be constantly changing. Extremely predictable observations based on the scientific method cannot determine truth because those observations can and often do change. Historical accounts show that our perspective on events or activities is greatly determined by the cultural context in which we live. Our interpretation of reality is shown to be made by the type of attention we give our observations and not found in some universal truth. Because of these changes in reality, if George Washington desired to own slaves today he would be arrested and convicted in accordance with the very Constitution he created.

excellent paper
well-argued & clearly written

ANNOTATED BIBLIOGRAPHY ASSIGNMENT AND MODEL

What Is an Annotated Bibliography?

An annotated bibliography is a list of references that have been summarized and reviewed in light of a particular position or claim a writer plans to make. The bibliography lists reference information of sources that have been researched in a conventionally accepted style (e.g., APA, MLA, or Chicago). Each reference is followed by a brief summary of the points pertinent to the writer's position and a review of that information in light of its usefulness (or lack of usefulness) to the writer's project.

Purpose of the Assignment

Annotated bibliographies are useful research tools. They can help you to collate and evaluate information for larger research projects.

Occasionally, a professor may ask you to write an annotated bibliography instead of a term paper. In this case, he or she may ask for an introduction, the annotated list of sources, and a conclusion. For example, your Early American History professor may ask that you research the achievements of women during the colonial and revolutionary periods. He asks you to find a number of sources, annotate and review their information. He also asks that you write an introduction, which introduces the nature of your investigation and the information you have found and a conclusion, which indicates a brief summary of your findings and an explanation of the significance of those findings, from your point of view. He then asks that you use this project as a basis for making a class presentation in which you will teach the other members of the class what you have learned. Although you are not specifically asked to write a paper, you have all the skeletal information from which you could go on to write a paper if it were assigned.

Assignment

Practice writing an annotated bibliography is typically combined with a re-searched argument assignment. If your instructor chooses to combine the two, he or she will explain the topics or projects you might consider investigating. After you have done some library research, you should clarify the direction and purpose of your project in your own mind. A review of the sources you have located through your library search will familiarize you with the current patterns of thought on your topic.

This assignment suggests that you write a review of at least 6 sources that address the topic you are researching. Let your review take the form of an annotated bibliography. It is a good idea to introduce your review with a paragraph or two that provides background information on the issue you are investigating. As you complete your annotations for the sources you identify in the bibliographic reference, list the author's points relevant to the issue you will address, comment on the position the author takes on the topic and briefly evaluate the source's potential usefulness for your own project. In other words, each annotation is a mini-review with the criteria of evaluation being a judgment of how relevant the article is to your research project.

A good way to organize your conclusion to the annotated bibliography as a whole is to pose questions that you still have on the issue. You might also at this point articulate the position or thesis that you plan to take on the topic and explain the significance of what you have learned from your research so far.

CHECKLIST

We are not providing student models for this assignment because the structure is so straightforward. But here is a visualization of the final paper:

Annotated Bibliography

Introduction: _____
_____
_____
_____

First Reference: publication information using MLA, APA, CBE, or other officially sanctioned documentation style.

Annotation: _____
_____
_____
_____
  _____
_____
_____
_____

Second Reference (and all additional references): Repeat format of first reference.

Conclusion: _____
_____
_____
_____

Here is a checklist to help you organize your annotated bibliography:

Introduction

Background to your topic and issue. The kinds of questions that you will ask yourself before writing this paragraph will include: What background does my audience need? What kinds of issues and evidence made me aware of this topic in the first place? What have I discovered in my initial research?

Annotations

- Title, author and publication information: Check a handbook for MLA, APA, CBE, and other documentation styles. Choose the style that most closely fits your topic area and follow it down to the last dot and squiggle. Once you have chosen a documentation style, there is no room for deviation (unless you are intentionally challenging or parodying the genre).
- Summary of article or source: What information does the source contain? What kinds of data or results are included? Identify the main point, then summarize subordinate points relating to your topic.
- Evaluation of source's value for your project: What kind of evidence have you discovered and how authoritative is it? Toward what conclusion does it lead? Which side of an issue does the evidence support? Does the source avoid or omit controversies about the issue?

Conclusion

The conclusion should provide a brief summary of what you have learned. It should also address the questions you may still have and suggest your direction for further research. You might include an articulation of the position or thesis you plan to take at this point.

RESEARCHED RHETORICAL ARGUMENT

What Is Argument?

In the "Appendix: Rhetorical Terms for Readers and Writers," you will find that the term "argument" carries a specialized meaning in rhetorical discourse. It is a form of discourse in which the writer defends a controversial claim with reasons and evidence in support of his views and refutes opposing views.

Your professors may ask you to write a research paper, or a position paper, or to argue a particular position based on research that you have completed in the library. For example, your philosophy professor may ask you to research views of deific power in existential, Romantic, and Marxist worldviews and argue a position for or against a "universal" power based on the reading that you have done. Or your professor in your World Cultures course asks you to research marriage rituals in Malaysian, North American, New Guinean, and West African cultures; and to present a position that argues for the most sensible rituals based on criteria that you are to define. In any of these cases, your professor is asking you to use both library sources and rhetorical strategies of argumentation to complete the assignment.

Purpose of the Assignment

The purpose of this assignment is twofold: (1) To become acquainted with the process of doing library research and using that research to support your ideas for an academic audience. (2) To use the rhetorical approach to reading and writing to analyze how writers construct arguments in relation to particular discourse communities.

For the purposes of this assignment, you will be making a claim about how writers adapt rhetorical strategies to a particular situation. This is a cumulative assignment in that it will require you to use many of the various types of writing already introduced in *Conversations* to support your claim. You will need to summarize certain features of the debate about your topic, rhetorically analyze terms of the debate, and synthesize sources and ideas about your claim. Finally, you will be arguing that the writers you analyze use certain rhetorical strategies for the purposes you claim they do.

We suggest that you select a topic within an academic discourse of particular interest to you or from the issues discussed in the readings in this text. The audience to whom you might imagine writing includes your instructor, your peers, and the academic discourse community in general. In this case, you will want to consider tailoring your language to demonstrate to this audience that you are familiar with their language and commonplaces.

The Assignment

While this assignment is provided to give you practice in writing a researched argument, we suggest that the claim you make and support with evidence and analysis is about the use of rhetorical strategies. In other words, rather than taking a position about whether a particular stance is right or wrong, good or bad, true or false, develop your thesis so it makes a claim about how writers use rhetorical strategies. The position that you take about the use of rhetorical strategies will require that you draw a conclusion or raise a significant question about how language constructs and shapes debates.

We suggest that you choose for analysis three articles on your topic. At least one of these ought to be written for an academic discipline. What you will want to do is analyze the relationship between the discourse community for which the articles were written and the rhetorical strategies employed by the writers. This task is likely to involve comparisons between the apparent expectations of given discourse communities and between rhetorical tactics of the writers.

You will want to do extensive library research to select articles appropriate for analysis. Your annotated bibliography skills will help you to conduct and write up your research.

Here is a checklist of rhetorical issues to consider as you research and write:

- What discourse community is the piece written for? What do you know or what can you figure out about that community's expectations for writing?
- How would you describe a typical format for writing in this community? What graphics or other non verbal signs seem to be acceptable or obligatory?
- Can you describe the text's structure or organizational pattern?
- What kinds of appeals does the writer make? How does she or he construct her or his ethos? Are there appeals to pathos? logos? Which of these seem appropriate for the audience and purpose? Which do not? Why?
- What kinds of evidence are presented in your sources? Where does that evidence come from? Are different kinds of sources represented, or are some privileged over others? How? Why? Are any sources omitted? Is there convincing support for the writer's claims? Explain your conclusions.
- What kinds of language do the writers use? Jargon? Colloquial? Slang? Formal? Figurative language? Emotionally charged language? What is the relationship between the audience and the kinds of language used?

This is a more open assignment than some of the others so you will need to make decisions about organization based on your topic, genre, and perspective. Keep in mind everything you have learned so far about writing informative papers and using evidence to support a position.

PEER RESPONSE QUESTIONS FOR RESEARCHED RHETORICAL ARGUMENT ASSIGNMENT

Name of Student Writer _____

Name of Student Responder _____

1. Is there enough background information in the introduction to give the reader a context for understanding the question at issue in this paper? Does the writer provide an overview of the relation between the range of the conversation and the rhetorical strategies used by writers participating in the conversation? If you are unsure about either the thesis or the rhetorical issues that the writer will be investigating, write what you think it should be given the information the writer has provided.

2. Does the writer provide adequate evidence to support the points he or she is trying to make? Are you persuaded by the writer's points? If not, what does the writer need to do to persuade you?

3. Has the writer used at least three different sources? Does the writer cite the sources properly? If not, show the writer where they need to check the accuracy of their citational references.

4. Does the writer analyze and explain their examples in terms of the rhetorical influence on the writer? Has the writer provided adequate analysis to be persuasive? If not, explain to the writer where they may need to analyze in more depth.

5. Is the paper organized so that one point builds on another? Is there logical flow from one idea to the next? Has the writer used transitions that help the reader to see the connections and relationships the writer is making among his or her points? If not, what is missing and how might the writer create a coherent paper?

6. Does the writer's conclusion reflect the points the writer has been making throughout the paper? Does the writer explain the significance of the conclusion? If not, what could the writer do to create a logical and persuasive conclusion?

STUDENT MODEL OF RESEARCHED RHETORICAL ARGUMENT

The writer of this paper introduces the topic with a summary of the major points of argument in the debate. The writer gives the reader sufficient information about the various positions at issue in order to adequately inform the reader about the question of concern. In the body of the paper, the writer identifies the rhetorical tools that will be analyzed in assessing the validity and credibility of the textual arguments, which represent the question at issue. The writer selects three or four predominant rhetorical strategies to examine in the paper. Additionally, the writer finds textual evidence that she can use to support her claims about the effectiveness of the strategies in convincing readers to take particular sides in the debate. The writer thoroughly analyzes the incorporation of these rhetorical strategies, gives examples as evidence to support her analysis, and shows how the use of the strategies serves to affect the readers' opinions on the subject. In her conclusion, the writer summarizes the points she has covered in the paper and explains the significance of using rhetorical devices that will persuade readers to accept particular positions in a controversial argument.

Points for Discussion

1. What sources might the writer need to have read in order to write the introduction to this paper? How might you go about finding sources when you investigate a topic of interest?

2. Prior to writing this paper, your instructor might ask you to write a proposal and annotated bibliography, which outlines the thesis of your argument and the sources you have read in order to make the claims you select to make in your paper. Because this writer has followed this process, she not only understands the content of the sources she has read, but also has analyzed the authors' use of rhetorical devices in making an argument. From what you have read and discussed in class so far, brainstorm a list of possible sources that you might turn to in order to investigate a topic of interest to you. What might be more appropriate? Less appropriate?

3. In your opinion, does this writer present a convincing argument? Why or why not?

4. Make a list of the points the writer makes in this paper. Note the evidence the writer uses to support those points. In your opinion, where does the writer give sufficient evidence in making a point and where might the writer need additional evidence in order to be convincing? How might you apply the knowledge gained from your analysis of this writer's paper to the writing of your own?

5. Notice how this writer creates transitions that help her to signal the reader about the points she is trying to make. Highlight the words and phrases the writer uses to construct these directional signals for the reader.

6. Find the sentences in each section of the paper in which the writer analyzes the rhetorical effectiveness of the authors' use of particular strategies. Notice how the writer explains the effectiveness of these strategies on the reader given the writer's purpose. Explain how you see this working to someone else in your class.

7. Make a list of possible topics of interest to you. Based on what you already know about that topic, list the questions at issue coming from different perspectives. What rhetorical strategies, that you know of, have been used to convince others to take a particular side in this debate? Write a paragraph that explains what your views are now and what questions you would wish to answer in a further investigation of the topic. Use these as a starting point in your research.

8. As you begin your research, sort the sources you find both by position in the argument and by use of rhetorical strategies. Do you see patterns emerging? In what ways might you use this information as you write the first draft of your paper?

Final Researched Assignment
Rhetoric and Writing

The main purpose of biomedical research is to improve the quality of human life. Using a variety of research methods, scientists are able to learn about, and more fully understand, the human body. One common, and effective means of scientific progression is animal research. Animal research is the process of using various animals for experimentation. Animals including rats, mice, dogs, cats, fish, and numerous others, are used for a variety of different testing and research projects. Experiments range from cosmetic testing, to the study of human fetal development, and beyond. Animals are even used by psychologists to study the human brain. Over the past several decades, animal research has been responsible for the obtainment of extensive amounts of scientific information, including many cures and vaccines for once fatal diseases. Despite its extensive benefits, animal research has always been associated with an enormous amount of controversy. This controversy has been sparked by extremists who are opposed to animal research. These extremists are often referred to as animal rights activists. Animal rights activists believe, for a variety of reasons, that animal testing is cruel and inhumane. The Animal Rights Movement (ARM) has existed for many years, and has recently accumulated an increase in its advocates. The ARM strongly believes that animal testing should be abolished completely. Scientists and researchers, however, are obviously supporters of animal research. Scientists argue that it is through animal research that they have made their greatest strides in biomedical advancement. They argue that animal research has been the predecessor of many great biomedical discoveries and that animal research is necessary in order for them to achieve their ultimate goal, which is that of completely understanding the human body, and curing its ailments. Finally there are those who are neutral, and suggest compromise. They feel that animal research should be reduced and alternative methods should be instigated whenever possible. However, they also feel that this reduction should not be done at the expense of biomedical discovery.

Due to the extreme controversy surrounding animal research, there has been a copious amount of literature written on this subject.

↑
*good
intro.*
↓

2

This literature has been written by authors from both sides of the spectrum in an effort to inform and persuade their colleagues, their antagonists and the general public about their views concerning animal research. The authors of this literature often use evidence as their greatest tool. Evidence is used to present and prove their viewpoint, and to establish their credibility as authorities on animal research. These writers also often write with a sarcastic tone and use condescending language in an effort to illustrate the absurdity of their opponents' viewpoints. Subsequently, the writer is able to bolster his own stand. A third strategy used by these writers to further the progression of their argument is to write in a manner that will appeal to their reader's logical reasoning, and/or emotional senses. By using a carefully crafted combination of evidence, language, tone, and by appealing to their audience's logical reasoning and emotional senses, these writers are able to effectively impose *wiw* upon their reader the benefits of animal research.

When writing about animal research, evidence can be an author's greatest tool. Evidence is usually composed of indisputable facts that clearly prove an author's argument. The foremost purpose of evidence in an academic writing is to support the author's argument. In May of 1993, *be consistent* a staff writer for a medical journal called The Lancet, wrote an article in which he discussed the controversies surrounding animal research. One of his arguments *in tense (stick to present)* was that animal research laws need to be reformed. He uses a federal court case as evidence, in which a judge ruled that, "the Department of Agriculture and other federal agencies had failed to set minimum standards for the care and treatment of research animals" *"Predator's"* (Lancet 1311). Using this evidence, the author is able to prove that the present animal research laws do not meet minimum requirements and √ that they need to be revised. By citing a federal judge, the author also creates credibility for his argument. Through the incorporation of a factual example, and by supporting it with a credible authority such as a federal judge, this author is able to effectively portray the need of reformation of √ the present animal research laws, to his reader.

One other method of implementing evidence that authors frequently employ is that of presenting facts and statistics in their

3

literature. By utilizing this type of evidence writers are able to confirm their argument, as well as generate credibility for themselves. In his article entitled, "Message in a Bottle," which is found in the April 22, 1995 issue of <u>The Economist,</u> the author uses more than fifteen separate statistics, and two graphs. Realizing that an economics magazine will be read primarily by those who are familiar with graphs and statistics, the author wisely interjected this type of evidence into his article. In this article, the author is attempting to depict the recent decline of world wide animal research. He states:

> National statistics . . . point to a substantial decline in animal use over the past decade. British research employed 2.8m animals in 1993, 100,000 fewer than the preceding year and 20% fewer than in 1987 (Message 83).

The author also includes a chart depicting this statistic. By incorporating this *persuasive form of* ~~indisputable~~ evidence, this author is able to credibly illustrate the recent decline in animal research.

good trans—   Although evidence is often an academic writer's greatest tool, authors often incorporate other rhetorical devices to further their convictions. Academic writers frequently employ the rhetorical strategies of <u>language and tone</u> in an attempt to persuade their reader on a deeper more personal level. The authors of animal research literature often write with a sarcastic tone and use condescending language in an effort to illustrate the absurdity of their opponents' viewpoint, and to sustain their own argument. In February of 1993 Walter E. Howard wrote an article for a medical journal called the Journal of Mammalogy in which he criticizes the ARM for their "uneducated and uncompromising" views. Howard begins his article in an attempt to demean the ARM, saying:

> . . . we must do more toward educating the public about nature to help counteract the biologically unsound animal rights movement, which wants to bring all new knowledge about mammals to a screeching halt (234).

4

good Obviously the ARM does not want to "bring all new knowledge about mammals to a screeching halt"(Howard 234), but by portraying the ARM in a condescending light, Howard is able to depict the "uneducated and uncompromising" faults of the ARM, thus unveiling the absurdity of the animal rights activists.

A second and more blatant example of an author using sarcasm is found in an article in a medical journal called <u>The Lancet.</u> In the article "A Predator's Compassion," the author addresses what he terms as "sentience" which he states: ". . . is used by some to draw the acceptability of swatting a wasp or putting slug pellets around the primulas and the impropriety of experimenting on a mouse"(Predator's 1311). He further states ". . . simple observations do not suggest that insects and gastropods are insentient"(Predator's 1311). He sarcastically demeans those who believe in this insentient hierarchy, saying: . . . those who use this argument are seemingly more influenced by children's stories featuring literate furry animals than by common sense or knowledge"(Predator's 1311). Here the author uses an obvious sarcastic, and condescending tone, thus bolstering his viewpoint that animal research cannot be regulated by the species of animals that are used. He also ridicules those who believe that it is acceptable to use wasps or slugs for research, but are opposed to using mice in laboratory experiments. By employing a sarcastic tone and utilizing a condescending voice, these two authors are able to communicate with their audience on an emotional level. At this level they are able to effectively exploit their opponents weaknesses and build their own arguments.

The third strategy used by these authors to further the progression of their argument, is to write in a manner that will appeal to their reader's logical reasoning, and/or their emotional senses. This *right* strategy is often used in combination with various other rhetorical strategies. It is perhaps the most effective method because logic and emotion are the two most prevalent faculties involved in the formation of an opinion. These writers recognize that in order to convince their

5

audience ~~of their convictions~~, they must appeal to their reader on a personal level.

In the article "Message in a Bottle", the author uses a very logical approach to convince his reader that animal research needs to gradually be "reduced, refined and replaced" (Lancet 83). *"Message"* He expresses that whenever possible, every effort is made to reduce the number of animals used in experiments. He also explains that alternative methods that do not require the use of animals are used when applicable. The author defines the "three R's", (reduce, refine, replace) as:

> . . . use fewer animals in tests and experiments; make the
> tests that remain necessary both more informative and
> more humane; and develop procedures in which animals no
> longer have to be used at all.(Lancet 83) *"Message"*

This authors use of "the three R's" is an example of a very straightforward, simple and logical means of informing his reader about the need to reduce, refine and replace animal experimentation. Knowing that he is writing this article for an economics magazine, the author also wisely interjects statistics, bar graphs and other logical evidence without contaminating the article with technical writing and medical jargon. His *good* audience, composed predominately of economists and other business men will appreciate statistics, bar graphs, and other factual evidence. The author knew that his particular audience would not comprehend medical terminology, scientific data or other technical information. By writing this article in a logical manner this author enables himself to relate to his business oriented audience. Once he has obtained this reader-writer relationship he is then able to *present* portray his evidence and opinions on a credible and a personal level.

In contrast, depending upon their purpose and their content, *choose* some authors chose to appeal to their readers emotional senses. In his article "Animal Research is Defensible", Walter E. Howard attempts to appeal to his readers emotional faculties. As opposed to the Lancet writer, Howard uses very few statistics, virtually no facts and little logic. He is writing with the sole intent of raising an emotional response from

6

his reader. Howard knows that animal research is a very controversial issue and that many people have strong feelings towards the topic, as is the case with most highly publicized controversies. Howard chooses to ignore the facts and merely appeal to his reader on purely an emotional level. He begins his article by saying:

> As mammalogists, we must do more toward educating the
> public about nature to help counteract the biologically
> unsound animal rights movement, which wants to bring all
> new knowledge about mammals to a screeching halt.
> (Howard 234)/

you've used this quote before, which is ok as long as you acknowledge that so it doesn't seem like an oversight.

Howard's main goal in writing this article is to instill within his audience the same antagonistic feelings which he feels for the ARM. It is unlikely that the ARM actually wants to ". . . bring all knew knowledge about mammals to a screeching halt . . .", but this is an energizing statement employed by Howard to arouse animosity towards the ARM. Howard knows that,if he can convince his audience to feel animosity for the ARM, then he has already succeeded in appealing to their emotional facets, thus increasing his chances of persuading them to agree that animal research must be continued, regardless of the ARM's strong opposition towards it.

Later on in the article Howard directly contrasts animal rights activists and animal researchers. Making solely an emotion appeal, Howard encourages his reader to "chose sides", or in other words to decide weather or not they will support his convictions. He says:

> If you try to debate with animal rightists you will find they
> usually behave like a religious cult where all human-benefit
> views have a negative value. Generally, they are very
> uncompromising and are anti-establishment types . . . On
> the contrary mammologists . . . and other researchers
> should and usually do demonstrate compassion and pity
> towards the animals they utilize.(Howard 234)

ad hominem argument

By making this statement, Howard draws from the emotional momentum that he has established to hopefully cement is reader into believing him; and in turn convincing them of the irrational and uncompromising aura

7

associated with the ARM. By appealing to his audience on an emotional level, Howard is able to effectively persuade his readers to form their opinions relating to animal research in accordance with his theories.

When writing to an audience that may be easily convinced to change their opinion, the strategic use of emotional appeal is perhaps the most effective petition that a writer can use. By incorporating a sarcastic tone, and condescending language into their argument, writers can reach their reader's on an emotional level and persuade them to agree with their theories. However, when writing to a more educated, fact-oriented audience, a logical appeal is usually more effective in persuading the audience. Using carefully selected evidence such as facts, statistics and graphs, an author is able to create an effective logical appeal. With the use of these strategies, the authors of the above discussed literature were able to effectively illustrate the absurdity of the ARM. More importantly, they were able to convey the importance of continued animal research.

8

Works Cited

"A Predator's Compassion." <u>The Lancet</u> 341 (1993): 1311-1312.

Howard, W. E. "Animal Research is Defensible." <u>Journal of Mammology</u>
    19 (1993): 234-235.

"Message in a Bottle." <u>The Economist</u> 22 April 1995: 83+

Excellent paper & well-written. Your occasional mechanical errors are redeemed by the quality of your argument.

SELF-REFLECTION ASSIGNMENT

What Is Self-Reflection?

Self-reflection is one of the most complex acts of cognition. It is multiply layered with tasks of analysis, argument, synthesis, summary, evaluation, and review. Different from self-expression, in which you might express whatever is on your mind, self-reflection requires interpretation of your experience through meaningful intellectual activity. Self-reflection expects that you take stock of your experience and learning and allow the writing to enact the shape of thought rather than presenting it as already arrived. Self-reflection demonstrates the transformation of thought played out in the process of writing and the resulting meaning discovered in factual materials. When you self-reflect, you attempt to draw together the roles of observer and maker, accommodating several viewpoints and thereby negotiating academic discourse. Self-reflection demonstrates your mind at work, the process of mindfulness working on the page itself; it portrays your subjective view of an objective phenomenon.

For example, you might be asked to reflect upon several readings you have completed in your African-American women's literature course and to demonstrate how your thoughts on a particular theme, topic, or idea have shifted in light not only of the reading you have done, but also in light of your own experiences inhabiting the represented textual worlds of African-American women's writing. Or you might be asked to reflect upon the genetic experiments on hybrid shrimp you have been studying in your Introduction to Aquaculture class in relation to the work of Gregor Mendel or Barbara McClintock, and to negotiate your own learning through the accounts of the inhabited worlds of their genetic revelations. Whatever the task, the job of self-reflection generally requires both inward musing and outward observation. It requires that you be of several minds on an issue, both subjectively inhabiting an idea and objectively reframing the possibilities. Self-reflection demonstrates the process of discursive negotiation on the page, and therefore is inherently more protean and tentative in its assertions than perhaps the work you might do to complete an analysis or argument assignment.

Purpose of the Assignment

To practice the skills of self-reflection and to get an idea about your progress as a college writer, this assignment asks you to assume a self-reflective stance on your growth and development as a college writer during the course of this composition class. Reconsider the conversations about knowing from Part Two and the conversations about writing from Part Three of this book. This assignment asks that you join in, continue, and/or transgress the ways in which professional compositionists (Spear, Bartholomae, Flower, Salvatori,

Haas, Corder) have accounted for "ways of behaving" like a college student writer with your own "self-reflective" representation of your experience as a college writer over the course of this class. What empirical evidence of your own experience do you wish to reflect upon and fold into the conversation college professors are engaged in about their students' writing? What questions, problems, assertions have arisen in your experience that you might wish them to consider as they prepare to teach the next group of college student writers in their classes? The purpose of this assignment is threefold: It is intended (1) to give you an opportunity to take stock of and interpret your writerly growth and development in this class and to reflect upon any transformation; (2) to provide you with an opportunity to represent your views of your own development as a beginning college writer on the objective phenomenon of professional compositionists' study, "the freshman writer"; and (3) to join in, continue, and/or transgress the conversations about freshman writers that appear in professional composition literature.

The organization for this essay should grow out of your reflection. You may find yourself following some of the suggestions given in any of the other assignments, depending on the form your reflection takes. This assignment allows for shifts in approach because of the transgressive nature of the form. You may find it helpful as you write to consider what form will best demonstrate your thought in progress on this topic.

Take the time to think about the purpose of the assignment (see above) and the audience, and write thoughtfully and critically about the issues the assignment asks you to address. Another way to think about this rhetorical situation is to consider that you are writing for professional compositionists . . . and your composition teacher. What do you think they should know about your growth as a college writer during this course [that will help to plan for class next year]? Tell your teacher where you think the class has succeeded, as well as where you think the class could use some improvement. Tell what you've learned about yourself as a college writer that you are pleased about and what you think you've learned about yourself as a college writer that might serve as a statement of your personal goals for growth.

PEER RESPONSE QUESTIONS FOR SELF-REFLECTION ASSIGNMENT

Name of Student Writer _____

Name of Student Responder _____

1. Does the writer interpret experience rather than just report it? If not, show the writer where interpretation might help the writer analyze and reflect on the significance of the experience they describe.

2. How does the writer allow the writing to take shape as the writer reflects? How does the writer demonstrate the transformation of thought played out in the process of writing?

3. Does the writer show evidence of taking a subjective view of an objective phenomena (in this case, the growth and development of the student writer)? Does the writer get close enough to his or her growth and development as a writer to demonstrate objective understanding of the subject of composition, the writer him or herself? There is a circularity here that is meaningful to self-reflection. It is stepping close and far in order to see the self and the experience from multiple perspectives. Do you see the writer doing this dance? If not, how might the writer think about broadening his or her views? Can you make any suggestions to the writer that would help him or her to make these moves?

4. Does the writer comment specifically on ideas learned in different parts of the course? If not, how might the writer bring this into his/her self-reflection?

5. Does the writer join in, continue, and/or transgress the ways in which professional compositionists have accounted for "ways of behaving" like a college student writer with his/her own "self-reflective" representation of experience as a college writer over the course of the class? If not, give the writer suggestions for how the reflection compares with ideas presented by Spear, Bartholomae, Flower, Salvatori, Haas, Elbow, Burke, and/or Corder. Ask the writer a question that might help him or her to identify any possible ways to bring the ideas of these writers to bear on his or her experience (either as affirmation, continuance, and/or transgression).

6. Does the organization of the essay seem to match the writer's reflective stance? In what ways or not? Describe how this seems to work or not for you as a reader. Any suggestions?

STUDENT MODELS OF SELF-REFLECTION ASSIGNMENT

The writers of these self-reflective essays discuss their growth and development as students and as writers as a result of their participation in a college writing class, which used an early version of *Conversations in Context* as their primary textbook. Although the two writers do different things in their self-reflections, there are some similarities. The first writer reflects upon the purpose of a college education and articulates a desire for a different orientation and a restructuring of approaches to college in which the goal of higher education becomes increased knowledge rather than high grades. Within this frame, the writer wonders about the ways it becomes difficult to imagine different teaching approaches that might foster such a goal. He ultimately concludes that the course has contributed to his goals for learning skills and knowledge, which he considers useful to his sense of a college education. The second writer discusses the specifics of what she has learned in the class. She compares writing as a high school student with writing as a college student and details her understanding of the demands of an academic discourse community. Although these two writers' reflections travel in different directions, both writers start with an articulation of changed perspectives. Both writers analyze their experiences in terms of a statement of the larger significance of such experiences in a college education. Both writers conclude in an open-ended fashion that begs a question rather than offering definitive solutions.

Points for Discussion

1. The introductions of both of these reflective essays begin with an "I used to think, but now I know . . ." format. There is no clear thesis statement. In what ways might both this introductory approach and the lack of a thesis statement serve the purposes of this assignment?

2. Both writers refer specifically to readings that have held significance for them in determining the direction of their growth and development. In what ways might the writers have developed further the connections between the readings and their statements of significance to the writers' learning?

3. Neither writer connects their experience as a freshman writer to the information about freshman writers given by professional compositionists represented in *Conversations*. In part, this oversight occurs because these particular models were written as first-and-only drafts during one class period. In what ways might the writers be directed to revise their drafts keeping in mind the requirement of the assignment which asks the writer to join in, continue, or transgress the ways in which professional compositionists (Spear, Bartholomae, Flower, Salvatori, Burke, Elbow, Haas, Corder) have accounted for "ways of behaving" like a college student writer with their own self-reflective representation of their experience as a college writer over the course of the class?

4. Both writers speak from the authority of their own experience as developing college writers. Analyze the rhetorical strategies they draw upon to construct this ethos.

5. Analyze the writers' organizational approaches to self-reflection. What similar structures do they use? Where do you see differences?

Self-Reflection Essay

Upon entering this class I felt that in order to be successful writing for my college career I was going to have to put in a good amount of work. I feel that this class has helped me to recognize what is important when writing in an academic setting. As you know, this was my first semester at the University and I wasn't sure what to expect from my classes, but when I realized the volume of writing I would be performing, it became important to me to begin exploring the different techniques of being a writer in an academic setting.

Looking back on this semester, I am convinced that although Bloom may have been a hypocrite he was right about some things. I do feel like I have a lack of direction and no hand is reaching in to guide me to where I need to go. But where I need to go is not definite. College to me is a place for a person to build knowledge and skills and then use those skills to either make a living for him/herself or we continue searching for more and more knowledge. I don't believe the purpose of college is to give a grade for performance and a diploma to its graduating students so that those students may be permitted a job. Too many diplomas and transcripts are speaking for students. While students know this, the skills do not become important to them; however, the grades do.

I feel that in order to be happy with my progress at this institution, I need to be confident that what I am learning is for the purpose of something greater than a grade or a "good mark." I am looking for skills and knowledge that will put me onto my own two feet so I may carve a living for myself out of the stagnant sludge of today's society. People go to this institution (it seems(so that they can eliminate (further) the risk of not "making it" in today's world. They want the ride to be easy through and through. They want there to be no stage in life where they struggle, in fact, they feel as though they are struggling now.

I hope to eliminate the buffer zone that stands between me (a protected member of the upper-middle class), and descend to the realm of living, of being (the realm of self-preservation and realization. I see all

2

around me the crutches that I use, that people use in order to effectively live in our world. I feel these crutches need to be done away with.

Maybe I'm taking this assignment in the wrong direction, but this is my self-reflection on "the freshman writer" (me). It is hard to say that you will a change in the approaches to teaching when you will a change in the approach and usefulness of a $27,000 per year education. Freshman writing should pursue the realization of the importance of building skills, as this course has. It should emphasize the uselessness of knowledge just for the sake of a grade, which this course has. Freshman writing should emphasize the importance of communication skills, and recognition of the conversations taking place around a particular community. Freshman writing is the construction of writing skills to be built on for the remainder of these students' lives.

Self-Reflection Essay

This class has taught me so much about writing (that I really don't know where to begin . . . Before I entered this class, I didn't know what the words "rhetoric" or "discourse communities" meant; nor did it even dawn on me that I am a part of one or many discourses that have helped shape me as a student. It really requires a leap (to begin reflecting about this part of my education) mainly because I feel I have grown out of an old way of thinking and learning, and into a new idea of what it means to write in the university.

Like many others that I have talked to in this class, I came in thinking I knew how to write an essay. That very idea makes me laugh now. I have learned that there is no place in the college discourse for the kind of writing my high school career taught me. Yes, that good old "form," (five ¶s): universal, boring, ineffective in persuading, good at summarizing, lacking synthesis, lacking analysis; these are the qualities of "the form." There is so much more to learn about writing when you enter college. Suddenly, professors want to know that you have learned something from them (that they have contributed, and you are recognizing this.

Some problems that have risen out of my "freshman writing experience" are my constant battle with over-summarizing. That "so what" factor is so much more important. The most valuable advice I believe I have ever heard is when you said, "Just tell your audience what they need to know." Simple advice, yes, but we all need to hear it. My advice to a class next semester might be to recognize this idea.

The most important thing I learned in this class was how to use rhetorical strategies. Also how to recognize them, synthesize them, and analyze them. The "rhetorical dictionary" in the back of the book was my greatest tool in writing an effective argument. Thus, I also learned that it is okay to think about a paper sentence-by-sentence. You told us how to go about it. It almost seemed as if we were cheating (, but this is where the growth started. I can look back on past essays and pick them apart sentence by sentence.

Something I think you should know is: this class has taught me more in the past semester than any other classes combined. Whether it

2

is the way you discuss, teach, critique, encourage, question, or answer (the way I think about writing has changed. The course readings have contributed to this also. Especially, Pratt, and her interpretations of the "contact zone." (Something I think every freshman should read). It really is that "puddle effect" we were talking about: The inner circle is what we came to college with, the second out is the utilization of course readings, the third is understanding the point of these readings. The outer circles are summary, then analysis, then system, etc. They keep rippling outward, building on each other. Basically, that is what this class has taught me, how to expand as a student: How to be elastic.

As far as improvements go, I can't think of much to say. I think a class like this demands diversity (something we unfortunately don't have a lot of here at our university). That is not to say I think we were all the same in here. I don't believe that to be true at all. Yet (I would be curious to know how this method of learning would play out in a more diverse environment . . .

Rhetorical Terms for Readers and Writers

The purpose of the rhetorical approach to reading and writing used in this book is to prepare you to write successfully in the rhetorical situation you are now entering—that of the academic community. In this part, we provide a rhetorical vocabulary for thinking and talking about *how* people read and write. Like most textbooks, this part presents an apparently objective summary of its subject (rhetoric). However, to present this information in textbook fashion was, like all writing decisions, a rhetorical decision related to our audience and purpose. Our purpose is not to provide an overview of the entire field of rhetoric, complete with all of its internal conflicts, but to provide a practical set of concepts for you to use as a vocabulary for thinking about college reading and writing. For this aim, the textbooklike distillation of information was our choice because it has the advantage of efficiency.

WHAT IS RHETORIC?

Rhetoric is perhaps the most ancient of disciplines. As modern members of the discipline, we editors have discussed and debated issues in the field of rhetoric among ourselves and with our colleagues and students. Our discussions joined written and oral conversations about rhetoric that extend from current professional journals like *Rhetoric Review* back to philosophers who lived before Socrates. In fact, when people refer to "classical rhetoric" they mean the systems of rhetoric developed by Greek thinkers beginning with a pre-Socratic group called the Sophists and including Aristotle and

Roman teachers and orators such as Quintilian and Cicero. These rhetoricians lived, taught, and wrote over a period of time extending from 500 BCE to the second century CE. You won't be surprised that in the course of discussions going back 2500 years, the term *rhetoric* has been defined in a variety of ways. Currently, it is often used pejoratively to designate words lacking substance, as in the following example:

> In the last analysis, his passionate promises boiled down to mere *rhetoric.*

As used here, rhetoric suggests words without meaning. But over its long history, rhetoric has been viewed much more broadly as a study of the uses of language for particular purposes. Aristotle defined rhetoric as the faculty of discovering all the available means of persuasion in any given situation. (Torture and bribes, of course, can be persuasive, but rhetoric is traditionally limited to verbal forms of persuasion.) The choices among strategies and techniques a speaker/writer can employ to communicate persuasively are the subject of rhetoric.

The term *persuasion* in Aristotle's definition has implications that might not be immediately apparent. If, as Aristotle assumed, all people (actually, he said "men") are reasonable creatures, then they will accept the truth of a proven proposition on the basis of the evidence—they will not need to be "persuaded." Therefore, for Aristotle, rhetoric was not needed to convince people of the truth of scientific knowledge. Rhetorical techniques were needed only for occasions when scientific proof was unavailable.

There were and are many such occasions. One, traditionally considered a special province of rhetoric, is the discourse of legislators. A legislator cannot scientifically prove that a particular law will be effective in ameliorating a social ill because the effects will come sometime in the future after the law is passed, and the legislator cannot know the future. Therefore, she must find means other than scientific proof to persuade her fellow legislators to adopt her law. Rhetoric deals with strategies for argument that are likely to be effective in such circumstances.

The courts are another forum where scientific proof is unavailable. There is frequently more than one plausible way to interpret evidence. An attorney must persuade the jury to accept her interpretation even though she has no irrefutable proof that the evidence points to her conclusion. It is clear why rhetoric, the study of how to argue persuasively, would be useful for anyone engaged in these activities.

However, it may not be so clear to you, and certainly was not clear to Aristotle, why rhetorical strategies for arguing would be useful in the sciences where factual "proof" is available. But you will learn, when you read the selections in Part Two of this text, that many people currently question whether scientific "facts" are self-evident. If the implications of scientific results indeed are not self-evident, but must be argued and defended, then scientists too must employ rhetorical means of persuasion. They must learn what rhetorical techniques are most appropriate to argue convincingly for their audience.

Rhetorical strategies that are very effective in one situation might be entirely unconvincing in another. Rhetorical analysis is the study of how to use language to affect, influence, or change a reader's view. The introductions and questions about readings and some of the writing assignments in this book are intended to help you become familiar with rhetorical terminology and to recognize the rhetorical nature of the readings themselves. We ask you to analyze rhetorically the techniques and strategies that other writers use so that, finally, you will be able to employ this knowledge to write more effectively yourself.

Because rhetorical choices are always made in a local situation in which already existing circumstances influence decisions, we have organized the terms hierarchically, with those pertaining to the *rhetorical situation,* including *audience* and *purpose,* coming first, and those addressing specific choices later. We do this to point out that specific choices are embedded like stacked dolls in larger contexts, but even the most minute element in the hierarchy can, conversely, affect any and all of the other parts. The components of rhetoric must be understood not as discrete entities, but as interdependent parts of the writing act. The terms are listed alphabetically in the index so that you can readily locate the definitions when you need them.

The Appendix omits some terms rhetoricians would usually include in an overview of rhetoric. As tools for analysis of writing, you will be able to use these terms in class to talk about the readings and about your own and your peers' drafts of writing assignments. Beyond this class, you will be able to use them to investigate the expectations for writing in any given situation. You will also be able to use many of these terms as a heuristic, or an exploratory guide, for inventing and organizing your own ideas for writing. The last section in the rhetoric, "Invention," is especially designed to help you apply the rhetorical vocabulary to your own writing processes.

Rhetoricians debate the relationship between speech and writing, and historically have described how to speak effectively rather than how to write. But because this book deals primarily with written work, we will refer to our subjects as writers and writing rather than speakers and speaking.

RHETORICAL SITUATION

The *rhetorical situation*—the particular context in and for which the writing is produced—constrains the writer's choices about how to present her ideas. Rhetoricians have identified several components of the rhetorical situation, including the *writer* herself, her *purpose,* her *audience,* or the *discourse community* for which she writes, and the *genre* in which she writes. The rhetorical situation comprises the givens in a writing situation, that is, the pre-existing conditions from which the impetus for writing emerges. For example, it would be rhetorically effective to use the highly specialized vocabulary and rigid format of the scientific report to write up a laboratory report for a grade in a cellular biology course, but to choose the same vocabulary and organization to talk about corn production to a farmer would not be effective. Factors already existing in the situation before you began writing or talking—in these examples, the differences in audience and purpose—control both the language and the logical moves one uses to communicate effectively in each situation.

Purpose: The purposes of writing can vary from being quite straightforward to being very complex. For instance, we could state Elizabeth Cody Newenhuyse's purpose for writing "De-Constructive Criticism" quite directly, while the purposes behind Kent Kirkpatrick's "Spandex Judge" might be more complex. As a student writing in the university, your purposes are at least two-fold: you have a purpose exterior to the writing itself (to get a good grade) and one internal to the writing (the purpose you work out in each paper, for instance, to explain what happens to a certain DNA molecule in the presence of a certain protein). Both purposes influence the further rhetorical decisions you make. It is important to identify a writer's purpose in order to understand the reasons for her rhetorical choices.

Audience: "Audience" usually refers to a group hearing and seeing a performance—the audience at a rock concert or a movie, for example. In rhetorical discourse, the term is left over from the classical rhetoric of ancient Greece and Rome, when all important discussions were carried on orally. Then audience referred to the specific listeners assembled before an orator. But now, with nearly universal literacy in developed countries, the term audience applies equally to readers. Because it refers to anyone who happens to hear or read a message, it is a more general term than *discourse community*.

Discourse Community: "Discourse community" is a useful term because it takes into account the local contingencies surrounding any writing occasion better than does the term "audience." A discourse community is a group of people who interact verbally as a result of a shared interest, and who generally abide by the same linguistic conventions during their interactions, though these conventions may be altered over time according to the dynamics of the group. Every person belongs to several different discourse communities. These may be physical communities, such as the managers and employees of Ben and Jerry's Ice Cream or Apple Computers, or they may comprise a much more dispersed community, say of ice cream chemists or computer systems specialists, who may never meet each other or read all the material produced by other community members. But they still share the interest and the specialized language needed to read anything written within the community.

Discourse: This term is difficult because it seems to encompass a broad range of meanings. In fact, you will see it used in some contexts where it seems synonymous with *language*. For our purposes, we will define it on two levels:

1. Discourse is the language shared among a group of people with specialized interests. It includes the subject matter available to the community and its vocabulary. For instance, Elizabeth Cody Newenhuyse makes logical moves in "De-Constructive Criticism" that would not be available to David Crews in "Animal Sexuality."
2. Discourse also refers to the individual utterances people make in conversation, whether written or spoken.

Conventions: This term has a specialized meaning for rhetoric and composition. In the discourse of rhetoric, conventions refer to all the generally accepted forms, rules, and procedures that describe acceptable writing for a particular community. For instance, one of the conventions of academic writing is always to use complete sentences. On the other hand, if you've ever examined sentence structure in advertising, you will have noted that sentence fragments are entirely *conventional* (the adjectival form of the term) in advertising.

Genre: "Genre" is a system of classification that we use when talking about writing, though other artistic fields are divided into genres as well. Genre is best defined through examples: novels, drama, poetry, short stories, letters, news articles, laboratory reports, and reviews are all writing genres. If you have a mental image of a specific kind of writing for each of these categories, you understand that genres are divided according to characteristics of writing such as form, style, and purpose.

The genres in academic discourse communities develop as ways of responding in writing to recurrent situations in the community. For instance, a recurrent need in the medical community (or any scientific community) is to publish the latest research in the development of new drugs (or in any research problem). Over the years, medicine and other sciences have developed well-defined genres for such publications. The conventions of a genre are shaped by the discourse community's rhetorical aims and ideology. These genres are not fixed; they are open to critique and can change over time as situations change. See, for instance, Mary Louise Pratt's "Arts of the Contact Zone" as an example of an essay that challenges the conventions of the academic essay genre.

As you work through this book, the reading and writing questions will help you to become aware of both the rationale for and critiques of the conventions of academic genres.

ARGUMENT

Argument has a specialized meaning in rhetoric. It is a form of discourse in which the writer defends a controversial claim with reasons and evidence in support of his own views, and refutes opposing views. The central concern of classical rhetoricians was how to argue effectively, so they discussed all of the persuasive techniques they identified—the appeals, the discovery of proofs or lines of argument, organization, stylistic analysis—in relation to argument. Because it is not the purpose of this Appendix to cover the rhetoric of argument comprehensively, but instead to provide you with a vocabulary for talking about your own reading and writing, we have organized the various terms not as components of argument but as an aid to understanding how some components of the rhetorical situation influence others.

Appeals: Aristotle identified three strategies that a speaker or writer could use to influence any audience's views. They were:

1. To create mutual trust between the audience and speaker by convincing the audience that the speaker is honest and knowledgeable,
2. To appeal to the audience's powers of reasoning, and
3. To appeal to the audience's emotions.

You don't need to be a writer to know that your audience and purpose will determine which appeals you use. For instance, if you have ever argued with a parent to allow you to use the family car, you know that the first and last of these strategies are probably most persuasive in this situation: You emphasize your own reliability, responsibility, and driving skill, and you appeal to your parent's sympathies for the impossibility of a social life without a car.

Each of these strategies has technical names and definitions. This Appendix defines them with reference to academic writing. Remember that all three appeals might be used in any single piece of writing, but some are generally more effective in college writing than others.

Appeal to Ethos, Ethical Appeal, or Appeal to Character: These terms refer to the choices writers make to create mutual trust between their audience and themselves. *Ethical* choices are the rhetorical strategies authors use to represent themselves as reliable, believable authorities.

In academic writing, it is important to establish one's credentials as a credible authority about the subject matter. Researchers and students often use the following strategies to portray themselves as reliable and knowledgeable:

1. Cite authorities and research in the discourse community for which you are writing. Your demonstration of thorough knowledge of the issue makes you more credible.

- Cite authorities considered reliable in the discourse community.
- Cite enough sources to demonstrate familiarity with the conversation about which you are writing.
- Acknowledge and explain contradictory sources.
- In some disciplines it is acceptable to cite relevant personal experience.

2. Establish common ground with the audience. The audience is more willing to believe someone they consider to be one of them.
   - Be aware of different perspectives among community members about your issue.
   - Begin with a position that most people in the community accept. (Note that among authors in this text, David Crews follows this advice, but Londa Shiebinger does not. A reader reading from a rhetorical perspective would view this as an interesting puzzle: What does each writer gain rhetorically with his or her particular choice?)

3. Demonstrate open-mindedness. Especially in the academic community where criticism is part of the process of making new knowledge, the consideration of several perspectives on the issue is highly valued.
   - Acknowledge the evidence from multiple perspectives within the community.
   - Acknowledge the feasibility of arguments from other perspectives.
   - Avoid attacks on personal character (*ad hominem* attacks).

Appeal to Logos, Logical Appeal: The appeal to logos, or logical appeal, refers to the rhetorical choices an author makes to appeal to the audience's reasoning powers. Writers often choose to convince their readers by demonstrating the reasonableness of their argument.

The logical appeal is as highly valued in academic writing as the ethical appeal. Here are some ways writers can demonstrate their logical thinking:

1. *To reason logically, define your terms.* It is a mistake to assume that a term you use has exactly the same meaning for your reader. To make sure that you and your reader are beginning at the same point, you need to define terms.

   The classical means of defining something is to provide its genus (the larger group to which it belongs) and to specify how this particular word differs from others in the genus. Here's an example:

   kit: a violin or rebec (genus, or larger group) small enough to be carried in the pocket, used by dance masters in the 17th and 18th centuries (specifying differences from other violins or rebecs).

   Other types of definitions include analogies, examples, synonyms, and descriptions.

2. *Make sure the evidence you use is sufficient, relevant, and timely.*
Before discussing how to judge whether evidence is sufficient, relevant, and timely, it is important to consider just what evidence *is.* Evidence is the information a writer provides in support of her reasons
or opinions. It's easy to distinguish evidence from reasons or opinions if you keep in mind the various forms that evidence can take. Evidence can take any of the following forms:

anecdote

extended definition

example

hypothetical example

historical or scientific fact

statistics

analogy

vivid descriptive details

the word of authorities

eyewitness account

Examine the three excerpts from articles about the bombing in
Saudi Arabia on pages 454–458 of this Appendix for examples of
these various kinds of evidence. You will note that the categories
overlap somewhat. It is not important to be able to categorize each
example of evidence as it is to be aware of the sorts of information
that constitute evidence. That's important for two reasons. First, in
your reading, you must remember that evidence never stands alone.
It is always present to support a larger point. Your professors will expect you to remember that larger point, though it usually helps to
cite evidence as well. Second, you need to be aware of what kind of
information constitutes evidence so you know when you have included it in your own writing. (*Note:* In summaries, by contrast, you
need to be able to recognize evidence so as NOT to include it.)

Now that you have a sense of what we mean by "evidence," we
can turn to the logical use of evidence.

Sufficient, relevant, and timely evidence: Various disciplines
have their own criteria for judging whether the evidence provided by
a writer is sufficient, relevant, and timely, and their criteria are part
of what you learn as a student of the field. Yet within those criteria,
you, the writer, must still make decisions. Some general rules of
thumb developed by rhetoricians about using evidence reasonably
include:

▪ *Sufficient evidence:* Sufficient evidence is particularly important
   for student writers, who tend to underestimate the amount of

evidence professors think is necessary to support a claim. As long as all the evidence you include is relevant and timely, you will seldom err by including too much.

Exactly how much evidence will be considered sufficient in any particular circumstance cannot be predetermined; however, rhetoricians have described a couple of typical fallacies, or errors in reasoning, having to do with using too little or no evidence:

—*Begging the question:* To beg the question is to assume something is true that still needs to be demonstrated. The sentence "Liberal Hollywood moguls promote pre-marital sex in movies and TV," sets up "Hollywood moguls promote pre-marital sex in movies and TV" as the claim to be proved or demonstrated. The sentence suggests to both the writer and reader that the writer will add, in the next sentence, some evidence from movies or TV that Hollywood moguls promote pre-marital sex. The question in the sentence that is *begged,* however, is whether Hollywood moguls are *liberal.* Though many people would disagree about this characterization, the statement simply assumes its accuracy without offering any evidence.

—*Jumping to a conclusion (hasty generalization):* This means to come to a conclusion prematurely on the basis of an unrepresentative sampling or too few examples. Polling organizations are examples of people who go to great statistical lengths *to avoid* this fallacy. They do all they can to ensure statistically that their population samples are both adequate and representative so that they can, for instance, accurately predict the outcome of an upcoming election. Otherwise, they risk looking silly. Stereotyping can be the result of hasty generalizations; people sometimes jump to a conclusion about an entire group of people on the basis of the actions of a very few.

■ *Relevant evidence:* What is relevant to your argument depends to a large extent on the particular purpose and discourse community for which you are writing. Writers often know of fascinating facts, statistics, or stories that are only tangentially related to the question at issue. Sometimes they must ruthlessly excise interesting material because it is not to the point.

Whether information is to the point is in part up to the writer's judgment. Some typical categories of irrelevant information that logicians have identified include:

—*Straw man:* To set up a straw man is to create a false target that is easily demolished. The audience is to believe that once the false target is destroyed, so is the real one. It is a diversionary tactic intended to draw attention away from the issue at hand. When politicians blame poor people for poverty, they create a straw man rather than address the real, more intractable issues of an economy that does not produce enough well-paying jobs to eliminate poverty.

—*Ad hominem (argument against the person):* This time the audience's attention is directed to the person making the argument rather than to the question at issue. When the writer cannot think of good arguments for the issue, she sometimes turns to the person behind the arguments. An example is to attack "religious fanatics" on one side of the abortion issue or "femi-nazis" on the other rather than arguing the ethics of the issue itself.

—*Red herring:* Sometimes a writer introduces an irrelevant point intentionally to throw readers off the trail—indeed, the source of the term red herring comes literally from throwing a tracker off the trail: In the days of fox hunting, it was believed that hounds could be thrown off the scent by dragging a stinky herring across the fox's trail.

- *Timely evidence:* How recent research must be to be considered timely depends on how fast knowledge in the discipline is developing. Sometimes significant advances are made in a very short time, so research more than a couple of years old may be out of date. Certain medical conditions like cystic fibrosis and AIDS are examples of areas where recent research has rendered work only a few years old obsolete. Astronomy after the repair of the Hubble telescope is another such field. Sometimes even a rather stable profession like law changes quite radically in certain areas, such as recent legal decisions about a person's right to determine her own moment of death. In other areas, like rhetoric and philosophy, modern work may exist side by side with ancient thinking but never eclipse it. Thus, to judge whether her evidence is timely, a student must learn the conditions and expectations of the discourse in which she is working.

3. *Be clear about your grounds for claiming cause/effect relationships.*
   - You must demonstrate that the cause you have identified is the only cause, or at least a significant cause of the outcome.
   - To reason logically about cause/effect relations, you must identify agency—the means by which a cause achieves its effects. The field of astrology is a well-known example of failure in this requirement. Scientists deride astrology because astrologists cannot show how the causes they identify—the positions of planets in the skies—have the effect they claim—changing particular events in an individual's life.
   - To discuss cause/effect relationships logically, you should indicate the strength of the causal relationship: Is it direct (funding cuts cause the university library to cancel subscriptions); incremental (every x grams of alcohol kills x brain cells); cumulative (a pack of cigarettes a day for 25 years causes lung cancer); or a threshold

issue (the effects may not be evident until we reach a "point of no return" when we are suddenly in deep trouble).

Here are some of the typical fallacies that occur in arguing cause/effect relations:

—*Post hoc ergo propter hoc:* Translated from the Latin, this phrase means "after this, therefore because of this." The typical example is to assume that the cause for being ill all night long was the dinner you ate shortly before getting sick. That dinner might be the cause, but so might the acute 24-hour flu virus that has been going around at school. It is a fallacy to assume that the dinner was the cause without further evidence.

—*Third cause:* Sometimes an event is attributed to a cause when in fact both the event and cause are linked to a third cause, another factor responsible for both. For instance, at one time, people may have thought that thunder was caused by lightning since it always seemed to follow lightning. But we now know that both result from a third cause, an electrical discharge.

—*Statistical correlations taken as cause/effect relations:* One of the most difficult relations to sort out is the difference between statistical correlations and cause/effect relations. For example, one statistic that is often cited is that birth rates decrease in underdeveloped countries as the years of education for women increase. It is tempting to conclude that more education causes women to have fewer children, but the statistics don't prove that. The statistics, for instance, have no way of telling us about other factors that may also be related, such as increase in wealth or decrease in infant mortality rates. The point to remember is that one cannot assume that one factor is the cause of another simply because the two always correlate statistically.

—*Slippery slope:* This is the unwarranted assumption that one event will set in motion an inevitable chain of events that will lead to disaster. Antisubstance abuse campaigns are often based on such arguments: The first sip of alcohol or puff of marijuana will inevitably lead to addiction and death.

Appeal to Pathos, Pathetic Appeal, Emotional Appeal: Though entirely acceptable in other areas, the emotional appeal is generally frowned upon in academic writing. In contexts where it is accepted, its effectiveness often depends on the writer's skillful use of language and narrative. The following choices enhance an emotional appeal:

- Vivid description.
- Figurative language.
- Emotional language.
- Personal stories or anecdotes.

Several of the selections in this text use emotional appeals. You might watch for similarities in audience or purpose among those articles that do so.

Arrangement

One of the decisions a writer makes is how to organize or arrange his material. Examining the arrangement of information in a piece of writing can reveal much about the writer's assumptions about his audience, subject matter, and the community's expectations. Recognizing the role of arrangement in the writing you read will also help you think through the organization of material in your own writing.

Material can be organized in about as many ways as there are people doing the organizing. But knowing a few of the common organizational patterns that have developed over the years can help you think and talk about organization in your reading and writing.

Point, Thesis, or Claim: According to current conventions of nonfiction writing, every piece of writing is unified under one main point, thesis, or claim. The piece can range in length from a paragraph to a book, and the main point can be quite straightforward or very complex, but one should be able to state it in a sentence or two. Book reviews recognize this when they summarize a text, as the following single-sentence review of a book titled *Distinction: A Social Critique of the Judgment of Taste* by Pierre Bourdieu demonstrates:

> With subtlety and sophistication, the great French sociologist analyzes the way social and economic classes are shaped and preserved by myriad tiny but amazingly precise difference—from preferences in food and art to body language and hairstyles.
>
> *Mother Jones,* August 1996

Here is an example of a single paragraph whose main point is stated in a single sentence. Which sentence states the main point?

> Fastidious writers determined to purge all fiction from their nonfiction concoct alternative terms they claim are more precise—"event-based imaginative writing versus non-event based imaginative writing," for example. But a lot of fiction is event-based, and a great deal of nonfiction is sheer imaginative speculation. Terminology is not the problem here. The problem is that the kind of imaginative writing known as "nonfiction" is, by any name, inextricably entangled in the kind of imaginative writing we call "fiction," and vice versa, and those who like their categories clean may as well start wringing their hands.
>
> *Orion,* Summer 1996, p. 55

The terms *main point, thesis,* and *claim* are synonymous enough that for practical use they do not need to be differentiated except to say that *claim* is more strictly applied to *argument* than the others. A *claim* states a controversial position to be defended in an argument.

Classical Argument Arrangement: Classical rhetoricians taught the following as the proper organization for arguments. What they said about speeches, we commonly apply to writing.

> *Exordium:* Introduction.
> The purpose of the introduction is to inform the audience of the topic and purpose of the writing and to convince them that it is worthy of their attention.
>
> *Narratio:* Narrative of background facts or circumstances.
> This part provides pertinent background information for understanding the issue at hand. It often includes what other people have thought and said about the issue.
>
> *Confirmatio:* The proof of the writer's case.
> This is what we commonly refer to as the body of an essay. Here the writer presents all of his reasons and the evidence he has gathered in support of his claim.
>
> *Refutatio:* Refutation.
> Here the writer anticipates objections to his position and refutes them. One of the decisions a writer must make is whether to present his own case or refute the opposing views first. Either is acceptable, and the writer must decide which will be more effective in his particular situation.
>
> *Peroratio:* Conclusion.
> The end is the part that stays with the audience longest, so here the writer should recapitulate his most important points and drive home the importance of the issue.

Academic Argument: Compositionists have identified this shortened formula as an organizational pattern found frequently in the writing of academics. It is an effective way for students to think about arrangement.

> *Introduction*
> Background information: what others have thought and said about the topic.
> > *Most people think . . .*
>
> Main point: the writer's thesis or claim, in some way differing from or adding to what others have said.
> > *But I assert . . .*

Body
The reasons and evidence for the writer's position.
   Here's why . . .

Conclusion
The significance of the issue. Answers the question
   So what?

Scientific Report Format: If you have written lab reports in science classes, you are familiar with the scientific research report. This format is prevalent in many disciplines outside as well as within the hard sciences. It usually consists of the following parts:

Introduction: The introduction states the problem that this researcher investigated. It often summarizes the work of other researchers who have studied the problem and points out that the particular issue considered here has not yet been resolved.

Methods: The researcher describes the methods used to investigate the problem.

Results: The researcher reports the immediate outcomes of the research.

Discussion: The researcher explains how this research contributes to understanding the problem and often points the way to further research questions.

Additional Organizational Patterns: Various patterns of arrangement are based on the principle of importance. Here are some of them:

Nestorian pattern: A Roman rhetorician named Nestor recommended that speakers organize the *confirmatio* of an argument as follows:
   First, give the second most important or convincing point in support of your argument.
   Second, give the least convincing point.
   End with the most convincing or most important point of your argument.

The rationale is that people remember longest what comes at the end, so that's where you put your most convincing point. But you don't want to begin with your weakest reason for fear of losing your audience early, so you bury that in the middle of the argument.

Climactic order: Build throughout the piece to the most important, most effective point at the end. The rationale here is to keep your audience with you by building suspense. You'll notice that this advice partially contradicts the Nestorian order. To use the climactic order, you would have to be able to construct your first, weakest point in a way that contributes to the suspense.

Inverted pyramid: This is the traditional organization for news writers. Just the opposite of the climactic order, here the most important information is given in the first paragraph and the rest of the details appear in the order of decreasing relevance and interest. The reason is that newspaper and magazine editors cut reporters' stories to fit the space available. Therefore, the important information has to appear upfront where it won't be cut.

The patterns based on importance seem to assume that relative levels of importance are self-evident. Yet a moment's reflection reveals that disagreements may well arise among reasonable people about which aspects of an issue or event are most important. In such cases, the patterns that writers employ can shape what readers view as important. The writer can actually construct the reader's view of the situation in part by how he arranges his information. See "Spandex Judge" as an example of a writer constructing the reader's notion of what is important about the subject of the article, Judge Nomoto.

SELECTION

The writer must always make selections from the material at hand. Some information is selected and emphasized, some included but downplayed, some omitted. A variety of ways exists to talk about selection processes:

Include/Omit: When a writer has more material at hand than can be included within a reasonable length for the project, she must select what to include and what to exclude. These decisions are made in light of the writer's knowledge of her immediate rhetorical situation. At the simplest level, she needs to select that material which is most relevant to her point and most likely to be persuasive to her audience.

A writer is often (though not always) aware of what she has omitted, but for a reader analyzing another writer's work, it can be difficult to think of information that is not present. Yet the reader's view of the subject may be radically altered if certain omitted information were included. Thus, the question of what to include can move rapidly from a practical issue of length to an ethical issue of arguing fairly.

Intensify/Downplay: Not all of the material a writer includes is treated equally. Some information is emphasized, or *intensified,* while other information is *downplayed.* As with the issue of inclusion and omission, the writer will, within the boundaries of ethicality, intensify that information most favorable to her point of view and downplay opposing information. Among the techniques a writer can use to intensify information are to elaborate on it by giving many details; to quote others extensively about it, especially respected authorities; to include the information in a position of importance in the piece as a whole; and to use vivid or emotionally charged language regarding it.

Examples

The following excerpts from national magazines published in July 1996 all concern the bombing of an apartment building housing American military personnel in Dhahran, Saudi Arabia. The excerpts include the first 500 words or so of each article. What aspects of the event does each report include and/or emphasize? Exclude or downplay? Whose voices are heard? How do these choices affect the readers' interpretation of the event? For the latter question, ask yourself how each article answers the following: What was the cause of the bombing? Who was responsible for the bombing? Why are American military personnel stationed in Dhahran? What is the significance of the bombing for Americans in general?

Gulf Shock Waves
The Bomb in Saudi Arabia Raises
Two Questions: How Safe Were the Troops?
How Safe Is the Regime?
Bruce W. Nelan

1 In the steamy darkness of a summer night on the Persian Gulf, Staff Sergeant Alfredo Guerrero was making the rounds of the observation posts under his command. He stepped onto the roof of one of the apartment buildings at the Khobar Towers near Dhahran and said hello to the two other members of the U.S. Air Force security police posted there. Then something caught his eye. Below he saw a white Chevrolet Caprice pulling into a public parking lot adjacent to the compound. Nothing odd about that, but the car was being followed closely by a large tanker truck, and the two vehicles were driving slowly along the edge of the lot. Directly opposite Building 131, where Guerrero stood watching, the Mercedes-Benz tanker backed up to the 10-ft.-high chain-link fence that separated the lot from the military area. Two men leaped out of the truck's cab, into the waiting Caprice, and roared away.

Excerpt from *Time,* July 8, 1996.

2   "That was the clicker," Guerrero later told TIME. "They were in a hurry. I felt something was going to happen very soon." He radioed a hasty report to his headquarters, and then he and the two lookouts dashed down to the residential floor below, where they began pounding on doors and yelling, "Get out! Get out!" They made it only to the seventh floor before what Guerrero had feared would happen did happen.

3   The force of the bomb sheared off the outer wall of Building 131 and left a smoking crater 85 ft. across and 35 ft. deep where the truck had been parked. The shock wave blew in windows and pulverized reinforced concrete, creating a blizzard of slashing, crushing projectiles. Windows in several other buildings, some half a mile away, were also shattered. In the midst of the carnage, Guerrero came upon a dazed and wounded man and helped him down seven flights of stairs to an emergency van that had pulled up outside. While many of the hundred or more officers and enlisted personnel in Building 131 had heard the shouting and headed into the stairwell, away from the blast, 19 airmen were killed and more than 50 were hospitalized.

4   The explosion prompted a painful review of what had gone wrong. Everyone had been aware of the danger since a smaller bomb killed seven people, including five Americans, at a U.S.-run training center in Riyadh, Saudi Arabia's capital, last November. Warnings of more outrages had been coming by phone and fax for months, and security measures at military facilities had been stepped up. Troubling long-range strategic questions also demand answers. Is the rule of the royal House of Saud in more danger than the West suspected? Does the presence of about 5,000 U.S. troops in Saudi Arabia bolster or undercut stability in the land? Could it go the way of Iran? Its future matters immensely because it produces 8 million bbl. of oil a day.

Target: America
The Saudis Need U.S. Protection

1 Outside the Khobar Towers complex, Saudi Arabians in white robes and headdresses stood staring at the shattered apartment building, some of them using binoculars to take in the scene. One of the men, wearing the scraggly beard and short robe of the more radical Muslim believers, suddenly turned to Faiza Saleh Ambah, a local correspondent for NEWSWEEK, smiled at her and recited a verse from the Koran: "Wherever ye are, death will find you out,

Excerpt from *Newsweek,* July 8, 1996.

even if ye are in towers built up strong and high." Without another word, he turned and walked away.

2   The 19 Americans who died in the explosion in Dhahran, and the hundreds more who suffered injuries, were pulling tough duty to protect Saudi Arabia. The royal House of Saud needs an American shield. Its vast oil wealth has not bought security from the vengeance of Iraq's Saddam Hussein or the machinations of Iran's ayatollahs and their friends. And although they preside over one of the world's most rigidly fundamentalist states, the high-living royals are denounced as hypocrites by ultramilitant Muslims. At any given moment, about 5,000 American military men and women are rotating through Saudi Arabia for 90 days at a time. More than 20,000 others stand guard elsewhere in the region (chart). For Saudis, the American presence is a painful paradox: they know they have to have it, but they resent the intrusion and are shamed by the need. And now, for the second time since five U.S. servicemen died in a bombing last November, Americans have become the target of what appears to be a homegrown conspiracy against the royal family.

BASIC INTERESTS

3 The American garrison may eventually become the problem, instead of the solution, for the House of Saud. But so far, no one in either government is talking about sending the GIs home. Bill Clinton took a condolence call from Saudi Arabia's King Fahd and said it would be "a mistake" to change the American mission. "Interests remain interests," said a senior U.S. official. "We have some very basic interests there." The most basic, of course, is that Saudi Arabia currently pumps 12 percent of the world's entire oil supply. Its stability is vital to the entire region, especially to the smaller, oil-producing emirates that fringe the Arabian Peninsula.

4   The day after the explosion, Clinton and his advisers considered a quick presidential visit to Saudi Arabia. The discussion continued during the flight to France for the summit of the G-7 industrial democracies. Clinton said he wanted to be sure a visit wouldn't interfere with the investigation of the blast. Finally, he and his staff decided to attend memorial services for the victims in Florida over the weekend, rather than descend on a country that already had more than enough on its hands.

5   Even without the irritant of an American presence, the Saudi regime would be in difficulty. For the first time in decades, economic problems have made many Saudis feel poor, and the air of discontent has never been stronger.

The Hard Questions
Blowback
Ronald Steel

1   The most surprising thing about last month's attack on the American base in Saudi Arabia was our surprise. Islamic fundamentalists and outlaw regimes have targeted the U.S. for more than a dozen years. In 1983, Shiite suicide bombers opposed to U.S. intervention in Lebanon's civil war killed 241 American servicemen in their Beirut barracks. In 1988, militants, whom the U.S. accused of working for Libya, blew up a Pan Am jet, killing 270 civilians. Three years ago, followers of a fundamentalist Egyptian cleric leveled part of the World Trade Center. Only last November, Saudi fundamentalists attacked a U.S. base in Riyadh and killed five Americans.

2   Such attacks are predictable. They are not, contrary to their depiction in the American press, random acts that defy logic. They are battles in a war that pits the strongest and most revolutionary power in the world against those determined to resist its authority and values. The U.S. is revolutionary in that our economy and culture are based on rendering every other form of social organization and belief obsolete. America not only practices democracy, individualism and capitalism at home but actively works to transform and even undermine regimes that it believes pursues these virtues insufficiently. Content with political influence and economic gain, older imperial powers like Britain and France have traditionally been less insistent on turning client states into images of themselves.

3   The global economy we dominate, the "international community" we organize, the cultural imperatives we transmit through Nike, McDonald's and Disney, enfold the world in an embrace as pervasive as it is, at least in our eye, seemingly irresistible. But what appears to us an embrace is to others a stranglehold. It is this conflict between modernizers and traditionalists, revolutionaries and defenders of the faith, that is being enacted so violently both within the Islamic states themselves and also along the fault lines between Islam and the West. This struggle runs far deeper than the cold war, which was, after all, simply a competition between two different versions of modernization.

4   The U.S. is under assault by those we label "Islamic fundamentalists" not because of what it is but for what it does. Countries such as Italy and Sweden are, after all, no less secular and "modern." But it is America that has the global military and economic reach to undermine traditional societies. Naturally, because of our unquestioning faith in technology, individualism, progress and consumption, we do not consider ourselves threatening. Puzzled

Excerpt from *The New Republic,* July 29, 1996.

when vilified, we assume our accusers must be demented. In truth, we and they live in different worlds.

5   This can be seen in many places, but perhaps nowhere more dramatically than in our relations with Saudi Arabia, a nation with which we are entwined by oil, money, politics and strategy, yet which is profoundly foreign to us culturally. We and the Saudis are linked, but in an uneasy and unstable union.

VOICE

Voice is a term used with a specialized meaning as well as its ordinary language meaning in the discourse of rhetoric. In its specialized sense, voice refers to the identity the writer assumes in the writing.

The Writer's Voice: One theory of language acquisition holds that people learn to speak in the ways they do from experiencing the many discourses in their environment. That is, an individual does not actually originate her own ways of talking, but picks up, reworks, and adapts the discourses of her surroundings. The various discourses and accents that teenagers adopt from music, sports, comedians, and ethnic and regional influences support this contention. What it suggests for writing is that, just as writers do not originate their own oral discourse, they do not originate what they write. What they write is adapted and reworked from discourses they have heard and read. Thus, a writer does not speak with just one authentic voice, but may speak with voices from any of the discourses she has learned.

The writer may use a *personal* voice to claim ideas or feelings as her own, or may adopt other voices for other reasons. The scientist adopts the voice of the *impersonal observer* when writing up her research in order to divorce the findings from personal prejudice and represent them as objective truth. When the dean welcomes the incoming class of freshmen, he speaks with an *institutional voice.* That is, he speaks at that occasion only because of the position he holds, and he speaks for the institution. In an extreme example, many news magazine articles are written by a team of reporters, but the article sounds as though it were written by just one person. In that case, the several authors strive for the single *reportorial voice* of none of them but of, say *Time* magazine.

As you read the selections in this book, think about the writers' voices. Does the writer adopt a personal voice, or is it the voice of an institution or a profession? As you write, consider which of the many voices available to you is most effective in the particular situation for which you are writing. Part of your college education is learning to appropriate new voices to fit the discourses you are moving into.

The Writer's Incorporation of Others' Voices: Besides his own voice, a writer usually incorporates the voices of many others into his writing. Some theorists think that writing is unavoidably interwoven with texts that have preceded it, so that any single sentence is only partially the utterance of the writer and is partly the traces and echoes of previous writing. Other voices can be interwoven into a new text so subtly that the writer is not even conscious of it; alternatively, the writer may name and directly quote another speaker. Here are some of the ways writers, sometimes unconsciously, incorporate the voices of others into a new text:

- *Embedded voice:* Some phrases that have originated in particular contexts become so common that we think of them as belonging to the basic vocabulary of the language. As Charles Bazerman notes, "When a writer uses the phrases *right to life* or *freedom of choice,* we know the author has not coined these phrases. We hear in them the echoes of two decades of debate on abortion and even wider echoes from past centuries' discussion of individual liberties and rights." (Bazerman, *The Informed Writer,* 4th ed., Boston: Houghton Mifflin, 1992). As the terms circulated among all those voices, they acquired the meanings we associate with them today, and as they continue to circulate among speakers and writers their meanings will continue to alter. When we use such terms, we are joining a longstanding conversation.

- *Privileged voice:* Writers *privilege* or emphasize certain voices for various reasons: The voice may belong to an authority who supports the writer's view, or to a person or group the writer feels deserves to be heard, or to an opponent whom the writer wishes to refute. A writer privileges a voice primarily by letting it speak for itself, that is, by quoting, sometimes extensively, the person or a representative of the group.

- *Marginalized voice:* The marginalized voice is de-emphasized, pushed to the margins. This happens intentionally when a writer feels for one reason or another that some voices in the discussion should not be heard, but sometimes it happens unintentionally because the writer is not aware of their existence or relevance.

- *Silenced voice:* This is a rhetorical term with especially political overtones. To say that a writer can silence voices suggests power. By ignoring what certain people or groups have to say about an issue, the writer excludes their position from the debate. Creationists argue that textbook publishers silence their viewpoint by excluding them from science books. American Indians argue that historians have silenced their position by ignoring them in narratives of American history.

Example

You might reread the previous magazine articles paying attention to the use of voices for a fuller understanding of how this device influenced your understanding of that situation. The article whose opening paragraphs are reprinted next provides a different kind of example. Though it is dated, published in 1985 when Madonna first burst onto the pop culture scene, it remains an intriguing example of the use of voice. How would you describe the voice of the writer? What persona does he appear to adopt? Where does it change? Whose voices are embedded in the article? privileged? marginalized? Can you think of any potential participants to this discussion whose voices have been silenced? What connections can you make between the writer's use of voice, the audience of *Time* magazine, the editorial aims of the magazine, and the subject matter of the article?

Madonna Rocks the Land
Sassy, Brassy and Beguiling, She Laughs Her Way to Fame
John Skow

1 Now then, parents, the important thing is to stay calm. You've seen Madonna wiggling on MTV—right, she's the pop-tart singer with the trashy outfits and the hi-there belly button. What is worse, your children have seen her. You tell your daughters to put on jeans and sweatshirts, like decent girls, and they look at you as if you've just blown in from the Planet of the Creeps. Twelve-year-old girls, headphones blocking out the voices of reason, are running around wearing T shirts labeled VIRGIN, which would not have been necessary 30 years ago. The shirts offer no guarantees, moreover; they merely advertise Madonna's first, or virgin, rock tour, now thundering across the continent, and her bouncy, love-it-when-you-do-it song *Like a Virgin.*

2 The bright side of this phenomenon is that these Wanna Be's (as in "We wanna be like Madonna!") could be out somewhere stealing hubcaps. Instead, all of them, hundreds of thousands of young blossoms whose actual ages run from a low of about eight to a high of perhaps 25, are saving up their baby-sitting money to buy cross-shaped earrings and fluorescent rubber bracelets like Madonna's, white lace tights that they will cut off at the ankles and black tube skirts that, out of view of their parents, they will roll down several turns at the waist to expose their middles and the waistbands of the pantyhose.

3 Does anyone remember underwear? The boldest of the Wanna Be's prowl thrift shops looking for ancient, bulletproof black lace bras and corsets, which they wear slapdash under any sort of gauzy shirt or found-in-the-attic

---

Excerpt from *Time,* May 27, 1985.

jacket. They tie great floppy rags in their frazzled hair, which when really authentic is blond with dark roots.

4   To Madonna Louise Ciccone, who is 26, and her Wanna Be's, such getups somehow suggest the '50s, now conceived on the evidence of old Marilyn Monroe movies to have been a quaint and fascinating though slightly tacky time, rich in flirtatious, pre-feminist sexuality. Although to her it's a joke, Madonna's "Boy Toy" belt buckle offends almost everyone except the Wanna Be's. Those who snoozed through the '50s the first time around are mystified. Some feminists clearly feel that Madonna's self-parody as an eye-batting gold digger, notably in her song *Material Girl,* is a joke too damaging to laugh at. Somebody has said that her high, thin voice, which is merely adequate for her energetic but not very demanding dance-pop songs, sounds like "Minnie Mouse on helium." Other detractors suggest that she *is* almost entirely helium, a gas-filled, lighter-than-air creation of MTV and other sinister media packagers (these doubters have not felt the power of Madonna's personality, which is as forceful and well organized as D-day). That mossy old (41) Rolling Stone Mick Jagger says that her records are characterized by "a central dumbness."

5   Kids born since the breakup of the Beatles, however, don't want to hear any of this. Can't hear anything else at this tick of the clock except brassy, trashy, junk-jingling, stage-stomping Madonna, who has been world famous for almost two months. Just now she is the hottest draw in show biz. Michael Jackson? History. Prince? The Peloponnesian Wars. Cyndi Lauper? Last week's flash, and besides, if you wanna be like Cyndi, you have to dye your hair orange and fuchsia, and your parents freak. No, Madonna is the full moon you see at this bend in the river, and never mind what is around the corner.

6   Her numbers, as they say, are spectacular. Her first album, a batch of dance tunes called simply *Madonna,* started slowly nearly two years ago, but now, at 2.8 million copies sold in the U.S., is closing in on triple platinum (in record-business jargon, 500,000 albums sold is gold, and 1 million is platinum). Her second, *Like a Virgin,* which includes five of her own songs, has gone quadruple platinum at 4.5 million copies in domestic sales, with 2.5 million more worldwide. Her singles have found 6.3 million buyers in the U.S. (or the same buyer 6.3 million times, exasperated parents may feel). *Like a Virgin* has sold 1.9 million copies as a single in the U.S., and the ballad *Crazy for You* recently dislodged USA (United Support of Artists) for Africa's *We Are the World* single from the top of the charts, though it has now slipped to sixth.

STYLE

Style is a difficult word to define. Generally, it refers to sentence-level and word-level features of writing that mark it as characteristic of a particular writer, group, publication, or occasion. We include the following elements of writing as having particular force in the making of a style, but style to some extent is affected by all of the rhetorical choices a writer can make.

Register: Register is the degree of formality of a piece of writing. It ranges from formal to informal to colloquial, and much variation exists within each of these levels.

- A *formal* register is generally characterized by a sophisticated vocabulary and complex sentence structure. It is used in important political documents (peace treaties or the U.S. Constitution), in some academic writing (Kenneth Burke's style in his article "Terministic Screens" in this text is written in a formal register) and speeches at formal political occasions (the president's annual State of the Union address to Congress).
- An *informal* register is characterized by standard grammar, more conversational sentences than the formal register, and a vocabulary that is comprehensible to people with a high school education. Popular magazines for the general educated public (*Time* magazine) and newscasters use an informal register.
- A *colloquial* register is what people use in ordinary conversation and friendly letters. It may include slang and nonstandard grammar.

Tone: Tone indicates the implied attitude toward the subject and the audience in a piece of writing. The tone may be solemn, playful, serious, ironic, humorous, authoritative, condescending, sympathetic, factual, polite, defensive, humble, proud, rude, irreverent—in fact, as many words as describe attitude can also describe tone.

Diction: Diction is a general term referring to choice of words. The choices can be as specific as using a word mistakenly, thinking it means something other than it does, or as broad as choosing appropriate words for a particular purpose and context.

Figures of Speech: Perhaps the most significant choices open to writers are provided by the patterns and words of language itself. A writer may choose to use *plain language*—the typical sentence patterns of the English language and the literal meanings of words—or may vary from the normal and the expected by arranging her sentences in unexpected patterns or using words in unexpected ways. When using language in unexpected ways, she is employing *figurative* language (figures of speech).

Figures of speech, according to the classical rhetorician, Quintilian, are any form of speech artfully varied from common usage. As such, they tend to draw attention to the language itself. They are divided into two main groups, *schemes* and *tropes*. A scheme is a variation from the ordinary pattern or arrangement of words in a sentence; a trope is a variation from the ordinary meaning of a word.

Remember that we can also talk about language that avoids figures of speech (language that consistently uses normal patterns and ordinary meanings) by calling it *plain language, plain speech,* or *ordinary language.*

Renaissance rhetoricians came up with 150 to 200 terms for naming different schemes or tropes. Our selection is admittedly pragmatic. We have chosen a few terms that we expect you to find helpful in talking about the prose style of readings in this text and about your own writing.

Schemes

- *Alliteration:* Repetition of initial sounds of two or more adjacent or closely positioned words.

  Perhaps we make a mistake to insist that the monarchy should be majestic . . . Perhaps Charles and Diana, in their follies, are simply enlarging the dramatic franchise of the family, giving it a contemporary feel.

  Lance Morrow, *Time* (July 22, 1996)

  Who often, but without success, have pray'd For apt Alliteration's artful aid.

  Charles Churchill, "The Prophecy of Famine"

- *Anaphora:* Repetition of the same word or group of words at the beginnings of a series of clauses.

  We see despair when social arrogance and indifference exist in the same person with the willingness to live at devastating levels of superficiality and self-trivialization. We see despair in the self-hatred that clogs the lives of so many materially comfortable citizens. We hear despair in the loss of vitality in our spoken language. . . . We see despair in the political activist who doggedly goes on and on, turning in the ashes of the same burnt-out rhetoric, the same gestures, all imagination spent.

  Adrienne Rich, "What Is Found There" (1993)

  And values, values fuel families, families that are bound together by love and commitment, families that then have the strength to withstand the assaults of contemporary life, to resist the images of violence and vulgarity that flood into our lives everyday, families that come together as communities to defeat the scourge of drugs and crime and incivility that threatens us. . . .

  Colin Powell's speech to the Republican National Convention, *New York Times* (Wednesday, August 14, 1996)

- *Antimetabole:* Repetition of words, in successive clauses, in reverse grammatical order.

  Not only does group membership shape language, but language also shapes group membership.

  Alan Wolfe, *The New Republic* (December 12, 1994)

- *Parallelism:* A pair or series of equivalent ideas in a sentence appearing in similar grammatical structures.

Some writers confuse authenticity, which they ought to aim at, with originality, which they should never bother about.

W. H. Auden, "The Dyer's Hand" (1962)

In the decades since World War II the old intellectual absolutisms have been dethroned: science, scientific history, and history in the service of nationalism. In their place—almost as an interim report—the postwar generation has constructed sociologies of knowledge, records of diverse peoples, and histories based upon group or gender identities.

Appleby, Joyce, et al., Introduction to
Telling the Truth About History (1993)

- *Antithesis:* The juxtaposition of contrasting ideas, often parallel in structure.

Form is finite, structure is infinite.

Charles Wright, "Halflife" (1988)

We have negative names, which stand not directly for positive ideas, but for their absence. . . . And thus one may truly be said to see darkness.

John Locke, "An Essay Concerning Human
Understanding" (1690)

How, then, has our knowledge of nature been influenced by struggles determining who is included in science and who is excluded, which projects are pursued and which ignored, whose experiences are validated and whose are not, and who stands to gain in terms of wealth or well-being and who does not?

Londa Schiebinger, Introduction to *Nature's Body* (1993)

- *Cumulative sentence:* This is the ordinary or plain language order of English sentences. It begins with the subject followed fairly closely by the verb, and adds detail at the end of the sentence.

Women have become an essential part of western history.

Patricia Limerick, "What on Earth Is the
New Western History?" (1991)

The new discovery opens exciting possibilities for treatment and prevention.

New York Times (August 14, 1996)

Since I can't fix either myself or rhetoric, I'd rather think about two or three small rhetorics, remembering to take the word as plural, trying to understand, for example, the consequences for rhetoric if one thinks of all speakers as remnants or leftovers, trying to understand the consequences for rhetoric if one decides, momentarily say, that all rhetoric is nostalgic, resonant with regret and loss, or trying to understand how one might make a rhetoric yonder on the other side of regret and loss.

Jim W. Corder, "Argument as Emergence,
Rhetoric as Love" (1994)

- *Anastrophe:* Inversion of the natural or usual word order.

    Answer came there none, nor ever can.
    > Paul Johnson, *The Birth of the Modern* (1991)

- *Parentheses:* Insertion of a phrase or clause that interrupts the normal syntax of the sentence, often to allow the author to comment in a voice different from that of the main discourse.

    We are—my father's family is (despite the evidence on my face)—of Europe.
    > Richard Rodriguez, *Days of Obligation: An Argument with My Mexican Father* (1992)

- *Periodic (climactic) sentence:* An arrangement that delays the subject and verb until the end of the sentence in order to create suspense. This pattern gives special emphasis to the end of the sentence.

    Going through experience, hooking some version of it to ourselves, accumulating what we know as evidence and insight, ignoring what does not look like evidence and insight to us, finding some pieces of life that become life for us, failing to find others, or choosing not to look, each of us creates the narrative that he or she is.
    > Jim W. Corder, "Argument as Emergence, Rhetoric as Love" (1994)

    Two days later, in Enniskillen, 80 miles southwest of Belfast, a bomb exploded and injured two people.
    > *Time* (July 22, 1996)

Tropes

- *Hyperbole:* Conscious exaggeration used to heighten effect or for comic effect.

    . . . A few miles up the trail, where the tree trunks are all cunningly disguised as hungry sows with cubs, the thought comes to me—evil, unbidden, seductive—why not just exterminate the pests? This, after all, is the human way: if you don't like it, rub it out, down to the last molecule of DNA. . . . Let a few hunters loose in the national parks with crossbows and Magnums, and it would be hasta la vista, bears.
    > Barbara Ehrenreich, *Time* (August 12, 1996)

- *Irony:* A figure of speech in which the intended meaning is expressed in words that have the opposite literal meaning. Irony is a subtle figure and easily missed if the reader is unfamiliar with the context or the writer's true views.

    You can't fight in here—this is the war room.
    > Stanley Kubrick's *Dr. Strangelove or: How I Learned to Stop Worrying and Love the Bomb* (1963)

- *Litotes:* Deliberate use of understatement.

My own sex will excuse me, if I treat them like rational creatures. . . .
> Mary Wollstonecraft, Introduction to
> *The Vindication of the Rights of Women* (1792)

- *Metaphor:* An implied comparison of two things of unlike nature.

A geometric proof is a mousetrap.
> Arthur Schopenhauer, *Complete Essays* (1942)

Science is a cemetery of dead ideas.
> Miguel de Unamuno, *The Tragic Sense of Life* (1954)

- *Metonymy:* To substitute a word closely associated for the word that is actually meant. For instance, the press often refers to the president of the United States as "the White House":

The equally historic nature of the decision facing Bill Clinton was clear not just to the White House but the whole nation.
> George J. Church, *Time* (August 12, 1996)

After the stock market tumbled on Friday, Wall Street tried to rebound yesterday, but came up short.
> *New York Times* (July 9, 1996)

- *Oxymoron:* A form of antithesis that brings together two contradictory terms for the sake of sharp emphasis.

A wild patience has taken me this far.
> Adrienne Rich, *A Wild Patience Has Taken Me This Far* (1984)

- *Personification:* To invest inanimate objects or abstract qualities with human qualities or abilities.

The cliche organizes life; it expropriates people's identity; it becomes ruler, defense lawyer, judge, and the law.
> Vaclav Havel, *Disturbing the Peace* (1986, translated 1990)

Money has no ears, no eyes, no respect; it is all gut, mouth, and ass.
> Guy Davenport, *Every Force Evolves a Form* (1987)

- *Simile:* A comparison between two things of unlike nature using the words *like* or *as*.

You may feel a little as if writing a novel is like trying to level Mount McKinley with a dentist's drill.
> Anne Lamott, *Bird by Bird* (1994)

Induction is working backward, like solving a maze by backtracking from the goal.
> William Poundstone, *Labyrinths of Reason* (1988)

- *Synecdoche:* A figure of speech in which the part stands for the whole.

Buddy had been knocked awake out of hiding in a washing machine while herds of policemen with dogs searched through a large building with many tiny rooms. When the arm came down, Buddy screamed because it had a blue cuff and sharp silver buttons.

Louise Erdrich, "American Horse" (1983)

INVENTION

For classical rhetoricians, *invention* was the first of the five "canons" or typical parts of the process of producing a speech. The other four were arrangement, style, memory, and delivery. The term *invention* has a specialized meaning in the discourse of rhetoric. In its most general sense, it refers to getting ideas for speaking or writing, so you might in part think of it as similar to its modern ordinary language use: you "invent" ideas to write about.

But few rhetoricians have believed that people simply invent ideas from scratch. In fact, differing views grounded in different theories about language and epistemology resulted in heated disagreements about where ideas come from and even whether it is possible to teach students how to get ideas. Although classical rhetoricians firmly believed that invention was an integral part of rhetoric, views had changed by the nineteenth century to the point that many rhetoricians argued that it wasn't a part of producing writing at all—that "getting" the ideas happened outside of or prior to the writing process itself, through means like scientific observation or poetic inspiration.

Our pragmatic view is that most if not all of the rhetorical concepts that you use to analyze what other writers have done can also serve as aids for getting ideas for your own writing. In this section, we first introduce the concepts traditionally identified with invention, and then review some of the central terms in the Appendix from the perspective of the writer, suggesting questions to ask yourself to help you apply them to your own writing.

Although it will be useful to explore these questions as you begin writing, you should think of invention as a continuing component of writing and return to these concepts for further stimulation throughout the process.

From the Ancients

Line of Reasoning (Topoi): Aristotle thought speakers should memorize a store of ways that ideas can relate to one another and, when preparing a speech, visit the "store" to find ways of talking about their topics. Over the years, these lines of reasoning have included cause to effect, analogy, definition, comparison and contrast, analysis, synthesis, opposition or antithesis, deductive reasoning, and inductive reasoning. You will find all of these terms defined elsewhere in this text. When you are getting ideas for writing, you can consider whether it would be useful to think of your topic in any of these ways. That is, you can ask yourself:

Do I wish to show the causes of X (my topic)?

Do I want to show the effects of X?

Can I explain X with an analogy?

Do I need to define X? If so, how shall I define it?

Can I compare or contrast X to something else?

Commonplace: The term commonplace sometimes refers to the lines of reasoning mentioned above, but it is also used to refer to common sayings, common ideas, or common wisdom that members of the audience are likely to share with each other and the writer. In this category, you would ask yourself:

What aphorisms or saying do I know related to X?

What people, accepted as wise or knowledgeable in my community, can I quote to support X?

From the Appendix

Rhetorical Situation Questions for Invention (These are especially relevant to the academic rhetorical situation.)

What do I know about the expectations of the discourse community for which I am writing?

What do I know about the expectations of the genre for which I am writing?

What do I know about the values and purposes of the discipline for which I am writing?

What do I know about the questions at issue in the discipline for which I am writing?

What do I know about the conversations that have already occurred about this topic in the discourse community for which I am writing?

Purpose Questions for Invention

What do I wish to achieve for myself by writing this paper?

What do I want to accomplish regarding my relationship with my professor?

What purpose do I want to accomplish within the paper? What point do I want to make in the paper?

Audience Questions for Invention

What do I know about the community for whom I am writing?

What are their values and beliefs?

Their central interests?

Their motives?

Discourse Community Questions for Invention

All those for Audience above, and

What do I know about the community's preferred genres and formats?

Their specialized language?

Genre Questions for Invention

What genre should I use?

What are the typical formats of this genre?

What parts, components or sections does this genre contain?

What levels of language does this genre typically use?

What are the aims or purposes typically embodied in this genre?

Should I parody a genre?

Appeals Questions for Invention

Which appeal(s) will be most effective for achieving my purpose with my audience?

If more than one kind of appeal would be effective, which one should be dominant?

What do I need to do in my writing in order to make a logical (emotional) appeal?

Emotional Appeal Questions for Invention

Will the emotional appeal be effective for my audience and purpose?

If so, how should I impart the emotional appeal? Should I tell anecdotes? use emotional language? vivid descriptive details? tropes?

Ethical Appeal Questions for Invention

What do I need to do to show my audience that they can believe me?

Should I summarize the ongoing conversation about X to show my familiarity with the field?

Should I quote authorities to show that I have read the respected voices in the field?

Do I need to include multiple perspectives on X?

Do I need to appear open-minded about X?

Do I need to do more reading to learn other perspectives?

Should I describe personal experience to show my sincere interest in X?

Logical Appeal Questions for Invention

Do I need to define my terms?

What kinds of evidence will my readers value?

Is it to my advantage to conform to readers' expectations for evidence, or should I surprise them in some ways? If so, for what purpose? And how should I go about it?

Am I supporting every claim with credible evidence?

Is my evidence relevant to the field? topic? points I want to make?

Is my evidence the most up-to-date in this field?

If I am arguing from cause to effect, how do I show the links between causes and effects? How do I demonstrate that the causes I identify are significant to the outcome?

Arrangement Questions for Invention

What pattern of arrangement will best support my purpose in this writing?

What patterns of arrangement fit the genre I am using?

Of what parts or components does my pattern of arrangement consist?

Do I want to play around with one of the typical patterns of arrangement? In what ways? What would the advantages be for achieving my purpose?

Voice Questions for Invention

What voice should I adopt for this paper?

What other voices should I emphasize to achieve my purposes with this audience?

Are there voices in this discussion with whose perspective I am unfamiliar? How can I learn about them?

Are there voices with which I disagree? How should I deal with them?

Language Questions for Invention

> What do I know about the language I am expected to imitate, adapt (adapt to) or adopt for this discourse?

> What is its register, tone, vocabulary, syntax (sentence structure)? How does it differ form my home language(s)?

> In what ways do I resist adopting the language of this discourse? Why?

> How can I accede to the features of this discourse without losing my own identity?

Register Questions for Invention

> What register will my audience expect? respect?

> Will I achieve my purposes by conforming to their expectations? What would I achieve by using a register that will surprise them?

Tone Questions for Invention

> What tone is appropriate to my audience, purpose, and subject matter?

> Do I want to play with tone in any way in this paper? for what effects?

Figures of Speech Questions for Invention

At various periods in rhetoric's history, writers and speakers have been encouraged to consider figures of speech early in the composing process and construct speeches or writing around them. Now, our advice is to be familiar with the stylistic and figurative options available to you because they may well provide you with felicitous ways to say things, and they may stimulate further things to say. So the same question for invention applies to all the figures of speech:

> Do I know this figure of speech well enough so that I will think of it if the appropriate occasion should arise?

LITERARY
ACKNOWLEDGEMENTS

Kent Kirkpatrick, "Spandex Judge." From *Face* May/June 1994, pp. 62-63, 71. Copyright © 1997 Transpacific Media Inc. Malibu, CA 90264-4260. Reprinted from Transpacific Magazine by express written permission. No part of this article may be reproduced for any purpose without express written consent.

Elizabeth Cody Newenhuyse, "Deconstructive Criticism." From *Today's Christian Woman,* May/June 1994, pp. 66-69. Reprinted by permission of author.

Allan Bloom, "Liberal Education." Reprinted with the permission of Simon & Schuster from THE CLOSING OF THE AMERICAN MIND by Allan Bloom. Copyright © 1987 by Allan Bloom.

Mike Rose, Selection from "The Politics of Remediation." Abridged and reprinted with the permission of The Free Press, a Division of Simon & Schuster from LIVES ON THE BOUNDARY: THE STRUGGLES AND ACHIEVEMENTS OF AMERICA'S UNDERPREPARED by Mike Rose. Copyright © 1989 by Mike Rose.

bell hooks, "Keeping Close to Home." From TALKING BACK, pp. 39-46, © 1989. Reprinted by permission of South End Press.

Conference on College Composition and Communication, "The Students' Right to Their Own Language." From *College Composition and Communication,* 1974. Copyright 1974 by the National Council of Teachers of English. Reprinted with permission.

Richard Rodriguez, Selection from "The Achievement of Desire." From *Hunger of Memory* by Richard Rodriguez. Reprinted by permission of David R. Godine, Publisher, Inc. Copyright © 1982 by Richard Rodriguez.

Mary Louise Pratt, "Arts of Contact Zone." Reprinted by permission of the Modern Language Associate of America from *Profession 91,* pp. 31-40, © 1991.

Kenneth Burke, "Terministic Screens." From LANGUAGE AND SYMBOLIC ACTION, © 1968, pp. 44-54, originally in Proceedings of the American Catholic Philosophical Association, Volume XXXIX, 1965.

David Bartholomae, "Inventing the University." Copyright © 1986 by the *Journal of Basic Writing,* Instructional Resource Center, Office of Academic Affairs, The City University of New York. Reprinted by permission.

Linda Flower, Victoria Stein, John Ackerman, Margaret Kantz, Kathleen McCormack, and Wayne Peck, "Reading-to-Write: Exploring a Cognitive and Social Process." Copyright © 1990 by Center for the Study of Writing. Used by permission of Oxford University Press, Inc.

Peter Elbow, "Writing for Teachers." From "Writing with Power: Techniques for Mastering the Writing Process" by Peter Elbow. Copyright © 1981 by Peter Elbow. Used by permission of Oxford University Press, Inc.

Karen Spear, "Sharing Writing." Reprinted by permission of Karen Spear "Sharing Writing: Peer Response Groups in English Classes," Boynton/Cook Publishers, a subsidiary of Greenwood Publishing Group, Portsmouth, NH, 1988.

Christina Haas, "Learning to Read Biology." From WRITTEN COMMUNICATION, pp. 43-74, copyright © 1994 by Sage Publications. Reprinted by permission of Sage Publications, Inc.

Mariolina Salvatori, "Conversations with Texts: Reading in the Teaching of Composition." *College English,* April 1996. Copyright 1996 by the National Council of Teachers of English. Reprinted with permission.

Jim Corder, "Argument as Emergence, Rhetoric as Love." From PROFESSING THE NEW RHETORICS: A SOURCEBOOK, pp. 412-428, Enos & Brown. Copyright © 1994 by *Rhetoric Review;* reprinted by permission of *Rhetoric Review.*

John Skow, "Madonna Rocks the Land," *Time Magazine* May 27, 1985. Copyright © 1985, Time Inc. Reprinted by permission.

"Target America" from *Newsweek,* July 8, 1996, pp. 23-24, © 1996, Newsweek, Inc. All rights reserved. Reprinted by permission.

Ronald Steel, "The Hard Questions: Blowback." From *The New Republic,* July 29, 1996. Reprinted by permission of THE NEW REPUBLIC, © 1996, The New Republic, Inc.

Bruce W. Nelan, "Gulf Shock Waves," *Time Magazine,* July 8, 1996, pp. 21-22. Copyright © 1996, Time Inc. Reprinted by permission.

ILLUSTRATION CREDITS

Page 4 © 1997 Transpacific Media, Inc.

Page 4 © 1997 Transpacific Media, Inc.

Page 5 © 1997 Transpacific Media, Inc.

Page 77 © Modern Language Association

Page 78 © Modern Language Association

Page 79 © Modern Language Association

Page 154 Courtesy of the National Library of Jamaica

Page 157 Staatsbibliothek zu Berlin—Preussischer Kulturbesitz, Abteilung Historische Drucke

Page 166 Courtesy of Patricia Wynne

Page 167 © David Crews

Page 171 © David Crews

Page 173 © David Crews

Page 173 © David Crews

Page 173 © David Crews

Page 175 Courtesy of Pauline Yahr

Page 175 Courtesy of Pauline Yahr

Page 177 © Laurence Frank

Page 177 © David Crews

INDEX